The Ultimate Spanish 101

Ronni L. Gordon, PhD
and David M. Stillman, PhD

Mc Graw Hill

New York Chicago San Francisco Athens London Madrid
Mexico City Milan New Delhi Singapore Sydney Toronto

1 2 3 4 5 6 7 8 9 LHS 24 23 22 21 20 19

ISBN 978-1-260-45363-8
MHID 1-260-45363-4

e-ISBN 978-1-260-45364-5
e-MHID 1-260-45364-2

McGraw-Hill Language Lab App

Audio recordings, review exercises, and flashcards that supplement this book can be found in the McGraw-Hill Language Lab app. Go to mhlanguagelab.com to access the online version of this application, or download the free mobile version from the Apple App store (for iPhone and iPad), or the Google Play store (for Android devices). Note: Internet connection required for audio content.

By the same authors

The Ultimate Spanish Review and Practice, Fourth Edition
The Ultimate Spanish Verb Review and Practice, Second Edition
The Big Red Book of Spanish Verbs, Second Edition
The Red Pocket Book of Spanish Verbs
Spanish Vocabulary Drills

The Ultimate French Review and Practice, Fourth Edition
The Ultimate French Verb Review and Practice, Second Edition
The Big Blue Book of French Verbs, Second Edition
The Blue Pocket Book of French Verbs
French Vocabulary Drills

Note

Significant content in this book was first published in *Practice Makes Perfect: Beginning Spanish with CD-ROM*, McGraw-Hill. The preliminary chapter, "Pronunciation and Spelling," first appeared in *Comunicando: A First Course in Spanish*, Second Edition, D.C. Heath and Company. Both titles are by Ronni L. Gordon, PhD and David M. Stillman, PhD.

For Alex and Mimi, whose brilliance, talents, and love illuminate and inspire every word we write

RLG and DMS

Preface

Almost seventy years later, I remember clearly how the magic of translating the words in books into images enriched my life, breaking the barriers of time and space.
—Mario Vargas Llosa, Nobel Prize in Literature 2010

¡Ahora pienso practicar lo más que pueda cada año!
—Plácido Domingo

The Ultimate Spanish 101 is a uniquely comprehensive, inviting, and user-friendly program designed for beginning learners of Spanish who want conversational proficiency based on a solid grammatical foundation and a broad, current vocabulary. Complete with textbook and app, the course provides abundant practice in all language skills—listening, speaking, reading, and writing. The conceptual features underpinning ***The Ultimate Spanish 101*** are practice and modularity.

"How do you get to Carnegie Hall? Practice, practice, practice!" How do you get to fluency in Spanish? Practice, practice, practice! ***The Ultimate Spanish 101*** audio component on the **Language Lab app** includes 170 *Diálogos*, all the *Variantes* of the textbook, 125 oral exercises called *Prácticas*, practice in pronouncing Spanish sounds, and flashcards for building vocabulary—all recorded by native speakers of Spanish with pauses for repetition. Practicing these exercises repeatedly until you have mastered the material will empower you to understand and speak Spanish better, resulting in more effective communication.

***The Ultimate Spanish 101* textbook** includes *Prácticas* that reinforce the grammatical structures and vocabulary presented in each chapter. Successful completion of the more than 300 structural, translation, and free expression exercises enables you to read simple Spanish prose and write short paragraphs on familiar topics in Spanish.

The modular organization of ***The Ultimate Spanish 101*** makes it easy for learners to adapt their practice time to their schedules. It is ideal for learners working on their own and as an ancillary for students learning Spanish in a classroom setting. The sections of each of the sixteen chapters of the book are conveniently listed on the app and can be accessed with a click. You can practice Spanish at your convenience and go at your own pace—on your computer, tablet, or cell phone.

Structure and Components of the Book

The Ultimate Spanish 101 opens with a Preliminary chapter, **Pronunciation and Spelling**, that describes the sounds of Spanish. Using the app, learners will be able to listen to and repeat these sounds after the native Spanish speakers. Mastering the sound system of Spanish will enable you to pronounce and understand better, which will result in enhanced communication skills.

The Ultimate Spanish 101 is comprised of sixteen chapters, all structured in the same way. Each chapter opens with **Communication Goals**, a statement of the chapter's objectives for learner achievement, and **Grammar Topics**, an outline of grammar points to be presented and practiced.

Each chapter has a series of interesting short **Diálogos** that present grammatical structures and vocabulary targeted in the chapter. There are between four and nineteen short *Diálogos* in each chapter, each one containing two to five exchanges that present conversations in authentic, current language on a variety of topics, such as family and relationships, work, entertainment, food, shopping, health, the daily routine, sports, holidays, business, technology, the economy, and life goals. Each *Diálogo* has an audio icon, indicating that it is recorded on the app. You will study the *Diálogo*, listen to the recording, and repeat each speech after the speaker.

The **Análisis** section that follows the *Diálogo* provides a linguistic breakdown, that is, an analysis of the sentence structures and vocabulary presented in the *Diálogo*. Each element is presented with an English translation.

The **Variantes** section following the *Análisis* presents new structures and vocabulary based on the content of the *Diálogo*. Like the *Diálogo*, the *Variantes* has an audio icon, indicating that it is recorded on the app. You will study the *Variantes*, listen to the recording, and repeat the structures after the speaker.

The Ultimate Spanish 101 presents essential Spanish tenses and the highest-frequency structures for a beginning learner of Spanish. The **Estructura y Práctica** sections present clear, concise explanations of the grammatical structures presented in the *Diálogos*, followed by exercises for practice of these structures. The explanations in the **Estructura** contrast Spanish and English grammar. Some grammatical topics appear in review, referencing the initial presentation, thereby reinforcing and improving your skills. In the **Práctica**, structural, writing, translation, and free expression exercises, some contextual or thematic, enable you to read simple Spanish prose and write short paragraphs on familiar topics in Spanish.

Un paso más (*A Step Further*), the culminating section of each chapter, encourages you to use what you have learned, applying it to activities that will expand your knowledge of the Spanish language (cognates, word families, synonyms and antonyms, and so on) and the Spanish-speaking world. You are encouraged to express yourself freely in Spanish by answering *Preguntas personales* (personal questions) and writing compositions on topics related to the content of each chapter—all in Spanish. You will learn about pre-Columbian civilizations in Mexico and take a virtual tour of the Museo Nacional de Antropología; read and explain a quote by Miguel de Cervantes's Don Quijote; and learn about holidays celebrated by Spanish speakers and write about the holidays you celebrate.

Language boxes, placed judiciously throughout the chapters, offer important information about the Spanish language, colorful idiomatic usage of Spanish, and interesting observations about Hispanic culture.

The Ultimate Spanish 101 provides **Verb Charts** you can consult when in doubt about a verb form or tense; an **Answer Key** so that you can check your answers to the exercises; and a **Glossary** of the words and expressions used in the sixteen chapters, each entry indicating in which chapter it appears for the first time.

The Ultimate Spanish 101 program will lead you to mastery of the Spanish language, empowering you to communicate with efficacy, confidence, and enjoyment, and through your knowledge of the language, develop a deep appreciation of the culture of Spanish-speaking peoples.

We are, as ever, grateful to Christopher Brown, our superlative publisher and esteemed friend, for his ultimate vision, wisdom, and guidance through this process of creation, and for all that came before.

Ronni L. Gordon, PhD
David M. Stillman, PhD

About the Authors

Ronni L. Gordon, PhD, is a prominent author of foreign language textbooks and materials for multimedia, including more than 30 titles in Spanish and other languages. She has taught and coordinated Spanish language programs and taught Spanish American literature at Harvard University, Boston University, and Drexel University. A foreign language consultant, she has read for the National Endowment for the Humanities, presented at the United States Department of Education, and consulted on states' K–12 academic standards for world languages. She has presented at conferences on foreign language pedagogy and Spanish American literature, as one of the first scholars to give a college course on Spanish American women writers.

David M. Stillman, PhD, is a well-known writer of foreign language textbooks and materials for multimedia, with a bibliography that includes titles in four languages. He teaches languages and linguistics at The College of New Jersey, where he also coordinates an innovative program of student-led oral proficiency classes. He has taught and coordinated foreign language programs at Boston University, Harvard University, and Cornell University. He has consulted on states' K–12 academic standards for world languages and presented at national and regional conventions of language educators, being appointed to national committees devoted to the improvement of teacher training.

Contents

Pronunciation and Spelling

PRONUNCIATION

Learning to speak a foreign language requires changing many of the pronunciation habits formed in learning your own language. Because these habits are so ingrained, acquiring acceptable pronunciation of a foreign language requires not only intensive practice, but also analysis of the individual sounds—how they are produced and how they compare to those of your own language. This introduction serves to aid your perception and production of the sounds of Spanish. The use of technical terms has been limited to allow you to concentrate on producing the sounds accurately.

To present Spanish sounds and their representation in Spanish spelling, certain symbols are used: Basic sounds of the language are written between slashes; variants of a sound in certain positions are written between square brackets; and letters used in spelling are in bold. Note that the symbol chosen to transcribe a sound may or may not be the letter that represents it in the Spanish spelling system.

This initial presentation will limit itself to "Standard Spanish" as spoken in Hispanic America, a set of pronunciation features devoid of regional peculiarities. Important dialect variations will be mentioned in individual chapters.

Vowels

Spanish has five vowel sounds, represented by the letters **a**, **e**, **i**, **o**, **u**. Listen to the speaker pronounce the following syllables. Notice that the Spanish vowels are shorter and tenser than their stressed counterparts in English.

ba	ka	fa	sa	ma
be	ke	fe	se	me
bi	ki	fi	si	mi
bo	ko	fo	so	mo
bu	ku	fu	su	mu

Now repeat each of the above syllables after the speaker. If you compare English *see* and Spanish **si** you will observe that the vowel sound in *see* really consists of two vowels pronounced as one syllable—the vowel of *sit* plus a glide similar to the *y* in *you*: /iy/. Diphthong is the technical term for two vowels pronounced together as a single syllable. The English vowels of the words *bay, bow, boo* are also diphthongs: /ey/, /ow/, /uw/, respectively. The similarity between Spanish and English diphthongs is limited, however. Diphthongs are far less frequent in Spanish than in English, where they are the norm in stressed syllables.

Repeat the following words and syllables after the speaker, taking care to produce a short, tense vowel and not a diphthong.

i si mi li pi bi bis mis fin sin
e se me le be pe fe mes les bes pes fes
o lo so fo mo los sos bos pos kos fos pon kon son
u bu ku tu lu nu mu su mus tus sus pus bun mun

English speakers should avoid pronouncing the letter **a** in Spanish like the English sound represented by the letter *a* in *class, cab, bag.*

a la pa ma sa ba ga bas las pas sas

In English, most unstressed vowels are reduced to a neutral vowel called "schwa" that is transcribed as /ə/. This is not reflected in English spelling, and many pairs of words that are pronounced alike, such as *affect/effect* and *accept/except*, are spelled differently. Any of the five written vowels may represent /ə/ in an unstressed syllable in English spelling. For example, the vowel of the first syllable of each of the following words is pronounced /ə/:

machine semantic mirage corrode supply

In Spanish, the sound /ə/ does not exist. All unstressed syllables have one of the five vowels **a**, **e**, **i**, **o**, **u**. Differences in unstressed vowels in Spanish not only distinguish countless pairs of words, but also signal some of the most fundamental grammatical functions of the language.

Correlated with the reduction of unstressed vowels to /ə/ in English is the shortening of unstressed syllables. In other words, stressed syllables in English take longer to say than unstressed syllables. In Spanish, however, stressed and unstressed syllables are the same length.

The following Spanish two-syllable words are all stressed on the first syllable. They have the vowel /a/ in both syllables. Repeat each one after the speaker, making sure to pronounce /a/ the same way in both syllables and to make the two syllables of equal length.

mala sala saca sana fama mapa matas
latas lana vana chata sacan sanan laman

The following Spanish two-syllable words have /e/ in both syllables and are stressed on the first syllable. To pronounce them correctly, concentrate on the following points:

1 · Avoid the diphthong /ey/, as in English *pay.*

2 · Pronounce the /e/ the same way in both syllables.

3 · Make the two syllables of equal length.

Repeat the following words after the speaker:

nene mece queme pele seque cheque
meten temen quemen peles seques meces

The following Spanish two-syllable words have /o/ in both syllables and are stressed on the first syllable. To pronounce them correctly, concentrate on the following points:

1 · Avoid the diphthong /ow/, as in English *toe.*

2 · Pronounce the /o/ the same way in both syllables.

3 · Make the two syllables of equal length.

Repeat the following words after the speaker:

como loco polo foso coso soso
cocos pocos somos lomos monos bonos

The following words are three syllables long, and they are all stressed on the middle syllable. Each word has the same vowel in all three syllables. Repeat each word after the speaker, concentrating on pronouncing the vowels of all three syllables in the same way and making all syllables of equal length.

/a/ batata macana canasta hamaca alpaca
/e/ demente pelele clemente deseque deseche
/o/ mocoso doloso conozco goloso coloco

The following pairs of words are distinguished solely by differences in the unstressed vowels. Repeat each pair of words after the speaker:

a / o	e / i	i / o
coma / como	pesó / pisó	mirar / morar
meta / meto	case / casi	pisando / posando
famosas / famosos	teces / tesis	misión / moción
calor / color	delatan / dilatan	timaron / tomaron
molina / molino	cemento / cimento	trincar / troncar

a / e	e / u
toma / tome	lechón / luchón
caminas / camines	regir / rugir
alemanas / alemanes	pechito / puchito
patinan / patinen	besito / busito
señoras / señores	hendir / hundir

e / o	o / u
pesó / posó	dorado / durado
velaron / volaron	fondita / fundita
tomes / tomos	goloso / guloso
quesito / cosito	mostela / mustela
velita / bolita	osamos / usamos

Consonants

b/v, d, g The Spanish letters **b** and **v** (which represent the same sound in Spanish), **d**, and **g** have more than one sound, depending on the letter's position in a word or sentence. After a pause and after **m** or **n**, Spanish **b/v**, **d**, and **g** represent sounds similar to those corresponding to English *b, d,* and *g* in *boy, does,* and *go.* Spanish /d/ is produced with the tip of the tongue touching the back of the upper front teeth rather than the gum ridge above them as in English. Spanish /g/ is spelled **gu** before **e** and **i**.

Repeat the following words after the speaker:

base donde goza vaso conde goma betún
dote hongo bomba dime tango invita demás
gasto bote anda gala voy lindo gusano
ambos dones ganga envase doy manga vino

These versions of Spanish /b/, /d/, and /g/ are called the hard variants of the sounds; they are transcribed in square brackets as [b], [d], and [g].

In all other positions, **b/v**, **d**, and **g** represent the soft variants of [b], [d], and [g], transcribed as [ƀ], [đ], and [ǥ].

[ƀ] is produced by forcing air through slightly parted lips, drawn back and not puckered.

coba cavamos tubo sabes lavas levantar

[đ] is pronounced similarly to the *th* in *rather, father,* and *other,* but with much less friction.

lodo desde podemos comida pierde guardan

Note that [d], not [đ], is used after /l/:

falda molde balde caldo peldaño celda

[ǥ] is produced similarly to [g], except that air is forced through a very narrow opening between the back of the tongue and the soft palate (back of the roof of the mouth).

pago digo agosto sigamos sagrado algo

The soft variants [ƀ], [đ], and [ǥ] are used between vowels, even when the vowels are in two different words.

yo bato yo doy yo gasto
tú vas tú dices tú gozas
la boca la danza la gota

r The sound represented by **r** in Spanish spelling is completely different from the one represented by *r* in English spelling. It consists of a single flap made by a rapid tap of the tongue against the gum ridge above the upper teeth. A similar sound exists in American English and is represented in English spelling by *t, d, tt, dd* between vowels (where the first vowel is stressed).

later spider batter ladder

Repeat the following words after the speaker, being careful to use a flap similar to the one appearing in the English words above.

cara cero poro toro cura lira

The flap occurring after an unstressed vowel is harder for English speakers to produce.

pirata parece morimos directo

The single flap /r/ is also used after consonants (written **r**).

preso traste cromo grande bravo drama frota

Spanish also has a trilled consonant /rr/ represented at the beginning of words by **r** and between vowels as **rr**. This sound consists of two or more flaps of the tongue against the upper gum ridge; it does not exist in American English. Repeat the following words after the speaker:

carro forro perro burrito ferrocarril amarramos
rato ropa reto rico ruso raqueta

Before another consonant or at the end of a word, the letter **r** may be pronounced either /r/ or /rr/, depending on the speaker and the degree of emphasis. Repeat the following words after the speaker:

puerta corto carpa tomar meter ser

j In Spanish spelling, the letter **j** and the letter **g** before **e** and **i** (but not before **a**, **o**, **u** or a consonant) represent a sound that does not exist in English and that we transcribe as /x/. The sound /x/ differs from /k/ in the same way that [g̶] differs from [g]: It is produced by forcing air through a narrow opening between the arched back of the tongue and the soft palate. For many Spanish speakers, especially those from the Caribbean, /x/ is usually replaced by /h/, as in English *hope*. Repeat the following words after the speaker:

jota jefe gente gime jale
lijo moja ajo teje caja
lijar mojar ají tejer cajera

ll/y Both **ll** and **y** represent the sound /y/. This sound is considerably tenser than the initial sound in English *yes*. English speakers must pay special attention to /y/, especially when it occurs between vowels. Repeat the following words after the speaker:

llamo hallo arroyo bello rayo yerno yodo

l Spanish **l** is pronounced very much like the /l/ sound in English *leak* and *less*. The tip of the tongue touches the gum ridge above the upper teeth, and air is forced out on the sides of the tongue. For final /l/ in English (as in *sell, tall, cool, full*), the tip of the tongue is lowered and the tongue is arched. In Spanish, final /l/ is pronounced exactly like initial /l/. Repeat the following words after the speaker:

lata lema liso losa luna
cal hiel gila col tul

p, t, k The sounds /p/, /t/, and /k/ before stressed vowels differ from their closest English counterparts by being unaspirated. The term "unaspirated" refers to the absence of the puff of air that follows these sounds in English. If you say English *pale, tale,* or *kale* while holding a lighted match at your mouth, the puff of air following /p/, /t/, or /k/ will extinguish the flame, because /p/, /t/, and /k/ are aspirated in English. However, when a Spanish speaker holds a lighted match at his mouth and says **pon**, **ten**, or **con**, the match does not go out, because /p/, /t/, and /k/ are unaspirated in Spanish.

While English /t/ is made by touching the gum ridge above the upper teeth, for Spanish /t/, the tip of the tongue touches the back of the upper teeth.

In Spanish, /k/ is spelled **qu** before **e** and **i**, but **c** is used elsewhere. Repeat the following words after the speaker:

panes pozo plano pica prado rompió toparon
tapa teme tripas tiza tope quitó votamos
cama queso quise clase creo coloqué cubre

s For all Spanish Americans and many Spaniards in southern Spain, the letters **s**, **z**, and **c** (when it appears before **e** and **i**) represent a sound similar to the one represented by *s* in English *sale*, *so*, and *see*. Repeat the following words after the speaker:

sala posa rosas comes cinco cacería
mozo luz luces haces zapato zurdo

f, m, n, ch These letters and combination of letters in Spanish represent sounds similar to their English counterparts. Repeat the following words after the speaker:

feo rifa mono lima nariz zona chato techo

h In Spanish spelling, **h** represents no sound—it is a silent letter, as in English *honor*. Repeat the following words after the speaker:

hablo haber han historia hombre humano

ñ The mark above the **n** is called a **tilde**. This letter represents a sound similar to the one written as *ni* in English *onion*. However, in English, the /n/ and the /y/ are pronounced in different syllables; in Spanish, the /ny/ goes with the following vowel. This sound is rare at the beginning of a word.

año piña uña mañas riñen ñame

c/z A major geographical variation in Spanish revolves around the pronunciation of the letter **c** before **e** and **i**, and the letter **z**. In Spanish America, these letters represent the sound /s/. However, in central and northern Spain, and in the speech of many speakers in southern Spain as well, these letters represent a sound similar to English *th* in *think*, *thank*, *cloth*. The phonetic symbol for this sound is the Greek letter theta, /θ/.

Dialects that distinguish the two sounds are described as having *distinción*. Dialects that do not have *distinción* pronounce **casa** and **caza** the same. Thus, in Spain, these pairs of words are pronounced differently, whereas in Spanish America, they are pronounced alike.

		SPAIN		SPANISH AMERICA	
casa *house*	caza *hunt*	/kasa/	/kaθa/	/kasa/	/kasa/
coser *sew*	cocer *cook*	/koser/	/koθer/	/koser/	/koser/
caso *case*	cazo *ladle*	/kaso/	/kaθo/	/kaso/	/kaso/

SPELLING

The Spanish Alphabet

a	a	**j**	jota	**r**	erre
b	be	**k**	ka	**s**	ese
c	ce	**l**	ele	**t**	te
d	de	**m**	eme	**u**	u
e	e	**n**	ene	**v**	uve
f	efe	**ñ**	eñe	**w**	doble uve
g	ge	**o**	o	**x**	equis
h	hache	**p**	pe	**y**	ye
i	i	**q**	cu	**z**	zeta

THE SPANISH ALPHABET

The Real Academia Española is Spain's official institution for overseeing the Spanish language. In 2010, it instituted a series of spelling reforms designed to standardize orthography. The Spanish alphabet was reduced to 27 letters, omitting the digraphs **ch** (**che** or **ce hache**) and **ll** (**doble ele**), which had been officially recognized letters. Today, the Spanish alphabet has the same letters as the English alphabet, plus **ñ**. In speech, many Spanish speakers disambiguate certain pairs of letters as follows: **b** = **be de burro, be grande, be larga** and **v** = **ve de vaca, ve chica, ve corta**; **i** = **i latina** and **y** = **i griega.** The digraph **rr** (**doble erre**) is not a letter of the alphabet.

Syllabification

A syllable in Spanish may consist of a single vowel, a diphthong, or a vowel or diphthong together with its preceding and following consonants. The following rules guide syllabification in Spanish.

1 · A single consonant between vowels goes with the following vowel.

rei-na a-mo ma-tan cau-sas te-mi-do

2 · Groups of two consonants that can begin a word (**p**, **t**, **c**, **b**, **d**, **g**, **f** + **l** or **r**) go with the following vowel.

co-pla ha-blo sue-gra pa-dre co-fre

3 · Other groups of two consonants are divided as follows:

him-no es-ta mun-do fal-ta sor-do

4 · Groups of three consonants are divided according to Rules 2 and 3. When the last two consonants of the three form one of the groups mentioned in Rule 2, they both go with the following vowel.

ram-bla ham-bre con-tra san-gre as-tro

If the last two consonants of a three-consonant cluster do not form one of the groups in Rule 2, only the third consonant goes with the following vowel.

ist-mo trans-ferir trans-porte

5 · Groups of four consonants are divided after the second consonant.

mons-truo ins-trumento ins-crito trans-plante

Accentuation

1 · Spanish words ending in a vowel or the letters **-n** or **-s** are stressed on the next-to-last syllable.

tri**s**te **ha**blan escri**ben** seño**ri**tas pro**vin**cias

2 · Spanish words ending in a consonant other than **-n** or **-s** (usually **-d**, **-l**, **-z**, **-r**) are stressed on the last syllable.

a**zul** ho**tel** Bra**sil** ve**jez** termi**nar** se**ñor** us**ted**

3 · When **i** or **u** precedes or follows **a**, **e**, or **o**, the two vowels are pronounced as one syllable.

estud**io** **sie**te **cien**c**ia** lim**pio** **seis** **cuan**do es**cue**la res**tau**rante

Combinations of **a**, **e**, and **o** form two syllables, not one.

tar**ea** mus**eo** m**ae**stro pr**eo**cupado des**ea**

4 · A written accent mark is required in Spanish when the stress of a word does not occur as presented above.

alemán inglés Canadá está cafés también
sábado jóvenes miércoles exámenes médico química
lápiz fácil Pérez rápido tránsito pantalón

In the following words, the combination of **i** or **u** + vowel forms two syllables, not one as in Rule 3, because here the /i/ and the /u/ are stressed. A written accent is therefore placed over the **i** or the **u**.

día tío economía biología reúne baúl actúa

5 · Words that are spelled the same but have different meanings are distinguished in writing by a written accent mark.

él *he, him*	el *the*
tú *you* (familiar)	tu *your*
más *more*	mas *but*
mí *me*	mi *my*
sí *yes*	si *if*
sólo *only*	solo *alone*

Punctuation and Capitalization

1 · Spanish questions are written with an inverted question mark (¿) at the beginning and a regular question mark (?) at the end.

¿Habla usted español?	*Do you speak Spanish?*

2 · Exclamations in Spanish begin with an inverted exclamation point (¡) and end with a regular exclamation point (!).

¡Qué va!	*You're kidding!*

3 · Interrogative words in Spanish are written with an accent mark.

¿Quién?	*Who?*
¿Qué?	*What?*
¿Cuándo?	*When?*
¿Dónde?	*Where?*

4 · Languages, nationalities, days of the week, and months of the year are written with an initial lowercase letter in Spanish, rather than with a capital letter as in English.

mexicano	*Mexican*
americano	*American*
viernes	*Friday*
marzo	*March*

5 · Subject pronouns in Spanish follow a different capitalization pattern than subject pronouns in English. **Yo** (*I*) is written with an initial lowercase letter when it is not the first word in a sentence. Likewise, **usted** (*you*, formal singular) and **ustedes** (*you*, formal plural; also informal plural in Spanish America) are written with an initial lowercase letter when they are not the first word in a sentence. However, they are often abbreviated in writing as **Ud.** and **Uds.**; when abbreviated, they begin with a capital **U**.

1

Getting Around Town—Where Is It?

Communication Goals

- Talking about gift-giving
- Asking for directions in a Spanish-speaking city
- Talking about shopping
- Getting attention to ask for information
- Vocabulary: everyday items, numbers 1 to 20

Grammar Topics

- **Hay** *there is, there are*
- **Ser** *to be* (third person singular)
- Articles and Gender of Nouns
- Question Formation
- Negative Sentences
- Plural Nouns
- Compound Nouns
- Numbers 1 to 20
- Noun Phrases

DIÁLOGO 1 · ¿Qué hay en la caja?

Study the dialogue, then listen to the recording and repeat each line.

ALEJANDRA	¿Qué hay en la caja?
BENJAMÍN	Una cámara.
ALEJANDRA	¿Es un regalo?
BENJAMÍN	Sí, es un regalo para Paula.

Análisis

Check that you understand the linguistic breakdown of each speech from *Diálogo 1.*

¿Qué hay en la caja?	*What is (there) in the box?*
¿Qué?	*What?*
hay	*is there*
en	*in*
la	*the* (feminine definite article)
caja	*box* (feminine noun)
en la caja	*in the box*
Una cámara.	*A camera.*
una	*a, an* (feminine indefinite article)
cámara	*camera* (feminine noun)
una cámara	*a camera*
¿Es un regalo?	*Is it a gift?*
es	*it is, he is, she is, you* (formal singular) *are* (**ser**)
un	*a, an* (masculine indefinite article)
un regalo	*a gift*
Sí, es un regalo para Paula.	*Yes, it's a gift for Paula.*
sí	*yes*
para	*for*
para Paula	*for Paula*

Variantes

Listen, and repeat the same structures from *Diálogo 1*, now with new vocabulary.

¿Qué hay en la caja ?	*What is* ***in the box?***
en la bolsa	*in the bag*
en la carpeta	*in the folder*
en la maleta	*in the suitcase*
en la gaveta	*in the drawer*
en la mochila	*in the backpack*
en el paquete	*in the package*
en el cartapacio	*in the briefcase*
en el armario	*in the closet*
en el maletín	*in the attaché case*
en el estante	*on the shelf*
Hay una cámara en la caja.	*There's* ***a camera*** *in the box.*
una computadora	*a computer*
una agenda electrónica	*an electronic appointment book*
un libro	*a book*
un CD (cedé)	*a CD*
un iPod	*an iPod*
un teléfono	*a telephone*
un (teléfono) celular	*a cell phone*

Hay una cámara en la caja.	*There's **a camera** in the box.*
un móvil	*a cell phone* (Spain)
una cartera	*a wallet* (for some speakers, *handbag*)
un bolso	*a handbag*
un billetero	*a wallet*
¿Qué hay en la caja? ¿Un regalo?	*What's in the box? A gift?*
No, no es un regalo.	*No, it's not a gift.*
¿Qué hay en la caja? ¿Un reloj?	*What's in the box? A wristwatch?*
No, es una pulsera.	*No, it's a bracelet.*
¿Es un regalo?	*Is it a gift?*
No, no es un regalo.	*No, it's not a gift.*
¿Es un regalo para Gabriela?	*Is it a gift for Gabriela?*
No, no es para Gabriela.	*No, it's not for Gabriela.*

Estructura y Práctica

Hay *there is, there are*

The word **hay** is an irregular verb form meaning *there is, there are.* It can be followed by either a singular or a plural noun.

Hay un regalo en la caja.	***There's a gift*** *in the box.*
Hay regalos en la caja.	***There are gifts*** *in the box.*

The noun that follows **hay** is considered to be the direct object of the verb. The direct object is a noun or pronoun that completes the thought of a verb by serving as the goal of the action.

¿Hay **regalos** en la caja? (*direct object noun*)	*Are there **gifts** in the box?*
Sí, **los** hay. (*direct object pronoun*)	*Yes, there are.*
¿Hay **carpetas** en la gaveta? (*direct object noun*)	*Are there **folders** in the drawer?*
Sí, **las** hay. (*direct object pronoun*)	*Yes, there are.*

Ser *to be* (third person singular)

The verb form **es** means *you are* (formal singular), as well as *he/she/it is.* It is a form of the irregular verb **ser** (*to be*). (See also Chapters 2, 3, and 4.)

¿Qué hay en el paquete?	*What is (there) in the package?*
Es un regalo.	***It's*** *a gift.*

A ***¿Qué hay?*** Express each dialogue exchange in Spanish.

1. *What's in the briefcase?*
   There's a cell phone in the briefcase.
2. *Are there folders in the drawer?*
   Yes, there are.

3. *What's on the shelf?*
   There are books on the shelf.
4. *Are there CDs in the package?*
   Yes, there are.
5. *Is there a computer in the backpack?*
   No, there's a camera.

B ***¿Qué hay en la caja?*** Write a sentence to tell what gift is in each box, using **es** and the noun provided. Include the corresponding indefinite article (**un**, **una**). Follow the *modelo.*

MODELO libro
→ Es un libro.

1. billetero
2. cartera
3. reloj
4. agenda electrónica
5. bolso
6. cámara
7. iPod
8. cartapacio

C ***¿Para quién es el regalo?*** **(Whom is the gift for?)** Write sentences stating that the gift mentioned is not for the person named in the first cue, but rather for the person named in the second cue. Follow the *modelo.*

MODELO libro: Ricardo / Tomás
→ El libro no es para Ricardo. Es para Tomás.

1. billetero: José / Juan
2. cartera: Matilde / Julia
3. reloj: Jorge / Alberto
4. agenda electrónica: Lorenzo / Nora
5. bolso: Rosa / Margarita
6. cámara: Luz / Daniel
7. iPod: Susana / Guillermo
8. cartapacio: Carlos / Roberto

SPELLING

After **g** and **q** and before the vowels **e** and **i**, the letter **u** does not represent a vowel, but is merely a spelling convention. The combinations of letters **gue** and **gui** represent the spoken syllables /ge/ and /gi/ (with the **g** pronounced as in English *go*), respectively: **juguete**, **guitarra**. The combinations of letters **que** and **qui** represent the spoken syllables /ke/ and /ki/, respectively: **paquete**, **embarque**, **aquí**.

Articles and Gender of Nouns

Articles

Like English, Spanish has a definite article equivalent to *the* and an indefinite article equivalent to *a, an*. The Spanish articles agree in gender and number with the noun they are associated with.

Here are the forms of the definite article in Spanish.

	MASCULINE	FEMININE
SINGULAR	**el** carro (*car*)	**la** caja
PLURAL	**los** carros	**las** cajas

Here are the forms of the indefinite article in Spanish.

	MASCULINE	FEMININE
SINGULAR	**un** carro	**una** caja
PLURAL	**unos** carros	**unas** cajas

The plural forms of the indefinite article in Spanish are sometimes not translated, and sometimes they are the equivalent of English *some*. They are also used before nouns that usually come in pairs, such as *eyes*, *ears*, or nouns that have no singular, such as *scissors*.

Gender of Nouns

Spanish nouns are divided into two broad classes, traditionally called masculine and feminine. Most (but not all) nouns referring to males are masculine, and most (but not all) nouns referring to females are feminine. Inanimate nouns such as **regalo** and **caja** are assigned to one of the two classes, usually (but not always) on the basis of their endings.

1 · Most nouns ending in -**o** are masculine, while most nouns ending in -**a** are feminine.

2 · Nouns ending in -**e** or a consonant typically give no clue as to gender (unless they refer to people), so their gender must be learned as you learn the noun.

The following nouns are all masculine.

el aceite *oil*
el aire *air*
el análisis *analysis*
el animal *animal*
el arete *earring*
el automóvil *car*
el bar *bar*
el billete *ticket, bill* (currency)
el café *café*
el cibercafé *internet café*
el cine *movie theater*
el coche *car*
el estante *shelf*
el examen *exam*
el hospital *hospital*
el hotel *hotel*
el informe *report*
el juguete *toy*
el lápiz *pencil*
el lugar *place*
el maletín *attaché case*
el mes *month*
el papel *paper*
el paquete *package*
el pez *fish*
el plan *plan*
el reloj *wristwatch*
el tren *train*

The following nouns are all feminine.

la base *base*
la calle *street*
la catedral *cathedral*
la ciudad *city*
la clase *class*
la crisis *crisis*
la flor *flower*
la gente *people*
la llave *key*
la luz *light*
la nariz *nose*
la paz *peace*
la piel *skin*
la pirámide *pyramid*
la red *web, internet*
la sed *thirst*
la suerte *luck*
la torre *tower*
la tos *cough*
la verdad *truth*
la vez *time* (*occasion*)
la voz *voice*

3 · The following suffixes indicate feminine nouns.

-ción, -ión la nación, la religión, la unión
-tad, -dad la libertad, la nacionalidad, la felicidad (*happiness*)
-tud la gratitud, la virtud, la juventud (*youth*)
-ie la serie (*series*), la superficie (*surface*)

4 · Some nouns have anomalous genders.

la mano *hand*
la moto (la motocicleta) *motorcycle*
la foto (la fotografía) *photograph*
el día *day*
el mapa *map*
el tranvía *trolley*

5 · Many nouns ending in **-ma** (usually international words borrowed from Greek) are masculine.

el clima *climate*
el drama *drama*
el idioma *language*
el poema *poem*
el problema *problem*
el programa *program*
el sistema *system*
el tema *subject*
el trauma *trauma*

D **Nouns and articles.** Write the correct definite and indefinite articles for each noun. Follow the *modelo.*

MODELO libro
→ el libro un libro

1. maleta
2. coche
3. reloj
4. clase
5. hotel
6. oficina
7. cosa (*thing*)
8. mano
9. cámara
10. paquete
11. teléfono
12. flor
13. problema
14. ciudad
15. maletín
16. tema

E Unscramble the letters in each item to form a Spanish noun. Write the noun and the definite article for each noun.

1. e m s
2. n e e g t
3. h o a m i l c
4. r a c o r
5. g e a o r l
6. t a m a l e
7. s l a e c
8. a o p r c a d m u t o
9. b o l r i
10. j e o l r

F **Sentence completion.** Select the correct word or phrase that completes each sentence. Write the word or phrase that you have selected.

1. Es un ______________ celular.
   a. teléfono b. computadora
2. ¿Qué hay en la ______________?
   a. paquete b. cartera
3. No hay gente en ______________.
   a. la gaveta b. el cibercafé
4. ¿Qué libros ______________ en el estante?
   a. hay b. es
5. —¿Hay documentos? —Sí, ______________ la carpeta.
   a. para b. en
6. Hay una ______________ en la caja.
   a. pulsera b. juguete
7. —¿Hay maletas en el armario? —Sí, ______________ hay.
   a. las b. los
8. Es un ______________.
   a. clase b. cartapacio

Question Formation: Information Questions, Yes/No Questions

There are two types of questions in Spanish: yes/no questions and information questions. In Spanish, all questions are written with an inverted question mark at the beginning of the sentence and a regular question mark at the end. Information questions begin with a question word. They expect a piece of information as an answer. (See also Chapters 2 and 3.)

¿**Qué** hay en la maleta?	***What*** *is in the suitcase?*
¿**Qué** es?	***What*** *is it?*
¿**Para quién** es el regalo?	***Whom*** *is the gift* ***for****?*

Questions not beginning with a question word are called yes/no questions, that is, they ask for either *yes* or *no* as an answer.

¿Hay libros en la mochila?	*Are there books in the backpack?*
Sí, los hay.	*Yes, there are.*
No, no los hay.	*No, there aren't.*

The most common way to ask a yes/no question is to change the intonation from statement intonation to rising question intonation. This is shown in writing by enclosing the sentence in question marks.

El bolso es para Raquel.	*The handbag is for Raquel.*
¿El bolso es para Raquel?	*Is the handbag for Raquel?*

The subject can also be placed after the verb.

Antonio trabaja por aquí.	*Antonio works around here.*
¿Trabaja Antonio por aquí? (**trabajar** (*to work*))	*Does Antonio work around here?*

When a question includes a form of the verb **ser** + an adjective, the subject is placed at the end of the sentence. The pattern of the question is thus verb + adjective + subject.

El hotel es cómodo.	*The hotel is comfortable.*
¿Es cómodo el hotel?	*Is the hotel comfortable?*

G ***Preguntas* (Questions).** Write a yes/no question or an information question from each string of elements. Follow the *modelo.*

MODELO una / es / bolsa
→ ¿Es una bolsa?

1. hay / en el armario / qué
2. regalo / es / un
3. cómodo / el hotel / es
4. flores / hay / qué
5. en / cafés / hay / la ciudad / qué
6. papeles / en / unos / hay / la mochila
7. hay / los estantes / qué / en / libros
8. para / el juguete / es / Juanito

Negative Sentences

Spanish sentences are made negative by placing **no** before the verb.

No hay restaurantes por aquí.	*There are* ***no*** *restaurants around here.*

To form negative questions (*isn't, aren't, doesn't,* etc.), the negative statement is spoken with rising intonation.

¿No hay un hotel por aquí?	*Isn't there a hotel around here?*

No is the equivalent of both the English response *no* and a marker of negation. Therefore, many negative responses to questions have two occurrences of **no**.

¿Hay unos bancos por aquí?	*Are there any banks around here?*
No, no hay.	*No, there aren't.*

H Restate each sentence in the negative.

1. La cámara es un regalo.
2. Hay una computadora en el armario.
3. Es un iPod.
4. El paquete es para Miguel.
5. Hay un cibercafé por aquí.
6. Hay maletas en el carro.
7. Es una oficina cómoda.
8. Hay dinero (*money*) en el billetero.

I *¡No!* Answer each question in the negative. Follow the *modelo*.

MODELO ¿Hay un banco por aquí?
→ No, no hay un banco por aquí.

1. ¿Es una agenda electrónica?
2. ¿Hay libros en el estante?
3. ¿El reloj es para Carlos?
4. ¿Hay un supermercado por aquí?
5. ¿Es un regalo para Julieta?
6. ¿Hay ropa (*clothing*) en la maleta?
7. ¿Hay un cartapacio en la oficina?
8. ¿Es un problema?

DIÁLOGO 2 · Hay dos farmacias.

Study the dialogue, then listen to the recording and repeat each line.

BENJAMÍN ¿Hay una farmacia por aquí?
ALEJANDRA Hay dos farmacias.
BENJAMÍN ¿Dónde?
ALEJANDRA Hay una en la esquina y otra en frente.

Análisis

Check that you understand the linguistic breakdown of each speech from *Diálogo 2*.

¿Hay una farmacia por aquí?	*Is there a drugstore around here?*
una farmacia	*a drugstore, a pharmacy*
por	*around, in the area of*
aquí	*here*
por aquí	*around here*
Hay dos farmacias.	*There are two drugstores.*
dos	*two*
farmacias	*drugstores*
¿Dónde?	*Where?*
Hay una en la esquina y otra en frente.	*There's one on the corner and another one across the street.*
una	*one* (feminine indefinite article)
la esquina	*street corner*
en la esquina	*on/at the corner*

y	*and*
otra	*another one* (feminine)
en frente	*across the street, opposite*
y otra en frente	*and another one across the street*

Variantes

Listen, and repeat the same structures from *Diálogo 2*, now with new vocabulary.

¿Hay una farmacia por aquí?	*Is there* ***a drugstore*** *around here?*
una oficina de turismo	*a tourist office*
un supermercado	*a supermarket*
una peluquería	*a hair salon, a barber shop*
un café	*a café*
un bar	*a bar*
un restaurante	*a restaurant*
una librería	*a bookstore*
un cine	*a movie theater*
un teatro	*a theater*
un hotel	*a hotel*
una heladería	*an ice cream shop*
un hospital	*a hospital*
Hay dos farmacias por aquí.	*There are* ***two drugstores*** *around here.*
dos oficinas de turismo	*two tourist offices*
tres hoteles	*three hotels*
cuatro supermercados	*four supermarkets*
cinco peluquerías	*five hair salons, five barber shops*
seis cafés	*six cafés*
siete teatros	*seven theaters*
ocho bares	*eight bars*
nueve restaurantes	*nine restaurants*
diez librerías	*ten bookstores*
¿Hay un supermercado por aquí?	*Is there a supermarket around here?*
No, no hay.	*No, there isn't.*
¿No hay un restaurante por aquí?	*Isn't there a restaurant around here?*
No, no hay.	*No, there isn't.*
¿Hay farmacias por aquí?	*Are there any drugstores around here?*
No, no hay.	*No, there aren't.*
¿No hay librerías por aquí?	*Aren't there any bookstores around here?*
No, no hay.	*No, there aren't.*

Estructura y Práctica

Plural Nouns

Spanish forms the plural of nouns by adding **-s** to nouns ending in a vowel and **-es** to nouns ending in a consonant. The **s** of the plural is always pronounced /s/, never /z/.

SINGULAR	PLURAL
cuarto (*room*)	cuarto**s**
persona	persona**s**
estante	estante**s**
cibercafé	cibercafé**s**
señor	señor**es**
catedral	catedral**es**

When the last syllable of a noun ending in a consonant has an accent mark, that accent mark is eliminated when the **-es** plural ending is added.

SINGULAR	PLURAL
maletín	maleti**nes**
nación (*nation*)	nacio**nes**
inglés (*Englishman*)	ingle**ses**
alemán (*German*)	alema**nes**

El país (*country*) is an exception: **los países.**

A singular noun that ends in a consonant and is stressed on the next-to-last syllable adds a written accent on the vowel of that stressed syllable when the **-es** plural ending is added. These apparent irregularities follow the rules for the placement of accent marks in Spanish.

SINGULAR	PLURAL
joven	j**ó**ven**es**
examen	ex**á**men**es**
origen	or**í**gen**es**

SPELLING

Nouns ending in **-z** change **-z** to **-c** when the plural ending **-es** is added.

el pez (*fish*) → los pe**ces**
la voz (*voice*) → las vo**ces**
el lápiz → los lápi**ces** (*retains the written accent*)

J **Nouns and articles in the plural.** Write the plural form of each noun with its corresponding definite and indefinite articles. Follow the *modelo*.

MODELO libro
→ los libros unos libros

1. maleta
2. cine
3. reloj
4. librería
5. problema
6. oficina
7. teatro
8. restaurante
9. papel
10. ciudad
11. teléfono
12. flor
13. mes
14. calle
15. maletín
16. luz

K Write the singular form of each noun with its corresponding definite and indefinite articles.

1. libros
2. bolsas
3. clases
4. lugares
5. hoteles
6. llaves
7. trenes
8. animales
9. cosas
10. veces
11. pulseras
12. cámaras
13. mapas
14. temas
15. cafés
16. hospitales

DIÁLOGO 3 · ¿Hay un cibercafé por aquí?

Study the dialogue, then listen to the recording and repeat each line.

BENJAMÍN	Perdón, ¿hay un cibercafé por aquí?
ALEJANDRA	Sí, hay uno en la esquina.
BENJAMÍN	Muchas gracias, señorita.
ALEJANDRA	De nada, señor. Adiós.

Análisis

Check that you understand the linguistic breakdown of each speech from *Diálogo 3*.

Perdón, ¿hay un cibercafé por aquí?	*Excuse me. Is there an internet café around here?*
Perdón	*Excuse me, Pardon me*
un cibercafé	*an internet café*

Sí, hay uno en la esquina. — *Yes, there's one on the corner.*
uno — *one* (masculine)

Muchas gracias, señorita. — *Thank you very much, miss.*
gracias — *thank you*
muchas gracias — *thank you very much*
señorita — *miss*

De nada, señor. Adiós. — *You're welcome, sir. Goodbye.*
de nada — *you're welcome*
señor — *sir*
adiós — *goodbye*

Variantes

Listen, and repeat the same structure from *Diálogo 3*, now with new vocabulary.

Perdón, señorita. — ***Excuse me**, miss.*
Oiga — *Say* (literally, *Hear, Listen*)
Por favor — *Please*

Estructura y Práctica

GETTING ATTENTION TO ASK FOR INFORMATION

Words such as **Perdón** (*Excuse me*) and **Oiga** (*Say, Hey* (literally, *Hear, Listen*)) can be used to get someone's attention when you want to ask a question. They are often followed by the appropriate form of address.

Perdón/Oiga, señor (*sir*), **señora** (*ma'am*), **señorita** (*miss*).

These expressions can often be used when stopping someone on the street to ask directions, as illustrated in the dialogues of this chapter.

Perdón, señorita. ¿Hay una oficina de turismo por aquí? — *Excuse me, miss. Is there a tourist office around here?*

L **Asking for and getting directions.** Express each dialogue in Spanish.

1. *Excuse me, sir. Is there a bank around here?*
   Yes, miss, there's one on the corner.
   Thank you, sir.
   You're welcome. Goodbye.

2. *Please, miss. Where* (¿Dónde?) *is there a hair salon?*
   There's one on the corner, ma'am.
   Thank you very much, miss.
   You're welcome, ma'am.

DIÁLOGO 4 · El centro comercial

Study the dialogue, then listen to the recording and repeat each line.

ALEJANDRA	Hay veinte tiendas en el centro comercial.
BENJAMÍN	¿Qué tiendas hay?
ALEJANDRA	Hay zapaterías, tiendas de ropa, jugueterías, una heladería, una tienda de deportes, una tienda por departamentos.
BENJAMÍN	¿Hay una tienda de electrodomésticos también?
ALEJANDRA	Claro que sí. Y una tienda de cómputo.

Análisis

Check that you understand the linguistic breakdown of each speech from *Diálogo 4*.

Hay veinte tiendas en el centro comercial.	*There are 20 stores in the shopping center.*
veinte	*20*
la tienda	*store*
veinte tiendas	*20 stores*
el centro comercial	*shopping center*
¿Qué tiendas hay?	*What stores are there?*
Hay zapaterías, tiendas de ropa, jugueterías, una heladería, una tienda de deportes, una tienda por departamentos.	*There are shoe stores, clothing stores, toy stores, an ice cream shop, a sporting goods store, a department store.*
el zapato	*shoe*
la zapatería	*shoe store*
la ropa	*clothing*
la tienda de ropa	*clothing store*
el juguete	*toy*
la juguetería	*toy store*
el helado	*ice cream*
la heladería	*ice cream shop*
el deporte	*sport*
la tienda de deportes	*sporting goods store*
el departamento	*department*
la tienda por departamentos	*department store*
¿Hay una tienda de electrodomésticos también?	*Is there an appliance store, too?*
el electrodoméstico	*household appliance*
los electrodomésticos	*household appliances*
la tienda de electrodomésticos	*appliance store*
también	*too*
Claro que sí. Y una tienda de cómputo.	*Yes, of course. And a computer store.*
claro	*of course*
sí	*yes*
claro que sí	*of course*
la tienda de cómputo	*computer store*

Variantes

Listen, and repeat the same structure from *Diálogo 4*, now with new vocabulary.

Hay once zapaterías en el centro.	*There are **11 shoe stores** downtown.*
doce librerías	*12 bookstores*
trece tiendas de deportes	*13 sporting goods stores*
catorce heladerías	*14 ice cream shops*
quince tiendas de ropa	*15 clothing stores*
dieciséis farmacias	*16 drugstores*
diecisiete teatros	*17 theaters*
dieciocho hoteles	*18 hotels*
diecinueve cibercafés	*19 internet cafés*
veinte restaurantes	*20 restaurants*

¿Hay helado?	*Is there any ice cream?*
No, no hay helado.	*No, there isn't any ice cream.*
No, no hay.	*No, there isn't.*

¿No hay helado?	*Isn't there any ice cream?*
No, no hay.	*No, there isn't.*

¿Hay una tienda de electrodomésticos también?	*Is there an appliance store, too?*
No, no hay.	*No, there isn't.*

¿No hay una joyería también?	*Isn't there a jewelry store, too?*
No, no hay.	*No, there isn't.*

Estructura y Práctica

Compound Nouns

Many Spanish compound nouns are formed with the preposition **de** (*of, from*). The English equivalent of these compound nouns usually consists of two juxtaposed nouns, but in the opposite order of that seen in Spanish.

tienda + zapatos → tienda de zapatos	*store + shoe(s) → shoe store*
tienda + electrodomésticos → tienda de electrodomésticos	*store + appliance(s) → appliance store*
museo + arte → museo de arte	*museum + art → art museum*
base + datos → base de datos	*base + data → database*
libro + texto → libro de texto	*book + text → textbook*
tarjeta + embarque → tarjeta de embarque	*pass + boarding → boarding pass*
tarjeta + crédito → tarjeta de crédito	*card + credit → credit card*
salón + belleza → salón de belleza	*salon + beauty → beauty salon*

Sometimes other prepositions are used instead of **de**.

la tienda **por** departamentos	*department store*

To make a compound noun plural, the noun preceding the preposition is made plural, but the noun following the preposition is not.

las quince nuevas **tiendas de cómputo**	*the 15 new **computer stores***

Compound nouns function like any other noun. They can be the subject or object of a verb, and they can be the object of a preposition.

La tienda por departamentos es muy grande.	*The department store is very big.*
Trabaja en la oficina de turismo.	*He works at the tourist office.*

M ***Las tiendas.*** Write the name of each store in Spanish; then write its plural form. Include the definite article for both singular and plural. Each one is a compound noun.

1. *the clothing store*
2. *the computer store*
3. *the shoe store*
4. *the appliance store*
5. *the sporting goods store*
6. *the department store*

N Select a noun from the second column that forms a compound noun with a noun from the first column. Join the nouns with the preposition **de**. Write each compound noun; then write the plural of each compound noun. Include the definite article for both singular and plural.

1. libro	a. datos
2. base	b. crédito
3. museo	c. turismo
4. tarjeta	d. texto
5. oficina	e. belleza
6. salón	f. arte

Numbers 1 to 20

Numerals (**los números**) in Spanish present few problems. Here are the numbers from one to twenty.

1	uno	11	once
2	dos	12	doce
3	tres	13	trece
4	cuatro	14	catorce
5	cinco	15	quince
6	seis	16	dieciséis
7	siete	17	diecisiete
8	ocho	18	dieciocho
9	nueve	19	diecinueve
10	diez	20	veinte

The numbers **uno, una** are identical with the indefinite article and agree with the following noun in gender.

un libro	*a book, one book*
una computadora	*a computer, one computer*

The numbers 16 through 19 may be written as three words each, but this is increasingly less common: **diez y seis, diez y siete, diez y ocho, diez y nueve**.

O ***Los números 1–20.*** Express these noun phrases in Spanish. Write all numbers as words.

1. *1 computer*
2. *2 cities*
3. *3 watches*
4. *4 things*
5. *5 movie theaters*
6. *6 clothing stores*
7. *7 hotels*
8. *8 gifts*
9. *9 cameras*
10. *10 ice cream shops*
11. *11 boxes*
12. *12 internet cafés*
13. *13 backpacks*
14. *14 telephones*
15. *15 days*
16. *16 supermarkets*
17. *17 photos*
18. *18 department stores*
19. *19 packages*
20. *20 sports*

P ***¿Cómo?*** **(What?!)** Use **¿Cómo?** (*What?!*) to express surprise or incredulity when your friend tells you how many there are of each item mentioned. Write your response to each statement, using the interrogative words **¿Cuántos?** or **¿Cuántas?** (*How many?*). Note that these interrogative words agree in number and gender with the noun they refer to. Follow the *modelo*.

MODELO Hay veinte carpetas en la gaveta.
→ ¿Cómo? ¿Cuántas?

1. Hay cuatro cibercafés por aquí.
2. Hay catorce regalos para Antonio.
3. Hay tres farmacias en la esquina.
4. Hay diez libros de texto en la mochila.
5. Hay dieciocho tiendas de cómputo en el centro comercial.
6. Hay seis museos de arte en la ciudad.
7. Hay ocho personas en el carro.
8. Hay dieciséis maletas en el armario.
9. Hay doce cuartos en la casa.
10. Hay tres cámaras en la caja.

Noun Phrases

A noun and the words directly associated with it (articles, numbers, adjectives, demonstratives, possessives) form a noun phrase. In Spanish, almost all of the components of noun phrases change their form to match the gender and number of the noun. This change in form to match the noun is called agreement. In Spanish, an adjective agrees in gender and number with its noun: **un carro cómodo, una oficina cómoda**. (See also Chapter 2.)

Q Express each English noun phrase in Spanish. Write all numbers as words.

1. *an art museum*
2. *six months*
3. *the department store*
4. *a credit card*
5. *the shopping center*
6. *eleven computer stores*
7. *twenty packages*
8. *some cities*

Un paso más

Are you ready to take your Spanish a step further? Here are exercises that will enhance your knowledge of the language and encourage you to express yourself freely.

R **Cognates.** An English speaker learning Spanish soon realizes that the two languages share many words. Borrowings from English are common in Spanish, as are borrowings from Spanish in English, and both languages have many words of common origin. **El programa** and **la persona** are two of the many cognates that appear in this chapter. However, some words—like **la librería** (*bookstore*), **la carpeta** (*folder*), and **el idioma** (*language*)—are false cognates. They are similar in form but different in meaning. Write the Spanish words (including the definite article) that are cognates of the following English words.

1. *camera*
2. *document*
3. *system*
4. *telephone*
5. *computer*
6. *analysis*
7. *tourism*
8. *art*
9. *theater*
10. *credit*
11. *pharmacy*
12. *museum*
13. *text*
14. *supermarket*
15. *problem*
16. *department*
17. *map*
18. *bank*

S ***Preguntas personales.*** Answer each question with a complete Spanish sentence. Replace **su** (*your*) with **mi** (*my*) in your answers.

1. ¿Qué hay en su cartapacio? ¿En su maletín? ¿En su maleta?
2. ¿Hay un (teléfono) celular en su mochila? ¿Qué cosas hay en su mochila?
3. ¿Cuánto dinero hay en su billetero? (**el dólar / los dólares** = *dollar/dollars*)
4. ¿Hay una farmacia por aquí? ¿Un café? ¿Un restaurante? ¿Dónde?
5. ¿Hay un centro comercial por aquí? ¿Qué tiendas hay? ¿Cuántas hay?
6. ¿Hay un regalo en la caja? ¿Qué es? ¿Para quién es?
7. ¿Es cómoda su oficina?
8. ¿Qué libros hay en los estantes?
9. ¿Qué hay en las gavetas?
10. ¿Cuántos cuartos hay en su casa (*house*)?
11. ¿Cuántas personas hay en su familia?

2

Describing Places and Things

Communication Goals

- Describing places and things
- Asking about hotel accommodations
- Indicating possession
- Vocabulary: qualities and attributes of things, colors, academic subjects

Grammar Topics

- Agreement of Adjectives
- Position of Adjectives
- Short Forms of Adjectives
- **Ser** *to be* (third person plural)
- Contraction **del**
- Possessive Adjectives
- More on Question Formation
- Intensifiers
- Noun Phrase Functions

DIÁLOGO 1 · ¿Cómo es el hotel?

Study the dialogue, then listen to the recording and repeat each line.

DANIEL ¿Es cómodo el hotel?
CAMILA Sí, muy cómodo y muy moderno.
DANIEL ¿Tu habitación es grande?
CAMILA Sí, es una habitación grande y muy bonita.

Análisis

Check that you understand the linguistic breakdown of each speech from *Diálogo 1.*

¿Es cómodo el hotel?	*Is the hotel comfortable?*
es	*it is, he is, she is, you* (formal singular) *are* (**ser**)
cómodo	*comfortable*
el hotel	*hotel*
Sí, muy cómodo y muy moderno.	*Yes, very comfortable and very modern.*
muy	*very*
muy cómodo	*very comfortable*
moderno	*modern*
muy moderno	*very modern*
¿Tu habitación es grande?	*Is your room big?*
tu	*your* (informal, before a singular noun)
la habitación	*room* (*especially in a hotel or dorm*)
tu habitación	*your room*
grande	*big*
Sí, es una habitación grande y muy bonita.	*Yes, it's a big room, and very pretty.*
y	*and*
bonito	*pretty*
muy bonita	*very pretty* (feminine)

Variantes

Listen, and repeat the same structures from *Diálogo 1*, now with new vocabulary.

Mi habitación es grande.	*My room is* ***big****.*
pequeña	*small*
chiquita	*small*
oscura	*dark*
clara	*bright, light*
hermosa	*beautiful*
fea	*ugly*
Mi habitación es grande.	*My* ***room*** *is big.*
casa	*house*
oficina	*office*
patio	*yard, patio*
jardín	*garden, yard*
garaje	*garage*
apartamento	*apartment*
condominio	*condominium*
cuarto	*room*

Mi casa es cómoda.	*My house is comfortable.*
Tu	*Your* (informal)
Su	*His, her, your* (formal), *their*
Nuestra	*Our*
Mis regalos son hermosos.	*My gifts are beautiful.*
Tus	*Your* (informal)
Sus	*His, her, your* (formal), *their*
Nuestros	*Our*
¿Es muy grande su jardín?	*Is their garden very big?*
No, no es muy grande.	*No, it's not very big.*
¿Es oscura nuestra oficina?	*Is our office dark?*
No, no es oscura.	*No, it's not dark.*

Estructura y Práctica

Agreement of Adjectives

Spanish adjectives are part of the noun phrase. They modify or describe the noun that is the head of the noun phrase. Like all modifiers of nouns, Spanish adjectives agree with the noun. Most adjectives agree in gender and number, while some agree only in number.

Spanish adjectives are divided into two broad categories: adjectives that have a masculine singular form ending in **-o** and adjectives that have a masculine singular form ending in a consonant or in a vowel other than **-o**.

Adjectives that have a masculine singular form ending in **-o** have four forms. They agree in both gender and number with the noun they modify or describe. An **-s** is added to the singular forms to form the plural. This **s** is pronounced /s/ like the double *s* in English *class*, not /z/ like the single *s* in *present.*

	MASCULINE	FEMININE
SINGULAR	un reloj **hermoso**	una pulsera **hermosa**
PLURAL	unos relojes **hermosos**	unas pulseras **hermosas**

Adjectives that have a masculine singular form ending in a consonant or in a vowel other than **-o** have two forms. They agree in number with the noun they modify or describe, but they have the same form for both masculine and feminine.

Adjectives ending in a consonant add **-es** to form the plural.

	MASCULINE	FEMININE
SINGULAR	un libro **difícil**	una situación **difícil**
PLURAL	unos libros **difíciles**	unas situaciones **difíciles**

Adjectives ending in **-e** add **-s** to form the plural.

	MASCULINE	FEMININE
SINGULAR	un documento **interesante**	una revista (*magazine*) **interesante**
PLURAL	unos documentos **interesantes**	unas revistas **interesantes**

More Adjectives

bueno *good*	barato *inexpensive, cheap*
malo *bad*	lindo *nice, lovely, pretty* (Spanish America)
nuevo *new*	inteligente *intelligent*
viejo *old*	maravilloso *wonderful*
caro *expensive*	estupendo *great, amazing*

A ***También.*** Write sentences stating that the noun asked about has the same quality as the noun in the original sentence. Make necessary changes in the form of the adjective. Follow the *modelo.*

MODELO El apartamento es cómodo. ¿Y la oficina?
→ La oficina es cómoda también.

1. La casa es nueva. ¿Y el condominio?
2. El barrio es comercial. ¿Y la zona?
3. El museo de arte es maravilloso. ¿Y la catedral?
4. La heladería es animada (*bustling*). ¿Y el café?
5. El supermercado es grande. ¿Y la tienda por departamentos?
6. La mochila es pequeña. ¿Y el cartapacio?
7. La agenda electrónica es útil. ¿Y el celular?
8. El cuarto es oscuro. ¿Y la habitación?
9. El teléfono es viejo. ¿Y la cámara?
10. El patio es bonito. ¿Y la calle?

B ***Son así* (like this).** Write sentences stating that the plural noun asked about has the same quality as the singular noun in the original sentence. Make necessary changes in the form of the adjective. Follow the *modelo.*

MODELO El patio es bonito. ¿Y los jardines?
→ Los jardines son bonitos también.

1. El problema es difícil. ¿Y los exámenes?
2. El paquete es chiquito. ¿Y las cajas?
3. La pulsera es hermosa. ¿Y los relojes?
4. El salón de belleza es moderno. ¿Y las tiendas de deportes?
5. El libro es interesante. ¿Y las películas (*films*)?
6. La ropa es cara. ¿Y las joyas?

7. El hospital es grande. ¿Y las farmacias?
8. La maleta es buena. ¿Y los cartapacios?
9. El teléfono celular es útil. ¿Y las computadoras?
10. El cibercafé es malo. ¿Y los restaurantes?

DIÁLOGO 2 · Las calles del centro

Study the dialogue, then listen to the recording and repeat each line.

CAMILA ¿Cómo son las calles del centro?
DANIEL Son bonitas, pero muy transitadas.
CAMILA ¿Hay mucho ruido?
DANIEL Sí, las calles del centro son muy ruidosas.

Análisis

Check that you understand the linguistic breakdown of each speech from *Diálogo 2.*

¿Cómo son las calles del centro?	*What are the downtown streets like?*
¿Cómo?	*How?* (here, *What?*)
son	*they are* (**ser**)
¿Cómo son?	*What are they like?*
la calle	*street*
del	*of the* (contraction of **de** + **el**)
las calles del centro	*the downtown streets*
Son bonitas, pero muy transitadas.	*They're pretty, but very heavily trafficked.*
bonito	*pretty*
bonitas	*pretty* (feminine plural)
pero	*but*
transitado	*heavily trafficked, with a lot of traffic*
muy transitadas	*very heavily trafficked* (feminine plural)
¿Hay mucho ruido?	*Is there a lot of noise?*
mucho	*much, a lot (of)*
el ruido	*noise*
Sí, las calles del centro son muy ruidosas.	*Yes, the downtown streets are very noisy.*
ruidoso	*noisy*
muy ruidosas	*very noisy* (feminine plural)

Variantes

Listen, and repeat the same structures from *Diálogo 2*, now with new vocabulary.

Es una calle ruidosa .	*It's a **noisy** street.*
tranquila	*quiet, calm, peaceful*
animada	*bustling, busy*
comercial	*commercial*
peatonal	*pedestrian (allowing no vehicular traffic)*

Es una calle comercial.	*It's a commercial **street**.*
un barrio	*neighborhood*
una zona	*area*
una avenida	*avenue*
un paseo	*boulevard*

Estructura y Práctica

Position of Adjectives

In Spanish, adjectives normally follow the noun, rather than precede it as in English.

un hotel **moderno**	*a **modern** hotel*
una casa **cómoda**	*a **comfortable** house*
unos informes **importantes**	*some **important** reports*
unas programadoras **inteligentes**	*some **intelligent** programmers*

However, certain types of adjectives precede the noun they modify.

- Adjectives that express quantity

mucho, mucha *much, a lot of*
muchos, muchas *many, a lot of*
poco, poca *little, not much*
pocos, pocas *few, not many*
bastante, bastantes *quite a lot of* (Spanish America); *enough* (Spain)
suficiente, suficientes *enough*
¿cuánto? ¿cuánta? *how much?*
¿cuántos? ¿cuántas? *how many?*
alguno, alguna, algunos, algunas *some*
ninguno, ninguna *no, none*
ambos, ambas *both*
varios, varias *several*

muchos hoteles viejos	*many old hotels*
pocos restaurantes baratos	*few inexpensive restaurants*
ambas zonas comerciales	*both commercial areas*
suficiente dinero	*enough money*

The adjective **todo** also belongs in this category. (See also Chapter 3.)

todo el dinero	*all the money*
toda la ropa	*all the clothing*
todos los condominios nuevos	*all the new condominiums*
todas las maletas grises	*all the gray suitcases*

- Ordinal numbers

primero *first*	sexto *sixth*
segundo *second*	séptimo *seventh*
tercero *third*	octavo *eighth*
cuarto *fourth*	noveno *ninth*
quinto *fifth*	décimo *tenth*

el **primer** día	*the **first** day*
la **primera** semana	*the **first** week*
el **tercer** día	*the **third** day*
la **tercera** semana	*the **third** week*

- Adjectives used in exclamations after **¡Qué!** (See also Chapter 3.)

¡Qué **lindo** barrio!	*What a **lovely** neighborhood!*
¡Qué **hermosa** ciudad!	*What a **beautiful** city!*
¡Qué **feo** día!	*What a **nasty** day!*
¡Qué **maravillosa** tienda!	*What a **wonderful** store!*

- Adjectives that express a subjective judgment made by the speaker, rather than an objective description. The adjectives **bueno** (*good*), **malo** (*bad*), **mejor** (*better/best*), and **peor** (*worse/worst*) fall into this category.

una **buena** persona	*a **good** person*
un **mal** día	*a **bad** day*
los **peores** problemas posibles	*the **worst** problems possible*
la **mejor** idea	*the **best** idea*
un **horrible** accidente	*a **horrible** accident*
una **magnífica** oportunidad	*a **magnificent** opportunity*
un **bonito** regalo	*a **pretty** gift*

- Adjectives that express a quality known to all, rather than new information about the noun.

la **verde** hierba	*the **green** grass*
la **blanca** nieve	*the **white** snow*

Some adjectives can appear either before or after the noun. In these cases, the meaning changes depending on the position of the adjective.

nuestro **antiguo** profesor	*our **former** teacher*
un cementerio **antiguo**	*an **ancient** cemetery*
cierto análisis	*a **certain** analysis*
una cosa **cierta**	*a **sure** thing*
un **nuevo** proyecto	***another** project*
un proyecto **nuevo**	*a **new** project*
este **pobre** país	*this **poor** country (unfortunate)*
un país **pobre**	*a **poor** country (economically depressed)*
un **gran** hombre	*a **great** man*
un hombre **grande**	*a **big** man*
diferentes posibilidades	***various** possibilities*
posibilidades **diferentes**	***different** possibilities*
Luis es **medio** español.	*Luis is **half** Spanish.*
el español **medio**	*the **average** Spaniard*
Es el **mismo** programa.	*It's the **same** program.*
El problema es el programa **mismo**.	*The problem is the program **itself**.*

Las bebidas allí son **pura** agua.	*The drinks there are **nothing but** water.*
Hay que beber agua **pura**.	*You should drink **pure** water.*
un **simple** empleado	*a **mere** employee*
una muchacha **simple**	*a **simple** girl*
cualquier persona	***any** person*
una persona **cualquiera**	*a **vulgar** person*
la **única** persona	*the **only** person*
una persona **única**	*a **unique** person*

Short Forms of Adjectives

The adjectives **bueno** (*good*) and **malo** (*bad*), the ordinal numbers **primero** (*first*) and **tercero** (*third*), the indefinite article **uno**, and **alguno** (*some*) and **ninguno** (*no*) lose their final **-o** before a masculine singular noun or before an adjective preceding a masculine singular noun.

un **buen** libro	*a **good** book*
BUT	
una **buena** revista	*a **good** magazine*
un **mal** día	*a **bad** day*
BUT	
una **mala** semana	*a **bad** week*
el **primer** día	*the **first** day*
el **tercer** mes	*the **third** month*

However, if these adjectives follow a masculine singular noun, the full form is used.

Felipe **Segundo**	*Philip **the Second***
el siglo **primero**	*the **first** century*

Alguno (*some*) and **ninguno** (*no*) add an accent mark over the **-u-** when the final **-o** is dropped. Notice that **alguno** and **ninguno** can stand before other adjectives.

algún buen vino chileno	***some** good Chilean wine*
No hay **ningún** restaurante caro.	*There is **no** expensive restaurant.*

The adjective **grande** shortens to **gran** before any singular noun, whether masculine or feminine. **Gran** means *great* when it precedes the noun.

una **gran** bailarina rusa	*a **great** Russian ballet dancer*

Grande does not shorten before plural nouns.

grandes artistas italianos	***great** Italian artists*

The adjective **cualquiera** (*any*) shortens to **cualquier** before any singular noun, whether masculine or feminine.

cualquier celular	***any** cell phone*
cualquier computadora	***any** computer*

C Write the form of the adjective in parentheses that correctly completes each sentence.

1. Es un ______________ chico. (bueno)
2. Lucía es su ______________ hija (*daughter*). (tercero)
3. Hay ______________ mapas en el maletín. (alguno)
4. Es el ______________ mes del año. (primero)
5. Son muy ______________ ideas. (malo)
6. Es una ______________ escritora. (grande)
7. No hay ______________ cibercafé por aquí. (ninguno)
8. ¿Hay ______________ paseo tranquilo? (alguno)

D Form noun phrases using the elements given. Some of the adjectives precede the noun and others follow it. Change the form of the adjectives and other elements to agree with the noun they refer to. Follow the *modelo.*

MODELO flores / mucho / hermoso
→ muchas flores hermosas

1. semana / primero / el
2. avenidas / animado / alguno
3. transitado / cierto / calles
4. peatonal / zona / bastante
5. periódico / cualquiera / importante
6. varios / pesado / revistas
7. computadora / ninguno / viejo
8. mucho / problemas / difícil
9. coche / ninguno / ruidoso
10. barato / poco / ropa

E Complete each sentence with the Spanish equivalent of the word in parentheses. Rewrite each sentence, placing the word either before or after the noun, depending on the meaning of the word.

1. Son unas ______________ niñas ______________. (*big*)
2. Es el ______________ perro ______________. (*same*)
3. Hay algunas ______________ personas ______________. (*poor, penniless*)
4. Es su ______________ oportunidad ______________. (*only*)
5. Es una ______________ civilización ______________. (*ancient*)
6. Es ______________ americano ______________. (*half*)
7. Es un ______________ científico ______________. (*great*)
8. Hay ______________ cosas ______________. (*certain*)

Ser *to be* (third person plural)

The verb form **son** means *you* (plural)/*they are*. It is a form of the irregular verb **ser** (*to be*). (See also Chapters 3 and 4).

¿Cómo **son** las oficinas? **Son** grandes y claras.	*What* ***are*** *the offices like?* ***They're*** *big and bright.*
¿El patio **es** lindo? Sí, y el jardín también. **Son** lindos.	***Is*** *the patio pretty?* *Yes, and the garden, too.* ***They're*** *pretty.*

F ***¿Cómo es tu barrio?*** Describe places and things in your neighborhood by writing sentences with **es** or **son** and the elements given. Change the form of the adjectives to agree with the nouns they refer to. Follow the *modelo.*

MODELO el hotel / cómodo / muy moderno
→ El hotel es cómodo y muy moderno.

1. la avenida / animado / muy transitado
2. las casas / hermoso / muy caro
3. las calles / comercial / muy ruidoso
4. la biblioteca (*library*) / viejo / muy importante
5. la tienda por departamentos / nuevo / muy grande
6. los condominios / pequeño / muy barato
7. la zona / tranquilo / muy bonito
8. los garajes / oscuro / muy feo
9. el salón de belleza / lindo / muy bueno
10. los jardines / peatonal / muy interesante

G Express the following dialogues in Spanish.

1. *Is there a lot of noise in the neighborhood?*
   No, the area is not very noisy.
2. *What is the house like?*
   It's modern and beautiful.
   And the rooms, what are they like?
   They're light and small.
3. *The gifts are for Raquel.*
   What's in this (esta) *pretty box?*
   It's a bracelet.
4. *Is there a shopping center around here?*
   Yes, there are twenty stores.
   It's not very big.
   No, but (pero) *the stores are very good.*
5. *The garden is lovely and there are many flowers.*
   Aren't they beautiful?
   The garden is very peaceful.
   Yes, it's a wonderful place (el lugar).

Contraction del

The preposition **de** contracts with the masculine singular definite article **el** to form **del**: **de** + **el** → **del**.

Es la farmacia **del** barrio.	*It's the neighborhood drugstore.*
Son los papeles **del** director.	*They're the director's papers.*
Salen **del** hotel. (**salir (de)** (*to go out, leave*))	*They're leaving the hotel.*
Es el problema **del banco**.	*It's the bank's problem.*

The preposition **de** does not contract with the other forms of the definite article.

Es el café **de la** esquina.	*It's the corner café.*
Son los papeles **de la** directora.	*They're the director's* (fem.) *papers.*
Salen **de los** jardines.	*They're leaving the gardens.*
Son los problemas **de los bancos**.	*They're the banks' problems.*
Es el cuarto **de las niñas**.	*It's the little girls' room.*

The preposition **de** does not contract with the pronoun **él** (*he, it*).

El condominio no es **de él**.	*It's not **his** condominium.*

H Join each pair of nouns with **de**. Write the corresponding form of the definite article for each noun and use the contraction **del** where needed. Follow the *modelo*.

MODELO habitación / hotel
→ la habitación del hotel

1. estantes / librería
2. maletín / director
3. cibercafé / esquina
4. temas / documento
5. supermercado / barrio
6. condominio / señorita
7. teatros / centro
8. computadoras / oficina
9. mapa / ciudad
10. luz / día
11. coches / garajes
12. electrodomésticos / casas
13. datos / libro
14. ruido / carro
15. problemas / museos
16. cámaras / banco

I Express the following phrases in Spanish, using **de**.

1. *the corner drugstore*
2. *the director's* [masc.] *office*
3. *the apartment keys*
4. *the toy store's toys*
5. *the garden's flowers*
6. *the (hotel) room's closets*
7. *the jewelry store's wristwatches*
8. *the neighborhood movie theater*
9. *the commercial area's stores*
10. *the electronic appointment book data*

DIÁLOGO 3 · ¿De qué color es tu carro?

Study the dialogue, then listen to the recording and repeat each line.

DANIEL	¿De qué color es tu carro?
CAMILA	Es azul.
DANIEL	¿Y el interior?
CAMILA	Es blanco.

Análisis

Check that you understand the linguistic breakdown of each speech from *Diálogo 3*.

¿De qué color es tu carro?	*What color is your car?*
el color	*color*
¿De qué color?	*What color?*
es	*is* (**ser**)
el carro	*car*
tu carro	*your car*
Es azul.	*It's blue.*
azul	*blue*
¿Y el interior?	*And what about the interior?*
y	*and (what about?)*
el interior	*the interior, the inside*
Es blanco.	*It's white.*
blanco	*white*

Variantes

Listen, and repeat the same structures from *Diálogo 3*, now with new vocabulary.

Mi carro es azul.	*My car is* ***blue.***
rojo	*red*
amarillo	*yellow*
gris	*gray*
verde	*green*
negro	*black*
anaranjado	*orange*
marrón	*brown*
beige	*beige*
morado	*purple*
violeta	*purple*
¿De qué color es tu coche?	*What color is your car?*
Mi coche es azul claro.	*My car is light blue.*
Mi coche es azul oscuro.	*My car is dark blue.*
¿De qué color son los zapatos?	*What color are the shoes?*
Son negros.	*They're black.*

¿De qué colores son las maletas?	*What colors are the suitcases?*
Son grises y rojas.	*They're gray and red.*

Estructura y Práctica

FORMS OF ADJECTIVES: COLORS

Some colors are four-form adjectives: **rojo/roja/rojos/rojas**. Other colors are two-form adjectives: **verde/verdes, azul/azules.** The colors **beige** and **violeta** are invariable, that is, they do not change for gender or number. The color *pink* is translated **rosado**, a four-form adjective, and also **rosa**, which is invariable. **Azul claro / azul oscuro** is invariable: **los pantalones** (*pants*) **azul claro, la camisa** (*shirt*) **azul oscuro.**

Possessive Adjectives

Here are the possessive adjectives in Spanish.

	SINGULAR	PLURAL
FIRST PERSON	mi(s)	nuestro/a/os/as
SECOND PERSON	tu(s)	vuestro/a/os/as
THIRD PERSON	su(s)	su(s)

The possessive adjectives **mi, tu, su** are used before singular nouns. They add an **-s** before plural nouns: **mis, tus, sus.**

mi carpeta	***my*** *folder*	**mis** carpetas	***my*** *folders*
tu mensaje	***your*** *message*	**tus** mensajes	***your*** *messages*
su perro	***his/her/your/its/ your*** (pl.)/***their*** *dog*	**sus** perros	***his/her/your/its/ your*** (pl.)/***their*** *dogs*

The possessive adjectives **nuestro** (*our*) and **vuestro** (*your*) are four-form adjectives. They agree in gender and number with the noun that follows.

nuestro/vuestro mensaje	nuestros/vuestros mensajes
nuestra/vuestra carpeta	nuestras/vuestras carpetas

Vosotros, the plural of **tú**, is used only in Spain, not in Spanish America. **Vosotros** verb forms and the possessive adjective **vuestro** will not be used actively in this book.

The possessive adjective **su/sus** refers to all third persons, both singular and plural. It can therefore mean *his, her, your, its, your* (plural), *their.* Be careful not to make the mistake of assuming that **su** means *his, her* and that **sus** means *their.* **Su** and **sus** agree with the noun that follows, not with the possessor.

su amigo	*his/her/your/its/your* (pl.)/*their friend*
sus amigos	*his/her/your/its/your* (pl.)/*their friends*

To focus on the referent of **su/sus**, a phrase beginning with **de** + subject pronoun is used. (For subject pronouns, see Chapter 3.)

el amigo de él/de ella/de Ud./de ellos/ de ellas/de Uds.	*his/her/your/their/their* (fem.)/*your* (pl.) *friend*
los amigos de él/de ella/de Ud./de ellos/ de ellas/de Uds.	*his/her/your/their/their* (fem.)/*your* (pl.) *friends*

J Express the following phrases with possessive adjectives in Spanish. Follow the *modelo.*

MODELO *his house*
→ su casa

1. *their class*
2. *my books*
3. *our neighborhood*
4. *her money*
5. *your dogs* (Uds.)
6. *their suitcases*
7. *your wallet* (tú)
8. *my cell phone*
9. *his problems*
10. *her credit cards*
11. *our folders*
12. *your street* (Uds.)
13. *your shoes* (tú)
14. *our city*
15. *its hotel*
16. *our toys*
17. *its computer stores*
18. *their boarding passes*

K ***Diálogos.*** Write the possessive adjectives that correctly complete each dialogue, using the cues in parentheses.

1. —¿De qué color es ______________ carro? (de ellas)

   —______________ carro es negro.
2. —¿Es animado ______________ barrio? (de él)

   —Sí, ______________ barrio es animado.
3. —¿Es nueva ______________ casa? (de Uds.)

   —No, ______________ casa es vieja.
4. —¿Son difíciles ______________ exámenes? (de ellos)

   —No, ______________ exámenes no son difíciles.
5. —¿De qué color son ______________ zapatos? (de ella)

   —______________ zapatos son marrones.
6. —¿Es pesado ______________ artículo? (de Ud.)

   —No, ______________ artículo es muy interesante.
7. —¿Cómo son ______________ perros? (de Ud.)

   —______________ perros son tranquilos.
8. —¿Son largos ______________ informes? (Uds.)

   —No, ______________ informes son cortos.

L ***¿De qué color es?*** Rewrite each phrase, including the Spanish equivalent of the word(s) in parentheses.

1. la ropa ________ (*black and white*)
2. unos carros ________ (*blue*)
3. mi cuarto ________ (*green*)
4. muchas flores ________ (*red and yellow*)
5. sus maletas ________ (*gray*)
6. tu mochila ________ (*purple*)
7. unas carteras ________ (*brown*)
8. su camiseta (*T-shirt*) ________ (*light blue*)
9. los abrigos (*overcoats*) ________ (*dark blue*)
10. unos bolsos ________ (*beige*)

DIÁLOGO 4 · ¿Qué hay en el maletín?

Study the dialogue, then listen to the recording and repeat each line.

CAMILA ¿Qué hay en tu maletín?
DANIEL Hay documentos importantes.
CAMILA ¿Son largos los documentos?
DANIEL Sí, son largos y muy pesados.

Análisis

Check that you understand the linguistic breakdown of each speech from *Diálogo 4*.

¿Qué hay en tu maletín?	*What's in your attaché case?*
tu	*your* (informal, before a singular noun)
Hay documentos importantes.	*There are important documents.*
importante	*important*
documentos importantes	*important documents*
¿Son largos los documentos?	*Are the documents long?*
largo	*long*
Sí, son largos y muy pesados.	*Yes, they're long and very boring.*
son	*they are* (**ser**)
muy	*very*
pesado	*heavy, boring*

Variantes

Listen, and repeat the same structures from *Diálogo 4*, now with new vocabulary.

Hay documentos en el maletín.	*There are **documents** in the attaché case.*
informes	*reports*
contratos	*contracts*
revistas	*magazines*
periódicos	*newspapers*
artículos	*articles*
folletos	*brochures*

El informe es largo.	*The report is **long**.*
corto	*short*
fácil	*easy*
aburrido	*boring*

Estructura y Práctica

More on Question Formation: Information Questions, Question Words (Interrogatives), Yes/No Questions

Information Questions

You learned in Chapter 1 that information questions expect a piece of information as an answer. Question words introduce information questions. They are always written with an accent mark in Spanish, and they carry stress in questions. Information questions in Spanish usually have the following word order: interrogative word + verb (+ subject) + other elements. The subject position may or may not be occupied, since verb endings indicate the subject.

¿**Qué** hay en la mochila?	***What** is (there) in the backpack?*
¿**Cómo** son las tiendas?	***What** are the stores **like**?*
¿**Cuántos** museos hay en la ciudad?	***How many** museums are (there) in the city?*

Question Words (Interrogatives)

The most important question words in Spanish are the following.

¿Cuál? ¿Cuáles?	*Which?*
¿Cuándo?	*When?*
¿Cuánto? ¿Cuánta?	*How much?*
¿Cuántos? ¿Cuántas?	*How many?*
¿Cómo?	*How?*
¿Dónde?	*Where?*
¿Adónde?	*(To) where?* (with verbs of motion)
¿De dónde?	*(From) where?*
¿Qué?	*What?*
¿Para qué?	*For what purpose?*
¿Por qué?	*Why?*
¿Quién? ¿Quiénes?	*Who?*
¿A quién? ¿A quiénes?	*Whom?*
¿De quién? ¿De quiénes?	*Whose?*

¿Qué? may be used before a verb or a noun.

¿**Qué hay** en la gaveta?	***What's (there)** in the drawer?*
¿**Qué tiendas** hay en esta calle?	***What stores** are there on this street?*

¿Cómo? asks for repetition when you don't hear something clearly.

Él llega mañana.	*He's arriving tomorrow.*
¿Cómo? ¿Cuándo llega?	***What?** When is he arriving?*

¿Cómo? is also used to express astonishment.

Carlos habla siete idiomas.	*Carlos speaks seven languages.*
¿Cómo? No lo puedo creer.	***What?!*** *I can't believe it.*

Prepositions associated with an interrogative word must precede it in Spanish. In English, they usually are separated from the question word and appear at the end of the sentence.

¿**De dónde** es Ud.?	***Where*** *are you* ***from****?*
¿**De quién** es el carro?	***Whose*** *car is it?*

M ***Preguntas informativas.*** Write the information question that would elicit the information given in each statement. There may be more than one response possible for some statements.

1. Nuestra casa es grande.
2. Hay tres tarjetas de crédito en su billetero.
3. Mi carro es azul oscuro.
4. Hay un CD en la caja.
5. El restaurante mexicano queda (*is*) en la esquina.
6. Las revistas son aburridas.
7. Los regalos son para Sofía.
8. El museo de arte queda (*is*) por aquí.
9. Hay dieciséis estudiantes (*students*) en la clase.
10. Es una agenda electrónica.
11. Son folletos y contratos.
12. El interior de su casa es blanco.
13. Hay tiendas de cómputo en esta (*this*) avenida.
14. Su (de ellos) jardín es lindo y tranquilo.

QUEDAR

Quedar means *to be located*, referring to things that do not change location.

El café **queda** por aquí.	*The café* ***is*** *around here.*
Mi hotel **queda** cerca.	*My hotel* ***is*** *nearby.*
Nuestra casa **queda** en la esquina.	*Our house* ***is*** *at the corner.*
Las tiendas de cómputo **quedan** en el centro.	*The computer stores* ***are*** *downtown.*

Yes/No Questions

You learned in Chapter 1 that questions not beginning with a question word are called yes/no questions; they ask for either *yes* or *no* as an answer.

When a sentence consists of a form of the verb **ser** and an adjective, the subject may be placed at the end of the sentence to form a question. The pattern of the question is thus verb + adjective + subject.

El artículo es corto.	*The article is short.*
¿Es corto el artículo?	*Is the article short?*
Los documentos son importantes.	*The documents are important.*
¿Son importantes los documentos?	*Are the documents important?*

N ***Preguntas de sí o no.*** Change each of the following statements into a yes/no question, using the pattern **ser** + adjective + subject. Follow the *modelo.*

MODELO El condominio es nuevo.
→ ¿Es nuevo el condominio?

1. Los teléfonos celulares son útiles.
2. Su reloj es caro.
3. Los paseos son muy transitados.
4. La catedral es vieja.
5. Las preguntas son difíciles.
6. Ana y Fernando son inteligentes.
7. El hotel es bueno.
8. Esta (*this*) calle es muy ruidosa.
9. Las flores son hermosas.
10. El profesor es aburrido.

DIÁLOGO 5 · Mis libros

Study the dialogue, then listen to the recording and repeat each line.

DANIEL Hay libros en la mesa, ¿no sabes?
CAMILA Ah, sí. Son mis libros de administración de empresas.
DANIEL ¿Son libros difíciles?
CAMILA Sí, son bastante difíciles, pero muy útiles.

Análisis

Check that you understand the linguistic breakdown of each speech from *Diálogo 5.*

Hay libros en la mesa, ¿no sabes?	*There are books on the table, you know?*
el libro	*book*
la mesa	*table*
en la mesa	*on the table*
¿no sabes?	*you know?* (literally, *don't you know?*)
Ah, sí. Son mis libros de administración de empresas.	*Oh, yes. They're my business books.*
mis	*my* (before a plural noun)
la administración	*administration*

la empresa	*firm, company, business*
la administración de empresas	*business (administration)*
¿Son libros difíciles?	*Are they difficult books?*
difícil	*difficult*
Sí, son bastante difíciles, pero muy útiles.	*Yes, they're quite difficult, but very useful.*
bastante	*quite, quite a lot*
bastante difícil	*quite difficult*
útil	*useful*

Variantes

Listen, and repeat the same structures from *Diálogo 5*, now with new vocabulary.

Son mis libros de administración de empresas.	*They're my* **business** *books.*
historia	*history*
economía	*economics*
derecho	*law*
ciencias políticas	*political science*
español	*Spanish*
inglés	*English*
computación	*computer science*
música	*music*
arte	*art*
medicina	*medical* (literally, *medicine*)
contabilidad	*accounting*
enfermería	*nursing*
matemáticas	*math*
química	*chemistry*
biología	*biology*
física	*physics*
¿Son libros difíciles?	*Are they* **difficult** *books?*
importantes	*important*
interesantes	*interesting*
nuevos	*new*
viejos	*old*

Estructura y Práctica

Intensifiers

An intensifier is a word, especially an adverb, that is used to emphasize, enhance, or add impact to another adjective, adverb, noun, or verb.

Su casa es **muy** fea.	*Their house is* **very** *ugly.*
Los exámenes son **bastante** fáciles.	*The exams are* **quite** *easy.*
Los gemelos son **completamente** diferentes.	*The twins are* **completely** *different.*

Many intensifiers are adverbs that end in **-mente**. They are formed by adding the suffix **-mente** to the feminine singular form of the adjective. (See also Chapter 8.)

MASCULINE SINGULAR	FEMININE SINGULAR	ADVERB	MEANING
completo	completa	completamente	*completely*

If the adjective has only one form for the masculine and feminine singular, then the suffix **-mente** is added to that form.

SINGULAR	ADVERB	MEANING
fácil	fácilmente	*easily*
suficiente	suficientemente	*sufficiently, adequately*

More adverbs ending in -mente

realmente *really*
relativamente *relatively*
sumamente *extremely*
verdaderamente *really*

O ***Intensificadores.*** Rewrite each of the following sentences, including the intensifier in parentheses to add emphasis to the adjective.

1. Mi clase de historia es interesante. (muy)
2. Las casas son hermosas. (tan (*so*))
3. El libro de arte es maravilloso. (realmente)
4. Es una ciudad grande. (bastante)
5. ¿Son largos los informes? (demasiado (*too*))
6. Nuestra empresa es nueva. (relativamente)
7. Unas calles son transitadas. (poco (*little, not much*))
8. Sus hijos son inteligentes. (sumamente)
9. ¿Es tranquilo tu barrio? (verdaderamente)
10. ¿No son modernas las oficinas? (suficientemente)

Noun Phrase Functions

Nouns and noun phrases function as the subject or object of the verb, as the object of a preposition, or as a short answer to a question. In Chapter 1, you saw examples of these functions. Noun phrases can also follow forms of the verb **ser** (*to be*) in the predicate of a sentence. In traditional grammar, this function is called the predicate nominative.

Es **una fiesta** para Juan.	*It's **a party** for Juan.*
Son **los amigos** de mi hijo.	*They're **friends** of my son.*

THE PREDICATE

The predicate consists of everything in a sentence except the subject. Thus, in the sentence *Philip studies business administration*, the words *studies business administration* form the predicate of the sentence. The predicate contains the verb and its objects, adverbs, prepositional phrases adding to the meaning of the verb, etc.

P **Noun phrases.** Create noun phrases from the elements given. Follow the *modelo.*

MODELO camisetas / sus / blancas
→ sus camisetas blancas

1. folletos / largos / quince
2. animadas / avenidas / unas
3. el / en / maletín
4. examen / de / química / mi
5. amarillas / flores / muchas
6. habitaciones / veinte / modernas
7. nuestros / para / amigos
8. rojo / el / carro
9. sus / matemáticas / de / clases
10. paseos / en / transitados / los

Q **Translation.** Express the following dialogues in Spanish.

1. *Is your* (tú) *neighborhood lively?*
   No, my neighborhood is quite quiet.
2. *Are your* (you [pl.]) *biology books interesting?*
   No, our biology books are boring.
3. *Is their company new?*
   Yes, their company is new and very important.
4. *Are her suitcases black?*
   No, her suitcases are brown.
5. *Are his articles difficult?*
   No, his articles are easy.

Un paso más

Are you ready to take your Spanish a step further? Here are exercises that will enhance your knowledge of the language and encourage you to express yourself freely.

R **Word families.** You have learned several adjectives that are derived from nouns, as well as some nouns that are derived from adjectives. Many of these words are cognates of English words. Nouns that end in **-dad**, **-tad**, **-cia**, **-eza**, **-ez** are usually feminine: **la novedad**, **la dificultad**, **la importancia**, **la grandeza**, **la vejez**. Increasing your recognition of word families and gender endings will make your study of the Spanish language more productive. In the exercise that follows, write the Spanish adjective that is related to the noun provided.

1. la importancia
2. la dificultad
3. el ruido
4. la tranquilidad
5. el comercio
6. la novedad
7. la claridad
8. el interés

9. la hermosura
10. la facilidad
11. la naranja (*orange*)
12. la grandeza
13. el tránsito
14. la oscuridad
15. la bondad
16. la utilidad
17. la comodidad
18. la modernidad
19. el peatón (*pedestrian*)
20. el ánimo (*spirit, energy*)
21. la vejez
22. la maldad
23. la verdad

S ***Preguntas personales.*** Answer each question with a complete Spanish sentence.

1. ¿Cómo es tu casa?
2. ¿De qué color es?
3. ¿Cuántos cuartos hay?
4. ¿Hay jardín, patio y garaje? ¿Cómo son?
5. ¿Dónde queda tu casa?
6. ¿Cómo es tu barrio?
7. ¿Cómo son las calles, avenidas y tiendas?
8. ¿Cómo es tu carro?
9. ¿De qué color es?
10. ¿Cuál es tu color favorito?

3

Nationalities, Professions, Food, and Films

Communication Goals

- Asking and telling about nationalities and origins
- Learning about the Spanish-speaking world
- Talking about restaurants and films
- Vocabulary: countries, foreign languages, food, professions

Grammar Topics

- Subject Pronouns
- **Ser** *to be*
- Adjectives of Nationality
- **¡Qué!** in Exclamations
- Information Questions
- Yes/No Questions
- Negative Sentences
- Position of Adjectives
- Prepositions
- Demonstrative Adjectives
- Gender of Nouns That Refer to People

DIÁLOGO 1 · ¿De dónde son?

Study the dialogue, then listen to the recording and repeat each line.

FERNANDA	¿Es Ud. mexicano?
ESTEBAN	No, no soy mexicano. Soy costarricense, de San José. ¿Y Ud.?
FERNANDA	¿Yo? Yo soy colombiana. Soy de Bogotá.

Análisis

Check that you understand the linguistic breakdown of each speech from *Diálogo 1.*

¿Es Ud. mexicano?	*Are you Mexican?*
es	*are* (third person singular) (**ser**)
Ud.	*you* (formal singular)
mexicano	*Mexican*
No, no soy mexicano. Soy costarricense, de San José. ¿Y Ud.?	*No, I'm not Mexican. I'm Costa Rican, from San José. And you?*
no	*no* (negative particle)
soy	*am* (first person singular) (**ser**)
costarricense	*Costa Rican*
de	*from*
San José	*San José* (*capital of Costa Rica*)
¿Yo? Yo soy colombiana. Soy de Bogotá.	*Me? I'm Colombian. I'm from Bogotá.*
yo	*I, me* (colloquial)
colombiana	*Colombian* (feminine)
Bogotá	*Bogotá* (*capital of Colombia*)

Variantes

Listen, and repeat the same structures from *Diálogo 1,* now with new vocabulary.

Soy mexicano.	Soy mexicana.	*I'm **Mexican**.*
costarricense	costarricense	*Costa Rican*
cubano	cubana	*Cuban*
colombiano	colombiana	*Colombian*
puertorriqueño	puertorriqueña	*Puerto Rican*
norteamericano	norteamericana	*American*
estadounidense	estadounidense	*American*
panameño	panameña	*Panamanian*
guatemalteco	guatemalteca	*Guatemalan*
salvadoreño	salvadoreña	*Salvadoran*
hondureño	hondureña	*Honduran*
nicaragüense	nicaragüense	*Nicaraguan*
dominicano	dominicana	*Dominican*
chileno	chilena	*Chilean*
argentino	argentina	*Argentinian, Argentine*
peruano	peruana	*Peruvian*
brasileño	brasileña	*Brazilian*
venezolano	venezolana	*Venezuelan*
uruguayo	uruguaya	*Uruguayan*
paraguayo	paraguaya	*Paraguayan*
ecuatoriano	ecuatoriana	*Ecuadoran*
boliviano	boliviana	*Bolivian*
canadiense	canadiense	*Canadian*
inglés	inglesa	*English*
español	española	*Spanish*

italiano	italiana	*Italian*
francés	francesa	*French*
portugués	portuguesa	*Portuguese*
alemán	alemana	*German*
polaco	polaca	*Polish*
irlandés	irlandesa	*Irish*
escocés	escocesa	*Scottish*
griego	griega	*Greek*
ruso	rusa	*Russian*
hindú	hindú	*Indian*
indio	india	*Indian*
vietnamita	vietnamita	*Vietnamese*
coreano	coreana	*Korean*
surcoreano	surcoreana	*South Korean*
norcoreano	norcoreana	*North Korean*
japonés	japonesa	*Japanese*
chino	china	*Chinese*
israelí	israelí	*Israeli*
iraquí	iraquí	*Iraqi*
iraní	iraní	*Iranian*
saudí, saudita	saudí, saudita	*Saudi*

Otras Nacionalidades

austríaco	austríaca	*Austrian*
holandés	holandesa	*Dutch*
belga	belga	*Belgian*
suizo	suiza	*Swiss*
luxemburgués	luxemburguesa	*Luxembourgian*
sueco	sueca	*Swedish*
noruego	noruega	*Norwegian*
danés	danesa	*Danish*
finlandés	finlandesa	*Finnish*
ucranio, ucraniano	ucrania, ucraniana	*Ukrainian*
paquistaní, pakistaní	paquistaní, pakistaní	*Pakistani*
filipino	filipina	*Philippine*
tailandés	tailandesa	*Thai*
taiwanés	taiwanesa	*Taiwanese*
sudafricano	sudafricana	*South African*
egipcio	egipcia	*Egyptian*
jordano	jordana	*Jordanian*
sirio	siria	*Syrian*
turco	turca	*Turkish*
libanés	libanesa	*Lebanese*
marroquí	marroquí	*Moroccan*
libio	libia	*Libyan*
afgano	afgana	*Afghan, Afghani*
australiano	australiana	*Australian*
neozelandés	neozelandesa	*New Zealander*

Estructura y Práctica

Subject Pronouns

Spanish and English have different sets of personal pronouns. Here are the English subject pronouns.

	SINGULAR	PLURAL
FIRST PERSON	*I*	*we*
SECOND PERSON	*you*	*you*
THIRD PERSON	*he, she, it*	*they*

Here are the Spanish subject pronouns.

	SINGULAR	PLURAL
FIRST PERSON	yo	nosotros, nosotras
SECOND PERSON	tú	vosotros, vosotras
THIRD PERSON	él, ella, usted	ellos, ellas, ustedes

NOTE Verb forms for **vosotros** will be presented but will not be practiced actively throughout the book.

There are several important differences between personal pronouns in English and in Spanish.

1 · The pronoun **yo** is not capitalized unless it is the first word of a sentence.

2 · The Spanish equivalents of *we* make a gender distinction that English does not require. **Nosotros** is used for groups of two or more males or for groups of two or more males and females. **Nosotras** is used for groups of two or more females.

3 · Spanish has four equivalents for English *you*. The pronouns **tú** and **vosotros/vosotras** are informal. **Tú** is used to address one person with whom you have a relationship that Hispanic culture defines as informal: family members, children, fellow students, etc. **Vosotros/vosotras** is used to address two or more people with whom you have an informal relationship. Note that **vosotros/vosotras** makes the same gender distinction as **nosotros/nosotras**, above. **Usted** and **ustedes** are used in formal situations. **Usted** is used to address one person with whom you have a relationship that Hispanic culture defines as formal: strangers, superiors at work, people not part of your usual network, etc. **Ustedes** is used to address two or more people with whom you have a formal relationship.

4 · In the third person plural, groups of two or more males or groups of two or more males and females are referred to as **ellos**. Groups of two or more consisting entirely of females are referred to as **ellas**.

5 · The equivalents of *you* (**vosotros/vosotras**) described in No. 3 above reflect the usage in Spain only. In Spanish America, **vosotros/vosotras** is not used. Instead, **ustedes** is used as the plural of both **tú** and **usted**.

6 · **Usted** is used with a third person singular verb. **Ustedes** is used with a third person plural verb. In writing, **usted** is usually written **Ud.**, and **ustedes** is usually written **Uds.** These abbreviations are pronounced **usted** and **ustedes**, respectively.

7 · The standards of formality that condition the choice of **tú** or **usted** vary within the Spanish-speaking world. Informal address is more frequent in Spain than in countries such as Mexico or Ecuador. Rural aristocratic milieus use **usted** much more than modern urban milieus.

8 · When in doubt, learners of Spanish should use formal address until asked to switch to **tú** by the native speaker they are talking to. American culture places a high value on informality, but in Spanish-speaking cultures, the inappropriate use of **tú** is considered rude, not friendly.

9 · Spanish has no equivalent for English *it* as a subject pronoun. All masculine nouns, whether referring to people or things, are replaced by **él**. All feminine nouns are replaced by **ella**.

10 · In many parts of Spanish America, **tú** is replaced by the pronoun **vos**, which has its own set of verb endings. This phenomenon, called *el voseo,* is characteristic of the speech of Argentina, Uruguay, Paraguay, Bolivia, Chile, Central America except for Panamá, and parts of Venezuela and Colombia. In Argentina, Uruguay, and Nicaragua, **vos** is acceptable in both speech and writing and has become a standard second person singular form.

11 · In Spanish, personal pronouns are not used as much as in English, because the ending of the verb shows who the subject is. The pronouns are used for focus or contrast, as in sentences such as the following.

Él es asesor, pero **ella** es abogada.	***He**'s a consultant, but **she**'s a lawyer.*
Uds. son italianos, pero **nosotros** somos ingleses.	***You** are Italian, but **we** are English.*

In the English equivalents of the sentences above, the subject pronouns are stressed.

12 · The pronoun **usted (Ud.)** is often used to add a note of politeness or formality to sentences.

A ***¿Quiénes son?*** Identify the subject or subjects of each of the following sentences. Write the correct subject pronoun or pronouns.

1. Es argentino.
2. Somos rusos.
3. Son panameñas.
4. Soy norteamericano.
5. Es india.
6. Son canadienses.
7. Eres israelí.
8. Somos venezolanas.

Ser to be

The verb **ser** is one of the two Spanish verbs meaning *to be.* An irregular verb, its conjugation in present tense is as follows:

ser *to be*	
SINGULAR	PLURAL
soy	somos
eres	sois
es	son

Uses of ser

1 · **Ser** links nouns and pronouns.

Yo **soy** ingeniero.	***I'm** an engineer.*
¿**Eres** dentista?	***Are you** a dentist?*
Alicia y José **son** amigos.	*Alicia and José **are** friends.*

Notice that, unlike English, Spanish omits the indefinite article **un/una** with a profession.

2 · **Ser** is used before (or, in information questions, after) a phrase beginning with **de** that expresses possession, origin, or the material of which something is made.

La oficina **es de** Jorge.	*The office **is** Jorge's.*
¿Uds. **son de** Chile?	***Are** you **from** Chile?*
¿**De quién es** este billetero?	***Whose** wallet **is** this?*
El reloj **es de** oro.	*The watch **is made of** gold.*

3 · **Ser** is used with color, nationality, aesthetic attributes, and age.

Mi carro **es** negro.	*My car **is** black.*
Somos norteamericanos.	***We are** American.*
Alonso y Nicolás **son** guapos.	*Alonso and Nicolás **are** handsome.*
El profesor **es** viejo.	*The professor **is** old.*

4 · **Ser** is used to tell time and to give the date. (See also Chapter 4.)

¿Qué hora **es**?	*What time **is it**?*
Es la una.	***It's** one o'clock.*
Son las dos y media.	***It's** two o'clock.*
Hoy **es** el once de marzo.	*Today **is** March 11.*

B ***Es de México.*** Write complete sentences, conjugating the verb **ser** to agree with each subject provided. Follow the *modelo.*

MODELO él → Es de México.

1. tú
2. ellos
3. yo
4. Uds.
5. ella
6. nosotros
7. Ud.
8. ellas

C ***De los Estados Unidos.*** Your new friend thinks that you, your family, and your friends are from other countries, but you're all from the United States. Write responses telling him so. Follow the *modelo.*

MODELO Claudio es francés, ¿no?
→ De Francia, no. Es de los Estados Unidos.

1. Tus papás son españoles, ¿no?
2. Tu primo es chino, ¿no?
3. Eres australiano, ¿no?
4. María Elena es colombiana, ¿no?
5. Uds. son alemanes, ¿no?
6. Tus amigos son irlandeses, ¿no?
7. Ud. es surcoreano, ¿no?
8. Diego y Fernanda son peruanos, ¿no?

The phrase **¿no?** added to a statement turns it into a question. This is called a tag question. In the *modelo* for Exercise C, it is translated as *isn't he?* The English translation will change based on the subject of the sentence. (See also Chapter 4.)

D ***Nacionalidades.*** Write a complete sentence to respond to each of the following questions, confirming the nationality of the people asked about. Follow the *modelo.*

MODELO ¿Lorenzo es de Bolivia?
→ Sí, es boliviano.

1. ¿Mateo es de Escocia?
2. ¿Tomás y Lucas son de Tailandia?
3. ¿Clara es de Vietnam?
4. ¿Uds. son de Costa Rica?
5. ¿Benjamín y Raquel son de Israel?
6. ¿Isabel es de Suecia?
7. ¿Joaquín es de Bélgica?
8. ¿Olivia y Amelia son de Taiwán?
9. ¿Josefa es de Irán?
10. ¿Esos estudiantes son de Egipto?

DIÁLOGO 2 · ¿De qué origen son?

Study the dialogue, then listen to the recording and repeat each line.

ESTEBAN ¿De dónde eres?
FERNANDA Soy de Puerto Rico. ¿Y tú?
ESTEBAN Yo soy de la Florida, pero de origen cubano.
FERNANDA ¡Qué casualidad! Yo también soy de origen cubano.

Análisis

Check that you understand the linguistic breakdown of each speech from *Diálogo 2.*

¿De dónde eres?	*Where are you from?*
de	*from*
¿dónde?	*where?*
eres	*you are* (second person singular) (**ser**)

Soy de Puerto Rico. ¿Y tú?	*I'm from Puerto Rico. What about you?*
soy	*I am* (first person singular) (**ser**)
Puerto Rico	*Puerto Rico (commonwealth of the U.S.;* Estado Libre Asociado de Puerto Rico)
tú	*you* (informal singular)
Yo soy de la Florida, pero de origen cubano.	*I'm from Florida, but of Cuban descent.*
yo	*I*
de	*from, of*
la Florida	*Florida*
pero	*but*
el origen	*origin, descent, background*
cubano	*Cuban*
de origen cubano	*of Cuban descent*
¡Qué casualidad! Yo también soy de origen cubano.	*What a coincidence! I am also of Cuban descent.*
¡Qué + *noun*!	*What a* + noun*!*
la casualidad	*chance, coincidence*
¡Qué casualidad!	*What a coincidence!*
también	*also, too*

Variantes

Listen, and repeat the same structures from *Diálogo 2*, now with new vocabulary.

Yo soy de Puerto Rico.	*I'm from* ***Puerto Rico****.*
los Estados Unidos	*the United States*
(el) Canadá	*Canada*
México	*Mexico*
Costa Rica	*Costa Rica*
Panamá	*Panama*
Guatemala	*Guatemala*
El Salvador	*El Salvador*
Honduras	*Honduras*
Nicaragua	*Nicaragua*
Colombia	*Colombia*
Chile	*Chile*
(la) Argentina	*Argentina*
(el) Perú	*Peru*
Venezuela	*Venezuela*
Paraguay	*Paraguay*
(el) Uruguay	*Uruguay*
(el) Ecuador	*Ecuador*
Bolivia	*Bolivia*
Cuba	*Cuba*

(el) Brasil	*Brazil*
Inglaterra	*England*
España	*Spain*
Italia	*Italy*
Francia	*France*
Portugal	*Portugal*
Alemania	*Germany*
Austria	*Austria*
Irlanda	*Ireland*
Escocia	*Scotland*
Grecia	*Greece*
Polonia	*Poland*
Rusia	*Russia*
(la) India	*India*
Vietnam	*Vietnam*
Corea	*Korea*
Corea del Sur	*South Korea*
Corea del Norte	*North Korea*
Japón	*Japan*
China	*China*
Israel	*Israel*
Irak	*Iraq*
Irán	*Iran*
Arabia Saudita	*Saudi Arabia*

Mi familia es de origen cubano.	*My family is of **Cuban** descent.*
inglés	*English*
español	*Spanish*
italiano	*Italian*
irlandés	*Irish*
escocés	*Scottish*
francés	*French*
alemán	*German*
griego	*Greek*
portugués	*Portuguese*
ruso	*Russian*
polaco	*Polish*
chino	*Chinese*
japonés	*Japanese*
coreano	*Korean*
indio	*Indian*
hindú	*Indian*
vietnamita	*Vietnamese*
iraquí	*Iraqi*
iraní	*Iranian*

Otros Países

(la) República Dominicana	*(the) Dominican Republic*
Holanda (Países Bajos)	*Holland (Netherlands)*
Bélgica	*Belgium*
Luxemburgo	*Luxembourg*
(la) Suiza	*Switzerland*
Suecia	*Sweden*
Noruega	*Norway*
Dinamarca	*Denmark*
Finlandia	*Finland*
Egipto	*Egypt*
Ucrania	*Ukraine*
Filipinas	*Philippines*
Paquistán, Pakistán	*Pakistan*
Taiwán	*Taiwan*
Sudáfrica	*South Africa*
Jordania	*Jordan*
Siria	*Syria*
Turquía	*Turkey*
el Líbano	*Lebanon*
Marruecos	*Morocco*
Libia	*Libya*
Afganistán	*Afghanistan*
Australia	*Australia*
Nueva Zelanda	*New Zealand*

Estructura y Práctica

Adjectives of Nationality

Some adjectives of nationality do not follow the pattern of other adjectives.

Adjectives of nationality ending in -**o** or -**e** have the expected number of forms. Adjectives of nationality ending in -**o** have four forms; those ending in -**e** have two forms. Note that adjectives of nationality are not capitalized in Spanish.

	MASCULINE	FEMININE
SINGULAR	un restaurante mexicano	una comida mexicana
PLURAL	unos restaurantes mexicanos	unas comidas mexicanas
SINGULAR	un periódico árabe	una revista árabe
PLURAL	unos periódicos árabes	unas revistas árabes

Most adjectives of nationality ending in -**e** end in the suffix -**ense**.

	MASCULINE	FEMININE
SINGULAR	un periódico canadiense	una revista canadiense
PLURAL	unos periódicos canadienses	unas revistas canadienses

Here are some two-form adjectives of nationality ending in vowels other than **-e**.

SINGULAR	PLURAL	MEANING
belga	belgas	*Belgian*
saudita	sauditas	*Saudi*
iraní	iraníes	*Iranian*
iraquí	iraquíes	*Iraqi*
israelí	israelíes	*Israeli*
marroquí	marroquíes	*Moroccan*
hindú	hindúes	*Hindu, Indian*

Adjectives of nationality ending in a consonant have four forms, not two like other adjectives ending in a consonant.

	MASCULINE	FEMININE
SINGULAR	español	español**a**
PLURAL	español**es**	español**as**

Adjectives of nationality having an accent mark on the final syllable in the masculine singular lose that written accent in the other three forms.

	MASCULINE	FEMININE
SINGULAR	francés	frances**a**
PLURAL	frances**es**	frances**as**
SINGULAR	alemán	aleman**a**
PLURAL	aleman**es**	aleman**as**

Other common adjectives of nationality ending in a consonant are the following:

danés *Danish*
escocés *Scottish*
finlandés *Finnish*
galés *Welsh*
holandés *Dutch*
inglés *English*
irlandés *Irish*
japonés *Japanese*
letón *Latvian*
libanés *Lebanese*
luxemburgués *Luxembourgian*
portugués *Portuguese*
tailandés *Thai*
taiwanés *Taiwanese*
ugandés *Ugandan*

"AMERICAN": ADJECTIVES OF NATIONALITY

A citizen of the United States is called **americano** or **norteamericano** (*North American*) in Spanish. In Spanish America, **americano** can also simply mean someone from the Americas. The term **norteamericano** is therefore clearer when referring to a United States citizen. The adjective **estadounidense** may be used in formal language to refer to someone or something from the United States (**los Estados Unidos**).

Adjectives of Nationality Used as Nouns

When accompanied by an article or other determiner, adjectives of nationality are used as nouns.

el **inglés**	*the Englishman*
la **griega**	*the Greek woman*
los **franceses**	*the French*

The masculine singular form of adjectives of nationality, when used with the definite article, also functions as a noun that refers to the language.

el inglés	*English*
el español	*Spanish*
el alemán	*German*
el ruso	*Russian*
el chino	*Chinese*

E ***Nacionalidad y origen.*** Write a complete sentence that tells the nationality and origin of the people indicated. The first country named is for nationality, the second for origin or descent. Follow the *modelo.*

MODELO Gonzalo: Puerto Rico / España
→ Gonzalo es puertorriqueño, pero de origen español.

1. Raquel: Ecuador / Alemania
2. Los señores (*Mr. and Mrs.*) Fuentes: Brasil / Dinamarca
3. Yo [*masc.*]: Escocia / Austria
4. María y Catalina: El Salvador / Líbano
5. Tú [*fem.*]: Bélgica / Irán
6. Regina y Mauricio: Uruguay / Ucrania
7. Uds. [*fem.*]: Francia / Paquistán
8. La señorita Rivas: Israel / Polonia
9. Victoria y yo [*masc.*]: Inglaterra / Marruecos
10. Ignacio y Alberto: Nicaragua / Vietnam

F ***Idiomas* (Languages).** Write the name of an official language spoken in each of the following countries. Write your answers in Spanish, and include the definite article.

1. Suecia
2. Portugal
3. Rusia
4. Finlandia
5. Francia
6. Alemania
7. Japón
8. Italia
9. Vietnam
10. Holanda
11. China
12. Egipto
13. Austria
14. Honduras
15. Corea del Sur
16. Tailandia

¡Qué! in Exclamations

¡Qué! is used in exclamations before both nouns and adjectives. The English equivalent is *What a!* when used before a singular noun, *What!* before a plural noun, and *How!* before an adjective.

¡**Qué** casualidad!	***What a*** *coincidence!*
¡**Qué** problemas!	***What*** *problems!*
¡**Qué** divertido!	***How*** *amusing!*
¡**Qué** estupendo!	***How*** *great!* / ***How*** *fantastic!*
¡**Qué** padre!	***How*** *great!* / ***How*** *fantastic!* (Mexico)
¡**Qué** chévere!	***How*** *great!* / ***How*** *fantastic!* (Puerto Rico)

To emphasize a characteristic of a noun, the pattern **¡Qué!** + adjective + noun may be used.

¡**Qué** buen amigo!	***What a*** *good friend!*
¡**Qué** mala suerte!	***What*** *bad luck!*
¡**Qué** lindos juguetes!	***What*** *nice toys!*
¡**Qué** ridículas ideas!	***What*** *ridiculous ideas!*

Perhaps more common in the above function is the pattern **¡Qué!** + noun + **más/tan** + adjective.

¡**Qué** país más interesante!	***What an*** *interesting country!*
¡**Qué** comida tan rica!	***What a*** *delicious meal!*
¡**Qué** películas más divertidas!	***What*** *entertaining films!*
¡**Qué** niños tan traviesos!	***What*** *mischievous children!*

G Rewrite each statement as an exclamation. Use **más** or **tan** in the exclamation, depending on which appears in parentheses. Follow the *modelo*.

MODELO El museo es muy grande. (más)
→ ¡Qué museo más grande!

1. Los hoteles son muy modernos. (más)
2. La comida es muy sabrosa. (tan)
3. El libro es muy interesante. (más)
4. Las señoras son muy simpáticas. (tan)
5. La ciudad es muy animada. (más)
6. Los temas son muy importantes. (tan)
7. El informe es muy aburrido. (más)
8. Las calles son muy ruidosas. (tan)
9. El jardín es muy tranquilo. (más)
10. Los estudiantes son muy inteligentes. (tan)

H Express the following exclamations with **¡Qué!** in Spanish.

1. *What a day!*
2. *How wonderful!*
3. *What a dessert!*
4. *How ugly!*
5. *How easy!*
6. *What a musician* [masc.]*!*
7. *How authentic!*
8. *What a painter* [fem.]*!*

DIÁLOGO 3 · Somos de Madrid.

Study the dialogue, then listen to the recording and repeat each line.

ESTEBAN	¿De dónde son Uds.?
FERNANDA	Somos españoles, de Madrid.
ESTEBAN	Pues mi esposa y yo también somos madrileños.
FERNANDA	¿De veras? ¿De qué parte de la ciudad?

Análisis

Check that you understand the linguistic breakdown of each speech from *Diálogo 3*.

¿De dónde son Uds.?	*Where are you from?*
Uds.	*you* (plural)
Somos españoles, de Madrid.	*We're Spaniards, from Madrid.*
somos	*we are* (first person plural) (**ser**)
español	*Spanish, Spaniard*
españoles	*Spanish, Spaniards*
Madrid	*Madrid* (*capital of Spain*)
Pues mi esposa y yo también somos madrileños.	*Well, my wife and I are also from Madrid.*
pues	*well* (interjection)
la esposa	*wife*
mi esposa	*my wife*
madrileño	*from Madrid*
¿De veras? ¿De qué parte de la ciudad?	*Really? Where in the city?*
de veras	*really*
la parte	*part*
¿de qué parte?	*where?, from which part?*
de la ciudad	*in the city, of the city*

Variantes

Listen, and repeat the same structures from *Diálogo 3*, now with new vocabulary.

Mi esposa y yo somos madrileños.	*My* ***wife*** *and I are from Madrid.*
esposo	*husband*
mujer	*wife*
marido	*husband*
novia	*girlfriend*
novio	*boyfriend*
amigo	*friend* (*male*)
amiga	*friend* (*female*)

Estructura y Práctica

MADRILEÑOS AND OTHER CITY DWELLERS

The residents of Madrid are known as **madrileños. Madrileño** is a gentilic (or demonym), a word that identifies the residents or natives of a particular place. You have learned the gentilics or adjectives of nationality of several countries, for example, **España → español(a)**. Here are some cities and their gentilics.

Ciudad de México	capitalino/a
Bogotá	bogotano/a
Buenos Aires	bonaerense, porteño/a
Caracas	caraqueño/a
La Habana	habanero/a
Lima	limeño/a
San Juan	sanjuanero/a
Santiago	santiaguino/a
Barcelona	barcelonés/barcelonesa
Sevilla	sevillano/a
Valencia	valenciano/a
Río de Janeiro	carioca
Nueva York	neoyorquino/a
Londres	londinense
París	parisiense, parisino/a
Roma	romano/a
Moscú	moscovita
Beijing (Pequín)	pequinés/pequinesa

Information Questions: Question Words (Interrogatives) with Prepositions

You learned about question formation in Spanish in Chapters 1 and 2. Remember that information questions are introduced by question words (interrogatives). A preposition associated with an interrogative word must precede it in Spanish. In English, a preposition is usually separated from the question word and appears at the end of the sentence.

¿**De dónde** son Uds.?	***Where** are you **from**?*
¿**De qué** parte del país?	***Where** in the country?*
¿**De quién** es el pasaporte?	***Whose** passport is it?*
¿**Para quién** son los paquetes?	***Who** are the packages **for**?* (literally, ***For whom** are the packages?*)
¿**De qué** origen eres?	***What** is your (country of) origin?*
¿**De qué** color es su carro?	***What** color is their car?*

I Express the following dialogues in Spanish.

1. *Where are you* (Ud.) *from?*
   I'm [masc.] *American, from Los Angeles.*
   What a coincidence! I'm also from California, from San Francisco.
2. *My husband and I are English, from London.*
   Really? My wife and I are also from London. Where in the city?

3. *What is your* (tú) *(country of) origin?*
   I'm of Irish descent. What about you (tú)*?*
   My family is of Scottish descent.
4. *Whose boarding pass is it?*
   It's Mr. Aguilar's.
5. *Who is the gift for?*
   It's for my girlfriend.

DIÁLOGO 4 · Los estudiantes chilenos

Study the dialogue, then listen to the recording and repeat each line.

FERNANDA	¿Los estudiantes son de Argentina?
ESTEBAN	No, no son argentinos. Son de Chile.
FERNANDA	¿De la capital?
ESTEBAN	No, de Santiago no. Son de Valparaíso.

Análisis

Check that you understand the linguistic breakdown of each speech from *Diálogo 4*.

¿Los estudiantes son de Argentina?	*Are the students from Argentina?*
el estudiante	*student*
los estudiantes	*students*
son	*(they) are* (third person plural) (**ser**)
Argentina	*Argentina*
son de Argentina	*(they) are from Argentina*
No, no son argentinos. Son de Chile.	*No, they're not Argentinian. They're from Chile.*
no	*no*
argentino	*Argentinian, Argentine*
son argentinos	*they're Argentinian(s), they're Argentine(s)*
no + *verb*	(negative particle: *not*) + verb
no son argentinos	*they're not Argentinian(s), they're not Argentine(s)*
Chile	*Chile*
Son de Chile.	*They're from Chile.*
¿De la capital?	*From the capital?*
la capital	*capital city*
No, de Santiago no. Son de Valparaíso.	*No, not from Santiago. They're from Valparaíso.*
Santiago	*Santiago (capital of Chile)*
de Santiago	*from Santiago*
de Santiago no	*not from Santiago*
Valparaíso	*Valparaíso (major port on the Pacific Ocean)*
Son de Valparaíso.	*They're from Valparaíso.*

Variantes

Listen, and repeat the same structures from *Diálogo 4*, now with new vocabulary.

¿De dónde son ellos?	*Where are they from?*
Son de Puerto Rico.	*They're from Puerto Rico.*
¿De San Juan?	*From San Juan?*
No, son de Ponce.	*No, they're from Ponce (second largest city).*

Estructura y Práctica

Yes/No Questions

As you learned in Chapters 1 and 2, yes/no questions (those that elicit *yes* or *no* as a response) are formed by changing the intonation from statement intonation to rising question intonation.

Los estudiantes son de Costa Rica.	*Los students are from Costa Rica.*
¿Los estudiantes son de Costa Rica?	*Are the students from Costa Rica?*

When a sentence consists of a form of the verb **ser** and an adjective, the subject may be placed at the end of the sentence to form a question. The pattern is thus verb + adjective + subject.

Los estudiantes son puertorriqueños.	*The students are Puerto Rican.*
¿Son puertorriqueños los estudiantes?	*Are the students Puerto Rican?*

J ***Latinoamérica.*** Transform the following statements about the nationalities of people from Latin America into yes/no questions. Follow the *modelo.*

MODELO Su amiga es colombiana.
→ ¿Es colombiana su amiga?

1. El marido de Anita es peruano.
2. Pilar es hondureña.
3. Los esposos (*husband and wife*) son guatemaltecos.
4. Mi mujer es chilena.
5. Rafael es ecuatoriano.
6. Los novios son costarricenses.
7. Mi marido y yo somos brasileños.
8. Blanca y Consuelo son panameñas.

Negative Sentences

As you learned in Chapter 1, a Spanish sentence is made negative by placing **no** before the verb. The word **no** often appears twice in a Spanish sentence that answers a question: The first **no** is the Spanish word for *no;* the second **no** is a marker of negation, referred to as a negative particle in English.

Ramón **no** es de Ecuador.	*Ramón is**n't** from Ecuador.*
¿Ramón es de Ecuador?	*Is Ramón from Ecuador?*
No, Ramón **no** es de Ecuador.	***No**, Ramón is**n't** from Ecuador.*

K ***No.*** Answer the following questions about these people in the negative. Follow the *modelo.*

MODELO ¿Perla es cubana?
→ No, Perla no es cubana.

1. ¿Jaime es de Venezuela?
2. ¿Tú eres de origen europeo (*European*)?
3. ¿Manuel es el esposo de Carolina?
4. ¿Sus (de él) estudiantes son hindúes?
5. ¿La profesora Arriaga es griega?
6. ¿Santiago y Emilia son novios?
7. ¿Uds. son de la capital?
8. ¿Su familia (de Uds.) es de Marruecos?

DIÁLOGO 5 · Unos restaurantes mexicanos

Study the dialogue, then listen to the recording and repeat each line.

FERNANDA ¿Hay un restaurante mexicano por aquí?
ESTEBAN Oh, sí, hay varios restaurantes mexicanos aquí en el centro.
FERNANDA ¿Son buenos?
ESTEBAN Sí, son buenos y no muy caros.

Análisis

Check that you understand the linguistic breakdown of each speech from *Diálogo 5.*

¿Hay un restaurante mexicano por aquí?	*Is there a Mexican restaurant around here?*
mexicano	*Mexican*
un restaurante mexicano	*a Mexican restaurant*
Oh, sí, hay varios restaurantes mexicanos aquí en el centro.	*Oh, yes, there are several Mexican restaurants downtown.*
varios	*several*
varios restaurantes mexicanos	*several Mexican restaurants*
¿Son buenos?	*Are they good?*
son	*they are* (**ser**)
bueno	*good*
buenos	*good* (masculine plural)
Sí, son buenos y no muy caros.	*Yes, they're good and not very expensive.*
no	*not*
muy	*very*
caro	*expensive*
caros	*expensive* (masculine plural)
no muy caros	*not very expensive*

Variantes

Listen, and repeat the same structures from *Diálogo 5*, now with new vocabulary.

El pollo es muy bueno aquí.	*The **chicken** is very good here.*
pavo	*turkey*
pescado	*fish*
cordero	*lamb*
pan	*bread*
arroz	*rice*
postre	*dessert*
pastel	*pastry, cake, pie*
helado	*ice cream*
La comida es muy buena aquí.	*The **food** is very good here.*
sopa	*soup*
ensalada	*salad*
fruta	*fruit*
torta	*cake*
pasta	*pasta*
pizza	*pizza*
salsa	*salsa, sauce*
salchicha	*sausage*
Los tacos son muy buenos aquí.	*The **tacos** are very good here.*
frijoles	*beans*
entremeses	*hors d'oeuvres*
sándwiches	*sandwiches*
perros calientes	*hot dogs*
huevos	*eggs*
mariscos	*shellfish*
quesos	*cheeses*
Las quesadillas son muy buenas aquí.	*The **quesadillas** are very good here.*
enchiladas	*enchiladas*
tapas	*tapas*
tortillas	*tortillas* (Mexico), *omelets* (Spain)
hamburguesas	*hamburgers*
papas fritas	*French fries*
legumbres	*vegetables*
¿Hay vino en la carta?	*Is there **wine** on the menu?*
cerveza	*beer*
café	*coffee*
té	*tea*
jugo	*juice*
chocolate caliente	*hot chocolate*
agua mineral	*mineral water*
leche	*milk*
limonada	*lemonade*

¿Hay refrescos en la carta? — *Are there **soft drinks** on the menu?*
bebidas sin alcohol — *nonalcoholic beverages*
batidos de fruta — *fruit shakes*

La comida es barata aquí. — *The food is **inexpensive** here.*
rica — *delicious*
deliciosa — *delicious*
sabrosa — *tasty*
picante — *spicy*

Otros Alimentos

el aceite de oliva	*olive oil*
la aceituna	*olive*
el aguacate	*avocado*
la albóndiga	*meatball*
los alimentos frescos	*fresh food*
el arroz con pollo	*chicken with rice*
el atún	*tuna*
las aves	*poultry* (el ave (*bird, chicken*))
el azúcar	*sugar*
la batata	*sweet potato*
el bistec/biftec	*steak*
la carne	*meat*
la carne de res/vaca	*beef*
la carne roja	*red meat*
la cebolla	*onion*
el cerdo	*pork*
la cereza	*cherry*
el chocolate	*chocolate*
la comida chatarra	*junk food*
la comida orgánica	*organic food*
la comida rápida	*fast food*
la comida vegetariana	*vegetarian food*
los dulces	*candy*
dulce	*sweet*
el durazno	*peach*
la galleta con chispas/pepitas de chocolate	*chocolate chip cookie*
las golosinas	*candy, sweets, treats*
goloso	*sweet-toothed*
ser goloso	*to have a sweet tooth*
los guisantes	*peas*
el jamón	*ham*
los lácteos	*dairy*
la lechuga	*lettuce*
la mantequilla	*butter*
la mantequilla de cacahuete	*peanut butter*
la manzana	*apple*

la naranja	*orange*
la nuez	*nut*
el pan integral	*whole grain bread*
la papa	*potato*
las pasas	*raisins*
la patata	*potato* (Spain)
la pera	*pear*
la pimienta	*pepper*
la piña	*pineapple*
el plátano	*banana*
el plato acompañante/adicional	*side dish*
la sal	*salt*
la soya/soja	*soy*
la ternera	*veal*
el tocino	*bacon*
el tomate	*tomato*
las uvas	*grapes*
las (uvas) pasas	*raisins*
las verduras	*greens, green vegetables*
el yogurt	*yogurt*
la zanahoria	*carrot*

Estructura y Práctica

NOUNS

Nouns that begin with stressed /a/ (written **a** or **ha**) are feminine and therefore take feminine adjectives. However, they take the masculine article in the singular and **las** in the plural. (See also Chapter 7.)

el agua **fría**	*cold water*
las aguas **frescas**	*cool waters*
el ave **blanca**	*white bird*
las aves **asadas**	*roasted poultry/chicken*
el haba **negra**	*black fava bean*
las habas **secas**	*dried fava beans*

Position of Adjectives

You have learned that, in Spanish, adjectives normally follow the noun, rather than precede it as in English. You also saw certain types of adjectives that precede the noun in Spanish. Preposed adjectives occur with postposed adjectives of nationality in noun phrases.

muchas compañías norteamericanas	*many American companies*
algunos cantantes italianos	*some Italian singers*
varios vinos españoles	*several Spanish wines*

L Write each noun phrase, completing it with the cues in parentheses in their correct positions. Make all necessary agreements when you write the complete phrase. Follow the *modelo.*

MODELO ________ carne ________ (mucho) (argentino)
→ mucha carne argentina

1. ________ queso ________ (suizo) (ninguno)
2. ________ jamones ________ (varios) (inglés)
3. ________ torta ________ (italiano) (bastante)
4. ________ uvas ________ (poco) (chileno)
5. ________ nueces ________ (alguno) (español)
6. ________ aceite de oliva ________ (griego) (suficiente)
7. ________ pescado ________ (alguno) (japonés)
8. ________ manzanas ________ (estadounidenses) (varios)

M ***¡Buen provecho!* (Enjoy your meal!)** Assign a category for each food on the list. Refer to the vocabulary in *Diálogo 5: Variantes* and *Otros Alimentos* as needed. Write the name of the correct category for each of the foods listed: **frutas**, **legumbres**, **lácteos**, **carnes y aves**, or **postres**.

1. el pollo
2. el queso
3. la manzana
4. la torta
5. la papa
6. la carne de res
7. la cebolla
8. el helado
9. la mantequilla
10. las uvas
11. el yogurt
12. el jamón
13. la piña
14. las galletas con chispas
15. los guisantes
16. las cerezas
17. las zanahorias
18. los dulces
19. la salchicha
20. la leche

DIÁLOGO 6 · Una película mexicana

Study the dialogue, then listen to the recording and repeat each line.

ESTEBAN ¿Hay cines aquí con películas en español?
FERNANDA Sí, en el cine Real hay una película mexicana.
ESTEBAN ¿Es buena la película?
FERNANDA Sí, es interesante y muy divertida.

Análisis

Check that you understand the linguistic breakdown of each speech from *Diálogo 6.*

¿Hay cines aquí con películas en español?	*Are there movie theaters here with films in Spanish?*
el cine	*movie theater*
la película	*film*
con	*with*
el español	*Spanish*
en español	*in Spanish*
Sí, en el cine Real hay una película mexicana.	*Yes, there's a Mexican film at the Real movie theater.*
mexicana	*Mexican* (feminine singular)
una película mexicana	*a Mexican film*
¿Es buena la película?	*Is the film good?*
Sí, es interesante y muy divertida.	*Yes, it's interesting and very entertaining.*
interesante	*interesting* (masculine and feminine)
divertido	*amusing, entertaining*
divertida	*amusing, entertaining* (feminine)

Variantes

Listen, and repeat the same structures from *Diálogo 6*, now with new vocabulary.

¿Hay películas en español?	*Are there films in* ***Spanish****?*
inglés	*English*
francés	*French*
italiano	*Italian*
alemán	*German*
portugués	*Portuguese*
ruso	*Russian*
chino	*Chinese*
japonés	*Japanese*
coreano	*Korean*
hindi	*Hindi*
hebreo	*Hebrew*
árabe	*Arabic*

Estructura y Práctica

Prepositions

Prepositions are words (such as *to, for, in, at, from* in English) that link nouns or pronouns to other elements of the sentence. The group of words consisting of a preposition + noun or pronoun is called a prepositional phrase. The prepositions of one language rarely correspond exactly to the prepositions of another. (See also Chapters 4, 5, and 6.)

In these chapters you have seen the prepositions **con** (*with*), **de** (*of, from, in, about*), **en** (*in, at, on*), and **para** (*for*). **Por** also means *for*, which you have learned as part of **por aquí** (*around here*) and **la tienda por departamentos** (*department store*).

Con *with*

Hay un cine **con** películas en español.	*There's a movie theater* ***with*** *films in Spanish.*
Hay arroz **con** pollo en la carta.	*There's chicken* ***with*** *rice on the menu.*

De *of, from, in, about*

De expresses possession, origin, and the material of which something is made.

Estos libros son **de** Consuelo.	*These are Consuelo****'s*** *books.*
Los programadores son **de** Chile.	*The programmers are* ***from*** *Chile.*
Marta es **de** origen polaco.	*Marta is* ***of*** *Polish descent.*
¿**De** qué parte eres?	*Where (****from*** *which part) are you* ***from****?*
¿**De** qué color es su casa?	*(****Of****) What color is their house?*
El reloj es **de** oro.	*The watch is (****made of****) gold.*
La comida **de** este restaurante es rica.	*The food* ***in*** *this restaurant is delicious.*
Es un libro **de** animales para niños.	*It's a book* ***about*** *animals for children.*

The preposition **de** is used to form compound nouns.

la administración **de** empresas	*business administration*
la tienda **de** cómputo	*computer store*
el museo **de** arte	*art museum*
la tarjeta **de** crédito	*credit card*
el libro **de** texto	*textbook*
la base **de** datos	*database*

The preposition **de** contracts with the masculine singular definite article **el** to form **del**.

Ana es la esposa **del** señor Vega.	*Ana is Mr. Vega****'s*** *wife.*
Es la ciudad más grande **del** país.	*It's the biggest city* ***in the*** *country.*

The preposition **de** occurs in many idiomatic expressions.

de veras	*really*
de nada	*you're welcome*

En *in, at, on*

Hay películas **en** francés.	*There are films* ***in*** *French.*
Hay informes **en** el maletín.	*There are reports* ***in*** *the attaché case.*
Hay muchos hoteles **en** el centro.	*There are many hotels downtown (****in*** *the downtown area).*
Hay un cibercafé **en** la esquina.	*There's an internet café* ***on/at*** *the corner.*
¿Qué hay **en** la carta?	*What's* ***on*** *the menu?*

To specify position, **en** can be replaced by **dentro de** (*inside of*) or **encima de** (*on, on top of*).

En specifies the period of time within which something happens.

Regresamos **en** diez minutos. (**regresar**) *We're coming back* ***in*** *ten minutes.*

Para *for*

Es un regalo **para** Miguel. *It's a gift* ***for*** *Miguel.*

N Complete each phrase with the missing preposition: **con**, **de**, **en**, **para**, or **por**. Write the correct prepositions, and remember to use the contraction **del** when necessary.

1. No hay pescado ________ la carta.
2. —¿________ quiénes son estos platos? —El sándwich ________ queso es ________ Daniel y la pasta ________ salsa es ________ Elena.
3. Son mis libros ________ administración ________ empresas.
4. El restaurante vegetariano queda (*is located*) ________ la esquina.
5. Sus amigos son ________ Madrid.
6. Hay un pastel ________ manzana ________ la mesa.
7. Perdón, ¿hay un cine ________ películas ________ inglés ________ aquí?
8. ¿________ qué origen eres?
9. ¿Hay tomate y lechuga ________ la hamburguesa?
10. La pulsera ________ oro es un regalo ________ Beatriz.
11. ________ favor, ¿hay una tienda ________ departamentos ________ este barrio?
12. Son los contratos ________ señor Maldonado.
13. ________ veras, ¿no hay una tienda ________ cómputo ________ el centro?
14. —Muchas gracias, señorita. —________ nada, señor.
15. El arroz ________ pollo es muy rico ________ este restaurante.
16. El helado ________ chocolate y el café ________ leche son muy buenos ________ este cibercafé.

DIÁLOGO 7 · Un restaurante auténtico

Study the dialogue, then listen to the recording and repeat each line.

FERNANDA ¿Cómo es la comida de este restaurante?
ESTEBAN Es muy buena y muy auténtica.
FERNANDA ¿Hay muchos platos diferentes?
ESTEBAN Sí, hay platos de todas las regiones del país.

Análisis

Check that you understand the linguistic breakdown of each speech from *Diálogo 7.*

¿Cómo es la comida de este restaurante?	*How's the food in this restaurant?*
¿Cómo?	*How?*
la comida	*food, meal*
¿Cómo es la comida?	*How's the food?*
de	*of, in*
este	*this* (masculine singular)
este restaurante	*this restaurant*
de este restaurante	*in this restaurant*
Es muy buena y muy auténtica.	*It's very good and very authentic.*
auténtico	*authentic*
auténtica	*authentic* (feminine)
¿Hay muchos platos diferentes?	*Are there many different dishes?*
mucho, mucha	*much*
muchos, muchas	*many*
el plato	*plate, dish*
muchos platos	*many dishes*
diferente	*different*
muchos platos diferentes	*many different dishes*
Sí, hay platos de todas las regiones del país.	*Yes, there are dishes from every region of the country.*
todo el, toda la, todos los, todas las	*all, every*
la región	*region*
las regiones	*regions*
todas las regiones	*all the regions, every region*
el país	*country*
del	*of the* (contraction of **de** + **el**)
del país	*of the country*
todas las regiones del país	*every region of the country*

Variantes

Listen, and repeat the same structures from *Diálogo 7*, now with new vocabulary.

Este café es bueno.	***This*** *café is good.*
Ese	*That*
Aquel	*That*
Estos platos son auténticos.	***These*** *dishes are authentic.*
Esos	*Those*
Aquellos	*Those*
Esta calle es bonita.	***This*** *street is pretty.*
Esa	*That*
Aquella	*That*

Estas maletas son grandes.	***These** suitcases are big.*
Esas	*Those*
Aquellas	*Those*

Estructura y Práctica

Demonstrative Adjectives

Spanish has a set of three demonstrative adjectives, whereas English has only two.

este	*this* (near the speaker)
ese	*that* (near the person spoken to)
aquel	*that* (removed from both the speaker and the person spoken to)

These demonstratives correspond to the Spanish division of place.

aquí	*here* (near the speaker)
ahí	*there* (near the person spoken to)
allí	*there* (removed from both the speaker and the person spoken to)

The demonstratives, like the definite and indefinite articles, agree with the noun they refer to in both gender and number. The masculine singular form is slightly irregular, as it does not end in **-o**. The other three forms look like any other adjective.

MASCULINE SINGULAR	MASCULINE PLURAL	FEMININE SINGULAR	FEMININE PLURAL
este	estos	esta	estas
ese	esos	esa	esas
aquel	aquellos	aquella	aquellas

Este café es bueno.	***This** café is good.*
Sí, pero **aquel** café es mejor.	*Yes, but **that** café (over there) is better.*
Esa mochila es linda.	***That** backpack is nice.*
Pero **esta** mochila es más útil.	*But **this** backpack is more useful.*

For many Spanish American speakers, **aquel** is replaced by **ese**.

O ***Estas cosas o esas cosas.*** Write the correct form of all three demonstrative adjectives for each of the following nouns. Follow the *modelo.*

MODELO libro
→ este ese aquel libro

1. comida
2. cine
3. países
4. calles
5. pizza
6. billete
7. flores
8. amigos
9. pan
10. región

P ***¿De dónde son?¿Cómo son?*** Rewrite each of the following sentences, changing the forms of the definite article to the corresponding forms of **este**. Follow the *modelo*.

MODELO La directora es canadiense.
→ Esta directora es canadiense.

1. Las programadoras son buenas.
2. El asesor es muy inteligente.
3. Los dentistas son viejos.
4. La cocinera es italiana.
5. El escritor es famoso.
6. Los músicos son de Cuba.
7. El cantante es brasileño.
8. La abogada es trabajadora (*hardworking*).
9. Las bailarinas son maravillosas.
10. Los médicos son hindúes.

When **todo** is used as an adjective, it is usually followed by the definite article. Notice the different translations in English.

todo el país	*the **whole** country, **all** the country*
toda la zona	*the **whole** area, the **entire** area*
todos los países	***every** country, **all** the countries*
todas las zonas	***every** area, **all** the areas*
todo el día	***all** day **long**, the **whole** day*
todos los días	***every** day*
toda la novela	*the **entire** novel*
todas las novelas	***all** the novels, **every** novel*

The forms **todo** and **toda** may precede a singular noun with the meaning *every*, especially in more formal style.

todo informe = todos los informes	***every** report*
toda tienda = todas las tiendas	***every** store*

Todo as a pronoun in Spanish means *everything*.

Todo es maravilloso aquí.	***Everything** is wonderful here.*
Todo es moderno en su casa.	***Everything** is modern in their house.*

When the pronoun **todo** is the object of a verb, the pronoun **lo** precedes the verb. Notice that **todo** as direct object may sometimes precede the verb.

Ahora **lo** comprendo **todo**. (**comprender**)	*Now I understand **everything**.*
Todo lo tiene. (**tener**)	*He has **everything**.*

Q Express the following phrases with **todo** in Spanish. Use **todo** as an adjective followed by the definite article.

1. *the whole city*
2. *every film*
3. *all the wines*
4. *all the downtown area*
5. *the entire country*
6. *all month long*
7. *the whole week*
8. *every meal*
9. *the entire neighborhood*
10. *all the actresses*

DIÁLOGO 8 · ¿De dónde son los profesores?

Study the dialogue, then listen to the recording and repeat each line.

ESTEBAN	¿De dónde es ese profesor? ¿De Santo Domingo?
FERNANDA	Sí, es dominicano.
ESTEBAN	¿Y aquella profesora?
FERNANDA	Ella es dominicana también.

Análisis

Check that you understand the linguistic breakdown of each speech from *Diálogo 8*.

¿De dónde es ese profesor? ¿De Santo Domingo?	*Where is that professor from? ¿Santo Domingo?*
¿dónde?	*where?*
¿de dónde?	*from where?*
el profesor	*university professor, secondary school teacher* (masculine)
ese profesor	*that teacher*
Santo Domingo	*Santo Domingo* (*capital of the Dominican Republic*)
Sí, es dominicano.	*Yes, he's Dominican.*
sí	*yes*
dominicano	*Dominican*
¿Y aquella profesora?	*What about that (female) professor?*
y	*and, and what about?*
la profesora	*university professor, secondary school teacher* (feminine)
aquella profesora	*that teacher*
Ella es dominicana también.	*She's Dominican, too.*
ella	*she*
dominicana	*Dominican* (feminine)

Variantes

Listen, and repeat the same structures from *Diálogo 8*, now with new vocabulary.

¿De dónde es ese profesor ?	*Where's that* ***professor*** *from?*
abogado	*lawyer*
dentista	*dentist*
médico	*doctor*
asesor	*consultant*
asesor financiero	*financial advisor*
ingeniero	*engineer*
escritor	*writer*
contador	*accountant*
enfermero	*nurse*
analista	*analyst*

¿De dónde es ese profesor ?	*Where's that **professor** from?*
programador	*programmer*
músico	*musician*
cantante	*singer*
bailarín	*dancer*
pintor	*painter*
cocinero	*cook, chef*
actor	*actor*
Aquella profesora es dominicana también.	*That **professor** is Dominican, too.*
abogada	*lawyer*
dentista	*dentist*
doctora	*doctor*
asesora	*consultant*
asesora financiera	*financial advisor*
ingeniera	*engineer*
escritora	*writer*
contadora	*accountant*
enfermera	*nurse*
analista	*analyst*
programadora	*programmer*
música	*musician*
cantante	*singer*
bailarina	*dancer*
pintora	*painter*
cocinera	*cook, chef*
actriz	*actress*

Otras Profesiones

el hombre de negocios *businessman*	la mujer de negocios *businesswoman*
el científico *scientist*	la científica *scientist*
el político *politician*	la política *politician*

Estructura y Práctica

Gender of Nouns That Refer to People

When a noun that refers to people ends in **-or**, **-és**, **-ón**, or **-ín**, the noun is usually masculine and adds **-a** to make the feminine form. The written accent is dropped when the suffix **-a** is added.

MASCULINE	FEMININE
el locutor *newscaster*	la locutora *newscaster*
el inglés	la inglesa
el anfitrión *host*	la anfitriona *hostess*
el bailarín	la bailarina

Some nouns that refer to people keep the same form for the feminine as for the masculine, changing only their article. Many of these nouns end in **-e**, **-a**, **-ista**, **-nte**, or a consonant.

el/la intérprete *performer*
el/la atleta *athlete*
el/la artista *artist, performing artist*
el/la dependiente *salesperson*
el/la agente *agent*
el/la albañil *mason, construction worker*

For some nouns ending in **-nte**, a feminine form ending in **-nta** is common: **el estudiante, la estudianta; el gerente, la gerenta.**

R ***Profesiones.*** Write the feminine form for each of the following nouns of profession.

1. el desarrollador de programas (*software developer*)
2. el desarrollador de web (*web developer*)
3. el administrador de bases de datos (*database administrator*)
4. el arquitecto de red (*computer network architect*)
5. el analista de seguridad de (la) información (*information security analyst*)
6. el enfermero practicante (*nurse practitioner*)
7. el médico asistente (*physician assistant*)
8. el gerente de marketing (mercadeo) (*marketing manager*)
9. el gerente de ventas (*sales manager*)
10. el diseñador de videojuegos (*video game designer*)

Un paso más

Are you ready to take your Spanish a step further? Here are exercises that will enhance your knowledge of the language and encourage you to express yourself freely.

S ***Oficios* (Occupations).** Write the English translation of each of the following nouns. Then write the feminine form of each of the nouns in Spanish. You have learned vocabulary words that will help you figure out the meanings of most of these words; other words will be familiar to you as cognates of English.

1. el hotelero
2. el electricista
3. el policía
4. el taxista
5. el uberista
6. el mesero
7. el florista
8. el jardinero
9. el panadero
10. el mecánico
11. el carpintero
12. el plomero
13. el periodista
14. el librero
15. el secretario
16. el recepcionista

17. el banquero
18. el estilista
19. el oficinista
20. el carnicero
21. el farmacéutico
22. el joyero

T ***Preguntas personales.*** Answer each question with a complete Spanish sentence.

1. ¿De dónde es Ud.?
2. ¿De qué origen es?
3. ¿De dónde son sus padres (*parents*)? ¿Y sus abuelos (*grandparents*)?
4. ¿Cuál es su profesión?
5. ¿Hay un restaurante mexicano en su barrio? ¿Qué platos hay en la carta? ¿Cómo es la comida?
6. ¿Hay un restaurante italiano (chino, japonés, francés, tailandés, vegetariano) en su ciudad? ¿Qué platos hay en la carta? ¿Cómo es la comida?
7. ¿Es Ud. vegetariano/vegetariana? ¿Qué alimentos come?
8. ¿Cuáles son sus alimentos favoritos?
9. ¿Cuáles son sus platos favoritos?
10. ¿Es goloso/golosa? ¿Qué dulces come?

4

Describing People, Emotions, and Health

Communication Goals

- Talking about one's physical state and frame of mind
- Locating people and places
- Telling time and days of the week
- Describing people
- Vocabulary: health, emotions, events, articles of clothing, the family

Grammar Topics

- **Estar** *to be*: Uses
- **Estar** vs. **ser**
- Adverbs of Place with Prepositions
- **Ser** *to be*: Uses
- **Ser** vs. **estar**: Describing Food
- Tag Questions
- **Estar** + Past Participle
- **Ser** and **estar** in Yes/No Questions

DIÁLOGO 1 · ¿Cómo estás?

Study the dialogue, then listen to the recording and repeat each line.

PACO	Hola, Carmen. ¿Cómo estás?
CARMEN	Estoy bien. Y tú, Paco, ¿qué tal?
PACO	Estoy acatarrado.
CARMEN	¡Pobre!

Análisis

Check that you understand the linguistic breakdown of each speech from *Diálogo 1.*

Hola, Carmen. ¿Cómo estás?	*Hi, Carmen. How are you?*
¿cómo?	*how?*
estás	*you are* (second person singular) (**estar**)
Estoy bien. Y tú, Paco, ¿qué tal?	*I'm fine. And how about you, Paco?*
estoy	*I am* (first person singular) (**estar**)
bien	*well, fine*
Estoy acatarrado.	*I have a cold.*
acatarrado	*sick with a cold*
¡Pobre!	*Poor guy! / You poor thing!*

Variantes

Listen, and repeat the same structures from *Diálogo 1,* now with new vocabulary.

Estoy bien .	*I'm (feeling)* ***fine.***
mal	*ill*
perfectamente	*very well, great*
regular	*so-so*
enfermo	*sick*
Diana está acatarrada .	*Diana has a* ***cold.***
un poco acatarrada	*slight cold*
¿Está enfermo tu hermano?	*Is your brother sick?*
Sí, está resfriado.	*Yes, he has a cold (is sick with a cold).*

Estructura y Práctica

Estar *to be*: Uses

The verbs **ser** and **estar** both mean *to be,* but they are not interchangeable. They are used in different contexts, as you will see in this chapter.

Estar (*to be*) is an irregular **-ar** verb. Its conjugation in the present tense is as follows.

estar *to be*

SINGULAR	PLURAL
estoy	estamos
estás	estáis
está	están

1 · **Estar** is used before adjectives that express a temporary physical state, such as health, or frame of mind, such as happiness.

Sara **está** bien.	*Sara* ***is (feeling)*** *fine.*
Estamos contentos.	***We're*** *happy.*
Mario, ¿por qué **estás** nervioso?	*Mario, why* ***are you*** *nervous?*

Only **estar** (not **ser**) can be used with **contento**.

2 · **Estar** is used to express location, whether temporary or permanent.

¿Dónde **están** los asesores?	*Where **are** the consultants?*
Están en su oficina.	***They're** in their office.*
Estoy en México.	***I'm** in Mexico.*
La heladería **está** cerca.	*The ice cream store **is** nearby.*

Remember that **queda**, from **quedar** (*to be located*), expresses location that is permanent only.

La biblioteca **queda** en la esquina.	*The library **is** on the corner.*
Las tiendas por departamentos **quedan** en el centro.	*The department stores **are** downtown.*

A Write the form of **estar** that correctly completes each of the following sentences.

1. Juan ____________ enfermo.
2. María y Consuelo ____________ bien.
3. Yo ____________ perfectamente.
4. ¿Por qué (tú) ____________ tan estresado?
5. Perla ____________ regular.
6. Daniel y yo ____________ cansados.
7. ¿Cómo ____________ Uds.?
8. Manolo y Luis ____________ mal.

DIÁLOGO 2 · Estoy inquieto.

Study the dialogue, then listen to the recording and repeat each line.

CARMEN	¿Cómo está Ud.?
PACO	Yo estoy bien, pero muy inquieto.
CARMEN	¿Inquieto? ¿Por qué?
PACO	¿No sabe? Fernando está en el hospital.

Análisis

Check that you understand the linguistic breakdown of each speech from *Diálogo 2.*

¿Cómo está Ud.?	*How are you?*
está	*you are, he is, she is* (third person singular) (**estar**)
Yo estoy bien, pero muy inquieto.	*I'm well, but very worried.*
inquieto	*worried*
¿Inquieto? ¿Por qué?	*Worried? Why?*
¿No sabe? Fernando está en el hospital.	*Then you don't know? Fernando is in the hospital.*

Variantes

Listen, and repeat the same structures from *Diálogo 2*, now with new vocabulary.

Juan está inquieto.	*Juan is* ***worried****.*
estresado	*stressed*
emocionado	*excited*
cansado	*tired*
contento	*happy*
deprimido	*depressed*
molesto	*annoyed*
Elena está preocupada.	*Elena is* ***worried****.*
triste	*sad*
asustada	*scared*
entusiasmada	*enthusiastic*
nerviosa	*nervous*
alegre	*cheerful*
angustiada	*distressed*
aburrida	*bored*

DIÁLOGO 3 · Estamos preocupados.

Study the dialogue, then listen to the recording and repeat each line.

CARMEN	Estamos preocupados. El perro no está en la casa.
PACO	¿No está en el jardín?
CARMEN	Tampoco.
PACO	Ahora yo estoy preocupado también.

Análisis

Check that you understand the linguistic breakdown of each speech from *Diálogo 3*.

Estamos preocupados. El perro no está en la casa.	*We're worried. The dog isn't in the house.*
estamos	*we are* (first person plural) (**estar**)
el perro	*dog*
¿No está en el jardín?	*Isn't he in the garden?*
el jardín	*garden*
Tampoco.	*No, he's not there either.*
tampoco	*neither*
Ahora yo estoy preocupado también.	*Now I'm worried, too.*
ahora	*now*

Variantes

Listen, and repeat the same structures from *Diálogo 3*, now with new vocabulary.

El perro está en el jardín.	*The* ***dog*** *is in the garden.*
gato	*cat*

Estructura y Práctica

B ***¿Cómo están?*** Write a sentence to describe the emotional state or frame of mind of each indicated member of your family. Use the correct form of **estar** plus the adjective provided. Make all necessary agreements. (For Spanish terms for family members, see the *Variantes* section of *Diálogo 19* in this chapter.) Follow the *modelo*.

MODELO mi primo / aburrido
→ Mi primo está aburrido.

1. mi mamá / entusiasmado
2. mis hijos / emocionado
3. yo [*fem.*] / contento
4. los tíos / triste
5. la cuñada / estresado
6. tú [*fem.*] / preocupado
7. la tía / deprimido
8. mis hermanos y yo / molesto
9. los abuelos / inquieto
10. mi papá / nervioso
11. mis nietas / alegre
12. las sobrinas / angustiado

DIÁLOGO 4 · Estamos muy atrasados.

Study the dialogue, then listen to the recording and repeat each line.

CARMEN El taxi ya está. ¿Ya están listos?
PACO No, no estamos listos todavía.
CARMEN ¡Caramba! Estamos muy atrasados ya.

Análisis

Check that you understand the linguistic breakdown of each speech from *Diálogo 4*.

El taxi ya está. ¿Ya están listos?	*The cab is here already. Are you ready?*
el taxi	*taxi, cab*
ya	*already*
están	*you* (plural) *are, they are* (third person plural) (**estar**)
listo	*ready* (when used with **estar**)
No, no estamos listos todavía.	*No, we're not ready yet.*
todavía	*still, yet*
¡Caramba! Estamos muy atrasados ya.	*My goodness! We're already very late.*
¡Caramba!	*My goodness!*
atrasado	*late, behind schedule*
estar atrasado	*to be behind schedule*

Variantes

Listen, and repeat the same structures from *Diálogo 4*, now with new vocabulary.

Están atrasados en la alta tecnología.	*They are* ***lagging*** *in high tech.*
adelantados	*advanced*

Estructura y Práctica

ADJECTIVES

Many of the adjectives you have seen in these *diálogos* end in **-ado** or **-ido**. For example, **emocionado, preocupado, acatarrado, atrasado, adelantado, aburrido, deprimido.**

These adjectives derive from the past participle (the **-do** form) of the present perfect tense. For **-ar** verbs, the ending is **-ado**; for **-er** and **-ir** verbs, the ending is **-ido**. (For the present perfect tense, see Chapter 13.)

DIÁLOGO 5 · ¿Dónde está el museo de arte?

Study the dialogue, then listen to the recording and repeat each line.

PACO	¿Dónde está el museo de arte?
CARMEN	Queda en la calle Robles al lado del parque.
PACO	¿Está lejos de la plaza?
CARMEN	En absoluto. Está a una cuadra de la plaza.

Análisis

Check that you understand the linguistic breakdown of each speech from *Diálogo 5*.

¿Dónde está el museo de arte?	*Where is the art museum?*
¿Dónde?	*Where?*
Queda en la calle Robles al lado del parque.	*It's on Robles Street, next to the park.*
queda	*it is* (to express the permanent location of places) (**quedar**)
al lado de	*next to*
el parque	*park*
al lado del parque	*next to the park*
¿Está lejos de la plaza?	*Is it far from the square?*
lejos de	*far from*
la plaza	*square*
lejos de la plaza	*far from the square*
En absoluto. Está a una cuadra de la plaza.	*Not at all. It's a block away from the square.*
En absoluto.	*Not at all.*
a	*at a distance of*
la cuadra	*(city) block*
a una cuadra	*a block away*
a una cuadra de la plaza	*a block away from the square*

Variantes

Listen, and repeat the same structures from *Diálogo 5*, now with new vocabulary.

¿Dónde está el museo de arte?	*Where is the **art museum**?*
el museo de ciencias	*science museum*
la biblioteca	*library*
la universidad	*university*
el colegio	*high school*
la escuela	*school*
el zoológico	*zoo*
el monumento	*monument*
la iglesia	*church*
la sinagoga	*synagogue*
la catedral	*cathedral*
el banco	*bank*
el club de jazz	*jazz club*
El hotel está a una cuadra de la plaza.	*The hotel is **a block** from the square.*
cinco cuadras	*five blocks*
una milla	*a mile*
diez kilómetros	*ten kilometers*
El edificio queda lejos de la plaza.	*The building is **far from** the square.*
cerca de	*near*
al lado de	*next to*
detrás de	*behind*
delante de	*in front of*
en frente de	*opposite*
a la derecha de	*to the right of*
a la izquierda de	*to the left of*
El perro está debajo de la mesa.	*The dog is **under** the table.*
encima de	*on top of*

DIÁLOGO 6 · Los gerentes están reunidos.

Study the dialogue, then listen to the recording and repeat each line.

CARMEN	Los gerentes no están en su oficina.
PACO	Es que están reunidos ahora.
CARMEN	¿Dónde es la reunión?
PACO	Es en la sala de conferencias.

Análisis

Check that you understand the linguistic breakdown of each speech from *Diálogo 6*.

Los gerentes no están en su oficina.	*The managers aren't in their offices.*
el gerente	*manager*
su	*their*

Es que están reunidos ahora.	*It's because they're having a meeting now.*
es que	*it's because, it's that, the fact is*
reunido	*at a meeting*
estar reunidos	*to be at a meeting, to be having a meeting*
¿Dónde es la reunión?	*Where is the meeting?*
¿Dónde es?	*Where is?* (of events)
la reunión	*meeting*
Es en la sala de conferencias.	*It's in the conference room.*
la sala de conferencias	*the conference room*

Variantes

Listen, and repeat the same structures from *Diálogo 6*, now with new vocabulary.

¿Dónde es la reunión ?	*Where is the* ***meeting****?*
la fiesta	*party*
el partido	*game*
la comida	*dinner*
el concierto	*concert*
el baile	*dance*
el espectáculo	*show*
el examen	*exam*
la conferencia	*lecture*
la boda	*wedding*

Estructura y Práctica

Estar vs. ser

As you have learned, **estar** is used to express location, whether temporary or permanent.

Estamos en Madrid.	***We're*** *in Madrid.*
¿Dónde **está** el banco?	*Where* ***is*** *the bank?*
El banco **está** enfrente del hotel.	*The bank* ***is*** *opposite the hotel.*

Ser is used to indicate where an event takes place. **Estar** cannot be used for this purpose.

¿Dónde **es** la conferencia?	*Where* ***is*** *the lecture?*
Es en la universidad.	***It's*** *at the university.*
¿Dónde **es** el concierto?	*Where* ***is*** *the concert?*
Es en el Teatro Real.	***It's*** *in the Teatro Real.*

C **Where is it?** Choose **ser** or **estar** to complete each of the following questions about where things or events are located. Follow the *modelos*.

MODELOS ¿Dónde ___*está*___ el billetero?

¿Dónde ___*es*___ la fiesta?

1. ¿Dónde ____________ el zoológico?
2. ¿Dónde ____________ el partido?
3. ¿Dónde ____________ el taxi?
4. ¿Dónde ____________ la boda?
5. ¿Dónde ____________ el bailarín?
6. ¿Dónde ____________ el jardín?
7. ¿Dónde ____________ la sala?
8. ¿Dónde ____________ el espectáculo?
9. ¿Dónde ____________ el informe?
10. ¿Dónde ____________ el paseo?
11. ¿Dónde ____________ la reunión?
12. ¿Dónde ____________ la joyería?

Adverbs of Place with Prepositions

Prepositions are words that link nouns or pronouns to other elements of the sentence. The group of words consisting of a preposition + a noun or pronoun is called a prepositional phrase.

Adverbs of place can combine with prepositions to form compound prepositions. In Chapter 1, you learned **enfrente** (*across the street*). The preposition **de** can be added to **enfrente**: **enfrente de** (*opposite, across the street from*).

El café está **enfrente**.	*The café is* ***across the street****.*
El café está **enfrente del** hotel.	*The café is* ***opposite / across the street from*** *the hotel.*

Here are some common adverbs of place with the preposition **de** (*of, from*).

a la derecha (de)	*on/to the right (of)*
a la izquierda (de)	*on/to the left (of)*
al lado (de)	*next to*
cerca (de)	*close (to)*
lejos (de)	*far (from)*
debajo (de)	*under*
delante (de)	*in front (of)*
detrás (de)	*behind*
encima (de)	*on top (of)*
al fondo (de)	*at/in the back (of)*

El colegio está **al lado del** museo.	*The high school is* ***next to*** *the museum.*
La sinagoga está **cerca de** la catedral.	*The synagogue is* ***near*** *the cathedral.*
El perro está **detrás de** su casa.	*The dog is* ***behind*** *their house.*

The preposition **a** (*to*) is used to express English *away from, at a distance of.*

La estación está **a tres cuadras** del hotel.	*The train station is* ***three blocks*** *from the hotel.*
El centro está **a diez minutos** de aquí.	*The downtown area is* ***ten minutes*** *from here.*

D ***¿Dónde está?*** Answer each of the following questions with a complete Spanish sentence. Use the cue provided and add the correct prepositions as necessary: **a, de, en, por**. Follow the *modelo.*

MODELO ¿Dónde está la heladería? (*on a pedestrian street*)
→ Está en una calle peatonal.

1. ¿Dónde está la universidad? (*nine miles from downtown*)
2. ¿Dónde queda el parque? (*behind the church*)
3. ¿Dónde está el perro? (*under the table*)
4. ¿Dónde están los edificios nuevos? (*near the business area*)
5. ¿Dónde está la tienda de deportes? (*at the corner*)
6. ¿Dónde están los documentos? (*on / on top of the shelf*)
7. ¿Dónde queda ese club de jazz? (*a block from the internet café*)
8. ¿Dónde queda el aeropuerto (*airport*)? (*far from the city*)
9. ¿Dónde están la escuela y el colegio? (*around here*)
10. ¿Dónde está la sala de conferencias? (*to the right of our office*)
11. ¿Dónde queda esa tienda de cómputo? (*next to an Italian restaurant*)
12. ¿Dónde está tu carro? (*in front of my house*)
13. ¿Dónde queda la farmacia? (*opposite the hospital*)
14. ¿Dónde están los gatos? (*behind the sofa* (el sofá))
15. ¿Dónde están nuestras maletas? (*in the back of the closet*)
16. ¿Dónde queda la catedral? (*to the left of the square*)

DIÁLOGO 7 · ¿A qué hora es la reunión?

Study the dialogue, then listen to the recording and repeat each line.

PACO ¿A qué hora es la reunión?
CARMEN A las dos y media.
PACO ¿Dos o doce?
CARMEN Dos. Es a las dos y media.

Análisis

Check that you understand the linguistic breakdown of each speech from *Diálogo 7*.

¿A qué hora es la reunión?	*At what time is the meeting?*
la hora	*hour, time*
¿A qué hora?	*At what time?*
A las dos y media.	*At two thirty.*
las dos	*two o'clock*
medio	*half*
y media	*and a half (hour)*
las dos y media	*two thirty, 2:30*

¿Dos o doce?	*(Did you say) Two or twelve?*
Dos. Es a las dos y media.	*(I said) Two. It's at 2:30.*

Variantes

Listen, and repeat the same structures from *Diálogo 7*, now with new vocabulary.

La reunión es a las dos .	*The meeting is at* ***two o'clock.***
tres y cuarto	*a quarter after three*
cuatro y quince	*4:15*
cinco y media	*5:30*
seis menos cuarto	*a quarter to six*
siete menos quince	*a quarter to seven*
ocho cincuenta	*8:50*
Es la una .	*It's* ***one o'clock.***
mediodía	*noon*
medianoche	*midnight*
Son las nueve de la mañana .	*It's* ***9:00 A.M.***
diez de la noche	*10:00 P.M.*
once en punto	*11:00 on the dot*
doce	*12 o'clock*

DIÁLOGO 8 · El museo no está abierto.

Study the dialogue, then listen to the recording and repeat each line.

CARMEN	El museo no está abierto todavía.
PACO	¡Qué raro! Ya son las once.
CARMEN	Ay, ¡qué tontos somos! Hoy es lunes.
PACO	Claro. Los lunes todos los museos están cerrados.

Análisis

Check that you understand the linguistic breakdown of each speech from *Diálogo 8*.

El museo no está abierto todavía.	*The museum isn't open yet.*
el museo	*museum*
abierto	*open*
estar abierto	*to be open*
todavía	*still, yet*
¡Qué raro! Ya son las once.	*How strange! It's 11 o'clock already.*
raro	*strange*
¡Qué raro!	*How strange!*
ya	*already*
las once	*eleven o'clock*
son las once	*it's eleven o'clock*

Ay, ¡qué tontos somos! Hoy es lunes.	*Oh, we're so stupid! Today is Monday.*
tonto	*stupid, silly, foolish*
¡qué tontos!	*how stupid!*
somos	*we are* (first person plural) (**ser**)
hoy	*today*
lunes	*Monday*
Claro. Los lunes todos los museos están cerrados.	*Of course. All the museums are closed on Mondays.*
claro	*of course*
los lunes	*on Mondays*
cerrado	*closed*
estar cerrado	*to be closed*

Variantes

Listen, and repeat the same structures from *Diálogo 8*, now with new vocabulary.

¿Qué día es hoy?	*What day is today?*
Hoy es lunes .	*Today is **Monday**.*
martes	*Tuesday*
miércoles	*Wednesday*
jueves	*Thursday*
viernes	*Friday*
sábado	*Saturday*
domingo	*Sunday*
¡Qué raro !	*How **strange**!*
interesante	*interesting*
ridículo	*ridiculous*
impresionante	*impressive, awesome*
tonto	*foolish, stupid, silly*
asombroso	*amazing*

Estructura y Práctica

Ser *to be*: Uses

1 · **Ser** (*to be*) is used to link nouns and pronouns.

Yo **soy** ingeniera.	***I'm** an engineer.*
Es arquitecto.	***He's** an architect.*
Somos norteamericanos.	***We're** American.*
Alicia y José **son** nuestros primos.	*Alicia and José **are** our cousins.*
El señor Pérez **es** el profesor.	*Mr. Pérez **is** the teacher.*

Because the verb ending tells who the subject is, subject pronouns do not appear in these sentences: **Es arquitecto. Somos norteamericanos.**

Unlike English, Spanish omits the indefinite article **un/una** with a profession: **Es arquitecto.** However, when the noun is modified, the indefinite article must be used: **Es un arquitecto exitoso** (*successful*).

2 · **Ser** is used before (or in questions, after) a phrase beginning with **de** that expresses possession, origin, or the material something is made of.

Esta oficina **es del** jefe.	*This office **is the** boss's.*
Somos de los Estados Unidos.	***We're from** the United States.*
Las chaquetas **son de** lana.	*The jackets **are made of** wool.*
¿De quién es este celular?	***Whose** cell phone **is** this?*

3 · **Ser** is used before adjectives that express inherent qualities and characteristics, such as physical and moral attributes, personality, nationality, age, religion, and color.

Felipe **es** inteligente.	*Felipe **is** intelligent.*
Sus hermanos **son** altos.	*His brother and sister **are** tall.*
Isabel y yo **somos** inglesas.	*Isabel and I **are** English.*
Juan **es** protestante, Samuel **es** judío, José **es** católico, and Alano **es** musulmán.	*Juan **is** Protestant, Samuel **is** Jewish, José **is** Catholic, and Alano **is** Muslim.*
Nuestro coche **es** gris.	*Our car **is** gray.*

4 · **Ser** is used to tell time, dates, and days of the week.

¿Qué hora **es**?	*What time **is it**?*
Es la una.	***It's** one o'clock.*
Son las dos y media.	***It's** two thirty.*
¿A qué hora **es** la comida?	*At what time **is** the dinner?*
Es a las siete.	***It's** at seven o'clock.*
Hoy **es** el siete de diciembre.	*Today **is** December seventh.*
Hoy **es** viernes.	*Today **is** Friday.*

E Write the form of **ser** that correctly completes each of the following sentences.

1. Roberto y Matilde __________ simpáticos.
2. Yo __________ científico.
3. ¿De dónde __________ tú?
4. El abrigo __________ de lana.
5. Nosotros __________ de Costa Rica.
6. Julio __________ muy gracioso.
7. Uds. __________ católicos, ¿no?
8. Elenita __________ mi hermana.
9. Sus zapatos __________ marrones.
10. Mi tía __________ canadiense.

Telling Time

To ask what time it is in Spanish, one says **¿Qué hora es? ¿Qué horas son?** is also used, especially in Spanish America. Phrases telling time begin with **Son las** + the hour. The one exception is **Es la una.** (*It's one o'clock.*). (For cardinal numbers, see Chapter 6.)

Here is the way Spanish tells time on the traditional analog clock.

Son las cinco.	*It's five o'clock.*
Son las cinco y cinco.	*It's five past five. / It's five after five.*
Son las cinco y diez.	*It's ten past five. / It's ten after five.*
Son las cinco y cuarto.	*It's a quarter past five. / It's a quarter after five.*
Son las cinco y veinte.	*It's twenty past five. / It's twenty after five.*
Son las cinco y veinticinco.	*It's twenty-five past five. / It's twenty-five after five.*
Son las cinco y media.	*It's half past five. / It's five thirty.*
Son las seis menos veinticinco.	*It's twenty-five to six.*
Son las seis menos veinte.	*It's twenty to six.*
Son las seis menos cuarto.	*It's a quarter to six.*
Son las seis menos diez.	*It's ten to six.*
Son las seis menos cinco.	*It's five to six.*
Son las seis.	*It's six o'clock.*

The preceding system is typical of Spain and Argentina. In the rest of Spanish America, the times from the half hour to the following hour are usually expressed as follows.

Faltan veinticinco para las seis.	*It's twenty-five to six.*
Faltan veinte para las seis.	*It's twenty to six.*
Faltan quince para las seis.	*It's a quarter to six.*
Faltan diez para las seis.	*It's ten to six.*
Faltan cinco para las seis.	*It's five to six.*

As in the United States, the use of digital clocks and watches in Spanish-speaking countries has changed the way people tell time. Phrases such as the following are replacing the traditional analog times.

Son las cinco y quince.	*It's five fifteen.*
Son las cinco y treinta.	*It's five thirty.*
Son las cinco (y) cuarenta y cinco.	*It's five forty-five.*

The conjunction **y** between the hour and minutes may be left out when stating times from thirty-one to fifty-nine minutes past the hour.

To specify the time at which something happens, the preposition **a** is used.

¿**A** qué hora llega el avión?	*At what time is the plane arriving?*
A las ocho cincuenta.	*At eight fifty.*

Spanish has two ways of expressing A.M. and P.M. In everyday speech, the phrases **de la mañana**, **de la tarde**, and **de la noche** are added to the expression of time.

La reunión es a las ocho **de la mañana**.	*The meeting is at 8* **A.M.**

For official time—train and airplane schedules, movie and show times, and class times—a twenty-four hour clock is used.

Hay un tren a las dieciocho (y) veinte.	*There's a train at 6:20 P.M.*
El avión llega a las veintidós (y) cuarenta.	*The plane is arriving at 10:40 P.M.*

Days of the Week

The days of the week are written with a lowercase letter in Spanish, rather than with a capital letter as in English.

lunes	*Monday*
martes	*Tuesday*
miércoles	*Wednesday*
jueves	*Thursday*
viernes	*Friday*
sábado	*Saturday*
domingo	*Sunday*

El domingo es el primer día de la semana.	***Sunday** is the first day of the week.*
El miércoles es un día ocupado.	***Wednesday** is a busy day.*

The singular definite article **el** means *on* before the days of the week.

Hay un concierto **el viernes**.	*There's a concert **on Friday**.*

The plural definite article **los** indicates repeated action or regular occurrence.

Este museo está cerrado **los martes**.	*This museum is closed **on Tuesdays**.*
No hay reunión **los jueves**.	*There's no meeting **on Thursdays**.*

DAYS AND TIME: EXPRESSIONS

el anochecer, el atardecer	*dusk, nightfall*
al anochecer, al atardecer	*at dusk, at nightfall*
ayer	*yesterday*
anteayer	*the day before yesterday*
el fin de semana	*weekend*
la madrugada	*early morning, dawn*
madrugador/madrugadora	*early riser*
mañana	*tomorrow*
pasado mañana	*the day after tomorrow*
la medianoche	*midnight*
el mediodía	*noon*
Es tarde.	*It's late.*
Es temprano.	*It's early.*
Mi reloj está adelantado.	*My watch is fast.*
Mi reloj está atrasado/retrasado.	*My watch is slow.*

F ***¿Qué hora es?*** Rewrite the following sentences in Spanish. Express the time in more than one way whenever possible. Follow the *modelo*.

MODELO It's 4:00.
→ Son las cuatro.

1. It's 7:00.
2. It's 1:00.
3. It's 9:30.
4. It's 2:15.
5. It's 4:45.
6. It's 10:20.
7. It's 3:50.
8. It's 6:00 A.M.
9. It's 5:25 P.M.
10. It's 11:10 P.M.
11. It's 8:05 A.M.
12. It's 12:00 A.M. It's 12:00 P.M.

G ***Diálogos.*** Write mini-dialogues in Spanish. First, ask where and at what time an event is taking place, then respond with the information requested. Write all numbers as words. Follow the *modelo*.

MODELO el espectáculo: el teatro / 8:00 P.M.
→ —¿Dónde es el espectáculo?
—Es en el teatro.
—¿A qué hora?
—Es a las ocho.

1. la reunión: la sala de conferencias / 11:30 A.M.
2. la fiesta de cumpleaños (*birthday*): la casa de Bernardo y Josefa / 7:00 P.M.
3. el partido de fútbol (*soccer*): el campo de fútbol (*soccer field*) / 1:30 P.M.
4. la boda: la iglesia / 4:00 P.M.
5. la comida: el hotel / 10:00 P.M.
6. el examen de historia: el salón de clase / 9:15 A.M.

H ***Los días de la semana.*** Express the following sentences in Spanish.

1. *There's a soccer game on Saturday.*
2. *What day is today?*
3. *The museums are closed on Mondays.*
4. *Their wedding is on Sunday.*
5. *This department store is open every day.*
6. *Mr. Paz is in the office from Monday to Thursday.*
7. *There are lectures at the university on Wednesdays.*
8. *We are having a meeting all day.*

DIÁLOGO 9 · Nuestro carro está descompuesto.

Study the dialogue, then listen to the recording and repeat each line.

PACO	¿Por qué está tu marido tan enojado?
CARMEN	Es que nuestro carro está descompuesto.
PACO	¿Dónde está el carro ahora?
CARMEN	Está en el taller mecánico.

Análisis

Check that you understand the linguistic breakdown of each speech from *Diálogo 9*.

¿Por qué está tu marido tan enojado?	*Why is your husband so angry?*
¿Por qué?	*Why?*
el marido	*husband*
tu	*your* (informal, before a singular noun)
tu marido	*your husband*
enojado	*angry*
tan	*so*
tan enojado	*so angry*
estar enojado	*to be angry*
Es que nuestro carro está descompuesto.	*It's that our car is broken.*
nuestro	*our*
nuestro carro	*our car*
descompuesto	*out of order, broken*
estar descompuesto	*to be out of order, to be broken*
¿Dónde está el carro ahora?	*Where is the car now?*
ahora	*now*
Está en el taller mecánico.	*It's in the mechanic's shop.*
el taller	*shop, workshop*
el taller mecánico	*mechanic's shop, garage (for repairs)*

Variantes

Listen, and repeat the same structures from *Diálogo 9*, now with new vocabulary.

¿Por qué está enojado?	*Why is he **angry**?*
enfadado	*angry*
molesto	*annoyed*
furioso	*furious*
El carro está en el taller mecánico.	*The car is in the **mechanic's shop**.*
el parqueo	*parking lot*
el estacionamiento	*parking lot*
el garaje	*garage (for parking, not repair)*
la gasolinera	*gas station*
La carretera está cerca de aquí.	***The highway** is near here.*
La autopista	*The turnpike*

DIÁLOGO 10 · La comida está rica.

Study the dialogue, then listen to the recording and repeat each line.

GABRIELA	Esta carne está hecha a la perfección.
HERNANDO	Yo estoy de acuerdo. Está muy rica.
GABRIELA	En realidad toda la comida está deliciosa.
HERNANDO	Por eso este restaurante es tan famoso.

Análisis

Check that you understand the linguistic breakdown of each speech from *Diálogo 10*.

Esta carne está hecha a la perfección.	*This meat is perfectly done.*
la carne	*meat*
hecho	*done*
estar hecho	*to be done*
la perfección	*perfection*
a la perfección	*perfectly, to perfection*
Yo estoy de acuerdo. Está muy rica.	*I agree. It's delicious.*
el acuerdo	*agreement*
de acuerdo	*in agreement*
estar de acuerdo	*to agree*
rico	*delicious*
estar rico	*to be delicious*
En realidad toda la comida está deliciosa.	*Actually, all the food is delicious.*
la realidad	*reality*
en realidad	*actually, really*
la comida	*food*
toda la comida	*all the food*
delicioso	*delicious*
estar delicioso	*to be delicious*
Por eso este restaurante es tan famoso.	*That's why this restaurant is so famous.*
por eso	*that's why*
famoso	*famous*
tan famoso	*so famous*

Variantes

Listen, and repeat the same structures from *Diálogo 10*, now with new vocabulary.

La carne está muy hecha.	*The meat is* ***too well done.***
poco hecha	*underdone*

Estructura y Práctica

Ser vs. estar: Describing Food

Ser and **estar** also contrast when describing food. **Ser** is used when referring to food in general. **Estar** is used when describing how a particular food tastes.

El pescado **es** rico.	*Fish **is** delicious.* (general statement)
El pescado **está** rico.	*The fish **is** delicious.* (*This particular fish tastes good.*)
Las legumbres **son** buenas para la salud.	*Vegetables **are** good for your health.* (general statement)
Estas legumbres **están** buenas.	*These vegetables **are** good.* (*These particular vegetables taste good.*)

DIÁLOGO 11 · ¡Yo estoy frito!

Study the dialogue, then listen to the recording and repeat each line.

GABRIELA ¿Por qué estás de mal humor?
HERNANDO Es que la impresora está descompuesta otra vez.
GABRIELA El técnico está en la oficina, ¿no?
HERNANDO No, el jueves es su día libre. ¡Yo estoy frito!

Análisis

Check that you understand the linguistic breakdown of each speech from *Diálogo 11.*

¿Por qué estás de mal humor?	*Why are you in a bad mood?*
de mal humor	*in a bad mood*
estar de mal humor	*to be in a bad mood*
Es que la impresora está descompuesta otra vez.	*Because the printer is broken again.*
la impresora	*printer*
otra vez	*again*
El técnico está en la oficina, ¿no?	*The technician is in the office, isn't he?*
el técnico	*technician*
¿no?	*isn't he?*
No, el jueves es su día libre. ¡Yo estoy frito!	*No, Thursday is his day off. I'm done for!*
el jueves	*Thursday*
el día	*day*
libre	*free*
el día libre	*day off*
frito	*done for, finished, doomed* (literally, *fried*)

Variantes

Listen, and repeat the same structures from *Diálogo 11*, now with new vocabulary.

Estás de mal humor.	*You're in a **bad** mood.*
buen	*good*
El técnico está en la oficina, ¿no?	*The technician is in the office, **isn't he?***
¿verdad?	*isn't he?*

Estructura y Práctica

I ***¿Ser o estar?*** Choose **ser** or **estar** to complete each of the following sentences, then write the correct form of the verb or verbs needed.

1. El arroz integral (*brown rice*) ____________ bueno para la salud.
2. Mi marido ____________ diseñador gráfico.
3. Estos platos ____________ muy sabrosos.
4. ____________ que yo no ____________ de acuerdo con Uds.
5. Aquel estacionamiento ____________ bastante caro.
6. La gasolinera ____________ al lado del parqueo.
7. El carro ____________ nuevo pero ____________ descompuesto otra vez.
8. Uds. ____________ muy atrasados ya.
9. El viernes ____________ su día libre.
10. ¿Por qué ____________ Eduardo de mal humor?
11. ¡Qué ridículos ____________ esos chicos!
12. La hamburguesa ____________ muy hecha.
13. Ese cantante ____________ muy famoso.
14. La tienda de cómputo ____________ abierto hasta (*until*) las nueve.

Tag Questions

Spanish adds phrases such as **¿no?**, **¿verdad?**, **¿no es verdad?**, and **¿no es cierto?** to statements to turn them into questions. These phrases are called tags. Tag questions signal that the speaker expects the answer *yes*. If the statement to be agreed with is negative, only **¿verdad?** can be used as a tag. English uses tags such as *isn't it?* and *aren't you?* to turn statements into questions.

Ya son las siete, **¿no?**	*It's already seven o'clock,* ***isn't it?***
Eres de origen francés, **¿no es cierto?**	*You're of French descent,* ***aren't you?***
El pollo está riquísimo, **¿verdad?**	*The chicken is delicious,* ***isn't it?***
No hay vuelo directo, **¿verdad?**	*There's no direct flight,* ***is there?***

J **Tag Questions.** Write a sentence from each string of elements given, adding the tag in parentheses to turn it into a tag question. Follow the *modelo*.

MODELO la / ya / una / es (¿no?)
→ Ya es la una, ¿no?

1. descompuesta / tu / impresora / está (¿no?)
2. esta / picante / está / salsa / muy (¿verdad?)
3. negocios / son / esos / de / costarricenses / hombres (¿no es cierto?)
4. queda / de / carretera / aquí / lejos / la / no (¿verdad?)

5. las / es / economía / a / clase / de / tres / la (¿no es verdad?)
6. el / es / béisbol / de / sábado / partido / el (¿no?)
7. humor / de / estás / no / mal (¿verdad?)
8. día / tu / es / libre / domingo / el (¿no es cierto?)

DIÁLOGO 12 · Pablo y su computadora

Study the dialogue, then listen to the recording and repeat each line.

HERNANDO	¿Dónde está Pablo?
GABRIELA	Está ocupado con su correo electrónico.
HERNANDO	Está sentado frente a su computadora como de costumbre. ¡Qué chico!

Análisis

Check that you understand the linguistic breakdown of each speech from *Diálogo 12.*

¿Dónde está Pablo?	*Where's Pablo?*
Está ocupado con su correo electrónico.	*He's busy with his email.*
ocupado	*busy*
estar ocupado	*to be busy*
con	*with*
su	*his*
el correo	*mail*
el correo electrónico	*email*
Está sentado frente a su computadora como de costumbre. ¡Qué chico!	*He's sitting in front of his computer as usual. What a kid!*
estar sentado	*to be sitting*
frente a	*in front of*
la computadora	*computer*
como	*like, as*
la costumbre	*custom, habit*
como de costumbre	*as usual*
el chico	*kid, boy, guy*
¡Qué chico!	*What a kid!*

Variantes

Listen, and repeat the same structures from *Diálogo 12*, now with new vocabulary.

Está ocupado con su correo electrónico .	*He's busy with his* ***email.***
sitio web	*website*
Está sentada frente a la computadora .	*She's sitting in front of* ***the computer.***
al televisor	*the television (set)*
a la televisión	*the television*
a la pantalla	*the screen*

Están sentados .	*They're **sitting**.*
parados	*standing*
de pie	*standing*
acostados	*lying down*
dormidos	*sleeping*
¡Qué muchacho !	*What a **boy**!*
muchacha	*girl*

DIÁLOGO 13 · Los señores Ortega están de vacaciones.

Study the dialogue, then listen to the recording and repeat each line.

HERNANDO ¿Dónde están los señores Ortega?
GABRIELA Están de vacaciones. Están en Cancún.
HERNANDO ¡Pobres! Estoy seguro que están tumbados en la playa todo el día.

Análisis

Check that you understand the linguistic breakdown of each speech from *Diálogo 13*.

¿Dónde están los señores Ortega?	*Where are Mr. and Mrs. Ortega?*
los señores Ortega	*Mr. and Mrs. Ortega*
Están de vacaciones. Están en Cancún.	*They're on vacation. They're in Cancún.*
las vacaciones	*vacation*
de vacaciones	*on vacation*
estar de vacaciones	*to be on vacation*
Cancún	*Cancún (world-famous tourist resort on Mexico's Yucatán Peninsula)*
¡Pobres! Estoy seguro que están tumbados en la playa todo el día.	*Poor people! I'm sure they're lying on the beach all day.*
pobre	*poor*
pobres	*poor people*
seguro	*sure*
estar seguro	*to be sure*
estar tumbado	*to be lying down*
la playa	*beach*
el día	*day*
todo el día	*all day*

Variantes

Listen, and repeat the same structures from *Diálogo 13*, now with new vocabulary.

Están de vacaciones .	*They're on **vacation**.*
viaje	*a trip*

Está en casa todo el día.	*She's at home* ***all day***.
toda la tarde	*all afternoon*
toda la noche	*all night*

Estructura y Práctica

Estar + Past Participle: Expressing Positions of the Body

Estar is used with the past participle to express positions of the body. The past participle functions as an adjective, thereby agreeing in gender and number with the noun it refers to. English uses the *-ing* form for this purpose. (For the past participle, see Chapter 13.)

Los invitados **están sentados** a la mesa.	*The guests* ***are sitting*** *at the table.*
Maite **está recostada**.	*Maite* ***is lying down***.

K Rewrite each of the following sentences. Include the correct form of **estar** plus the past participle (cue in parentheses) to describe positions of the body. Make all necessary changes. Follow the *modelo*.

MODELO La niña ya ______________. (acostado)
→ La niña ya está acostada.

1. Julio y Laura ______________________________ en la sala de conferencias. (sentado)
2. Las hermanas ______________________________ en la cama. (tumbado)
3. El bebé ______________________________. (dormido)
4. Los jardineros (*gardeners*) ______________________________. (arrodillado (*kneeling*)) (la rodilla (*knee*))
5. Algunos pasajeros (*passengers*) ______________________________ en el autobús. (parado)
6. Virginia ______________________________ en el sofá. (echado (*lying down*))
7. El receptor (*catcher*) ______________________________. (agachado (*crouching*))

L ***Estoy seguro que...*** Express each of the following sentences in Spanish, stating your certainty that some people are doing certain things.

1. *I'm sure that Marta is busy with her website.*
2. *I'm sure that Mr. and Mrs. Martínez are on vacation.*
3. *I'm sure that Paco is lying on the beach as usual.*
4. *I'm sure that my friends* [fem.] *are sitting in front of the television.*
5. *I'm sure that the boys are on a trip.*
6. *I'm sure that Lorenzo is lying down.*
7. *I'm sure that your* (tú) *computer is broken.*
8. *I'm sure that you're* (Uds.) *in the office all day.*

DIÁLOGO 14 · ¿Cómo es el novio de Laura?

Study the dialogue, then listen to the recording and repeat each line.

GABRIELA	¿Cómo es el novio de Laura?
HERNANDO	Miguel es alto, delgado y moreno. Es muy guapo.
GABRIELA	Es simpático, ¿verdad?
HERNANDO	Ah sí. Es un tipo encantador y gracioso.

Análisis

Check that you understand the linguistic breakdown of each speech from *Diálogo 14*.

¿Cómo es el novio de Laura?	*What does Laura's boyfriend look like?*
¿cómo?	*how?*
¿Cómo es?	*What is he like? / What does he look like?*
el novio	*boyfriend, fiancé*
Miguel es alto, delgado y moreno. Es muy guapo.	*Miguel is tall, thin, and dark. He's very handsome.*
alto	*tall*
delgado	*thin*
moreno	*dark-haired, dark-skinned*
guapo	*handsome, good-looking*
Es simpático, ¿verdad?	*He's nice, isn't he?*
simpático	*nice*
la verdad	*truth*
¿verdad?	*isn't he?* (tag question)
Ah sí. Es un tipo encantador y gracioso.	*Oh, yes. He's a charming and funny guy.*
el tipo	*guy*
encantador	*charming*
gracioso	*funny, witty*

Variantes

Listen, and repeat the same structures from *Diálogo 14*, now with new vocabulary.

Roberto es bajo.	*Roberto is* ***short****.*
gordo	*fat*
amable	*kind*
antipático	*unpleasant*
honrado	*honest*
divertido	*amusing*
Marta es encantadora.	*Marta is* ***charming****.*
flaca	*thin*
rubia	*blond*
arrogante	*arrogant*
alegre	*cheerful (by nature)*
atenta	*considerate*

DIÁLOGO 15 · ¿Cómo es Isabel?

Study the dialogue, then listen to the recording and repeat each line.

HERNANDO	Isabel es trabajadora y emprendedora.
GABRIELA	Es muy inteligente también.
HERNANDO	Por eso es directora de la compañía.

Análisis

Check that you understand the linguistic breakdown of each speech from *Diálogo 15*.

Isabel es trabajadora y emprendedora.	*Isabel is hardworking and enterprising.*
trabajador	*hardworking*
emprendedor	*enterprising*
Es muy inteligente también.	*She's also very intelligent.*
inteligente	*intelligent*
Por eso es directora de la compañía.	*That's why she's president of the company.*
la directora	*director, president* (feminine)
la compañía	*company*
la directora de la compañía	*president of the company*

Variantes

Listen, and repeat the same structures from *Diálogo 15*, now with new vocabulary.

¿Es trabajadora Isabel?	*Is Isabel hardworking?*
Sí, es muy trabajadora.	*Yes, she's very hardworking.*
¿Es rico el director?	*Is the director rich?*
Sí, es rico.	*Yes, he's rich.*

Estructura y Práctica

M *¿Cómo son?* Write complete sentences to describe some of Santiago's family members. Make all necessary changes. Follow the *modelo.*

MODELO mi prima: joven / bonito
→ Mi prima es joven y bonita.

1. mis sobrinos: rubio / bajo
2. mis papás: inteligente / simpático
3. mi hermano: alto / moreno
4. mis hijos: guapo / encantador
5. mis cuñadas: antipático / arrogante
6. mi hermana: emprendedor / rico
7. mis nietos: moreno / delgado
8. mi tía: flaco / lindo
9. mi esposa: honrado / amable
10. mis primas: alegre / atento
11. mis abuelos: trabajador / divertido
12. mi cuñado: gordo / feo

DIÁLOGO 16 · ¿De quién es?

Study the dialogue, then listen to the recording and repeat each line.

HERNANDO	¿De quién es esta bufanda?
GABRIELA	Es del niño.
HERNANDO	Y esos guantes, ¿de quién son?
GABRIELA	Son de la niña.

Análisis

Check that you understand the linguistic breakdown of each speech from *Diálogo 16*.

¿De quién es esta bufanda?	*Whose scarf is this?*
¿De quién?	*Whose?*
la bufanda	*scarf*
Es del niño.	*It's the boy's.*
el niño	*male child, boy*
del niño	*of the boy, belonging to the boy*
Y esos guantes, ¿de quién son?	*And what about those gloves? Whose are they?*
el guante	*glove*
Son de la niña.	*They're the girl's.*
la niña	*female child, girl*
de la niña	*of the girl, belonging to the girl*

Variantes

Listen, and repeat the same structures from *Diálogo 16*, now with new vocabulary.

¿De quiénes es esta cámara?	*Whose camera is this?*
Es de ellos.	*It's theirs.*
¿De quiénes son esos discos compactos?	*Whose compact discs are those?*
Son de ellas.	*They're theirs.* (feminine)

Estructura y Práctica

N ***¿De quién es?*** Express the following dialogues in Spanish.

1. *Whose book is this?*
   It's the teacher's [masc.].
2. *These shoes. Whose are they?*
   They're hers.
3. *Whose wallet is that?*
   It's Doctor Lara's.
4. *These socks* (las medias). *Whose are they?*
   They're hers.
5. *Whose* [pl.] *car is it?*
   It's theirs.

DIÁLOGO 17 · ¿De qué son los suéteres?

Study the dialogue, then listen to the recording and repeat each line.

HERNANDO	Señorita, por favor, ¿de qué son estos suéteres?
GABRIELA	Son de algodón.
HERNANDO	¿Hay suéteres de lana?
GABRIELA	Cómo no. Están al fondo, a la derecha.

Análisis

Check that you understand the linguistic breakdown of each speech from *Diálogo 17.*

Señorita, por favor, ¿de qué son estos suéteres?	*Miss, please, what are these sweaters made of?*
señorita	*miss*
por favor	*please*
¿De qué son?	*What are they made of?*
el suéter	*sweater*
Son de algodón.	*They're cotton.*
el algodón	*cotton*
¿Hay suéteres de lana?	*Are there wool sweaters?*
la lana	*wool*
Cómo no. Están al fondo, a la derecha.	*Of course. They're in the back, on the right.*
Cómo no.	*Of course.*
estar al fondo	*to be in the back*
a la derecha	*on the right, to the right*

Variantes

Listen, and repeat the same structures from *Diálogo 17,* now with new vocabulary.

¿De qué es el suéter ?	*What's the* ***sweater*** *made of?*
la blusa	*blouse*
la camisa	*shirt*
el traje	*suit*
el abrigo	*coat*
la chaqueta	*jacket*
la falda	*skirt*
el vestido	*dress*
el pantalón	*pants*
el bluejean	*jeans*
la camiseta	*T-shirt*
la corbata	*necktie*
el sombrero	*hat*
el gorro	*cap*
¿De qué son estos zapatos ?	*What are* ***these shoes*** *made of?*
estos guantes	*these gloves*
estos pantalones	*these pants*
estas botas	*these boots*

Estructura y Práctica

O ***¿De qué es?*** Express each of the following sentences in Spanish, using the cue in parentheses to describe what the item of clothing is made of. Follow the *modelo*.

MODELO ¿De qué es el gorro (*cap*)? (lana)
→ Es de lana.

1. ¿De qué es esta corbata? (seda (*silk*))
2. ¿De qué son las botas? (cuero (*leather*))
3. ¿De qué son esas camisetas? (poliéster)
4. ¿De qué es el vestido? (lino (*linen*))
5. ¿De qué son los pantalones? (pana (*corduroy*))
6. ¿De qué es esta falda? (algodón)

DIÁLOGO 18 · Mi trabajo es aburrido.

Study the dialogue, then listen to the recording and repeat each line.

GABRIELA ¿Cuál es su profesión?
HERNANDO Soy programador.
GABRIELA ¿Es interesante su trabajo?
HERNANDO No. En realidad es muy aburrido.

Análisis

Check that you understand the linguistic breakdown of each speech from *Diálogo 18*.

¿Cuál es su profesión?	*What is your profession?*
la profesión	*profession*
Soy programador.	*I'm a computer programmer.*
el programador	*computer programmer*
¿Es interesante su trabajo?	*Is your work interesting?*
interesante	*interesting*
el trabajo	*work, job*
No. En realidad es muy aburrido.	*No. Actually, it's very boring.*
en realidad	*actually, really*
ser aburrido	*to be boring*

Variantes

Listen, and repeat the same structures from *Diálogo 18*, now with new vocabulary.

¿Cuál es su profesión?	*What is your **profession**?*
dirección	*address*
número de teléfono	*telephone number*
nacionalidad	*nationality*
religión	*religion*
fecha de nacimiento	*date of birth*
estado civil	*marital status*
Soy casado.	*I'm **married**.*
divorciado	*divorced*

Estoy casado. — *I'm **married**.*
divorciado — *divorced*

Soy programador. — *I'm **a computer programmer**.*
hombre de negocios — *a businessman*
arquitecto — *an architect*

Estructura y Práctica

¿CUÁL? AND ¿QUÉ?

¿Cuál? before **ser** is used for English *what?* when an identification is asked for.

¿Cuál es la fecha de hoy? — *What's today's date?*
¿Cuál es la capital de España? — *What is the capital of Spain?*
¿Cuál es su apellido? — *What is your last name?*

¿Qué? before **ser** asks for a definition.

¿Qué es el ciberespacio? — *What is cyberspace?*

P Express the following dialogues in Spanish.

1. *Whose suitcase is this?*
   It's his.
2. *What are those suits made of?*
   They're wool.
3. *Please, miss, where are the silk* (seda) *ties?*
   They're next to the shirts.
4. *Whose* [pl.] *coats are those?*
   They're theirs.
5. *What is your* (Uds.) *nationality?*
   We're Peruvian.
6. *What is your* (Ud.) *profession?*
   I'm a lawyer [fem.].
   What is your nationality?
   I'm Panamanian.
   And your (country of) origin?
   I'm of English descent.

DIÁLOGO 19 · Regalos para mi familia

Study the dialogue, then listen to the recording and repeat each line.

HERNANDO ¿Para quién son estos regalos?
GABRIELA Bueno, este regalo es para mis padres.
HERNANDO ¿Y los otros?
GABRIELA Son para mis hermanos.

Análisis

Check that you understand the linguistic breakdown of each speech from *Diálogo 19*.

¿Para quién son estos regalos? — *Whom are these gifts for?*
¿Para quién? — *For whom?*

Bueno, este regalo es para mis padres. — *Well, this gift is for my parents.*
los padres — *parents*

¿Y los otros?	*And what about the other ones?*
Son para mis hermanos.	*They're for my brother and sister.*
los hermanos	*brother(s) and sister(s), brothers*

Variantes

Listen, and repeat the same structures from *Diálogo 19*, now with new vocabulary.

El iPod es para mi madre .	*The iPod is for my* ***mother****.*
padre	*father*
mamá	*mom*
papá	*dad*
hijo	*son*
hija	*daughter*
hermano	*brother*
hermana	*sister*
abuela	*grandmother*
abuelo	*grandfather*
tía	*aunt*
tío	*uncle*
cuñado	*brother-in-law*
cuñada	*sister-in-law*
madrastra	*stepmother*
padrastro	*stepfather*

Estos regalos son para nuestros padres .	*These gifts are for our* ***parents****.*
papás	*parents*
hijos	*children*
abuelos	*grandparents*
nietos	*grandchildren*
tíos	*aunt(s) and uncle(s), uncles*
primos	*cousins*
sobrinos	*niece(s) and nephew(s), nephews*

Estructura y Práctica

Ser and estar in Yes/No Questions

In Chapter 1, you learned that when a yes/no question includes a form of the verb **ser** + an adjective, the subject is placed at the end of the sentence. The pattern of the question is thus verb + adjective + subject.

Estos programadores son trabajadores.	*These computer programmers are hardworking.*
¿Son trabajadores estos programadores?	*Are these computer programmers hardworking?*
Eugenia es simpática.	*Eugenia is pleasant.*
¿Es simpática Eugenia?	*Is Eugenia pleasant?*

Similarly, in questions containing a form of the verb **estar** + an adjective, the subject is placed at the end of the sentence.

Los chicos están contentos.	*The kids are happy.*
¿Están contentos los chicos?	*Are the kids happy?*
La tienda de cómputo está abierta.	*The computer store is open.*
¿Está abierta la tienda de cómputo?	*Is the computer store open?*

For information questions in Spanish, a preposition associated with an interrogative word must precede it. In English, prepositions are usually separated from the question word and appear at the end of the sentence.

¿**De quién** es aquella casa?	***Whose** house is that?*
¿**De dónde** son tus abuelos?	***Where** are your grandparents **from**?*
¿**De qué** es el traje?	***What** is the suit **made of**?*
¿**Para quién** es el reloj?	***Whom** is the watch **for**?*

Q ***¿Cuál es la pregunta?*** Write the information question that would elicit each of the following responses. Follow the *modelo*.

MODELO Estas maletas son de Daniel.
→ ¿De quién son estas maletas?

1. Los señores Arriaga están de vacaciones en Europa.
2. Es ingeniero mecánico.
3. Las chicas están perfectamente.
4. Es la una y media.
5. Las camisetas son de algodón.
6. Santiago es la capital de Chile.
7. La novia de Arturo es encantadora.
8. Hoy es viernes.
9. La reunión es en la oficina del director.
10. La fiesta es a las nueve.
11. Los zapatos son del niño.
12. La pulsera es para Emilia.
13. Estos platos están muy sabrosos.
14. Estoy casado.
15. Calle Flores, número dieciocho.
16. Son protestantes.

R Transform the following sentences with **ser** and **estar** into yes/no questions. Follow the *modelo*.

MODELO Sus primos son argentinos.
→ ¿Son argentinos sus primos?

1. Las tiendas por departamentos están abiertas.
2. Su trabajo es aburrido.
3. Sus hijos están emocionados.
4. La novia de Juan Antonio es atenta.
5. Los niños están asustados.
6. Este contador está muy ocupado.
7. Sus papás son simpáticos.
8. Tu coche está descompuesto.
9. Esos museos son impresionantes.
10. Lola y Diego son casados.
11. Su hermano es emprendedor.
12. Estos países están muy adelantados.

Un paso más

Are you ready to take your Spanish a step further? Here are exercises that will enhance your knowledge of the language and encourage you to express yourself freely.

S Here is a list of nouns related to adjectives that appear in Chapter 4. Write the adjective related to each of the nouns. Learning the adjective related to the noun will help you increase your vocabulary.

1. el aburrimiento
2. el catarro
3. el adelanto
4. la alegría
5. la angustia
6. el susto
7. la reunión
8. el cansancio
9. la emoción
10. la enfermedad
11. el entusiasmo
12. el estrés
13. la inquietud
14. la molestia
15. el nervio
16. la preocupación
17. el atraso
18. la tristeza
19. el divorcio
20. la gracia

T ***Preguntas personales.*** Answer each question with a complete Spanish sentence.

1. ¿Qué día es hoy?
2. ¿Qué hora es?
3. ¿Hay una reunión (un concierto, una fiesta, un partido) hoy?
4. ¿Dónde es? ¿A qué hora es?
5. ¿Dónde queda tu casa?
6. ¿Dónde queda tu lugar de trabajo (*workplace*)?
7. ¿Cómo es tu carro? ¿Está descompuesto?
8. ¿Hay un taller mecánico cerca de tu casa? ¿Dónde está?

U Write a paragraph in Spanish telling about yourself and some family members. Use these questions as a guide.

1. ¿Cómo eres?
2. ¿Cuál es tu profesión?
3. ¿Cuál es tu estado civil?
4. ¿Cuál es tu nacionalidad?
5. ¿De qué origen eres?
6. ¿Cuál es tu religión?
7. ¿Cuál es tu fecha de nacimiento?
8. ¿Cómo estás actualmente (*these days*)? (la salud (*health*); el ánimo (*spirits*))
9. ¿Cómo son tus papás (hijos, hermanos, abuelos, nietos, tíos, primos, cuñados)?
10. ¿Cómo están actualmente?

5

Work and Leisure

Communication Goals

- Talking about work, vacation and travel, and leisure activities
- Telling how you celebrate your birthday
- Telling when things happen
- Vocabulary: sports, music, the computer, the seasons, months, meals

Grammar Topics

- The Present Tense of Regular **-ar** Verbs
- Uses of the Present Tense
- **Hacer** *to do, make*
- **Ir** *to go*
- **Ir** + **a** + Infinitive
- Contraction **al**
- Direct Objects and the Personal **a**
- Relative Pronoun **que**
- Negative Words
- Compound Nouns
- Nouns
- Adverbs of Time

DIÁLOGO 1 · Hacen ejercicio.

Study the dialogue, then listen to the recording and repeat each line.

JUAN	¿Haces mucho ejercicio?
ISABEL	Sí, troto cinco veces por semana y levanto pesas.
JUAN	Yo troto también, pero no levanto pesas.
ISABEL	Pues vamos a trotar juntos mañana.

Análisis

Check that you understand the linguistic breakdown of each speech from *Diálogo 1.*

¿Haces mucho ejercicio?	*Do you exercise a lot?*
hacer	*to do, make*
haces	*you do*
el ejercicio	*exercise, workout*
mucho ejercicio	*a lot of exercise*

Sí, troto cinco veces por semana y levanto pesas.	*Yes, I jog five times a week and I lift weights.*
trotar	*to jog*
troto	*I jog*
la vez	*time (occasion, occurrence)*
las veces	*times (occasions, occurrences)*
cinco veces	*five times*
la semana	*week*
por semana	*weekly*
levanto	*I lift*
la pesa	*weight*
las pesas	*weights, dumbbells*

Yo troto también, pero no levanto pesas.	*I jog, too, but I don't lift weights.*

Pues vamos a trotar juntos mañana.	*Well, let's jog together tomorrow.*
pues	*well* (interjection)
vamos	*we go, we're going*
vamos a + *infinitive*	*let's (do something)*
vamos a trotar	*let's jog*
juntos	*together*
mañana	*tomorrow*

Variantes

Listen, and repeat the same structures from *Diálogo 1*, now with new vocabulary.

Vamos a trotar juntos mañana.	*Let's **jog** together tomorrow.*
nadar	*swim*
patinar	*skate*
caminar	*walk*
montar en bicicleta	*take a bicycle ride*
montar a caballo	*go horseback riding*

Vamos al gimnasio.	*We're going **to the gym**.*
al estadio	*to the stadium*
a la piscina	*to the pool*
a la pista	*to the track*
a la cancha de tenis	*to the tennis court*
a la cancha de baloncesto	*to the basketball court*
al campo de fútbol americano	*to the football field*
a la playa	*to the beach*

al bosque nacional	*to the national park*
al campo	*to the countryside*
al mar	*to the seashore*

¿Haces ejercicio ?	*Do you* ***exercise?***
deportes	*play sports, do sports*
yoga	*do yoga*
camping	*go camping*
jogging	*jog, go jogging*

Estructura y Práctica

The Present Tense of Regular -ar Verbs

The Spanish verb system is characterized by a large number of forms, each one of which shows person and tense. This is very different from English, where person and tense are signaled by separate words that are often contracted.

SPANISH	ENGLISH
llego	*I arrive, I am arriving, I'm arriving*
estudiamos	*we study, we are studying, we're studying*

Spanish verbs are divided into three classes, called conjugations, distinguished by the vowel of the infinitive. The infinitive is the form of the verb that does not show person or tense and is the form used for listing verbs in dictionaries and vocabularies. Spanish infinitives may end in **-ar**, **-er**, or **-ir**. When the infinitive ending is removed, the stem of the verb is left. Endings are added to the stem.

The present indicative tense in Spanish is formed by adding the present tense endings to the stem of the verb. You will learn the **-ar** conjugation in this chapter. In Chapter 6, you will learn the **-er** and **-ir** conjugations.

comprar *to buy*

yo	compr**o**	nosotros	compr**amos**
tú	compr**as**	vosotros	compr**áis**
él/ella/Ud.	compr**a**	ellos/ellas/Uds.	compr**an**

Note that **-ar** verbs have the vowel **a** in all the endings except the **yo** form.

Stress is a very important feature of the Spanish verb system. The forms of **-ar**, **-er**, and **-ir** verbs are stressed on the stem in the singular (**yo/tú/él/ella/Ud.**) and the third person plural (**ellos/ellas/Uds.**) forms, and on the ending in the **nosotros** and **vosotros** forms.

hablo, hablas, habla, hablan, hablamos, habláis

Uses of the Present Tense

1 · The present tense forms of Spanish verbs express both the English simple present (*I speak*) and the English present progressive (*I'm speaking*).

Tocas el piano.	***You play*** *the piano.* ***You're playing*** *the piano.*
¿**Trabajan** Uds. en casa?	***Do you work*** *at home?* ***Are you working*** *at home?*

2 · The **yo** form and the **nosotros** form of the present tense are often used to ask for instructions.

¿**Entrego** los documentos hoy?	***Shall I submit*** *the documents today?*
¿**Tomamos** un vino tinto?	***Shall we have*** *a red wine?*

3 · After **¿Por qué no...?**, the present tense is used to make a suggestion.

¿**Por qué no** cenas con nosotros?	***Why don't*** *you have dinner with us?*
¿**Por qué no** vamos de vacaciones en mayo?	***Why don't*** *we go on vacation in May?*

4 · The present tense may be used to express the future when another element of the sentence (such as an adverb of time) makes the future reference clear.

Mañana **montan** a caballo.	*Tomorrow* ***they'll go*** *horseback* ***riding****.*

Hacer *to do, make*

You will see in Chapter 6 that **-er** verbs are conjugated like **-ar** verbs, except that they have **-e-** in the ending where **-ar** verbs have **-a-**. **Hacer**, like a number of common **-er** verbs, has an irregular **yo** form: a **-g-** inserted before the **-o** ending. Verbs with this irregularity are called **-g-** verbs. Thus, the **yo** form of **hacer** (**hago**) is irregular, but the rest of its present tense forms are regular.

hacer *to do, make*

yo	hago	nosotros	hacemos
tú	haces	vosotros	hacéis
él/ella/Ud.	hace	ellos/ellas/Uds.	hacen

¿Haces mucho ejercicio?	*Do you exercise a lot?*
Hago deportes pero no mucho.	*I play sports, but not a lot.*

A ***Los deportes.*** Write sentences using the string of elements given to tell what sports and exercises you and your friends do. Follow the *modelo.*

MODELO Pablo / trotar
→ Pablo trota.

1. tú / montar en bicicleta
2. Uds. / nadar
3. yo / patinar sobre hielo (*ice-skate*)
4. mis amigos y yo / montar a caballo
5. Ud. / caminar ocho millas diarias (*daily*)
6. Marta y Simón / trotar
7. Nicolás / levantar pesas
8. Diana / patinar sobre ruedas (*roller-skate*)

B ***¡No hacen nada!*** Write the form of **hacer** that correctly completes each of the following sentences about the sports and workouts these people refuse to do!

1. Uds. no ______________ camping.
2. Yo no ______________ deportes.
3. Él no ______________ jogging.
4. Ellos no ______________ una caminata (*walk around*).
5. Ud. no ______________ ejercicio.
6. Tú no ______________ yoga.
7. Nosotros no ______________ rafting.
8. Ella no ______________ Pilates.

C Express the following sentences in Spanish.

1. *I swim twice a week.*
2. *Shall we take a bicycle ride today?*
3. *I'll exercise tomorrow.*
4. *Why don't we go to the gym together?*
5. *My friends don't play sports.*
6. *Let's walk to the basketball court.*

DIÁLOGO 2 · Vamos al club.

Study the dialogue, then listen to the recording and repeat each line.

ISABEL ¿Por qué no vamos al club Maracas?
JUAN Ah, tú hablas del club donde tocan música latina, ¿no?
ISABEL Precisamente. Vamos a tomar una copa y escuchar música.
JUAN ¡Y bailar salsa! ¿Qué esperamos? Vamos ahora mismo.

Análisis

Check that you understand the linguistic breakdown of each speech from *Diálogo 2*.

¿Por qué no vamos al club Maracas?	*Why don't we go to Club Maracas?*
vamos	*we go*
no vamos	*we don't go*
¿Por qué no vamos?	*Why don't we go?*
el club	*club*
al	*to the* (contraction of **a** + **el**)
al club	*to the club*
Ah, tú hablas del club donde tocan música latina, ¿no?	*Ah, you mean the club where they play Latin music, right?*
hablar	*to speak, talk*
de	*about*
del	*of the, about the* (contraction of **de** + **el**)
tocar	*to play (a musical instrument)*
la música	*music*
latino	*Latin*
Precisamente. Vamos a tomar una copa y escuchar música.	*Exactly. We'll have a drink and listen to music.*
precisamente	*exactly*
tomar	*to take; to drink*

una copa	*an alcoholic drink* (literally, *wine glass, stem glass*)
tomar una copa	*to have a drink*
escuchar	*to listen to*
¡Y bailar salsa! ¿Qué esperamos?	*And dance salsa! What are we waiting for?*
Vamos ahora mismo.	*Let's go right now.*
bailar	*to dance*
la salsa	*salsa dance music* (literally, *sauce*)
esperar	*to wait for*
¿Qué esperamos?	*What are we waiting for?*
Vamos.	*Let's go.*
ahora	*now*
ahora mismo	*right now*

Variantes

Listen, and repeat the same structures from *Diálogo 2*, now with new vocabulary.

Vamos al club.	*Let's go **to the club**.*
a la discoteca	*to the discotheque*
al bar	*to the bar*
al concierto	*to the concert*
a la exposición de arte	*to the art exhibit*
¿De qué hablas?	*What are you talking about?*
Hablo del club.	*I'm talking **about the club**.*
de la discoteca	*about the discotheque*
del cine	*about the movie theater*
de la galería de arte	*about the art gallery*
del espectáculo	*about the show*
de la obra de teatro	*about the play*
Tocan música latina en el iPod.	***They play** Latin music on the iPod.*
Escuchan	*They listen to*
Disfrutan de	*They enjoy*
Graban	*They record*
Cargan	*They upload*
Descargan	*They download*
Toco el piano.	*I play **the piano**.*
el clarinete	*the clarinet*
la flauta	*the flute*
la guitarra	*the guitar*
el violín	*the violin*
el saxofón	*the saxophone*
Vamos a tomar una copa.	*Let's have **a drink**.*
algo	*something*
el desayuno	*breakfast*
el almuerzo	*lunch*
la merienda	*a snack*

Estructura y Práctica

Ir *to go*

Ir (*to go*) is an irregular verb and one of the small number of verbs ending in **-oy** in the first person singular: **voy**.

ir *to go*

yo	**voy**	nosotros	vamos
tú	vas	vosotros	vais
él/ella/Ud.	va	ellos/ellas/Uds.	van

¿Adónde van Uds.? — *Where are you going?*
Yo voy a la cancha de tenis y Diego va a la piscina. — *I'm going to the tennis court and Diego is going to the pool.*

D ***¿Adónde van?*** Write sentences using the verb **ir** with the elements given to tell where these people are going. Follow the *modelo*.

MODELO los chicos / la discoteca
→ Los chicos van a la discoteca.

1. Felipe y yo / el campo
2. Uds. / la cancha de tenis
3. Mercedes / la piscina
4. los señores Vargas / la playa
5. yo / el concierto
6. tú / el bar
7. Mauricio / el bosque nacional
8. Ud. / la galería de arte

Ir + a + Infinitive

In both English and Spanish, the infinitive can follow a conjugated verb. In the **ir** + **a** + infinitive construction, the verb **ir** is conjugated and connected to the infinitive by the preposition **a**.

Van a tomar el almuerzo. — *They're going to have lunch.*

Ir + **a** + infinitive is a frequent substitute for the future tense.

¿Cuándo vamos a cenar? — *When are we going to have dinner?*
Voy a servir (*to serve*) la cena a las ocho. — *I'm going to serve dinner at eight o'clock.*

Vamos a + infinitive often means *let's (do something)*. However, when used in the negative, it can only mean *we are not going to do something.*

Vamos a hacer un viaje en mayo. — *Let's take a trip in May.*
No vamos a hacer un viaje en mayo. — *We're not going to take a trip in May.*

E ***¿Qué van a hacer?*** Expand each of the following sentences using the **ir** + **a** + infinitive construction to state what people are going to do at the party. Follow the *modelo.*

MODELO Ellos hacen una pizza.
→ Ellos van a hacer una pizza.

1. Uds. toman una copa.
2. Mario descarga música brasileña.
3. Yo hago las tapas.
4. Manuel y Leticia bailan el tango.
5. Tú hablas con los invitados (*guests*).
6. Alicia y yo tocamos el piano.
7. Clara graba un video.
8. ¡Nosotros disfrutamos de una fiesta muy divertida!

Contraction al

You learned in Chapter 2 that the preposition **de** contracts with the masculine singular definite article **el** to form **del: de** + **el** → **del.**

Es la oficina **del** gerente. *It's the manager's office.*

Similarly, the preposition **a** contracts with the masculine singular definite article **el** to form **al: a** + **el** → **al.**

Voy **al** museo. *I'm going **to the** museum.*

The preposition **a**, like **de**, does not contract with other forms of the definite article or with the pronoun **él** (*he, it*).

¿Vas **a los** conciertos pop? *Do you go **to** pop concerts?*
Van **a la** playa. *They're going **to the** beach.*
¿Por qué se lo entregaste **a él**? *Why did you hand it **to him**?*

F ***A o al.*** Rewrite each of the following sentences, completing each one by writing the preposition **a** or the contraction **al** as necessary. Make any necessary changes.

1. —¿Uds. van ______ ir ______ el mar mañana?
   —Sí, vamos ______ ir ______ la playa mañana en la tarde.
2. —¿Vas ______ el gimnasio?
   —No, voy ______ el club.
3. —¿Ud. camina ______ la tienda de cómputo?
   —Sí, pero primero voy ______ la heladería.
4. —¿Tus amigos van ______ la universidad?
   —No, van ______ el campo de fútbol.
5. —La reunión es ______ las dos, ¿verdad?
   —No, es ______ la una.
6. —El teatro está ______ una cuadra de aquí, ¿no?
   —Ah sí. Queda ______ el lado de una galería de arte.

G Express the following sentences in Spanish.

1. *I'm going to have lunch.*
2. *Let's go to the museum.*
3. *What are you* (Uds.) *talking about?*
4. *We're talking about the show.*
5. *What are you* (tú) *listening to?*
6. *I'm downloading Spanish music.*
7. *Why don't we ice-skate* (patinar sobre hielo)*?*

DIÁLOGO 3 · ¿Esperas a alguien?

Study the dialogue, then listen to the recording and repeat each line.

JUAN ¿Qué haces? ¿Esperas a alguien?
ISABEL Sí, espero a mi amigo Gabriel.
JUAN Ah claro, Gabriel, tu amigo que hace programación.
ISABEL Sí, él y yo trabajamos juntos. Mira, ya llega.

Análisis

Check that you understand the linguistic breakdown of each speech from *Diálogo 3*.

¿Qué haces? ¿Esperas a alguien?	*What are you doing? Are you waiting for someone?*
esperar	*to wait for*
esperas	*you wait for*
a	(personal **a** required before an animate direct object)
alguien	*someone*
esperar a alguien	*to wait for someone*
Sí, espero a mi amigo Gabriel.	*Yes, I'm waiting for my friend Gabriel.*
Ah claro, Gabriel, tu amigo que hace programación.	*Oh, of course, Gabriel, your friend who does computer programming.*
claro	*of course*
que	*who, which, that*
hacer	*to do, make*
hace	*he does*
la programación	*(computer) programming*
Sí, él y yo trabajamos juntos. Mira, ya llega.	*Yes, he and I work together. Look, here he comes.*
trabajar	*to work*
trabajamos	*we work*
juntos	*together*
mirar	*to look at*
Mira	*look* (**tú** command form of **mirar**)
ya	*already, now*
llegar	*to arrive*
llega	*he arrives*
ya llega	*here he comes*

Variantes

Listen, and repeat the same structures from *Diálogo 3*, now with new vocabulary.

¿Esperas a alguien?	***Are you waiting for** someone?*
Llevas	*Are you taking*
Ayudas	*Are you helping*
Visitas	*Are you visiting*
Buscas	*Are you looking for*
Llamas	*Are you calling*
¿A quién esperas?	*Whom are you **waiting for**?*
llevas	*taking*
ayudas	*helping*
visitas	*visiting*
buscas	*looking for*
llamas	*calling*
miras	*looking at*
Busco al programador.	*I'm looking for **the computer programmer**.*
a la cocinera	*the chef*
a los asesores	*the consultants*
a las profesoras	*the teachers*
a Juan Carlos	*Juan Carlos*
a sus primos	*their cousins*
al señor Machado	*Mr. Machado*
a la señorita Salinas	*Ms. Salinas*
a mi perro	*my dog*
Busco el correo electrónico.	*I'm looking for **the email**.*
la estación de tren	*the train station*
una tienda de cómputo	*a computer store*
mis llaves	*my keys*
nuestros discos compactos	*our compact discs*
Es mi amigo que hace programación.	*It's my friend who **does programming**.*
diseña sitios web	*designs websites*
desarrolla software	*develops software*
navega en la red	*surfs the internet*
toma fotos	*takes pictures*
¿Llamas a alguien?	*Are you calling someone?*
No, no llamo a nadie.	*No, I'm not calling anyone.*
¿Miras algo?	*Are you looking at something?*
No, no miro nada.	*No, I'm not looking at anything.*

Estructura y Práctica

Direct Objects and the Personal *a*

The direct object is a noun or pronoun that completes the idea of a verb by labeling the goal of the action. Spanish distinguishes between two kinds of direct objects.

1 · Inanimate direct objects are connected to the verb without a preposition.

Llevo **los paquetes** a casa.	*I'm taking* ***the packages*** *home.*
El cocinero hace **un plato** rico.	*The chef is making* ***a*** *delicious* ***dish.***
Toca **la flauta**.	*She plays* ***the flute.***

2 · Animate direct objects are connected to the verb by means of the preposition **a**. This use of **a** is called personal **a**. The animate object must be specific and identifiable to require the use of personal **a**.

Llevo **a mis hijos** a casa.	*I'm taking* ***my children*** *home.*
Llamo **a Carmen** más tarde.	*I'll call* ***Carmen*** *later.*

Some English verbs that require a preposition (for example, *for, to, at*) before the direct object have Spanish verb equivalents that are followed immediately by a direct object.

buscar otro empleo	***to look for*** *another job*
escuchar música	***to listen to*** *music*
esperar el autobús	***to wait for*** *the bus*
mirar estos contratos	***to look at*** *these contracts*

If, however, the direct object is a definite animate being, it is preceded by the personal **a**.

Busca **al** programador.	*He's looking for the computer programmer.*
Escuchamos **a** la cantante.	*We're listening to the singer.*
Esperan **a** sus amigos.	*They're waiting for their friends.*
¿Por qué miras **a** ese tipo?	*Why are you looking at that guy?*

The words **alguien** (*somebody, someone*) and **nadie** (*nobody, no one*) are also preceded by personal **a** when they are the direct object of the verb.

¿Buscas **a alguien**?	*Are you looking for someone?*
No, no busco **a nadie**.	*No, I'm not looking for anyone.*

H ***¿La a personal o no?*** Determine whether or not the personal **a** is needed in each of the following sentences. Rewrite the sentences that require the personal **a**, making any necessary changes. Write an X if the sentence does not need the personal **a**.

1. Busco ______ mi celular.
2. ¿Vas a visitar ______ tus primos?
3. Esperan ______ el tren.
4. Voy a llamar ______ mis suegros (*in-laws*).
5. Llevan ______ muchas cajas.
6. ¿______ quién miras?
7. Vamos a ayudar ______ el asesor.
8. No miramos ______ nada.
9. Buscan ______ su perro.
10. Armando lleva ______ su esposa al centro.
11. Escucho ______ música clásica.
12. ¿Esperas ______ alguien?

Relative Pronoun que

Relative pronouns introduce relative clauses. A relative clause is a sentence that is incorporated into a larger sentence and that functions as an adjective within the larger sentence. In other words, it describes a noun. Relative clauses are also called adjective clauses. See the following English examples.

They live in a ***new*** *house.*
They live in a house ***that they bought last year****.*

Both *new* and *that they bought last year* modify the noun *house*. *New* is an adjective and *that they bought last year* is a relative clause that functions as an adjective.

The Spanish relative pronoun **que** can refer to people or things and can be either the subject or object of its clause.

1 · **Que** as the subject of the verb

mi amigo **que** trabaja en Inglaterra	*my friend* ***who*** *works in England*
un programa **que** es innovador	*a program* ***that*** *is innovative*

2 · **Que** as the direct object of the verb

la señora **que** voy a llamar	*the woman (****that****) I'm going to call*
los sitios web **que** diseñan	*the websites (****that****) they design*

In English, when the relative pronoun is the object of the verb in the relative clause, the pronoun is often omitted. It is never omitted in Spanish.

la casa **que** van a comprar	*the house (****that****) they're going to buy*
los asesores **que** contratamos	*the consultants (****that****) we hired*

When **que** is the object of the verb in the relative clause and it refers to people, it may be replaced by **a quien** or **a quienes**, depending on whether it refers to a singular or plural noun. **A quien** and **a quienes** are more formal in style than **que**.

el asesor **a quien** contratamos	*the consultant (****whom****) we hired*
los asesores **a quienes** contratamos	*the consultants (****whom****) we hired*

I ***Mis amigos.*** Write sentences using a relative clause introduced by the relative pronoun **que** to tell about your friends. Use the cues in parentheses. Follow the *modelo.*

MODELO Ana es mi amiga. (Mi amiga habla italiano.)
→ Ana es mi amiga que habla italiano.

1. Pedro es mi amigo. (Mi amigo toca el saxofón.)
2. Rebeca y Nora son mis amigas. (Mis amigas estudian física.)
3. Lorenzo es mi amigo. (Mi amigo diseña sitios web.)
4. Elena es mi amiga. (Mi amiga cocina muy bien.)
5. Antonio y Matilde son mis amigos. (Mis amigos trabajan en mi oficina.)
6. Ricardo es mi amigo. (Mi amigo hace programación.)

J ***¿Qué es precisamente?*** Use a relative clause to tell which person or object is being referred to in each question. Use the cues in parentheses. Follow the *modelo*.

MODELO ¿Qué libro? (El libro está en el estante.)
→ El libro que está en el estante.

1. ¿Qué museo? (El museo está abierto los lunes.)
2. ¿Qué mujeres de negocios? (Las mujeres de negocios ganan mucho dinero.)
3. ¿Qué asesor? (El asesor habla tres idiomas.)
4. ¿Qué coche? (El coche negro está descompuesto.)
5. ¿Qué estudiantes? (Los estudiantes hacen deportes.)
6. ¿Qué cancha de tenis? (La cancha de tenis queda enfrente de la piscina.)
7. ¿Qué profesores? (Los profesores enseñan (*teach*) administración de empresas.)
8. ¿Qué trajes? (Los trajes son de lana.)

Negative Words

Nada (*nothing*) and **nadie** (*no one*) are negative words. They have negative meaning when used in isolation.

¿Qué buscas? **Nada.**	*What are you looking for?* ***Nothing.***
¿Quién hace la cena? **Nadie.**	*Who's making dinner?* ***No one.***

Nada and **nadie** can function as the subject of a verb.

Nada es imposible.	***Nothing*** *is impossible.*
Nadie habla inglés aquí.	***No one*** *speaks English here.*

Nada and **nadie** can also function as the object of a verb. When a negative word follows the verb in Spanish, **no** must be used before the verb. When **nadie** is the direct object of a verb, it is preceded by the personal **a**.

No hago **nada** hoy.	*I'm not doing anything today.*
Ellos **no** ayudan **a nadie**.	*They don't help anyone.*

Here is a list of the most common negative words in Spanish, together with their affirmative counterparts.

NEGATIVE WORDS	AFFIRMATIVE COUNTERPARTS
nada *nothing*	algo *something*
nadie *no one, nobody*	alguien *someone, somebody*
ninguno (ningún), ninguna *no, none*	alguno (algún), alguna *some* algunos, algunas *some*
nunca, jamás *never*	algunas veces, a veces, alguna vez *sometimes* siempre *always* muchas veces, a menudo *often*

NEGATIVE WORDS	AFFIRMATIVE COUNTERPARTS
tampoco *neither*	o *or*
ni... ni *neither . . . nor*	o... o *either . . . or*
ya no *no longer*	todavía *still*

Ninguno and **alguno** are used before nouns, functioning as adjectives or pronouns. (For the forms **ningún** and **algún** before a masculine singular noun, see Chapter 2.)

ninguna calle	***no*** *street,* ***no*** *streets*
ningún medico	***no*** *doctor,* ***no*** *doctors*

Ninguno is only used in the plural when the following noun is inherently plural and has no singular. For all other nouns, the singular is used.

ningunos anteojos	***no*** *eyeglasses* (los anteojos)
ningunas tijeras	***no*** *scissors* (las tijeras)

Spanish, unlike English, allows two or more negative words in a sentence.

Nadie hace **nada nunca**.	*Nobody ever does anything.*

EXPRESSIONS WITH NEGATIVE WORDS

EXPRESSIONS WITH NEGATIVE WORDS	AFFIRMATIVE COUNTERPARTS
en/por ninguna parte *nowhere*	en/por alguna parte *somewhere*
en/por ningún lado *nowhere*	en/por algún lado *somewhere*
de ninguna manera *in no way, not at all*	de alguna manera *somehow, in some way*
de ningún modo *in no way*	de algún modo *somehow, in some way*

casi nunca *hardly ever*
nunca jamás *never ever*
nunca más *never again, no more*
¡Hasta nunca! *Goodbye forever!*
ni hablar *nothing doing*
ni modo *nothing doing*
nada de eso *nothing of the sort*
nada de extraordinario *nothing unusual*
nada más *that's all*
por nada del mundo *for nothing in the world*
nadie más *nobody else*
Es un don nadie. *He's a nobody.*

K ***¡Siempre negativo!*** Write negative responses to each of the following questions, using **no** plus the negative words that correspond to their affirmative counterparts. Follow the *modelo*.

MODELO ¿Vas a tomar algo?
→ No, no voy a tomar nada.

1. ¿Uds. esperan a alguien?
2. ¿Roberto va a bailar salsa alguna vez?

3. ¿Los cocineros preparan algunos platos de pollo?
4. ¿Leonor habla ruso también?
5. ¿Siempre estudias en la biblioteca?
6. ¿Todavía patinas sobre hielo?
7. ¿Julio busca o a su perro o a su gato?
8. ¿Algunas abogadas trabajan los sábados?

DIÁLOGO 4 · Una fiesta de cumpleaños

Study the dialogue, then listen to the recording and repeat each line.

ISABEL	¿Vas a celebrar tu cumpleaños con una fiesta?
JUAN	Sí, y voy a invitar a todos mis amigos.
ISABEL	¿Vas a invitar a Jaime Sandoval también?
JUAN	¡Qué va! Él es muy antipático y siempre toma demasiado.

Análisis

Check that you understand the linguistic breakdown of each speech from *Diálogo 4*.

¿Vas a celebrar tu cumpleaños con una fiesta?	*Are you going to celebrate your birthday with a party?*
ir a + *infinitive*	*to be going to (do something)*
celebrar	*to celebrate*
vas a celebrar	*you're going to celebrate*
el cumpleaños	*birthday*
la fiesta	*party*
Sí, y voy a invitar a todos mis amigos.	*Yes, and I'm going to invite all my friends.*
voy a invitar	*I'm going to invite*
a	(personal **a** required before an animate direct object)
todos mis amigos	*all my friends*
¿Vas a invitar a Jaime Sandoval también?	*Are you going to invite Jaime Sandoval, too?*
¡Qué va! Él es muy antipático y siempre toma demasiado.	*Are you kidding? He is very unpleasant and always drinks too much.*
¡Qué va!	*Are you kidding?*
antipático	*unpleasant*
siempre	*always*
tomar	*to take; to drink*
demasiado	*too much*
toma demasiado	*he drinks too much*

Variantes

Listen, and repeat the same structures from *Diálogo 4*, now with new vocabulary.

Jaime toma demasiado.	*Jaime* ***drinks*** *too much.*
habla	*talks*
trabaja	*works*
viaja	*travels*
¿A quiénes vas a invitar?	*Whom are you going to invite?*
Voy a invitar a todos mis amigos.	*I'm going to invite all my friends.*
¿No vas a invitar a Susana?	*Aren't you going to invite Susana?*
No, y no voy a invitar a Laura tampoco.	*No, and I'm not going to invite Laura either.*

Estructura y Práctica

Compound Nouns

The compound nouns you learned in Chapter 1 consisted of two nouns with the preposition **de**: **el museo de arte**, **la tienda de zapatos**. The compound nouns in this chapter are composed of a verb in third person singular of the present tense + a plural noun. The verb precedes the noun in Spanish, unlike its English counterpart. These compound nouns function as a masculine singular noun and take the definite article **el**. The plural of these compound nouns uses the plural form of the article, but the noun remains the same.

el cumpleaños *birthday* (cumplir (*to turn, reach*)) + años (*years*)
los cumpleaños *birthdays*

el aguafiestas *wet blanket, party pooper, spoilsport* (aguar (*to spoil*)) + fiestas (*parties*)
los aguafiestas *wet blankets, party poopers, spoilsports*

L **Compound nouns.** For each of the following items, form a compound noun by combining the third person singular form of the given verb with the plural of the given noun. Write each compound noun with its definite article, then write the English translation of each noun. Note that the third person singular form of **-ir** verbs in present tense ends in **-e**. Follow the *modelo*.

MODELO quitar (*to remove*) + mancha (*stain*)
→ el quitamanchas (*stain remover*)

1. lavar (*to wash*) + el plato (*dish*)
2. rascar (*to scrape*) + el cielo (*sky*)
3. cortar (*to cut*) + la uña (*fingernail*)
4. cubrir (*to cover*) + la cama (*bed*) [*cama* remains singular]
5. parar (*to stop*) + la caída (*fall*)
6. abrir (*to open*) + la lata (*can*)
7. cortar (*to cut*) + el césped (*grass, lawn*) [*césped* remains singular]
8. sacar (*to take out, get out*) + el corcho (*cork*)

DIÁLOGO 5 · Vamos a ir de vacaciones.

Study the dialogue, then listen to the recording and repeat each line.

JUAN Ud. va a ir de vacaciones en el verano, ¿verdad?
ISABEL Sí, hago un viaje con mis amigos a España en julio. ¡Ya hacemos las maletas!
JUAN ¡Qué estupendo! ¿Uds. van a hacer turismo entonces?
ISABEL Ah sí, vamos a viajar por todo el país. Y vamos a tomar muchas fotos.

Análisis

Check that you understand the linguistic breakdown of each speech from *Diálogo 5*.

Ud. va a ir de vacaciones en el verano, ¿verdad? — *You're going to go on vacation in the summer, aren't you?*
- las vacaciones — *vacation*
- de vacaciones — *on vacation*
- ir de vacaciones — *to go on vacation*
- el verano — *summer*
- ¿verdad? — *aren't you?*

Sí, hago un viaje con mis amigos a España en julio. ¡Ya hacemos las maletas! — *Yes, I'm taking a trip with my friends to Spain in July. We're already packing!*
- el viaje — *trip*
- hacer un viaje — *to take a trip*
- hago un viaje — *I'm taking a trip*
- España — *Spain*
- julio — *July*
- la maleta — *suitcase*
- hacer las maletas — *to pack*
- hacemos las maletas — *we're packing*

¡Qué estupendo! ¿Uds. van a hacer turismo entonces? — *How wonderful! So you are going to go sightseeing?*
- estupendo — *terrific, wonderful, great*
- ¡Qué + *adjective*! — *How +* adjective*!*
- hacer turismo — *to go sightseeing*
- entonces — *then, so, in that case*

Ah sí, vamos a viajar por todo el país. Y vamos a tomar muchas fotos. — *Oh, yes, we are going to travel around the whole country. And we are going to take a lot of pictures.*
- viajar — *to travel*
- vamos a viajar — *we are going to travel*
- por — *through, around*
- todo el país — *the whole country, the entire country*
- la foto — *photograph, picture*
- tomar fotos — *to take pictures*

Variantes

Listen, and repeat the same structures from *Diálogo 5*, now with new vocabulary.

¿Ud. va a ir de vacaciones en el verano?	*Are you going to go on vacation in* ***the summer****?*
el otoño	*the fall*
el invierno	*the winter*
la primavera	*the spring*
Hago un viaje en julio.	*I'll be taking a trip in* ***July****.*
agosto	*August*
septiembre	*September*
octubre	*October*
noviembre	*November*
diciembre	*December*
enero	*January*
febrero	*February*
marzo	*March*
abril	*April*
mayo	*May*
junio	*June*
Toman un avión.	*They're taking* ***a plane****.*
un tren	*a train*
un taxi	*a taxi*
un autobús	*a bus*
el metro	*the subway*
un barco	*a boat*

Estructura y Práctica

Nouns

Some nouns in Spanish have unpredictable genders. (See Chapter 1.)

la foto (la fotografía) *photograph*
la moto (la motocicleta) *motorcycle*
la mano *hand*
el día *day*
el mapa *map*

Some nouns in Spanish are always plural.

los anteojos *eyeglasses*
las gafas *eyeglasses*
los gemelos *twins, binoculars, cufflinks*
las tijeras *scissors*
los auriculares *earphones*

Some nouns in Spanish are usually plural.

las vacaciones *vacation*
las elecciones *election*
los bienes *goods*
las afueras *outskirts*
los celos *jealousy*

M ***¡De vacaciones!*** Choose the item from the second column that correctly completes the phrase in the first column to learn about the López's family trip. Write the complete phrase.

1. preparan	a. varios museos
2. viajan	b. en la piscina
3. visitan	c. turismo
4. llegan	d. las maletas
5. sacan	e. al aeropuerto
6. hacen	f. salsa
7. bailan	g. en avión
8. nadan	h. las tarjetas de embarque

DIÁLOGO 6 · Encargamos una pizza.

Study the dialogue, then listen to the recording and repeat each line.

ISABEL ¿Qué vamos a cenar esta noche? ¿Cenamos fuera o preparamos algo en casa?

JUAN Vamos a cenar en casa, pero sin cocinar. ¿Por qué no encargamos una pizza?

ISABEL ¡Estupendo! Ahora mismo yo llamo al restaurante Roma para encargar la pizza.

JUAN Y yo voy a comprar una botella de vino y alquilar una película.

Análisis

Check that you understand the linguistic breakdown of each speech from *Diálogo 6*.

¿Qué vamos a cenar esta noche?	*What are we going to have for dinner?*
¿Cenamos fuera o preparamos algo en casa?	*Shall we eat out or shall we prepare something at home?*
cenar	*to have dinner*
cenar algo	*to have something for dinner*
la noche	*night*
esta noche	*tonight*
fuera	*out, outside*
cenar fuera	*to have dinner out*
¿Cenamos fuera?	*Shall we have dinner out?*
preparar	*to prepare*
¿Preparamos algo?	*Shall we prepare something?*
la casa	*house*
en casa	*at home*

Vamos a cenar en casa, pero sin cocinar. ¿Por qué no encargamos una pizza?	*Let's eat at home, but without cooking. Why don't we order a pizza?*
vamos a + *infinitive*	*let's (do something)*
vamos a cenar	*let's have dinner*
sin	*without*
cocinar	*to cook*
sin cocinar	*without cooking*
encargar	*to order*
¿Por qué no encargamos?	*Why don't we order?*
la pizza	pizza
¡Estupendo! Ahora mismo yo llamo al restaurante Roma para encargar la pizza.	*Great! I'll call the Roma restaurant right now to order the pizza.*
estupendo	*terrific, wonderful, great*
ahora mismo	*right now*
llamar	*to call*
yo llamo	*I call, I'll call*
llamar a un lugar	*to call a place*
para + *infinitive*	*in order (to do something)*
para encargar la pizza	*(in order) to order the pizza*
Y yo voy a comprar una botella de vino y alquilar una película.	*And I'm going to buy a bottle of wine and rent a movie.*
comprar	*to buy*
la botella	*bottle*
el vino	*wine*
una botella de vino	*a bottle of wine*
alquilar	*to rent*
la película	*movie, film*

Variantes

Listen, and repeat the same structures from *Diálogo 6*, now with new vocabulary.

¿Preparamos un plato vegetariano?	***Should we prepare** a vegetarian dish?*
Hacemos	*Should we make*
Cocinamos	*Should we cook*
Compramos	*Should we buy*
Encargamos	*Should we order*
Yo llamo al restaurante ahora mismo.	*I'll call **the restaurant** right now.*
a la empresa	*the firm*
al número (de teléfono)	*the number*
a la oficina	*the office*
al bufete	*the lawyer's office*

Vamos a ir de compras ahora . — *Let's go shopping **now**.*
tarde — *late*
temprano — *early*
más tarde — *later*
más temprano — *earlier*
pronto — *soon*
después — *afterwards*
hoy — *today*
mañana — *tomorrow*
pasado mañana — *the day after tomorrow*

Estructura y Práctica

Adverbs of Time

Adverbs of time only modify verbs. They are usually not derived from adjectives in Spanish or English.

¿Tomas el desayuno **temprano**? — *Do you have breakfast **early**?*
Vamos al concierto **mañana**. — *We're going to the concert **tomorrow**.*
¿Uds. **ya** ganan mucho dinero? — *Are you **already** earning a lot of money?*

N ***¿Cuándo?*** Express each sentence in Spanish to find out when things are happening.

1. *Let's go sightseeing tomorrow.*
2. *I'm packing right now.*
3. *I always help my parents.*
4. *Shall we take a trip in the summer?*
5. *Why don't we have dinner out on Friday?*
6. *Are you* (Uds.) *going to the national park early?*
7. *Yes, we're going to go at seven in the morning.*
8. *Emilia is visiting her brother the day after tomorrow.*
9. *The web designers are going to work together very soon.*
10. *We'll take the children to the shoe store later.*

DIÁLOGO 7 · En tus horas libres

Study the dialogue, then listen to the recording and repeat each line.

JUAN ¿Qué haces en tus horas libres?
ISABEL Dibujo, canto en una banda y hago deportes. ¿Tú?
JUAN Yo cuando estoy libre hago programas y páginas web para pequeñas empresas.
ISABEL ¡Qué emprendedor eres! Así ganas dinero en tus ratos libres.

Análisis

Check that you understand the linguistic breakdown of each speech from *Diálogo 7*.

¿Qué haces en tus horas libres?	*What do you do in your free time?*
la hora	*hour, time*
libre	*free*
las horas libres	*free time* (literally, *free hours*)
en tus horas libres	*in your free time, when you are free*
Dibujo, canto en una banda y hago deportes. ¿Tú?	*I draw, I sing in a band, and I play sports. How about you?*
dibujar	*to draw*
dibujo	*I draw*
cantar	*to sing*
canto	*I sing*
la banda	*band*
el deporte	*sport*
hacer deportes	*to play sports*
hago deportes	*I play sports*
Yo cuando estoy libre hago programas y páginas web para pequeñas empresas.	*When I'm free, I do programs and web pages for small businesses.*
estar libre	*to be free, be at leisure*
estoy libre	*I'm free*
el programa	*program*
la página	*page*
la página web	*web page*
pequeño	*small*
la empresa	*business, firm*
la pequeña empresa	*small business*
¡Qué emprendedor eres! Así ganas dinero en tus ratos libres.	*How enterprising you are! That way you earn money in your free time.*
emprendedor	*enterprising*
así	*that way, in that way, thus*
ganar	*to earn*
el dinero	*money*
ganar dinero	*to earn money*
ganas dinero	*you earn money*

Variantes

Listen, and repeat the same structures from *Diálogo 7*, now with new vocabulary.

Ganas mucho dinero.	***You earn** a lot of money.*
Gastas	*You spend*
Ahorras	*You save*
Pagas	*You pay*

Llevas	*You carry*
Deseas	*You want*
Haces	*You make*

En mis horas libres, canto en una banda.	*In my free time,* ***I sing in a band.***
saco fotos	*I take pictures*
practico mi español	*I practice my Spanish*
saco a pasear a mi perro	*I take my dog out for a walk*
pinto cuadros	*I paint pictures*

Estructura y Práctica

O ***Las actividades de ocio* (Leisure activities).** Write the present tense form of the verb that correctly completes each of the following sentences to tell what you and your friends do as leisure activities. Follow the *modelo.*

MODELO Alonso *pasea* por las calles del centro. (pasear (*to go for a walk*))

1. Maite ______________ en la red. (navegar)
2. Yo ______________ música. (escuchar)
3. Tú ______________ una clase en línea. (tomar)
4. Ignacio y Héctor ______________ bricolaje (*do-it-yourself projects*). (hacer)
5. Ud. ______________ a la gente en los cafés. (observar (*to watch*))
6. Uds. ______________ en bicicleta. (montar)
7. Juanita ______________ sitios web. (diseñar)
8. ¡Todos nosotros ______________ de la vida! (disfrutar (*to enjoy*))

Un paso más

Are you ready to take your Spanish a step further? Here are exercises that will enhance your knowledge of the language and encourage you to express yourself freely.

P **Forming nouns from verbs.** Nouns are formed from verbs in multiple ways. (1) Some nouns related to verbs consist of the verb stem + **-o** or **-a**. (2) Many nouns are formed from **-ar** verbs with the suffix **-ción**. Most of these have English cognates ending in *-tion*. (3) Many nouns are formed from the past participle of verbs. They consist of the verb stem + the suffix **-ada** (for **-ar** verbs) or **-ida** (for **-er** and **-ir** verbs). Write the English translation for each of the following nouns; then write the Spanish verb from which it derives.

1. el trabajo
2. la canción
3. la espera
4. la invitación
5. la mirada
6. la ayuda
7. la visita
8. el desarrollo

9. la práctica
10. la celebración
11. el dibujo
12. la llegada
13. la preparación
14. la compra
15. la cocina
16. el ahorro
17. el gasto
18. la navegación
19. el pago
20. la grabación
21. la llamada
22. el diseño

Q ***Preguntas personales.*** Answer each question with a complete Spanish sentence.

1. ¿Qué deportes hace Ud.?
2. ¿Qué ejercicio hace?
3. ¿Escucha música latina? ¿Qué otra música escucha?
4. ¿Toca un instrumento musical? ¿Cuál? ¿Cuánto practica todos los días?
5. ¿Cuándo es su cumpleaños? ¿Cómo celebra su cumpleaños?
6. ¿Cuándo va Ud. de vacaciones? ¿Adónde va? ¿Con quién(es) va?
7. ¿Qué meses son buenos para viajar? ¿Cuál es su estación (*season*) favorita?
8. ¿Cocina platos de alta cocina (*haute cuisine, gourmet*)? ¿Cuáles son?
9. ¿A qué restaurantes va?
10. ¿Encarga comida a domicilio (encargar comida a domicilio (*to order take out*))? ¿Qué comida encarga?
11. ¿Qué hace en sus horas libres?
12. ¿Cómo gana dinero? ¿Cuánto dinero gasta al mes? ¿Cuánto dinero ahorra al mes?
13. ¿A qué tiendas va para comprar comida (ropa, libros, zapatos, medicamentos y productos de belleza y cuidado personal (*medicine and beauty and personal care products*), dispositivos electrónicos (*electronic devices*))?
14. ¿Usa el e-comercio? ¿Qué compra por internet?

6

The Weather, Foreign Languages, and Sports

Communication Goals

- Talking about learning a foreign language, making plans, cooking and eating
- Telling what you want, need, prefer, are able, intend, and know how to do
- Telling how long you have been doing something
- Vocabulary: foreign languages, weather expressions, business, numbers, sports

Grammar Topics

- The Present Tense of Regular **-er** and **-ir** Verbs
- Review: Uses of the Present Tense
- **Hace** + Expression of Time + Verb in Present Tense
- Stem-changing Verbs
- **Tener** *to have*
- Verb + Infinitive Construction, Verb + Connector + Infinitive Construction
- **Para** vs. **por**
- **Saber** and **conocer**
- Direct Object Pronouns
- Stem-changing Verbs: **servir** and **pedir**
- Prepositional Pronouns
- Numbers
- **Seguir**
- **Jugar**

DIÁLOGO 1 · Estudiamos español.

Study the dialogue, then listen to the recording and repeat each line.

LAURA	Yo comienzo a tomar una clase de español a distancia.
MATEO	¿Necesitas usar el español en tu trabajo?
LAURA	Sí, y hace cinco años que yo estudio español, pero no hablo muy bien el idioma.
MATEO	Pues hay que practicar mucho para dominar un idioma.

Análisis

Check that you understand the linguistic breakdown of each speech from *Diálogo 1*.

Yo comienzo a tomar una clase de español a distancia.	*I'm starting to take an online Spanish course.*
comenzar (**e** > **ie**)	*to begin*
comenzar a + *infinitive*	*to start to (do something), begin (doing something)*
tomar una clase	*to take a class*
comienzo a tomar	*I'm starting to take*
la distancia	*distance*
a distancia	*at a distance*
una clase a distancia	*an online course, a distance learning course*
¿Necesitas usar el español en tu trabajo?	*Do you need to use Spanish in your work?*
necesitar	*to need*
necesitar + *infinitive*	*to need to (do something)*
usar	*to use*
en	*in*
el trabajo	*work, job*
Sí, y hace cinco años que yo estudio español, pero no hablo muy bien el idioma.	*Yes, and I've been studying Spanish for five years, but I don't speak the language very well.*
hace + *expression of time*	*for* + expression of time
hace cinco años	*for five years*
estudio	*I study* (here, *I have been studying*)
bien	*well*
muy bien	*very well*
el idioma	*language*
Pues hay que practicar mucho para dominar un idioma.	*Well, you have to practice a lot to master a language.*
pues	*well* (interjection)
hay que + *infinitive*	*one must (do something), it is necessary to (do something), you have to (do something)*

mucho	*a lot*
para	*for, in order to*
dominar	*to master*

Variantes

Listen, and repeat the same structures from *Diálogo 1*, now with new vocabulary.

Comienzo a hablar español.	***I'm beginning to** speak Spanish.*
Empiezo a	*I'm beginning to*
Aprendo a	*I'm learning to*
Voy a	*I'm going to*
¿Necesitas usar el español?	***Do you need to** use Spanish?*
Debes	*Should you*
Puedes	*Can you*
Prefieres	*Do you prefer to*
Quieres	*Do you want to*
Piensas	*Do you intend to*
Deseas	*Do you want to*
Esperas	*Do you hope to, Do you expect to*
Sabes	*Do you know how to*
Hay que practicar el español todos los días.	*You have to **practice Spanish every day**.*
comprender su punto de vista	*understand her point of view*
compartir las ideas	*share the ideas*
pensar en el problema	*think about the problem*
meter la tarjeta en el parquímetro	*put the card into the parking meter*
¿Cuánto (tiempo) hace que estudias español?	*How long have you been **studying Spanish**?*
vives en el centro	*living downtown*
asistes a estos conciertos	*attending these concerts*
escribes novelas	*writing novels*
recibes sus correos electrónicos	*receiving their emails*
Hace cinco años que estudio español.	***I've been studying Spanish** for five years.*
vivo en el centro	*I've been living downtown*
asisto a estos conciertos	*I've been attending these concerts*
escribo novelas	*I've been writing novels*
recibo sus correos electrónicos	*I've been receiving their emails*
Hace cinco años que estudio español.	*I've been studying Spanish **for five years**.*
Hace un año	*for a year*
Hace ocho meses	*for eight months*
Hace mucho tiempo	*for a long time*
Hace poco tiempo	*for a short time*
Hace un semestre	*for a semester*

Estructura y Práctica

The Present Tense of Regular -er and -ir Verbs

As you learned in Chapter 5, Spanish verbs are divided into three classes, called conjugations, distinguished by the vowel of the infinitive. Spanish infinitives may end in **-ar**, **-er**, or **-ir**.

The present indicative tense in Spanish is formed by adding the present tense endings to the stem of the verb. You learned the **-ar** conjugation in Chapter 5. Here are the **-er** and **-ir** conjugations.

comprender *to understand*	
comprend**o**	comprend**emos**
comprend**es**	comprend**éis**
comprend**e**	comprend**en**

escribir *to write*	
escrib**o**	escrib**imos**
escrib**es**	escrib**ís**
escrib**e**	escrib**en**

Note that the endings of the **-er** and **-ir** verbs are identical except in the first and second person plural (**nosotros** and **vosotros** forms). The endings of the three conjugations are similar. The characteristic difference is the vowel of the ending: **-ar** verbs have an **-a-** in five of the six endings, while **-er** verbs have an **-e-**. **-Ir** verb endings are identical to **-er** verb endings in all but two persons, as shown.

A **Regular *-er* and *-ir* verbs.** Write the present tense form of the regular **-er** or **-ir** verb that correctly completes each of the following sentences. Use the verbs in parentheses.

1. Ellos ________________ (correr) diez millas todos los días.
2. Nosotros ________________ (vivir) en el centro.
3. Ella ________________ (romper) con su novio.
4. Yo ________________ (creer) que va a llover más tarde.
5. ¿Ya (tú) ________________ (subir) al tren?
6. Él no ________________ (compartir) sus ideas con nadie.
7. ¿Cuándo ________________ (vender) Uds. su casa?
8. Ud. no ________________ (resistir) a la tentación, ¿verdad?

B ***¿Qué hacen en la universidad?*** Write sentences from the strings of elements given to tell what you and other people are doing in the university today. Follow the *modelo*.

MODELO los problemas / discutir / los estudiantes
→ Los estudiantes discuten los problemas.

1. un informe / escribir / Mario
2. en la biblioteca / leer / nosotros
3. yo / una conferencia / asistir a
4. abrir / Uds. / los libros de texto

5. las teorías de la física / comprender / tú
6. imprimir / un artículo / María Elena
7. subir (*to upload*) / Rodrigo y Mateo / unos archivos
8. Ud. / para el laboratorio / salir

Review: Uses of the Present Tense

You learned the uses of the present tense in Chapter 5. Here is a brief review.

1 · The present tense forms of Spanish verbs express both the English simple present (*I speak*) and the English present progressive (*I'm speaking*).

Lee libros de cocina.	***She reads*** *cookbooks.* ***She's reading*** *cookbooks.*
Escribo libros de texto.	***I write*** *textbooks.* ***I'm writing*** *textbooks.*

2 · The **yo** form and the **nosotros** form of the present tense are often used to ask for instructions.

¿**Asisto** al concierto?	***Shall I attend*** *the concert?*
¿**Vivimos** en este barrio?	***Shall we live*** *in this neighborhood?*

3 · After **¿Por qué no…?**, the present tense is used to make a suggestion.

¿Por qué no compartes tu idea?	***Why don't you share*** *your idea?*
¿Por qué no corren el maratón?	***Why don't you run*** *the marathon?*

4 · The present tense may be used to express the future when another element of the sentence (such as an adverb of time) makes the future reference clear.

Vuelven de su viaje el jueves.	***They'll return*** *from their trip on Thursday.*
Servimos la cena a las ocho.	***We'll serve*** *dinner at 8 o'clock.*

Hace + Expression of Time + Verb in Present Tense

The present tense is used in Spanish to express actions beginning in the past but continuing into the present (English *have/has been doing something*). The period of time during which the action has been going on is expressed in a phrase beginning with **hace**.

Hace seis meses que trabajo aquí.	*I have been working here* ***for six months.***
Él estudia español **hace tres años.**	*He's been studying Spanish* ***for three years.***

Note that the time phrase with **hace** can be placed either at the beginning of the sentence or at the end. When it is placed at the beginning, the conjunction **que** is used to connect it to what follows.

To ask a question using this construction, the form **¿Cuánto (tiempo) hace que** + verb in present tense? is used. (The word **tiempo** is optional.)

¿Cuánto (tiempo) hace que Ud. vive en la ciudad?	***How long*** *have you been living in the city?*

C *¿Cuánto tiempo hace...?* Form questions using **¿Cuánto tiempo hace que...?** and the elements given. Then answer each question in two ways, using the time phrase in parentheses. Follow the *modelo*.

MODELO Ana / estudiar español (siete años)
→ —¿Cuánto tiempo hace que Ana estudia español?
—Hace siete años que estudia español.
—Estudia español hace siete años.

1. tú / esperar / a tus amigos (quince minutos)
2. los niños / buscar a su perro (dos días)
3. Uds. / vivir en este barrio (dieciséis años)
4. Pedro / tomar clases a distancia (un año)
5. Uds. / hacer deportes (cuatro meses)
6. Susana y Fernando / buscar casa (varios meses)
7. nosotros / asistir a estos conciertos (mucho tiempo)
8. Ud. / mandar emails (una hora)

Stem-changing Verbs

Many Spanish verbs show a change in the vowel of the stem in the present tense. This occurs in those forms where the vowel of the stem is stressed—all three singular forms and the third person plural; only the **nosotros** and **vosotros** forms are not affected. These are called stem-changing verbs. For **-ar** and **-er** verbs, the stem changes are **e** > **ie** and **o** > **ue**. Stem changes in **-ir** verbs are **e** > **i**, **e** > **ie**, and **o** > **ue**.

You cannot predict from the infinitive which verbs will have a stem change and which will not, so you must memorize the verbs that have a stem change. These changes are indicated in infinitive listings in this book as follows.

pensar (**e** > **ie**)
volver (**o** > **ue**)
servir (**e** > **i**)

1 · Here are present tense forms of the **-ar** and **-er** stem-changing verbs **pensar** (*to think*), **querer** (*to want*), **contar** (*to count, tell*), and **volver** (*to return*).

pensar (e > ie) *to think*	
pi**e**nso	pensamos
pi**e**nsas	pensáis
pi**e**nsa	pi**e**nsan

querer (e > ie) *to want*	
qui**e**ro	queremos
qui**e**res	queréis
qui**e**re	qui**e**ren

contar (o > ue) *to count, tell*	
c**ue**nto	contamos
c**ue**ntas	contáis
c**ue**nta	c**ue**ntan

volver (o > ue) *to return*	
v**ue**lvo	volvemos
v**ue**lves	volvéis
v**ue**lve	v**ue**lven

Additional verbs that pattern like **pensar** and **querer** (**e** > **ie**) are **cerrar** (*to close*), **comenzar** (*to begin*), **empezar** (*to begin*), **entender** (*to understand*), **helar** (*to freeze*), **merendar** (*to have an afternoon snack*), **nevar** (*to snow*), and **reventar** (*to burst*). Impersonal verbs like **helar** and **nevar** are conjugated only in the third person singular.

Additional verbs that pattern like **contar** and **volver** (**o** > **ue**) are **almorzar** (*to have lunch*), **costar** (*to cost*), **devolver** (*to return (something), to give back (something)*), **encontrar** (*to find*), **jugar** (*to play (a sport or game)*), **llover** (*to rain*), **poder** (*to be able, can*), **probar** (*to try, taste*), and **tronar** (*to thunder*). **Jugar** is conjugated as if it had **-o-** as its stem vowel. Impersonal verbs like **llover** and **tronar** are conjugated only in the third person singular.

2 · Here are present tense forms of the **-ir** stem-changing verbs **servir** (*to serve*), **preferir** (*to prefer*), and **dormir** (*to sleep*).

servir (e > i) *to serve*	
s**i**rvo	servimos
s**i**rves	servís
s**i**rve	s**i**rven

preferir (e > ie) *to prefer*	
pref**ie**ro	preferimos
pref**ie**res	preferís
pref**ie**re	pref**ie**ren

dormir (o > ue) *to sleep*	
d**ue**rmo	dormimos
d**ue**rmes	dormís
d**ue**rme	d**ue**rmen

Additional verbs that pattern like **servir** (**e** > **i**) are **pedir** (*to ask for, request*) and **seguir** (*to follow, continue*). The verb **morir** (*to die*) is conjugated like **dormir**. The verb **sentir** (*to feel*) is conjugated like **preferir**. (For more on **seguir**, see *Diálogo 10* in this chapter.)

D **Stem-changing verbs.** Write the present tense form of the stem-changing verb that correctly completes each of the following sentences. Use the verbs in parentheses.

1. El concierto ______________ (comenzar) a las siete y media.
2. Ellos ______________ (volver) de su viaje el domingo.
3. Yo ______________ (querer) más carne, por favor.
4. ¿No (tú) ______________ (encontrar) tus llaves?
5. ¿Uds. ______________ (pedir) algo de postre?
6. Él ______________ (pensar) en su futuro.
7. ¿Cuánto ______________ (costar) esos trajes?
8. Ella ______________ (preferir) la falda azul de lana.
9. ¿Por qué no ______________ (probar) Ud. este plato?
10. El bebé ______________ (dormir) muy poco.

11. ¿A qué hora ______________ (empezar) los partidos?
12. Es que nosotros no ______________ (entender) el problema.
13. Yo ______________ (almorzar) con Uds. pasado mañana.
14. Ellas no ______________ (servir) la cena hasta las seis.
15. ¿Tú ______________ (jugar) al golf o al tenis?
16. Nosotros ______________ (merendar) hoy a las cuatro y media.

DIÁLOGO 2 · ¿Tú sabes francés?

Study the dialogue, then listen to the recording and repeat each line.

LAURA	Tú sabes francés, ¿verdad?
MATEO	Yo leo y escribo francés, pero no entiendo muy bien el francés hablado.
LAURA	Dominar el idioma hablado es difícil.
MATEO	Por eso espero pasar unos meses en Francia el año que viene.

Análisis

Check that you understand the linguistic breakdown of each speech from *Diálogo 2.*

Tú sabes francés, ¿verdad?	*You know French, don't you?*
saber	*to know*
sabes	*you know*
el francés	*French*
¿verdad?	*don't you?*
Yo leo y escribo francés, pero no entiendo muy bien el francés hablado.	*I read and write French, but I don't understand spoken French very well.*
leer	*to read*
escribir	*to write*
entender (**e** > **ie**)	*to understand*
hablado	*spoken* (past participle of **hablar**)
el francés hablado	*spoken French*
Dominar el idioma hablado es difícil.	*It's difficult to master the spoken language.*
dominar	*to master*
el idioma hablado	*the spoken language*
difícil	*difficult*
Por eso espero pasar unos meses en Francia el año que viene.	*That's why I hope to spend a few months in France next year.*
por eso	*that's why, therefore*
esperar + *infinitive*	*to hope to (do something)*
el mes	*month*
unos meses	*a few months*
Francia	*France*
el año	*year*
que viene	*next* (literally, *that's coming*)
el año que viene	*next year*

Variantes

Listen, and repeat the same structures from *Diálogo 2*, now with new vocabulary.

¿Sabes francés?	*Do you know **French**?*
inglés	*English*
español	*Spanish*
italiano	*Italian*
alemán	*German*
ruso	*Russian*
chino	*Chinese*

DIÁLOGO 3 · Hace mal tiempo.

Study the dialogue, then listen to the recording and repeat each line.

MATEO Llueve fuerte. Yo no tengo ganas de salir.
LAURA Yo tampoco. Además, hace frío y viento.
MATEO Y ahora yo creo que empieza a nevar. ¡Qué día más feo!
LAURA Menos mal que no tenemos que ir a ninguna parte hoy.

Análisis

Check that you understand the linguistic breakdown of each speech from *Diálogo 3*.

Llueve fuerte. Yo no tengo ganas de salir.	*It's raining hard. I don't feel like going out.*
llover (**o** > **ue**)	*to rain*
fuerte	*strong, hard, loud*
tengo	*I have*
no tengo ganas de + *infinitive*	*I don't feel like (doing something)*
Yo tampoco. Además, hace frío y viento.	*Neither do I. Besides, it's cold and windy.*
tampoco	*neither*
yo tampoco	*neither do I*
además	*besides*
hacer	*to do, make*
el frío	*cold*
hace frío	*it's cold*
el viento	*wind*
hace viento	*it's windy*
Y ahora yo creo que empieza a nevar. ¡Qué día más feo!	*And now I think it's beginning to snow. What an awful day!*
creer	*to believe*
creo	*I believe*
empezar (**e** > **ie**)	*to begin*
empezar a hacer algo	*to begin to do something, start to do something*
nevar (**e** > **ie**)	*to snow*
feo	*ugly*
¡Qué día más feo!	*What an awful day!*

Menos mal que no tenemos que ir a ninguna parte hoy.	*It's lucky that we don't have to go anywhere today.*
menos mal	*fortunately, at least*
menos mal que	*it's lucky that*
tener que + *infinitive*	*to have to (do something)*
ir	*to go*
tenemos que ir	*we have to go*
a ninguna parte	*anywhere, nowhere* (with verb of motion)

Variantes

Listen, and repeat the same structures from *Diálogo 3*, now with new vocabulary.

Yo no tengo ganas de salir .	*I don't feel like **going out**.*
entrar	*going in*
regresar	*going back*
discutir	*arguing, discussing*
subir	*going up*
dormir	*sleeping*
Hace frío .	*It's **cold**.*
calor	*hot*
fresco	*cool*
viento	*windy*
sol	*sunny*
Empieza a nevar .	*It's beginning to **snow**.*
llover	*rain*
tronar	*thunder*
despejar	*clear up*
No tenemos que ir .	*We don't have to **go**.*
seguir	*continue*
volver	*go back*
comenzar	*begin*
correr	*run*
¿Qué tiempo hace?	*What's the weather like?*
Hace buen/mal tiempo.	*The weather's good/bad.*
¿Qué temperatura hace?	*What's the temperature?*
Hace setenta grados.	*It's seventy degrees.*

Estructura y Práctica

E ***¿Qué tiempo hace?*** Express the following sentences in English to describe the weather in some American cities. Write numbers as words.

1. *It's hot in Miami.*
2. *It's raining in Seattle.*
3. *It's cool in Philadelphia.*
4. *The weather's good in San Diego.*

5. *It's very windy in Chicago.*
6. *It's snowing in Boston.*
7. *It's very cold in Anchorage.*
8. *It's 75 degrees in Washington, D.C.*
9. *It's thundering in New York.*
10. *It's sunny in Dallas.*
11. *The weather's bad in Baton Rouge.*

Tener *to have*

Tener is an irregular verb—one that does not follow the standard pattern of formation. The most common pattern of irregular verbs in the present tense is an irregular **yo** form, most often a **-g-** inserted before the **-o** ending. Verbs with this irregularity, called **-g-** verbs, may also have irregularities in the other forms. **Tener** is one such verb.

tener *to have*	
ten**g**o	tenemos
tienes	tenéis
tiene	tienen

Tener is used in the verb + connector + infinitive construction **tener que** (*to have to* (*do something*)).

Verb + Infinitive Construction, Verb + Connector + Infinitive Construction

In both Spanish and English, the infinitive can follow a conjugated verb. In this function, the infinitive serves as a complement, much like an object. Depending on the first verb (the conjugated verb) in this construction, the infinitive may follow the verb directly or be linked to it by a connector, most commonly the preposition **a** or **de**. All the examples that follow appear in Chapter 6.

1 · Here are some of the most common verbs that are followed directly by the infinitive.

deber *should, ought to, must*
Debemos ayudarlo. — *We should / ought to / must help him.*

desear *to want to*
Desea vivir en este barrio. — *She wants to live in this neighborhood.*

esperar *to hope to*
Esperamos graduarnos en mayo. — *We hope to graduate in May.*

lograr *to succeed in, manage to*
A ver si logro salir un poco antes. — *Let's see if I can manage to get out a little early.*

necesitar *to need to*
Necesitas estudiar un poco más. — *You have to study a little more.*

pensar *to intend to*
Pienso ir de vacaciones en junio. — *I intend to go on vacation in June.*

poder *to be able to, can*
¿Ud. no puede terminar el informe hoy? *Can't you finish the report today?*

preferir *to prefer to*
Prefiere ir por tren. *He prefers to go by train.*

querer *to want to*
Quiero buscar otro empleo. *I want to look for another job.*

saber *to know how to*
Esos niños ya saben nadar. *Those children already know how to swim.*

2 · Here are some of the most common verbs that are followed by **a** + infinitive.

aprender a *to learn to*
¿Dónde aprendió Ud. a hablar español? *Where did you learn to speak Spanish?*

ayudar (a uno) a *to help (someone) to*
Ayúdeme a elaborar el presupuesto. *Help me draw up the budget.*

comenzar a *to begin to, start to*
¿Cuándo comienza Ud. a trabajar? *When do you start to work?*

empezar a *to begin to, start to*
Empiezo a comprender el problema. *I'm beginning to understand the problem.*

ir a *to be going to*
Voy a servir la cena a las ocho. *I'm going to serve dinner at eight o'clock.*

3 · Here are some of the most common verbs that are followed by **de** + infinitive.

acabar de *to have just*
Acabo de entregarle los datos. *I have just submitted the data to him.*

tener ganas de *to feel like*
No tenemos ganas de salir esta noche. *We don't feel like going out tonight.*

tratar de *to try to*
Trate Ud. de comprenderme. *Try to understand me.*

4 · There are two verbs that use **que** as the connector to the following infinitive.

tener que *to have to*
¿Qué tienes que hacer hoy? *What do you have to do today?*

hay que *one has to, one must*
Hay que estudiar idiomas. *One has to study languages.*

F **Connectors.** Write the connector (**a**, **de**, or **que**) that correctly completes each of the following sentences. Write an X if no connector is required.

1. Piensa ______ tomar una clase a distancia.
2. ¿Vas ______ asistir a la reunión?

3. Debemos ______ ahorrar más dinero.
4. Comienzo ______ escribir el informe.
5. No quieren ______ salir todavía.
6. Tienes ______ conocer bien el mercado.
7. Acaba ______ regresar de la playa.
8. Esperan ______ tener éxito en los negocios.
9. Trata ______ dominar el idioma.
10. Empiezas ______ comprender el problema, ¿no?
11. ¡No pueden ______ discutir más!
12. Aprendes ______ jugar al béisbol, ¿verdad?
13. Hay ______ aprovechar las ofertas.
14. Necesita ______ practicar el español todos los días.
15. Prefieren ______ ir de vacaciones en abril.
16. ¿No tienes ganas ______ hacer nada?
17. Sabemos ______ bailar salsa muy bien.
18. No logra ______ devolver la pelota.

G ***Expansión.*** Rewrite each sentence, using the verb in parentheses to expand it. Add the correct connector as necessary. Follow the *modelo.*

MODELO Compro un libro de recetas de cocina. (necesitar)
→ Necesito comprar un libro de recetas de cocina.

1. Es experto en su campo. (querer)
2. ¿No encuentras tus gafas? (poder)
3. ¿Escribes el informe en español? (tener)
4. Conozco a los asesores chilenos. (acabar)
5. Entiende el inglés muy bien. (empezar)
6. Hago programación. (saber)
7. El niño cuenta hasta cien. (aprender)
8. Tienen mucho éxito con su empresa. (esperar)
9. Vuelven de México la semana entrante. (pensar)
10. Prueba las tapas, ¿no? (ir)
11. Juegan al fútbol. (preferir)
12. Resisten a la tentación. (tratar)

DIÁLOGO 4 · Quiero aprender a cocinar.

Study the dialogue, then listen to the recording and repeat each line.

LAURA	Quiero aprender a cocinar pero no sé por dónde empezar.
MATEO	¿Conoces un buen libro de recetas de cocina?
LAURA	Acabo de comprar este libro. Tiene cien recetas.
MATEO	Pues vamos a probar esta receta sencilla para hacer huevos revueltos.

Análisis

Check that you understand the linguistic breakdown of each speech from *Diálogo 4*.

Quiero aprender a cocinar pero no sé por dónde empezar.	*I want to learn how to cook, but I don't know where to begin.*
querer (**e** > **ie**)	*to want*
querer + *infinitive*	*to want to (do something)*
aprender	*to learn*
aprender a + *infinitive*	*to learn how to (do something)*
cocinar	*to cook*
aprender a cocinar	*to learn how to cook*
sé	*I know*
por	*for, through, around*
por dónde	*where, in what place*
¿Conoces un buen libro de recetas de cocina?	*Do you know a good cookbook?*
conocer	*to know, be familiar with*
buen	*good*
la receta	*recipe*
la cocina	*kitchen, cooking*
un libro de recetas de cocina	*a cookbook*
Acabo de comprar este libro. Tiene cien recetas.	*I've just bought this book. It has one hundred recipes.*
acabar de + *infinitive*	*to have just (done something)*
cien	*one hundred*
Pues vamos a probar esta receta sencilla para hacer huevos revueltos.	*Well, let's try this simple recipe to make scrambled eggs.*
pues	*well, in that case* (interjection)
vamos a + *infinitive*	*let's (do something)*
probar (**o** > **ue**)	*to try; to taste*
vamos a probar	*let's try*
sencillo	*simple*
para + *infinitive*	*in order to (do something)*
hacer	*to do, make*
el huevo	*egg*
revuelto	*scrambled*
huevos revueltos	*scrambled eggs*

Variantes

Listen, and repeat the same structures from *Diálogo 4*, now with new vocabulary.

Quiero aprender a cocinar.	*I want to learn to* ***cook.***
coser	*sew*
manejar	*drive*
programar	*program*
Acabo de comprar el libro.	***I've just bought*** *the book.*
Acabo de leer	*I've just read*
Acabo de vender	*I've just sold*
Acabo de escribir	*I've just written*
Acabo de abrir	*I've just opened*
Acabo de romper	*I've just torn*
Prueban la comida.	*They're trying the food. / They're tasting the food.*
Ahora comen.	*They're* ***eating*** *now.*
almuerzan	*having lunch*
meriendan	*having a snack* (usually in the afternoon)

Estructura y Práctica

Para vs. por

The prepositions **para** and **por** are often confusing to English-speaking students of Spanish, because both of them can be translated as *for*.

1 · **Para** labels the goal of an action. This goal may be the destination of motion, the time by which something is done, or the beneficiary of the action.

Daniel salió **para** la oficina.	*Daniel left* ***for*** *the office.*
Tiene que terminar el informe **para** el jueves.	*He has to finish the report* ***by*** *Thursday.*
El anillo es **para** Fernanda.	*The ring is* ***for*** *Fernanda.*
Lo hago **para** ti.	*I'm doing it* ***for*** *you.* (*for your benefit*)

Para is used before an infinitive to label the purpose of an action.

Ahorro dinero **para** comprar una casa.	*I'm saving money* (***in order***) *to buy a house.*
Estudia mucho **para** sacar buenas notas.	*She studies a lot* ***in order*** *to get good grades.*

Para appears in several idiomatic expressions.

para siempre	*forever*
para variar	*for a change*
estar **para**	*to be about to*

2 · **Por** expresses motion through a place or imprecise location.

Deben seguir **por** esta calle.	*You should continue* ***along*** *this street.*
¿Vas a caminar **por** el parque?	*Are you going to walk* ***through*** *the park?*
Creo que viven **por** aquí.	*I think they live* ***around*** *here.*

Por expresses duration in time.

Trabajó con nosotros **por** muchos meses.	*He worked with us* ***for*** *many months.*

Por expresses the cause or reason for an action.

Se enoja **por** cualquier cosa.	*He gets angry* ***for*** *any little thing.*
No quieren vivir aquí **por** el frío.	*They don't want to live here* ***because of*** *the cold.*
Lo hacemos **por** ti.	*We're doing it* ***because of*** *you.*

Por appears in many idiomatic expressions.

por ahora	*for now*
por aquí	*around here*
por casualidad	*by chance*
por ciento	*percent*
por desgracia	*unfortunately*
por eso	*therefore, that's why*
por favor	*please*
por todas partes	*everywhere*
por todos lados	*everywhere*

3 · **Para** and **por** contrast with each other in the following contexts.

¿**Para** quién trabaja Ud.?	***For*** *whom are you working?*
Trabajo **para** el señor López.	*I'm working* ***for*** *Mr. López. (He's my boss.)*
¿**Por** quién trabaja Ud.?	***For*** *whom are you working?*
Trabajo **por** el señor López.	*I'm working* ***for*** *Mr. López. (I'm working in his place.)*

H ***Para y por.*** Choose either **para** or **por** to correctly complete each of the following sentences.

1. Estos regalos son ______ mis sobrinos.
2. Tienes que seguir ______ aquella avenida.
3. Necesito ganar dinero ______ pagar la matrícula (*tuition*).
4. Ni sabemos ______ dónde comenzar el proyecto.
5. ¿Piensas regresar a la ciudad ______ la semana entrante?
6. ¿A qué hora debemos salir ______ el teatro?
7. Mi hija va a estudiar español en Madrid ______ un año.

8. Los Ortega no quieren vivir aquí ______ el calor.
9. Uds. están ______ merendar, ¿no?
10. Ya salgo ______ la oficina. Necesito estar ______ las nueve.
11. ¿Sabes ______ casualidad dónde está el perro? Lo acabo de buscar ______ todos lados.

DIÁLOGO 5 · No conozco al nuevo gerente.

Study the dialogue, then listen to the recording and repeat each line.

MATEO ¿Tú conoces al hombre que acaba de entrar?
LAURA No, no lo conozco pero creo que es el nuevo gerente.
MATEO ¿Sabes si tiene mucha experiencia?
LAURA Yo sé que conoce bien el mercado. Es reconocido como experto en su campo.

Análisis

Check that you understand the linguistic breakdown of each speech from *Diálogo 5*.

¿Tú conoces al hombre que acaba de entrar?	*Do you know the man who has just come in?*
conocer	*to know a person*
conoces al hombre	*you know the man*
que	*who*
acabar de + *infinitive*	*to have just (done something)*
acaba de entrar	*he has just come in*
No, no lo conozco pero creo que es el nuevo gerente.	*No, I don't know him, but I think he's the new manager.*
lo	*him* (masculine direct object pronoun)
conozco	*I know*
creer	*to believe, think*
que	*that* (conjunction)
el gerente	*manager*
¿Sabes si tiene mucha experiencia?	*Do you know whether he has a lot of experience?*
sabes	*you know*
si	*if, whether*
la experiencia	*experience*
Yo sé que conoce bien el mercado. Es reconocido como experto en su campo.	*I know that he knows the market well. He is recognized as an expert in his field.*
sé	*I know*
conoce	*he knows*
el mercado	*market*

reconocido	*recognized*
ser reconocido	*to be recognized*
como	*as*
el experto	*expert*
el campo	*field*

Variantes

Listen, and repeat the same structures from *Diálogo 5*, now with new vocabulary.

¿Conoces al hombre que acaba de entrar?	*Do you know **the man** who has just come in?*
a la mujer	*the woman*
a la persona	*the person*
a ese señor	*that man*
a esa señorita	*that young woman*
al tipo	*the guy*
a aquel joven	*that young man*
al empleado	*the employee*
No lo conozco.	*I don't **know** him.*
comprendo	*understand*
visito	*visit*
No lo llevo.	*I'm not **taking** him.*
llamo	*calling*
busco	*looking for*
espero	*waiting for*
miro	*looking at*
ayudo	*helping*
Creo que es el nuevo gerente.	*I think **he's the new manager**.*
conoce bien el mercado	*he knows the market well*
está en su oficina	*he's in his office*
hace programación	*he does programming*
diseña sitios web	*he designs websites*
desarrolla software	*he develops software*
Sé que conoce bien el mercado.	*I know **he knows the market well**.*
tiene buenas ideas	*he has good ideas*
sabe resolver problemas	*he knows how to solve problems*
vuelve de un viaje de negocios hoy	*he's returning from a business trip today*
habla tres idiomas	*he speaks three languages*
va a tener mucho éxito	*he's going to be very successful*
¿Sabes si tiene mucha experiencia?	*Do you know if **he has a lot of experience**?*
habla español	*he speaks Spanish*
gana mucho dinero	*he earns a lot of money*
conoce a los asesores	*he knows the consultants*
puede trabajar los fines de semana	*he can work on weekends*
piensa cerrar unas tiendas	*he intends to close some stores*

Estructura y Práctica

Saber and conocer

Spanish has two verbs that mean *to know*: **saber** and **conocer**. Both are irregular verbs.

1 · **Saber** has an irregularity in the first person singular (**yo** form) but is regular in the rest of the conjugation.

saber *to know*	
sé	sabemos
sabes	sabéis
sabe	saben

Saber means to know something that you have learned or can repeat or state.

Sé la fecha.	***I know*** *the date.*
Sabemos la respuesta.	***We know*** *the answer.*

Saber is used before a following clause beginning with **si** or **que**.

¿**Sabes** si van a venir?	***Do you know*** *if they are going to come?*
Sé que ella enseña en esta escuela.	***I know*** *that she teaches at this school.*

Saber is used before an infinitive with the meaning *to know how to (do something).*

Esta niña ya **sabe** leer.	*This child already* ***knows how to*** *read.*

2 · **Conocer** has **-zc-** before the **-o** ending of the **yo** form. All other forms are regular.

conocer *to know*	
cono**zc**o	conocemos
conoces	conocéis
conoce	conocen

Conocer means *to know* in the sense of being familiar with or having an acquaintance with. It is used with people and places.

¿**Conocen** Uds. a mi primo Javier?	***Do you know*** *my cousin Javier?*
Él **conoce** muy bien Madrid.	*He* ***knows*** *Madrid very well.*
No **conozco** la República Dominicana.	*I* ***haven't been to*** *the Dominican Republic.*

The phrases **conocer la dirección** (*to know the address*) and **conocer el número de teléfono** (*to know the phone number*) are also very common.

I ***Saber y conocer.*** Write the present tense form of **saber** or **conocer** that correctly completes each of the following sentences.

1. Pienso que él no ______________ nada.
2. Tú ______________ que Olivia es una compradora compulsiva.
3. Yo no ______________ a nadie en esta ciudad.

4. Ellos no ______________ por dónde empezar.
5. Ud. ______________ aquella tienda de cómputo, ¿no?
6. Yo ______________ que tú me ______________ muy bien.
7. ¿Quién ______________ la dirección de Carlos?
8. Nosotros no ______________ al nuevo ingeniero pero ______________ quién es.
9. ¿Ud. ______________ qué tiempo va a hacer mañana?
10. Uds. no ______________ Costa Rica, ¿verdad?
11. ¿Tú ______________ si debemos seguir por esta carretera?
12. ¿Los señores Álvarez? Claro que yo los ______________.

Direct Object Pronouns

Direct object nouns may be replaced by direct object pronouns once it is clear to whom or what they refer. In this chapter, we present **lo**, the third person singular direct object pronoun that refers to people and things that are grammatically masculine. **Lo** means *him* and *it*; **lo** also means *you* when referring to **Ud.** (For more on direct object pronouns, see Chapter 7.)

J ***Lo.*** Write sentences to answer each of the following questions, changing the direct object noun in the question to a direct object pronoun in your answer. Answer *yes* or *no*, based on the cue in parentheses. Follow the *modelos*.

MODELOS ¿Ella prepara el pollo? (sí)
→ Sí, lo prepara.

¿Ella prepara el pollo? (no)
→ No, no lo prepara.

1. ¿Ellos leen el chino? (sí)
2. ¿Ud. conoce al profesor de historia? (no)
3. ¿Llamas al diseñador de sitios web? (sí)
4. ¿Uds. sirven el pastel? (no)
5. ¿Ella visita al abuelo? (sí)
6. ¿Él busca a su perro? (no)
7. ¿Ayudas a tu hermano? (sí)
8. ¿Uds. empiezan el proyecto? (sí)
9. ¿Él cuenta el dinero? (no)
10. ¿Uds. encuentran su maletín? (no)

DIÁLOGO 6 · ¡Yo no puedo comer nada más!

Study the dialogue, then listen to the recording and repeat each line.

LAURA	¡Qué comida más rica! Siempre comemos muy bien aquí.
MATEO	Y sirven los mejores postres del mundo. ¿Qué pides de postre?
LAURA	¿De postre? Yo no puedo comer nada más. ¡Estoy para reventar!

Análisis

Check that you understand the linguistic breakdown of each speech from *Diálogo 6*.

¡Qué comida más rica! Siempre comemos muy bien aquí.	*What delicious food! We always eat very well here.*
comer	*to eat*
comemos	*we eat*
siempre	*always*
Y sirven los mejores postres del mundo. ¿Qué pides de postre?	*And they serve the best desserts in the world. What are you having for dessert?*
servir (**e** > **i**)	*to serve*
sirven	*they serve*
mejor	*better, best*
el postre	*dessert*
los mejores postres	*the best desserts*
de	*in* (after a superlative)
del mundo	*of the world, in the world*
pedir (**e** > **i**)	*to ask for, order*
pides	*you ask for, you order*
de postre	*for dessert*
¿De postre? Yo no puedo comer nada más. ¡Estoy para reventar!	*For dessert? I can't eat anything else. I'm about to burst!*
poder (**o** > **ue**)	*to be able, can*
poder + *infinitive*	*to be able to (do something)*
nada	*nothing*
más	*more, else*
nada más	*nothing else*
estar para + *infinitive*	*to be about to (do something)*
reventar (**e** > **ie**)	*to burst*
¡Estoy para reventar!	*I'm about to burst!*

Variantes

Listen, and repeat the same structures from *Diálogo 6*, now with new vocabulary.

Yo no puedo comer nada más.	*I can't **eat** another thing.*
beber	*drink*
tomar	*drink*
probar	*try, taste*
¿Qué pides de postre?	*What are you **ordering** for dessert?*
sirves	*serving*

Estructura y Práctica

Stem-changing Verbs: servir and pedir

Here are the present tense forms of the **-ir** stem-changing verbs **servir** (*to serve*) and **pedir** (*to ask for, request*).

servir (e > i) *to serve*	
sirvo	servimos
sirves	servís
sirve	sirven

pedir (e > i) *to ask for, request*	
pido	pedimos
pides	pedís
pide	piden

K Write the form of the verb **servir** or **pedir** that correctly completes each of the following sentences.

1. Este jugador ________________ bien la pelota.
2. Nosotros ________________ unos libros por internet.
3. Las meseras ________________ la cena.
4. ¿Por qué no (tú) ________________ la cuenta (*bill*)?
5. Yo no ________________ postre porque no puedo comer nada más.
6. Nosotros ________________ a la patria (*native country*).
7. Tú ________________ de ejemplo (*set an example*) para los niños.
8. El culpable (*culprit*) ni ________________ perdón (*to apologize*).
9. Hago un pastel y lo ________________ con helado.
10. ¿Uds. ________________ pizza a domicilio? (*takeout*)

DIÁLOGO 7 · No puedo imprimir el informe.

Study the dialogue, then listen to the recording and repeat each line.

MATEO Oye, trabajas muy tarde hoy. ¿Lees tu correo electrónico?
LAURA Ya no. Ahora tengo que terminar mi informe.
MATEO Y luego vas a imprimir el informe, ¿verdad?
LAURA Por desgracia no puedo. La impresora está descompuesta.

Análisis

Check that you understand the linguistic breakdown of each speech from *Diálogo 7*.

Oye, trabajas muy tarde hoy. ¿Lees tu correo electrónico?	*Hey, you're working very late today. Are you reading your email?*
oye	*say, hey* (literally, *hear*)
leer	*to read*
lees	*you read, you are reading*

el correo	*mail*
electrónico	*electronic*
el correo electrónico	*email*
Ya no. Ahora tengo que terminar mi informe.	*Not anymore. Now I have to finish my report.*
ya no	*no longer, not anymore*
tener que + *infinitive*	*to have to (do something)*
terminar	*to finish*
tengo que terminar	*I have to finish*
el informe	*report*
Y luego vas a imprimir el informe, ¿verdad?	*And then you are going to print the report, aren't you?*
luego	*then, later, afterward*
ir a + *infinitive*	*to be going to (do something)*
imprimir	*to print*
vas a imprimir	*you are going to print*
¿verdad?	*aren't you?*
Por desgracia no puedo. La impresora está descompuesta.	*Unfortunately, I can't. The printer is broken.*
por desgracia	*unfortunately*
poder (**o** > **ue**)	*to be able, can*
puedo	*I can, I am able*
la impresora	*printer*
descompuesto	*out of order, broken*
estar descompuesto	*to be out of order, be broken*

Variantes

Listen, and repeat the same structures from *Diálogo 7*, now with new vocabulary.

Tengo que terminar el informe.	*I have to* ***finish*** *the report.*
escribir	*write*
leer	*read*
imprimir	*print*
comenzar	*begin*
guardar	*save (computer file)*
descargar	*download*
¿Vas a imprimir el informe?	***Are you going to*** *print the report?*
Tienes que	*Do you have to*
Debes	*Must you*
Prefieres	*Do you prefer to*
Puedes	*Are you able to*
Empiezas a	*Are you beginning to*
Tratas de	*Are you trying to*

DIÁLOGO 8 · Tenemos planes para el fin de semana.

Study the dialogue, then listen to the recording and repeat each line.

LAURA	¿Ya tienes planes para el fin de semana?
MATEO	Sí. Felipe y yo pensamos visitar a Elena y Tomás.
LAURA	¿Tus amigos que viven en la costa? Entonces vas al mar.
MATEO	No, ellos vuelven a su apartamento en la ciudad el sábado.

Análisis

Check that you understand the linguistic breakdown of each speech from *Diálogo 8*.

¿Ya tienes planes para el fin de semana?	*Do you have plans for the weekend already?*
ya	*already*
tienes	*you have*
el plan	*plan*
para	*for*
fin	*end*
el fin de semana	*weekend*
Sí. Felipe y yo pensamos visitar a Elena y Tomás.	*Yes, Felipe and I intend to visit Elena and Tomás.*
pensar (**e** > **ie**)	*to think*
pensar + *infinitive*	*to intend to (do something)*
pensamos visitar	*we intend to visit*
¿Tus amigos que viven en la costa? Entonces vas al mar.	*Your friends who live at the shore? So you're going to the ocean.*
que	*who*
vivir	*to live*
la costa	*coast, shore*
el mar	*sea, ocean*
No, ellos vuelven a su apartamento en la ciudad el sábado.	*No, they're coming back to their apartment in the city on Saturday.*
volver (**o** > **ue**)	*to return, come back*
el apartamento	*apartment*
la ciudad	*city*
el sábado	*Saturday, on Saturday*

Variantes

Listen, and repeat the same structures from *Diálogo 8*, now with new vocabulary.

¿Tienes planes para el fin de semana?	*Do you have plans for **the weekend**?*
el sábado	*Saturday*
el domingo	*Sunday*
mañana	*tomorrow*

esta noche	*tonight*
la semana entrante	*next week*
el mes próximo	*next month*
el verano	*the summer*

Pensamos visitar a Elena.	***We intend to*** *visit Elena.*
Queremos	*We want to*
Preferimos	*We prefer to*
Debemos	*We should*
Necesitamos	*We need to*
Podemos	*We're able to*
Esperamos	*We hope to*
Tenemos que	*We have to*

DIÁLOGO 9 · Las gangas—¡no puedo resistir a la tentación!

Study the dialogue, then listen to the recording and repeat each line.

MATEO Pienso ir al centro comercial hoy. ¿Quieres ir conmigo? Podemos aprovechar las ofertas de enero.

LAURA No necesito ropa ni nada para la casa. Debo ahorrar mi dinero para comprar un coche.

MATEO Mujer, tú sabes que eres una compradora compulsiva. Anda, vamos.

LAURA Qué bien me conoces. Cuando hay gangas, ¡no puedo resistir a la tentación!

Análisis

Check that you understand the linguistic breakdown of each speech from *Diálogo 9*.

Pienso ir al centro comercial hoy. ¿Quieres ir conmigo? Podemos aprovechar las ofertas de enero.	*I intend to go to the shopping center today. Do you want to go with me? We can take advantage of the January sales.*
pensar (**e** > **ie**)	*to think*
pensar + *infinitive*	*to intend to (do something)*
pienso ir	*I intend to go*
el centro comercial	*shopping center, mall*
al	*to the* (contraction of **a** + **el**)
querer (**e** > **ie**)	*to want*
querer + *infinitive*	*to want to (do something)*
conmigo	*with me*
¿Quieres ir conmigo?	*Do you want to go with me?*
poder (**o** > **ue**)	*to be able, can*
poder + *infinitive*	*to be able to (do something)*
aprovechar	*to take advantage of*
la oferta	*sale*

podemos aprovechar las ofertas	*we can take advantage of the sales*
enero	*January*
las ofertas de enero	*the January sales*
No necesito ropa ni nada para la casa. Debo ahorrar mi dinero para comprar un coche.	*I don't need clothing or anything for the house. I should save my money to buy a car.*
la ropa	*clothing*
ni	*nor*
nada	*nothing*
deber	*ought to, should, must*
deber + *infinitive*	*ought to / should / must (do something)*
ahorrar	*to save*
el dinero	*money*
debo ahorrar mi dinero	*I should save my money*
para	*in order to*
el coche	*car* (Spain, Argentina)
Mujer, tú sabes que eres una compradora compulsiva. Anda, vamos.	*Oh, you know that you are a compulsive shopper. Come on, let's go.*
mujer	*oh; oh, come on now; well; hey* (interjection) (literally, *woman*; addressed to a woman)
sabes	*you know*
que	*that*
la compradora	*shopper* (feminine)
compulsivo	*compulsive*
anda	*come on* (**tú** command form of **andar**)
vamos	*let's go* (**nosotros** command form of **ir**)
Qué bien me conoces. Cuando hay gangas, ¡no puedo resistir a la tentación!	*How well you know me. When there are bargains, I can't resist the temptation!*
qué bien	*how well*
me	*me* (direct object pronoun)
me conoces	*you know me*
la ganga	*bargain*
puedo	*I can*
resistir	*to resist*
resistir a algo	*to resist something*
la tentación	*temptation*
resistir a la tentación	*to resist temptation*

Variantes

Listen, and repeat the same structures from *Diálogo 9*, now with new vocabulary.

Pienso ir al centro comercial hoy.	***I intend to** go to the mall today.*
Prefiero	*I prefer to*
Puedo	*I can*
Espero	*I hope to*
Necesito	*I need to*
Deseo	*I want to*
Debo	*I ought to*
¿Quieres ir ?	*Do you want to **go**?*
subir	*go up*
bajar	*go down*
regresar	*go back*
volver	*go back*
¿Quieres ir conmigo ?	*Do you want to go **with me**?*
con él	*with him*
con ella	*with her*
con nosotros	*with us*
con ellos	*with them*
Quiero ir contigo .	*I want to go **with you**.*
con Ud.	*with you*
con Uds.	*with you*
con ellas	*with them*
Cuentan conmigo .	*They count **on me**.*
contigo	*on you*
con nosotros	*on us*
con Uds.	*on you*
con él	*on him*
¿Cuánto cuesta esta camisa?	*How much does this shirt cost?*
Cuesta sesenta y cinco dólares.	*It costs **sixty-five** dollars.*
noventa y un	*ninety-one*
¿Cuánto cuestan los zapatos?	*How much do the shoes cost?*
Cuestan cien dólares.	*They cost **one hundred** dollars.*
ciento cuarenta	*one hundred forty*
El carro cuesta treinta y cinco mil dólares.	*The car costs **thirty-five thousand** dollars.*
cincuenta y un mil	*fifty-one thousand*
La casa cuesta trescientos mil dólares.	*The house costs **three hundred thousand** dollars.*
setecientos cincuenta mil	*seven hundred fifty thousand*
un millón de	*a million*
dos millones de	*two million*

Hay veintiún paquetes y veintiuna cajas.	*There are twenty-one packages and twenty-one boxes.*
Hay quinientos paquetes y setecientas cajas.	*There are five hundred packages and seven hundred boxes.*

Estructura y Práctica

Prepositional Pronouns

In Spanish, there is a special set of pronouns that is used after prepositions. These pronouns are identical with the subject pronouns except in the first and second persons singular.

Here is the set of prepositional pronouns after **para**.

para **mí**	para **nosotros/nosotras**
para **ti**	para **vosotros/vosotras**
para **él/ella/Ud.**	para **ellos/ellas/Uds.**

Note that the prepositional pronoun **mí** has a written accent, though the prepositional pronoun **ti** does not.

After **con** there are three irregular forms.

con + mí → **conmigo**	*with me*
con + ti → **contigo**	*with you* (informal singular)
consigo	*with himself, with herself, with yourself* (formal singular), *with yourselves* (formal plural), *with themselves*

L **Prepositional pronouns.** Write each preposition with the correct prepositional pronoun indicated by the subject pronoun in parentheses. Follow the *modelo.*

MODELO de (yo)
→ de mí

1. para (ella)
2. con (tú)
3. de (él)
4. para (yo)
5. con (nosotros)
6. de (Uds.)
7. por (yo)
8. con (yo)
9. a (tú)
10. para (tú)
11. por (Ud.)
12. a (yo)
13. por (tú)
14. en (él)
15. de (tú)
16. en (ellos)

Numbers

Here's a review of the numbers from one to twenty as presented in Chapter 1.

1	uno	11	once
2	dos	12	doce
3	tres	13	trece
4	cuatro	14	catorce
5	cinco	15	quince
6	seis	16	dieciséis
7	siete	17	diecisiete
8	ocho	18	dieciocho
9	nueve	19	diecinueve
10	diez	20	veinte

Here are the numbers from twenty-one through thirty-nine.

21	veintiuno (-una)	31	treinta y uno (una)
22	veintidós	32	treinta y dos
23	veintitrés	33	treinta y tres
24	veinticuatro	34	treinta y cuatro
25	veinticinco	35	treinta y cinco
26	veintiséis	36	treinta y seis
27	veintisiete	37	treinta y siete
28	veintiocho	38	treinta y ocho
29	veintinueve	39	treinta y nueve
30	treinta		

All numbers ending in *one* have a masculine and a feminine form: **veintiuno, veintiuna; treinta y uno, treinta y una**. They agree with the following noun in gender. Before a masculine noun, **veintiuno** shortens to **veintiún** and **uno** shortens to **un**.

veintiún libros	***twenty-one*** *books*
treinta y un libros	***thirty-one*** *books*
veintiuna páginas	***twenty-one*** *pages*
treinta y una páginas	***thirty-one*** *pages*

However, the masculine form is sometimes used colloquially before feminine nouns as well.

veintiún páginas	*twenty-one pages*
treinta y un páginas	*thirty-one pages*

The numbers 21 through 29 may be written as three words each, but this is increasingly less common: **veinte y uno/una**, **veinte y dos**, **veinte y tres**, etc.

The numbers 31 through 39 are occasionally written as one word each in some countries: **treintiuno/treintiuna**, **treintidós**, **treintitrés**, etc.

Note that the forms **veintiún**, **veintidós**, **veintitrés**, and **veintiséis** have written accents, according to the rules for the placement of accent marks in Spanish.

Here are the numbers from 40 to 99.

40	cuarenta	70	setenta
41	cuarenta y uno (una)	71	setenta y uno (una)
42	cuarenta y dos	80	ochenta
43	cuarenta y tres	81	ochenta y uno (una)
50	cincuenta	90	noventa
51	cincuenta y uno (una)	91	noventa y uno (una)
52	cincuenta y dos	99	noventa y nueve
60	sesenta		
61	sesenta y uno (una)		

Here are the hundreds in Spanish.

100	cien	600	seiscientos/seiscientas
200	doscientos/doscientas	700	setecientos/setecientas
300	trescientos/trescientas	800	ochocientos/ochocientas
400	cuatrocientos/cuatrocientas	900	novecientos/novecientas
500	quinientos/quinientas		

The forms **quinientos/quinientas**, **setecientos/setecientas**, and **novecientos/novecientas** are irregular in their formation.

The numeral **cien** becomes **ciento** before another number. **Ciento** has no feminine form. **Ciento** + number is used before both masculine and feminine nouns.

101	ciento uno (una)
102	ciento dos
110	ciento diez
155	ciento cincuenta y cinco

The word **y** is not used between **ciento** and a following number.

Multiples of **cien** agree in gender and number with the noun they refer to. They agree even when another number intervenes.

doscient**os** cafés	*two hundred cafés*
doscient**os** cincuenta y ocho cafés	*two hundred fifty-eight cafés*
doscient**as** tiendas	*two hundred stores*
doscient**as** cincuenta y ocho tiendas	*two hundred fifty-eight stores*
quinient**os** pesos	*five hundred pesos*
quinient**os** dieciocho pesos	*five hundred eighteen pesos*
quinient**as** computadoras	*five hundred computers*
quinient**as** dieciocho computadoras	*five hundred eighteen computers*
novecient**os** archivos	*nine hundred files*
novecient**os** treinta y un archivos	*nine hundred thirty-one files*
novecient**as** calles	*nine hundred streets*
novecient**as** treinta y un**a** calles	*nine hundred thirty-one streets*

The word for 1,000 is **mil**.

1,000	mil
1,050	mil cincuenta

1,200	mil doscientos/doscientas
1,278	mil doscientos/doscientas setenta y ocho
2,000	dos mil
2,100	dos mil cien
2,912	dos mil novecientos/novecientas doce
3,000	tres mil
4,000	cuatro mil
5,000	cinco mil
6,000	seis mil
7,000	siete mil
8,000	ocho mil
9,000	nueve mil
10,000	diez mil
20,000	veinte mil
100,000	cien mil
200,000	doscientos/doscientas mil
500,000	quinientos/quinientas mil
1,000,000	un millón

NOTES

1 · The word **un** is not used before **cien** or **mil** to mean 100 or 1,000. Contrast this with English *one hundred, one thousand.*

2 · Agreements of multiples of 100,000 take place across intervening numbers.

trescient**os** mil mensajes	*three hundred thousand messages*
trescient**os** cincuenta mil mensajes	*three hundred fifty thousand messages*
trescient**as** mil viviendas	*three hundred thousand dwellings*
trescient**as** cincuenta mil viviendas	*three hundred fifty thousand dwellings*

3 · **Un, una** do not agree with the noun when they precede **mil** directly. Only **un** is used even if the noun is feminine.

trescientas cincuenta y **un mil** viviendas	*three hundred fifty-one thousand dwellings*

However, agreement with a feminine noun is not uncommon in colloquial usage.

treinta y **una mil** cuentas de banco	*thirty-one thousand bank accounts*

4 · In some countries of the Spanish-speaking world, a period is used to separate thousands when writing numbers, and the comma serves as a decimal point.

1.500.000	un millón quinientos mil
$10,25	diez dólares veinticinco centavos

5 · The word **millón** is a masculine noun. It is preceded by **un** and followed by **de** when a noun follows directly. It is made plural (**millones**) after numbers higher than *one.*

un millón de dólares	*a million dollars*
diez millones de dólares	*ten million dollars*

The preposition **de** is not used if another number intervenes.

un millón quinientos mil dólares	*one million five hundred thousand dollars*
diez millones quinientos mil dólares	*ten million five hundred thousand dollars*

6 · In most Spanish-speaking countries, **un billón** means *a trillion. A billion* is **mil millones**.

M ***¿Cuántos hay?*** Express each of the following numbers in Spanish words.

1. 41 ______________________ días
2. 84 ______________________ idiomas
3. 100 ______________________ años
4. 731 ______________________ zonas
5. 976 ______________________ edificios
6. 1,000 ______________________ empresas
7. 1,495 ______________________ ciudades
8. 3,581 ______________________ ciudadanos (*citizens*)
9. 10,729 ______________________ mujeres
10. 265,000 ______________________ hombres
11. 1,000,000 ______________________ habitantes (*inhabitants*)
12. 92,000,000 ______________________ dólares

DIÁLOGO 10 · No sé dónde queda su casa.

Study the dialogue, then listen to the recording and repeat each line.

LAURA Sé que Victoria y Pablo viven en la calle Castaño. ¿Sabes su dirección?
MATEO Creo que es el número setenta y tres.
LAURA Pues no encuentro su calle en el plano.
MATEO No tienes que leer el plano. Yo conozco la calle Castaño. Si sigues por la avenida Conde vas a llegar.

Análisis

Check that you understand the linguistic breakdown of each speech from *Diálogo 10*.

Sé que Victoria y Pablo viven en la calle Castaño. ¿Sabes su dirección?	*I know that Victoria and Pablo live on Castaño Street. Do you know their address?*
sé	*I know*
que	*that*
vivir	*to live*
viven	*they live*

en	*in, on*
la calle	*street*
la calle Castaño	*Castaño Street*
sabes	*you know*
su	*their*
la dirección	*address*
Creo que es el número setenta y tres.	*I think it is number seventy-three.*
creer	*to believe, think*
creo	*I believe, I think*
que	*that*
el número	*number*
setenta y tres	*seventy-three*
Pues no encuentro su calle en el plano.	*Well, I can't find their street on the city map.*
encontrar (**o** > **ue**)	*to find*
encuentro	*I find*
no encuentro	*I don't find, I can't find*
el plano	*street map, city map*
No tienes que leer el plano. Yo conozco la calle Castaño. Si sigues por la avenida Conde vas a llegar.	*You don't have to read the map. I know Castaño Street. If you continue along Conde Avenue, you'll get there.*
tener que	*to have to*
leer	*to read*
no tienes que leer el plano	*you don't have to read the map*
conozco	*I know*
seguir (**e** > **i**)	*to follow, continue*
por	*for, through*
seguir por	*to continue along*
la avenida	*avenue*
ir a + *infinitive*	*to be going to (do something)*
llegar	*to arrive, get there*
vas a llegar	*you'll get there*

Variantes

Listen, and repeat the same structures from *Diálogo 10*, now with new vocabulary.

Sé que viven en la calle Castaño.	*I know **they live on Castaño Street**.*
es una calle tranquila	*it's a quiet street*
hay un museo de arte en frente	*there's an art museum opposite*
sus vecinos son simpáticos	*their neighbors are nice*
¿Sabes su dirección?	*Do you know her **address**?*
número de teléfono	*telephone number*
dirección electrónica	*email address*
fecha de nacimiento	*date of birth*

No tienes que leer el plano.	***You don't have to*** *read the street map.*
No debes	*You shouldn't*
No puedes	*You can't*
No necesitas	*You don't need to*
No logras	*You don't manage to*
No sabes	*You don't know how to*
No quieres	*You don't want to*
Yo conozco la calle Castaño.	*I'm familiar with* ***Castaño Street.***
este barrio	*this neighborhood*
Ciudad de México	*Mexico City*
Madrid	*Madrid*
Puerto Rico	*Puerto Rico*

Estructura y Práctica

Seguir

Seguir (**e** > **i**) (*to follow, continue*) is a stem-changing verb that also has a spelling change in the present tense. For verbs that end in **-guir**, **gu** changes to **g** before **o** and **a**. In the present tense, the change occurs only in the first person singular (**yo** form). Here is the conjugation of **seguir** in present tense.

seguir (**e** > **i**) *to follow, continue*	
sigo	seguimos
sigues	seguís
sigue	siguen

Verbs ending in **-seguir** are conjugated like **seguir**: **conseguir** (*to get, acquire*), **perseguir** (*to pursue, persecute*), **proseguir** (*to proceed*). Their respective first person singular forms are **consigo**, **persigo**, and **prosigo**.

N Rewrite each of the following sentences, changing the verb + infinitive construction to the correct present tense form of **seguir**. Follow the *modelo.*

MODELO Ellos deben seguir por esa avenida.
→ Siguen por esa avenida.

1. Uds. van a seguir por la autopista.
2. Puedes seguir la conversación.
3. El perro trata de seguir a los niños.
4. ¿Ud. espera seguir un curso de inglés a distancia?
5. Pienso seguir los consejos (*advice*) de mis padres.
6. Acabamos de seguir por una avenida bajo construcción.
7. Él tiene que seguir las órdenes (*orders*) del médico.
8. Quieren seguir el ejemplo (*example*) de su abuelo.

DIÁLOGO 11 · Pablo juega al tenis.

Study the dialogue, then listen to the recording and repeat each line.

LAURA	Hola, Pablo, veo que tienes tu raqueta de tenis. ¿Vas a jugar ahora?
PABLO	No, yo vuelvo de la cancha de tenis. Juego al tenis todas las tardes.
LAURA	Yo sé que eres un magnífico jugador. ¿Con quién juegas?
PABLO	Con Rafa. Es mejor que yo. Cuando él sirve yo no puedo devolver la pelota.

Análisis

Check that you understand the linguistic breakdown of each speech from *Diálogo 11.*

Hola, Pablo, veo que tienes tu raqueta de tenis. ¿Vas a jugar ahora?	*Hi, Pablo, I see that you have your tennis racket. Are you going to play now?*
ver	*to see*
veo	*I see*
que	*that*
tienes	*you have*
la raqueta	*racket*
el tenis	*tennis*
la raqueta de tenis	*tennis racket*
ir a + *infinitive*	*to be going to (do something)*
jugar (**u** > **ue**)	*to play (a sport or game)*
vas a jugar	*you are going to play*
ahora	*now*
No, yo vuelvo de la cancha de tenis. Juego al tenis todas las tardes.	*No, I'm coming back from the tennis court. I play tennis every afternoon.*
volver (**o** > **ue**)	*to return, come back*
vuelvo	*I return, I come back*
de	*from*
la cancha	*court*
la cancha de tenis	*tennis court*
la tarde	*afternoon*
todas las tardes	*every afternoon*
Yo sé que eres un magnífico jugador. ¿Con quién juegas?	*I know that you are a great player. Who do you play with?*
sé	*I know*
que	*that*
ser	*to be*
eres	*you are*
magnífico	*magnificent, terrific, great*
el jugador	*player*
un magnífico jugador	*a great player*
con	*with*
quién	*who, whom*

con quién	*with whom*
juegas	*you play*
Con Rafa. Es mejor que yo. Cuando él sirve yo no puedo devolver la pelota.	*With Rafa. He's better than I am. When he serves, I can't return the ball.*
Rafa	(nickname of *Rafael*)
mejor	*better*
que	*than*
mejor que yo	*better than I*
servir (**e** > **i**)	*to serve*
sirve	*he serves*
puedo	*I can*
devolver (**o** > **ue**)	*to give back (something), return (something)*
devolver la pelota	*to return the ball*

Variantes

Listen, and repeat the same structures from *Diálogo 11*, now with new vocabulary.

Juego al tenis .	*I play* ***tennis.***
béisbol	*baseball*
fútbol	*soccer*
fútbol americano	*football*
baloncesto	*basketball*
golf	*golf*
¿Con quién juegas ?	*Whom* ***do you play*** *with?*
vas	*do you go*
compartes	*do you share*
discutes	*do you argue*
vives	*do you live*
comes	*do you eat*
hablas	*do you talk*
trabajas	*do you work*

Estructura y Práctica

Jugar

Jugar (*to play* (*a sport or game*)), a stem-changing verb, is conjugated as if it had **-o-** as its stem vowel.

jugar (u > ue) *to play (a sport or game)*

j**ue**go	jugamos
j**ue**gas	jugáis
j**ue**ga	j**ue**gan

Jugar is used with the preposition **a** and the definite article to indicate the game or sport played.

jugar al tenis	*to play tennis*
jugar al béisbol	*to play baseball*
jugar a las cartas	*to play cards*

Some Spanish speakers omit the preposition **a** and the definite article before the name of the game: **jugar tenis, jugar béisbol, jugar cartas**.

JUGAR AND TOCAR: *TO PLAY*

Remember that Spanish has another word meaning *to play*. **Tocar**, not **jugar**, is used to express *to play a musical instrument.*

Toco el clarinete.	*I play the clarinet.*
Sofía toca el violín.	*Sofía plays the violin.*
¿Tocas un instrumento de viento o de cuerda?	*Do you play a wind or a string instrument?*

O ***¡Vamos a jugar!*** Rewrite each of the following sentences, changing the verb + infinitive construction to the correct present tense form of **jugar**. Follow the *modelo*.

MODELO Los chicos desean jugar al baloncesto.
→ Juegan al baloncesto.

1. Joaquín y yo sabemos jugar al ajedrez (*chess*).
2. Estos dos equipos (*teams*) logran jugar en la Serie Mundial (*World Series*).
3. Nunca quiero jugar al tenis de mesa (*Ping-Pong*).
4. Carlitos comienza a jugar a los videojuegos.
5. ¿Tienes ganas de jugar a las cartas?
6. Ud. sabe jugar al vólibol, ¿no?
7. Uds. aprenden a jugar al dominó.
8. Blanca acaba de jugar un juego de sociedad (*board game*).

Un paso más

Are you ready to take your Spanish a step further? Here are exercises that will enhance your knowledge of the language and allow you to express yourself freely.

P **Synonyms and antonyms.** A synonym is a word that means the same or nearly the same as another word. An antonym is a word having the meaning opposite to that of another word. As you study Spanish, you will learn nuance in meaning and be able to select the precise word in any given situation. Learning synonyms and antonyms will increase your vocabulary, thereby expanding your freedom of expression in the language.

Sinónimos. Write a synonym for each of the following verbs, using a verb from Chapter 6.

1. empezar
2. volver
3. bajar
4. tomar
5. subir
6. querer
7. entender

Antónimos. Write the adjective from the second column that is an antonym for each adjective in the first column.

1. feliz	a. pobre
2. adelantado	b. tranquilo
3. abierto	c. barato
4. inquieto	d. claro
5. delgado	e. aburrido
6. caro	f. cerrado
7. interesante	g. triste
8. joven	h. gordo
9. feo	i. antipático
10. rico	j. atrasado
11. oscuro	k. hermoso
12. simpático	l. viejo

Q **Translation.** Express the following sentences in Spanish.

1. *The weather is nasty. It's cold and windy.*
2. *And it's beginning to rain.*
3. *Benjamín has been working in this field for twenty-one years.*
4. *He knows the market very well.*
5. *The students intend to take an online Spanish course.*
6. *They know they have to practice a lot to master the spoken language.*
7. *This restaurant serves the best desserts in the city.*
8. *That's why I'm ordering two. I can't resist the temptation!*
9. *Do you* (tú) *know how to play tennis?*
10. *No, but I want to learn to play.*
11. *I feel like going to the beach. Do you* (tú) *want to go with me?*
12. *I've just come back from the shore. I prefer to go to the country.*

R ***Preguntas personales.*** Answer each question with a complete Spanish sentence.

1. ¿Cuánto tiempo hace que Ud. estudia español?
2. ¿Qué otros idiomas estudia (habla, lee, escribe)?
3. ¿Necesita usar el español en su trabajo? ¿Cómo lo usa?
4. ¿Qué hace para dominar el idioma?
5. ¿Qué tiempo hace hoy?
6. ¿Ud. prefiere el calor o el frío? ¿Por qué?
7. ¿Qué deportes juega en verano (invierno)? ¿Juega bien?
8. ¿Con quiénes juega?
9. ¿Sabe cocinar? ¿Qué cocina?
10. ¿Qué planes tiene para el fin de semana?
11. ¿Es un comprador compulsivo / una compradora compulsiva?
12. Cuando va de compras (*shopping*), ¿trata de aprovechar las ofertas? ¿Busca gangas?
13. ¿Cuánto dinero gasta en comida, ropa y otras cosas todos los meses?

7

Entertaining at Home

Communication Goals

- Talking about being hungry, thirsty, warm, cold, sleepy
- Telling how you prepare for a dinner party
- Talking about television and the movies
- Vocabulary: home appliances, entertainment

Grammar Topics

- Irregular Verbs
- Expressions with **tener**
- **El** with Feminine Nouns
- Direct Object Pronouns
- **Haber** *to have*
- Direct Object Pronouns with Verb + Infinitive Constructions
- Word Order

DIÁLOGO 1 · Los invitados vienen a cenar.

Study the dialogue, then listen to the recording and repeat each line.

OLIVIA Son las siete. Pronto vienen los invitados.
NICOLÁS Eso espero. Yo tengo mucha hambre.
OLIVIA Paciencia, chico. El arroz con pollo ya está y voy a hacer la ensalada.
NICOLÁS Y yo pongo la mesa ahora mismo. Ah, oigo el timbre. Ya están. ¡Por fin!

Análisis

Check that you understand the linguistic breakdown of each speech from *Diálogo 1.*

Son las siete. Pronto vienen los invitados.	*It's seven o'clock. The guests are coming soon.*
las siete	*seven o'clock*
son las siete	*it's seven o'clock*
pronto	*soon*
venir	*to come*
el invitado	*guest*
vienen los invitados	*the guests are coming*
Eso espero. Yo tengo mucha hambre.	*I hope so. I am very hungry.*
eso	*that*
esperar	*to hope*
eso espero	*that's what I hope, I hope so*
tener	*to have*
el hambre	*hunger* (feminine)
tener hambre	*to be hungry* (literally, *to have (feel) hunger)*
tener mucha hambre	*to be very hungry* (literally, *to have (feel) a lot of hunger)*
Paciencia, chico. El arroz con pollo ya está y voy a hacer la ensalada.	*Patience. The chicken with rice is already done and I'm going to make the salad.*
la paciencia	*patience*
chico	*boy* (interjection; often not translated in this usage)
el arroz	*rice*
el pollo	*chicken*
el arroz con pollo	*chicken with rice* (*traditional Hispanic dish*)
ya	*already*
estar	*to be ready, be done*
la ensalada	*salad*
Y yo pongo la mesa ahora mismo. Ah, oigo el timbre. Ya están. ¡Por fin!	*And I'll set the table right now. Oh, I hear the bell. They're here now. At last!*
poner	*to put*
pongo	*I put*
poner la mesa	*to set the table*
ahora mismo	*right now*
oír	*to hear*
oigo	*I hear*
el timbre	*doorbell*
estar	*to be here*
ya están	*they're here now*
por fin	*finally, at last*

Variantes

Listen, and repeat the same structures from *Diálogo 1*, now with new vocabulary.

Los invitados vienen.	*The guests **are coming**.*
salen	*are leaving*
van	*are going*
vuelven	*are coming back*
Yo tengo hambre.	*I'm **hungry**.*
sed	*thirsty*
calor	*warm*
frío	*cold*
sueño	*sleepy*
razón	*right*
Él tiene mucha prisa.	*He's **in a big hurry**.*
mucho miedo	*very afraid*
mucha paciencia	*very patient*
muchos celos	*very jealous*
mucha suerte	*very lucky*
Oigo el timbre.	*I hear **the doorbell**.*
un ruido	*a noise*
un sonido	*a sound*
una voz	*a voice*
gritos	*shouts, screams*
¿Oyes al profesor?	*Do you hear the professor?*
Sí, lo oigo.	*Yes, I hear him.*
¿Oyes esos anuncios?	*Do you hear those announcements?*
No, no los oigo.	*No, I don't hear them.*
¿Oyes su voz?	*Do you hear her voice?*
Sí, la oigo.	*Yes, I hear it.*
¿Oyes a las actrices?	*Do you hear the actresses?*
No, no las oigo.	*No, I don't hear them.*

Estructura y Práctica

Irregular Verbs

Many Spanish verbs do not follow the standard pattern of formation in the present tense. These are called irregular verbs.

1 · Most irregular verbs in the present tense show an irregular **yo** form, with the rest of the forms being regular. The most common **yo** form irregularity is a **-g-** inserted before the **-o** ending. Verbs with this irregularity are called **-g-** verbs. (For the irregular verbs **ser** and **estar**, see Chapters 1, 3, and 4; for the irregular verbs **hacer** and **ir**, see Chapter 5.)

caer *to fall*	
caigo	caemos
caes	caéis
cae	caen

hacer *to do, make*	
hago	hacemos
haces	hacéis
hace	hacen

poner *to put*	
pongo	ponemos
pones	ponéis
pone	ponen

salir *to go out, leave*	
salgo	salimos
sales	salís
sale	salen

traer *to bring*	
traigo	traemos
traes	traéis
trae	traen

valer *to be worth, cost*	
valgo	valemos
vales	valéis
vale	valen

2 · Some **-g-** verbs show other irregularities or have stem changes in the present.

decir *to say, tell*	
digo	decimos
dices	decís
dice	dicen

oír *to hear*	
oigo	oímos
oyes	oís
oye	oyen

tener *to have*	
tengo	tenemos
tienes	tenéis
tiene	tienen

venir *to come*	
vengo	venimos
vienes	venís
viene	vienen

3 · A variant of **-g-** verbs shows **-zc-** before the **-o** ending of the **yo** form. These verbs have infinitives that end in **-cer** or **-cir** preceded by a vowel.

conocer *to know*	
cono**zc**o	conocemos
conoces	conocéis
conoce	conocen

parecer *to seem*	
pare**zc**o	parecemos
pareces	parecéis
parece	parecen

traducir *to translate*	
tradu**zc**o	traducimos
traduces	traducís
traduce	traducen

4 · A few verbs have other irregularities in the first person singular, but regular forms in the rest of the conjugation.

caber *to fit*	
quepo	cabemos
cabes	cabéis
cabe	caben

saber *to know*	
sé	sabemos
sabes	sabéis
sabe	saben

ver *to see*	
veo	vemos
ves	veis
ve	ven

5 · Verbs ending in **-uir** (not including those ending in **-guir**) add **-y-** between the **u** and the ending in all forms of the singular and in the third person plural, that is, in all forms except the **nosotros** and **vosotros** forms.

construir *to build*	
construyo	construimos
construyes	construís
construye	construyen

Other verbs that pattern like **construir** are **concluir** (*to conclude*), **destruir** (*to destroy*), **huir** (*to flee*), and **incluir** (*to include*).

6 · A small number of verbs end in **-oy** in the first person singular. **Estar** and **ser** show additional irregularities in their conjugations; the form **estoy** is stressed on the second syllable. Notice that in **vosotros** forms of one syllable (**dais**, **vais**, **sois**, and also **veis**, above), the written accent mark is omitted.

dar *to give*	
doy	damos
das	dais
da	dan

estar *to be*	
estoy	estamos
estás	estáis
está	están

ir *to go*	
voy	vamos
vas	vais
va	van

ser *to be*	
soy	somos
eres	sois
es	son

A **Irregular verbs.** Write the present tense form of the verb that correctly completes each of the following dialogues. Use the irregular verbs in parentheses.

1. —______________ mal tiempo. Va a nevar. (hacer)

   —Mira. La nieve ya ______________. (caer)

2. —¿Qué regalo ______________ Ud.? (traer)

   —Yo ______________ una cámara digital. (traer)

3. —Eva, Mateo ______________ tu novio, ¿no? (ser)

   —Ya no. ______________ con Jacobo. (salir)

4. —¿Uds. no ______________ el timbre? (oír)

   —No, no ______________ nada. (oír)

5. —Tú ______________ a verme mañana, ¿no? (venir)

   —No, ______________ pasado mañana. (venir)

6. —¿Qué película ______________ en el cine Metro? (poner)

   —Es un nuevo film inglés. Todo el mundo ______________ que es fabuloso. (decir)

7. —¿Tú ______________ las noticias ahora? (ver)

   —No, ______________ una telenovela. (ver)

8. —Yo ______________ la comida pronto. (hacer)

   —Y yo ______________ a poner la mesa. (ir)

9. —¿Todos nosotros ______________ en el taxi? (caber)

   —No todos. Yo no ______________. (caber)

10. —¿Cómo se ______________ *car* en español? (decir)

—Bueno, en México nosotros ______________ "carro". (decir)

11. —¿De dónde (tú) ______________? (ser)

—______________ español. (ser)

12. —¿Cómo ______________ Uds.? (estar)

—Yo ______________ perfectamente, pero Elena ______________ acatarrada. (estar)

Expressions with **tener**

Many English phrases consisting of *to be* + adjective and referring to mental or physical states have Spanish equivalents consisting of **tener** + noun. These expressions are used only for people, not for things.

NOUN	IDIOM	MEANING
el hambre *hunger*	tener hambre	*to be hungry*
la sed *thirst*	tener sed	*to be thirsty*
el calor *heat*	tener calor	*to be warm*
el frío *cold*	tener frío	*to be cold*
la prisa *hurry, haste*	tener prisa	*to be in a hurry*
la vergüenza *shame*	tener vergüenza	*to be ashamed*
el éxito *success*	tener éxito	*to be successful*
el cuidado *care, caution*	tener cuidado	*to be careful*
la razón *right, reason*	tener razón	*to be right*
la suerte *luck*	tener suerte	*to be lucky*
el sueño *sleep, sleepiness*	tener sueño	*to be sleepy*
las ganas *desire*	tener ganas de + *infinitive*	*to feel like (doing something)*

Since the word following **tener** in these idioms is a noun, it cannot be modified by **muy**, but must be modified by quantity words such as **mucho**, **poco**, **tanto**, and **demasiado**. These modifiers agree with the noun in gender and number.

¿Tienes **mucha** sed?	*Are you* ***very*** *thirsty?*
Hoy tengo **poca** hambre.	*Today I'm* ***not very*** *hungry.*
Tenemos **muchas** ganas de conocerla.	*We're* ***very*** *eager to meet her.*
¡Tengo **tanto** sueño!	*I am* ***so*** *sleepy!*
Tengo **demasiado** frío aquí.	*I am* ***too*** *cold here.*
Debes tener **mucho** cuidado.	*You must be* ***very*** *careful.*
¿Por qué tiene Ud. **tanta** prisa?	*Why are you in* ***such a*** *hurry?*

B ***Tener: Expresiones.*** Express each sentence in Spanish, using the correct form of the verb **tener** to describe the physical state or frame of mind of these people. Follow the *modelo*.

MODELO *You* (Ud.) *are very patient.*
→ Tiene mucha paciencia.

1. *They are very hungry.*
2. *Are you* (tú) *not very thirsty?*
3. *We're right.*
4. *He is very lucky.*

5. *Why are you* (Ud.) *so ashamed?*
6. *I am not in a hurry.*
7. *Are you* (Uds.) *too cold?*
8. *She is too careful.*
9. *Why are they so sleepy?*
10. *We're very eager to see him.*
11. *I hope to be successful.*
12. *Are you* (tú) *not very warm?*

El with Feminine Nouns

When a feminine noun begins with a stressed /a/ sound (written **a** or **ha**), it takes the singular article **el**, not **la**.

el agua *water*
el hambre *hunger*

Adjectives that modify these nouns are feminine singular.

el agua fría *cold water*
tanta hambre *so much hunger*

In the plural, **las** is used: **las aguas**.

C Write a noun phrase for each of the following nouns beginning with a stressed /a/. Include the correct definite article and the correct form of the adjective in parentheses.

1. ______ agua ______________ (potable (*drinking*))
2. ______ aguas ______________ (destilado)
3. ______ hambre ______________ (extremo)
4. ______ ave ______________ (negro)
5. ______ aves ______________ (rapaz (*of prey*))
6. ______ alma (*soul*) ______________ (divino)
7. ______ almas ______________ (humano)
8. ______ área ______________ (grande)
9. ______ áreas ______________ (protegido)
10. ______ haba (*fava bean*) ______________ (blanco)
11. ______ habas ______________ (fresco)
12. ______ hacha (*hatchet*) ______________ (afilado (*sharp*))

ESO *THAT*

Spanish has several forms ending in **-o** that are called neuters. There are three neuter demonstrative pronouns: **esto**, **eso**, and **aquello**. These pronouns refer to situations or ideas, not to specific nouns.

Paco no dice la verdad.	*Paco doesn't tell the truth.*
Eso es muy malo.	***That's** very bad.* (**eso** = *the fact that he doesn't tell the truth*)

(For demonstrative adjectives, see Chapter 3; for demonstrative pronouns, see Chapter 12.)

DIÁLOGO 2 · Vemos televisión.

Study the dialogue, then listen to the recording and repeat each line.

NICOLÁS	Ya es hora de ver la telenovela. Prendo la tele.
OLIVIA	Ah sí, quiero verla. Pero ponen una película muy buena a la misma hora.
NICOLÁS	Pues, ¿por qué no vemos la película ahora? Y...
OLIVIA	¡Claro! Podemos grabar la telenovela y verla después. Perfecto.

Análisis

Check that you understand the linguistic breakdown of each speech from *Diálogo 2*.

Ya es hora de ver la telenovela. Prendo la tele.	*It's already time to watch the soap opera. I'll turn on the TV.*
la hora	*hour, time*
ser hora de	*to be time to*
ver	*to see, watch*
la telenovela	*serialized TV drama, soap opera*
es hora de ver la telenovela	*it's time to watch the soap opera*
prender	*to turn on, put on*
prendo	*I'll turn on, I'll put on*
prender la tele	*to turn on the TV*
Ah sí, quiero verla. Pero ponen una película muy buena a la misma hora.	*Yes, I want to see it. But they're showing a very good movie at the same time.*
la	*it* (feminine singular pronoun)
verla	*to see it, watch it*
quiero verla	*I want to see it*
la película	*movie, film*
mismo	*same*
a la misma hora	*at the same time*
Pues, ¿por qué no vemos la película ahora? Y...	*Well then, why don't we watch the movie now? And . . .*
pues	*well, well now, well then* (interjection)
vemos	*we see, we watch*
¿por qué no vemos?	*why don't we watch?*
¡Claro! Podemos grabar la telenovela y verla después. Perfecto.	*Of course! We can record the soap opera and watch it afterward. Perfect.*
¡Claro!	*Of course!*
grabar	*to record*
podemos grabar	*we can record*
la	*it* (feminine singular pronoun)
verla	*to see it, watch it*
después	*afterward*

Variantes

Listen, and repeat the same structures from *Diálogo 2*, now with new vocabulary.

Prendo la tele.	*I'll turn **the TV** on.*
la radio	*the radio*
el microondas	*the microwave*
la lavadora	*the washing machine*
la secadora	*the dryer*
el lavaplatos	*the dishwasher*
el aire acondicionado	*the air conditioning*
la calefacción	*the heat*
¿La tele? Sí, quiero verla.	*TV? Yes, I want to watch it.*
¿El documental? Sí, quiero verlo.	*The documentary? Yes, I want to watch it.*
¿Las noticias? Sí, quiero verlas.	*The news? Yes, I want to watch it.*
¿Los programas? Sí, quiero verlos.	*The programs? Yes, I want to watch them.*

Estructura y Práctica

Ver *to see*

Review the conjugation of **ver** in present tense.

ver *to see*	
veo	vemos
ves	veis
ve	ven

D *¿Qué ven?* Write the form of the verb **ver** that correctly completes each of the following sentences to find out what people are watching on television.

1. Yo ______________ un documental.
2. Carlitos ______________ dibujos animados (*cartoons*).
3. Uds. ______________ una película.
4. Claudia ______________ las noticias.
5. Tú ______________ un programa de cocina (*cooking show*).
6. Ud. ______________ un programa de detectives (*crime show*).
7. Nosotros ______________ una telenovela (*serial drama*).
8. Ellos ______________ una comedia de situación (*sitcom*).

Poner *to put*

Review the conjugation of **poner** in present tense.

poner *to put*	
pongo	ponemos
pones	ponéis
pone	ponen

Direct Object Pronouns

Direct object nouns may be replaced by direct object pronouns once it is clear to whom or what they refer.

Here are the direct object pronouns in standard Spanish American usage.

	SINGULAR	PLURAL
FIRST PERSON	me	nos
SECOND PERSON	te	(os)
THIRD PERSON	lo, la	los, las

Note that **lo** and **la** refer to both people and things. The direct object pronoun **lo** replaces both people and things that are grammatically masculine singular: **lo** means both *him* and *it*. The direct object pronoun **la** replaces both people and things that are grammatically feminine singular: **la** means both *her* and *it*. In the plural, note that Spanish **los, las** refer to both people and things just like English *them*, but Spanish **los, las** reflect the gender of the nouns they replace as well. (The pronoun **os** appears in parentheses because the **vosotros** form is not used in Spanish America.)

The direct object pronouns **lo, la, los, las** also mean *you* when referring to **usted** or **ustedes**.

Creo que **lo** conozco, señor.	*I think I know **you**, sir.*
Creo que **la** conozco, señora.	*I think I know **you**, ma'am.*
Creo que **los** conozco, señores.	*I think I know **you**, gentlemen.*
Creo que **las** conozco, señoras.	*I think I know **you**, ladies.*

REGIONAL USAGE

In parts of Spain, **lo** is replaced by **le** when referring to a person, but not when referring to an object. In these varieties of Spanish, the following sentences are distinct.

¿Qué es ese libro? No **lo** conocemos.	*What book is that? We are not familiar with **it**.*
¿Quién es ese señor? No **le** conocemos.	*Who is that man? We don't know **him**.*

In Spanish America, both sentences would read **No lo conocemos.**

The plural **los** may be replaced by **les** when referring to people, but this is less common.

In many parts of Spanish America, **le** and **les** are used as the direct object pronouns corresponding to **Ud.** and **Uds.**, respectively.

Si hay un problema, nosotros **le** contactamos.	*If there is a problem, we will contact **you**.*

E **Direct object nouns to pronouns.** Write sentences to answer each of the following questions, changing the direct object nouns to pronouns in your responses. Use the cues in parentheses, which indicate whether your response should be affirmative or negative. Follow the *modelo.*

MODELO ¿Lees el ruso? (sí)
→ Sí, lo leo.

¿Lees el ruso? (no)
→ No, no lo leo.

1. ¿Sara pone la mesa? (sí)
2. ¿Ellos venden su casa? (no)
3. ¿Uds. sirven estas galletas? (sí)
4. ¿Martín sube los archivos? (no)
5. ¿Ud. comprende esta idea? (no)
6. ¿Conoces a mis compañeros de trabajo? (sí)
7. ¿Isabel y Ud. prefieren esos vestidos? (sí)
8. ¿Sabes la dirección de los Fernández? (no)
9. ¿Uds. oyen el ruido? (sí)
10. ¿Ud. me [*masc.*] entiende? (sí)
11. ¿Ud. nos [*fem.*] lleva al centro? (no)
12. ¿Alonso comienza la base de datos? (sí)

F ***¡Ponemos a Cristóbal por las nubes!*** **(We praise Cristóbal to the skies!)** Write the form of **poner** that correctly completes each of the following sentences to tell who is a fan of Cristóbal's music (**la nube** = *cloud*).

1. Ricardo lo ____________ por las nubes.
2. Uds. lo ____________ por las nubes.
3. Yo lo ____________ por las nubes.
4. Ud. lo ____________ por las nubes.
5. Margarita lo ____________ por las nubes.
6. Tú lo ____________ por las nubes.
7. Todos sus aficionados (*fans*) lo ____________ por las nubes.
8. Ud. y yo lo ____________ por las nubes.

G ***Lo, la, los, las*** **referring to** ***Ud.*** **and** ***Uds.*** Write sentences that correctly answer the questions, using the direct object pronouns that replace **Ud.** and **Uds.** Write the answers in two ways where possible. Follow the *modelo.*

MODELO ¿Me lleva Ud.?
→ No, señor, no lo llevo.

1. ¿Me conoce Ud.?

   No, señora, ____________________.
2. ¿Nos busca Ud.?

   No, señores, ____________________.
3. ¿Nos llama Ud.?

   No, señoras, ____________________.
4. ¿Me comprende Ud.?

   No, señorita, ____________________.

5. ¿Me ayuda Ud.?

   No, señor, ____________________.

6. ¿Nos conoce Ud.?

   No, señoritas, ____________________.

7. ¿Me quiere Ud. visitar?

   No, señor, ____________________.

8. ¿Nos piensa Ud. invitar?

   No, señores, ____________________.

9. ¿Me va Ud. a llevar?

   No, señora, ____________________.

10. ¿Nos necesita ver?

    No, señor, ____________________.

H **Translation.** Express the following sentences in Spanish, using the correct form of the direct object pronoun. Write the answers in two ways where possible.

1. *I see her.*
2. *He's calling me.*
3. *We're going to take them* [fem.].
4. *Are you* (tú) *looking for him?*
5. *Do you* (Uds.) *want to wait for us?*
6. *She hopes to meet you* (tú).
7. *Do you* (Ud.) *intend to help them* [masc.]*?*
8. *They* [fem.] *can't understand you* (Ud.) [fem.].
9. *I want to invite you* (Uds.) [masc.].
10. *I'm not going to visit her.*

DIÁLOGO 3 · Dan una película.

Study the dialogue, then listen to the recording and repeat each line.

OLIVIA	Quiero ver la película que dan en el cine Ritz.
NICOLÁS	Yo también la quiero ver. Dicen que es excelente.
OLIVIA	Si quieres verla hoy, más vale salir ahora porque va a haber mucha gente.
NICOLÁS	Es cierto. De todas formas vamos a tener que hacer cola.

Análisis

Check that you understand the linguistic breakdown of each speech from *Diálogo 3*.

Quiero ver la película que dan en el cine Ritz.	*I want to see the movie that they're showing at the Ritz movie theater.*
dar una película	*to show a movie*
que	*that* (conjunction)
que dan	*that they are showing*
el cine	*movie theater*
Yo también la quiero ver. Dicen que es excelente.	*I want to see it, too. They say it's excellent.*
la	*it* (replacing feminine singular noun)
decir	*to say, tell*
que	*that* (conjunction)
excelente	*excellent*

Si quieres verla hoy, más vale salir ahora porque va a haber mucha gente.	*If you want to see it today, we should leave now, because there will be a lot of people (there).*
la	*it*
verla	*to see it, watch it*
quieres verla	*you want to see it*
más vale + *infinitive*	*it's better to (do something)*
salir	*to leave, go out*
haber	*to be there* (infinitive of **hay**)
la gente	*people* (singular in Spanish)
mucha gente	*a lot of people*
va a haber mucha gente	*there will be a lot of people (there)*
Es cierto. De todas formas vamos a tener que hacer cola.	*That's right. In any case, we're going to have to stand in line.*
cierto	*correct, true, right*
de todas formas	*in any case*
ir a + *infinitive*	*to be going to (do something)*
tener que + *infinitive*	*to have to (do something)*
la cola	*line (of people)*
hacer cola	*to stand in line, wait in line*
vamos a tener que hacer cola	*we're going to have to stand in line*

Variantes

Listen, and repeat the same structures from *Diálogo 3*, now with new vocabulary.

¿La película? La quiero ver.	*The film? I want to see it.*
¿El film? Lo quiero ver.	*The film? I want to see it.*
¿Los videos? Los quiero ver.	*The videos? I want to see them.*
¿Las diapositivas? Las quiero ver.	*The slides? I want to see them.*
Dicen que es excelente.	*They say **it's excellent**.*
que va a llover	*it's going to rain*
que vienen el sábado	*they're coming on Saturday*
que sí	*yes*
que no	*no*
Va a haber mucha gente.	*There will be **many people**.*
muchas personas	*many people*
una gran cantidad de gente	*a great many people*
mucho público	*a big audience*

Estructura y Práctica

Dar *to give*

Review the conjugation of **dar** in present tense.

dar *to give*	
doy	damos
das	dais
da	dan

I *¿Dan consejos?* Write sentences using the elements given to say that these people never give advice. Make all necessary changes. Follow the *modelo.*

MODELO Ud. / nunca / dar consejos (*to give advice*)
→ Ud. nunca da consejos.

1. Antonio y yo / nunca / dar consejos
2. Juan / nunca / dar consejos
3. María y Susana / nunca / dar consejos
4. yo / nunca / dar consejos
5. tú / nunca / dar consejos
6. la hermana de Pablo / nunca / dar consejos
7. Uds. / nunca / dar consejos

Decir *to say, tell*

Review the conjugation of **decir** in present tense.

decir *to say, tell*	
d**ig**o	decimos
d**i**ces	decís
d**i**ce	d**i**cen

J *¡Todos callados!* **(Everyone quiet!)** Write sentences using the elements given to explain that nobody is saying anything. Make all necessary changes. Follow the *modelo.*

MODELO nosotros / no decir / nada
→ Nosotros no decimos nada.

1. tú / no decir / nada
2. nuestros amigos / no decir / nada
3. Raúl / no decir / nada
4. Ud. / no decir / nada
5. yo / no decir / nada
6. Camila / no decir / nada
7. Uds. / no decir / nada
8. Ana María y yo / no decir / nada

Salir *to go out, leave*

Review the conjugation of **salir** in present tense.

salir *to go out, leave*	
sal**g**o	salimos
sales	salís
sale	salen

K *¿Cuándo salen?* Write sentences using the elements given to tell when people are leaving the office. Use the correct form of **salir** with the time cue. Follow the *modelo.*

MODELO ellos / en una hora
→ Ellos salen en una ahora.

1. nosotros / a las seis y media
2. Roberto / dentro de unos minutos
3. yo / en veinte minutos
4. Ud. / muy pronto
5. los empleados / ahora mismo
6. tú / un poco tarde
7. Uds. / a la hora de cenar
8. Timoteo y Rebeca / temprano

Valer *to be worth, cost*

Review the conjugation of **valer** in present tense.

valer *to be worth, cost*	
val**g**o	valemos
vales	valéis
vale	valen

L Express the following sentences in Spanish. Use the expression **más vale...** to say that it's better to do something.

1. *It's better to leave at noon.*
2. *It's better to discuss the problems.*
3. *It's better not to go.*
4. *It's better to share the information.*

Haber *to have*

Haber (*to have*) is used almost exclusively as an auxiliary verb to form the compound tenses. (See Chapter 13.) In this chapter, we introduce **haber** in its infinitive form as part of the verb + **a** + infinitive construction.

haber *to have*	
he	hemos
has	habéis
ha	han

Va a haber mucha gente. — ***There will be*** *many people.*
Va a haber muchos invitados. — ***There will be*** *many guests.*

Haber is also the infinitive of **hay** (*there is, there are*), which you learned in Chapter 1. **Hay** is a modified form of the third person singular form **ha**. **Hay** may be followed by either a singular or a plural noun. The noun that follows **hay** is considered to be the direct object of the verb.

Hay un concierto hoy a las ocho. — ***There's*** *a concert today at eight o'clock.*
¿**Hay** suficientes médicos? — ***Are there*** *enough doctors?*
No, no los **hay**. — *No,* ***there aren't*** *(enough of them).*

Hay is used in the expression **hay que** (*one must / you must / it is necessary to* (*do something*)). In this expression, **hay** is linked to an infinitive by the connector **que**.

Hay que practicar el español.	***You must*** *practice Spanish.*
Hay que hacer cola.	***It's necessary to*** *wait in line.*
Hay que tener cuidado.	***One must*** *be careful.*

M Express the following sentences in Spanish. Use the expression **hay que...** to say that it's necessary to do something.

1. *It's necessary to master a language.*
2. *You must be lucky.*
3. *Sometimes you must resist temptation.*
4. *It's necessary to be patient.*

Direct Object Pronouns with Verb + Infinitive Constructions

Direct object pronouns precede the conjugated verb. In verb + infinitive constructions, direct object pronouns may either precede the conjugated verb or follow the infinitive. When they follow, they are attached to the infinitive in writing.

Lo quiero ver. / Quiero ver**lo**.	*I want to see it.*
Las vamos a traer. / Vamos a traer**las**.	*We're going to bring them.*

N **Direct object pronouns with the verb + infinitive construction.** Expand each sentence using the verb (or verb + connector) that appears in parentheses to make a verb + infinitive construction. Change the direct object noun to a pronoun. Write each expanded sentence in two ways, according to the *modelo*.

MODELO Daniel imprime el informe. (necesitar)
→ Daniel necesita imprimirlo.
→ Daniel lo necesita imprimir.

1. Devuelves la pelota. (deber)
2. ¿Uds. no prueban las quesadillas? (querer)
3. Tienen mucho éxito. (empezar a)
4. No traduzco los documentos. (poder)
5. Vemos a nuestros primos. (esperar)
6. Traigo las flores. (ir a)
7. Ayudamos a los niños. (tener que)
8. Ud. domina el idioma. (lograr)
9. Alicia diseña páginas web. (saber)
10. ¿Ud. la llama? (pensar)
11. Entiendo su punto de vista. (tratar de)
12. Encuentra su cartera. (acabar de)

DIÁLOGO 4 · ¿Oímos música?

Study the dialogue, then listen to the recording and repeat each line.

NICOLÁS ¿Oímos música? Traigo unos viejos discos de vinilo. Están rayados pero la música es increíble.

OLIVIA ¡Fabuloso! Y yo tengo una app para descargar música en el iPod. También podemos transmitir videos musicales de YouTube a la tele.

Análisis

Check that you understand the linguistic breakdown of each speech from *Diálogo 4.*

¿Oímos música? Traigo unos viejos discos de vinilo. Están rayados pero la música es increíble.	*Shall we listen to music? I have some old vinyl records. They're scratched, but the music is incredible.*
oír	*to hear, listen to*
¿oímos?	*shall we listen to?*
traer	*to bring, have with one*
traigo	*I'm bringing (something), I have (something) with me*
el disco de vinilo	*vinyl record*
rayado	*scratched*
están rayados	*they're scratched*
increíble	*incredible*
¡Fabuloso! Y yo tengo una app para descargar música en el iPod. También podemos transmitir videos musicales de YouTube a la tele.	*Terrific! And I have an app for downloading music to the iPod. We can also send music videos from YouTube to the TV.*
fabuloso	*fabulous, terrific*
una app	*app (application)*
descargar	*to download*
transmitir	*to transmit, send*
el video musical	*music video*

Estructura y Práctica

Oír *to hear*

Review the conjugation of **oír** in present tense.

oír *to hear*	
oigo	oímos
oyes	oís
oye	oyen

O ***¿Qué oyen?*** Write sentences using the correct form of **oír** and the elements given to find out what people are hearing or listening to. Follow the *modelo.*

MODELO Miguel / los ruidos de la calle
→ Miguel oye los ruidos de la calle.

1. Marta y yo / el timbre
2. Ud. / música
3. ellos / unos sonidos
4. yo / voces
5. tú / gritos
6. Uds. / el teléfono
7. Leonor / una conversación

DIÁLOGO 5 · ¿Cómo se dice?

Study the dialogue, then listen to the recording and repeat each line.

OLIVIA	Traduzco mi sitio web al inglés. ¿Quieres verlo?
NICOLÁS	Claro. Oye, ¿cómo se dice "sitio web" en inglés?
OLIVIA	Se dice *website.*

Análisis

Check that you understand the linguistic breakdown of each speech from *Diálogo 5.*

Traduzco mi sitio web al inglés. ¿Quieres verlo?	*I'm translating my website into English. Do you want to see it?*
traducir	*to translate*
traduzco	*I translate, I'm translating*
el sitio	*place, site*
el sitio web	*website*
el inglés	*English (language)*
traducir al inglés	*to translate into English*
lo	*it* (replacing masculine singular noun)
verlo	*to see it*
Claro. Oye, ¿cómo se dice "sitio web" en inglés?	*I certainly do. Say, how do you say "website" in English?*
claro	*of course*
oye	*say, hey* (literally, *hear*)
se dice	*you say, one says*
¿cómo se dice?	*how do you say?*
Se dice *website.*	*You say "website."*

Variantes

Listen, and repeat the same structures from *Diálogo 5*, now with new vocabulary.

¿Cómo se dice *computer* en español?	*How do you say "computer" in Spanish?*
Se dice "computadora". Y en España, "ordenador".	*You say* computadora. *And in Spain,* ordenador.

Estructura y Práctica

Conocer *to know*

Review the conjugation of **conocer** in present tense.

conocer *to know*	
cono**zc**o	conocemos
conoces	conocéis
conoce	conocen

Traducir *to translate*

Review the conjugation of **traducir** in present tense.

traducir *to translate*	
tradu**zc**o	traducimos
traduces	traducís
traduce	traducen

DIÁLOGO 6 · Cae la nieve.

Study the dialogue, then listen to the recording and repeat each line.

NICOLÁS Hace muy mal tiempo. Está nublado. Parece que va a llover.
OLIVIA ¿Llover? ¿No ves? Cae la nieve.

Análisis

Check that you understand the linguistic breakdown of each speech from *Diálogo 6*.

Hace muy mal tiempo. Está nublado. Parece que va a llover.	*The weather is very bad. It's cloudy. It looks like it's going to rain.*
el tiempo	*weather*
mal tiempo	*bad weather*
hace mal tiempo	*the weather is bad*
nublado	*cloudy*
estar nublado	*to be cloudy*
parecer	*to seem, look like*
que	*that* (conjunction)
llover (**o** > **ue**)	*to rain*
va a llover	*it's going to rain*
¿Llover? ¿No ves? Cae la nieve.	*Rain? Can't you see? Snow is falling.*
ves	*you see*
¿No ves?	*Can't you see? / Don't you see?*
caer	*to fall*
la nieve	*snow*
Cae la nieve.	*Snow is falling.*

Variantes

Listen, and repeat the same structures from *Diálogo 6*, now with new vocabulary.

La nieve cae.	***Snow** is falling.*
La lluvia	*Rain*
La noche cae.	*It's nightfall.*

Estructura y Práctica

Parecer *to seem*

Review the conjugation of **parecer** in present tense.

parecer *to seem*	
pare**z**co	parecemos
pareces	parecéis
parece	parecen

Caer *to fall*

Review the conjugation of **caer** in present tense.

caer *to fall*	
ca**ig**o	caemos
caes	caéis
cae	caen

DIÁLOGO 7 · Los libros no caben.

Study the dialogue, then listen to the recording and repeat each line.

OLIVIA ¿Y aquellos libros? Los vas a meter en la caja, ¿verdad?
NICOLÁS ¿No ves? No cabe ni un solo libro más.

Análisis

Check that you understand the linguistic breakdown of each speech from *Diálogo 7*.

¿Y aquellos libros? Los vas a meter en la caja, ¿verdad?	*And what about those books? You're going to put them into the box, aren't you?*
y	*and, and what about?*
aquel	*that*
los	*them*
meter	*to put inside of*
los vas a meter	*you're going to put them in*
¿verdad?	*aren't you?*

¿No ves? No cabe ni un solo libro más.	*Can't you see? Not even one more book can fit.*
ves	*you see*
¿No ves?	*Can't you see?*
caber	*to fit*
no cabe	*it doesn't fit*
ni	*not even*
solo	*single*
un solo	*one single*
ni un solo libro	*not even one single book*
más	*more*
ni un solo libro más	*not even one more book*

Estructura y Práctica

Caber *to fit*

Review the conjugation of **caber** in present tense.

caber *to fit*	
quepo	cabemos
cabes	cabéis
cabe	caben

DIÁLOGO 8 · Una chica pesada

Study the dialogue, then listen to the recording and repeat each line.

NICOLÁS	Yo no tengo ganas de ver a Lorenza.
OLIVIA	¿Por qué? ¿No la encuentras simpática?
NICOLÁS	De ningún modo. La chica es muy pesada. Siempre da consejos.

Análisis

Check that you understand the linguistic breakdown of each speech from *Diálogo 8*.

Yo no tengo ganas de ver a Lorenza.	*I don't feel like seeing Lorenza.*
tener ganas de + *infinitive*	*to feel like (doing something)*
¿Por qué? ¿No la encuentras simpática?	*Why? Don't you find her to be nice?*
la	*her*
encontrar (**o** > **ue**)	*to find*
la encuentras	*you find her*
simpático	*nice, appealing, pleasant* (of people)

De ningún modo. La chica es muy pesada. Siempre da consejos.	*Not at all. The girl is very annoying. She's always giving advice.*
de ningún modo	*not at all*
la chica	*girl*
pesado	*annoying, boring*
siempre	*always*
el consejo	*piece of advice*
consejos	*advice*
dar consejos	*to give advice*

Variantes

Listen, and repeat the same structures from *Diálogo 8*, now with new vocabulary.

La encuentro simpática.	*I find her nice.*
Lo encuentro simpático.	*I find him nice.*
Las encuentro simpáticas.	*I find them nice.* (females)
Los encuentro simpáticos.	*I find them nice.* (males or males and females)

DIÁLOGO 9 · ¿A qué hora vienes?

Study the dialogue, then listen to the recording and repeat each line.

OLIVIA	Tengo que verte. Paso por tu casa mañana.
NICOLÁS	Muy bien. ¿A qué hora vienes a verme?

Análisis

Check that you understand the linguistic breakdown of each speech from *Diálogo 9*.

Tengo que verte. Paso por tu casa mañana.	*I've got to see you. I'll come by your house tomorrow.*
tener que + *infinitive*	*to have to (do something)*
te	*you*
verte	*to see you*
tengo que verte	*I have to see you*
pasar	*to pass, come by*
pasar por tu casa	*to come by your house*
mañana	*tomorrow*
Muy bien. ¿A qué hora vienes a verme?	*That's fine. What time are you coming to see me?*
¿a qué hora?	*at what time?*
vienes	*you're coming*
venir a + *infinitive*	*to be coming to (do something)*
me	*me*
verme	*to see me*

Variantes

Listen, and repeat the same structures from *Diálogo 9*, now with new vocabulary.

Tengo que verte.	*I have to* ***see you.***
verlo	*see him, you* (**Ud.**, male)
verla	*see her, you* (**Ud.**, female)
verlos	*see them* (males or males and females), *you* (**Uds.**, males or males and females)
verlas	*see them* (females), *you* (**Uds.**, females)
¿Vienes a verme?	*Are you coming to* ***see me?***
vernos	*see us*
verlo	*see him*
verlas	*see them* (females)

Estructura y Práctica

Venir *to come*

Review the conjugation of **venir** in present tense.

venir *to come*	
vengo	venimos
vienes	venís
viene	vienen

P ***¿Cuándo vienen?*** Write sentences using the correct form of **venir** and the time cue given to find out when these people are coming. Follow the *modelo.*

MODELO Alberto / mañana
→ Alberto viene mañana.

1. los chicos / en la tarde
2. Ud. / el jueves
3. yo / a las ocho
4. Uds. / por la mañana
5. Anita y yo / esta noche
6. tú / el miércoles
7. Javier / a la una y media

DIÁLOGO 10 · No los puedo llevar.

Study the dialogue, then listen to the recording and repeat each line.

NICOLÁS Nos llevas al centro comercial esta tarde, ¿no?
OLIVIA Lo siento. Hoy no los puedo llevar. Mañana, quizás.

Análisis

Check that you understand the linguistic breakdown of each speech from *Diálogo 10.*

Nos llevas al centro comercial esta tarde, ¿no?	*You'll take us to the mall this afternoon, won't you?*
llevar	*to take (someone somewhere)*
nos	*us*
nos llevas	*you'll take us*
¿no?	*won't you?, right?*
Lo siento. Hoy no los puedo llevar. Mañana, quizás.	*I'm sorry. I can't take you today. Maybe tomorrow.*
sentir (**e** > **ie**)	*to feel, feel sorry about*
Lo siento.	*I'm sorry.*
los	*you* (**Uds.**)
no los puedo llevar	*I can't take you*
quizás	*maybe, perhaps*

Variantes

Listen, and repeat the same structures from *Diálogo 10*, now with new vocabulary.

Los puedo llevar.	*I* ***can*** *take you.*
quiero	*want to*
debo	*should*
necesito	*need to*
pienso	*intend to*
prefiero	*prefer to*
espero	*hope to*

DIÁLOGO 11 · Yo lo llamo a Ud.

Study the dialogue, then listen to the recording and repeat each line.

NICOLÁS Ud. me va a llamar mañana, ¿verdad?
OLIVIA Sí, señor, yo lo llamo mañana por la mañana.

Análisis

Check that you understand the linguistic breakdown of each speech from *Diálogo 11.*

Ud. me va a llamar mañana, ¿verdad?	*You're going to call me tomorrow, aren't you?*
me	*me*
llamar	*to call*
me va a llamar	*you're going to call me*
¿verdad?	*aren't you?*

Sí, señor, yo lo llamo mañana por la mañana.	*Yes, sir. I'll call you tomorrow morning.*
lo	*you* (**Ud.**)
yo lo llamo	*I'll call you*
mañana por la mañana	*tomorrow morning*

Variantes

Listen, and repeat the same structures from *Diálogo 11*, now with new vocabulary.

Ud. me va a llamar.	*You're going to call* ***me****.*
nos	*us*
lo	*him*
la	*her*
los	*them* (males or males and females)
las	*them* (females)
Yo lo llamo mañana.	*I'll call* ***you*** *tomorrow.*
la	*you* (**Ud.**, female)
los	*you* (**Uds.**, males or males and females)
las	*you* (**Uds.**, females)

DIÁLOGO 12 · Yo la ayudo.

Study the dialogue, then listen to the recording and repeat each line.

OLIVIA	Por favor, ¿puede Ud. ayudarme con la base de datos?
NICOLÁS	Claro que sí, señorita. Yo la ayudo en seguida.

Análisis

Check that you understand the linguistic breakdown of each speech from *Diálogo 12*.

Por favor, ¿puede Ud. ayudarme con la base de datos?	*Excuse me, can you help me with the database?*
por favor	*please, excuse me*
me	*me*
ayudar	*to help*
ayudarme	*to help me*
la base de datos	*database*
Claro que sí, señorita. Yo la ayudo en seguida.	*Certainly, miss. I'll help you right away.*
claro que sí	*of course I can, of course I will*
señorita	*miss*
la	*you* (**Ud.**)
yo la ayudo	*I'll help you*
en seguida	*right away*

Variantes

Listen, and repeat the same structures from *Diálogo 12*, now with new vocabulary.

¿Puede Ud. ayudarme ?	*Can you **help me**?*
ayudarnos	*help us*
ayudarlos	*help them* (males or males and females)
ayudarlas	*help them* (females)

DIÁLOGO 13 · No lo conozco.

Study the dialogue, then listen to the recording and repeat each line.

OLIVIA	¿Verdad que conoces a mi amigo Eduardo?
NICOLÁS	No, no lo conozco. Espero conocerlo algún día.

Análisis

Check that you understand the linguistic breakdown of each speech from *Diálogo 13*.

¿Verdad que conoces a mi amigo Eduardo?	*You know my friend Eduardo, don't you?*
¿Verdad que...?	*Is it true that . . . ?*
conocer	*to know (a person)*
a	(personal **a**)
No, no lo conozco. Espero conocerlo algún día.	*No, I don't know him. I hope to meet him someday.*
lo	*him*
no lo conozco	*I don't know him*
esperar	*to hope*
esperar + *infinitive*	*to hope to (do something)*
conocer	*to meet (a person)*
conocerlo	*to meet him*
espero conocerlo	*I hope to meet him*
alguno	*some*
algún día	*someday*

Variantes

Listen, and repeat the same structures from *Diálogo 13*, now with new vocabulary.

No lo conozco.	*I don't know **him**.*
la	*her*
los	*them* (males or males and females)
las	*them* (females)

DIÁLOGO 14 · Tienes prisa.

Study the dialogue, then listen to the recording and repeat each line.

NICOLÁS	¿Por qué tienes tanta prisa?
OLIVIA	Es que el avión sale a las siete.

Análisis

Check that you understand the linguistic breakdown of each speech from *Diálogo 14.*

¿Por qué tienes tanta prisa?	*Why are you in such a hurry?*
la prisa	*hurry, haste*
tanta prisa	*such a hurry*
tener prisa	*to be in a hurry*
tener tanta prisa	*to be in such a hurry*
Es que el avión sale a las siete.	*Because the plane leaves at seven.*
es que	*the fact is that, because*
el avión	*airplane*
salir	*to go out, leave*
las siete	*seven o'clock*
a las siete	*at seven o'clock*

DIÁLOGO 15 · ¿Quién trae el vino?

Study the dialogue, then listen to the recording and repeat each line.

OLIVIA	Yo traigo tapas a la fiesta. Tú traes el vino, ¿no?
NICOLÁS	No, yo no. Lo trae Diego.

Análisis

Check that you understand the linguistic breakdown of each speech from *Diálogo 15.*

Yo traigo tapas a la fiesta. Tú traes el vino, ¿no?	*I'm bringing hors d'oeuvres to the party. You're bringing the wine, aren't you?*
traer	*to bring*
traigo	*I bring, I'm bringing*
las tapas	*hors d'oeuvres*
la fiesta	*party*
traes	*you're bringing*
el vino	*wine*
¿no?	*aren't you?*
No, yo no. Lo trae Diego.	*No, not me. Diego is bringing it.*
yo no	*not I, not me*
lo	*it* (replacing masculine singular noun)
lo trae Diego	*Diego is bringing it*

Variantes

Listen, and repeat the same structures from *Diálogo 15*, now with new vocabulary.

¿El vino? Lo trae Diego.	*The wine? Diego is bringing it.*
¿Los sándwiches? Los trae Diego.	*The sandwiches? Diego is bringing them.*
¿La torta? La trae Diego.	*The cake? Diego is bringing it.*
¿Las tapas? Las trae Diego.	*The tapas? Diego is bringing them.*

Estructura y Práctica

Word Order

The typical Spanish word order in a sentence is the same as English: subject-verb-object. However, word order in Spanish often appears freer than word order in English. Spanish uses word order the way English uses intonation—to focus on the new information or key information in a sentence. English word order is relatively fixed, so a rise in intonation signals the focus of the sentence.

*I think **Susan** is going out.*
*No, **Philip** is going out.*

In Spanish, new information is placed at the end of the sentence, even if it is the subject.

Creo que sale **Susana**.	*I think **Susana** is going out.*
No, sale **Felipe**.	*No, **Felipe** is going out.*

The words **sale** and **llega** go at the end of the sentences when the verb is what is focused on.

¿Felipe **sale**?	***Is** Felipe **going out**?*
No, Felipe **llega**.	*No, Felipe **is arriving**.*

Q **Word order.** Write sentences to tell who is bringing each item to the party by correcting your friend's incorrect information. Note that the subject is placed at the end of the sentence in the response. Change each direct object noun to a pronoun. Follow the *modelo*.

MODELO Alfredo trae los refrescos, ¿no? (Rafael)
→ No, los trae Rafael.

1. Patricia trae los sándwiches, ¿no? (Lucas y Laura)
2. Paco y Lidia traen el vino, ¿no? (yo)
3. Tú traes las ensaladas, ¿no? (Uds.)
4. Nosotros traemos la pizza, ¿no? (Guillermo)
5. Tú y Franco traen los postres, ¿no? (tú)
6. Santiago trae la cerveza, ¿no? (nosotros)
7. Luz trae las empanadas, ¿no? (Uds.)

Un paso más

Are you ready to take your Spanish a step further? Here are exercises that will enhance your knowledge of the language and allow you to express yourself freely.

Expressions and Idioms with Irregular Verbs

There are many expressions and idioms formed with some of the irregular verbs you learned in this chapter: **tener**, **dar**, **poner**, **valer**, **oír**, and **ver**. Using these colorful idiomatic expressions will make your Spanish sound more authentic!

tener *to have*
- **tener la culpa de** *to be to blame for* (la culpa = *blame, fault*)
- **tener lugar** *to take place*
- **tener mala cara** *to look bad* (la cara = *face*)
- **no tener ni pies ni cabeza** *to not make sense, have no rhyme or reason* (el pie = *foot*; la cabeza = *head*)

dar *to give*
- **dar guerra** *to cause, make trouble* (la guerra = *war*)
- **dar (la) lata** *to pester, make a nuisance of oneself* (la lata = *can*)
- **dar una vuelta** *to take a walk/ride* (la vuelta = *walk, ride*)

poner *to put*
- **poner las cartas sobre la mesa** *to put one's cards on the table*

valer *to be worth, cost*
- **valer la pena** *to be worthwhile, be worth it* (la pena = *effort, trouble*)

oír *to hear*
- **Las paredes oyen.** *The walls have ears.* (la pared = *wall*)

ver *to see*
- **Ojos que no ven, corazón que no siente.** *Out of sight, out of mind.* (el ojo = *eye*; el corazón = *heart*)

R ***Expresiones y modismos* (Expressions and idioms).** Express each of the following sentences in Spanish, using the expressions and idioms above. Make all necessary changes.

1. *The meeting is taking place in the director's office.*
2. *It's necessary to put one's cards on the table.*
3. *Clara no longer has a boyfriend. Out of sight, out of mind.*
4. *An excellent job? It's worth waiting for it.*
5. *Juanito always causes trouble. And his sister makes a nuisance of herself.*
6. *Their plan doesn't make sense.*
7. *We shouldn't say anything. The walls have ears.*
8. *Nobody is to blame for that.*

9. *Diego, are you sick? You look bad.*
10. *I'm taking a walk in the park. Are you* (tú) *coming with me?*

S ***Preguntas personales.*** Answer each question with a complete Spanish sentence.

1. ¿Tienes hambre? ¿Qué quieres comer?
2. ¿Tienes sed? ¿Qué vas a beber?
3. ¿Qué haces para preparar una comida para tus invitados?
4. ¿Qué comida sirves?
5. ¿Qué programas prefieres ver en la televisión?
6. Si tus amigos te invitan a una fiesta en su casa, ¿qué traes de regalo?
7. ¿Qué tiempo hace hoy? ¿Qué tiempo va a hacer mañana?
8. ¿Tienes paciencia (éxito, suerte, miedo, celos)? Explica (*Explain*).

T **Translation.** Express the following dialogues in Spanish.

1. *It's time for lunch. Are you* (tú) *hungry?*
   No, I'm not hungry, but I'm very thirsty.
2. *Sir, can you please help me with my computer?*
   Of course, ma'am, I'll help you right away.
3. *Our friends say the film they're showing in that movie theater is terrific. I'm very eager to see it.*
   They're right. I just saw it.
4. *It's twenty-five degrees and very windy. I'm cold.*
   Yes, it's cold and snow is falling, but I'm not very cold.
5. *I want to see the crime show.*
   I want to see it, too.
6. *Do you* (Ud.) *know the businessmen who are coming this afternoon?*
   No, I don't know them, but I intend to meet them.
7. *There will be a lot of people at the theater.*
   I know. We're going to have to stand in line. And I'm not patient!
8. *How do you say "advice" in Spanish?*
   You say consejos.

8

The Daily Routine

Communication Goals

- Talking about your daily routine
- Telling how you take care of yourself by eating well and exercising
- Talking about feelings and relationships
- Understanding Hispanic naming customs
- Vocabulary: emotional states such as feeling happy, excited, or angry, falling in love; everyday activities such as getting up, getting dressed

Grammar Topics

- Reflexive Verbs: Formation
- Reflexive Verbs: Uses
- Reflexive Verbs and Their Non-reflexive (Transitive) Counterparts
- Reflexive Verbs Existing Only as Reflexives
- Reflexive Verbs: Reciprocal Meaning
- Reflexive Pronouns
- Reflexive Verbs: Verb + Infinitive Construction
- Adverbs with the Suffix **-mente**
- **Al** + Infinitive
- Prepositions with Reflexive Verbs
- Ordinal Numbers

DIÁLOGO 1 · Carlos el aguafiestas

Study the dialogue, then listen to the recording and repeat each line.

PALOMA ¡Qué fiesta más divertida! Parece que todos los invitados se divierten mucho.

CARLOS No todos. Yo me aburro rotundamente.

PALOMA Carlos, tú me exasperas. Siempre eres el aguafiestas.

Análisis

Check that you understand the linguistic breakdown of each speech from *Diálogo 1*.

¡Qué fiesta más divertida! Parece que todos los invitados se divierten mucho.	*What a fun party! It looks like all the guests are having a very good time.*
la fiesta	*party*
divertido	*amusing, fun*
parecer	*to seem*
parece que	*it seems that*
el invitado	*guest*
todos los invitados	*all the guests*
divertirse (**e** > **ie**)	*to have a good time, have fun*
mucho	*a lot*

No todos. Yo me aburro rotundamente.	*Not all. I am bored stiff.*
todos	*all, everyone*
aburrirse	*to be bored*
rotundo	*definite, emphatic*
rotundamente	*definitely, emphatically*

Carlos, tú me exasperas. Siempre eres el aguafiestas.	*Carlos, you exasperate me. You are always the party pooper.*
exasperar	*to exasperate*
siempre	*always*
el aguafiestas	*party pooper, wet blanket*

Variantes

Listen, and repeat the same structures from *Diálogo 1*, now with new vocabulary.

Todos se divierten .	*Everyone* ***is having a good time.***
se alegran	*is happy*
se entusiasman	*is getting excited, is feeling thrilled*
se ríen	*is laughing*
se emocionan	*is getting excited*
se animan	*is cheering up*

Yo me aburro .	*I* ***am getting bored.***
me asusto	*am getting frightened*
me enfado	*am getting angry*
me enojo	*am getting angry*
me molesto	*am getting annoyed*
me ofendo	*am getting insulted*

Tú me exasperas .	*You're* ***making me lose my patience.***
me aburres	*boring me*
me asustas	*frightening me*
me enfadas	*making me angry*
me enojas	*making me angry*
me molestas	*annoying me*
me ofendes	*insulting me*

Estructura y Práctica

Reflexive Verbs: Formation

Reflexive verbs are a class of verbs in Spanish that always appear with an object pronoun that refers to the subject. This pronoun is called the reflexive pronoun. English also has reflexive verbs. In English, reflexive pronouns end in *-self* or *-selves*: *I hurt myself, they hurt themselves.* English reflexive verbs are a limited class and stress that the subject performs the action upon himself. In Spanish, however, reflexive verbs are a broad category with several different functions that do not correspond at all to English reflexives. Reflexive verbs appear in vocabulary lists with **-se** attached to the infinitive: **levantarse**, **enojarse**, **ofenderse**, **divertirse** (**e** > **ie**), **reírse** (**e** > **i**), **aburrirse**.

Study the conjugation of the reflexive verb **levantarse** (*to get up*) in the present tense. Note that the reflexive pronouns are the same as the direct object pronouns in the first and second persons (**yo**, **tú**, **nosotros**, and **vosotros** forms). In the third person, the reflexive pronoun is **se** in both the singular and the plural.

levantarse *to get up*	
me levanto	**nos** levantamos
te levantas	**os** levantáis
se levanta	**se** levantan

Some reflexive verbs are also stem-changing verbs. Study the conjugation of **reírse** (**e** > **i**) in the present tense.

reírse (**e** > **i**) *to laugh*	
me río	nos reímos
te ríes	os reís
se ríe	se ríen

Reflexive Verbs: Uses

Spanish reflexive verbs correspond most often to intransitive verbs or verb phrases in English. Their English equivalents often contain *get* or *be*. Intransitive verbs in Spanish are those that cannot take a direct object, for example, **ir** (*to go*) and **llegar** (*to arrive*).

aburrirse *to get bored, be bored*
asustarse *to get scared*
divertirse *to have a good time*
enojarse *to get angry*
marearse *to get dizzy*
ofenderse *to get insulted, be offended*
pasearse *to stroll*
sorprenderse *to be surprised*
tranquilizarse *to calm down, stop worrying*

Me aburro en la oficina.	*I get bored at the office.*
Ella se marea en el avión.	*She gets dizzy on the plane.*
Él se ofende por tonterías.	*He gets insulted by silly things.*
Me divierto mucho en Costa Rica.	*I'm having a very good time in Costa Rica.*

A ***¿Cómo reaccionan?*** Write sentences that describe how people are feeling and reacting. Use the reflexive verbs in parentheses. Follow the *modelo*.

MODELO yo (alegrarse)
→ Yo me alegro.

1. Julio (molestarse)
2. Uds. (aburrirse)
3. Victoria y yo (entusiasmarse)
4. tú (reírse)
5. Alfonso y Edit (asustarse)
6. Ud. (emocionarse)
7. yo (divertirse)
8. Consuelo y Javier (ofenderse)
9. María Elena (enojarse)
10. Juan Carlos y yo (animarse)

B **Reflexive verbs.** Express the following dialogues in Spanish.

1. *I'm getting bored. And you* (tú)*?*
   Are you kidding? I'm having a great time.
2. *Does he get insulted easily?*
   Yes, and he often gets annoyed.
3. *The children are getting excited.*
   Yes, they're laughing a lot.
4. *Why are you* (Uds.) *getting angry?*
   We're not getting angry but, yes, we're losing our patience.

Reflexive Verbs and Their Non-reflexive (Transitive) Counterparts

Many reflexive verbs have a non-reflexive counterpart. The non-reflexive verb is transitive and is used with a direct object. Compare the following pairs of expressions.

acostar (**o** > **ue**) al niño *to put the child to bed*	acostarse (**o** > **ue**) *to go to bed*
asustar al gato *to scare the cat*	asustarse *to get scared*
calmar a las víctimas *to calm the victims down*	calmarse *to calm down*
lavar el carro *to wash the car*	lavarse *to wash up*
pasear al perro *to walk the dog*	pasearse *to take a walk*
sentar (**e** > **ie**) a la gente *to seat people*	sentarse (**e** > **ie**) *to sit down*

Acuesto a los niños y después me acuesto.	*I put the children to bed and then I go to bed.*
Juan se despierta y luego despierta a su hermana.	*Juan wakes up and then he wakes his sister up.*

C **Reflexive or transitive verb?** Select one of the verbs in parentheses (reflexive or transitive) to correctly complete each of the following sentences, then write its correct form.

1. Nos ________________ (aburrir / aburrirse) esta obra de teatro.
2. Parece que Uds. ________________ (enojar / enojarse) por algo.
3. Rafael y yo ________________ (emocionar / emocionarse) en los partidos de fútbol.
4. Últimamente Luisa me ________________ (exasperar / exasperarse) mucho.
5. Esas películas de terror te ________________ (asustar / asustarse), ¿verdad?
6. Yo ________________ (divertir / divertirse) mucho en los conciertos.
7. ¿Por qué ________________ (preocupar / preocuparse) Ud. por ellos?
8. Ramón los ________________ (animar / animarse) con sus chistes (*jokes*) tontos.
9. Su actitud me ________________ (sorprender / sorprenderse) mucho.
10. ¿Por qué no (Uds.) ________________ (sentar / sentarse) en esta fila (*row*)?

D **Transitive verbs.** Express the following sentences in Spanish.

1. *You* (tú) *are frightening us.*
2. *We're calming her down.*
3. *She's raising her hand.*
4. *I'm cheering him up.*
5. *You* (Uds.) *are annoying me.*
6. *They're boring their friends.*

DIÁLOGO 2 · Comprometerse y casarse

Study the dialogue, then listen to the recording and repeat each line.

PALOMA ¿No sabes? Liliana y Jorge acaban de comprometerse.
CARLOS Me alegro de saberlo. Yo sé que los prometidos están muy enamorados.
PALOMA Es verdad. Dicen que van a casarse en julio.

Análisis

Check that you understand the linguistic breakdown of each speech from *Diálogo 2.*

¿No sabes? Liliana y Jorge acaban de comprometerse.	*You know? Liliana and Jorge have just gotten engaged.*
¿No sabes?	*You know?*
acabar de + *infinitive*	*to have just (done something)*
comprometerse	*to get engaged*
Me alegro de saberlo. Yo sé que los prometidos están muy enamorados.	*I'm glad to know that. I know that the engaged couple is very much in love.*
alegrarse de + *infinitive*	*to be happy to (do something), glad to (do something)*
los prometidos	*engaged couple*
estar enamorado	*to be in love*

Es verdad. Dicen que van a casarse en julio. — *It's true. They say that they are going to get married in July.*
la verdad — *truth*
es verdad — *it's true*
casarse — *to get married*

Variantes

Listen, and repeat the same structures from *Diálogo 2*, now with new vocabulary.

Acaban de comprometerse. — *They've just* ***gotten engaged.***
casarse — *gotten married*
reunirse — *gotten together*
mudarse — *moved (changed residence)*
instalarse — *moved in*

Van a casarse en julio. — *They're going to* ***get married*** *in July.*
comprometerse — *get engaged*
divorciarse — *get divorced*

Liliana se casa con Jorge. — *Liliana* ***is getting married to*** *Jorge.*
se compromete con — *is getting engaged to*

Ella se enamora de él. — *She* ***falls in love with*** *him.*
se acuerda de — *remembers*
se olvida de — *forgets*
se fía de — *trusts*
se ocupa de — *takes care of*
se despide de — *says goodbye to*

Estructura y Práctica

Reflexive Verbs Existing Only as Reflexives

A small number of Spanish verbs exist only as reflexives.

arrepentirse (**e** > **ie**) de algo *to regret something*
atreverse a hacer algo *to dare to do something*
desmayarse *to faint*
divorciarse *to get divorced*
jactarse de algo *to boast about something, brag about something*
quejarse de algo *to complain about something*
suicidarse *to commit suicide*

E **Reflexive verbs existing only as reflexives.** Write a sentence for each of the following strings of elements. Follow the *modelo*.

MODELO Gustavo / arrepentirse de / su comportamiento (*behavior*)
→ Gustavo se arrepiente de su comportamiento.

1. yo / jactarse de / mis hijos
2. tú / quejarse de / todo

3. nosotros / no atreverse a / hablar de eso
4. Pedro y Elena / divorciarse / por falta de comunicación
5. Maite y su hermano / desmayarse / por tener la tensión baja (*low blood pressure*)

F ***Oraciones con verbos reflexivos* (Sentences with reflexive verbs).** Express the following dialogues in Spanish.

1. *They say that Lucía is getting engaged to Benjamín.*
   And it seems that Margarita is getting married to Leonardo.
2. *Do you* (Ud.) *remember Armando's address?*
   I'm sorry. I forget everything!
3. *You know? We're moving into our new house today.*
   I'm very glad to know that.
4. *Who is taking care of the details* (los detalles) *of the meeting?*
   I'm taking care of the reports and Diego is tending to the other documents.
5. *Why are you* (tú) *saying goodbye to all the guests?*
   It's that the party is very boring. I'm leaving!

DIÁLOGO 3 · Los novios se quieren.

Study the dialogue, then listen to the recording and repeat each line.

CARLOS	Benjamín y Jimena se entienden perfectamente.
PALOMA	Los novios se ven y se hablan por celular todos los días.
CARLOS	Y se escriben correos electrónicos todo el día.
PALOMA	Es obvio que se quieren, ¿no?

Análisis

Check that you understand the linguistic breakdown of each speech from *Diálogo 3*.

Benjamín y Jimena se entienden perfectamente.	*Benjamín and Jimena get along perfectly.*
entenderse (**e** > **ie**)	*to get along*
perfecto	*perfect*
perfectamente	*perfectly*
Los novios se ven y se hablan por celular todos los días.	*They see each other and talk to each other by cell phone every day.*
los novios	*the boyfriend and girlfriend, the couple*
verse	*to see each other*
se ven	*they see each other*
hablarse	*to talk to each other*
se hablan	*they talk to each other*
por celular	*by cell phone*

Y se escriben correos electrónicos todo el día. — *And they write each other emails all day long.*
escribirse — *to write to each other*
se escriben — *they write to each other*
se escriben correos electrónicos — *they write emails to each other*

Es obvio que se quieren, ¿no? — *It's obvious that they love each other, isn't it?*
obvio — *obvious*
es obvio que — *it's obvious that*
quererse — *to love each other*
se quieren — *they love each other*

Variantes

Listen, and repeat the same structures from *Diálogo 3*, now with new vocabulary.

Se entienden. — *They understand each other.*
Se comprenden. — *They understand each other.*
Se conocen. — *They know each other.*
Se ayudan. — *They help each other.*
Se quieren. — *They love each other.*
Se besan. — *They kiss each other.*
Se abrazan. — *They hug each other.*

Nos entendemos. — *We understand each other.*
Nos comprendemos. — *We understand each other.*
Nos conocemos. — *We know each other.*
Nos ayudamos. — *We help each other.*
Nos queremos. — *We love each other.*
Nos besamos. — *We kiss each other.*
Nos abrazamos. — *We hug each other.*
Nos tuteamos. — *We address each other as* tú *(informally).*

Estructura y Práctica

Reflexive Verbs: Reciprocal Meaning

Reflexive verbs used in the plural may convey a reciprocal meaning equivalent to English "each other."

Pablo y Beatriz **se ven** todos los días. — *Pablo and Beatriz* ***see each other*** *every day.*
Ellos **se quieren**. — *They* ***love each other****.*
¿Por qué no **nos tuteamos**? — *Why don't* ***we use the* tú *form with each other****?*
Nos enviamos emails. — ***We send each other*** *emails.*

G **Reflexive verbs with reciprocal meaning.** Express the following sentences in Spanish.

1. *You* (Ud.) *and Jorge understand each other very well.*
2. *Micaela and I see each other every day.*
3. *Why don't we address each other as* tú*?*
4. *The children are hugging each other.*
5. *Shall we help each other with the project?*
6. *Roberto and Alejandra love each other a lot.*
7. *We know each other quite well.*
8. *Eunice and her cousin write to each other once a year.*

DIÁLOGO 4 · Nos damos prisa.

Study the dialogue, then listen to the recording and repeat each line.

CARLOS	Se hace tarde. Debemos darnos prisa.
PALOMA	Me visto, me peino, me pinto la cara y nos vamos.
CARLOS	Bueno, yo me pongo el abrigo y te espero abajo.

Análisis

Check that you understand the linguistic breakdown of each speech from *Diálogo 4*.

Se hace tarde. Debemos darnos prisa.	*It's getting late. We should hurry.*
hacerse	*to become*
hacerse tarde	*to get late*
darse prisa	*to hurry up, get moving*
Me visto, me peino, me pinto la cara y nos vamos.	*I'll get dressed, comb my hair, put on makeup, and we'll leave.*
vestirse (**e** > **i**)	*to get dressed*
peinarse	*to comb one's hair*
pintar	*to paint*
la cara	*face*
pintarse la cara	*to put on makeup*
irse	*to go away, leave*
nos vamos	*we'll leave*
Bueno, yo me pongo el abrigo y te espero abajo.	*OK, I'll put on my coat and I'll wait for you downstairs.*
ponerse + *article of clothing*	*to put (article of clothing) on*
el abrigo	*coat*
ponerse el abrigo	*to put one's coat on*
abajo	*downstairs*

Variantes

Listen, and repeat the same structures from *Diálogo 4*, now with new vocabulary.

Debemos darnos prisa.	*We should **hurry up**.*
levantarnos	*get up*
sentarnos	*sit down*

pasearnos	*go for a walk*
apresurarnos	*hurry up*

Me visto.	*I'm getting dressed.*
Me pongo la ropa.	*I'm putting my clothes on.*
Me desnudo.	*I'm getting undressed.*
Me quito la ropa.	*I'm taking my clothes off.*
Me arreglo.	*I'm getting ready.*
Me maquillo.	*I'm putting on makeup.*
Nos vamos.	*We're leaving.*
Nos quedamos.	*We're staying.*
Nos acercamos.	*We're approaching.*
Nos alejamos.	*We're moving far away.*
Yo me pongo el abrigo.	*I'm putting on **my coat**.*
la chaqueta	*my jacket*
los pantalones	*my pants*
la camisa	*my shirt*
los guantes	*my gloves*
Ella se quita el suéter.	*She's taking off **her sweater**.*
el vestido	*her dress*
la falda	*her skirt*
la blusa	*her blouse*
el reloj	*her watch*
Yo me pruebo el traje.	*I'm trying the suit on.*
Él se prueba los zapatos.	*He's trying the shoes on.*

Estructura y Práctica

Reflexive Pronouns

Spanish reflexive pronouns are often the equivalent of English possessive adjectives with parts of the body or articles of clothing. Note that, in this case, the reflexive pronoun is an indirect object and the definite article is used before the noun. Spanish uses a singular noun for articles of clothing and parts of the body, even with plural subjects. It is assumed that each person has one item, unless the item comes in pairs. (For more on indirect objects, see Chapter 9.)

lastimarse el pie *to hurt one's foot*
lavarse las manos *to wash one's hands*
limpiarse los dientes *to brush one's teeth, clean one's teeth*
ponerse los zapatos *to put on one's shoes*
quitarse el abrigo *to take off one's coat*
romperse el brazo *to break one's arm*

Nos ponemos el abrigo.	*We're putting on our coats.*
Se lavan la cara.	*They're washing their faces.*

Paco acaba de lastimarse el pie. — *Paco has just hurt his foot.*
¿Por qué no te pruebas el traje azul? — *Why don't you try on the blue suit?*

H Express the following sentences in Spanish.

1. *I'm trying the blouse and skirt on.*
2. *The children are taking their shoes off.*
3. *María Elena is combing her hair.*
4. *Are you* (tú) *getting dressed right now?*
5. *We get up at 7:00 A.M. every day.*
6. *It's getting late. You* (Uds.) *have to hurry up!*
7. *Each time Samuel plays soccer, he hurts his foot.*
8. *We're getting ready and we're leaving.*

PONER

The reflexive verb **ponerse** is used in the following ways in Chapter 8.

ponerse *to put on (clothing)*
ponerse a + *infinitive* *to begin to (do something)*
ponerse en contacto *to get in touch*
ponerse en forma *to get into shape*

Ponerse is also used with an adjective to mean *to become* when referring to a physical or emotional change.

Me pongo feliz al ver a mis hijos. — ***I get** happy when I see my children.*
Se pone roja cuando siente vergüenza. — ***She** blushes (**gets** red) when she feels ashamed.*
¿Por qué **se ponen** tan nerviosos? — *Why **are you getting** so nervous?*

DIÁLOGO 5 · Cómo cuidarte mejor

Study the dialogue, then listen to the recording and repeat each line.

CARLOS Te acatarras con frecuencia. Debes cuidarte mejor.
PALOMA Es verdad que no me mantengo en forma y no me alimento bien.
CARLOS Bueno, debes comenzar a hacer ejercicio lo antes posible.
PALOMA ¡Y voy a dejar de comer comida basura hoy mismo!

Análisis

Check that you understand the linguistic breakdown of each speech from *Diálogo 5*.

Te acatarras con frecuencia. Debes cuidarte mejor. — *You often catch colds. You should take better care of yourself.*
acatarrarse — *to catch a cold*
la frecuencia — *frequency*
con frecuencia — *often, frequently*
cuidarse — *to take care of oneself*
mejor — *better*

Es verdad que no me mantengo en forma y no me alimento bien. — *It's true that I don't keep in shape and I don't eat right.*

mantener	*to keep* (conjugated like **tener**)
mantenerse	*to keep oneself*
la forma	*shape*
mantenerse en forma	*to keep in shape*
alimentarse	*to feed oneself, eat*
alimentarse bien/mal	*to eat well/badly, eat right/poorly*
bien	*well, right*
mal	*badly, poorly*

Bueno, debes comenzar a hacer ejercicio lo antes posible. — *Well, you should begin exercising as soon as possible.*

bueno	*well, okay*
comenzar (**e** > **ie**) a + *infinitive*	*to begin (doing something)*
hacer ejercicio	*to exercise*
antes	*before*
lo antes posible	*as soon as possible*

¡Y voy a dejar de comer comida basura hoy mismo! — *And I'm going to stop eating junk food this very day!*

dejar de + *infinitive*	*to stop (doing something)*
la comida basura	*junk food*
hoy	*today*
mismo	*very, same*
hoy mismo	*this very day*

Variantes

Listen, and repeat the same structures from *Diálogo 5*, now with new vocabulary.

Te acatarras con frecuencia.	***You catch a cold** frequently.*
Te resfrías	*You catch a cold*
Te enfermas	*You get sick*
Te sientes mal	*You feel ill*

Debes cuidarte .	*You should **take care of yourself**.*
relajarte	*relax*
tranquilizarte	*calm down*
calmarte	*calm down*
ponerte en forma	*get into shape*
pasearte	*go for a walk*

Hago ejercicio con frecuencia .	*I exercise **frequently**.*
con cuidado	*carefully*
con facilidad	*easily*
con dificultad	*with difficulty*

¿Hacen ejercicio frecuentemente ?	*Do they exercise **frequently**?*
cuidadosamente	*carefully*
fácilmente	*easily*
difícilmente	*with difficulty*

Estructura y Práctica

Reflexive Verbs: Verb + Infinitive Construction

When a reflexive verb appears in its infinitive form in a verb + infinitive construction, the **se** of the infinitive must change to agree with the subject of the sentence. Like other object pronouns, the reflexive pronoun may be placed either before the first verb or after the infinitive, in which case it is attached to it in writing. There is no difference in meaning.

Me debo calmar.	Debo calmar**me**.
Te debes calmar.	Debes calmar**te**.
Se debe calmar.	Debe calmar**se**.
Nos debemos calmar.	Debemos calmar**nos**.
Os debéis calmar.	Debéis calmar**os**.
Se deben calmar.	Deben calmar**se**.

I **Reflexive Verbs: Expansion.** Expand each sentence using the verb + infinitive or verb + connector + infinitive construction. Use the verb that appears in parentheses. Write all sentences, following the word order in the *modelo*.

MODELO Se quedan unos días más. (desear)
→ Desean quedarse unos días más.

1. Se dan prisa. (deber)
2. ¿Te despiertas temprano? (ir a)
3. Manolo se prueba el traje. (acabar de)
4. Ud. se alimenta bien. (comenzar a)
5. Nos cuidamos lo más posible. (tratar de)
6. Se divierten mucho en la playa. (querer)
7. Me mantengo en forma. (tener que)
8. ¿Arturo no se pone en forma? (poder)
9. Las chicas se acatarran. (empezar)
10. Nos relajamos un poco. (necesitar)
11. ¿Te duchas por la mañana? (preferir)
12. Se instalan en el condominio. (lograr)

J **Reflexive Verbs: Expansion.** Expand each sentence using the verb + infinitive or verb + connector + infinitive construction. Use the verb that appears in parentheses. Write all sentences, following the word order in the *modelo*.

MODELO No te enfadas. (deber)
→ No te debes enfadar.

1. Me gradúo en junio. (ir a)
2. Se sientan cerca de nosotros. (querer)
3. El niñito se viste solo. (saber)
4. No se meten en todo. (deber)
5. Me reúno con Uds. la semana próxima. (preferir)
6. Nos apresuramos o perdemos el avión. (tener que)
7. Se ríen. (empezar a)
8. ¿Te casas con Federico? (pensar)
9. Nos vemos pronto. (esperar)
10. ¿Catalina se enamora? (volver a)
11. Se acuerda de la fecha. (acabar de)
12. Pablo se coloca en una empresa importante. (lograr)

Adverbs with the Suffix -mente

Most adverbs of manner in Spanish are formed by adding the suffix -**mente** to the feminine singular form of the adjective.

MASCULINE SINGULAR	FEMININE SINGULAR	ADVERB	MEANING
cómodo	cómoda	cómodamente	*comfortably*
cuidadoso	cuidadosa	cuidadosamente	*carefully*
generoso	generosa	generosamente	*generously*
lento	lenta	lentamente	*slowly*
nervioso	nerviosa	nerviosamente	*nervously*

If the adjective has only one form for the masculine and feminine singular, then the suffix -**mente** is added to that form.

SINGULAR	ADVERB	MEANING
fácil	fácilmente	*easily*
inteligente	inteligentemente	*intelligently*
regular	regularmente	*regularly*

Adverbs ending in -**mente** have two stresses in speech, one on the original stressed syllable of the adjective and one on the first **e** of the suffix -**mente**.

intelig**e**ntem**e**nte	*intelligently*
gener**o**sam**e**nte	*generously*

If the adjective itself has a written accent mark, the accent mark is retained when the suffix -**mente** is added.

difí**í**cilm**e**nte	*with difficulty*
r**í**gidam**e**nte	*rigidly*

Spanish often uses a phrase consisting of **con** + a noun instead of an adverb ending in -**mente**.

Lo hacen **con cuidado.**	*They do it* ***carefully.***
Ella se viste **con elegancia.**	*She dresses* ***elegantly.***
Trabajan **con entusiasmo.**	*They work* ***enthusiastically.***

Adverbs modify verbs or adjectives. They add the idea of time, place, quantity, doubt, or manner to the sentence. Adverbs of time, place, quantity, doubt, and manner are usually not derived from adjectives in Spanish or in English.

hoy *today*

No sé si vienen **hoy.**	*I don't know if they're coming* ***today.***

aquí *here*

Todos se reúnen **aquí.**	*Everyone gets together* ***here.***

mucho *a lot*

Ese hombre trabaja **mucho.**	*That man works* ***a lot.***

bien *well*
La niña lee **bien**. — *The little girl reads **well**.*

tal vez *perhaps*
Tal vez se arreglan. — ***Perhaps** they're getting ready.*

The masculine singular form of adjectives is often used as an adverb, especially in informal speech.

¿Es mejor jugar **feo** y ganar o jugar **bonito** y perder?	*Is it better to play **dirty** and win or play **fair** and lose?*
No te entienden porque no hablas **claro**.	*They don't understand you, because you don't speak **clearly**.*

K ***Adverbios.*** Write the adverb with the suffix **-mente** that is derived from each of the following adjectives.

1. hermoso
2. estupendo
3. inteligente
4. honrado
5. regular
6. alegre
7. nervioso
8. compulsivo
9. comercial
10. triste
11. cómodo
12. fácil
13. atento
14. arrogante
15. asustado

L ***Adverbios.*** Write the masculine singular form of the adjective (the base form) from which each adverb is derived.

1. perfectamente
2. generalmente
3. cuidadosamente
4. recientemente
5. últimamente
6. difícilmente
7. frecuentemente
8. rotundamente
9. pesadamente
10. fríamente
11. normalmente
12. graciosamente
13. pobremente
14. amablemente
15. tranquilamente

M Write the adverb ending in **-mente** that is equivalent to each of the following phrases with **con** + a noun.

1. con frecuencia
2. con claridad
3. con inteligencia
4. con dificultad
5. con alegría
6. con tranquilidad
7. con atención
8. con comodidad
9. con tristeza
10. con amabilidad
11. con arrogancia
12. con felicidad
13. con sinceridad
14. con oscuridad
15. con ruido

DIÁLOGO 6 · La rutina diaria

Study the dialogue, then listen to the recording and repeat each line.

PALOMA	¿Qué haces al despertarte por la mañana?
CARLOS	Me cepillo los dientes, me ducho, me visto y me peino.
PALOMA	Yo también, y me limpio los dientes dos veces—al despertarme y después de desayunar.
CARLOS	¿Te lavas el pelo todos los días? Yo sí.

Análisis

Check that you understand the linguistic breakdown of each speech from *Diálogo 6*.

¿Qué haces al despertarte por la mañana?	*What do you do when you wake up in the morning?*
al + *infinitive*	*when (doing something), upon (doing something)*
despertarse (**e** > **ie**)	*to wake up*
al despertarte	*when you wake up*
por la mañana	*in the morning*
Me cepillo los dientes, me ducho, me visto y me peino.	*I brush my teeth, I shower, I get dressed, and I comb my hair.*
cepillar	*to brush*
cepillarse los dientes	*to brush one's teeth*
ducharse	*to shower, take a shower*
vestirse (**e** > **i**)	*to get dressed*
peinarse	*to comb one's hair*
Yo también, y me limpio los dientes dos veces—al despertarme y después de desayunar.	*Me, too, and I brush my teeth twice—when I get up and after having breakfast.*
limpiar	*to clean*
limpiarse los dientes	*to brush one's teeth*
la vez	*time (occurrence)*
dos veces	*twice, two times*
después de + *infinitive*	*after (doing something)*
¿Te lavas el pelo todos los días? Yo sí.	*Do you wash your hair every day? I do.*
lavar	*to wash*
lavarse el pelo	*to wash one's hair*

Variantes

Listen, and repeat the same structures from *Diálogo 6*, now with new vocabulary.

¿Qué haces al despertarte?	*What do you do when you wake up?*
Al despertarme, me limpio los dientes.	*When I wake up, I brush my teeth.*
¿Qué hace Elena al levantarse?	*What does Elena do when she gets up?*
Al levantarse, se lava la cara.	*When she gets up, she washes her face.*

¿Qué hacen Uds. al reunirse?	*What do you do when you get together?*
Al reunirnos, nos ponemos a trabajar.	*When we get together, we begin to work.*
¿Qué vas a hacer al graduarte?	*What are you going to do when you graduate?*
Al graduarme, voy a colocarme en una empresa.	*When I graduate, I'm going to get a position in a company.*
¿Te limpias los dientes antes de desayunar?	*Do you brush your teeth before you have breakfast?*
Claro, y después de desayunar también.	*Of course, and after I have breakfast, too.*
Se duchan.	*They take a shower.*
Se bañan.	*They take a bath.*
Se afeitan.	*They shave.*
Se pintan.	*They put on makeup.*
Se pinta la cara.	*She puts on* ***makeup*** *(face).*
los labios	*lipstick (lips)*
las uñas	*nail polish (nails)*
Me cepillo los dientes.	*I brush* ***my teeth.***
el pelo	*my hair*
Te lavas el pelo.	***You wash*** *your hair.*
Te cortas	*You cut*
Te secas	*You dry*
Nos lavamos el pelo.	*We're washing* ***our hair.***
la cabeza	*our hair*
la cara	*our faces*
las manos	*our hands*
los pies	*our feet*

Estructura y Práctica

N ***Al levantarse por la mañana.*** Write sentences using reflexive verbs to describe what people do when they get up in the morning. Follow the *modelo.*

MODELO los niños / bañarse
→ Los niños se bañan.

1. tú / cepillarse los dientes
2. Pilar y yo / lavarse la cabeza
3. Roberto / afeitarse
4. Uds. / secarse el pelo
5. Ignacio / ponerse la ropa
6. yo / pasarse el hilo dental (*to floss*)
7. Marisol y Julieta / pintarse los labios
8. Ud. / ducharse

MORE VOCABULARY

El aseo personal (*personal grooming*): **productos de belleza y cuidado personal** (*beauty and personal care products*)

los aceites de baño *bath oils*
el acondicionador (para el pelo) *hair conditioner*
la afeitadora *razor*
el aftershave *aftershave (lotion)*
el agua de colonia *cologne*
el bronceador *suntan lotion*
el cepillo de dientes *toothbrush*
el cepillo para el pelo *hairbrush*
el champú *shampoo*
el cortaúñas *nail clippers*
la crema de afeitar *shaving cream*
la crema hidratante *moisturizing cream*
el depilatorio *depilatory, hair remover*
el desodorante *deodorant*
el enjuague (bucal) *mouthwash* (bucal < boca (*mouth*))
el esmalte de uñas *nail polish*
el hilo dental *dental floss*
la hoja de afeitar *razor blade*
el jabón *soap*
el lápiz para los labios *lipstick*
la lima de uñas *nail file*
la loción para después del afeitado *aftershave (lotion)*
el maquillaje *makeup*
la máquina (maquinilla) de afeitar *electric razor*
la pasta de dientes *toothpaste*
el peine *comb*
el perfume *perfume*
las pinzas *tweezers*
el protector solar *sunscreen*
la rasuradora *razor*
las sales de baño *bath salts*
el secador de pelo/cabello *hair dryer*
el suavizante (para el pelo) *hair conditioner*
el tinte para el cabello *hair coloring*

Al + Infinitive

The **al** + infinitive phrase can replace a clause beginning with **cuando** when the subjects of the two clauses are the same. Note that the **al** + infinitive phrase can occur either after the main clause or at the beginning of the sentence.

Siempre lo veo **cuando salgo**. Siempre lo veo **al salir**.	*I always see him when I go out.*
Cuando me levanto, me cepillo los dientes. **Al levantarme**, me cepillo los dientes.	*When I get up, I brush my teeth.*

Note that the English construction consisting of *upon* plus the *-ing* form of the verb is the equivalent of the Spanish **al** + infinitive phrase.

Al oír esto, me enfado.	***Upon hearing this***, *I get angry.*

This English construction, however, is typical of formal or literary language. The Spanish **al** + infinitive phrase is used in informal as well as formal language.

O ***Al*** **+ infinitive.** Rewrite each of the following sentences, replacing the clauses that begin with **cuando** with the **al** + infinitive construction. Write each sentence in two ways. Follow the *modelo.*

MODELO Cuando hablo con ese tipo, me molesto mucho.
→ Me molesto mucho al hablar con ese tipo.
→ Al hablar con ese tipo, me molesto mucho.

1. Cuando oigo música, me emociono mucho.
2. Cuando Mario sale de la oficina, va a casa.
3. Cuando te acuestas, ¿te duermes en seguida?
4. Cuando Eva sabe qué pasa, se enoja.
5. Cuando Uds. terminan de ducharse, se visten.
6. Cuando te despiertas, te limpias los dientes.
7. Cuando los niños llegan del parque, se bañan.
8. Cuando Ud. se levanta, ¿se lava el pelo?
9. Cuando me reúno con mis amigos, me divierto mucho.
10. Cuando vemos que todo está bien, nos tranquilizamos.

DIÁLOGO 7 · No se llevan bien.

Study the dialogue, then listen to the recording and repeat each line.

PALOMA Me fijo en que Javier y Pablo no se llevan bien últimamente.
CARLOS Tú conoces a Javier. Se enoja fácilmente y se ofende por cualquier cosa.
PALOMA Y Pablo lo enoja y lo ofende.
CARLOS En efecto. ¡Qué dos!

Análisis

Check that you understand the linguistic breakdown of each speech from *Diálogo 7.*

Me fijo en que Javier y Pablo no se llevan bien últimamente.	*I notice that Javier and Pablo aren't getting along lately.*
fijarse en	*to notice*
bien	*well, right*
llevarse bien	*to get along*
mal	*badly*
llevarse mal	*not to get along*
últimamente	*lately*

Tú conoces a Javier. Se enoja fácilmente y se ofende por cualquier cosa.	*You know Javier. He gets angry easily and takes offense at every little thing.*
enojar	*to anger*
enojarse	*to get angry*
fácilmente	*easily*
ofender	*to offend, insult*
ofenderse	*to get offended, get insulted*
la cosa	*thing*
cualquier	*any*
por cualquier cosa	*for any little thing*
Y Pablo lo enoja y lo ofende.	*And Pablo makes him angry and insults him.*
lo enoja	*angers him*
lo ofende	*offends him, insults him*
En efecto. ¡Qué dos!	*That's right. What a pair!*

Variantes

Listen, and repeat the same structures from *Diálogo 7*, now with new vocabulary.

¿En qué te fijas?	*What are you noticing?*
Me fijo en que se llevan mal.	*I'm noticing that they don't get along.*
Lo enoja.	*He makes him angry.*
Lo ofende.	*He insults him.*
Lo molesta.	*He annoys him.*
Lo preocupa.	*He worries him.*
Las tranquilizamos.	*We're calming them down.*
Las preocupamos.	*We're worrying them.*
Las animamos.	*We're encouraging them.*
Las asustamos.	*We're frightening them.*
Uds. se quejan de todo.	*You **complain about** everything.*
se ocupan de	*take care of*
se interesan en	*are interested in*
se meten en	*meddle in*
No se reúnen últimamente.	*They don't get together **lately**.*
recientemente	*recently*
generalmente	*generally*
normalmente	*normally*

Estructura y Práctica

Prepositions with Reflexive Verbs

You have learned many reflexive verbs that appear with certain prepositions. It is important to learn the prepositions that are used with specific reflexive verbs.

Nos acercamos **a** la carretera.	*We're approaching the highway.*
Se olvida **de** unas fechas importantes.	*He forgets some important dates.*

P **Prepositions.** Write the preposition that correctly completes each of the following sentences.

1. Ya nos despedimos ____________ los invitados.
2. ¿Por qué no te fías ____________ él?
3. Me pongo ____________ trabajar.
4. Nos interesamos ____________ la música clásica.
5. Beatriz se casa ____________ Esteban.
6. Nadie se atreve ____________ hablar del asunto.
7. ¿____________ qué se fijan?
8. Nunca se acuerda ____________ los cumpleaños.
9. Marco se compromete ____________ Sofía.
10. Siempre te quejas ____________ algo.
11. No te enamoras ____________ nadie, ¿verdad?
12. Nos alegramos ____________ verlos.
13. El perro se aleja ____________ la casa.
14. Daniel se ocupa ____________ la oficina.

DIÁLOGO 8 · Matricularse o graduarse

Study the dialogue, then listen to the recording and repeat each line.

PALOMA	Tengo que matricularme para el segundo semestre. Tú también, ¿no?
CARLOS	Nada de matrícula para mí. ¡Yo me gradúo en junio!
PALOMA	Felicidades, chico. Así que vas a despedirte de todos nosotros.
CARLOS	¡Qué va! Claro que nos vamos a mantener en contacto.

Análisis

Check that you understand the linguistic breakdown of each speech from *Diálogo 8*.

Tengo que matricularme para el segundo semestre. Tú también, ¿no?	*I have to register for the second semester. You do, too, don't you?*
matricularse	*to register (for classes)*
tengo que matricularme	*I have to register*
el semestre	*semester*
segundo	*second*
Nada de matrícula para mí. ¡Yo me gradúo en junio!	*No registration for me. I'm graduating in June!*
nada de + *noun*	*no* + noun, *none of* + noun
la matrícula	*registration*
graduarse	*to graduate*
yo me gradúo	*I graduate, I'm graduating*
Felicidades, chico. Así que vas a despedirte de todos nosotros.	*Congratulations, buddy. So you're going to say goodbye to all of us.*
felicidades	*congratulations*
chico	*man, buddy, guy* (interjection)
despedirse de uno	*to say goodbye to someone*
vas a despedirte	*you'll say goodbye*
todos nosotros	*all of us*
¡Qué va! Claro que nos vamos a mantener en contacto.	*Not true! Of course we will stay in touch with each other.*
¡Qué va!	*Are you kidding? / Not true! / Of course not!*
claro que + *verb*	*of course* + verb
el contacto	*contact*
mantenerse en contacto	*to keep in touch, stay in touch*

Variantes

Listen, and repeat the same structures from *Diálogo 8*, now with new vocabulary.

Tengo que matricularme.	*I have to* ***register****.*
inscribirme	*register*
suscribirme	*subscribe*
Es el primer año.	*It's the* ***first*** *year.*
segundo	*second*
tercer	*third*
cuarto	*fourth*
quinto	*fifth*
sexto	*sixth*
séptimo	*seventh*
octavo	*eighth*
noveno	*ninth*
décimo	*tenth*

Es la primera semana.	*It's the **first** week.*
segunda	*second*
tercera	*third*
cuarta	*fourth*
quinta	*fifth*
sexta	*sixth*
séptima	*seventh*
octava	*eighth*
novena	*ninth*
décima	*tenth*
¿Te gradúas este año?	*Are you graduating this year?*
No, me gradúo el año próximo.	*No, I'm graduating next year.*
¿Te despides de nosotros?	*Are you saying goodbye to us?*
Sí, ya me voy.	*Yes, I'm going away.*
Nos vamos a mantener en contacto.	*We're going to **stay in touch** (with each other).*
poner en contacto	*get in touch*

Estructura y Práctica

Ordinal Numbers

You learned about ordinal numbers in Chapter 2, where they were presented as a type of adjective that precedes the noun it modifies. Here is a review of the ordinal numbers in Spanish from first to tenth.

primero	*first*	sexto	*sixth*
segundo	*second*	séptimo	*seventh*
tercero	*third*	octavo	*eighth*
cuarto	*fourth*	noveno	*ninth*
quinto	*fifth*	décimo	*tenth*

NOTES

1 · The ordinals **primero** and **tercero** are shortened to **primer** and **tercer**, respectively, before a masculine singular noun.

el **primer** mensaje	*the **first** message*
el **tercer** mes	*the **third** month*

2 · The ordinal numbers, except for **primero**, are not used in giving the date. The cardinal numbers (**dos, tres, cuatro, cinco**, etc.) are used instead.

el **cuatro** de julio	*the **fourth** of July*
el **once** de enero	*January **eleventh***
el **veinticinco** de agosto	*August **twenty-fifth***
el **seis** de junio	*June **sixth***
el **veintinueve** de marzo	*March **twenty-ninth***

BUT

el **primero** de febrero — *February **first***

Some speakers say **el uno de febrero.**

3 · After *tenth*, Spanish usually uses the cardinal number in place of the ordinal.

Ellos viven en el piso **doce.** — *They live on the **twelfth** floor.*

Q **Ordinal numbers.** Replace the cardinal number with the ordinal number in each sentence. Follow the *modelo.*

MODELO Es la reunión número dos.
→ Es la segunda reunión.

1. Leemos el libro número cinco.
2. Juego en el partido número ocho.
3. Escribo el correo electrónico número seis.
4. Siguen el plan número tres.
5. Es la semana número siete del viaje.
6. Hacen la práctica número dos.
7. Tomas la clase a distancia número nueve.
8. Se reúnen el miércoles número uno del mes.
9. Es la vez número cuatro que los visitamos.
10. Es la conferencia número uno de la serie.
11. Es el año número diez de la empresa.
12. ¿Conoces a su hija número tres?

DIÁLOGO 9 · ¿Cuál es su nombre?

Study the dialogue, then listen to the recording and repeat each line.

PALOMA Señor, ¿cómo se llama Ud.?
JOSÉ Me llamo José Arias Herrera.
PALOMA Y su esposa, ¿cómo se llama?
JOSÉ Ella se llama Beatriz Paz Arroyo.

Análisis

Check that you understand the linguistic breakdown of each speech from *Diálogo 9.*

Señor, ¿cómo se llama Ud.? — *Sir, what is your name?*
llamarse — *to be called, be named*
se llama — *his/her/your name is*

Me llamo José Arias Herrera. me llamo	*My name is José Arias Herrera.* *my name is*
Y su esposa, ¿cómo se llama?	*And what is your wife's name?*
Ella se llama Beatriz Paz Arroyo.	*Her name is Beatriz Paz Arroyo.*

Variantes

Listen, and repeat the same structures from *Diálogo 9*, now with new vocabulary.

Y sus hijos, ¿cómo se llaman? Mi hijo se llama Miguel Arias Paz y mi hija se llama Maite Arias Paz.	*And what are your children's names?* *My son's name is Miguel Arias Paz and* *my daughter's name is Maite Arias Paz.*
Niño, ¿cómo te llamas? Me llamo Juanito Fuentes.	*Little boy, what's your name?* *My name is Juanito Fuentes.*

Estructura y Práctica

HISPANIC NAMES

Hispanic naming customs are different from those in the Anglo-Saxon world. Many Spanish speakers have compound first names: **Juan Carlos**, **Ana María**, **José Luis. María**, honoring the Virgin Mary, may appear as the second name in compound names for males as well as for females: **José María**. Women having one of these names are usually called by the latter part of the compound: **Carmen** for **María del Carmen**, **Dolores** for **María de los Dolores**.

Hispanic family names (*apellidos*) also have different patterns. In most Spanish-speaking countries, people use their mother's maiden name after their father's family name. Thus, if you meet someone named **Ricardo Solana Cabreras**, you can assume that **Solana** is his father's family name and **Cabreras** his mother's. For someone named **Susana Durán Ribera**, **Durán** would be her father's family name and **Ribera** her mother's maiden name. In most Spanish-speaking countries, women do not change their names when they marry. Sometimes, for more formal social purposes, **Susana Durán Ribera** would use her husband's name and would be called **Susana Durán de Solana**. The children of **Ricardo Solana Cabreras** and **Susana Durán Ribera** would be **Diego Solana Durán** and **Jimena Solana Durán.**

R ***¿Cómo se llama Ud.?*** Express the following dialogues in Spanish, using the correct forms of **llamarse**.

1. *Ma'am, what is your* (Ud.) *name?*
   My name is Isabel Ortega Castellanos.
2. *What is his name?*
   His name is Antonio Herrera Calderón.
3. *Little boy, what is your* (tú) *name?*
   My name is Juan Manuel Echevarría.
4. *What is her name?*
   Her name is Alicia Marqués Goya.

Un paso más

Are you ready to take your Spanish a step further? Here are exercises that will enhance your knowledge of the language and allow you to express yourself freely.

S **More reflexive verbs.** Select a verb from the list below to complete each of the following sentences. Write the form of the verb that correctly completes each one.

aprovecharse (de) *to take advantage of*
burlarse (de) *to make fun of*
callarse *to become quiet*
equivocarse (al) *to be wrong*
hacerse + *profession* *to become* + profession
mejorarse *to get better*
morirse (**o** > **ue**) *to die*
portarse bien/mal *to behave well/badly*

1. Los estudiantes ________________ cuando entra el profesor.
2. Berta ________________ al casarse con ese tipo.
3. Hace una semana que Paco está resfriado pero ya ________________.
4. Debemos ________________ de esta gran oportunidad.
5. Esteban ________________ ingeniero.
6. Están muy tristes porque su perro ________________.
7. Estos niños nos exasperan. Los tres ________________ mal.
8. Es muy feo ________________ de la gente.

T **Translation.** Express the following first person narratives in Spanish.

1. **La rutina diaria**

   My name is Gabriela Torres Ribera. Upon waking up, I brush my teeth, take a shower, and wash my hair. After I get dressed, I put on makeup and comb my hair. My husband Fernando showers, shaves, and gets dressed. After having breakfast, I dress the children and Fernando takes them to school. My husband and I leave for the office.

2. **Hago planes**

   My name is Antonio Lapesa Mondragón. I've just graduated from the university and I'm looking for a job. I'm an accountant. I hope to get a position with a large firm. I've also just gotten engaged. My fiancée Pilar, who is a web designer, wants to get married this year, but I think we shouldn't hurry. We have to work a few years in order to be able to buy a house. We don't worry because we love each other, we understand each other, and we always help each other. We know we'll be successful.

3. **Necesito cuidarme**

   My name is Mario Sánchez Vargas. I catch colds frequently. I've been feeling sick for six weeks. The doctor tells me I'm fine but that I should take better care of myself. That's why I'm going to start exercising. I want to get into shape. I'm going to jog and lift weights. I have to stop eating junk food and start to eat well. I know that I should relax more, go to bed earlier, and live more calmly. I'm going to get bored, but I'll feel great!

U ***Preguntas personales.*** Answer each question with a complete Spanish sentence.

1. ¿Cómo se llama Ud.?
2. ¿Está casado/casada? ¿Cómo se llama su esposo/esposa? (¿Piensa casarse? ¿Con quién?)
3. ¿Cómo se llaman sus amigos y colegas?
4. ¿Uds. se llevan bien? ¿Cuándo se ven (se hablan por teléfono, se escriben)?
5. ¿Ud. se mantiene en contacto con sus amigos de la universidad? ¿Se mandan textos o emails?
6. ¿Cómo es su rutina diaria?
7. ¿Qué productos de belleza y cuidado personal usa para su aseo personal?
8. ¿Qué hace para cuidarse bien y mantener una buena salud física y mental?
9. ¿En qué cosas o actividades se interesa mucho?
10. ¿Qué lo/la emociona (aburre, entusiasma, molesta, asusta, alegra, enoja)?
11. ¿Es Ud. quejumbroso/quejumbrosa (*a complainer*)? ¿De qué se queja? ¿Tiene aversión (*pet peeve*)? ¿A qué cosas?
12. ¿Ud. se matricula en la universidad? ¿En qué universidad? ¿Cuándo se gradúa?

9

Travel, Likes and Dislikes

Communication Goals

- Talking about past events
- Describing airplane, train, and car trips
- Talking about likes and dislikes
- Vocabulary: travel, the airport, traffic, cardinal points and geographical regions

Grammar Topics

- The Preterit Tense: Formation
- Preterit of **-er** and **-ir** Verbs with Stems Ending in a Vowel
- Preterit of Verbs with Stem Changes
- Irregular Preterits
- Preterit of Verbs with Spelling Changes
- The Indirect Object
- Reverse Construction Verbs
- Verbs with a Different Meaning in the Preterit

DIÁLOGO 1 · Un vuelo directo

Study the dialogue, then listen to the recording and repeat each line.

ROBERTO	¿Encontraste un vuelo a Madrid? ¿Pudiste reservar los billetes en línea?
SOFÍA	Sí, encontré un vuelo directo. Hice todos los trámites en línea.
ROBERTO	Menos mal. La última vez que viajamos tuvimos que hacer escala.
SOFÍA	¡Fue un viaje interminable! No nos gustó para nada.

Análisis

Check that you understand the linguistic breakdown of each speech from *Diálogo 1.*

¿Encontraste un vuelo a Madrid? ¿Pudiste reservar los billetes en línea?	*Did you find a flight to Madrid? Could you make the reservations online?*
encontrar (**o** > **ue**)	*to find*
encontraste	*you found*
el vuelo	*flight*
pudiste	*you could*
reservar	*to reserve*
el billete	*ticket*
la línea	*line*
en línea	*online*
Sí, encontré un vuelo directo. Hice todos los trámites en línea.	*Yes, I found a nonstop flight. I did the whole procedure online.*
encontré	*I found*
el vuelo directo	*nonstop flight*
hice	*I did*
el trámite	*step, procedure*
Menos mal. La última vez que viajamos tuvimos que hacer escala.	*That's fortunate. The last time we traveled, we had to make a stopover.*
menos mal	*that's fortunate, fortunately*
la vez	*time (occasion)*
último	*last*
viajamos	*we traveled*
tuvimos	*we had*
tuvimos que	*we had to*
la escala	*stopover*
hacer escala	*to make a stopover*
¡Fue un viaje interminable! No nos gustó para nada.	*It was an endless trip! We didn't like it at all.*
fue	*it was*
el viaje	*trip*
interminable	*endless*
un viaje interminable	*an endless trip*
gustó	*it was appealing*
nos	*to us, for us*
no nos gustó	*we didn't like it*
para nada	*(not) at all*

Variantes

Listen, and repeat the same structures from *Diálogo 1*, now with new vocabulary.

Encontré un vuelo directo.	***I found*** *a direct flight.*
Tomé	*I took*
Reservé	*I reserved*
Pedí	*I asked for*
Preferí	*I preferred*
Elegí	*I chose*
¿Pudiste reservar los billetes en línea?	*¿Did you manage* ***to reserve*** *the tickets online?*
comprar	*to buy*
pagar	*to pay for*
¿Hiciste los trámites en línea?	*Did you make the arrangements online?*
Sí, lo hice todo a través de internet.	*Yes, I did everything online.*
Viajamos a España.	***We traveled to*** *Spain.*
Regresamos a	*We went back to*
Volvimos a	*We went back to*
Conocimos	*We got to know*
Recorrimos	*We traveled around*
Tuvimos que hacer escala.	*We had to* ***make a stopover****.*
hacer vuelo de conexión	*make a connecting flight*
cambiar el vuelo	*change the flight*
Hicimos preparativos para el viaje.	*We* ***got ready for the trip****.*
un viaje	*took a trip*
las maletas	*packed*
escala en Barcelona	*made a stopover in Barcelona*
Fue un viaje interminable.	*It was* ***a very long trip****.*
un vuelo agotador	*an exhausting flight*
un avión grande	*a big airplane*
No nos gustó.	*We didn't like it.*
No nos importó.	*We didn't care about it. / We didn't mind it.*
No nos interesó.	*We weren't interested in it.*
No nos convino.	*It wasn't good for us.*
¿Te gustó el viaje?	*Did you like the trip?*
Sí, me gustó.	*Yes, I liked it.*
¿Te gustan los vuelos directos?	*Do you like direct flights?*
Sí, me gustan.	*Yes, I like them.*
¿Te gusta viajar?	*Do you like to travel?*
Sí, me gusta viajar.	*Yes, I like to travel.*
¿Les conviene viajar la semana próxima?	*Is it good for you to travel next week?*
No, no nos conviene.	*No, it's not good for us.*

Estructura y Práctica

The Preterit Tense: Formation

The preterit tense in Spanish is used to express completed actions in the past.

The preterit is signaled by sets of endings added to the verb stem. The characteristic feature of the preterit is that its endings are all stressed.

The preterit of **-er** and **-ir** verbs have the same endings. They differ from the preterit endings of the **-ar** verbs in having an **i** rather than an **a** as the characteristic vowel.

Here are the preterit conjugations of regular verbs.

comprar *to buy*		**vender** *to sell*		**escribir** *to write*	
compr**é**	compr**amos**	vend**í**	vend**imos**	escrib**í**	escrib**imos**
compr**aste**	compr**asteis**	vend**iste**	vend**isteis**	escrib**iste**	escrib**isteis**
compr**ó**	compr**aron**	vend**ió**	vend**ieron**	escrib**ió**	escrib**ieron**

Note that in the **nosotros** form of **-ar** and **-ir** verbs, the preterit forms are identical with those of the present tense.

PRESENT AND PRETERIT

compramos	*we buy* OR *we bought*
escribimos	*we write* OR *we wrote*

Context clarifies whether the verb form is in the present or preterit tense.

For **-er** verbs, the present and preterit forms are distinct.

PRESENT	PRETERIT
vend**emos** *we sell*	vend**imos** *we sold*

A **Preterit of regular verbs.** Write the preterit form of the verb that corresponds with each present tense form given.

1. trabaja
2. esperas
3. comprendemos
4. miro
5. imprimen
6. llevan
7. compra
8. comen
9. viajo
10. debes
11. corres
12. aprendo
13. bebe
14. abrimos
15. vende
16. manejo
17. escribe
18. regresamos
19. vives
20. toman

Preterit of -er and -ir Verbs with Stems Ending in a Vowel

-Er and **-ir** verbs whose stems end in a vowel change the endings -**ió** to -**yó** and -**ieron** to -**yeron**. These verbs also add a written accent to the -**i**- of the endings of the **tú, nosotros**, and **vosotros** forms of the preterit.

caer *to fall*

ca**í**	ca**ímos**
ca**íste**	ca**ísteis**
ca**yó**	ca**yeron**

leer *to read*

le**í**	le**ímos**
le**íste**	le**ísteis**
le**yó**	le**yeron**

construir *to build*

constru**í**	constru**ímos**
constru**íste**	constru**ísteis**
constru**yó**	constru**yeron**

oír *to hear*

o**í**	o**ímos**
o**íste**	o**ísteis**
o**yó**	o**yeron**

Verbs ending in -**guir** do not follow this pattern.

seguir *to follow*

seguí	seguimos
seguiste	seguisteis
siguió	siguieron

Preterit of Verbs with Stem Changes

In the preterit, there are no stem changes in -**ar** and -**er** verbs, even if they have a stem change in the present. (For more on stem-changing verbs, see Chapter 6.)

pensar *to think*

PRESENT		PRETERIT	
p**ie**nso	pensamos	pensé	pensamos
p**ie**nsas	pensáis	pensaste	pensasteis
p**ie**nsa	p**ie**nsan	pensó	pensaron

volver *to return*

PRESENT		PRETERIT	
v**ue**lvo	volvemos	volví	volvimos
v**ue**lves	volvéis	volviste	volvisteis
v**ue**lve	v**ue**lven	volvió	volvieron

-**Ir** verbs that have a change in the vowel of the stem in the present have a vowel change in the third person forms of the preterit. Verbs that change **e** > **ie** or **e** > **i** in the present have -**i**- in the third person singular and plural of the preterit. The verbs **morir** and **dormir** have -**u**- in the third person singular and plural of the preterit.

sentirse *to feel*

PRESENT		PRETERIT	
me s**ie**nto	nos sentimos	me sentí	nos sentimos
te s**ie**ntes	os sentís	te sentiste	os sentisteis
se s**ie**nte	se s**ie**nten	se s**i**ntió	se s**i**ntieron

pedir *to ask for*

PRESENT		PRETERIT	
p**i**do	pedimos	pedí	pedimos
p**i**des	pedís	pediste	pedisteis
p**i**de	p**i**den	p**i**dió	p**i**dieron

morir *to die*

PRESENT		PRETERIT	
m**ue**ro	morimos	morí	morimos
m**ue**res	morís	moriste	moristeis
m**ue**re	m**ue**ren	m**u**rió	m**u**rieron

dormir *to sleep*

PRESENT		PRETERIT	
d**ue**rmo	dormimos	dormí	dormimos
d**ue**rmes	dormís	dormiste	dormisteis
d**ue**rme	d**ue**rmen	d**u**rmió	d**u**rmieron

Irregular Preterits

A number of common verbs in Spanish have irregular preterit forms. Almost all of these verbs have the following characteristics.

1 · The preterit is formed from an irregular stem.

2 · The endings are those of **-er** and **-ir** verbs except in the first and third person singular forms: the **yo** and **él/ella/Ud.** forms.

3 · The **yo** and **él/ella/Ud.** forms are stressed on the stem, not on the endings.

4 · The ending for the **yo** form is **-e** and the ending for the **él/ella/Ud.** form is **-o**.

5 · In most cases, the irregular stem has the vowel **-i-** or **-u-**.

venir *to come*		**tener** *to have*		**hacer** *to do, make*	
vin**e**	vin**imos**	tuv**e**	tuv**imos**	hic**e**	hic**imos**
vin**iste**	vin**isteis**	tuv**iste**	tuv**isteis**	hic**iste**	hic**isteis**
vin**o**	vin**ieron**	tuv**o**	tuv**ieron**	hiz**o**	hic**ieron**

poder *to be able, can*	
pud**e**	pud**imos**
pud**iste**	pud**isteis**
pud**o**	pud**ieron**

poner *to put*	
pus**e**	pus**imos**
pus**iste**	pus**isteis**
pus**o**	pus**ieron**

andar *to walk*	
anduv**e**	anduv**imos**
anduv**iste**	anduv**isteis**
anduv**o**	anduv**ieron**

querer *to want, love*	
quis**e**	quis**imos**
quis**iste**	quis**isteis**
quis**o**	quis**ieron**

caber *to fit*	
cup**e**	cup**imos**
cup**iste**	cup**isteis**
cup**o**	cup**ieron**

saber *to know*	
sup**e**	sup**imos**
sup**iste**	sup**isteis**
sup**o**	sup**ieron**

The verbs **decir**, **traer**, and verbs ending in **-ducir** have preterit stems ending in **-j-**. In the **ellos/ellas/Uds.** form of these verbs, the ending is **-eron**, not **-ieron**.

decir *to say, tell*	
dij**e**	dij**imos**
dij**iste**	dij**isteis**
dij**o**	dij**eron**

traer *to bring*	
traj**e**	traj**imos**
traj**iste**	traj**isteis**
traj**o**	traj**eron**

conducir *to drive*	
conduj**e**	conduj**imos**
conduj**iste**	conduj**isteis**
conduj**o**	conduj**eron**

NOTES

1 · In the third person singular form of **hacer** in the preterit, the stem is spelled **hiz-** (**hizo**). The spelling change **c** > **z** before **o** retains the pronunciation /s/.

2 · Compound forms of the verbs **hacer** (**rehacer**, etc.), **poner** (**proponer**, etc.), **tener** (**mantener**, etc.), **traer** (**atraer**, etc.), **venir** (**convenir**, etc.) are conjugated in the same way as the main verb.

3 · The preterit of **hay** is **hubo**.

The verb **dar** is conjugated like an **-er**/**-ir** verb in the preterit. The preterit forms of **dar** and **ver** have no written accent marks.

dar *to give*	
di	**dimos**
diste	**disteis**
dio	**dieron**

ver *to see*	
v**i**	v**imos**
v**iste**	v**isteis**
v**io**	v**ieron**

The verbs **ser** (*to be*) and **ir** (*to go*) have identical conjugations in the preterit. Context usually clarifies which verb is intended.

ser *to be* / **ir** *to go*	
fui	fuimos
fuiste	fuisteis
fue	fueron

Preterit of Verbs with Spelling Changes

-**Ar** verbs whose stem ends in **c**, **g**, or **z** change those letters to **qu**, **gu**, and **c**, respectively, in the **yo** form of the preterit. These forms are regular in speech; the written changes in the **yo** form are in accordance with the rules of Spanish spelling. The following list includes verbs that you have learned through Chapter 9.

INFINITIVE	**yo** FORM OF THE PRETERIT
buscar	bus**qué**
colocar	colo**qué**
explicar	expli**qué**
sacar	sa**qué**
tocar	to**qué**
apagar	apa**gué**
entregar	entre**gué**
jugar	ju**gué**
llegar	lle**gué**
madrugar	madru**gué**
navegar	nave**gué**
pagar	pa**gué**
actualizar	actuali**cé**
almorzar	almor**cé**
analizar	anali**cé**
comenzar	comen**cé**
empezar	empe**cé**
organizar	organi**cé**
tranquilizar	tranquili**cé**

B ***Viajes.*** Rewrite each sentence, changing the verb from the present tense to the preterit. Follow the *modelo.*

MODELO Regresan a los Estados Unidos.
→ Regresaron a los Estados Unidos.

1. Subes al avión.
2. Prefiere un vuelo directo.
3. Viajamos a Ciudad de Panamá.
4. Voy al aeropuerto en taxi.
5. Hacen escala en Miami.
6. Saco mi tarjeta de embarque.
7. Facturan el equipaje.
8. Vuelve de Panamá el domingo.
9. Pago los billetes en línea.
10. ¿No puedes encontrar tu maleta?
11. Se abrochan el cinturón de seguridad.
12. Pierde el vuelo.
13. Llego a la terminal A.
14. ¡Es un viaje maravilloso!

DIÁLOGO 2 · En el aeropuerto

Study the dialogue, then listen to the recording and repeat each line.

SOFÍA	¿Te salió bien en el aeropuerto? ¿Nada de líos?
ROBERTO	Pan comido. Llegué temprano, facturé mi equipaje y saqué mi tarjeta de embarque.
SOFÍA	¿Luego seguiste a la puerta de embarque?
ROBERTO	Primero fui a comer algo y compré unas revistas.

Análisis

Check that you understand the linguistic breakdown of each speech from *Diálogo 2.*

¿Te salió bien en el aeropuerto? ¿Nada de líos?	*Did everything go all right for you at the airport? No problems?*
te	*to you*
le	*to him, to her, to you*
salirle bien/mal a uno	*to turn out well/badly for someone*
el aeropuerto	*airport*
nada de + *noun*	*no* + noun
el lío	*problem, complication, bit of trouble*
Pan comido. Llegué temprano, facturé mi equipaje y saqué mi tarjeta de embarque.	*Piece of cake. I got there early, checked my luggage, and got my boarding pass.*
pan comido	*easy as pie, piece of cake*
llegué	*I arrived*
facturar	*to check (baggage)*
facturé	*I checked*
el equipaje	*luggage*
sacar	*to take out, get*
saqué	*I got*
la tarjeta	*card*
el embarque	*boarding*
la tarjeta de embarque	*boarding pass*
¿Luego seguiste a la puerta de embarque?	*Then you went on to the boarding gate?*
luego	*then, after that*
seguir (**e** > **i**)	*to follow, continue on to*
seguiste	*you continued on to*
la puerta	*gate*
la puerta de embarque	*boarding gate*
Primero fui a comer algo y compré unas revistas.	*First I went to eat something, and I bought some magazines.*
primero	*first*
fui	*I went*
algo	*something*
compré	*I bought*
la revista	*magazine*

Variantes

Listen, and repeat the same structures from *Diálogo 2*, now with new vocabulary.

¿Te salió bien en el aeropuerto?	*Did it go smoothly for you at the airport?*
Sí, me salió muy bien.	*Yes, very smoothly (for me).*
¿Les salió bien en el aeropuerto?	*Did it go smoothly for you at the airport?*
Sí, nos salió muy bien.	*Yes, very smoothly (for us).*
¿Le salió bien en el aeropuerto?	*Did it go smoothly for him at the airport?*
Sí, le salió muy bien.	*Yes, very smoothly (for him).*
¿Le salió bien en el aeropuerto?	*Did it go smoothly for her at the airport?*
Sí, le salió muy bien.	*Yes, very smoothly (for her).*
Llegué temprano.	***I arrived** early.*
Fui	*I went*
Salí	*I left*
Vine	*I came*
Coloqué mi equipaje.	***I placed** my luggage.*
Busqué	*I looked for*
Saqué	*I took out*
Toqué	*I touched*
Fui a comer algo.	*I went to **eat** something.*
tomar	*have*
beber	*drink*
comprar	*buy*
buscar	*look for*
Compré unas revistas.	***I bought** some magazines.*
Leí	*I read*
Vi	*I saw*
Llegamos anoche.	*We arrived **last night**.*
ayer	*yesterday*
anteayer	*the day before yesterday*
la semana pasada	*last week*
el mes pasado	*last month*
el año pasado	*last year*
hace una semana	*a week ago*
hace un mes	*a month ago*
hace un año	*a year ago*
hace varios días	*several days ago*

Estructura y Práctica

The Indirect Object

The indirect object labels the secondary goal of the action of the verb. The primary goal is the direct object. The direct object is connected directly to the verb without the aid of a preposition. In Spanish, the indirect object is connected to the verb by the preposition **a** (usually *to* or *for* in English). Indirect objects almost always refer to people. (For more on direct object pronouns, see Chapter 7.)

For example, in the sentence *Michael sends an email,* the first goal of the action is *an email.* It is the direct object of the verb. A second goal can be added: *Michael sends an email to Emily.* In this sentence, *Emily* is the indirect object (the secondary goal of the action), joined to the verb *sends* by the preposition *to.* In English, the indirect object can also be placed before the direct object, and when this word order is used, the preposition *to* is omitted: *Michael sends Emily an email.*

Indirect Object Pronouns

Here are the indirect object pronouns in Spanish.

	SINGULAR	PLURAL
FIRST PERSON	me	nos
SECOND PERSON	te	os
THIRD PERSON	le	les

Note that the indirect object pronouns for first and second persons are the same as the corresponding direct object pronouns.

Position of Indirect Object Pronouns

Both direct object pronouns and indirect object pronouns follow the same rules for placement in the sentence.

Indirect object pronouns precede the conjugated verb.

Ella **me** trajo un lindo regalo.	*She brought* ***me*** *a lovely gift.*
Le escribí una vez por semana.	*I wrote to* ***him*** *once a week.*
No **les** mandamos nada.	*We didn't send* ***them*** *anything.*

In verb + infinitive constructions, the indirect object pronoun may precede the first verb or follow the infinitive. When it follows the infinitive, it is attached to it in writing. There is no difference in meaning.

Te quiero **mostrar** mi carro nuevo. Quiero **mostrarte** mi carro nuevo.	*I want to* ***show you*** *my new car.*
Les va a **decir** la verdad. Va a **decirles** la verdad.	*He's going to* ***tell them*** *the truth.*

Use of Indirect Object Pronouns with Indirect Object Nouns

In Spanish, an indirect object noun is usually accompanied by the corresponding indirect object pronoun.

Jaime **le** envió el texto **a Inés**.	*Jaime sent the text* ***to Inés****.*

Here are some additional examples.

Le contamos **a Magdalena** lo que pasó.	*We told* ***Magdalena*** *what happened.*
Les expliqué el problema **a mis colegas.**	*I explained the problem* ***to my colleagues****.*
Le voy a pedir un aumento de sueldo **al gerente**.	*I'm going to ask* ***the manager*** *for a raise.*

C **Indirect object pronouns.** Rewrite each of the following sentences, changing the indirect object pronoun based on the cue in parentheses. Follow the *modelo.*

MODELO Le escribió un texto. (a ellos)
→ Les escribió un texto.

1. Le mandó un email. (a mí)
2. Te expliqué mi idea. (a ella)
3. Me recordaron la fecha. (a nosotros)
4. Le entregó los documentos. (a Uds.)
5. Nos vendiste tu carro. (a él)
6. Les devolvimos el dinero. (a ti)
7. Le contó la historia. (a Ud.)
8. Me enseñaron la casa. (a ellas)

D **Indirect object pronouns.** Write sentences that have a verb in the preterit and an indirect object pronoun, using the elements given. Use the cue in parentheses to determine the indirect object pronoun. Follow the *modelo.*

MODELO ella / preguntar / la dirección (a ellos)
→ Ella les preguntó la dirección.

1. ellos / pedir / un favor (a nosotros)
2. tú / leer / un libro (a él)
3. yo / traer / el periódico (a Uds.)
4. nosotros / decir / lo que pasó (a ti)
5. Ud. / explicar / el plan (a ella)
6. él / regalar / unas flores (a mí)
7. ellas / hacer / una comida muy rica (a Ud.)
8. Uds. / dar / un regalo (a ellas)

E **Indirect object pronouns.** Write sentences that have a verb in the preterit, an indirect object (noun), and its corresponding indirect object pronoun, using the elements given. Follow the *modelo.*

MODELO él / enviar / un regalo / a sus papás
→ Él les envió un regalo a sus papás.

1. tú / entregar / el informe / al director
2. Manolo / mostrar / su nuevo apartamento / a sus amigos
3. yo / hacer / unas preguntas / al asesor

4. ellos / pedir / la cuenta / a la mesera
5. Daniela / servir / unas tapas / a los invitados
6. Uds. / dar / el software / al programador
7. ella / decir / la verdad / a su abogada
8. tú / escribir / un email / a tus abuelos
9. nosotros / vender / el coche / a nuestra vecina
10. los profesores / explicar / los problemas / a sus estudiantes

Reverse Construction Verbs

Reverse construction verbs usually appear with an indirect object pronoun. They are called reverse construction verbs because the English subject in equivalent sentences corresponds to the Spanish indirect object, and the English direct object corresponds to the subject of the corresponding Spanish sentence.

For instance, the verb **gustar** is the equivalent of English *to like*, but the structure of sentences containing **gustar** is very different from those containing *to like* in English.

In the following English sentence, the subject of the sentence is *I*: *I like this computer.* The noun phrase *this computer* is the direct object of the verb *like*. The Spanish equivalent of this sentence is **Me gusta esta computadora.** In the Spanish sentence, **me** is the indirect object of the verb **gustar**. The subject of the sentence is **la computadora**, and therefore the verb must be in the third person singular to agree with the subject.

Note that the verb changes to the third person plural when the subject is plural.

Me gustan estas computadoras.	*I like these computers.*

Reverse construction verbs are usually in third person singular or plural; they appear only rarely in first or second person.

When the subject of a reverse construction verb is an infinitive, the verb is in the third person singular.

Me gusta ver las noticias antes de acostarme.	***I like to watch*** *the news before going to bed.*
¿**Te interesa trabajar** en Chile?	***Are you interested in working*** *in Chile?*

Note that subject nouns used with **gustar** are usually preceded by the definite article or some other determiner. This can create ambiguity in the meaning of the sentence, as illustrated in the first example below.

Le gusta **el** helado.	*He likes ice cream.* (general statement) *He likes the ice cream.* (*what he's eating now*)
Nos gustan **los** documentales.	*We like documentaries.*

Here are some common reverse construction verbs. The phrase **a uno** represents the indirect object.

caerle bien/mal a uno *to like/dislike (usually a person)*
convenirle a uno *to be suitable for someone*
encantarle a uno *to love something*
entusiasmarle a uno *to be/get excited about something*
faltarle a uno *to be short of something, not have something*
fascinarle a uno *to charm/captivate someone, to love something*
hacerle falta a uno *to need something*
importarle a uno *to matter to someone*
interesarle a uno *to be interested in something*
quedarle a uno *to have something left*
sobrarle a uno *to have more than enough of something*
tocarle a uno *to be someone's turn*

Les cae bien su profesor.	***They like*** *their professor.*
Creo que **te conviene** esta universidad.	*I think this university* ***is good for you.***
Me encanta el café colombiano.	***I love*** *Colombian coffee.*
Nos entusiasmó mucho el partido.	***We got very excited about*** *the game.*
Le falta paciencia.	***He has no*** *patience.*
Nos fascina el teatro.	***We're captivated by*** *the theater.*
Me hace falta tu apoyo.	***I need*** *your support.*
¿**No te importa** el medio ambiente?	***Don't you care about*** *the environment?*
Me interesan los altibajos de la economía.	***I'm interested in*** *the fluctuations of the economy.*
¿Cuánto dinero **les queda**?	*How much money* ***do you have left?***
Me sobra trabajo.	***I have more than enough*** *work.*
A ti te toca ahora.	***It's your turn*** *now.*

To focus on the person involved in sentences with reverse construction verbs, a phrase consisting of the preposition **a** + prepositional pronoun is used.

A mí me importa el futuro, pero **a él**, nada.	*I care about the future, but* ***he*** *doesn't at all.*

Some reverse construction verbs can be used in other constructions with a difference in meaning.

REVERSE CONSTRUCTION	**A ella le falta** paciencia.	*She lacks patience.*
REGULAR CONSTRUCTION	**Ella falta** mucho a clase.	*She is often absent from class.*
REVERSE CONSTRUCTION	**Me quedó** poco dinero.	*I had little money left.*
REGULAR CONSTRUCTION	**Quedé** en verlo mañana.	*I agreed to see him tomorrow.*
REVERSE CONSTRUCTION	**Les toca** jugar ahora.	*It's their turn to play now.*
REGULAR CONSTRUCTION	**Ellos tocan** la guitarra.	*They play the guitar.*

F **Reverse construction verbs.** Rewrite each sentence, changing the subject from singular to plural. Make all necessary changes. Follow the *modelo.*

MODELO Le gusta la cámara.
→ Le gustan las cámaras.

1. Me interesa tu idea.
2. Les encanta esta novela.
3. Le falta una reservación.
4. Nos entusiasma el partido de béisbol.
5. Me gusta este concierto.
6. ¿Te cae bien el gerente?
7. Le queda un proyecto.
8. Nos hace falta otra computadora.
9. Les fascina aquella tienda de ropa.
10. ¿No te importa su problema?

G **Reverse construction verbs.** Rewrite each sentence, changing the verb from present to preterit. Follow the *modelo.*

MODELO Les sobra trabajo.
→ Les sobró trabajo.

1. Nos interesa esa película.
2. Le gustan los programas.
3. ¿Te cae mal este tipo?
4. Les hace falta más dinero.
5. Me encanta la obra de teatro.
6. Nos falta tiempo para terminar el proyecto.
7. Le queda el examen de química.
8. Les entusiasman las conferencias.

H **Translation.** Express each of the following sentences in Spanish, using a reverse construction verb in the preterit.

1. *I liked it.*
2. *She didn't care about them.*
3. *They loved it.*
4. *Did you* (tú) *need them?*
5. *It was good for them.*
6. *We were very interested in it.*
7. *You* (Uds.) *had more of them than you needed.*
8. *I was excited to see them.*
9. *They disliked him.*
10. *Was he interested in working in Europe?*
11. *We loved driving through the desert.*
12. *Did you* (tú) *mind going through security?*

I **Expansion of reverse construction verbs.** Expand each sentence by adding the **ir a** + infinitive construction to the reverse construction verb. Follow the *modelo.*

MODELO Le gusta la excursión.
→ Le va a gustar la excursión.

1. Nos interesan esos libros.
2. Le hace falta un mapa.
3. Les sobra comida.
4. Te caen bien nuestros amigos.
5. Me encanta viajar en tren.
6. No les importa llegar tarde.
7. Te conviene conocer al director de mercadeo.
8. Le toca jugar pronto.

DIÁLOGO 3 · A bordo del avión

Study the dialogue, then listen to the recording and repeat each line.

ROBERTO	Luego subí al avión y el auxiliar de vuelo me ayudó a colocar mi equipaje de mano arriba.
SOFÍA	Entonces te acomodaste en tu asiento. ¿Un asiento de ventana?
ROBERTO	No, un asiento de pasillo. Me abroché el cinturón de seguridad. A los quince minutos el avión despegó.

Análisis

Check that you understand the linguistic breakdown of each speech from *Diálogo 3.*

Luego subí al avión y el auxiliar de vuelo me ayudó a colocar mi equipaje de mano arriba.	*Then I got on the plane and the flight attendant helped me put my carry-on overhead.*
subir	*to go up, get on*
subí	*I got on*
subir al avión	*to get on the plane*
el auxiliar de vuelo	*flight attendant*
ayudar	*to help*
ayudó	*he/she helped*
colocar	*to place, put*
la mano	*hand*
el equipaje de mano	*hand luggage, carry-on (bag)*
arriba	*above, upstairs, overhead*
Entonces te acomodaste en tu asiento. ¿Un asiento de ventana?	*Then you settled into your seat. A window seat?*
acomodarse	*to get comfortable in, settle in(to)*
te acomodaste	*you settled into*
el asiento	*seat*
la ventana	*window*
el asiento de ventana	*window seat*
No, un asiento de pasillo. Me abroché el cinturón de seguridad. A los quince minutos el avión despegó.	*No, an aisle seat. I buckled my seatbelt. Fifteen minutes later, the plane took off.*
el pasillo	*aisle*
el asiento de pasillo	*aisle seat*
abrocharse el cinturón	*to buckle one's (seat)belt, fasten one's (seat)belt*
me abroché	*I buckled, I fastened*
me abroché el cinturón de seguridad	*I buckled my seatbelt, I fastened my seatbelt*
a los quince minutos	*fifteen minutes from then, fifteen minutes later*
despegar	*to take off*
despegó	*it took off*

Variantes

Listen, and repeat the same structures from *Diálogo 3*, now with new vocabulary.

¿Dónde colocó su equipaje de mano?	*Where did you put your carry-on bag?*
Lo coloqué arriba.	*I placed it above.*
Se acomodó en el asiento.	*She settled into **the seat**.*
el sofá	*the couch*
el sillón	*the armchair*
su cama	*her bed*
los brazos de su mamá	*her mother's arms*
Se abrochó el cinturón de seguridad.	*He fastened his seatbelt.*
Se desabrochó el cinturón de seguridad.	*He unfastened his seatbelt.*
El avión despegó.	*The plane took off.*
Dos horas después, el avión aterrizó.	*Two hours later, the plane landed.*
Me falta mi equipaje de mano.	*I'm missing my carry-on bag.*
Le faltan sus maletas.	*She's missing her suitcases.*
Me cayó bien el auxiliar de vuelo.	*I liked the flight attendant.*
Y yo le caí bien a él.	*And he liked me.*
A los auxiliares de vuelo les caen bien los pasajeros.	*The flight attendants like the passengers.*

DIÁLOGO 4 · El vuelo

Study the dialogue, then listen to the recording and repeat each line.

SOFÍA	¿Qué tal el vuelo? ¿Agradable? Yo sé que despegó con un poco de retraso.
ROBERTO	Ah sí, pero una vez en el aire, todo bien.
SOFÍA	¿Qué hiciste? ¿Te dormiste?
ROBERTO	No, pedí un vino, me puse los auriculares para oír música y leí unas revistas.

Análisis

Check that you understand the linguistic breakdown of each speech from *Diálogo 4*.

¿Qué tal el vuelo? ¿Agradable? Yo sé que despegó con un poco de retraso.	*How was the flight? Pleasant? I know that it took off a little late.*
el vuelo	*flight*
agradable	*pleasant*
un poco de	*a little, some*
el retraso	*delay*
un poco de retraso	*a little delay*
Ah sí, pero una vez en el aire, todo bien.	*Oh, yes, but once we were in the air, everything was fine.*
una vez	*once*
en el aire	*in the air, airborne*
todo bien	*everything is/was fine*

¿Qué hiciste? ¿Te dormiste?	*What did you do? Did you fall asleep?*
hiciste	*you did*
dormir (**o** > **ue**)	*to sleep*
dormirse (**o** > **ue**)	*to fall asleep*
te dormiste	*you fell asleep*
No, pedí un vino, me puse los auriculares para oír música y leí unas revistas.	*No, I ordered a glass of wine, put on the earphones to listen to music, and read some magazines.*
pedir (**e** > **i**)	*to order, ask for*
pedí	*I ordered*
puse	*I put*
me puse	*I put on*
los auriculares	*earphones*
leí	*I read*

Variantes

Listen, and repeat the same structures from *Diálogo 4*, now with new vocabulary.

Una vez en el aire, todo bien.	*Once we were **in the air**, everything was fine.*
en la tierra	*on the ground (landed)*
a bordo	*on board*
en la puerta de embarque	*at the gate*
¿Qué hiciste?	*What did you do?*
No hice nada.	*I didn't do anything.*
¿Qué dijiste?	*What did you say?*
No dije nada.	*I didn't say anything.*
¿Qué trajiste?	*What did you bring?*
No traje nada.	*I didn't bring anything.*
¿Qué viste?	*What did you see?*
No vi nada.	*I didn't see anything.*
¿Qué tuviste?	*What did you get?*
No tuve nada.	*I didn't get anything.*
¿Uds. se durmieron?	*Did you fall asleep?*
No, no nos dormimos.	*No, we didn't fall asleep.*
¿Se dieron prisa?	*Did you rush?*
No, no nos dimos prisa.	*No, we didn't rush.*
¿Se pusieron de pie?	*Did you stand up?*
No, no nos pusimos de pie.	*No, we didn't stand up.*
¿Se sintieron mareados?	*Did you feel dizzy?*
No, no nos sentimos mareados.	*No, we didn't feel dizzy.*
¿Se fueron?	*Did you go away?*
No, no nos fuimos.	*No, we didn't go away.*

¿Se perdieron?	*Did you get lost?*
No, no nos perdimos.	*No, we didn't get lost.*
Le pidió un vino.	***He asked her for** a glass of wine.*
Le sirvió	*He served her*
Le dio	*He gave her*
Le trajo	*He brought her*
Le ofreció	*He offered her*
Me puse los auriculares.	***I put on** the headphones.*
Me quité	*I took off*
¿Ud. leyó la revista?	*Did you read the magazine?*
Sí, la leí.	*Yes, I read it.*
¿Ud. oyó la música?	*Did you listen to the music?*
Sí, la oí.	*Yes, I listened to it.*
¿Ud. siguió el camino?	*Did you follow the path?*
No, no lo seguí.	*No, I didn't follow it.*

Estructura y Práctica

J ***El pretérito.*** Review the preterit of **-er** and **-ir** verbs with stems ending in a vowel, verbs with stem changes, and irregular preterits. Write the preterit form of the verb that corresponds with each present tense form given.

1. cree
2. construyo
3. leen
4. distribuimos
5. cuenta
6. vuelven
7. quiero
8. entendemos
9. comenzamos
10. llueve
11. piensas
12. digo
13. pueden
14. sé
15. traemos
16. viene
17. sigues
18. duermen
19. estoy
20. da
21. pongo
22. vamos
23. haces
24. son
25. pide
26. hay
27. conduzco
28. tienen
29. ves
30. prefiere

K ***Ya pasó.*** Write answers to each of the following questions, using a verb in the preterit to explain that the things being asked about already happened. For questions that include a direct object noun, change the noun to a pronoun in your answer. Follow the *modelo.*

MODELO ¿Miguel va a comer las enchiladas?
→ Ya las comió.

1. ¿Julia va a ver a sus primos?
2. ¿Ud. y sus colegas van a reunirse el miércoles?
3. ¿Ellos van a pedir el vino?
4. ¿Vas a matricularte para el segundo semestre?
5. ¿Ana va a casarse con su prometido?
6. ¿Uds. van a traer los documentos?
7. ¿Ud. va a comenzar el proyecto este mes?
8. ¿Ellos van a construir la casa?
9. ¿Vas a hacer los trámites para el viaje?
10. ¿Esteban va a ponerse en contacto contigo?
11. ¿Los empleados van a seguir las instrucciones?
12. ¿Ud. va a almorzar ahora?
13. ¿Uds. van a ir al museo de arte?
14. ¿Vas a buscar al gato?
15. ¿Marcos va a recoger el equipaje?

L ***Una narrativa.*** Write the correct preterit form of each of the following verbs in parentheses to learn about Daniel Arriaga's day.

La alarma de Daniel no (1) _______________ (sonar) esta mañana. Él (2) _______________ (asustarse) al ver la hora. Él (3) _______________ (levantarse), (4) _______________ (afeitarse), (5) _______________ (ducharse) y (6) _______________ (vestirse). (7) _______________ (Darse) prisa por llegar a la estación de tren. (8) _______________ (Llegar) a la oficina justo a tiempo (*just in time*). (9) _______________ (Correr) a la sala de conferencias donde (10) _______________ (tener) una reunión con su equipo de asesores.

DIÁLOGO 5 · Recuerdos: Viaje de vuelta a Estados Unidos

Study the dialogue, then listen to the recording and repeat each line.

ROBERTO	¿Te acuerdas del aterrizaje? Tomamos tierra en el aeropuerto de Filadelfia pero no nos dejaron bajar del avión por una hora.
SOFÍA	Ah sí, fue horrendo. Por fin pudimos bajar y fuimos a recoger nuestro equipaje.
ROBERTO	Luego pasamos por la aduana donde mostramos el pasaporte. Cogimos un taxi para irnos a casa.
SOFÍA	¡Qué jetlag tuvimos al día siguiente! ¡Y qué lindos recuerdos de nuestro viaje!

Análisis

Check that you understand the linguistic breakdown of each speech from *Diálogo* 5.

¿Te acuerdas del aterrizaje? Tomamos tierra en el aeropuerto de Filadelfia pero no nos dejaron bajar del avión por una hora.	*Do you remember the landing? We landed at the Philadelphia airport, but they didn't let us get off the plane for an hour.*
acordarse de (**o** > **ue**)	*to remember*
el aterrizaje	*landing*
tomar tierra	*to land, touch down*
el aeropuerto	*airport*
dejar	*to leave, let*
dejar a uno hacer algo	*to let someone do something*
dejaron	*they let*
no nos dejaron bajar	*they didn't let us get off*
bajar de	*to get off (a conveyance)*
bajar del avión	*to get off the plane*
por + *time expression*	*for/during* + a period of time
por una hora	*for an hour*

Ah sí, fue horrendo. Por fin pudimos bajar y fuimos a recoger nuestro equipaje.	*Oh, yes, it was horrible. We finally were able to get off and get our luggage.*
fue	*it was*
horrendo	*horrible, awful*
por fin	*finally*
pudimos	*we were able to*
fuimos	*we went*
recoger	*to pick up, get* (not used in all countries)
el equipaje	*luggage*
fuimos a recoger nuestro equipaje	*we went to get our luggage*

Luego pasamos por la aduana donde mostramos el pasaporte. Cogimos un taxi para irnos a casa.	*Then we went through customs, where we showed our passports. We took a cab to go home.*
luego	*then*
pasar por	*to go through*
pasamos	*we went through*
la aduana	*customs*
mostrar (**o** > **ue**)	*to show*
mostramos	*we showed*
el pasaporte	*passport*
coger	*to take, grab* (not used in all countries)
cogimos	*we took*
el taxi	*taxi*
para	*in order to*
irse	*to leave*
irse a	*to leave for, go to*
irse a casa	*to go home, leave for home, depart for home*
¡Qué jetlag tuvimos al día siguiente! ¡Y qué lindos recuerdos de nuestro viaje!	*What jet lag we had the next day! And what lovely memories of our trip!*
el jetlag	*jet lag*
tuvimos	*we had*
siguiente	*following*
al día siguiente	*the next day*
lindo	*pretty, lovely*
el recuerdo	*memory, remembrance*

Variantes

Listen, and repeat the same structures from *Diálogo 5*, now with new vocabulary.

¿Te acuerdas del aterrizaje?	*Do you remember* ***the landing****?*
del despegue	*the takeoff*
No nos dejaron bajar del avión.	*We weren't allowed* ***to get off the plane****.*
subir al avión	*to get on the plane*
Por fin pudimos bajar.	*Finally we could* ***get off****.*
subir	*get on*
sentarnos	*sit down*
ponernos de pie	*stand up*
prender el celular	*turn our cell phones on*
apagar el celular	*shut off our cell phones*
Pasamos por la aduana.	*We went/passed through* ***customs****.*
el control de seguridad	*security*
la terminal	*the terminal*
Le mostramos los pasaportes al aduanero.	*We showed our passports to the customs inspector.*

Les mostramos los pasaportes a los aduaneros.	*We showed our passports to the customs inspectors.*
Le entregué mi billete.	*I handed him my ticket.*
Él me entregó la tarjeta de embarque.	*He handed me my boarding pass.*

Estructura y Práctica

M ***Una narrativa.*** Write the correct preterit form of each of the following verbs in parentheses to learn about Isabel Rubio's trip.

El año pasado yo (1) ______________ (hacer) un viaje a Europa con mi esposo y mis dos hijos. Primero nosotros (2) ______________ (viajar) a Inglaterra donde (3) ______________ (pasar) una semana en Londres. Después (4) ______________ (tomar) el tren del Eurotúnel (del Canal de la Mancha) a Francia y (5) ______________ (quedarse) cinco días en París. Por fin nosotros (6) ______________ (llegar) a España donde (7) ______________ (tener) que quedarnos tres semanas porque tenemos mucha familia en Madrid. Claro que no (8) ______________ (poder) irnos sin verlos a todos. (9) ¡______________ (Ser) un viaje maravilloso!

DIÁLOGO 6 · Nuestro viaje al sudoeste

Study the dialogue, then listen to the recording and repeat each line.

SOFÍA	Hace dos años Juan, Pedro y yo alquilamos una furgoneta para recorrer el suroeste de Estados Unidos.
ROBERTO	Pedro me dijo que hicieron un viaje maravilloso. Se divirtieron mucho, ¿no?
SOFÍA	Como nunca. Vimos desiertos, montañas y cactos. ¡Qué paisajes más impresionantes!
ROBERTO	Creo que el suroeste te interesó mucho.

Análisis

Check that you understand the linguistic breakdown of each speech from *Diálogo 6.*

Hace dos años Juan, Pedro y yo alquilamos una furgoneta para recorrer el suroeste de Estados Unidos.	*Two years ago, Juan, Pedro, and I rented a station wagon to travel through the southwest United States.*
hace + *time expression* + *verb in preterit*	*ago*
hace dos años	*two years ago*
alquilar	*to rent*
alquilamos	*we rented*
la furgoneta	*station wagon*
recorrer	*to travel through*
el suroeste	*the southwest*

Pedro me dijo que hicieron un viaje maravilloso. Se divirtieron mucho, ¿no?	*Pedro told me that you had a wonderful trip. You had a very good time, didn't you?*
me	*to me, for me*
dijo	*he said, he told*
me dijo	*he told me*
que	*that* (subordinating conjunction)
me dijo que...	*he told me that . . .*
hicieron	*you made, you did*
hacer un viaje	*to take a trip*
hicieron un viaje	*you took a trip, you had a trip*
maravilloso	*wonderful*
se divirtieron	*you had a good time*
Como nunca. Vimos desiertos, montañas y cactos. ¡Qué paisajes más impresionantes!	*You can't imagine. We saw deserts, mountains, and cacti. What impressive scenery!*
como nunca	*you can't imagine*
vimos	*we saw*
el desierto	*desert*
la montaña	*mountain*
el cacto	*cactus*
el paisaje	*scenery, landscape*
impresionante	*impressive*
Creo que el suroeste te interesó mucho.	*I think you found the Southwest very interesting.*
el suroeste	*the Southwest*
te	*to you, for you*
interesó	*it interested*
te interesó	*it interested you*
te interesó mucho	*you found it very interesting*

Variantes

Listen, and repeat the same structures from *Diálogo 6*, now with new vocabulary.

Alquilamos una furgoneta.	***We rented*** *a van.*
Compramos	*We bought*
Manejamos	*We drove*
Condujimos	*We drove*
Recorrimos el suroeste.	*We toured* ***the Southwest****.*
el sur	*the South*
el oeste	*the West*
el norte	*the North*
el este	*the East*
el sudeste	*the Southeast*
el nordeste	*the Northeast*
el noroeste	*the Northwest*

El suroeste te interesó mucho, ¿no?	*You were very interested in the Southwest, weren't you?*
Sí, me encantó.	*Yes, I loved it.*
Me encantaron los paisajes. ¿Y a ti? A mí me encantaron también.	*I loved the landscapes. How about you? I loved them, too.*

Estructura y Práctica

N ***Una narrativa.*** Write the correct preterit form of each of the following verbs in parentheses to learn about a birthday party.

Mi amiga Sofía (1) ______________ (cumplir) veintisiete años ayer. Anoche yo (2) ______________ (asistir) a su fiesta de cumpleaños. Todos nosotros los invitados (3) ______________ (comer) platos riquísimos y (4) ______________ (beber) mucho vino. Sofía (5) ______________ (alegrarse) al abrir sus regalos. Yo le (6) ______________ (traer) flores y una linda cartera. A la una de la mañana, Javier (7) ______________ (tener) la idea de ir a un club de salsa. Todo el mundo (8) ______________ (entusiasmarse) mucho. Nosotros (9) ______________ (ir) a un club donde (10) ______________ (oír) música y (11) ______________ (bailar) hasta las cuatro de la mañana. ¡Nosotros (12) ______________ (divertirse) mucho!

DIÁLOGO 7 · Los viajes de negocios

Study the dialogue, then listen to the recording and repeat each line.

SOFÍA	¿Cuándo volvió de su viaje de negocios?
ROBERTO	Del viaje a la ciudad de México, el miércoles. Pero al día siguiente me fui de viaje otra vez. Esta vez viajé a Santiago de Chile.
SOFÍA	Conoció a los directores de la compañía, ¿verdad?
ROBERTO	Sí, y les expliqué nuestro plan de mercadeo. Todos los días madrugué y me acosté muy tarde. ¡Estoy agotado!

Análisis

Check that you understand the linguistic breakdown of each speech from *Diálogo* 7.

¿Cuándo volvió de su viaje de negocios?	*When did you get back from your business trip?*
volver de	*to come back from*
volvió	*you got back*
el viaje de negocios	*business trip*
Del viaje a la ciudad de México, el miércoles. Pero al día siguiente me fui de viaje otra vez. Esta vez viajé a Santiago de Chile.	*From my trip to Mexico City, on Wednesday. But the next day I left on another trip. This time I traveled to Santiago, Chile.*

la ciudad de México	*Mexico City*
al día siguiente	*next day*
irse de viaje	*to leave on a trip*
me fui	*I left*
viajar	*to travel*

Conoció a los directores de la compañía, ¿verdad? — *You met the directors of the company, didn't you?*

conoció	*you met*
el director	*director*
la compañía	*company*

Sí, y les expliqué nuestro plan de mercadeo. Todos los días madrugué y me acosté muy tarde. ¡Estoy agotado! — *Yes, and I explained our marketing plan to them. Every day I got up very early and went to bed very late. I'm exhausted!*

les	*to them*
explicar	*to explain*
expliqué	*I explained*
el plan	*plan*
el mercadeo	*marketing*
el plan de mercadeo	*marketing plan*
madrugar	*to get up very early*
madrugué	*I got up very early*
agotado	*exhausted*
estar agotado	*to be exhausted*

Variantes

Listen, and repeat the same structures from *Diálogo 7*, now with new vocabulary.

Viajaron a la ciudad de México.	***They traveled** to Mexico City.*
Volvieron	*They returned*
Fueron	*They went*
Vinieron	*They came*
Hicieron un viaje	*They took a trip*

Les expliqué nuestro plan de mercadeo.	***I explained** our marketing plan to them.*
mostré	*I showed*
traje	*I brought*
di	*I gave*

Les actualicé el plan de mercadeo.	***I updated** the marketing plan for them.*
organicé	*I organized*
escribí	*I wrote*
conseguí	*I got*

Me acosté.	*I **went to bed**.*
desperté	*woke up*
levanté	*got up*
coloqué	*got a job*
vestí	*got dressed*
tranquilicé	*stopped worrying*

Estructura y Práctica

O ***Una narrativa.*** Write the correct preterit form of each of the following verbs in parentheses to learn about Felipe and Blanca's life.

Felipe y Blanca (1) ______________ (estudiar) administración de empresas en la universidad. Ellos (2) ______________ (graduarse) hace siete años. Blanca (3) ______________ (colocarse) en una empresa de mercadeo y Felipe (4) ______________ (empezar) a trabajar en una compañía de software. Felipe y Blanca (5) ______________ (comprometerse) y al año siguiente (6) ______________ (casarse). Ellos (7) ______________ (comprar) una casa y (8) ______________ (tener) un hijo. ¡Son muy felices!

DIÁLOGO 8 · ¡Qué tráfico!

Study the dialogue, then listen to the recording and repeat each line.

SOFÍA ¡Qué embotellamiento! Nunca vamos a llegar a la estación. Creo que ya perdimos el tren.

ROBERTO No te preocupes. Yo descubrí un atajo el otro día. Y ya tenemos reservaciones.

SOFÍA Bueno, podemos sacar los boletos en la máquina. En la taquilla lleva más tiempo.

Análisis

Check that you understand the linguistic breakdown of each speech from *Diálogo 8*.

¡Qué embotellamiento! Nunca vamos a llegar a la estación. Creo que ya perdimos el tren.	*What a traffic jam! We'll never get to the station. I think we missed the train already.*
el embotellamiento	*traffic jam*
la estación	*station*
perder el tren	*to miss the train*
perdimos	*we missed*
No te preocupes. Yo descubrí un atajo el otro día. Y ya tenemos reservaciones.	*Don't worry. I discovered a shortcut the other day. And we already have reservations.*
preocuparse	*to worry*
no te preocupes	*don't worry*
descubrir	*to discover*
descubrí	*I discovered*
la reservación	*reservation*
Bueno, podemos sacar los boletos en la máquina. En la taquilla lleva más tiempo.	*Well, we can buy the tickets from the machine. It's faster than at the ticket window.*
sacar	*to take out*
sacar los boletos	*to buy the tickets, get the tickets*
la máquina	*machine*

la taquilla	*box office, ticket window*
llevar más tiempo	*to take more time*
En la taquilla lleva más tiempo.	(literally) *At the ticket window, it takes more time.*

Variantes

Listen, and repeat the same structures from *Diálogo 8*, now with new vocabulary.

Tomé un atajo en las horas punta.	*I took a shortcut at rush hour.*
Nos faltó tiempo.	*We didn't have enough time.*
Nos sobró tiempo.	*We had more than enough time.*
¿Cuánto dinero le falta?	*How much money is he short?*
Le faltan mil dólares.	*He's a thousand dollars short.*
Nos queda mucho dinero. ¿Y a ti?	*We have a lot of money left. How about you?*
A mí también.	*I do, too.*
¿Les hacen falta los boletos?	*Do you need the tickets?*
Sí, nos hace falta comprarlos.	*Yes, we need to buy them.*

DIÁLOGO 9 · Una excursión a Toledo

Study the dialogue, then listen to the recording and repeat each line.

ROBERTO Hicimos una excursión de Madrid a Toledo. Tomamos el tren de alta velocidad y llegamos en media hora.

SOFÍA Vieron la casa y la pintura de El Greco, ¿verdad?

ROBERTO Claro. Para eso fuimos. Además, conocimos las iglesias, las sinagogas y El Alcázar. Y caminamos por las espléndidas calles medievales.

Análisis

Check that you understand the linguistic breakdown of each speech from *Diálogo 9*.

Hicimos una excursión de Madrid a Toledo. Tomamos el tren de alta velocidad y llegamos en media hora.	*We took a trip from Madrid to Toledo. We took the high-speed train and got there in half an hour.*
hicimos	*we did, we made*
la excursión	*tour, trip*
la velocidad	*speed*
alta velocidad	*high speed*
media hora	*half hour*
Vieron la casa y la pintura de El Greco, ¿verdad?	*You saw El Greco's house and paintings, didn't you?*
vieron	*you saw*
la pintura	*painting, paintings*

Claro. Para eso fuimos. Además, conocimos las iglesias, las sinagogas y El Alcázar. Y caminamos por las espléndidas calles medievales.	*Of course. That's why we went. In addition, we visited the churches, the synagogues, and the Alcázar. And we walked along the splendid medieval streets.*
para eso	*for that purpose*
fuimos	*we went*
Para eso fuimos.	*That's why we went.*
además	*besides, in addition*
conocimos	*we visited* (of places)
la iglesia	*church*
la sinagoga	*synagogue*
El Alcázar	*El Alcázar (fortress overlooking Toledo)*
caminamos	*we walked*
por	*through, along*
medieval	*medieval*

Variantes

Listen, and repeat the same structures from *Diálogo 9*, now with new vocabulary.

Para eso fuimos.	*That's why* ***we went****.*
volvimos	*we returned*
vinimos	*we came*
salimos	*we left*
No conoció nada.	*She didn't become familiar with anything.*
No supo nada.	*She didn't find out anything.*
¿A quién le van a gustar estas calles medievales?	*Who is going to like these medieval streets?*
A mí.	*I am.*
¿A quiénes les va a interesar esta pintura?	*Who is going to be interested in this painting?*
A ellos.	*They are.*

Estructura y Práctica

P **Translation: Reverse construction verbs.** Express the following sentences in Spanish, using reverse construction verbs. Note that the verbs have a noun or an infinitive as the subject.

1. *They're short one aisle seat.*
2. *They have three window seats left.*
3. *It's your* (Ud.) *turn to pass through customs.*
4. *It's not good for us to make a stopover.*
5. *I like these flight attendants.*
6. *Does he need to get his boarding pass?*
7. *You* (tú) *like to travel by plane, but I love to take the high-speed train!*

Verbs with a Different Meaning in the Preterit

Some verbs take on a different meaning when they are used in the preterit. The distinction in meaning will be especially important when you study the difference between the preterit tense and the imperfect tense, which are two ways of looking at past time. (See Chapters 10 and 11.) In the case of the following verbs, when used in the preterit they focus on the beginning or completion of an action. For example, **supe** means *I began to know,* that is, *I found out.*

VERB	SPANISH	ENGLISH
saber *to know*	Supe su nombre hoy.	*I found out his name today.*
conocer *to know*	Los conocimos ayer.	*We met them yesterday.*
tener *to have*	Tuvo una idea.	*He got an idea.*
poder *to be able to*	¿No pudiste verla?	*Didn't you manage to see her?*
querer *to want*	No quiso ir.	*He refused to go.*

Q **Verbs with a different meaning in the preterit.** Express each of the following sentences in Spanish, using a verb from the list above.

1. *We managed to tour six countries.*
2. *I finally found out their address.*
3. *He got a great idea.*
4. *The passenger* [fem.] *refused to shut off her cell phone.*
5. *Did you* (tú) *manage to check your luggage?*
6. *When did you* (tú) *meet Mr. and Mrs. Díaz?*

Un paso más

Are you ready to take your Spanish a step further? Here are exercises that will enhance your knowledge of the language and allow you to express yourself freely.

R **Compound nouns.** Select a noun in the second column that forms a compound noun with a noun in the first column. Join the nouns with the preposition **de** and then write each compound noun with its definite article.

1. viaje	a. embarque
2. asiento	b. seguridad
3. auxiliar	c. negocios
4. puerta	d. conexión
5. equipaje	e. mano
6. control	f. vuelo
7. vuelo	g. mercadeo
8. tren	h. ventana
9. plan	i. alta velocidad

S ***Diálogos.*** Express the following dialogues about travel in Spanish.

1. *We took a trip to Chile five years ago.*
   It was an exhausting flight, wasn't it?
2. *The plane took off, and twenty minutes later, I unbuckled my seatbelt.*
   And I settled into my seat and fell asleep immediately.
3. *Did you* (tú) *like the scenery in the Southwest?*
   Yes, I loved it. We drove through the desert and saw impressive cactuses.
4. *Did you* (Uds.) *have to make a stopover?*
   No, it was a direct flight.
5. *What did you* (Ud.) *do when you got off the plane?*
   I picked up my luggage and went through customs.
6. *Did you* (tú) *show your passport at the gate?*
   No, but I handed the boarding pass to the young woman.
7. *Did you* (Ud.) *check your suitcase?*
   No, the flight attendant put it in the overhead compartment (el compartimiento de arriba).
8. *What a traffic jam! We're going to miss our flight.*
   Nonsense! I know a shortcut.

T ***Preguntas personales.*** Answer each question with a complete Spanish sentence.

1. ¿Qué cosas o actividades te gustan?
2. ¿Qué te importa más que nada en la vida? ¿Por qué?
3. ¿Te gusta viajar? ¿Por qué?

U ***Una narrativa personal.*** Write a personal narrative in Spanish about a plane, train, or car trip you took, using words and expressions from Chapter 9. Use the following questions as a guide.

1. ¿Fue un viaje de vacaciones o de negocios?
2. ¿Qué preparativos y trámites hiciste?
3. ¿Adónde fuiste?
4. ¿Cuándo fuiste?
5. ¿Cómo viajaste?
6. ¿Con quiénes viajaste?
7. ¿Hiciste turismo? ¿Qué viste?
8. ¿Qué comiste? ¿Te gustó la comida?
9. ¿El viaje te salió bien/mal? Explica (*Explain*).

10

Childhood, Family History, University

Communication Goals

- Talking about time, weather, and repeated actions in the past
- Talking about what you did as a child and your family history
- Telling about pre-Columbian peoples and the pyramids in Mexico
- Vocabulary: childhood memories, university, working in a restaurant, immigrants

Grammar Topics

- The Imperfect Tense
- Long-form Possessive Adjectives
- The Passive Voice
- **Se** Construction
- Double Object Pronouns
- The Reflexive Pronoun as Indirect Object
- Imperfect vs. Preterit: Two Aspects of Past Time
- Double Object Pronouns in Verb + Infinitive Constructions
- Verbs with Different Meanings in Imperfect and Preterit
- Expressions with **dar**
- **Hacía** + Expression of Time + **que** + Verb in Imperfect Tense
- Preterit and Imperfect in Indirect Discourse (Reported Speech)

DIÁLOGO 1 · Cuando yo era niño...

Study the dialogue, then listen to the recording and repeat each line.

JOSÉ Cuando yo era niño, mi familia y yo íbamos al mar todos los veranos. ¿Cómo pasabas tú los veranos?

ELENA Cuando yo era niña, mis papás me llevaban de viaje. Yo conocía las grandes capitales del mundo.

JOSÉ Disfrutabas de unas vacaciones muy interesantes.

ELENA Y las vacaciones tuyas eran muy tranquilas y relajadas.

Análisis

Check that you understand the linguistic breakdown of each speech from *Diálogo 1*.

Cuando yo era niño, mi familia y yo íbamos al mar todos los veranos. ¿Cómo pasabas tú los veranos?	*When I was a child, my family and I used to go to the seashore every summer. How did you spend the summers?*
era	*I was*
el niño	*child*
la familia	*family*
mi familia	*my family*
íbamos	*we used to go*
el mar	*sea*
el verano	*summer*
todos los veranos	*every summer*
pasar	*to spend (time)*
pasabas	*you spent, you used to spend*
Cuando yo era niña, mis papás me llevaban de viaje. Yo conocía las grandes capitales del mundo.	*When I was a child, my parents took me traveling. I visited the great capitals of the world.*
la niña	*child*
mis papás	*my parents* (especially in Spanish America)
llevar	*to take (someone somewhere)*
llevar a uno de viaje	*to take someone on a trip*
llevaban	*they used to take*
me llevaban de viaje	*used to take me traveling*
conocer + *place*	*to visit* + place
yo conocía	*I visited*
la capital	*capital city*
el mundo	*world*

Disfrutabas de unas vacaciones muy interesantes.	*You had very interesting vacations.*
disfrutar de algo	*to enjoy something*
disfrutabas	*you enjoyed, you had*
las vacaciones	*vacation* (always plural in Spanish)
interesante	*interesting*
Y las vacaciones tuyas eran muy tranquilas y relajadas.	*And your vacations were very calm and relaxed.*
las vacaciones tuyas	*your vacation*
tranquilo	*quiet, calm*
relajado	*relaxed*

Variantes

Listen, and repeat the same structures from *Diálogo 1*, now with new vocabulary.

Íbamos al mar todos los veranos.	***We went** to the seashore every summer.*
Viajábamos	*We traveled*
Manejábamos	*We drove*
Conducíamos	*We drove*
Las vacaciones tuyas eran tranquilas.	***Your** vacation was restful.*
mías	*My*
suyas	*His, Her, Your, Their*
nuestras	*Our*

Estructura y Práctica

The Imperfect Tense

The forms of the imperfect tense are almost entirely regular. Two sets of endings are used, one for **-ar** verbs and another for **-er** and **-ir** verbs. **-Ar** verbs have **-aba-** in all forms; **-er** and **-ir** verbs have **-ía-** in all forms.

tomar *to take; to drink*	
tom**aba**	tom**ábamos**
tom**abas**	tom**abais**
tom**aba**	tom**aban**

comer *to eat*	
com**ía**	com**íamos**
com**ías**	com**íais**
com**ía**	com**ían**

vivir *to live*	
viv**ía**	viv**íamos**
viv**ías**	viv**íais**
viv**ía**	viv**ían**

NOTES

1 · The first and third person singular forms are identical for all verbs in the imperfect: **yo/él/ella/Ud. hablaba/aprendía/escribía.**

2 · For **-ar** verbs, the **nosotros** form is the only one with a written accent: **hablábamos.**

3 · For **-er** and **-ir** verbs, all forms have a written accent over the **-í-** of the imperfect ending.

4 · The imperfect of **hay** is **había** (*there was, there were*).

Only the verbs **ser**, **ir**, and **ver** are irregular in the imperfect.

ser *to be*	
era	éramos
eras	erais
era	eran

ir *to go*	
iba	íbamos
ibas	ibais
iba	iban

ver *to see*	
veía	veíamos
veías	veíais
veía	veían

Uses of the Imperfect

The imperfect tense is used to express an event or action going on in the past without any reference to its beginning or end. Therefore, it is the tense used to express repeated actions in past time. Adverbs and adverbial phrases such as **todos los días**, **siempre**, and **muchas veces** are often clues for the selection of the imperfect rather than the preterit.

The imperfect is therefore also the tense used for description and expressing background in the past. Common English equivalents for the Spanish imperfect are *used to do, was doing.*

¿**Jugabas** al tenis todos los días? — ***Did you play** tennis every day?*
No, **jugaba** solamente los sábados. — *No, **I** only **played** on Saturdays.*

¿Qué tiempo **hacía**? — *What **was** the weather like?*
Hacía calor y **estaba** nublado. — ***It was** warm and (**it was**) cloudy.*

The imperfect tense is used to tell what time it was in the past. The preterit is never used in this function. (See *Diálogo 14* in this chapter.)

¿Qué hora **era**? — *What time **was it**?*
Eran las tres de la tarde. — ***It was** 3:00 P.M.*

The imperfect tense is used in indirect discourse, or reported speech (reporting what someone said), after the preterit form of verbs such as **decir** and **escribir**. (See *Diálogo 17* in this chapter.)

¿Qué te **dijo** Mario? — *What **did** Mario **tell** you?*
Me **dijo** que **volvía** tarde. — ***He told** me **he was coming back** late.*

¿Le **escribiste** a Carmen? — ***Did** you **write** to Carmen?*
Sí, le **escribí** que **me mudaba**. — *Yes, **I wrote** her that **I was moving**.*

(For the presentation of the preterit tense, see Chapter 9. For an explanation of the imperfect vs. the preterit, see *Diálogo 5* of this chapter.)

A Write the imperfect form of the verb that corresponds with each present tense form given.

1. hablo
2. comen
3. escribimos
4. son
5. crees
6. tengo
7. vuelven
8. sé

9. dices
10. ve
11. vienen
12. hay
13. tomamos
14. hago
15. vives
16. puede
17. quieren
18. pide
19. voy
20. juegas
21. suben
22. entiendo
23. leemos
24. damos
25. estoy
26. pongo
27. piensan
28. almuerzas
29. sigo
30. construye

B ***¿Qué hacían?*** Write the imperfect form of the verb in parentheses that correctly completes each of the following sentences. Follow the *modelo*.

MODELO Ella *abría* las cajas. (abrir)

1. Ellos ________________ en una tienda de deportes. (trabajar)
2. ¿Tú ________________ las grandes capitales? (recorrer)
3. Él ________________ a ir de vacaciones en agosto. (ir)
4. Nosotros ________________ en mi oficina. (reunirse)
5. ________________ muy buen tiempo. (Hacer)
6. Yo ________________ unos pájaros hermosos. (ver)
7. Esos inmigrantes ________________ de origen griego. (ser)
8. Uds. ________________ comida sana. (servir)
9. Ella nos ________________ una foto de su familia. (enseñar)
10. No ________________ tren hasta las cuatro de la tarde. (haber)
11. Les ________________ el mar. (encantar)
12. Ella y yo ________________ un paseo todas las tardes. (dar)
13. Los niños ________________ ir al jardín zoológico, ¿verdad? (querer)
14. Yo ________________ una clase a distancia. (tomar)
15. Tú ________________ aprovechar las ofertas de enero, ¿verdad? (pensar)
16. ¿Ud. ________________ jugar al fútbol? (saber)
17. Nos ________________ merendar al aire libre. (gustar)
18. La abuela ________________ a sus nietecitas. (vestir)
19. Los Sánchez ________________ en pleno centro. (vivir)
20. Nosotros no ________________ de acuerdo con ellos. (estar)

C ***Todos los días.*** Rewrite each sentence in the imperfect, adding the adverb or adverbial phrase of frequency in parentheses. Follow the *modelo.*

MODELO Jorge se despierta a las siete. (todos los días)
→ Jorge se despertaba a las siete todos los días.

1. Yo me reúno con mis amigos. (todos los domingos)
2. ¿Uds. van a la sierra? (todos los inviernos)
3. María Elena almuerza con nosotros. (cada semana)
4. Rodrigo y yo asistimos a un concierto. (todas las semanas)
5. ¿No puedes hacer un viaje? (cada año)
6. Les doy muchos regalos. (todos los años)
7. Se divierten mucho en las fiestas. (siempre)
8. Los chicos ven ese programa. (a menudo)

Long-form Possessive Adjectives

Most Spanish speakers don't stress possessive adjectives to contrast them the way we do in English.

He likes ***his*** *computer, not* ***my*** *computer.*
Your *house is bigger than* ***their*** *house.*

In order to stress possessive adjectives, Spanish uses long-form possessives. These consist of the definite article + noun + long-form possessive. All the long-form possessive adjectives agree with the noun in gender and number.

el boleto **mío**	la oficina **mía**	el boleto **nuestro**	la oficina **nuestra**
los boletos **míos**	las oficinas **mías**	los boletos **nuestros**	las oficinas **nuestras**
el boleto **tuyo**	la oficina **tuya**	el boleto **vuestro**	la oficina **vuestra**
los boletos **tuyos**	las oficinas **tuyas**	los boletos **vuestros**	las oficinas **vuestras**
el boleto **suyo**	la oficina **suya**	el boleto **suyo**	la oficina **suya**
los boletos **suyos**	las oficinas **suyas**	los boletos **suyos**	las oficinas **suyas**

A prepositional phrase beginning with **de** can replace forms of **suyo** to provide a focus on the person referred to.

el boleto de él / de ella / de Ud. / de ellos / de ellas / de Uds.
los boletos de él / de ella / de Ud. / de ellos / de ellas / de Uds.

In noun phrases with long-form possessive adjectives, the indefinite article, a demonstrative adjective, or a numeral can replace the definite article.

una oficina nuestra	*an office of ours*
estos boletos suyos	*these tickets of yours*
dos amigos míos	*two friends of mine*

(For possessive adjectives, see Chapter 2.)

D ***¿De quién es?*** Write phrases using long-form possessive adjectives to tell whose items these are. Follow the *modelo*.

MODELO el billetero (él)
→ el billetero suyo

1. los maletines ______________ (nosotros)
2. el cartapacio ______________ (yo)
3. las cámaras ______________ (ellos)
4. el gorro ______________ (Ud.)
5. el celular ______________ (tú)
6. el abrigo ______________ (ella)
7. las tarjetas de crédito ______________ (Uds.)
8. el coche ______________ (él)
9. la cartera ______________ (yo)
10. la pintura ______________ (nosotras)
11. los aretes (*earrings*) ______________ (tú)
12. la casa de campo ______________ (Uds.)

E Express the following phrases in Spanish, using long-form possessive adjectives. Follow the *modelo*.

MODELO *that farm of his*
→ esa finca suya

1. *these reports of yours* (tú)
2. *three friends* [fem.] *of hers*
3. *an apartment of theirs*
4. *an idea of mine*
5. *these problems of yours* (Uds.)
6. *that car of his*
7. *a company of ours*
8. *some plans of yours* (Ud.)
9. *this watch of mine*
10. *that sister-in-law of hers*

DIÁLOGO 2 · En la finca

Study the dialogue, then listen to the recording and repeat each line.

JOSÉ Todos los años mi esposa y yo llevábamos a nuestros hijos a una finca.
ELENA Me imagino que a los niños les gustaba ver los animales.
JOSÉ Sí, muchísimo. Había vacas, caballos, gallinas, cabras y ovejas.
ELENA Supongo que toda la comida fue cultivada en la finca misma. ¡Qué vida más sana!

Análisis

Check that you understand the linguistic breakdown of each speech from *Diálogo 2.*

Todos los años mi esposa y yo llevábamos a nuestros hijos a una finca.	*Every year, my wife and I used to take our children to a farm.*
todos los años	*every year*
llevábamos	*we used to take*
los hijos	*children*
a nuestros hijos	*our children*
la finca	*farm*
Me imagino que a los niños les gustaba ver los animales.	*I imagine that the children liked to see the animals.*
imaginarse	*to imagine*
me imagino	*I imagine*
a los niños	*the children*
les gustaba	*they liked*
les gustaba ver	*they liked to see*
el animal	*animal*
Sí, muchísimo. Había vacas, caballos, gallinas, cabras y ovejas.	*Yes, very much. There were cows, horses, chickens, goats, and sheep.*
muchísimo	*very much*
había	*there was, there were*
la vaca	*cow*
el caballo	*horse*
la gallina	*hen, chicken*
la cabra	*goat*
la oveja	*sheep*
Supongo que toda la comida fue cultivada en la finca misma. ¡Qué vida más sana!	*I suppose that all the food was grown right there on the farm. What a healthy life!*
suponer	*to suppose* (conjugated like **poner**)
supongo	*I suppose*
la comida	*food*
toda la comida	*all the food*
cultivar	*to grow* (transitive)
fue cultivada	*was grown*
mismo	*the very* (when it follows the noun)
en la finca misma	*on the very farm, on the farm itself, right there on the farm*
la vida	*life*
sano	*healthy*
¡Qué vida más sana!	*What a healthy life!*

Variantes

Listen, and repeat the same structures from *Diálogo 2*, now with new vocabulary.

Comían comida sana.	***They ate** healthy food.*
Pedían	*They ordered*
Servían	*They served*
Hacían	*They made*
Cocinaban	*They cooked*
Preparaban	*They prepared*
La comida fue cultivada por el agricultor.	***The food was grown** by the farmer.*
Las papas fueron cultivadas	*The potatoes were grown*
El maíz fue cultivado	*The corn was grown*
Los frijoles fueron cultivados	*The beans were grown*

Estructura y Práctica

F ***Una narrativa.*** Write the correct imperfect form of each of the following verbs in parentheses to create a narrative.

Habla Ricardo. Cuando yo (1) ________________ (ser) niño, mis hermanos y yo (2) ________________ (ir) a una finca que (3) ________________ (quedar) en la sierra. A veces a mis papás les (4) ________________ (gustar) tomar las vacaciones en verano, a veces (5) ________________ (preferir) tomarlas en invierno. Es que nos (6) ________________ (encantar) los deportes de verano y también los de invierno. Cuando (7) ________________ (hacer) calor, nosotros (8) ________________ (nadar) en el río y cuando (9) ________________ (nevar), nosotros (10) ________________ (esquiar). En verano, yo (11) ________________ (montar) a caballo todos los días. Mi caballo favorito (12) ________________ (llamarse) Campeón. A mis hermanos menores les (13) ________________ (fascinar) darles de comer a los animales.

POSITION OF ADJECTIVES

In Chapter 2, you learned that some adjectives can appear either before or after the noun and that the meaning changes depending on the position of the adjective.

In *Diálogo 2*, **en la finca misma** is translated as *right there on the farm, on the farm itself.* If the adjective **mismo** precedes the noun—**en la misma finca**—the meaning changes to *on the same farm.* Here are some other examples.

cierta tradición	*a certain tradition*	una cosa **cierta**	*a sure thing*
un **gran** hombre	*a great man*	un hombre **grande**	*a large man*
esa **pobre** gente	*those poor people (unfortunate)*	esa gente **pobre**	*those poor people (lacking money)*
la **única** persona	*the only person*	una persona **única**	*a unique person*

The Passive Voice

The passive voice in Spanish consists of a form of **ser** + the past participle. In Spanish, the past participle agrees in gender and number with the subject of the sentence. Similarly, English forms the passive voice with a form of the auxiliary verb *to be* + the past participle.

You will learn about the past participle in Chapter 13. For now, it is enough to know that for regular verbs, the past participle in Spanish ends in **-do**. (Some irregular verbs have past participles ending in **-to** or **-cho**.)

The past participle consists of the following elements:

verb stem + { the vowel **a** for **-ar** verbs / the vowel **i** for **-er** and **-ir** verbs } + **-do**

tomar	tom + a + do →	**tomado**	*taken*
comer	com + i + do →	**comido**	*eaten*
vivir	viv + i + do →	**vivido**	*lived*

La computadora **fue reparada** ayer.	*The computer **was fixed** yesterday.*
Los archivos **fueron descargados** ya.	*The files **were downloaded** already.*
El informe no **fue recibido**.	*The report **was** not **received**.*
¿**Fueron pagadas** las cuentas?	***Were** the bills **paid**?*

The passive voice sometimes uses an agent phrase beginning with **por**.

Los cheques **fueron cobrados**.	*The checks **were cashed**.*
Los cheques **fueron cobrados por el contador**.	*The checks **were cashed by the accountant**.*

The passive is used to move the focus of the sentence to the direct object of the verb by making it the subject. The passive voice thus deemphasizes the performer of the action.

El jefe despidió **a los empleados**. → **Los empleados** fueron despedidos por el jefe.
La profesora explicó **el problema**. → **El problema** fue explicado por la profesora.

The passive voice is much more common in English than in Spanish. Spanish prefers the **se** construction to remove the focus from the performer of the action. (See *Diálogo 3* in this chapter.)

G **Passive voice.** Write the preterit form of **ser** + the past participle (verb in parentheses) that correctly completes each of the following sentences in the passive voice. Note the agent phrase in each sentence. Follow the *modelo.*

MODELO La cena *fue preparada* por el cocinero. (preparar)

1. Los cuartos ________________ por el pintor. (pintar)
2. La computadora ________________ por el programador. (prender)
3. Las cartas ________________ por el secretario. (entregar)
4. El condominio ________________ por los señores Ayala. (vender)
5. Los niños ________________ por sus papás. (acostar)

6. El pescado ______________________ por el mesero. (servir)
7. Las manzanas ______________________ por el agricultor. (cultivar)
8. La empresa ______________________ por mis abuelos. (fundar)
9. Los problemas ______________________ por los abogados del bufete. (discutir)
10. El maletín ______________________ por el auxiliar de vuelo. (subir)
11. Los empleados ______________________ por el gerente. (despedir)
12. La canción ______________________ por la soprano. (cantar)

H ***La voz pasiva.*** Rewrite each of the following sentences, changing the active construction to a passive construction. Follow the *modelo.*

MODELO Raúl grabó las canciones.
→ Las canciones fueron grabadas por Raúl.

1. El director firmó los papeles.
2. La doctora Vega explicó la teoría.
3. Los asesores terminaron el informe.
4. Los turistas italianos tomaron las fotos.
5. Un amigo mío diseñó mi sitio web.
6. Consuelo cosió el botón.
7. Los estudiantes aprendieron todas las fechas.
8. El desarrollador de programas entró los datos.
9. El equipo peruano ganó el partido.
10. Guillermo prendió la tele.

DIÁLOGO 3 · De vacaciones en Costa Rica

Study the dialogue, then listen to the recording and repeat each line.

ELENA Uds. hacían ecoturismo en Costa Rica durante el verano, ¿verdad?
JOSÉ Sí. Recorríamos varias selvas tropicales donde había una gran cantidad de mariposas hermosas.
ELENA ¿Visitaban los cafetales?
JOSÉ Desde luego. Veíamos cómo se producía el café. Nos interesaba mucho.

Análisis

Check that you understand the linguistic breakdown of each speech from *Diálogo 3*.

Uds. hacían ecoturismo en Costa Rica durante el verano, ¿verdad?	*You used to do ecotourism in Costa Rica during the summer, didn't you?*
hacer turismo	*to go sightseeing*
hacer ecoturismo	*to do ecotourism*
hacían	*used to do*
durante	*during*
el verano	*summer*
¿verdad?	*didn't you?*

Sí. Recorríamos varias selvas tropicales donde había una gran cantidad de mariposas hermosas.	*Yes, we traveled around several tropical jungles where there was a large number of beautiful butterflies.*
recorrer	*to travel around, travel through*
recorríamos	*we traveled around*
varios	*several*
la selva	*jungle*
tropical	*tropical*
la cantidad	*quantity*
una gran cantidad de	*a large amount of, a large number of*
la mariposa	*butterfly*
hermoso	*beautiful*
¿Visitaban los cafetales?	*Did you (use to) visit the coffee plantations?*
visitaban	*you used to visit*
el cafetal	*coffee plantation*
Desde luego. Veíamos cómo se producía el café. Nos interesaba mucho.	*Of course. We would see how coffee was produced. We were very interested in that.*
desde luego	*of course*
veíamos	*we would see, we used to see*
cómo	*how*
producir	*to produce*
se produce el café	*coffee is produced*
se producía el café	*coffee was produced*
interesarle a uno	*to be interested in something*
nos interesaba	*we were interested in it*

Variantes

Listen, and repeat the same structures from *Diálogo 3*, now with new vocabulary.

Recorríamos una selva tropical.	***We traveled around** a tropical forest.*
Visitábamos	*We visited*
Veíamos	*We saw*
¿Visitaban los cafetales?	***Did you visit** the coffee plantations?*
Veían	*Did you see*
Recorrían	*Did you travel around*
Se producía petróleo.	*They produced oil.*
Se producía vino.	*They produced wine.*
Se producían automóviles.	*They produced cars.*
Se producían productos petroquímicos.	*They produced petrochemical products.*
Se habla español en Costa Rica.	*Spanish is spoken in Costa Rica.*

¿Cómo se dice *coffee plantation* en español?	*How do you say "coffee plantation" in Spanish?*
Se dice "cafetal".	*You say* cafetal.
¿Cómo se deletrea la palabra "verano"?	*How do you spell the word* verano?
Se escribe ve chica, e, ere, a, ene, o.	*It's written v, e, r, a, n, o.*
Se come bien en esta ciudad.	*You eat well in this city.*
Se comen granos integrales.	*You eat whole grains.*
Se debe comer granos integrales.	*You should eat whole grains.*
Uno se divierte mucho en Madrid.	*People have a great time in Madrid.*
Nos interesaba.	***We were interested in** it.*
Nos gustaba.	*We liked*
Nos encantaba.	*We loved*
Nos fascinaba.	*We were fascinated by*
Nos entusiasmaba.	*We were enthusiastic about*

Estructura y Práctica

Se Construction

To understand the **se** construction, it is important to understand the difference between the subject of the sentence and the performer of the action. Subject is a grammatical category. The subject of a sentence determines the ending of the verb.

Usually, the subject is also the performer of the action, but not always. In the examples below, the subjects of the sentences are the nouns *water* and *meat.*

The water boiled.
The meat was cooking.

The performers of the actions, however, are left unspecified.

Spanish removes the focus from the performer of the action by using the **se** construction. The **se** construction consists of the pronoun **se** and the third person singular or plural of the verb, depending on whether the grammatical subject is singular or plural. The usual translation of the **se** construction in English is the passive voice.

Se terminó el proyecto.	*The project was finished.*
Se toman unas decisiones importantes.	*Important decisions are made.*
Se vendieron las computadoras viejas.	*The old computers were sold.*
Se va a construir una carretera.	*A highway is going to be built.*

For intransitive verbs, the verb is always third person singular in the **se** construction.

Se vive bien en esta ciudad.	*People live well in this city. / You live well in this city.*
¿Por dónde se sale?	*Where is the exit?*

When an intransitive infinitive is the subject of the **se** construction, the verb is third person singular.

Se puede salir por aquí. — *You can go out this way.*
Se debe manejar con cuidado. — *One should drive carefully.*

If the verb has a reflexive **se**, then the **se** construction cannot be used. **Uno** is used instead.

Uno se divierte mucho en Barcelona. — *People have a great time in Barcelona.*
Uno no se aburre en esta ciudad. — *People don't get bored in this city.*
Uno se debe cuidar bien. — *You should take good care of yourself.*

The agent phrase with **por** cannot be used in the **se** construction.

I ***Se* construction.** Rewrite each sentence using the **se** construction + verb in the present tense. Follow the *modelos*.

MODELOS Recorren el país.
→ Se recorre el país.
Recorren los países.
→ Se recorren los países.

1. Visitan la zona histórica.
2. Sacas fotos.
3. Cultiva verduras.
4. Hago turismo.
5. Resolvemos el problema.
6. Oímos música.
7. Realizan el proyecto.
8. Produzco vinos.
9. Servimos platos vegetarianos.
10. Ves mariposas.

J ***Se* construction with intransitive verbs.** Rewrite each sentence using the **se** construction + verb in the present tense. Follow the *modelo*.

MODELO Entran por la puerta principal.
→ Se entra por la puerta principal.

1. Navegamos en la red.
2. Abren a las nueve y media.
3. Vivimos muy bien en nuestro país.
4. Hablamos por celular.
5. Trabajan de lunes a jueves.
6. Salimos para el centro.
7. Suben en el ascensor.
8. Llegan a la puerta de embarque.
9. Manejan con cuidado.
10. Bajamos en la escalera mecánica.

K ***Se* construction.** Rewrite each of the following sentences, expanding each sentence with a **se** construction by adding the verb in parentheses. Follow the *modelo*.

MODELO Se baja del avión. (necesitar)
→ Se necesita bajar del avión.

1. Se cambia el vuelo. (poder)
2. Se sube a la pirámide. (permitir)
3. No se come comida basura. (deber)
4. Se apaga el celular. (necesitar)
5. No se ve nada por la niebla. (poder)
6. No se fuma en este edificio. (permitir)
7. Se deja una propina. (deber)
8. Se pasa por el control de seguridad. (necesitar)

DIÁLOGO 4 · Las fotos del cafetal

Study the dialogue, then listen to the recording and repeat each line.

JOSÉ	¿No ibas a enseñarme las fotos del cafetal?
ELENA	Naturalmente. Te las enseño ahora mismo.

Análisis

Check that you understand the linguistic breakdown of each speech from *Diálogo 4.*

¿No ibas a enseñarme las fotos del cafetal?	*Weren't you going to show me the photos of the coffee plantation?*
ibas	*you were going*
enseñar	*to show*
enseñarme	*to show me*
ibas a enseñarme	*you were going to show me*
la foto	*photo*
Naturalmente. Te las enseño ahora mismo.	*Of course. I'll show them to you right now.*
te las	*them to you*
te las enseño	*I'll show them to you*
ahora mismo	*right now*

Variantes

Listen, and repeat the same structures from *Diálogo 4*, now with new vocabulary.

¿Las fotos? Te las enseño.	*The photos? I'll show them to you.*
¿La foto? Te la enseño.	*The photo? I'll show it to you.*
¿El regalo? Te lo enseño.	*The gift? I'll show it to you.*
¿Los regalos? Te los enseño.	*The gifts? I'll show them to you.*
¿Ibas a enseñarme el cafetal?	*Were you going to show me the coffee plantation?*
Sí, quería enseñártelo antes, pero te fuiste.	*Yes, I was going to show it to you before, but you left.*

Estructura y Práctica

Double Object Pronouns

In standard English, direct and indirect object pronouns do not occur together. When a direct and indirect object are present in the same sentence, the indirect object must appear in a prepositional phrase.

*I give it **to him**.*

In this sentence, *it* is the direct object and *to him* is the indirect object in a prepositional phrase.

In Spanish, however, an indirect object pronoun and a direct object pronoun always appear together when they are dependent on the same verb. The indirect object pronoun precedes the direct object pronoun. Here are the possible combinations with a first or second person indirect object pronoun.

me lo, me la	*it to me*	**nos lo, nos la**	*it to us*
me los, me las	*them to me*	**nos los, nos las**	*them to us*
te lo, te la	*it to you*	**os lo, os la**	*it to you*
te los, te las	*them to you*	**os los, os las**	*them to you*

The indirect object pronouns of the third person, **le** and **les**, change to **se** before the direct object pronouns.

le/les + lo → se lo	le/les + la → se la
le/les + los → se los	le/les + las → se las

se lo, se la	*it to him / to her / to you / to them / to you* (plural)
se los, se las	*them to him / to her / to you / to them / to you* (plural)

If speakers need to focus on the person **se** refers to, they add a phrase beginning with the preposition **a.**

Se lo presté **a ella,** no **a él.**	*I lent it* ***to her,*** *not* ***to him.***
Él se los pidió **a Ud.**	*He asked* ***you*** *for them.*

L **Double object pronouns.** Rewrite each sentence, changing the direct object noun to a pronoun. Make all necessary changes. Retain the original tense of the verb. Follow the *modelo.*

MODELO Le explicaba la idea.
→ Se la explicaba.

1. Les enseñábamos el cafetal.
2. Te consigo los billetes.
3. Le cuenta la historia.
4. Me trajeron las flores.
5. Le entregué el pasaporte.
6. Nos mostraban sus fotos.
7. Les mandabas los informes.
8. Les sirvió la torta.
9. No le presta el dinero.
10. Me enviaba las cartas.

The Reflexive Pronoun as Indirect Object

Certain reflexive verbs can appear with direct objects. Most of these verbs express actions that have an effect on articles of clothing or parts of the body. (For reflexive verbs, see Chapter 8.)

ponerse + *article of clothing*	*to put on*
probarse (**o** > **ue**) + *article of clothing*	*to try on*
quitarse + *article of clothing*	*to take off*
romperse + *article of clothing*	*to tear*
lavarse + *part of the body*	*to wash*
quemarse + *part of the body*	*to burn*
romperse + *part of the body*	*to break*

For these verbs, the reflexive pronoun **se** is an indirect object, not a direct object.

Remember that an indirect object pronoun and a direct object pronoun always appear together if they are dependent on the same verb. The indirect object pronoun precedes the direct object pronoun.

Me puse los zapatos.	*I put on my shoes.*
Me los puse.	*I put them on.*
Se lavó el pelo.	*She washed her hair.*
Se lo lavó.	*She washed it.*
Se quitaron la chaqueta.	*They took off their jackets.*
Se la quitaron.	*They took them off.*

In English, the equivalent of the indirect object reflexive pronoun is usually a possessive adjective.

Se lavó el pelo.	*She washed **her** hair.*

Spanish uses a singular noun for articles of clothing and parts of the body, even with plural subjects. It is assumed that each person has one item, unless the item comes in pairs like shoes or gloves, in which case Spanish uses a plural noun.

Se quitaron **la chaqueta**.	*They took off **their jackets**.*
Se quitaron **los guantes**.	*They took off **their gloves**.*

M **Double object pronouns and reflexive verbs.** Write a response to each question, changing the direct object noun to a pronoun. Make all necessary changes. Retain the tense of the question in your answer. Follow the *modelo.*

MODELO ¿Pedro se lavaba las manos?
→ Sí, se las lavaba.

1. ¿Te pusiste la camisa nueva?
2. ¿Inés se prueba las botas?
3. ¿Los pasajeros se abrocharon el cinturón de seguridad?
4. ¿Alfonso se corta el pelo?
5. ¿Uds. se cepillaban los dientes?
6. ¿Tus amigas se maquillan la cara?
7. ¿El jugador se rompió el tobillo?
8. ¿Ud. se secó el pelo?

DIÁLOGO 5 · Las pirámides

Study the dialogue, then listen to the recording and repeat each line.

JOSÉ Las pirámides de San Juan de Teotihuacán fueron construidas por los aztecas, ¿verdad?

ELENA No, chico, las pirámides ya estaban cuando los aztecas fundaron su imperio en Tenochtitlán, hoy Ciudad de México.

JOSÉ Pues eso no lo sabía. ¿Quién las construyó entonces?

ELENA Los toltecas.

Análisis

Check that you understand the linguistic breakdown of each speech from *Diálogo 5.*

Las pirámides de San Juan de Teotihuacán fueron construidas por los aztecas, ¿verdad?	*The pyramids in San Juan de Teotihuacán were built by the Aztecs, weren't they?*
la pirámide	*pyramid*
San Juan de Teotihuacán	*San Juan de Teotihuacán* (*town northeast of Mexico City where the Pyramid of the Sun and Pyramid of the Moon are located*)
construir	*to build*
fueron construidas	*they were built*
los aztecas	*Aztecs* (*the most advanced pre-Columbian culture in Mexico at the time of the Spanish conquest; Aztec empire overthrown by Hernán Cortés in 1520*)
No, chico, las pirámides ya estaban cuando los aztecas fundaron su imperio en Tenochtitlán, hoy Ciudad de México.	*Well, no, the pyramids were already there when the Aztecs founded their empire in Tenochtitlán, today (known as) Mexico City.*
chico	*boy* (used as interjection)
estar	*to be there, exist*
ya estaban	*they were already there*
fundar	*to found*
el imperio	*empire*
Pues eso no lo sabía. ¿Quién las construyó entonces?	*Well, I didn't know that. Then who built them?*
eso	*that* (neuter demonstrative pronoun)
sabía	*I knew*
construyó	*built*
Los toltecas.	*The Toltecs.*
los toltecas	*Toltecs* (*indigenous people of Mexico, in decline by the thirteenth century*)

Variantes

Listen, and repeat the same structures from *Diálogo 5,* now with new vocabulary.

Me interesaban las pirámides.	***I was interested in*** *the pyramids.*
Me gustaban	*I liked*
Me encantaban	*I loved*
Me fascinaban	*I was fascinated by*
Me entusiasmaban	*I was enthusiastic about*
Las pirámides fueron construidas por los toltecas.	*The pyramids were built by the Toltecs.*
La Gran Muralla fue construida por los chinos.	*The Great Wall was built by the Chinese.*

El Coliseo fue construido por los romanos.	*The Coliseum was built by the Romans.*
Los Jardines Colgantes fueron construidos por los babilonios.	*The Hanging Gardens were built by the Babylonians.*

Estructura y Práctica

Imperfect vs. Preterit: Two Aspects of Past Time

The imperfect and the preterit are both past tenses. The difference between them is not a difference in time, but a difference in how past actions are viewed. The preterit views past actions as completed or as having happened once. The imperfect views past actions as ongoing processes in past time.

When Spanish speakers refer to a past action, they have to choose between these two tenses. In English this distinction is not mandatory.

Cuando yo era joven, **dormía** bien.	*When I was young, **I slept** well.*
Anoche **dormí** bien.	*Last night **I slept** well.*

The imperfect has several common translations in English, such as *used to do something* or *was/were doing something.*

Mauricio **trabajaba** en aquella empresa.	*Mauricio **used to work** at that firm.*
¿Sabes lo que **hacía** en México?	*Do you know what **he was doing** in Mexico?*

The imperfect is the tense most often selected to express repeated actions in the past.

Yo me levantaba temprano todos los días.	***I got up** early every day.*
Nosotros siempre **pasábamos** el verano allí.	***We** always **spent** the summer there.*

The imperfect expresses the background of events. The events themselves are in the preterit.

Eran las tres cuando **terminé** mi informe.	***It was** three o'clock when **I finished** my report.*
Hacía buen tiempo cuando **salieron**.	*The weather **was** good when **they left**.*
Empezó a llover mientras **nos paseábamos**.	***It began** to rain while **we were taking a walk**.*
No **fui** a la oficina porque **me sentía** mal.	***I didn't go** to the office because **I felt** sick.*
Yo **entraba** datos en la computadora cuando el jefe me **llamó**.	*I **was entering** data on the computer when the boss **called** me.*

It is possible to have sentences with all verbs in the imperfect or all verbs in the preterit.

Leíamos mientas ellos **navegaban** en la red.	***We were reading** while **they were surfing** the web.*
Rita **se maquilló, se peinó** y **se vistió**.	*Rita **put on makeup, combed her hair,** and **got dressed**.*

N ***¿Imperfecto o pretérito?*** Write either the imperfect or the preterit form of each verb in parentheses to correctly complete each of the following sentences. Each sentence has two verbs, one of which will be in the imperfect and the other in the preterit.

MODELO Carmen *estaba* estresada hasta que *cambió* su estilo de vida. (estar, cambiar)

1. Yo no ________________ a nadie en la fiesta hasta que ________________ mis amigos. (conocer, llegar)
2. Tú ________________ veintiocho años cuando ________________, ¿no? (tener, casarse)
3. Nosotros ________________ la ciudad hasta que ________________ a llover. (recorrer, empezar)
4. Julio ________________ al médico porque le ________________ la garganta. (ir, doler)
5. Margarita ________________ mientras ________________ música. (dormirse, escuchar)
6. Juan Pedro y yo ________________ un taxi cuando ________________ un accidente de tráfico. (buscar, ver)
7. ________________ las once de la noche cuando ellos ________________ del teatro. (Ser, regresar)
8. Cuando yo ________________ niña, mis papás me ________________ a Inglaterra. (ser, llevar)
9. ________________ sol y calor cuando Uds. ________________ del hotel, ¿verdad? (Hacer, salir)
10. Las pirámides ya ________________ cuando los aztecas ________________ su imperio. (estar, fundar)
11. Paula no ________________ el problema hasta que Gabriel se lo ________________. (comprender, explicar).
12. Ellos le ________________ a Marcos que ________________ darle una beca. (decir, pensar)
13. Nosotros ________________ cola en la aduana hasta que los aduaneros nos ________________ el pasaporte. (hacer, pedir)
14. Rafael no ________________ jugar al fútbol porque ________________ el pie. (poder, romperse)
15. Tú ________________ en el lago hasta que ellos ________________ la merienda campestre. (nadar, servir)

NEUTER PRONOUNS

In *Diálogo 5*, you saw the sentence **Pues eso no lo sabía**. **Eso** is a neuter demonstrative pronoun that refers to the information about the pyramids in the previous line of dialogue. The three neuter demonstrative pronouns in Spanish—**esto**, **eso**, and **aquello**—refer to situations or ideas, not to specific nouns.

Mi hijo consiguió una beca de investigación.	*My son got a research grant.*
¡**Eso** es estupendo!	***That's** great!* (**eso** = *the fact that he got the grant*)
Miguel está resentido porque lo despidieron.	*Miguel is resentful because they fired him.*
Pero **aquello** fue hace mucho tiempo.	*But **that** was a long time ago.* (**aquello** = *the fact that he was fired*)

DIÁLOGO 6 · El profesor explica sus ideas.

Study the dialogue, then listen to the recording and repeat each line.

JOSÉ El profesor les iba a explicar a Uds. sus ideas sobre las civilizaciones precolombinas.

ELENA En efecto. Creo que nos las va a explicar la semana entrante.

Análisis

Check that you understand the linguistic breakdown of each speech from *Diálogo 6*.

El profesor les iba a explicar a Uds. sus ideas sobre las civilizaciones precolombinas.	*The professor was going to explain his ideas about pre-Columbian civilizations to you.*
iba a + *infinitive*	*was going to (do something)*
la idea	*idea*
sobre	*about, on the topic of*
la civilización	*civilization*
precolombino	*pre-Columbian (before the arrival of Christopher Columbus)*
En efecto. Creo que nos las va a explicar la semana entrante.	*That's right. I think he's going to explain them to us next week.*
en efecto	*that's right, indeed*
creer	*to believe*
nos las	*them* (feminine) *to us*
nos las va a explicar	*he's going to explain them to us*
entrante	*next*
la semana entrante	*next week*

Variantes

Listen, and repeat the same structures from *Diálogo* 6, now with new vocabulary.

¿Les iba a explicar sus ideas a Uds.? Sí, nos las iba a explicar.	*Was he going to explain his ideas to you?* *Yes, he was going to explain them to us.*
¿Les iba a explicar sus ideas a ellos? Sí, se las iba a explicar.	*Was he going to explain his ideas to them?* *Yes, he was going to explain them to them.*
¿Le iba a explicar sus ideas a él? Sí, se las iba a explicar.	*Was he going to explain his ideas to him?* *Yes, he was going to explain them to him.*
¿Le iba a explicar sus ideas a ella? Sí, se las iba a explicar.	*Was he going to explain his ideas to her?* *Yes, he was going to explain them to her.*

Estructura y Práctica

Double Object Pronouns in Verb + Infinitive Constructions

Like single object pronouns, double object pronouns precede the conjugated verb. In verb + infinitive constructions, double object pronouns may either precede the conjugated verb or follow the infinitive. When they follow, they are attached to the infinitive in writing and an accent mark is added to the vowel before the **-r** of the infinitive.

¿**Me lo** vas a explicar?
¿Vas a explicár**melo**? } *Are you going to explain* ***it to me****?*

O **Double object pronouns: expanded sentences.** Rewrite each of the following sentences to include either **ir a** or **acabar de** as indicated in parentheses. Make necessary changes to the verb and the object pronouns. Write each sentence in two ways. Follow the *modelo.*

MODELO Se lo piden. (acabar de)
→ Acaban de pedírselo.
→ Se lo acaban de pedir.

1. Se la vendemos. (ir a)
2. Nos los regala. (acabar de)
3. Se lo digo. (ir a)
4. Te lo escribimos. (acabar de)
5. Me las llevan. (ir a)
6. Se la devuelves. (acabar de)
7. Se los hago. (ir a)
8. Nos lo dan. (acabar de)

P **Double object pronouns.** Write answers to each of the following questions, adding **ir a** to the original sentence to say that you didn't help the children do certain things, but you are going to help them soon. Write each answer expressing the **ir a** + infinitive construction in two ways. Follow the *modelo*.

MODELO ¿Ya le lavaste la cabeza a Juanita?
→ No, pero se la voy a lavar pronto.
→ No, pero voy a lavársela pronto.

1. ¿Ya les abrochaste el abrigo a Carlitos y Tere?
2. ¿Ya le limpiaste los dientes a Fede?
3. ¿Ya le pusiste las medias a Carlita?
4. ¿Ya le ataste los zapatos a Luisito?
5. ¿Ya les secaste el pelo a las niñas?
6. ¿Ya le quitaste el pijama al bebé?
7. ¿Ya les cepillaste el pelo a los gemelos?
8. ¿Ya le cortaste el pelo al niño?

DIÁLOGO 7 · Los abuelos

Study the dialogue, then listen to the recording and repeat each line.

ELENA ¿Te acuerdas bien de tus abuelos? ¿Cómo eran?
JOSÉ Eran muy simpáticos y cariñosos. Y los abuelos tuyos, ¿cómo eran?
ELENA Por desgracia yo nunca los conocí.
JOSÉ Qué triste. Yo quería mucho a mis abuelos. Ellos hacían un papel muy importante en mi vida.

Análisis

Check that you understand the linguistic breakdown of each speech from *Diálogo 7*.

¿Te acuerdas bien de tus abuelos? ¿Cómo eran?	*Do you remember your grandparents well? What were they like?*
acordarse de (**o** > **ue**)	*to remember*
los abuelos	*grandparents*
eran	*they were*
Eran muy simpáticos y cariñosos. Y los abuelos tuyos, ¿cómo eran?	*They were very nice and loving. What about your grandparents? What were they like?*
simpático	*nice, likeable*
cariñoso	*loving, affectionate*
los abuelos tuyos	*your grandparents*
Por desgracia yo nunca los conocí.	*Unfortunately, I never met them.*
por desgracia	*unfortunately*
conocí	*I met*
Qué triste. Yo quería mucho a mis abuelos. Ellos hacían un papel muy importante en mi vida.	*How sad. I loved my grandparents very much. They played a very important role in my life.*
qué triste	*how sad*
querer	*to love*
quería	*I loved*

hacían	*they did, they made*
hacer un papel	*to play a role*
ellos hacían un papel	*they played a role*
la vida	*life*
en mi vida	*in my life*

Variantes

Listen, and repeat the same structures from *Diálogo 7*, now with new vocabulary.

¿Cómo eran los abuelos tuyos?	*What were **your** grandparents like?*
suyos	*his, her, your, their*
Los abuelos míos eran muy cariñosos.	***My** grandparents were very loving.*
nuestros	*Our*

Estructura y Práctica

Verbs with Different Meanings in Imperfect and Preterit

Some Spanish verbs have very different translations in the imperfect and the preterit. English may even use different verbs to express the difference between the imperfect and the preterit of some Spanish verbs.

Yo **tenía** una idea.	***I had** an idea.*
Yo **tuve** una idea.	***I got** an idea.*
Sabía su nombre.	***He knew** her name.*
Supe su nombre.	***He found out** her name.*
Conocíamos a sus abuelos.	***We knew** his grandparents.*
Conocimos a sus abuelos.	***We met** his grandparents.*
No podían volver hasta las ocho.	***They couldn't** return until eight o'clock. (It doesn't say whether they returned by eight or not.)*
No pudieron volver hasta las ocho.	***They couldn't** return by eight o'clock. (They didn't return by eight.)*
No querías ir, ¿verdad?	***You didn't want** to go, did you?*
No quisiste ir, ¿verdad?	***You refused** to go, didn't you? (You didn't want to go, and you didn't.)*

Q ***¿Imperfecto o pretérito?*** Express the following sentences in Spanish, choosing either the imperfect or the preterit tense.

1. *We wanted to (and did) go sightseeing.*
2. *They found out their nationality.*
3. *The contract? She refused to give it to them.*
4. *I had (was in the process of having) a plan.*
5. *Did you* (tú) *meet those friends* [masc.] *of his?*
6. *He couldn't (and didn't) meet with me.*

DIÁLOGO 8 · La historia de la familia

Study the dialogue, then listen to the recording and repeat each line.

JOSÉ	Me parece que Uds. saben mucho sobre la historia de su familia.
ELENA	Es que nuestros abuelos siempre nos contaban cosas de su vida.
JOSÉ	Entonces Uds. sabían mucho de su vida.
ELENA	Sí. Nos hablaban de su lucha, de sus sueños, de sus triunfos y desilusiones.

Análisis

Check that you understand the linguistic breakdown of each speech from *Diálogo 8*.

Me parece que Uds. saben mucho sobre la historia de su familia.	*I think that you know a lot about the history of your family.*
me parece que	*I think that, it seems to me that*
sobre	*about (on the topic of)*
la historia	*history, story*
la familia	*family*
Es que nuestros abuelos siempre nos contaban cosas de su vida.	*That's because our grandparents always told us things about their lives.*
es que	*that's because, the fact is that*
contar (**o** > **ue**)	*to tell, relate, narrate*
contaban	*they told*
la cosa	*thing*
cosas de su vida	*things about their lives*
Entonces Uds. sabían mucho de su vida.	*So you knew a lot about their lives.*
sabían	*you knew*
Sí. Nos hablaban de su lucha, de sus sueños, de sus triunfos y desilusiones.	*Yes. They spoke to us about their struggle, their dreams, their successes and disappointments.*
hablaban	*they spoke*
la lucha	*struggle*
el sueño	*dream*
el triunfo	*success, triumph*
la desilusión	*disappointment*

Variantes

Listen, and repeat the same structures from *Diálogo 8*, now with new vocabulary.

¿Sus abuelos les contaban la historia de su familia?	*Did your grandparents tell you about your family history?*
Sí, les encantaba contárnosla.	*Yes, they loved to tell us about it.*
¿Quieres contarles la historia a los niños?	*Do you want to tell the story to the boys?*
Sí, quiero contársela.	*Yes, I want to tell it to them.*
¿Les quieres contar el cuento a las niñas?	*Do you want to tell the story to the girls?*
Sí, quiero contárselo.	*Yes, I want to tell it to them.*

DIÁLOGO 9 · Merienda al aire libre

Study the dialogue, then listen to the recording and repeat each line.

ELENA Yo no pude ir a la merienda campestre. ¿Fue divertida?
JOSÉ Mucho. Éramos como veinte personas. Hacía sol y calor. Era un día ideal.
ELENA ¿Nadaron en el lago y jugaron al béisbol y al vólibol?
JOSÉ Ah sí. El ejercicio nos dio hambre. Comimos todo lo que había pero seguíamos con hambre.

Análisis

Check that you understand the linguistic breakdown of each speech from *Diálogo 9.*

Yo no pude ir a la merienda campestre. ¿Fue divertida?	*I couldn't go to the picnic. Was it fun?*
pude	*I could*
no pude ir	*I couldn't (and didn't) go*
la merienda campestre	*picnic*
fue	*it was*
divertido	*fun, amusing*
Mucho. Éramos como veinte personas. Hacía sol y calor. Era un día ideal.	*It really was. We were about twenty people. It was sunny and hot. It was a perfect day.*
mucho	*very much so* (from **muy divertido**, with **divertido** omitted)
éramos	*we were*
como	*about* (*approximately*)
hacía sol	*it was sunny*
hacía calor	*it was hot*
era	*it was*
ideal	*ideal, perfect*
¿Nadaron en el lago y jugaron al béisbol y al vólibol?	*Did you swim in the lake and play baseball and volleyball?*
nadar	*to swim*
el lago	*lake*
jugar (**u** > **ue**)	*to play*
jugar + a + *definite article* + *name of game*	*to play* + name of game
jugar al béisbol	*to play baseball*
jugar al vólibol	*to play volleyball*
Ah sí. El ejercicio nos dio hambre. Comimos todo lo que había pero seguíamos con hambre.	*Oh, yes. The exercise made us hungry. We ate all there was, but we were still hungry.*
el ejercicio	*exercise*
darle hambre a uno	*to make someone hungry*
nos dio hambre	*it made us hungry*
había	*there was, there were*
todo lo que había	*everything that there was*

seguir (**e** > **i**)	*to follow*
seguíamos	*we were following*
seguir con hambre	*to still be hungry*
seguíamos con hambre	*we were still hungry*

Variantes

Listen, and repeat the same structures from *Diálogo 9*, now with new vocabulary.

¿Qué tiempo hacía?	*What was the weather like?*
Hacía calor .	*It was* ***hot****.*
frío	*cold*
setenta grados	*seventy degrees*
viento	*windy*
Estaba nublado .	*It was* ***cloudy****.*
despejado	*clear*
Llovía.	*It was raining.*
Nevaba.	*It was snowing.*
Nos daba hambre .	*It was making us* ***hungry****.*
sed	*thirsty*
calor	*warm*
frío	*cold*
sueño	*sleepy*
miedo	*afraid / It was scaring us.*

Estructura y Práctica

Uses of the Imperfect: Describing the Weather

The imperfect is the tense used for description and expressing background in the past against which completed actions or events occur. For example, when weather expressions provide the background for an event that occurred in the past, the imperfect is used for the weather expression, and the preterit is used for the event or action that occurred in the past.

Hacía buen tiempo cuando **fui** al centro comercial.	***It was nice weather*** *when* ***I went*** *to the mall.*

R ***¿Qué tiempo hacía?*** Express the following sentences in Spanish, using imperfect or preterit verb forms.

1. *It was very cloudy when we got to the beach.*
2. *When the tourists went to see the pyramids, it was very hot.*
3. *It was ninety degrees when he got back to the coffee plantation.*
4. *When the plane took off, it was very windy.*
5. *It was clear when the picnic began.*
6. *Was it raining when you* (tú) *left the theater?*
7. *It was snowing when she came by.*
8. *It was cold when they woke up.*

Uses of the Verb seguir

In *Diálogo 9*, the verb **seguir** is used with the preposition **con** in the expression **seguir con hambre** (*to still be hungry*).

Seguían con sed.	*They were still thirsty.*
¿Sigues con dolor?	*Do you still have pain?*

Seguir con can also mean *to continue / go on / carry on with.*

Los peloteros **siguieron con** el partido.	*The baseball players **went on with** the game.*

Seguir con la vista means *to keep in view, keep one's eye on, not take one's eye off.*

Seguía al tipo sospechoso **con la vista**.	***He kept his eye on** the suspicious guy.*

Seguir means *to still be* before an adjective.

Seguían preocupados/enojados/ molestos.	***They were still** worried/angry/annoyed.*

Expressions with dar

Some idioms with **tener** can be constructed with **dar** + indirect object to express the idea of *to make someone feel something*. One such expression appeared in *Diálogo 9*. Here are some others.

darle envidia *to make someone feel envious*
darle celos a uno *to make someone jealous*
darle la razón a uno *to agree that someone is right*
darle ganas a uno *to make someone feel like doing something*
darle confianza a uno *to give someone confidence*
darle vergüenza a uno *to make someone feel ashamed*
darle dolor a uno *to make someone feel pain*

Le di la razón.	*I agreed that he was right.*
Eso les dio ganas de llorar.	*That (situation) made them feel like crying.*

(For idioms with **tener**, see Chapter 7.)

S ***Tengo... → Me dio...*** Rewrite each of the following sentences, replacing the **tener** + noun idiom with a **dar** + indirect object expression. Follow the *modelo.*

MODELO Tenía frío.
→ Le dio frío.

1. Teníamos hambre.
2. Ellos tenían miedo.
3. Tenías sueño.
4. Él tenía vergüenza.
5. Yo tenía confianza.
6. Ud. tenía calor.
7. Uds. tenían celos.
8. Ella tenía dolor.
9. Ellas tenían envidia.
10. Teníamos frío.

T Express the following sentences in Spanish, using a **dar** + indirect object expression. Use the imperfect of the verb **dar**.

1. *The boring film was making him sleepy.*
2. *The songs were making us feel like dancing.*
3. *Our support was giving them confidence.*
4. *Her handsome friend was making her boyfriend jealous.*
5. *The good aroma of the soup was making me feel hungry.*
6. *The behavior* (el comportamiento) *of their little boy was making his parents feel ashamed.*
7. *What was making you* (tú) *feel envious?*
8. *The rain was making us feel cold.*

DIÁLOGO 10 · ¡Qué olvidadizos somos!

Study the dialogue, then listen to the recording and repeat each line.

PABLO Uds. nos dijeron que iban a hacernos los sándwiches y las ensaladas para la merienda campestre, ¿verdad?

JULIA Ay, ¡qué olvidadizos somos! Se los preparamos ahora.

Análisis

Check that you understand the linguistic breakdown of each speech from *Diálogo 10*.

Uds. nos dijeron que iban a hacernos los sándwiches y las ensaladas para la merienda campestre, ¿verdad?	*You told us that you were going to make the sandwiches and the salads for the picnic (for us), didn't you?*
nos dijeron que	*you told us that*
iban	*you were going*
iban a hacernos	*you were going to make for us*
el sándwich	*sandwich*
la ensalada	*salad*
la merienda campestre	*picnic*
Ay, ¡qué olvidadizos somos! Se los preparamos ahora.	*Oh, how forgetful we are! We'll prepare them for you now.*
olvidadizo	*forgetful*
se los	*them for you*
se los preparamos	*we'll prepare them for you*

Variantes

Listen, and repeat the same structures from *Diálogo 10*, now with new vocabulary.

¿Debemos servirles la torta y el café ahora?	*Should we serve you the cake and coffee now?*
No, ahora no. ¿Por qué no nos los sirven más tarde?	*No, not now. Why don't you serve them to us later?*

DIÁLOGO 11 · Días universitarios

Study the dialogue, then listen to the recording and repeat each line.

JULIA	Yo asistí a una universidad privada. ¿Y tú?
PABLO	Yo no. La universidad mía era estatal. Costaba menos.
JULIA	Yo no tenía beca. Trabajaba en una librería para ganar dinero.
PABLO	Y yo trabajaba de mesero en un café cuando no tenía clases.

Análisis

Check that you understand the linguistic breakdown of each speech from *Diálogo 11.*

Yo asistí a una universidad privada. ¿Y tú?	*I attended a private university. How about you?*
asistir a	*to attend*
la universidad	*university*
privado	*private*
Yo no. La universidad mía era estatal. Costaba menos.	*Not me. My university was a state university. It cost less.*
la universidad mía	*my university*
era	*it was*
costar (**o** > **ue**)	*to cost*
costaba menos	*it cost less*
Yo no tenía beca. Trabajaba en una librería para ganar dinero.	*I didn't have a scholarship. I worked in a bookstore to earn money.*
tenía	*I had*
la beca	*scholarship (monetary award)*
trabajaba	*I used to work*
la librería	*bookstore*
ganar	*to earn*
para ganar dinero	*in order to earn money*
Y yo trabajaba de mesero en un café cuando no tenía clases.	*And I worked as a waiter in a café when I didn't have classes.*
trabajar de	*to work as*
el mesero	*waiter*
trabajar de mesero	*to work as a waiter*
yo trabajaba de mesero	*I used to work as a waiter*
el café	*café*
la clase	*class*

Variantes

Listen, and repeat the same structures from *Diálogo 11*, now with new vocabulary.

La universidad mía era estatal.	***Mine** was a state university.*
tuya	*Yours*
suya	*His, Hers, Yours, Theirs*
nuestra	*Ours*

Estructura y Práctica

U ***Una narrativa.*** Write the correct imperfect form of each of the following verbs in parentheses to create a narrative.

Habla Mercedes. Todos los días yo (1) ________________ (despertarse) a las seis y media de la mañana. Al levantarme, yo (2) ________________ (cepillarse) los dientes, (3) ________________ (ducharse), (4) ________________ (maquillarse) y (5) ________________ (vestirse). Después yo (6) ________________ (desayunar) con mis compañeras de cuarto y (7) ________________ (salir) para la universidad. Yo (8) ________________ (asistir) a una universidad privada donde (9) ________________ (hacer) la carrera de economía. Al graduarme (10) ________________ (esperar) trabajar en finanzas. Aunque yo (11) ________________ (tener) beca me (12) ________________ (faltar) dinero así que (13) ________________ (trabajar) de mesera en el café universitario.

DIÁLOGO 12 · Se da una propina.

Study the dialogue, then listen to the recording and repeat each line.

JULIA Yo pagué la cuenta. ¿Por qué no le dejas tú la propina al mesero?
PABLO Mira. Ya se la dejé.
JULIA ¿Esta miserable propina? ¡Qué poco generoso eres! Se debe dejar el veinte por ciento de propina.
PABLO ¿Tanto? Bueno, tienes razón. Yo también fui mesero una vez.

Análisis

Check that you understand the linguistic breakdown of each speech from *Diálogo 12.*

Yo pagué la cuenta. ¿Por qué no le dejas tú la propina al mesero?	*I paid the check. Why don't you leave the tip for the waiter?*
la cuenta	*bill, check* (restaurant)
dejarle algo a uno	*to leave something for someone*
dejarle una propina al mesero	*to leave the waiter a tip*
Mira. Ya se la dejé.	*Look. I already left it for him.*
se la	*it for him*
se la dejé	*I left it for him*
¿Esta miserable propina? ¡Qué poco generoso eres! Se debe dejar el veinte por ciento de propina.	*This meager tip? How ungenerous you are! One should leave a tip of twenty percent.*
miserable	*miserable, meager*
generoso	*generous*
poco	*little, not much* (negates adjectives)
poco generoso	*stingy, ungenerous*

se debe dejar	*one should leave*
por ciento	*percent*
el veinte por ciento	*twenty percent*
de propina	*as a tip*

¿Tanto? Bueno, tienes razón. Yo también fui mesero una vez. — *That much? Well, you're right. I was also a waiter once.*

tanto	*so much*
bueno	*well*
tener razón	*to be right*
tienes razón	*you're right*
una vez	*once*

Variantes

Listen, and repeat the same structures from *Diálogo 12*, now with new vocabulary.

¿Piensas dejarle una propina a la mesera?	*Do you intend to leave a tip for the waitress?*
Mira. Acabo de dejársela.	*Look. I've just left it for her.*
Se debe hacer ejercicio.	*You should exercise.*
Se puede entrar por esa puerta.	*One can go in through that door.*
No se permite fumar en este edificio.	*Smoking is not allowed in this building.*
Se necesita hacer cola en la aduana.	*You have to stand in line at customs.*

DIÁLOGO 13 · La beca fue suspendida.

Study the dialogue, then listen to the recording and repeat each line.

JULIA Cien estudiantes iban a recibir esa beca. ¿Qué pasó?

PABLO La beca fue suspendida porque no había suficiente dinero. Así que no se la dieron a nadie.

Análisis

Check that you understand the linguistic breakdown of each speech from *Diálogo 13*.

Cien estudiantes iban a recibir esa beca. ¿Qué pasó? — *One hundred students were going to receive that scholarship. What happened?*

iban a recibir	*they were going to receive*
¿Qué pasó?	*What happened?*

La beca fue suspendida porque no había suficiente dinero. Así que no se la dieron a nadie. — *The scholarship was discontinued because there wasn't enough money. So they didn't give it to anyone.*

suspender	*to discontinue, suspend*
fue suspendido	*it was discontinued, it was suspended*
suficiente	*enough*
se la	*it to him, it to her, it to you, it to them*
no se la dieron a nadie	*they didn't give it to anyone*

Variantes

Listen, and repeat the same structures from *Diálogo 13*, now with new vocabulary.

¿Le dieron la beca a Jaime? No, no se la dieron.	*Did Jaime get the scholarship?* *No, they didn't give it to him.*
¿Le dieron el puesto a Susana? No, no se lo dieron.	*Did Susana get the position?* *No, they didn't give it to her.*
¿Le dieron la pasantía a Ud.? No, no me la dieron.	*Did you get the internship?* *No, they didn't give it to me.*
El proyecto fue suspendido. La reunión fue suspendida. Los programas fueron suspendidos. Las becas fueron suspendidas.	*The project was postponed.* *The meeting was adjourned.* *The programs were discontinued.* *The scholarships were discontinued.*

DIÁLOGO 14 · Dificultades en la carretera

Study the dialogue, then listen to the recording and repeat each line.

PABLO ¿Qué hora era cuando Uds. llegaron a casa?
JULIA Eran las diez y media. Había mucho tráfico y no conocíamos la carretera. ¿Y Uds.?
PABLO Era medianoche. Había tormenta y manejábamos muy lentamente. No se podía ver nada por la lluvia y la niebla.

Análisis

Check that you understand the linguistic breakdown of each speech from *Diálogo 14*.

¿Qué hora era cuando Uds. llegaron a casa?	*What time was it when you got home?*
¿Qué hora era?	*What time was it?*
llegar a casa	*to get home, arrive home*
Eran las diez y media. Había mucho tráfico y no conocíamos la carretera. ¿Y Uds.?	*It was ten thirty. There was a lot of traffic and we weren't familiar with the highway. How about you?*
eran las diez y media	*it was ten thirty*
había	*there was*
el tráfico	*traffic*
no conocíamos	*we were not familiar with, we didn't know*
la carretera	*the highway*
Era medianoche. Había tormenta y manejábamos muy lentamente. No se podía ver nada por la lluvia y la niebla.	*It was midnight. There was a storm and we were driving very slowly. You couldn't see anything because of the rain and the fog.*
la medianoche	*midnight*
era medianoche	*it was midnight*

había	*there was*
la tormenta	*storm*
había tormenta	*there was a storm*
manejar	*to drive*
manejábamos	*we were driving*
lento	*slow, slowly*
lentamente	*slowly*
podía	*was able*
no se podía ver nada	*you couldn't see anything*
por	*because of*
la lluvia	*rain*
la niebla	*fog*

Variantes

Listen, and repeat the same structures from *Diálogo 14*, now with new vocabulary.

¿Qué hora era cuando regresaron?	*What time was it when you came back?*
Era la una.	*It was one o'clock.*
Era mediodía.	*It was noon.*
Eran las siete.	*It was seven o'clock.*
Era tarde.	*It was late.*
Había un embotellamiento.	*There was a traffic jam.*
Había tantos líos de tráfico.	*There were so many traffic jams.*
Había una gran cantidad de carros.	*There were loads of cars.*
No se podía ver por la nieve.	*We couldn't* ***see*** *because of the snow.*
manejar	*drive*
caminar	*walk*
aparcar	*park*
Manejaban muy lentamente.	*They were driving very* ***slowly****.*
rápidamente.	*fast*
¿Cuánto (tiempo) hacía que manejaban?	*How long had you been driving?*
Hacía tres horas que manejábamos.	*We had been driving for three hours.*
Manejábamos hacía tres horas.	*We had been driving for three hours.*

Estructura y Práctica

Uses of the Imperfect: Telling Time

The imperfect tense is used to tell what time it was in the past. The preterit is never used.

¿Qué hora **era**?	*What time* ***was*** *it?*
Eran las tres de la tarde.	***It was*** *3:00 P.M.*

V ***¿Qué hora era?*** Write sentences telling at what time certain things happened, using the elements given. The imperfect tense is used to tell the time, and the preterit is used to tell what happened. Follow the *modelo.*

MODELO las dos de la tarde / ella / tomar el almuerzo
→ Eran las dos de la tarde cuando ella tomó el almuerzo.

1. las nueve de la noche / ellos / volver de las pirámides
2. las siete y media de la mañana / tú / levantarse
3. la una de la tarde / nosotros / ir a la merienda campestre
4. las tres cuarenta y cinco de la tarde / los directores de la empresa / reunirse
5. las cinco de la tarde / yo / empezar a jugar al tenis
6. las ocho menos veinte de la noche / Uds. / llegar a la finca
7. casi las once de la noche / Ud. / terminar de escribir su informe
8. las diez de la mañana / él / salir para el cafetal

DIÁLOGO 15 · Se realizaba un sueño.

Study the dialogue, then listen to the recording and repeat each line.

JULIA En aquella época venían muchos inmigrantes a los Estados Unidos.
PABLO En efecto. Había muchos italianos, irlandeses, alemanes y polacos.
JULIA Soñaban con mejorar su vida.
PABLO Y en este país muchos pudieron realizar su sueño.

Análisis

Check that you understand the linguistic breakdown of each speech from *Diálogo 15.*

En aquella época venían muchos inmigrantes a los Estados Unidos.	*At that time, many immigrants were coming to the United States.*
la época	*time, era, epoch, period of time*
en aquella época	*at that time, during that period*
venían	*they were coming*
el inmigrante	*immigrant*
los Estados Unidos	*United States*
En efecto. Había muchos italianos, irlandeses, alemanes y polacos.	*That's right. There were many Italians, Irish, Germans, and Poles.*
en efecto	*that's right, indeed*
había	*there was, there were* (imperfect of **hay**)
el italiano	*Italian*
el irlandés	*Irish*
el alemán	*German*
el polaco	*Pole*

Soñaban con mejorar su vida.	*They dreamed of improving their lives.*
soñar con	*to dream of*
mejorar	*to improve*
soñar con mejorar	*to dream of improving*
la vida	*life*
Y en este país muchos pudieron realizar su sueño.	*And in this country, many were able to realize their dream.*
en este país	*in this country*
pudieron	*they could, they were able*
realizar	*to achieve, realize*
el sueño	*dream*

Variantes

Listen, and repeat the same structures from *Diálogo 15*, now with new vocabulary.

Soñaban con mejorar su vida.	*They used to dream about* ***making their lives better.***
llevar una vida mejor	*leading a better life*
vivir mejor	*living better*
triunfar en la vida	*getting ahead, succeeding in life*
una vida mejor	*a better life*
¿Cuánto tiempo llevaban en los Estados Unidos?	*How long had they been in the United States?*
Llevaban diez años en el país.	*They had been living in the country for ten years.*

Estructura y Práctica

W ***Una narrativa.*** Write the correct imperfect form of each of the following verbs in parentheses to complete this paragraph about immigrants.

A principios del siglo veinte (*In the early twentieth century*) (1) ________________ (llegar) mucha gente a los Estados Unidos de otros países. Muchos de esos inmigrantes (2) ________________ (ser) pobres y (3) ________________ (esperar) encontrar empleo. Ellos (4) ________________ (soñar) con llevar una vida mejor y por lo tanto (5) ________________ (tener) que aprender inglés para poder trabajar. Ellos (6) ________________ (trabajar) en fábricas (*factories*) y tiendas pequeñas. La vida (7) ________________ (ser) muy difícil para ellos pero (8) ________________ (saber) que (9) ________________ (vivir) en un país que les (10) ________________ (dar) la oportunidad de realizar sus sueños y triunfar en la vida.

DIÁLOGO 16 · Lo que hacíamos

Study the dialogue, then listen to the recording and repeat each line.

PABLO	¿Qué hacían Uds.?
JULIA	Yo escribía unos correos electrónicos mientras Marisol leía una novela. ¿Y Uds.?
PABLO	Pues yo oía música en mi cuarto mientras Felipe veía televisión en la sala.

Análisis

Check that you understand the linguistic breakdown of each speech from *Diálogo 16*.

¿Qué hacían Uds.?	*What were you doing?*
hacían	*you were doing*
Yo escribía unos correos electrónicos mientras Marisol leía una novela. ¿Y Uds.?	*I was writing some emails while Marisol was reading a novel. How about you?*
escribía	*I was writing*
unos	*some*
unos correos electrónicos	*some emails*
mientras	*while*
leía	*she was reading*
Pues yo oía música en mi cuarto mientras Felipe veía televisión en la sala.	*Well, I was listening to music in my room while Felipe was watching television in the living room.*
oía	*I was hearing, I was listening to*
veía	*he was seeing, he was watching*
ver televisión	*to watch television*
la sala	*living room*

Variantes

Listen, and repeat the same structures from *Diálogo 16*, now with new vocabulary.

Ellos dormían la siesta mientras nosotros navegábamos en la red.	*They were taking a nap while we were surfing the web.*
¿Cuánto (tiempo) hacía que navegabas en la red?	*How long had you been surfing the web?*
Hacía una hora que navegaba en la red.	*I had been surfing the web for an hour.*
¿Desde cuándo navegabas en la red?	*Since when had you been surfing the web?*
Navegaba en la red desde las tres.	*I had been surfing the web since three o'clock.*

Estructura y Práctica

Hacía + Expression of Time + que + Verb in Imperfect Tense

Spanish uses the imperfect tense to refer to past actions that are seen as continuing at another point of time in the past. English uses a *had been doing something* construction for this function.

To tell how long something had been going on, the following constructions are used:

hacía + expression of time + **que** + verb in imperfect

Hacía dos años que vivía en Madrid. — ***I had been living*** *in Madrid* ***for two years.***

OR

verb in imperfect + **hacía** + expression of time

Vivía en Madrid **hacía dos años.** — ***I had been living*** *in Madrid* ***for two years.***

To ask a question about how long something had been going on, the following construction is used (the word **tiempo** is optional).

¿Cuánto (tiempo) hacía que + verb in the imperfect?

¿Cuánto tiempo hacía que vivías en Madrid? — ***How long had you been living*** *in Madrid?*

Desde is used to specify the starting point of an action that began in the past and continues to another point in the past.

¿Desde cuándo trabajabas con ellos? — ***Since when had you been working*** *with them?*

Trabajaba con ellos **desde** enero. — ***I had been working*** *with them* ***since*** *January.*

(For equivalent time expressions in present tense, see Chapter 6.)

X ***Diálogos. ¿Cuánto tiempo hacía que...?*** Write questions using the construction **¿Cuánto tiempo hacía que...?** and answer them using the construction **hacía** + expression of time + **que** + verb in the imperfect. Follow the *modelo.*

MODELO Ud. / estudiar español / viajar a Costa Rica (tres años)
→ —¿Cuánto tiempo hacía que Ud. estudiaba español cuando viajó a Costa Rica?
→ —Hacía tres años que estudiaba español.

1. tú / tocar el piano / ellos / darte una beca (ocho años)
2. ella / jugar al golf / comenzar a llover (dos horas)
3. Uds. / esperar / sus primos / ellos / llegar (media hora)
4. él / trabajar en Chile / su empresa / mandarlo al Perú (cinco meses)

Y Express the following sentences in Spanish, using the appropriate time expression and the imperfect tense.

1. *I had been looking for the dog for an hour.*
2. *Since when had the farmers been growing corn?*
3. *How long had you* (tú) *been interested in modern art?*
4. *Cars had been produced in this plant for fifty years.*
5. *We had been doing ecotourism since June.*
6. *They had been serving healthy food for many years.*
7. *How long had it been snowing?*
8. *He had been attending a state university since last year.*

DIÁLOGO 17 · La dirección electrónica

Study the dialogue, then listen to the recording and repeat each line.

JULIA	Ud. nos dijo que iba a mandarnos la dirección electrónica de Franco.
PABLO	Se la mandé ayer.
JULIA	¿De veras? Pero no la encontré en nuestro buzón.
PABLO	Se la voy a mandar otra vez. No entiendo por qué no la recibieron.

Análisis

Check that you understand the linguistic breakdown of each speech from *Diálogo 17.*

Ud. nos dijo que iba a mandarnos la dirección electrónica de Franco.	*You said that you would send us Franco's email address.*
iba a	*you were going to*
Se la mandé ayer.	*I sent it to you yesterday.*
se la	*it to you*
se la mandé	*I sent it to you*
¿De veras? Pero no la encontré en nuestro buzón.	*Really? But I didn't find it in our inbox.*
¿De veras?	*Really?*
encontrar (**o** > **ue**)	*to find*
el buzón	*mailbox, inbox*
Se la voy a mandar otra vez. No entiendo por qué no la recibieron.	*I'll send it to you again. I don't understand why you didn't get it.*
se la voy a mandar	*I'm going to send it to you*
otra vez	*again*
entender (**e** > **ie**)	*to understand*
recibir	*to receive, get*

Variantes

Listen, and repeat the same structures from *Diálogo 17*, now with new vocabulary.

Ellos nos dijeron que iban a casarse.	*They **told** us they were going to get married.*
contaron	*told*
escribieron	*wrote*
informaron	*informed*
¿El número de teléfono? Se lo mandé ayer.	*The telephone number? I sent it to you yesterday.*
¿Las fechas? Se las voy a mandar esta tarde.	*The dates? I'm going to send them to you this afternoon.*

Estructura y Práctica

Preterit and Imperfect in Indirect Discourse (Reported Speech)

The imperfect tense is used in indirect discourse, or reported speech (reporting what someone said), after the preterit form of verbs such as **decir** and **escribir**.

¿Qué te dijo Mario?	*What did Mario tell you?*
Me **dijo** que **volvía** tarde.	***He told** me **he was coming back** late.*
¿Le escribiste a Carmen?	*Did you write to Carmen?*
Sí, le **escribí** que **me mudaba**.	*Yes, **I wrote** her that **I was moving**.*

Z **Reported speech.** Write answers to the following questions, using the elements given, to show reported speech. Follow the *modelo*.

MODELO ¿Qué te dijo Alonso? (venir a visitarme)
→ Me dijo que venía a visitarme.

1. ¿Qué le dijeron a Ud. sus tíos? (mi primo / casarse)
2. ¿Qué les escribió Anita a Uds.? (ella / ir al extranjero)
3. ¿Qué te escribieron tus papás? (disfrutar de sus vacaciones)
4. ¿Qué te texteó tu amigo? (estar en camino)
5. ¿Qué le dijiste a tu novia? (quererla mucho)
6. ¿Qué le preguntó Ud. a su colega? (él / trabajar todavía en la base de datos)
7. ¿Qué te contó tu hijo? (interesarle estudiar administración de empresas)
8. ¿Qué les informó a Uds. el jefe de producción? (él / hacer un estudio de mercado)

DIÁLOGO 18 · ¿Quién tiene el iPod?

Study the dialogue, then listen to the recording and repeat each line.

PABLO ¿Me prestas tu iPod, por favor?
JULIA Se lo presté a Esteban la semana pasada. ¿Por qué no se lo pides a él?
PABLO ¿Y todavía no te lo devolvió?
JULIA No. Pero si él te lo da a ti, tú me lo puedes devolver.

Análisis

Check that you understand the linguistic breakdown of each speech from *Diálogo 18*.

¿Me prestas tu iPod, por favor?	*Can you lend me your iPod, please?*
prestarle algo a uno	*to lend something to someone*
Se lo presté a Esteban la semana pasada. ¿Por qué no se lo pides a él?	*I lent it to Esteban last week. Why don't you ask him for it?*
se lo	*it to him*
se lo presté	*I lent it to him*
se lo presté a Esteban	*I lent it to Esteban*
pedirle algo a uno	*to ask someone for something*
pedírselo a él	*to ask him for it*
¿Y todavía no te lo devolvió?	*And he still hasn't returned it to you?*
devolverle algo a uno	*to return something to someone*
todavía	*still, yet*
No. Pero si él te lo da a ti, tú me lo puedes devolver.	*No. But if he gives it to you, you can return it to me.*
darle algo a uno	*to give something to someone*
te lo da a ti	*he gives it to you*

Variantes

Listen, and repeat the same structures from *Diálogo 18*, now with new vocabulary.

¿Me prestas tu cámara, por favor?	*Will you lend me your camera, please?*
Claro. Pero tienes que devolvérmela para el fin de semana.	*Of course. But you have to return it to me by the weekend.*

Estructura y Práctica

AA ***Fue ayer.*** Express the following sentences in Spanish, explaining that everything happened yesterday. Use double object pronouns. Follow the *modelo.*

MODELO *The suitcase? I lent it to Antonio yesterday.*
→ ¿La maleta? Se la presté a Antonio ayer.

1. *The folders? We returned them to her yesterday.*
2. *The contract? He sent it to the lawyers yesterday.*
3. *The ticket? They gave it to me yesterday.*
4. *The gardens? She showed them to us yesterday.*
5. *The package? They wrapped* (envolver) *it for you* (Uds.) *yesterday.*
6. *The money? You* (Ud.) *asked me for it yesterday.*
7. *The earrings? We gave them to her as a gift yesterday.*
8. *The wallet? I brought it to you* (tú) *yesterday.*
9. *The documents? I handed them to him yesterday.*
10. *The cookies? I made them for him yesterday.*

Un paso más

Are you ready to take your Spanish a step further? Here are exercises that will enhance your knowledge of the language and allow you to express yourself freely.

BB ***Preguntas personales.*** Answer each question with a complete Spanish sentence.

1. Cuando eras niño/niña, ¿cómo eras?
2. ¿Qué hacías todos los días?
3. ¿Quiénes formaban parte de tu familia?
4. ¿Era muy unida (*close*) tu familia?
5. ¿Convivías con tus abuelos? ¿Cómo eran? ¿Hacían un papel importante en tu vida?
6. ¿Te reunías mucho con tus tíos y primos?
7. ¿Dónde vivías de niño/niña?
8. ¿Adónde ibas de vacaciones?
9. ¿Cuáles son los recuerdos más vivos de tu niñez?

CC ***Narrativas personales***

Narrativa personal 1. Write a paragraph about your family history. Use the following questions as a guide to discuss a relative or relatives who emigrated to the United States.

1. ¿Tus abuelos o bisabuelos (*great-grandparents*) eran inmigrantes a los Estados Unidos?
2. ¿De dónde eran?
3. ¿En qué año llegaron a los Estados Unidos?
4. ¿Por qué o para qué emigraron a los Estados Unidos?
5. Describe (*Describe*) su experiencia, sus sueños y su lucha. ¿Pudieron triunfar en la vida?
6. ¿Qué idioma(s) hablaban?
7. ¿Se habla el idioma en tu familia todavía?

Narrativa personal 2. Write a paragraph about your visit—either real or imaginary—to the *Museo Nacional de Antropología. Diálogo 5* of this chapter talks about pre-Columbian civilizations in Mexico—the Aztecs, the Toltecs, and the pyramids of San Juan de Teotihuacán. To learn more and view impressive artifacts, visit the *Museo Nacional de Antropología* in Mexico City via the website http://www.mna.inah.gob.mx/. Use information from the museum website and the following questions as a guide.

Cuando estaba en México, visité el Museo Nacional de Antropología...

1. ¿Por qué estabas en México?
2. ¿Cuándo hiciste el viaje?
3. ¿Cómo era el museo?

4. ¿Qué había en las salas *(rooms)*?
5. ¿Qué viste en las salas dedicadas a la cultura tolteca y la cultura azteca?
6. ¿Qué aprendiste de las culturas precolombinas?
7. ¿También conociste las pirámides de San Juan de Teotihuacán? ¿Cómo eran?

Narrativa personal 3. Write a paragraph about your college experience, using the following questions as a guide.

Cuando yo era universitario/universitaria...

1. ¿Asistías a una universidad privada o estatal? ¿A cuál?
2. ¿Qué carrera hacías?
3. ¿Qué materias tomabas? ¿En qué te especializabas?
4. ¿Qué título(s) universitario(s) (*degree*(*s*)) tienes?
5. ¿Tenías beca?
6. ¿Trabajabas mientras estudiabas? ¿Qué hacías?
7. ¿Vivías en un apartamento o en una residencia universitaria (*dormitory*)?

11

Health and Accidents

Communication Goals

- Talking about health, accidents, and unplanned events
- Describing a visit to the doctor
- Vocabulary: healthy lifestyle, illnesses, parts of the body

Grammar Topics

- The Imperfect and the Preterit: Two Aspects of Past Time
- Reflexive Verbs with Reciprocal Meaning
- Augmentatives
- Diminutives
- Reverse Construction Verbs: **doler** *to hurt, ache*
- Unplanned Occurrences (Use of the Indirect Object Pronoun)

DIÁLOGO 1 · En el centro comercial

Study the dialogue, then listen to the recording and repeat each line.

RAQUEL Entonces, ¿viste a Gonzalo en el centro comercial?
MIGUEL Sí, él me saludó cuando yo subía en la escalera mecánica.
RAQUEL Pero cuando nosotros le dijimos que íbamos, él dijo que no podía acompañarnos.
MIGUEL No sé qué decirte. A lo mejor cambió de idea.

Análisis

Check that you understand the linguistic breakdown of each speech from *Diálogo 1.*

Entonces, ¿viste a Gonzalo en el centro comercial? — *So you saw Gonzalo at the mall?*

viste — *you saw*

Sí, él me saludó cuando yo subía en la escalera mecánica.	*Yes, he said hello to me when I was going up the escalator.*
saludar	*to say hello to, greet*
saludó	*he said hello*
subir	*to go up*
subía	*I was going up*
la escalera mecánica	*escalator*
Pero cuando nosotros le dijimos que íbamos, él dijo que no podía acompañarnos.	*But when we told him that we were going, he told us that he couldn't go with us.*
dijimos	*we said, we told*
íbamos	*we were going*
dijo	*he said, he told*
no podía	*he couldn't*
acompañar	*to accompany, go with*
No sé qué decirte. A lo mejor cambió de idea.	*I don't know what to say (to you). Maybe he changed his mind.*
qué decirte	*what to say to you*
a lo mejor	*maybe*
cambiar	*to change*
cambiar de idea	*to change one's mind*

Variantes

Listen, and repeat the same structures from *Diálogo 1*, now with new vocabulary.

Él nos dijo que no podía acompañarnos.	*He **told** us he wasn't able to go with us.*
contó	*told*
escribió	*wrote*
informó	*informed*
Él nos dijo que no podía acompañarnos.	*He told us he **wasn't able** to go with us.*
no quería	*didn't want*
no pensaba	*didn't intend*
no esperaba	*didn't expect*
no necesitaba	*didn't need*
no tenía que	*didn't have*
Él me saludó cuando yo subía en la escalera mecánica.	*He **waved** to me when I was going up the escalator.*
llamó	*called*
gritó	*shouted*
Él me saludó cuando yo subía en la escalera mecánica.	*He waved to me when I **was going up** the escalator.*
bajaba	*was going down*

¿Subieron por las escaleras o por el ascensor?	*Did they walk up or take the elevator?*
Subieron a pie porque el ascensor no funcionaba.	*They walked up because the elevator wasn't working.*
Bajaron a pie porque el elevador estaba descompuesto.	*They walked down because the elevator was broken.*
Cuando llegué al tercer piso, no había nadie.	*When I got to the third floor, nobody was there.*

Estructura y Práctica

The Imperfect and the Preterit: Two Aspects of Past Time

In Chapter 10, you learned the imperfect tense and how it contrasts with the preterit. (See also Chapter 9.) This chapter provides a more extensive study of this complicated topic: imperfect and preterit as two aspects of past time.

A **Imperfect or preterit.** Write either the imperfect or the preterit for each verb in parentheses to correctly complete each of the following sentences. Each sentence has two verbs; one might be in the imperfect and the other in the preterit, or both might be in the same tense. Follow the *modelo*.

MODELO Nosotros *salíamos* (salir) de casa cuando *sonó* (sonar) el teléfono.

1. Mercedes ________________ (ir) a pie porque no ________________ (poder) encontrar un taxi.
2. Ellos ________________ (pensar) acompañarnos pero ________________ (cambiar) de idea.
3. Felipe ________________ (bajar) en la escalera mecánica mientras yo ________________ (subir) en el ascensor.
4. Alonso ________________ (entrar) en la oficina y nos ________________ (saludar).
5. ¿Ud. les ________________ (decir) que ________________ (querer) trasladarse a otra oficina?
6. Yo ________________ (almorzar) fuerte, pero ________________ (seguir) con hambre toda la tarde.
7. Todos los años nosotros ________________ (visitar) la finca donde ________________ (montar) a caballo.
8. Hoy Uds. ________________ (levantarse) a las siete y ________________ (arreglarse) a las ocho.
9. Ayer yo ________________ (despertarse) temprano porque ________________ (tener) mucho que hacer.

DIÁLOGO 2 · Un partido de béisbol

Study the dialogue, then listen to the recording and repeat each line.

MIGUEL ¿Qué tal el partido de béisbol? ¿Ganó tu equipo?
RAQUEL ¿No sabes qué pasó? Veíamos el partido y comíamos unos perros calientes cuando de repente hubo un tremendo aguacero.
MIGUEL Entonces el partido fue suspendido por la lluvia.
RAQUEL Esperábamos hasta que dejó de llover. ¡Siguió el partido, dos horas más tarde!

Análisis

Check that you understand the linguistic breakdown of each speech from *Diálogo 2*.

¿Qué tal el partido de béisbol? ¿Ganó tu equipo?	*How was the baseball game? Did your team win?*
el partido	*game, sports match*
el partido de béisbol	*baseball game*
ganó	*he won*
el equipo	*team*
¿No sabes qué pasó? Veíamos el partido y comíamos unos perros calientes cuando de repente hubo un tremendo aguacero.	*Don't you know what happened? We were watching the game and eating hot dogs when suddenly there was a huge downpour.*
pasó	*it happened*
veíamos	*we were watching*
comíamos	*we were eating*
de repente	*suddenly*
hubo	*there was, there were*
tremendo	*tremendous, huge, terrible*
el aguacero	*shower, downpour*
Entonces el partido fue suspendido por la lluvia.	*So the game was suspended because of the rain.*
suspender	*to suspend*
fue suspendido	*was suspended*
por	*because of*
por la lluvia	*because of the rain*
Esperábamos hasta que dejó de llover. ¡Siguió el partido, dos horas más tarde!	*We waited until it stopped raining. The game went on, two hours later!*
esperar	*to wait*
esperábamos	*we waited*
hasta que	*until*
dejar de + *infinitive*	*to stop (doing something)*
dejó de llover	*it stopped raining*
seguir	*to continue*
siguió el partido	*the game continued*
más tarde	*later*

Variantes

Listen, and repeat the same structures from *Diálogo 2*, now with new vocabulary.

Veíamos el partido cuando comenzó a llover.	***We were watching*** *the game when it started to rain.*
Oíamos	*We were listening to*
Esperábamos	*We were waiting for*
Veíamos el partido cuando comenzó a llover.	*We were watching the game when* ***it started*** *to rain.*
empezó a	*it began*
Esperábamos hasta que dejó de llover.	*We waited until* ***it stopped raining****.*
salió el sol	*the sun came out*
Cenábamos cuando Paco pasó por la casa.	*We were having dinner when Paco stopped by.*

Estructura y Práctica

B **Imperfect or preterit.** Write either the imperfect or the preterit for each verb in parentheses to correctly complete each of the following sentences. Each sentence has two verbs; one might be in the imperfect and the other in the preterit, or both might be in the same tense. Follow the *modelo*.

MODELO El lanzador (*pitcher*) se hizo (hacerse) daño mientras se jugaba (jugar) la quinta entrada (*inning*).

1. ____________ (Llover) tanto que ellos ____________ (tener) que suspender el partido.
2. Nosotros ____________ (esperar) en el café hasta que ____________ (dejar) de nevar.
3. Yo ____________ (comer) un perro caliente mientras Esteban ____________ (tomar) su cerveza.
4. ____________ (Estar) despejado todo el día hasta que por fin ____________ (haber) un aguacero.
5. Cuando el jugador ____________ (pegar (*to hit*)) un jonrón, los aficionados ____________ (ponerse) a gritar de alegría.

DIÁLOGO 3 · Al señor Reyes lo trasladaron.

Study the dialogue, then listen to the recording and repeat each line.

MIGUEL Por favor, ¿está el señor Reyes?
RAQUEL No, señor. José Reyes trabajaba en esta sucursal hasta que lo trasladaron en mayo.
MIGUEL ¿Ud. sabe cómo puedo ponerme en contacto con él?
RAQUEL Lo siento. El número de teléfono que yo tenía ya no sirve porque lo cambiaron.

Análisis

Check that you understand the linguistic breakdown of each speech from *Diálogo 3*.

Por favor, ¿está el señor Reyes?	*Excuse me, is Mr. Reyes in?*
por favor	*please; excuse me (to get someone's attention)*
estar	*to be in, be there*
No, señor. José Reyes trabajaba en esta sucursal hasta que lo trasladaron en mayo.	*No, sir. José Reyes worked at this branch until they transferred him in May.*
trabajaba	*he worked, he used to work*
la sucursal	*branch (of a company,* etc.*)*
hasta que	*until*
trasladar	*to transfer*
trasladaron	*they transferred*
¿Ud. sabe cómo puedo ponerme en contacto con él?	*Do you know how I can get in touch with him?*
el contacto	*contact*
ponerse en contacto con	*to get in touch with*
Lo siento. El número de teléfono que yo tenía ya no sirve porque lo cambiaron.	*I'm sorry. The telephone number I had is no good anymore because they changed it.*
lo siento	*I'm sorry*
el número de teléfono	*telephone number*
tenía	*I had*
ya no	*no longer, no more*
servir	*to be useful*
ya no sirve	*is no good, is not valid anymore*
cambiaron	*they changed*

Variantes

Listen, and repeat the same structures from *Diálogo 3*, now with new vocabulary.

Marta trabajaba aquí hasta que la trasladaron.	*Marta used to work here until she was* ***transferred****.*
despidieron	*fired*

Hasta que Juan se jubiló era gerente de sucursal.	*Until Juan retired, he was branch manager.*
El número de teléfono que yo tenía fue cambiado.	*The telephone number I had was changed.*

Estructura y Práctica

C **Translation.** Express the following sentences in Spanish, selecting either the imperfect or the preterit for each verb.

1. *I was secretary* [masc.] *to the CEO* (director ejecutivo) *until he got sick.*
2. *Elena and Mercedes stopped working at that branch.*
3. *The telephone number was changed so* (así que) *we couldn't call them.*
4. *Did the manager transfer or fire Joaquín?*
5. *Víctor didn't finish the report because there wasn't enough data.*

SERVIR (E > I)

You are familiar with the verb **servir (e > i)** meaning *to serve*. The verb has different meanings in different structures and contexts. For example, in this chapter, **servir** is used in the sentence **ya no sirve**, meaning *it's no good* or *it's not valid anymore*. Note these uses of **servir**.

No **sirve quejarse/llorar.**	*There's no use in complaining/crying.*
Eso **no sirve para nada.**	*That's no good at all. / It's useless.*
Tener una rabieta no **te sirve para nada.**	*It's no use for you to throw a tantrum.*
¿Para qué **sirve esperar**?	*What's the point in waiting?*
¿**Sirven de** algo estos documentos?	*Do these documents have a purpose?*
Juan Diego **nos servía de** traductor.	*Juan Diego was our translator.*
Ellos no **sirven para** esas cosas.	*They're not good at those things.*
Me sirvo más arroz.	*I'll help myself to more rice.*
Se servía de estos sitios web todos los días.	*He used these websites every day.*
¿**En qué puedo servirle**?	*What can I do for you? / May I help you? (in a store)*
Sírvete. / Sírvase Ud.	*Help yourself.* (to food)

DIÁLOGO 4 · Compañeros de clase

Study the dialogue, then listen to the recording and repeat each line.

RAQUEL ¿Cuánto tiempo hacía que conocías a Isabel cuando Uds. se casaron?
MIGUEL Casi seis años. Nos conocimos mientras los dos estudiábamos en el extranjero.
RAQUEL Eran compañeros de clase en la Universidad de Sevilla, ¿verdad?
MIGUEL Sí. Mientras tomábamos clases de español, comenzamos a salir juntos.

Análisis

Check that you understand the linguistic breakdown of each speech from *Diálogo 4.*

¿Cuánto tiempo hacía que conocías a Isabel cuando Uds. se casaron?	*How long had you known Isabel when you two got married?*
¿Cuánto tiempo?	*How long?*
conocías a Isabel	*you knew Isabel*
¿Cuánto tiempo hacía que (tú) + *imperfect*?	*How long had (you) been (doing something)?*
se casaron	*you got married*
Casi seis años. Nos conocimos mientras los dos estudiábamos en el extranjero.	*Almost six years. We met (each other) while we were both studying abroad.*
casi	*almost*
conocerse	*to meet each other*
nos conocimos	*we met*
mientras	*while*
estudiábamos	*we were studying*
extranjero	*foreign*
en el extranjero	*abroad*
Eran compañeros de clase en la Universidad de Sevilla, ¿verdad?	*You were classmates at the University of Seville, right?*
el compañero	*companion, friend*
el compañero de clase	*classmate*
Sí. Mientras tomábamos clases de español, comenzamos a salir juntos.	*Yes. While we were taking Spanish classes, we began to go out together.*
tomábamos	*we were taking*
comenzar a + *infinitive*	*to begin to (do something)*
comenzamos	*we began*
salir	*to go out*
juntos	*together*

Variantes

Listen, and repeat the same structures from *Diálogo 4*, now with new vocabulary.

¿Cuánto tiempo hacía que conocías a Isabel cuando Uds. se casaron?	*How long had you known Isabel when you got married?*
Hacía tres años que yo conocía a Isabel cuando nos casamos.	*I had known Isabel for three years when we got married.*
Nos conocimos mientras estábamos en el extranjero.	***We met** while we were abroad.*
Nos enamoramos	*We fell in love*
Nos comprometimos	*We got engaged*

Mientras estudiábamos , Raquel prendió la tele.	*While **we were studying**, Raquel turned on the TV.*
leíamos	*we were reading*
comíamos	*we were eating*
dormíamos	*we were sleeping*
Yo salí mientras tú navegabas en la red.	*I **went out** while you were surfing the web.*
regresé	*came back*
me fui	*left*
Yo salí mientras tú oías música.	*I went out while **you were listening to** music.*
descargabas	*you were downloading*
componías	*you were composing*

Estructura y Práctica

Reflexive Verbs with Reciprocal Meaning

You learned in Chapter 8 that the plural forms of reflexive verbs are used to express reciprocal action corresponding to the English phrase *each other*.

¿**Se escribían** todos los meses?	***Did you write to each other** every month?*
¡Qué va! **Nos escribíamos** una vez al año.	*Are you kidding! **We wrote to each other** once a year.*

D **Translation.** Express the following sentences in Spanish, selecting either the imperfect or the preterit for each verb. Pay special attention to the reflexive verbs with reciprocal meaning.

1. *How long had you* (Uds.) *known each other when you got engaged?*
2. *We had been seeing each other for a week when we began to address each other as* tú.
3. *How long had we been helping each other with the project when you* (Ud.) *moved?*
4. *While Lola and Juan were hugging and kissing each other, Lola's little brother started to laugh.*
5. *They understood each other very well until something happened.*
6. *We met when we were working at a high tech company.*

DIÁLOGO 5 · Alguien se equivocó de número.

Study the dialogue, then listen to the recording and repeat each line.

RAQUEL	Chico, ¡qué ojeras tienes! ¿No dormiste anoche?
MIGUEL	Al contrario. Dormía profundamente cuando sonó el teléfono a las cinco de la mañana.
RAQUEL	Ay, te despertaste sobresaltado. ¿Quién fue?
MIGUEL	Alguien se equivocó de número. Yo estaba tan alterado que no pude volver a dormirme.

Análisis

Check that you understand the linguistic breakdown of each speech from *Diálogo 5.*

Chico, ¡qué ojeras tienes! ¿No dormiste anoche?	*Wow, what dark circles you have under your eyes! Didn't you sleep last night?*
chico	*wow* (interjection)
la ojera	*dark circle under the eye*
dormiste	*you slept*
anoche	*last night*
Al contrario. Dormía profundamente cuando sonó el teléfono a las cinco de la mañana.	*Just the opposite. I was in a deep sleep when the telephone rang at five o'clock in the morning.*
al contrario	*on the contrary, just the opposite*
dormía	*I was sleeping*
profundo	*deep*
profundamente	*deeply*
sonar (**o** > **ue**)	*to ring*
sonó	*it rang*
Ay, te despertaste sobresaltado. ¿Quién fue?	*Oh, you woke up startled. Who was it?*
despertarse (**e** > **ie**)	*to wake up*
te despertaste	*you woke up*
sobresaltado	*startled*
fue	*it was*
Alguien se equivocó de número. Yo estaba tan alterado que no pude volver a dormirme.	*Someone dialed the wrong number. I was so unnerved that I couldn't fall asleep again.*
equivocarse	*to be mistaken*
equivocarse de	*to get the wrong thing, do the wrong thing*
equivocarse de número	*to dial the wrong number*
se equivocó de número	*he dialed the wrong number*
estaba	*I was*
alterado	*unnerved, upset*
no pude	*I couldn't (and didn't)*
volver a hacer algo	*to do something again*
volver a dormirse	*to fall asleep again*
No pude volver a dormirme.	*I couldn't fall asleep again.*

Variantes

Listen, and repeat the same structures from *Diálogo 5,* now with new vocabulary.

Dormía cuando sonó el teléfono.	***I was sleeping** when the phone rang.*
Me dormía	*I was falling asleep*
Me duchaba	*I was taking a shower*
Me lavaba la cabeza	*I was washing my hair*
Me relajaba	*I was relaxing*

Volví a dormirme.	*I* ***fell asleep*** *again.*
peinarme	*combed my hair*
ducharme	*showered*

Estructura y Práctica

E **Interruptions.** Write either the imperfect or the preterit for each verb in parentheses to correctly complete each of the following sentences, explaining how some people were interrupted from what they were doing. Follow the *modelo.*

MODELO Rafael *dormía* (dormir) la siesta cuando *llamó* (llamar) su hermano.

1. Nosotros ________________ (imprimir) unos papeles cuando la impresora ________________ (dejar) de funcionar.
2. Mateo ________________ (leer) una novela policíaca (*crime novel*) cuando ________________ (oír) unos ruidos raros en la casa.
3. Yo ________________ (ver) las noticias en la tele cuando mis amigos ________________ (venir) a buscarme.
4. Laura ________________ (preparar) la cena cuando alguien ________________ (tocar) el timbre.
5. Los chicos ________________ (jugar) al béisbol cuando su perro ________________ (comenzar) a ladrar (*bark*).

DIÁLOGO 6 · Un niño prodigio

Study the dialogue, then listen to the recording and repeat each line.

MIGUEL	Me dijeron que Julio era un niño prodigio.
RAQUEL	Es cierto. Tenía doce años cuando se graduó en la universidad.
MIGUEL	¿Lo conociste cuando era niño? ¿Cómo era?
RAQUEL	Era un niño encantador, superdotado pero nada presumido.

Análisis

Check that you understand the linguistic breakdown of each speech from *Diálogo 6.*

Me dijeron que Julio era un niño prodigio.	*They told me that Julio was a child prodigy.*
dijeron	*they said, they told*
era	*he was*
prodigio	*wonder, prodigy*
el niño prodigio	*child prodigy*

Es cierto. Tenía doce años cuando se graduó en la universidad.	*It's true. He was twelve years old when he graduated from the university.*
tenía	*he had*
tenía doce años	*he was twelve years old*
graduarse en	*to graduate from*
graduarse en la universidad	*to graduate from college, graduate from the university*
se graduó	*he graduated*
¿Lo conociste cuando era niño? ¿Cómo era?	*Did you meet him when he was a child? What was he like?*
conociste	*you met*
era	*he was*
Era un niño encantador, superdotado pero nada presumido.	*He was a delightful child, extremely gifted, but not at all conceited.*
era	*he was*
encantador	*delightful*
dotado	*gifted*
superdotado	*extremely gifted*
nada	*not at all* (when it precedes an adjective)
presumido	*conceited*
nada presumido	*not at all conceited*

Variantes

Listen, and repeat the same structures from *Diálogo 6*, now with new vocabulary.

Me dijeron que Julio era un niño prodigio.	***They told me*** *Julio was a child prodigy.*
Me informaron	*They informed me*
Tenía veinticinco años cuando se graduó.	*He was twenty-five years old* ***when he graduated****.*
cuando se hizo ingeniero	*when he became an engineer*
cuando se recibió de ingeniero	*when he got his engineering degree*
¿Camila era estudiante cuando la conociste?	*Was Camila a student when you met her?*
No, ya era física cuando la conocí.	*No, she was already a physicist when I met her.*
Manolo era un niño mandón.	*Manolo was* ***a bossy child****.*
un niño llorón	*a crybaby*
un niño preguntón	*an inquisitive child, a nosey child*
un niño dormilón	*a sleepyhead*
¿Raúl nunca se casó?	*Raúl never married?*
No, es solterón.	*No, he's a confirmed bachelor.*

Sofía tiene mucho dinero, ¿no?	*Sofía has a lot of money, doesn't she?*
¡Muchísimo! Es una ricachona.	*Loads! She's a very rich woman.*
¡Qué niñito más adorable!	*What a cute* ***little boy****!*
chiquita	*little girl*
bebito	*little baby*

Estructura y Práctica

F **Translation.** Express the following sentences in Spanish, selecting either the imperfect or the preterit for each verb.

1. *They told me their daughter was going to graduate from college.*
2. *Alonso was a confirmed bachelor until he met and married Sofía.*
3. *Victoria became a lawyer when she was twenty-seven.*
4. *You* (tú) *were very young when you got your medical degree.*
5. *The twins* [masc.] *were very gifted and nice, but also somewhat conceited.*

Augmentatives

Augmentatives indicate largeness, but they also have other meanings, such as disparagement. The most common augmentative ending in Spanish is **-ón/-ona**. It is often added to nouns and adjectives.

el hombre	→ el hombrón	*big man*
la mujer	→ la mujerona	*big woman*
rico	→ ricachón	*very rich, loaded*
inocente	→ inocentón	*naïve, gullible*

When the suffixes **-ón/-ona** are added to a verb root, they denote *given to performing the action of the verb.*

preguntar	→ preguntón	*always asking questions, inquisitive, nosey*
comer	→ comilón	*big eater, gluttonous*

The suffixes **-ote/-ota** and **-azo** are also used to form augmentatives, sometimes with the added connotation of contempt.

el libro	→ el librote	*big book*
grande	→ grandote, grandota	*very big, enormous*

In addition, **-azo** added to a noun can denote a blow or a strike with the object (or body part) indicated by the noun.

el codo (*elbow*)	→ el codazo	*elbow jab*
la cabeza	→ el cabezazo	*head butt*
el puño	→ el puñetazo	*fist punch*

Sometimes the addition of an augmentative suffix creates a new word. There is usually no suggestion of size.

la palabra	→ la palabrota	*swear word*
el éxito	→ el exitazo	*smash hit*
el soltero	→ el solterón	*confirmed bachelor*
la cintura (*waist*)	→ el cinturón	*belt*
la caja	→ el cajón	*drawer*
la rata (*rat*)	→ el ratón	*mouse*

G ***Aumentativos.*** Rewrite each of the following words with the augmentative ending **-ón/-ona**.

1. la casa
2. contestar
3. fácil
4. llorar
5. mirar
6. la muchacha
7. matar

Rewrite each of the following words with the augmentative ending **-azo**.

8. el martillo (*hammer*)
9. el perro
10. el puño (*fist*)
11. los ojos
12. el catarro

DIÁLOGO 7 · Paquito estaba enfermo.

Study the dialogue, then listen to the recording and repeat each line.

MIGUEL	Oye, ¿no me dijiste que Paquito estaba enfermo?
RAQUEL	Sí. Lo llevé al pediatra porque le dolía el oído y tenía fiebre.
MIGUEL	Pobrecito. ¿Qué dijo el pediatra?
RAQUEL	Me dijo que mi hijito tenía infección. Le recetó un antibiótico.

Análisis

Check that you understand the linguistic breakdown of each speech from *Diálogo 7*.

Oye, ¿no me dijiste que Paquito estaba enfermo?	*Say, didn't you tell me that Paquito was sick?*
oye	*say, hey* (attention-getting word, informal)
dijiste	*you said, you told*
estaba	*he was*
enfermo	*sick*
estar enfermo	*to be sick*

Sí. Lo llevé al pediatra porque le dolía el oído y tenía fiebre.	*Yes, I took him to the pediatrician because his ear hurt and he had a fever.*
llevar	*to take (someone somewhere)*
llevé	*I took*
el pediatra	*pediatrician*
doler (**o** > **ue**)	*to hurt* (patterns like **gustar**)
le dolía	*it hurt him*
le dolía el oído	*his ear hurt (him)*
tenía	*he had*
la fiebre	*fever*
Pobrecito. ¿Qué dijo el pediatra?	*Poor kid. What did the pediatrician say?*
pobrecito	*poor kid, poor guy*
dijo	*he said, he told*
Me dijo que mi hijito tenía infección. Le recetó un antibiótico.	*He told me that my son had an infection. He prescribed an antibiotic for him.*
me dijo	*he told me*
mi hijito	*my son*
tenía	*he had*
la infección	*infection*
recetar	*to prescribe*
recetarle algo a uno	*to prescribe something for someone*
le recetó	*he prescribed for him*
el antibiótico	*antibiotic*

Variantes

Listen, and repeat the same structures from *Diálogo 7*, now with new vocabulary.

Paquito estaba enfermo.	***Paquito** was sick.*
Juanito	*Juanito*
Carlitos	*Carlitos*
Dieguito	*Dieguito*
A Paquita le dolía la cabeza.	***Paquita** had a headache.*
Juanita	*Juanita*
Paulita	*Paulita*
A Carmencita le dolía la garganta.	***Carmencita** had a sore throat.*
Lolita	*Lolita*
Rosita	*Rosita*
Al abuelito le duele la espalda.	*Grandpa's **back** hurts.*
el cuello	*neck*
la rodilla	*knee*
el tobillo	*ankle*
A la abuelita le duelen los ojos.	*Grandma's **eyes** hurt.*
las piernas	*legs*
los dedos	*fingers*

Su hermanito tenía dolor de estómago.	*Their **little brother** had a stomachache.*
nietecito	*little grandson*
sobrinito	*little nephew*
primito	*little cousin*
Su hermanita tenía dolor de cabeza.	*Their **little sister** had a headache.*
nietecita	*little granddaughter*
sobrinita	*little niece*
primita	*little cousin*
El jovencito tomaba aspirinas.	*The young man took **aspirins**.*
vitaminas	*vitamins*
Florecita tenía catarro.	*Florecita had **a cold**.*
resfriado	*a cold*
gripe	*the flu*
alergia	*an allergy*
¿Quieres tomar un cafecito?	*Do you want to have a quick cup of coffee?*
Ahora tengo cita con el médico.	*I have a doctor's appointment now.*
Quizás después.	*Maybe afterwards.*

Estructura y Práctica

Diminutives

Spanish makes wide use of diminutives. The most common diminutive ending in Spanish is **-ito/-ita**. Diminutive endings are most commonly added to nouns, but they may appear also with adjectives.

libro	librito
casa	casita
viejo	viejito

Diminutives in Spanish express a variety of meanings, not only small size. They can express affection, sarcasm, politeness, etc.

Tienen una casita en el campo.	*They have a small house in the country.*
El perrito de ellos es muy cariñoso.	*Their dog is very affectionate.*
Él es timidito.	*He's somewhat shy.*

Diminutives are very common with proper names. Notice that in writing, the letters **c** and **g** change to **qu** and **gu**, respectively, before the diminutive ending.

Luis → Luisito
Paco → Paquito
Elena → Elenita
Diego → Dieguito
Sara → Sarita

Several groups of words take the ending -**cito**: words that end in -**e**, -**n**, or -**r**; words that end in a stressed vowel; and words of one syllable.

pobre → pobrecito
tren → trencito
pan → pancito
dolor → dolorcito
papá → papacito

Two-syllable nouns that have a first syllable containing -**ie**- or -**ue**- and that end in -**o** or -**a** pattern differently. They drop the -**o** or -**a** and add -**ecito**/-**ecita**. The same is true of many one-syllable nouns ending in a consonant.

tienda → tiendecita
puerta → puertecita
flor → florecita

However, the rules vary from country to country, especially for words of one syllable. **Papito**, **trenecito**, and **panecito** are also current.

TICO

Tico, a colloquial term for a native of Costa Rica, derives from the prominent use of the diminutive ending -**ico** rather than -**ito** in Costa Rica. -**Ico** is also used in Cuba, the Dominican Republic, and other countries, but it appears most widely in Costa Rica.

H ***Diminutivos.*** Rewrite each of the following words as a diminutive ending in -**ito** or -**ita**.

1. la ropa
2. el dedo
3. la niña
4. el pájaro
5. la voz
6. el chico
7. fresco
8. el joven
9. la botella
10. el calor
11. la fiesta
12. Miguel
13. poco
14. la nieta
15. el abuelo
16. cerca
17. la cabeza
18. Rodrigo
19. mismo
20. el choque
21. el pez
22. la luz
23. la tos

Reverse Construction Verbs: **doler** *to hurt, ache*

In Chapter 9, you learned about reverse construction verbs. These verbs appear with an indirect object pronoun and pattern like **gustar** (*to like*). The verb **doler** (**o** > **ue**) fits into this pattern.

Me gusta este barrio.	*I like this neighborhood.*
Me gustan estos barrios.	*I like these neighborhoods.*
Le duele el pie.	*His foot hurts.*
Le duelen los pies.	*His feet hurt.*
Le duele una muela.	*She has a toothache.*

Doler also means *to distress.*

Nos duele verlo en una silla de ruedas.	***We're distressed to see him** in a wheelchair. / **It distresses us to see him** in a wheelchair.*

I ***¡Ay, qué dolor!*** Express the following sentences in Spanish, using either the present or the imperfect tense of the verb **doler** in your answers.

1. *Juanita has a stomachache.*
2. *Pedro had a backache.*
3. *Their knees are aching.*
4. *Our little niece has a sore throat.*
5. *You* (tú) *had a headache.*
6. *The player's ankles are painful.*
7. *Paco's little grandson had an earache.*
8. *Their eyes were hurting.*

DIÁLOGO 8 · Un chequeo médico

Study the dialogue, then listen to the recording and repeat each line.

MIGUEL	Fui al médico porque me sentía mal y tenía mucho estrés.
RAQUEL	Entonces tuviste un chequeo. ¿Te hicieron un análisis de sangre?
MIGUEL	Sí. Parece que tengo el colesterol alto. Tengo que ponerme a dieta.
RAQUEL	Yo también tuve que bajar de peso porque tenía la presión sanguínea alta.

Análisis

Check that you understand the linguistic breakdown of each speech from *Diálogo 8.*

Fui al médico porque me sentía mal y tenía mucho estrés.	*I went to the doctor because I felt sick and I had a lot of stress.*
fui al médico	*I went to the doctor*
sentirse (**e** > **ie**)	*to feel*
me siento mal	*I feel sick*
me sentía mal	*I was feeling sick*
tenía	*I had*
el estrés	*stress*

Entonces tuviste un chequeo. ¿Te hicieron un análisis de sangre?	*So you had a checkup. Did they do a blood test (on you)?*
tuviste	*you had*
el chequeo	*checkup*
hicieron	*they did*
el análisis	*analysis, study, test*
la sangre	*blood*
el análisis de sangre	*blood test*
Sí. Parece que tengo el colesterol alto. Tengo que ponerme a dieta.	*It seems that my cholesterol is high. I have to go on a diet.*
parece que	*it seems that*
el colesterol alto	*high cholesterol*
ponerse a dieta	*to go on a diet*
Yo también tuve que bajar de peso porque tenía la presión sanguínea alta.	*I also had to lose weight because I had high blood pressure.*
tuve que	*I had to*
el peso	*weight*
bajar de peso	*to lose weight*
tuve que bajar de peso	*I had to (and did) lose weight*
tenía	*I had*
la presión	*pressure*
sanguíneo	*blood* (adjective)
la presión sanguínea	*blood pressure*

Variantes

Listen, and repeat the same structures from *Diálogo 8*, now with new vocabulary.

Empecé a comer sano porque me sentía cansado.	***I started to eat healthy food*** *because I was feeling tired.*
Cambié mi estilo de vida	*I changed my lifestyle*
Comencé a hacer ejercicio	*I started to exercise*
Dejé de comer tanta grasa	*I stopped eating so much fat*
¿Viste a Javier? Se puso gordo. Sí, engordó mucho porque es comilón.	*Did you see Javier? He got fat. Yes, he got very fat because he's a big eater.*
¿Viste a Rosa? Se puso delgada. Sí, adelgazó porque come como un pajarito.	*Did you see Rosa? She got thin. Yes, she got thin because she eats like a (little) bird.*
Tuve que bajar de peso porque la ropa me quedaba pequeña.	*I had to lose weight because my clothing didn't fit.* (literally, *my clothing was small on me)*
Tuve que aumentar de peso porque la ropa me quedaba grande.	*I had to gain weight because my clothing didn't fit.* (literally, *my clothing was big on me)*

DIÁLOGO 9 · Los mosquitos le comían vivo.

Study the dialogue, then listen to the recording and repeat each line.

RAQUEL Oye chico, ¿qué tienes en la piel? ¿Es un sarpullido?
MIGUEL Son picaduras de mosquito. Los mosquitos me comían vivo cuando acampábamos la semana pasada.
RAQUEL ¿No dormiste en una tienda de campaña?
MIGUEL Claro, pero me olvidé de ponerme el repelente contra mosquitos. ¡Mira tú el resultado!

Análisis

Check that you understand the linguistic breakdown of each speech from *Diálogo 9*.

Oye chico, ¿qué tienes en la piel? ¿Es un sarpullido?	*Hey, what have you got on your skin? Is it a rash?*
oye, chico	*hey* (interjection) (literally, *listen, guy*; addressed to a male)
la piel	*skin*
el sarpullido	*rash*
Son picaduras de mosquito. Los mosquitos me comían vivo cuando acampábamos la semana pasada.	*They're mosquito bites. The mosquitos were eating me alive when we went camping last week.*
la picadura	*bite*
el mosquito	*mosquito*
la picadura de mosquito	*mosquito bite*
comer vivo	*to eat (someone) alive*
me comían vivo	*they were eating me alive*
acampar	*to camp, go camping*
acampábamos	*we were camping*
¿No dormiste en una tienda de campaña?	*Didn't you sleep in a tent?*
dormiste	*you slept*
la tienda de campaña	*tent*
Claro, pero me olvidé de ponerme el repelente contra mosquitos. ¡Mira tú el resultado!	*Of course, but I forgot to put on mosquito repellent. And look what happened!*
olvidarse de hacer algo	*to forget to do something*
ponerse	*to put on*
el repelente	*repellent*
contra	*against*
el repelente contra mosquitos	*mosquito repellent*
el resultado	*the result*
¡Mira tú el resultado!	*Look what happened!* (literally, *Look at the result!*)

Variantes

Listen, and repeat the same structures from *Diálogo 9*, now with new vocabulary.

Me pica mucho la picadura de abeja.	*The bee sting itches a lot.*
Debes tratar de no rascártela.	*You should try not to scratch it.*
El champú me entró en los ojos.	*I got shampoo in my eyes.*
Están rojos. Te pican, ¿no?	*They look red. They sting, don't they?*
Tomaba el sol y ahora tengo quemadura de sol.	*I was sunbathing, and now I have a sunburn.*
¿Te olvidaste de ponerte el filtro solar?	*Did you forget to put sunblock on? / Did you forget to put sunscreen on?*
Uso lentes .	*I wear* ***glasses****.*
lentes de sol	*sunglasses*
lentes de contacto	*contact lenses*

Estructura y Práctica

Unplanned Occurrences (Use of the Indirect Object Pronoun)

In Spanish, unplanned occurrences—such as forgetting, breaking, losing, or dropping something—can be expressed by adding the indirect object pronoun to a **se** construction with certain verbs. These constructions focus on the object affected rather than on the person involved. These are high frequency structures heard in everyday speech.

acabársele

Se les acabó el repelente contra mosquitos.	***They ran out of*** *mosquito repellent.*

caérsele

Se me cayeron los lentes de contacto.	***I dropped*** *my contact lenses.*

rompérsele

Se le rompió el meñique al beisbolista.	*The baseball player* ***broke*** *his pinky.*

olvidársele

Se nos olvidó llevar el paraguas.	***We forgot*** *to bring the umbrella.*

ocurrírsele

¿Por qué no **se te ocurrió** llevar el paraguas?	*Why* ***didn't you think of*** *taking an umbrella?*

Here are some other verbs used in this construction.

descomponérsele a uno *to have something break down*
perdérsele a uno *to lose*
quebrársele a uno *to break*
quedársele a uno *to leave something behind*

J ***Sucesos inesperados* (Unplanned occurrences).** Rewrite each of the following sentences, transforming the **se** construction into an unplanned occurrence structure. Use the correct indirect object pronoun, as indicated by the cue in parentheses. Follow the *modelo.*

MODELO Se rompió la botella de champú. (á el)
→ Se le rompió la botella de champú.

1. Se acabó el filtro solar. (a ella)
2. Se olvidaron las toallas de playa (*beach towels*). (a nosotros)
3. ¿Se quedó el repelente contra mosquitos en casa? (a Uds.)
4. Se cayeron los lentes de sol. (a mí)
5. Se descompuso el carro. (a ellos)
6. Se perdieron las gafas oscuras. (a ti)
7. Se quebraron los platos. (a Ud.)

K Express the following sentences in Spanish.

1. *The mosquitos were eating us alive.*
2. *What a bite! You* (tú) *shouldn't scratch it.*
3. *Catalina was sunbathing until a bee stung her.* (*picar* (to sting))
4. *Pedro lost his sunglasses in the sand* (la arena).
5. *They left the tent at the campsite* (el campamento).
6. *Poor thing* [fem.]*! She got shampoo in her eyes.*

DIÁLOGO 10 · Aurora tuvo un niño.

Study the dialogue, then listen to the recording and repeat each line.

MIGUEL ¿Sabes que Aurora tuvo un niño?
RAQUEL ¿De veras? Yo ni sabía que estaba embarazada.
MIGUEL Aurora me contó que su esposo regresaba de un viaje de negocios cuando ella dio a luz.
RAQUEL ¡Ay, ese Santiago! ¡Hasta al nacimiento de su hijo llega tarde!

Análisis

Check that you understand the linguistic breakdown of each speech from *Diálogo 10*.

¿Sabes que Aurora tuvo un niño?	*Do you know that Aurora had a baby boy?*
tener un niño	*to have a child, to have a boy child*
tuvo un niño	*she had a baby boy*

¿De veras? Yo ni sabía que estaba embarazada.	*Really? I didn't even know that she was pregnant.*
ni	*not even*
sabía	*I knew*
ni sabía	*I didn't even know*
estar embarazada	*to be pregnant*
Aurora me contó que su esposo regresaba de un viaje de negocios cuando ella dio a luz.	*Aurora told me that her husband was coming back from a business trip when she gave birth.*
contar (**o** > **ue**)	*to tell, recount*
me contó que...	*she told me that . . .*
regresar	*to return, come/go back*
regresaba	*he was returning*
regresaba de un viaje de negocios	*he was coming back from a business trip*
dar a luz	*to give birth*
dio a luz	*she gave birth*
¡Ay, ese Santiago! ¡Hasta al nacimiento de su hijo llega tarde!	*Oh, that Santiago! He even comes late to the birth of his son!*
el nacimiento	*the birth*
el nacimiento de su hijo	*the birth of his son*

Variantes

Listen, and repeat the same structures from *Diálogo 10*, now with new vocabulary.

Nos contó que estaba embarazada .	*She told us **that she was pregnant**.*
que iba al médico	*that she was going to the doctor*
que tenía una enfermedad	*that she had an illness*

Estructura y Práctica

L **Imperfect or preterit.** Write either the imperfect or the preterit for each verb in parentheses to correctly complete each of the following sentences.

1. Hace unos días yo ________________ (saber) que Claudia ________________ (estar) embarazada.
2. Los Arriaga nos ________________ (decir) que su hija ________________ (ir) a tener un hijo.
3. Nosotros ________________ (esperar) en la sala de espera hasta que Matilde ________________ (dar) a luz.
4. Cuando Jorge ________________ (estar) en el consultorio del médico, la enfermera le ________________ (hacer) un análisis de sangre.
5. Los papás de Fernandito lo ________________ (llevar) al pediatra porque al niño le ________________ (doler) el estómago y ________________ (tener) fiebre.

DIÁLOGO 11 · Falsa alarma

Study the dialogue, then listen to the recording and repeat each line.

RAQUEL	¿No sabes? Mientras Mateo y yo subíamos en el ascensor, sonó la alarma.
MIGUEL	Dios mío, ¡qué susto! ¿Creían que había un incendio?
RAQUEL	Sí. Llegaron los bomberos y la policía. Por suerte fue una falsa alarma.

Análisis

Check that you understand the linguistic breakdown of each speech from *Diálogo 11*.

¿No sabes? Mientras Mateo y yo subíamos en el ascensor, sonó la alarma.	*You know? While Mateo and I were going up in the elevator, the alarm went off.*
subíamos	*we were going up*
el ascensor	*elevator*
sonó	*it sounded, it went off*
la alarma	*the alarm*
Dios mío, ¡qué susto! ¿Creían que había un incendio?	*My gosh, what a scare! Did you think there was a fire?*
Dios	*God*
Dios mío	*my gosh, my goodness*
el susto	*fright*
¿creían?	*did you think?*
había	*there was*
el incendio	*fire (accidental)*
Sí. Llegaron los bomberos y la policía. Por suerte fue una falsa alarma.	*Yes. The firefighters and the police arrived. Luckily, it was a false alarm.*
llegaron	*they arrived*
el bombero	*firefighter*
los bomberos	*firefighters*
la policía	*the police*
la suerte	*luck*
por suerte	*luckily*
fue	*it was*
una falsa alarma	*a false alarm*

Variantes

Listen, and repeat the same structures from *Diálogo 11*, now with new vocabulary.

Mientras subíamos en el ascensor, sonó la alarma.	*While we were going up in the elevator,* ***the alarm sounded.***
llegaron los bomberos	*the firefighters arrived*
Mientras estaban en el banco, hubo un atraco.	*While they were in the bank, there was a holdup.*
Mientras viajaban, estalló una guerra en su país.	*While they were traveling, a war broke out in their country.*
La policía atrapó al ladrón mientras él se escapaba.	*The police caught the thief while he was escaping.*

Estructura y Práctica

M **Imperfect or preterit.** Write either the imperfect or the preterit for each verb in parentheses to correctly complete each of the following sentences.

1. Mientras nosotros ________________ (bajar) en la escalera mecánica,
   ________________ (ver) un atraco (*mugging*) a un paseante (*passerby*).
2. Mientras la familia ________________ (estar) de vacaciones,
   ________________ (sonar) la alarma de su casa.
3. El incendio ________________ (arder (*to burn*)) hasta que los bomberos lo
   ________________ (apagar).
4. Su vida ________________ (ser) tranquila hasta que ________________ (estallar) la guerra.

DIÁLOGO 12 · Un choque de carros

Study the dialogue, then listen to the recording and repeat each line.

MIGUEL	Hoy, mientras yo retiraba dinero del cajero automático, hubo un choque de carros delante del banco.
RAQUEL	¿Hubo heridos? ¿Llegó una ambulancia?
MIGUEL	Sí, dos paramédicos atendieron a las víctimas. Afortunadamente sólo tenían heridas leves.

Análisis

Check that you understand the linguistic breakdown of each speech from *Diálogo 12*.

Hoy, mientras yo retiraba dinero del cajero automático, hubo un choque de carros delante del banco.	*Today, while I was withdrawing money from the ATM, there was a car crash in front of the bank.*
retirar dinero	*to withdraw money*
retiraba	*I was withdrawing*
el cajero automático	*the ATM*
hubo	*there was, there were*
el choque	*collision*
un choque de carros	*a car crash*
delante de	*in front of*
delante del banco	*in front of the bank*
¿Hubo heridos? ¿Llegó una ambulancia?	*Were any people injured? Did an ambulance arrive?*
el herido	*injured or wounded person*
la ambulancia	*ambulance*

Sí, dos paramédicos atendieron a las víctimas. Afortunadamente sólo tenían heridas leves. — *Yes, two paramedics tended to the victims. Fortunately, they only had light injuries.*

el paramédico	*paramedic*
atender a	*to tend to, look after*
la víctima	*victim* (always feminine in Spanish)
afortunadamente	*fortunately*
sólo	*only*
tenían	*they had*
la herida	*injury, wound*
leve	*light, slight*

Variantes

Listen, and repeat the same structures from *Diálogo 12*, now with new vocabulary.

Yo estaba en la esquina cuando chocaron dos coches.	*I was at the corner when **two cars crashed**.*
vi un accidente de tráfico	*I saw a traffic accident*
un coche atropelló a un peatón	*a car ran a pedestrian over*
Todo el mundo miraba mientras los paramédicos atendían a las víctimas.	*Everyone was watching while the paramedics **were tending to the victims**.*
daban primeros auxilios	*were giving first aid*

Estructura y Práctica

N ***Una narrativa.*** Write either the imperfect or the preterit for each of the following verbs in parentheses to create a narrative about an accident.

Samuel (1) ________________ (ir) todas las semanas al banco para retirar dinero del cajero automático. El miércoles pasado él (2) ________________ (llegar) a la esquina donde (3) ________________ (quedar) el banco y (4) ________________ (acercarse) al cajero automático. De repente él (5) ________________ (oír) el ruido de sirenas y una ambulancia y (6) ________________ (ver) a muchos policías y bomberos. Le (7) ________________ (preguntar) a un policía qué (8) ________________ (pasar). El policía le (9) ________________ (decir) que un peatón (*pedestrian*) (10) ________________ (cruzar) la calle sin mirar y un taxi lo (11) ________________ (atropellar). Los paramédicos (12) ________________ (atender) a la víctima que afortunadamente sólo (13) ________________ (tener) heridas leves.

Un paso más

Are you ready to take your Spanish a step further? Here are exercises that will enhance your knowledge of the language and allow you to express yourself freely.

Phrases, expressions, and filler words

To make your Spanish sound more like a native speaker's in conversation, it is important to use words, phrases, and expressions that a Spanish speaker uses automatically and repeats often in speech. Among these are *fillers*—words, phrases or sounds that mark a pause or hesitation in speech. In everyday English conversation, we use fillers such as *ah, um,* and *er,* and words and phrases including *okay, well, hey, right?, y'know, that is, I mean, like, so, actually,* and *basically.*

Spanish also has phrases, expressions, and filler words (**muletillas**) that you would want to use to make your conversation more colloquial. These include **este** (like *um* or *er,* this is a delaying or hesitating technique); **bueno**, **pues**, **oye**, **mira**, **chico**, **entonces**, **¿no sabes?**, **¡ah sí!**, **¡Dios mío!**, **vale**, **no me digas**, **menos mal**, **claro (que sí/que no)**, **cómo no**, **¡caramba!**, **¡ni hablar!**, **¡ya lo creo!**, **en realidad**, **o sea**, **¿de veras?**, **fíjate**, **me imagino**, **¿entiendes?**, **¿me explico?**; tags like **¿verdad?**, **¿no?**, and **¿no es cierto?**; **¡vaya!** (wow!); and exclamations such as **¡Qué bien!**, **¡Qué maravilloso!**, **¡Qué pena!**, and **¡Qué horror!**

O To make the following dialogues more authentic, rewrite the speeches, choosing phrases and fillers from the above list (or others you learned in previous chapters) and placing them anywhere in the sentences you think appropriate. Add punctuation and capital or lowercase letters as needed. You'll be surprised what a difference these little words and phrases make!

1. —¿Quieres ir conmigo al partido de béisbol mañana?
   —¡Van a jugar mis equipos favoritos!
   —Vamos a comer perros calientes y cacahuetes.
   —¡Y tomar unas cervecitas también!

2. —¡Qué sarpullido tienes en las piernas! ¿Qué te pasó?
   —Daba una caminata con unos amigos y pisamos hiedras venenosas (*poison ivy*).
   —Te pica mucho. Pero no debes rascarte.
   —La loción de calamina me alivia un poco la picazón.
   —Se ve feíto. ¡Por ahora debes usar un pantalón largo!

3. —Hubo un accidente en el centro comercial.
   —¿Qué pasó?
   —Parece que dos personas se cayeron en la escalera mecánica.
   —¿Tenían heridas graves?
   —No sé. Espero que no.

P ***Preguntas personales.*** Answer each question with a complete Spanish sentence.

1. ¿Ud. prefiere comprar ropa y otros artículos en una tienda o en línea? ¿Qué cosas compra en las tiendas? ¿Y por internet?

2. ¿Cuánto tiempo hacía que conocía a su prometido/prometida cuando se casaron?

3. ¿Cómo se conocieron?
4. ¿Cómo era de niño/niña? ¿Mandón/mandona, llorón/llorona, preguntón/preguntona?
5. ¿Tiene un hijo? ¿Es un niño / una niña prodigio? ¿Cómo es?
6. ¿Ud. va de campamento (*to go camping*)? ¿Adónde va? ¿Con quiénes va?
7. ¿Qué es lo que le gusta del camping?
8. ¿Cómo puede describir su "estilo de vida"?

Q Write a paragraph about a medical experience you had. Use the following questions as a guide.

1. ¿Ud. tuvo un accidente o sufría de una enfermedad?
2. ¿Tenía dolor? ¿Otros síntomas?
3. ¿Los paramédicos lo/la atendieron? ¿Le dieron primeros auxilios?
4. ¿Fue al médico o a una sala de emergencias?
5. ¿Fue al hospital en ambulancia?
6. ¿Le hicieron un análisis de sangre?
7. ¿Le tomaron la presión arterial?
8. ¿Cuál fue el diagnóstico?
9. ¿Qué le recomendaron?
10. ¿Le recetaron un medicamento?
11. ¿Va al médico por un chequeo todos los años?
12. ¿Qué hace para mantener la salud física y emocional?

R Write a paragraph about the medical personnel you and your family members see, choosing words from the following list. Most of these words are cognates of English words, and others are words you learned in previous chapters. You already know how to derive the feminine forms of the nouns, so you'll be able to talk about female counterparts.

el cardiólogo
el cirujano
el/la dentista
el dermatólogo
el enfermero practicante
el/la especialista
el gastroenterólogo
el ginecólogo
el médico asistente
el médico de cabecera, el médico de familia
el neurólogo
el/la obstetra
el oftalmólogo
el oncólogo
el/la osteópata
el otorrinolaringólogo
el/la pediatra
el/la periodontista
el/la psiquiatra
el reumatólogo
el urólogo

12

People: Character and Personality, Societal Problems

Communication Goals

- Comparing people and things
- Talking about character and personality
- Vocabulary: environmental pollution and other problems of society

Grammar Topics

- Comparative of Adjectives, Adverbs, and Nouns
- Adverbs of Manner
- Superlative of Adjectives: Absolute Superlative
- Nominalization of Adjectives (Adjectives Used as Nouns)
- Conjunctions: **y** *and,* **o** *or*
- Review: Prepositional Pronouns

DIÁLOGO 1 · ¿Quién es más terco?

Study the dialogue, then listen to the recording and repeat each line.

MANUEL	¿No te parece que Sofía es terca?
TERESA	Ah sí, pero tú no conoces a su hermana Julia. Es más terca que ella.
MANUEL	Y su hermano, ¿es tan terco como ellas?
TERESA	¿Pepe? Pepe les gana y con mucho. Él es el más terco de la familia.

Análisis

Check that you understand the linguistic breakdown of each speech from *Diálogo 1.*

¿No te parece que Sofía es terca?	*Don't you think that Sofía is stubborn?*
no te parece que	*don't you think that, doesn't it seem to you that*
terco	*stubborn*

Ah sí, pero tú no conoces a su hermana Julia. Es más terca que ella.	*Oh, yes, but you don't know her sister Julia. She is more stubborn than she is.*
más + *adjective* + que	*more* + adjective + *than*
Y su hermano, ¿es tan terco como ellas?	*And their brother? Is he as stubborn as they are?*
tan + *adjective* + como	*as* + adjective + *as*
¿Pepe? Pepe les gana y con mucho. Él es el más terco de la familia.	*Pepe? Pepe is the champ. He's the most stubborn one in the family.*
ganarle a uno	*to have someone beat*
les gana	*has them beat* (literally, *beats them all*)
con mucho	*by a lot*
el más terco	*the most stubborn one*
el más terco de la familia	*the most stubborn one in the family*

Variantes

Listen, and repeat the same structures from *Diálogo 1*, now with new vocabulary.

Ella es más despistada que su hermana.	*She is* ***more absentminded than*** *her sister.*
más caprichosa que	*more unpredictable than*
más atractiva que	*more attractive than*
más entrometida que	*more meddlesome than*
más comprensiva que	*more understanding than*
más pesada que	*more annoying than*
más coqueta que	*more flirtatious than*
más cortés que	*more polite than*
Él es menos serio que su hermano.	*He is* ***not as serious as*** *his brother.*
menos presumido que	*not as conceited as*
menos maleducado que	*not as rude as*
menos tímido que	*not as shy as*
menos mentiroso que	*not as deceitful as*
menos egoísta que	*not as selfish as*
menos calculador que	*not as calculating as*
menos raro que	*not as strange as, not as weird as*
Ellos no son tan ambiciosos como Uds.	*They are not* ***as ambitious as*** *you are.*
tan optimistas como	*as optimistic as*
tan pesimistas como	*as pessimistic as*
tan realistas como	*as realistic as*
tan trabajadores como	*as hardworking as*
tan sensatos como	*as sensible as*
Yo estoy tan ocupada como tú.	*I'm* ***as busy as*** *you are.*
tan contenta como	*as happy as*
tan preocupada como	*as worried as*
tan aburrida como	*as bored as*
tan decepcionada como	*as disappointed as*
tan emocionada como	*as excited as*
tan estresada como	*as stressed as*

tan entusiasmada como	*as enthusiastic as*
tan deprimida como	*as depressed as*
José es el más gruñón de la familia.	*José is **the grouchiest one** in his family.*
el más amable	*the kindest one*
el más sincero	*the sincerest one*
el más considerado	*the most thoughtful one*
el más cascarrabias	*the most cantankerous one*
Carmen es la más alegre de la familia.	*Carmen is **the most cheerful one** in her family.*
la más sensible	*the most sensitive one*
la más ingenua	*the most naïve one*
la más falsa	*the most two-faced one*
la más perezosa	*the laziest one*
Esteban te gana y con mucho.	*Esteban beats **you** by a lot.*
me	*me*
nos	*us*
le	*him, her, you* (Ud.)
les	*them, you* (Uds.)

Estructura y Práctica

Comparative of Adjectives, Adverbs, and Nouns

Adjectives

The comparative of adjectives is relatively simple in Spanish. Here is the basic pattern for comparisons of inequality.

más + adjective + **que**
menos + adjective + **que**

Más + adjective is the equivalent of English *more* + adjective, or the adjective with the suffix *-er*.

más inteligente que	*more intelligent than*
más bonito que	*prettier than*

Menos means *less*, but it is usually translated as *not as*.

menos interesante que	*less interesting than, not as interesting as*

Spanish uses **tan** + adjective + **como** to express the comparison of equality.

tan terco como	*as stubborn as*
tan aburrido como	*as boring as*

The adjectives **bueno** and **malo** have irregular comparative forms.

mejor *better*
peor *worse*

Este hotel es **mejor** que el otro.	*This hotel is **better** than the other one.*
Su situación es **peor** que la nuestra.	*Their situation is **worse** than ours.*

Más bueno and **más malo** refer to moral qualities.

Ese chico es más bueno que el pan.	*That boy is as good as gold.* (literally, *better than bread*)
Aquella mujer es más mala que su hermana.	*That woman is worse than her sister.*

The comparatives **más grande** and **más pequeño** are replaced by **mayor and menor,** respectively, when referring to age.

Mi hermano es **mayor** que yo.	*My brother is* ***older*** *than I.*
Mi hermano es **más grande** que yo.	*My brother is* ***bigger*** *than I.*
Su esposa es **menor** que él.	*His wife is* ***younger*** *than he.*
Su esposa es **más pequeña** que él.	*His wife is* ***shorter*** *than he.*

Superlative of Adjectives

Spanish has no particular superlative form. Usually, the definite article (or possessive adjective) is used with the noun that the adjective modifies to imply a superlative.

Quiero hablar con una persona más comprensiva.	*I want to speak with a more understanding person.*
Julia es **la persona más comprensiva** que conozco.	*Julia is* ***the most understanding person*** *I know.*

After a superlative, *in* is translated as **de**.

Es la ciudad más importante **del** país.	*It's the most important city* ***in*** *the country.*
Miguel es el alumno más dotado **de la** clase.	*Miguel is the most gifted student* ***in*** *the class.*

Adverbs

Adverbs are compared in the same way as adjectives. Here is the pattern for the comparison of inequality.

más + adverb + **que**
menos + adverb + **que**

Se viaja **más cómodamente** en tren **que** en autobús.	*One travels* ***more comfortably*** *by train* ***than*** *by bus.*
Se viaja **menos cómodamente** en burro **que** en carro.	*One travels* ***less comfortably*** *by donkey* ***than*** *by car.*

Spanish uses **tan** + adverb + **como** to express the comparison of equality.

Se viaja **tan cómodamente** en tren **como** en avión.	*One travels* ***as comfortably*** *by train* ***as*** *by plane.*

Nouns

When nouns are the object of comparison, the patterns **más** + noun + **que** and **menos** + noun + **que** are used.

Él escribe **más informes que** yo.	*He writes* ***more reports than*** *I.*
Él escribe **menos informes que** yo.	*He writes* ***fewer reports than*** *I.*

For the comparison of equality, **tan** changes to **tanto** before a noun and agrees with the noun in gender and number.

Él escribe **tantos informes como** yo.	*He writes **as many reports as** I do.*

Verbs

Más que, **menos que**, and **tanto como** can also modify verbs.

Ella trabaja **más que** yo.	*She works **more than** I do.*
Ella trabaja **menos que** yo.	*She works **less than** I do.*
Ella trabaja **tanto como** yo.	*She works **as much as** I do.*

Note that in colloquial English, speakers often use an object pronoun after *than*, even when a subject pronoun would be required grammatically—for example, *She works more than me.* This usage is impossible in Spanish.

Comparisons with Numerals

In comparisons involving numbers, **que** is replaced by **de** before a numeral.

En esta oficina trabajan **más de cincuenta** personas.	***More than fifty** people work in this office.*

However, if the meaning is *only* or *no more than*, **más que** is used. In this case, the verb is usually negative.

No cursa **más que dos** materias.	*He's **only** taking **two** subjects.* (literally, *He's not taking more than two subjects.*)
No me quedan **más que cuatro** dólares.	*I have **only four** dollars left.* (literally, *I don't have more than four dollars left.*)

Que (*Than*) + Negative Words

After **que** (*than*), Spanish uses negative words such as **nada**, **nadie**, and **nunca** after a comparative where English uses indefinite words such as *anything*, *anyone*, and *ever*.

La salud es más importante **que nada**.	*Health is more important **than anything**.*
Él estudia más **que nadie**.	*He studies more **than anyone**.*
Ahora la comida cuesta más **que nunca**.	*Now food costs more **than ever**.*

A **Comparisons of inequality and equality: Adjectives.** Write two new sentences that show comparisons of inequality by combining the two sentences given. Write one new sentence that shows a comparison using **más que** (*more than*) and a second sentence that shows a comparison using **menos que** (*less than*). Follow the *modelo.*

MODELO Gonzalo es trabajador. / Diego es más trabajador.
→ Diego es más trabajador que Gonzalo.
→ Gonzalo es menos trabajador que Diego.

1. Aurora es presumida. / Consuelo es más presumida.
2. Jaime y Federico están entusiasmados. / Nosotros estamos más entusiasmados.
3. El profesor de física es exigente. / La profesora de química es más exigente.

4. Los pantalones son caros. / La chaqueta es más cara.
5. Tú eres optimista. / Yo soy más optimista.
6. La casa es moderna. / El condominio es más moderno.
7. Juan Manuel es cortés. / Uds. son más corteses.
8. Los tamales están ricos. / Los tacos están más ricos.

B **Comparisons of equality: Adjectives.** Write sentences from the elements given to show comparisons of equality. Follow the *modelo.*

MODELO Timoteo / amable / su hermano
→ Timoteo es tan amable como su hermano.

1. Elena / caprichosa / Victoria
2. Pedro / ingenuo / tú
3. ellos / egoístas / Rodrigo
4. Paquita / coqueta / su prima
5. los empleados / trabajadores / el director
6. Uds. / estresados / sus amigos
7. Ana María / calculadora / su cuñada
8. Bernardo / emocionado / Beatriz
9. nuestros hijos / ocupados / nosotros
10. tú / comprensiva / tus papás

Adverbs of Manner

As you learned in Chapter 8, most adverbs of manner in Spanish are formed by adding the suffix **-mente** to the feminine singular form of the adjective.

MASCULINE SINGULAR	FEMININE SINGULAR	ADVERB	MEANING
ingenuo	ingenua	ingenuamente	*naively*
caprichoso	caprichosa	caprichosamente	*unpredictably*
rígido	rígida	rígidamente	*rigidly*
estricto	estricta	estrictamente	*strictly*

If the adjective has only one form for the masculine and feminine singular, then the suffix **-mente** is added to that form.

SINGULAR	ADVERB	MEANING
amable	amablemente	*kindly*
inflexible	inflexiblemente	*inflexibly*
alegre	alegremente	*happily*
indulgente	indulgentemente	*leniently*

Adverbs ending in **-mente** have two stresses in speech, one on the original stressed syllable of the adjective and one on the first **e** of the suffix **-mente**.

If the adjective itself has a written accent mark, the accent mark is retained when the suffix **-mente** is added.

cortés	cortésmente
tímido	tímidamente
fácil	fácilmente

C **Comparisons of inequality and equality: Adverbs.** Write sentences from the elements given to show comparisons of inequality and equality using **más, menos,** and **tan**. Use the preterit tense. Follow the *modelo.*

MODELO él / hablar / tímidamente / ella
→ Él habló más tímidamente que ella.
→ Ella habló menos tímidamente que él.
→ Él habló tan tímidamente como ella.

1. Guillermo / escuchar / atentamente / Josefa
2. Alberto / trabajar / ambiciosamente / Santiago
3. Uds. / ir de compras / frecuentemente / nosotros
4. la familia Suárez / vivir / cómodamente / la familia Morales
5. nosotros / manejar / lentamente / tú
6. Antonio / ofenderse / fácilmente / su hermano
7. Damián / correr / rápidamente / Uds.
8. tú / pensar / profundamente / yo
9. Blanca / contestar / amablemente / Pepe
10. Ud. / reaccionar / sensible / Daniela

D **Comparisons of inequality and equality: Nouns.** Write sentences from the elements given to show comparisons of inequality and equality using **más, menos,** and **tan.** Use the imperfect tense. Follow the *modelo.*

MODELO Arturo / recibir / textos / Celeste
→ Arturo recibía más textos que Celeste.
→ Celeste recibía menos textos que Arturo.
→ Arturo recibía tantos textos como Celeste.

1. yo / cursar / materias / tú
2. el niño / tener / hambre / su hermanita
3. Uds. / comprar / libros de texto / los otros estudiantes
4. Eva / ver / películas / María Elena
5. tú / comer / comida chatarra / tus amigos
6. nosotros / leer / obras maestras / ellos
7. Sofía / recorrer / países / su marido
8. Ignacio / hacer / ejercicio / Mateo

E ***¿Cómo son sus parientes?*** Write sentences from the elements given to describe what these members of the Vargas family are like. Use the superlative of each adjective. Make all necessary changes. Follow the *modelo.*

MODELO la tía Olivia / ingenuo
→ La tía Olivia es la más ingenua.

1. la abuela Raquel / sensato
2. el tío Rodrigo / cascarrabias
3. los primos Laura y Martín / calculador
4. las nietas Teresita y Paquita / coqueta
5. la cuñada Lucía / entrometido
6. los sobrinos Ramón y Eugenia / terco
7. el yerno (*son-in-law*) Manolo / realista
8. la nuera (*daughter-in-law*) Montserrat / pesado

F **Translation.** Express the following sentences in Spanish.

1. *Anita is more conceited than her sister.*
2. *Jorge is less rude than his friends.*
3. *Cristóbal was as stressed as you* (tú) *were.*
4. *My brother and sister are as thoughtful as I.*
5. *Matilde is the shyest person in her family.*
6. *Juanito is the strangest student in his class.*

DIÁLOGO 2 · La primera novela es la mejor de todas.

Study the dialogue, then listen to the recording and repeat each line.

TERESA Dicen que la nueva novela de Fuentes es buenísima.
MANUEL Es cierto. Yo la leí y creo que es mejor que su última novela.
TERESA Pero no es tan buena como la primera que escribió, ¿verdad?
MANUEL Claro que no. Ésa es una obra maestra. Es la mejor de todas.

Análisis

Check that you understand the linguistic breakdown of each speech from *Diálogo 2*.

Dicen que la nueva novela de Fuentes es buenísima.	*They say that Fuentes's new novel is very good.*
buenísimo	*very good*
Es cierto. Yo la leí y creo que es mejor que su última novela.	*It's true. I read it, and I think that it is better than his last novel.*
mejor que	*better than*
último	*last*

Pero no es tan buena como la primera que escribió, ¿verdad?	*But it's not as good as the first one he wrote, is it?*
la primera	*the first one*
no es tan buena como	*it's not as good as*
Claro que no. Ésa es una obra maestra. Es la mejor de todas.	*Of course not. That one is a masterpiece. It's the best one of all.*
claro que no	*of course not*
ésa	*that one*
la obra	*work (literary, musical,* etc.)
la obra maestra	*masterpiece*
la mejor	*the best one*

Variantes

Listen, and repeat the same structures from *Diálogo 2*, now with new vocabulary.

El nuevo libro no es tan bueno como el último.	*The new book is not* ***as good as*** *the last one.*
tan interesante como	*as interesting as*
tan divertido como	*as entertaining as*
tan atractivo como	*as engaging as*
tan largo como	*as long as*
Su novela es buenísima.	*His novel is* ***very good****.*
interesantísima	*very interesting*
divertidísima	*very entertaining*
larguísima	*very long*
aburridísima	*very boring*
Este libro es el mejor de todos.	*This book is the best one of all.*
Paz es el mejor autor del mundo.	*Paz is the best author in the world.*

Estructura y Práctica

Superlative of Adjectives: Absolute Superlative

The absolute superlative is a term used for the suffix **-ísimo** in Spanish, a suffix that is the equivalent of *very*. The addition of the suffix **-ísimo** creates a new four-form adjective. The final vowel of the masculine singular form of the adjective is dropped before the **-ísimo** ending. If the masculine singular form of the adjective ends in a consonant, the suffix **-ísimo** is added directly to the adjective.

caro	→	carísimo	*very expensive*
contento	→	contentísimo	*very happy*
raro	→	rarísimo	*very strange*
tonto	→	tontísimo	*very silly*
inteligente	→	inteligentísimo	*very intelligent*
potente	→	potentísimo	*very powerful*
difícil	→	dificilísimo	*very difficult*

Adverbs can be formed by adding **-mente** to the feminine singular form of the absolute superlative.

rarísimamente	*very strangely*
tontísimamente	*very stupidly*

Adverbs of quantity also have absolute superlative forms.

mucho	→ muchísimo	*very much*
poco	→ poquísimo	*very little*

Adjectives or adverbs of quantity whose last consonant is **c** or **g** show a spelling change before adding the ending **-ísimo**: The **c** changes to **qu** and **g** changes to **gu** before the ending **-ísimo** is added.

poco	→ poquísimo	*very little*
simpático	→ simpatiquísimo	*very nice, very pleasant*
largo	→ larguísimo	*very long*

G **The absolute superlative.** Write the absolute superlative of the adjective in parentheses to correctly complete each of the following sentences. Follow the *modelo*.

MODELO La clase de matemáticas es *dificilísima*. (difícil)

1. Carolina lleva ropa ______________. (elegante)
2. Todos los platos que probamos estuvieron ______________. (rico)
3. Los informes que escribieron son ______________. (largo)
4. Este museo de arte es ______________. (interesante)
5. Se presentaban unas obras de teatro ______________. (bueno)
6. Los paisajes que vieron eran realmente ______________. (hermoso)
7. Conocimos a unas personas ______________. (simpático)
8. Estos exámenes son ______________. (fácil)
9. El profesor dio una explicación ______________. (claro)
10. Los programadores van a estar ______________ todo el día. (ocupado)

H **Translation.** Express the following sentences in Spanish. Write all numbers as words.

1. *It's the best book in our library.*
2. *It's the most famous brand on the market.*
3. *We were working more than ever.*
4. *Enrique used to travel as frequently as we did.*
5. *Last year Perla earned more than 200,000 dollars.*
6. *Pablo has only 1,700 dollars left in his savings account* (la cuenta de ahorros).
7. *Our team beat the other team by a lot.*

8. *They bought as many pens and pencils as we.*
9. *Do you* (Ud.) *think this manager is more demanding than the former one?*
10. *Are you kidding? He's the most lenient manager in the company.*
11. *Health is more important than anything.*
12. *Raquel complains more than anyone.*

DIÁLOGO 3 · Busco una nueva computadora.

Study the dialogue, then listen to the recording and repeat each line.

MANUEL	Esta computadora es más potente que la mía.
TERESA	También es más cara que la tuya.
MANUEL	¿Y aquélla? Es aún más cara que ésta.
TERESA	Me imagino que funciona mejor que ésta.

Análisis

Check that you understand the linguistic breakdown of each speech from *Diálogo 3*.

Esta computadora es más potente que la mía.	*This computer is more powerful than mine.*
potente	*powerful*
la mía (< la computadora mía)	*mine*
También es más cara que la tuya.	*It's also more expensive than yours.*
la tuya (< la computadora tuya)	*yours*
¿Y aquélla? Es aún más cara que ésta.	*And that one? It's even more expensive than this one.*
aquélla (< aquella computadora)	*that one*
aún	*even*
ésta (< esta computadora)	*this one*
Me imagino que funciona mejor que ésta.	*I imagine that it works better than this one.*
imaginarse	*to imagine*
funcionar	*to work, function*
mejor que	*better than*
ésta (< esta computadora)	*this one*

Variantes

Listen, and repeat the same structures from *Diálogo 3*, now with new vocabulary.

Esta computadora es más potente que la tuya .	*This computer is* ***more powerful than yours.***
más potente que la suya	*more powerful than his/hers/yours* (Ud., Uds.)/*theirs*
más potente que la nuestra	*more powerful than ours*

Este teléfono celular es menos caro que el mío.	*This cell phone **isn't as expensive as mine**.*
es menos caro que el tuyo	*isn't as expensive as yours*
es menos caro que el suyo	*isn't as expensive as his/hers/yours* (Ud., Uds.)/*theirs*
es menos caro que el nuestro	*isn't as expensive as ours*
Estos bolígrafos son tan baratos como ésos.	*These **pens** are as cheap as those.*
lápices	*pencils*
cuadernos	*notebooks*
disquetes	*diskettes*
cartuchos de tinta	*ink cartridges*
Esta marca es tan buena como ésa.	*This brand is as good as that one.*
Estas plumas son tan buenas como ésas.	*These pens are as good as those.*
¿Ese software es más fácil de usar que éste?	*Is that software more user friendly than this one?*
No, este software es tan fácil de usar como ése.	*No, this software is as user friendly as that one.*
Este iPod funciona mejor que aquél.	*This iPod works better than that one.*

Estructura y Práctica

Nominalization of Adjectives (Adjectives Used as Nouns)

Nominalization is the process by which a part of speech, such as an adjective, is made to function as a noun or pronoun. In English, there are several processes that accomplish this. In Spanish, however, there is only one: deletion of the noun. Nominalization takes place in several types of structures.

1 · A noun may be deleted from a phrase consisting of a determiner + noun + adjective. In this structure, the adjective plus the definite article (or other determiner) can function as a noun. The definite article is not stressed in the nominalized phrase, but the indefinite article is.

el modelo nuevo y el **modelo** antiguo	*the new model and the old model*
→ el modelo nuevo y **el antiguo**	*the new model and **the old one***
las ciudades grandes y las **ciudades** pequeñas	*the big cities and the little cities*
→ las ciudades grandes y **las pequeñas**	*the big cities and **the little ones***
una computadora barata y una **computadora** cara	*a cheap computer and an expensive computer*
→ una computadora barata y **una cara**	*a cheap computer and **an expensive one***

2 · A noun may be deleted in a prepositional phrase beginning with **de**, including phrases expressing possession. In this structure, the definite article (or other determiner) becomes a pronoun and is stressed.

la casa de María y la **casa** de Juan	*María's house and John's house*
→ la casa de María y **la de Juan**	*María's house and* ***John's***
los zapatos de cuero y los **zapatos** de tela	*the leather shoes and the cloth shoes*
→ los zapatos de cuero y **los de tela**	*the leather shoes and* ***the cloth ones***

3 · A noun may be deleted after a demonstrative adjective. In this structure, an accent mark was traditionally added to the demonstrative adjective when the noun was deleted, but the accent mark is optional in current usage. The resultant structure is a demonstrative pronoun.

ese vuelo y este **vuelo**	*that flight and this flight*
→ ese vuelo y **éste/este**	*that flight and* ***this one***
estas dietas y esa **dieta**	*these diets and that diet*
→ estas dietas y **ésa/esa**	*these diets and* ***that one***
estos documentos y aquellos **documentos**	*these documents and those documents*
→ estos documentos y **aquéllos/aquellos**	*these documents and* ***those***
aquella sucursal y estas **sucursales**	*that branch and these branches*
→ aquella sucursal y **éstas/estas**	*that branch and* ***these***

4 · A noun may be deleted from a phrase containing a long-form possessive. The resultant structure is called a possessive pronoun.

el tráfico nuestro y el **tráfico** suyo	*our traffic and their traffic*
→ el tráfico nuestro y **el suyo**	*our traffic and* ***theirs***
la universidad tuya y la **universidad** mía	*your university and my university*
→ la universidad tuya y **la mía**	*your university and* ***mine***
los consejos suyos y los **consejos** tuyos	*his advice and your advice*
→ los consejos suyos y **los tuyos**	*his advice and* ***yours***
la pasantía mía y las **pasantías** de Uds.	*my internship and your internships*
→ la pasantía mía y **las de Uds.**	*my internship and* ***yours***

I ***¿Cuál te gusta más?*** Write a response to each of the following questions, eliminating the nouns that are being compared. Follow the *modelo.*

MODELO ¿Cuál te gusta más, la primera novela o la segunda novela?
→ Prefiero la primera, pero me gusta la segunda también.

1. ¿Cuál te gusta más, el abrigo marrón o el abrigo negro?
2. ¿Cuáles te gustan más, los libros de cuentos o los libros de poesía?
3. ¿Cuál te gusta más, la oficina de enfrente o la oficina de al lado?
4. ¿Cuáles te gustan más, los museos de arte o los museos de ciencias?
5. ¿Cuál te gusta más, el restaurante italiano o el restaurante mexicano?

6. ¿Cuáles te gustan más, los carros fabricados en los Estados Unidos o los carros fabricados en el extranjero?
7. ¿Cuál te gusta más, la mochila grande o la mochila pequeña?
8. ¿Cuáles te gustan más, las asignaturas obligatorias o las asignaturas optativas?
9. ¿Cuáles te gustan más, los sándwiches vegetarianos o los sándwiches de carne?
10. ¿Cuál te gusta más, el suéter de lana o el suéter de algodón?

J **Possessive pronouns used in comparisons.** Rewrite each sentence, replacing the underlined phrase with the corresponding possessive adjective. Follow the *modelo.*

MODELO Mi casa es más grande que <u>la casa de Fernanda</u>.
→ Mi casa es más grande que la suya.

1. Nuestra calle es más tranquila que <u>la calle de ellos</u>.
2. Tu proyecto era tan interesante como <u>mi proyecto</u>.
3. Sus cursos son menos difíciles que <u>nuestros cursos</u>.
4. Nuestras empresas ganaron tanto dinero como <u>las empresas de Ud.</u>
5. Su equipo juega tan bien como <u>tu equipo</u>.
6. La novia de Ricardo es tan alegre como <u>la novia de su hermano</u>.
7. Este celular funcionaba mejor que <u>el celular de Susana</u>.
8. Tus profesores son tan exigentes como <u>mis profesores</u>.

K **Demonstrative pronouns.** Write a response to each of the following questions, using demonstrative pronouns to say that you like the first item better than the second. Follow the *modelo.*

MODELO ¿Qué sopa le gusta más? ¿Esta sopa o esa sopa?
→ Me gusta ésta más que ésa.
OR
→ Me gusta esta más que esa.

1. ¿Qué tienda de ropa le gusta más? ¿Esta tienda de ropa o aquella tienda de ropa?
2. ¿Qué hotel le gusta más? ¿Aquel hotel o este hotel?
3. ¿Qué cuadernos le gustan más? ¿Esos cuadernos o estos cuadernos?
4. ¿Qué camisas le gustan más? ¿Estas camisas o aquellas camisas?
5. ¿Qué libro de texto le gusta más? ¿Este libro de texto o aquel libro de texto?
6. ¿Qué lentes de sol te gustan más? ¿Estos lentes de sol o esos lentes de sol?

DIÁLOGO 4 · ¿El traje negro o el gris?

Study the dialogue, then listen to the recording and repeat each line.

TERESA	Me parece que este traje negro es más fino que ese gris.
MANUEL	Pero fíjate que el gris cuesta tanto como el negro. ¿Cómo puede ser?
TERESA	Chico, a veces el precio engaña.

Análisis

Check that you understand the linguistic breakdown of each speech from *Diálogo 4.*

Me parece que este traje negro es más fino que ese gris.	*I think that this black suit is of better quality than that gray one.*
fino	*fine, of good quality*
más fino que	*of better quality than*
ese gris (< ese traje gris)	*that gray one*
Pero fíjate que el gris cuesta tanto como el negro. ¿Cómo puede ser?	*But notice that the gray one costs as much as the black one. How can that be?*
fijarse	*to notice*
fíjate que	*notice that*
el gris (< el traje gris)	*the gray one*
costar (**o** > **ue**)	*to cost*
tanto como	*as much as*
el negro (< el traje negro)	*the black one*
Chico, a veces el precio engaña.	*Well, sometimes the price doesn't tell you everything.*
chico	*well* (interjection)
a veces	*sometimes*
el precio	*the price*
engañar	*to deceive, fool*
el precio engaña	(literally) *the price fools you*

Variantes

Listen, and repeat the same structures from *Diálogo 4*, now with new vocabulary.

Esta camisa blanca es más fina que esa azul.	*This white shirt is of better quality than that blue one.*
Aquellos suéteres de lana son más finos que éstos de algodón.	*Those wool sweaters are of better quality than these cotton ones.*
Los zapatos españoles no cuestan tanto como los italianos.	*The Spanish shoes cost less than the Italian ones.*

Estructura y Práctica

L **Translation.** Express each of the following sentences in Spanish. All sentences are in the present tense.

1. *These ink cartridges cost more than those.*
2. *The silk gloves are of better quality than the leather ones.*
3. *This red coat is longer than that navy blue one.*
4. *I think you* (tú) *got to know as many Latin American cities as we did.*

DIÁLOGO 5 · La contaminación del ambiente

Study the dialogue, then listen to the recording and repeat each line.

MANUEL Me pican los ojos. Creo que hay muchísima contaminación del ambiente aquí.

TERESA Pues fíjate que yo no la noto. En realidad creo que hay menos polución en esta ciudad que en la nuestra.

Análisis

Check that you understand the linguistic breakdown of each speech from *Diálogo 5.*

Me pican los ojos. Creo que hay muchísima contaminación del ambiente aquí.	*My eyes are itching. I think there's an awful lot of environmental pollution here.*
picarle a uno	*to itch*
me pican los ojos	*my eyes itch*
muchísimo	*very much, an awful lot*
la contaminación	*pollution*
el ambiente	*environment*
la contaminación del ambiente	*environmental pollution*
Pues fíjate que yo no la noto. En realidad creo que hay menos polución en esta ciudad que en la nuestra.	*Can you imagine, I don't notice it. Actually, I think that there is less pollution in this city than in ours.*
fijarse	*to notice*
fíjate que	*notice that, imagine that, can you imagine*
notar	*to notice*
yo no la noto	*I don't notice it*
en realidad	*actually*
menos	*less*
la polución	*pollution*
menos polución que	*less pollution than*
la ciudad	*city*
la nuestra (< la ciudad nuestra)	*ours*

Variantes

Listen, and repeat the same structures from *Diálogo* 5, now with new vocabulary.

Hay muchísimo ruido ambiental aquí.	*There's an awful lot of* ***noise pollution*** *here.*
espíritu cívico	*civic spirit*
reciclaje	*recycling*
Hay muchísima basura aquí.	*There's an awful lot of* ***garbage*** *here.*
drogadicción	*drug addiction*
pobreza	*poverty*
Hay poquísimo crimen aquí.	*There's very little* ***crime*** *here.*
abuso de drogas	*drug abuse*
Ésta es la ciudad más contaminada del país.	*This is the most polluted city in the country.*
Éste es el país más contaminado del mundo.	*This is the most polluted country in the world.*

Estructura y Práctica

M **Translation.** Express each of the following sentences in Spanish.

1. *There's more noise pollution than ever in our society.*
2. *This is the most polluted region in the state.*
3. *There are people who think that recycling is more important than anything.*
4. *There's less crime in our city than in yours* (Uds.).
5. *There was a great deal of civic spirit in the country during the fifties* (los años cincuenta).
6. *There's more drug addiction than ever.*

DIÁLOGO 6 · Un nuevo puesto

Study the dialogue, then listen to the recording and repeat each line.

TERESA	Me gusta tu nueva oficina. Es más amplia que la anterior.
MANUEL	Sí, y entra más luz en ésta que en la que tenía.
TERESA	Entonces estás más contento aquí que en tu otro puesto.
MANUEL	No completamente. Mi nuevo jefe es mucho más exigente que el antiguo.

Análisis

Check that you understand the linguistic breakdown of each speech from *Diálogo* 6.

Me gusta tu nueva oficina. Es más amplia que la anterior.	*I like your new office. It's more spacious than your previous one.*
amplio	*spacious, broad, ample*
más amplio que	*more spacious than*
anterior	*previous*
la anterior (< la oficina anterior)	*the former one*

Sí, y entra más luz en ésta que en la que tenía.	*Yes, and this one is brighter than the one I had.*
entra luz	*it's bright* (literally, *light comes in*)
ésta (< esta oficina)	*this one*
entra más luz en ésta que la que tenía (< la oficina que tenía)	*it's brighter in this one than the one I had*
Entonces estás más contento aquí que en tu otro puesto.	*So you're happier here than in your other job.*
estar contento	*to be happy*
estás más contento aquí que	*you're happier here than*
tu otro puesto	*your other job*
No completamente. Mi nuevo jefe es mucho más exigente que el antiguo.	*Not entirely. My new boss is much more demanding than the former one.*
completamente	*completely, entirely*
mi nuevo jefe	*my new boss*
exigente	*demanding, strict*
más exigente que	*more demanding than*
mucho más exigente que	*much more demanding than*
antiguo	*former* (when it precedes a noun)
el antiguo (< el antiguo jefe)	*the former one*

Variantes

Listen, and repeat the same structures from *Diálogo 6*, now with new vocabulary.

Tu nuevo apartamento es más amplio que el anterior.	*Your new apartment is more spacious than your previous one.*
Entra más luz en éste que en el que tenía.	*This one has more light than the one I had before.*
Éste tiene más dormitorios que el que tenía.	*This one has more* **bedrooms** *than the one I had before.*
cuartos de baño	*bathrooms*
armarios	*closets*
ventanas	*windows*
¿Estás más contento aquí que en tu puesto anterior?	*Are you happier here than in your former position?*
Ah sí, ¡estoy contentísimo!	*Oh, yes, I'm very happy!*
Me gusta tu nueva oficina.	*I like your new office.*
Entonces a ti te gusta más que a mí.	*Then you like it more than I do.*
Yo tengo más trabajo que Ud.	*I have* **more** *work than you do.*
menos	*less*
Uds. tenían tanto trabajo como yo.	*You had as much work as I had.*
Ellos escribieron tantos informes como nosotros.	*They wrote as many reports as we did.*

¿Navegas en la red tanto como yo?	*Do you surf the web as much as I do?*
No, yo navego más que tú.	*No, I surf* ***more*** *than you do.*
menos	*less*
¿Tu nueva jefa es tan exigente como el antiguo?	*Is your new boss as demanding as your old one?*
Es más exigente que él. Yo trabajo más que nunca.	*She's more demanding than he. I work harder than ever.*

Estructura y Práctica

N **Translation.** Express each of the following sentences in Spanish.

1. *This apartment is more spacious than the ones you* (Ud.) *saw previously.*
2. *That condominium is bigger and less expensive than mine.*
3. *This house has as many bedrooms as theirs, but it has fewer bathrooms than ours.*
4. *This computer is more powerful than the one I had.*
5. *The previous computer was more user friendly than the one I have now.*

DIÁLOGO 7 · Curso cinco asignaturas.

Study the dialogue, then listen to the recording and repeat each line.

MANUEL	Este semestre curso cinco asignaturas. Tengo más trabajo que nunca.
TERESA	¿Para cuál materia estudias más? ¿Para historia?
MANUEL	No, para química. La materia es dificilísima y estudio con el doctor Figueroa.
TERESA	¿Con Figueroa? Pobre de ti. Es el profesor más estricto e inflexible de la universidad.

Análisis

Check that you understand the linguistic breakdown of each speech from *Diálogo 7*.

Este semestre curso cinco asignaturas. Tengo más trabajo que nunca.	*This semester I'm taking five subjects. I have more work than ever.*
el semestre	*semester*
cursar	*to take (academic subjects)*
la asignatura	*(school) subject*
más trabajo que nunca	*more work than ever*
¿Para cuál materia estudias más? ¿Para historia?	*For which subject do you study the most? For history?*
cuál	*which*
la materia	*(school) subject*
para cuál materia	*for which subject*
más	*more, the most*
la historia	*history*

No, para química. La materia es dificilísima y estudio con el doctor Figueroa.	*No, for chemistry. The subject is very difficult and I'm studying with Dr. Figueroa.*
la química	*chemistry*
dificilísimo	*very difficult*
¿Con Figueroa? Pobre de ti. Es el profesor más estricto e inflexible de la universidad.	*With Figueroa? Poor you. He's the strictest and most rigid professor in the university.*
pobre de ti	*poor you*
estricto	*strict*
inflexible	*rigid, inflexible*
el profesor más estricto e inflexible	*the strictest and most rigid professor*
de	*in* (when it follows a superlative)

Variantes

Listen, and repeat the same structures from *Diálogo 7*, now with new vocabulary.

Yo estudié más que nunca .	*I studied* ***harder than ever****.*
más que nadie	*harder than anyone*
más que nada	*harder than anything*
La materia es dificilísima .	*The subject is* ***very difficult****.*
facilísima	*very easy*
importantísima	*very important*
interesantísima	*very interesting*
Yo siempre cursaba más de cinco asignaturas.	*I always took more than five subjects.*
Siempre escribíamos más de dos composiciones.	*We always wrote more than two compositions.*
Yo no tomaba más que cuatro cursos.	*I took only four courses.*
No escribíamos más que dos composiciones.	*We wrote only two compositions.*
Las asignaturas obligatorias son las más fáciles.	***The required subjects*** *are the easiest ones.*
Las asignaturas optativas	*The electives*
Pobre de mí .	*Poor* ***me****.*
ti	*you*
Ud.	*you*
él	*guy*
ella	*girl*
nosotros	*us*
Uds.	*you*
ellos/ellas	*guys*
¿Vas a ir conmigo a la librería?	*Are you going to go to the bookstore with me?*
Claro que voy contigo.	*Of course I'll go with you.*

¿Tienes que comprar un libro de texto para la clase de filosofía?	*Do you have to buy a textbook for philosophy class?*
Sí, para ella y también para la de biología.	*Yes, for that class and also for biology.*
Es la profesora más indulgente de la universidad.	*She's the most* ***lenient*** *professor in the university.*
popular	*popular*
Los cursos de matemáticas son los más difíciles de la facultad de ciencias.	*The math courses are the most difficult ones in the (school of) sciences.*
Son más difíciles que los de física.	*They are harder than the physics (courses).*
Yo resolví el problema más fácilmente que tú.	*I solved the problem* ***more easily than*** *you.*
menos fácilmente que	*less easily than*
Ellos trabajan tan cuidadosamente como nosotros.	*They work as carefully as we do.*

Estructura y Práctica

Conjunctions: y and, o or

The conjunction **y** (*and*) is written and pronounced **e** when it immediately precedes a word that begins with the sound /i/: **guapos e inteligentes**, **padres e hijos**. There is no change when a word begins with a diphthong such as /ie/: **fuego y hielo** (*fire and ice*).

Similarly, **o** (*or*) is written and pronounced **u** when it immediately precedes a word that begins with the sound /o/: **siete u ocho**, **minutos u horas**.

O **Conjunctions *y* and *o*.** Rewrite each of the following phrases, reversing the order of the two items and adding the correct form of the conjunction to each new phrase. Follow the *modelos*.

MODELOS inglés y español → español e inglés

hoy o mañana → mañana u hoy

1. idiomas y lingüística
2. Honduras o Costa Rica
3. ingenua y sensible
4. hombres o mujeres
5. optimista o pesimista
6. italianos y franceses
7. oeste o este
8. iglesias y sinagogas
9. hidrógeno y oxígeno
10. igualdad y libertad
11. hipopótamos y rinocerontes
12. holandés o escocés

Review: Prepositional Pronouns

In Chapter 6, you learned the special set of pronouns used after prepositions. These pronouns are identical with the subject pronouns except in the first and second persons singular.

para **mí**	para **nosotros/nosotras**
para **ti**	para **vosotros/vosotras**
para **él/ella**	para **ellos/ellas**
para **Ud.**	para **Uds.**

Note that after **con** there are three irregular forms.

con + mí → conmigo	*with me*
con + ti → contigo	*with you* (**tú**)
consigo	*with himself, with herself, with yourself* (**Ud.**), *with yourselves* (**Uds.**), *with themselves*

P ***Te equivocas.*** Write a response to each of the following questions to tell your friend that he's wrong about who you were going to do things with or for. Use prepositional pronouns in your responses. Follow the *modelo.*

MODELO Ibas a almorzar con Rosa, ¿verdad?
→ No, con ella, no.

1. Ibas a comprar un regalo para los Fernández, ¿verdad?
2. Ibas a pasar por nosotros, ¿verdad?
3. Ibas a jugar al tenis con tus amigas, ¿verdad?
4. Ibas a preparar unos platos para mí, ¿verdad?
5. Ibas a casarte con Juan Antonio, ¿verdad?
6. Ibas a hacer las investigaciones por tu jefa, ¿verdad?
7. Ibas a reunirte conmigo, ¿verdad?
8. Ibas a ver la obra de teatro conmigo, ¿verdad?

Un paso más

Are you ready to take your Spanish a step further? Here are exercises that will enhance your knowledge of the language and allow you to express yourself freely.

Q ***Preguntas personales.*** Answer each question with a complete Spanish sentence.

1. ¿Cómo eres?
2. ¿Cómo son los miembros de tu familia?
3. Para ti, ¿quién es el mejor escritor / la mejor escritora (actor, actriz, dramaturgo/a, director(a) de cine)? ¿Por qué crees que son los mejores?

4. ¿Cuáles son los mejores libros que leíste? ¿Las mejores películas que viste? ¿Por qué crees que son los mejores?
5. ¿Qué asignaturas cursas/cursabas en la universidad? ¿Son/Eran obligatorias u optativas?
6. ¿Cómo son/eran tus profesores?

R Write a paragraph about American ideals and principles. You may want to include discussion of some issues in American society today. Resources to help you with this topic, including useful vocabulary, appear below. You will be able to read and understand much of the material because you are already familiar with it and many words are cognates of English words. Use the following questions as a guide.

1. ¿Cuáles son los principios e ideas fundamentales de los Estados Unidos de América reflejados (*reflected*) en sus documentos fundacionales?
2. ¿Hay mucho espíritu cívico en el país?
3. ¿Cuáles son algunos ejemplos del espíritu cívico en su ciudad o su pueblo?
4. ¿Cuáles son los problemas más graves de la sociedad estadounidense actualmente?
5. ¿Tú crees que se pueden resolver? ¿Cómo?

Resources

The Declaration of Independence
https://www.archives.gov/espanol/la-declaracion-de-independencia.html

The Constitution of the United States of America
https://www.archives.gov/espanol/constitucion

Vocabulario útil

el bien común *the common good, the public good*
el bienestar *general welfare*
la caridad *charity*
la ciudadanía *citizenship*
el ciudadano *citizen*
la Constitución de los Estados Unidos de América *Constitution of the United States of America*
la cultura política *political culture*
el deber *obligation*
la Declaración de Derechos *the Bill of Rights*
la Declaración de la Independencia *the Declaration of Independence*
la democracia *democracy*
el derecho *right*
los documentos fundacionales *founding documents*
la enmienda *amendment*
las diez primeras enmiendas a la Constitución de los Estados Unidos de América *the first ten amendments to the Constitution of the United States of America* (*the Bill of Rights*)
el estado de derecho *rule of law*
el gobierno *government*
el gobierno estatal *state government*
el gobierno federal *federal government*
el gobierno municipal *city government*
la igualdad *equality*
los impuestos *taxes*
la justicia *justice*
la ley *law*
la libertad *freedom*
"Nosotros el Pueblo" *"We the People"*
el orgullo *pride*
la responsabilidad *responsibility, accountability*

13

Business and the Growth of Cities

Communication Goals

- Talking about things that have happened in the recent past
- Talking about things that had happened
- Describing a business plan and a budget
- Vocabulary: business and the economy, religious rites and traditions, urban growth

Grammar Topics

- Past Participle: Formation
- Past Participle: Uses
- Present Perfect
- Present Perfect: Position of Object Pronouns
- **Estar** + Past Participle: Expressing Positions of the Body
- Past Perfect (Pluperfect)
- The Progressive Tenses

DIÁLOGO 1 · Un día de mucho ajetreo

Study the dialogue, then listen to the recording and repeat each line.

MARÍA ¿Por qué no has contestado mi email? ¿No lo has recibido acaso?
FELIPE Hoy ha sido un día de mucho ajetreo. No he tenido ni un solo minuto para respirar.

Análisis

Check that you understand the linguistic breakdown of each speech from *Diálogo 1.*

¿Por qué no has contestado mi email?	*Why haven't you answered my email?*
¿No lo has recibido acaso?	*Maybe you didn't receive it?*
has (< *auxiliary verb* **haber**)	*you have*
contestar	*to answer*
contestado	*answered*

has contestado	*you have answered*
el email	*email*
recibir	*to get, receive*
recibido	*received*
has recibido	*you have received*
lo has recibido	*you have received it*
acaso	*maybe, perhaps*

Hoy ha sido un día de mucho ajetreo. No he tenido ni un solo minuto para respirar.	*Today has been a very hectic day. I haven't had even a minute to breathe.*
ha (< *auxiliary verb* **haber**)	*it has*
ser	*to be*
sido	*been*
ha sido	*it has been*
el ajetreo	*intense activity, hustle and bustle*
de mucho ajetreo	*hectic*
he (< *auxiliary verb* **haber**)	*I have*
tener	*to have*
tenido	*had*
he tenido	*I have had*
ni	*not even*
solo	*alone, single*
ni un solo	*not even one single*
ni un solo minuto	*not even one (single) minute*
respirar	*to breathe*

Variantes

Listen, and repeat the same structures from *Diálogo 1*, now with new vocabulary.

¿Por qué no has contestado el email?	*Why haven't you* ***answered*** *the email?*
escrito	*written*
leído	*read*
mandado	*sent*

No lo he recibido.	*I haven't* ***received*** *it.*
enviado	*sent*
abierto	*opened*
visto	*seen*

Ha sido un día difícil.	*It has been a* ***difficult*** *day.*
largo	*long*
corto	*short*
duro	*hard*
maravilloso	*wonderful*

Estructura y Práctica

Past Participle: Formation

The past participle in Spanish ends in **-do**. Some irregular verbs have past participles ending in **-to** or **-cho**.

The past participle consists of the following elements.

verb stem + { the vowel **a** for **-ar** verbs / the vowel **i** for **-er** and **-ir** verbs } + do

tomar	→ tom + a + do	→ **tomado**	*taken*
comer	→ com + i + do	→ **comido**	*eaten*
vivir	→ viv + i + do	→ **vivido**	*lived*

The past participles of **ir** and **ser** are regular.

ir → **ido**
ser → **sido**

The past participle of **haber** is **habido**. The present perfect of the irregular verb form **hay** (*there is, there are*) is **ha habido**.

Ha habido un gran cambio.	***There has been*** *a great change.*
Ha habido unos problemas graves.	***There have been*** *some serious problems.*

-Er and **-ir** verbs whose stems end in a vowel add an accent mark over the **i**.

caer → caído
creer → creído
leer → leído
oír → oído
traer → traído

The following verbs have irregular past participles.

abrir	**abierto**	morir	**muerto**
cubrir	**cubierto**	poner	**puesto**
decir	**dicho**	resolver	**resuelto**
escribir	**escrito**	romper	**roto**
hacer	**hecho**	ver	**visto**
imprimir	**impreso**	volver	**vuelto**

When a prefix is added to these verbs, the past participle of the new verb shows the same irregularities.

contradecir *to contradict*	**contradicho**
describir *to describe*	**descrito**
descubrir *to discover*	**descubierto**
devolver (**o** > **ue**) *to give back*	**devuelto**
rehacer *to redo*	**rehecho**
suponer *to suppose*	**supuesto**
prever *to foresee*	**previsto**

Past Participle: Uses

1 · The past participle is frequently used as an adjective. It may either follow a noun or a form of **estar** or **ser**. When used as an adjective, it agrees in gender and number with the noun it refers to.

un documento **roto**	*a* ***torn*** *document*
los mensajes **escritos**	*the* ***written*** *messages*
una reunión **aburrida**	*a* ***boring*** *meeting*
las puertas **cerradas**	*the* ***closed*** *doors*
El profesor está **enojado**.	*The teacher is* ***angry***.
La cena está **servida**.	*Dinner is* ***served***.
Los turistas están **cansados.**	*The tourists are* ***tired***.
Las ventanas están **abiertas**.	*The windows are* ***open***.

2 · The past participle is used with **estar** to express positions of the body such as sitting or standing. The past participle functions as an adjective, thereby agreeing in gender and number with the noun it refers to. (See also *Diálogo 10* in this chapter.)

Alicia **está sentada** en la mecedora.	*Alicia* ***is sitting*** *in the rocking chair.*

3 · The past participle is used with **ser** to form the passive voice. In the passive voice, the past participle agrees in gender and number with the noun it refers to. (For more on the passive voice, see Chapter 10.)

Mi sitio web **fue diseñado** por Carlos.	*My website* ***was designed*** *by Carlos.*
Los datos **fueron analizados** ayer.	*The data* ***was analyzed*** *yesterday.*

4 · The past participle is used with **haber** to form the present perfect, the past perfect, and the other perfect tenses. In the perfect tenses, the past participle is invariable—it does not agree in gender or number.

A **Past participle used as adjective.** Write the adjective form derived from the verb in parentheses to correctly complete each noun phrase. Follow the *modelo.*

MODELO los datos *guardados* (guardar)

1. el lavaplatos ________________ (descomponer)
2. una lengua ________________ (escribir)
3. unos soldados ________________ (*fallen, dead*) (caer)
4. el suéter ________________ (romper)
5. el sueldo ________________ (aumentar)
6. la carne poco ________________ (hacer)
7. unos paisajes ________________ (ver)
8. las obras maestras más ________________ (leer)
9. las hojas (*leaves*) ________________ (morir)
10. unos proyectos ________________ a cabo (llevar) (llevar a cabo (*to carry out, achieve*))

B **Past participle as adjective with *estar.*** Write sentences using **estar** and the elements given to describe the physical or emotional state of each person. Make all necessary changes. Follow the *modelo.*

MODELO Federico / resfriado
→ Federico está resfriado.

1. Carmen / angustiado
2. Rodrigo y Diego / aburrido
3. nosotras / emocionado
4. tú [*fem.*] / estresado
5. Juanita / deprimido
6. Carlos y Mateo / entusiasmado
7. yo [*masc.*] / preocupado
8. Esteban y Vera / acatarrado
9. Ud. [*fem.*] / cansado
10. Fernando / confundido

Present Perfect

The present perfect tense in Spanish consists of the present tense of the auxiliary verb **haber** + the past participle. In the perfect tenses, the past participle is invariable—it does not agree in gender or number. The Spanish present perfect usually corresponds to the English present perfect, which consists of *have* + past participle.

SINGULAR		PLURAL	
he comido	*I have eaten*	hemos comido	*we have eaten*
has comido	*you have eaten*	habéis comido	*you have eaten*
ha comido	*he/she has eaten, you* (Ud.) *have eaten*	han comido	*they/you* (Uds.) *have eaten*

The negative word **no** precedes the form of **haber** in the perfect tenses.

Hoy **no** he visto a nadie. — *Today I haven't seen anyone.*
¿Por qué **no** han llamado? — *Why haven't they called?*

No words can be placed between the auxiliary verb and the past participle, including in questions. This is different from English usage.

¿**Han terminado** Uds.? — ***Have** you **finished**?*
¿**Han llegado** los invitados? — ***Have** the guests **arrived**?*
¿**Ha leído** el estudiante el libro? — ***Has** the student **read** the book?*

C ***Haber* or past participle?** Write either a form of the auxiliary verb **haber** or the past participle to correctly complete each of the following phrases, using the cue in parentheses. Follow the *modelo.*

MODELO has <u>escrito</u> (escribir)

1. ______________ contestado (yo)
2. han ______________ (volver)
3. hemos ______________ (oír)
4. ______________ comprendido (Ud.)
5. ha ______________ (decir)
6. ______________ comido (Uds.)
7. he ______________ (ver)
8. ______________ subido (nosotros)
9. ______________ ido (tú)
10. han ______________ (dar)

D Rewrite each sentence, changing the verb from the present tense to the present perfect. Follow the *modelo*.

MODELO Venden su casa.
→ Han vendido su casa.

1. Cursa dos asignaturas optativas.
2. Quieren visitarnos.
3. Ponemos la mesa.
4. Llueve todo el día.
5. Es difícil adelgazar.
6. Se incluyen los ingresos y los gastos.
7. Abro las ventanas.
8. No ves a nadie, ¿verdad?
9. Hay mucho ajetreo hoy.
10. Estamos tan emocionados como Uds.
11. Tienen que pagar el seguro de salud.
12. ¿Pides más vino?

E Write a sentence with the verb in present perfect, using the string of elements given. Then write a second sentence with **estar** + the past participle to show the resulting condition of the first sentence. Follow the *modelo*.

MODELO él / terminar / el proyecto
→ Él ha terminado el proyecto.
→ El proyecto está terminado.

1. yo / escribir / los documentos
2. nosotros / hacer / el plan de negocios
3. ella / pagar / la hipoteca
4. Uds. / recibir / la invitación
5. ellos / abrir / las fábricas
6. tú / facturar / el equipaje
7. él / alquilar / el apartamento
8. ellas / poner / la mesa
9. Ud. / descargar / su canción favorita
10. ellos / construir / los rascacielos

DIÁLOGO 2 · Han empezado el proyecto.

Study the dialogue, then listen to the recording and repeat each line.

FELIPE ¿Uds. ya han elaborado el presupuesto?
MARÍA No todavía. Apenas hemos comenzado a recoger los datos.
FELIPE ¿Entonces no han podido seguir con el proyecto?
MARÍA Bueno, hemos hecho un plan de negocios, eso es todo hasta ahora.

Análisis

Check that you understand the linguistic breakdown of each speech from *Diálogo 2*.

¿Uds. ya han elaborado el presupuesto?	*Have you already drawn up the budget?*
han (< *auxiliary verb* **haber**)	*you* (Uds.) *have*
elaborar	*to draw up, develop*
elaborado	*drawn up, developed*
Uds. han elaborado	*you have drawn up, you have developed*
el presupuesto	*budget*

No todavía. Apenas hemos comenzado a recoger los datos.	*Not yet. We've barely begun to collect the data.*
todavía	*still, yet*
no todavía	*not yet*
apenas	*hardly, barely*
hemos (< *auxiliary verb* **haber**)	*we have*
comenzar (**e** > **ie**)	*to begin*
comenzado	*begun*
hemos comenzado	*we have begun*
recoger	*to collect, gather*
los datos	*data*
¿Entonces no han podido seguir con el proyecto?	*So you haven't been able to go on with the project?*
han (< *auxiliary verb* **haber**)	*you* (Uds.) *have*
poder (**o** > **ue**)	*to be able to, can*
podido	*been able to*
han podido	*have been able to*
seguir (**e** > **i**) con	*to go on with, continue* (*with*)
el proyecto	*the project*
Bueno, hemos hecho un plan de negocios, eso es todo hasta ahora.	*Well, we have made a business plan, that's all up to now.*
hemos (< *auxiliary verb* **haber**)	*we have*
hacer (*irreg.*)	*to do, make*
hecho	*done, made*
hemos hecho	*we have made*
el plan	*plan*
los negocios	*business*
el plan de negocios	*business plan*
eso	*that*
todo	*everything*
hasta	*until*
hasta ahora	*up to now, so far*

Variantes

Listen, and repeat the same structures from *Diálogo 2*, now with new vocabulary.

Hemos comenzado a recoger los datos.	*We've begun* ***to collect the data.***
entrar los datos	*to enter the data*
analizar los datos	*to analyze the data*
guardar los datos	*to save the data*
Han podido seguir.	***You have been able to*** *continue.*
Han querido	*You have wanted to*
Han necesitado	*You have needed to*
Han preferido	*You have preferred to*
Han pensado	*You have intended to*
Han tenido que	*You have had to*

Hemos elaborado el presupuesto.	***We've drawn up*** *the budget.*
Hemos estudiado	*We've studied*
Hemos cambiado	*We've changed*
Hemos mirado	*We've looked at*
¿Ud. ha incluido los ingresos?	*Have you included* ***income****?*
los gastos	*expenses*
El presupuesto incluye su sueldo.	*The budget includes* ***his salary****.*
la hipoteca	*the mortgage*
el seguro de salud	*health insurance*
Lo han hecho.	***They have done*** *it.*
han dicho	*They have said*
han visto	*They have seen*
han devuelto	*They have returned*
han roto	*They have broken*
han traído	*They have brought*
han leído	*They have read*

Estructura y Práctica

F ***Un proyecto.*** Write a sentence using the string of elements given to tell what you and your colleagues have recently done on your project. Use the present perfect tense. Follow the *modelo.*

MODELO todos nosotros / empezar / el proyecto
→ Todos nosotros hemos empezado el proyecto.

1. el equipo / hacer / el plan de negocios
2. Alejo y yo / elaborar / el presupuesto
3. los asesores / recoger / los datos
4. el artista gráfico / dibujar / el logo
5. yo / crear / diapositivas (*slides*) en PowerPoint
6. tú / mandar / los emails
7. Uds. / reunirse / en la sala de conferencias
8. Leonardo / diseñar / el folleto (*brochure*)
9. Claudia y su asistente / leer / todos los documentos
10. Ud. / imprimir / el volante (*flyer*)

DIÁLOGO 3 · Ha muerto Ramón Fernández.

Study the dialogue, then listen to the recording and repeat each line.

MARÍA ¿Has oído la noticia? Ha muerto Ramón Fernández.
FELIPE Sí, yo sé. He ido al velorio y le he dado el pésame a su viuda.
MARÍA ¿Sabes cuándo va a ser el entierro?
FELIPE Me han dicho que va a tener lugar el jueves.

Análisis

Check that you understand the linguistic breakdown of each speech from *Diálogo 3*.

¿Has oído la noticia? Ha muerto Ramón Fernández.	*Have you heard the news? Ramón Fernández has died.*
has (< *auxiliary verb* **haber**)	*you* (**tú**) *have*
oír	*to hear*
oído	*heard*
has oído	*you have heard*
la noticia	*(piece of) news*
ha (< *auxiliary verb* **haber**)	*he has*
morir	*to die*
muerto	*died*
ha muerto	*he has died*
Sí, yo sé. He ido al velorio y le he dado el pésame a su viuda.	*Yes, I know. I went to the wake and I paid my condolences to his widow.*
he (< *auxiliary verb* **haber**)	*I have*
ir	*to go*
ido	*gone*
he ido	*I have gone*
el velorio	*wake*
el pésame	*condolences*
dar el pésame	*to pay condolences*
he (< *auxiliary verb* **haber**)	*I have*
dar	*to give*
dado	*given*
he dado	*I have given*
le he dado el pésame	*I expressed my condolences to her widow*
la viuda	
¿Sabes cuándo va a ser el entierro?	*Do you know when the funeral will be?*
el entierro	*funeral, burial*
Me han dicho que va a tener lugar el jueves.	*I've been told that it will take place on Thursday.*
han (< *auxiliary verb* **haber**)	*they have*
decir	*to say, tell*
dicho	*said*
han dicho	*they have said, they have told*
el lugar	*place*
tener lugar	*to take place*

Variantes

Listen, and repeat the same structures from *Diálogo 3*, now with new vocabulary.

He ido al velorio.	*I've gone* ***to the wake.***
al entierro	*to the funeral*
al cementerio	*to the cemetery*
a la sinagoga	*to the synagogue*
a la iglesia	*to the church*
Le he dicho "mi más sentido pésame" al viudo.	*I said "you have my deepest sympathy" to the widower.*
¿Qué te han dicho?	*What have they told you?*
No me han dicho nada.	*They haven't told me anything.*

Estructura y Práctica

Present Perfect: Position of Object Pronouns

In the perfect tenses, direct and indirect object pronouns, as well as reflexive pronouns, precede the form of **haber**. The negative word **no** precedes the object pronouns.

Buscamos a Ana. ¿**No la has** visto?	*We're looking for Ana. Haven't you seen her?*
¿El iPod? **Se lo he** dado a Lorenzo.	*The iPod? I've given it to Lorenzo.*

G Write an answer to each of the following questions, using the present perfect of the verb from the question. Add object pronouns in your response as needed. Follow the *modelo*.

MODELO ¿Vas a visitar a tus primos?
→ Ya los he visitado.

1. ¿Vas a regalarle unas flores a tu novia?
2. ¿Uds. van a pedirles un aumento de sueldo a los jefes?
3. ¿Su mamá va a leerle un cuento al niño?
4. ¿Ud. va a darles el pésame a los dolientes (*mourners*)?
5. ¿Vas a llevar a tus amigas a la universidad?
6. ¿Ellas van a decirles a Uds. lo que pasó?
7. ¿Tina va a prestarte la sartén?
8. ¿Uds. van a hacer el café?

DIÁLOGO 4 · Son puros chismes.

Study the dialogue, then listen to the recording and repeat each line.

FELIPE ¿Vas a decirle a Teresa lo que oíste?
MARÍA Ya se lo he dicho.
FELIPE ¿Cómo ha reaccionado?
MARÍA Me ha asegurado que son puros chismes.

Análisis

Check that you understand the linguistic breakdown of each speech from *Diálogo 4*.

¿Vas a decirle a Teresa lo que oíste?	*Are you going to tell Teresa what you heard?*
decirle a Teresa	*to tell Teresa*
lo que	*what*
oíste	*you heard*
Ya se lo he dicho.	*I've already told (it to) her.*
ya	*already*
he (< *auxiliary verb* **haber**)	*I have*
decir (*irreg.*)	*to say, tell*
dicho	*said, told*
he dicho	*I have told*
se lo he dicho	*I have told it to her*
¿Cómo ha reaccionado?	*How did she react?*
ha (< *auxiliary verb* **haber**)	*she has*
reaccionar	*to react*
reaccionado	*reacted*
ha reaccionado	*she has reacted*
Me ha asegurado que son puros chismes.	*She (has) assured me that it's nothing more than gossip.*
ha (< *auxiliary verb* **haber**)	*she has*
asegurar	*to assure*
asegurado	*assured*
ha asegurado	*she has assured*
me ha asegurado	*she has assured me*
puro	*just, merely, only* (when it appears before a noun)
el chisme	*gossip*
puros chismes	*nothing more than gossip*

Variantes

Listen, and repeat the same structures from *Diálogo 4*, now with new vocabulary.

Yo se lo he dicho.	*I've said it to her.*
Yo se lo he contado.	*I've told it to her.*
Yo se lo he asegurado.	*I've assured her of it.*
Me la ha dado.	*She **has given** it to me.*
ha entregado	*has handed*
ha mandado	*has sent*

Estructura y Práctica

H **Translation.** Express each of the following sentences in Spanish.

1. *She has already told them what she heard.*
2. *Have you* (tú) *already paid your condolences to Daniel's widow?*
3. *The budget? We've drawn it up for them.*
4. *The contract? They haven't explained it to us yet.*
5. *The coffee pot* (la cafetera)*? I haven't had time to return it to him.*
6. *The income and expenses? Have you* (Ud.) *shown them to the accountant* [fem.]*?*
7. *There has been a lot of hustle and bustle in the company.*

DIÁLOGO 5 · Antonio no tiene pelos en la lengua.

Study the dialogue, then listen to the recording and repeat each line.

FELIPE ¡Qué barbaridad! ¿Antonio se ha atrevido a decir tal cosa?
MARÍA Tú sabes cómo es. No tiene pelos en la lengua.
FELIPE Es cierto. Siempre ha sido así.

Análisis

Check that you understand the linguistic breakdown of each speech from *Diálogo 5*.

¡Qué barbaridad! ¿Antonio se ha atrevido a decir tal cosa?	*How outrageous! Antonio dared to say something like that?*
la barbaridad	*outrageous thing*
¡Qué barbaridad!	*How outrageous! / How awful!*
ha (< *auxiliary verb* **haber**)	*he has*
atreverse a + *infinitive*	*to dare to (do something)*
atrevido	*dared*
se ha atrevido	*he has dared*
tal	*such a*
tal cosa	*such a thing, something like that*
Tú sabes cómo es. No tiene pelos en la lengua.	*You know what he's like. He doesn't mince his words.*
no tener pelos en la lengua	*not to mince one's words*
Es cierto. Siempre ha sido así.	*It's true. He's always been like that.*
siempre	*always*
ha (< *auxiliary verb* **haber**)	*he has*
ser	*to be*
sido	*been*
ha sido	*he has been*
así	*like that*

Variantes

Listen, and repeat the same structures from *Diálogo 5*, now with new vocabulary.

¿Ellos siempre han sido así?	*Have they always been like that?*
Ella, sí, siempre ha sido así. Él no.	*Yes, she has always been like that. But he hasn't.*

Estructura y Práctica

IDIOMS WITH TENER

In this chapter, you learned the idiom **no tener pelos en la lengua** (*to not mince one's words*), adding to the many idioms with **tener** that you learned in previous chapters. Here are idioms with the verb **tener** that use parts of the body.

tener en la punta de la lengua

¿La palabra? Este... La tengo en la punta de la lengua.	*The word? Um . . . It's on the tip of my tongue.*

no tener pelo de tonto

Carlos no tiene pelo de tonto.	*Carlos is nobody's fool.*

no tener ni pies ni cabeza

Este plan no tiene ni pies ni cabeza.	*This plan doesn't make any sense at all.*

tener pájaros en la cabeza

Ese tipo tenía pájaros en la cabeza.	*That guy had crazy ideas, he acted so foolishly.*

Present Perfect of Reflexive Verbs

In the perfect tenses, all object pronouns, including reflexive pronouns, precede the form of **haber**. The negative word **no** precedes the object pronouns.

¿Vas a ponerte los zapatos?	*Are you going to put your shoes on?*
Ya me los he puesto.	*I've already put them on.*
No, no me los he puesto.	*No, I haven't put them on yet.*

(For more on reflexive pronouns, see Chapter 8.)

I ***Ya ha pasado.*** Write an answer to each of the following questions, using the present perfect of the reflexive verb in the question to explain that these things have already happened. Change direct object nouns to pronouns and make all necessary changes. Follow the *modelo.*

MODELO ¿Cuándo va María a arreglarse?
→ Se ha arreglado ya.

1. ¿Cuándo van Uds. a matricularse?
2. ¿Cuándo va Pedro a graduarse?
3. ¿Cuándo vas a lavarte la cabeza?
4. ¿Cuándo van ellos a reunirse?
5. ¿Cuándo va Ud. a probarse las camisas?
6. ¿Cuándo van Camila y Samuel a casarse?

7. ¿Cuándo vas a comprometerte con Julián?
8. ¿Cuándo van Uds. a mudarse al nuevo condominio?
9. ¿Cuándo van los niños a cepillarse los dientes?
10. ¿Cuándo va Olivia a maquillarse la cara?

DIÁLOGO 6 · No nos han invitado.

Study the dialogue, then listen to the recording and repeat each line.

FELIPE	¿Uds. van a asistir al bautizo del bebé de Margarita y Leonardo?
MARÍA	No nos han invitado todavía. ¿Y Uds.?
FELIPE	Nosotros tampoco hemos recibido la invitación.

Análisis

Check that you understand the linguistic breakdown of each speech from *Diálogo 6.*

¿Uds. van a asistir al bautizo del bebé de Margarita y Leonardo?	*Are you going to attend the baptism of Margarita and Leonardo's baby?*
asistir a	*to attend*
el bautizo	*baptism*
asistir al bautizo	*to attend the baptism*
No nos han invitado todavía. ¿Y Uds.?	*They haven't invited us yet. How about you?*
han (< *auxiliary verb* **haber**)	*they have*
invitar	*to invite*
invitado	*invited*
han invitado	*they've invited*
no nos han invitado	*they haven't invited us*
Nosotros tampoco hemos recibido la invitación.	*We haven't received the invitation either.*
tampoco	*neither*
recibir	*to get, receive*
recibido	*received*
hemos recibido	*we have received*
tampoco hemos recibido la invitación	*we haven't received the invitation either*

Variantes

Listen, and repeat the same structures from *Diálogo 6*, now with new vocabulary.

No nos han invitado.	*They **haven't invited** us.*
han preguntado	*haven't asked*
han contestado	*haven't answered*
han llamado	*haven't called*
han visitado	*haven't visited*
han comprendido	*haven't understood*
han creído	*haven't believed*

DIÁLOGO 7 · La mesa está puesta.

Study the dialogue, then listen to the recording and repeat each line.

MARÍA	¿Cuándo vas a poner la mesa? Pronto llegan los invitados.
FELIPE	Mira, ya está puesta.
MARÍA	Muy bien, pero faltan los vasos.
FELIPE	Los he sacado del lavaplatos. ¿Por qué no los colocas tú en la mesa?

Análisis

Check that you understand the linguistic breakdown of each speech from *Diálogo 7*.

¿Cuándo vas a poner la mesa? Pronto llegan los invitados.	*When are you going to set the table? The guests will be arriving soon.*
poner la mesa	*to set the table*
pronto	*soon*
pronto llegan	*they'll soon be arriving*
el invitado	*guest*
Mira, ya está puesta.	*Look, it's already set.*
puesto	*put; set* (past participle of **poner**)
estar puesta	*to be set* (*of the table*)
Muy bien, pero faltan los vasos.	*Great, but there are no glasses.*
faltar	*to be missing*
el vaso	*(drinking) glass*
faltan los vasos	*the glasses are missing, there are no glasses*
Los he sacado del lavaplatos. ¿Por qué no los colocas tú en la mesa?	*I have taken them out of the dishwasher. Why don't you put them on the table?*
he	*I have*
sacar	*to take out*
sacado	*taken out*
he sacado	*I have taken out*
los he sacado	*I have taken them out*
el lavaplatos	*dishwasher*
colocar	*to place, put*
tú los colocas	*you place them, you put them*

Variantes

Listen, and repeat the same structures from *Diálogo 7*, now with new vocabulary.

El almuerzo está servido.	*Lunch is served.*
La cena está servida.	*Dinner is served.*
Los vasos están rotos.	*The glasses are broken.*
Las tazas están rotas.	*The cups are broken.*
He sacado las cucharas de la gaveta.	*I've taken* ***the spoons*** *out of the drawer.*
las cucharitas	*the teaspoons*
los tenedores	*the forks*
los cuchillos	*the knives*
las servilletas	*the napkins*

Estructura y Práctica

J ***Ya está hecho.*** Write answers to each of the following questions, explaining that these things have already been done. Use the past participle as an adjective in your responses. Make all necessary changes. Follow the *modelo.*

MODELO Rita, ¿cuándo vas a peinarte?
→ Ya estoy peinada.

1. ¿Cuándo va Gerardo a levantarse?
2. Gabriela, ¿cuándo vas a enamorarte?
3. ¿Cuándo van ellos a acostarse?
4. Nora y Clara, ¿cuándo van a vestirse?
5. Chicos, ¿cuándo van Uds. a bañarse?
6. Marta, ¿cuándo vas a arreglarte?
7. ¿Cuándo van los Rivera a instalarse en su nueva casa?
8. ¿Cuándo van Armando y Carolina a divorciarse?

DIÁLOGO 8 · Las ventanas están abiertas.

Study the dialogue, then listen to the recording and repeat each line.

FELIPE Me muero de calor. ¿Has abierto las ventanas?
MARÍA Sí, están abiertas.

Análisis

Check that you understand the linguistic breakdown of each speech from *Diálogo 8.*

Me muero de calor. ¿Has abierto las ventanas?	*I'm dying of the heat. Have you opened the windows?*
morirse de	*to die of, die from* (often figurative)
el calor	*heat*
morirse de calor	*to be dying of the heat*
has	*you have*
abrir	*to open*
abierto	*opened* (past participle of **abrir**)
has abierto	*you have opened*
Sí, están abiertas.	*Yes, they're open.*
estar abierto	*to be open*

Variantes

Listen, and repeat the same structures from *Diálogo 8,* now with new vocabulary.

¿Has cerrado la puerta?	*Have you closed the door?*
Sí, está cerrada.	*Yes, it's closed.*

DIÁLOGO 9 · Los informes están impresos.

Study the dialogue, then listen to the recording and repeat each line.

MARÍA Hay que imprimir los informes.
FELIPE Ya están impresos.

Análisis

Check that you understand the linguistic breakdown of each speech from *Diálogo 9*.

Hay que imprimir los informes.	*It's necessary to print the reports.*
hay que + *infinitive*	*one must (do something), you have to (do something)*
el informe	*report*
Ya están impresos.	*They're already printed.*
impreso	*printed* (past participle of **imprimir**)
estar impreso	*to be printed*

Variantes

Listen, and repeat the same structures from *Diálogo 9*, now with new vocabulary.

Hay que resolver este problema.	*It's necessary to solve this problem.*
Ya está resuelto.	*It's solved already.*

DIÁLOGO 10 · Los niños no se han acostado.

Study the dialogue, then listen to the recording and repeat each line.

FELIPE ¿Los niños se han acostado?
MARÍA No, no están acostados todavía.

Análisis

Check that you understand the linguistic breakdown of each speech from *Diálogo 10*.

¿Los niños se han acostado?	*Have the children gone to bed?*
han	*they have*
acostarse (**o** > **ue**)	*to go to bed*
acostado	*gone to bed*
se han acostado	*they have gone to bed*
No, no están acostados todavía.	*No, they're not in bed yet.*
estar acostado	*to be in bed, be lying down*

Variantes

Listen, and repeat the same structures from *Diálogo 10*, now with new vocabulary.

¿La niña se ha acostado?	*Has the little girl gone to bed?*
No, no está acostada.	*No, she's not in bed.*

¿El niño se ha levantado? No, no está levantado.	*Has the little boy gotten up?* *No, he's not up.*
¿Te aburres? No, no estoy aburrido.	*Are you bored?* *No, I'm not bored.*
¿Uds. se preocupan mucho? Sí, siempre estamos preocupados.	*Do you worry a lot?* *Yes, we're always worried.*
¿Ellas se enojan mucho? Sí, siempre están enojadas.	*Do they get angry a lot?* *Yes, they're always angry.*
Ellos están sentados en el sofá. Ellas están paradas en la cola.	*They're sitting on the couch.* *They're standing in line.*

Estructura y Práctica

Estar + Past Participle: Expressing Positions of the Body

As you learned in Chapter 4, **estar** is used with the past participle to express positions of the body such as sitting or standing. The past participle functions as an adjective, thereby agreeing in gender and number with the noun it refers to. English uses the *-ing* form for this purpose.

Raquel **está sentada** en el sillón.	*Raquel* ***is sitting*** *in the armchair.*
Los niños **estaban acostados**.	*The children* ***were lying down.***

K ***¿Sentado o parado?*** Write the form of **estar** plus past participle that correctly completes each of the following sentences describing how these people are positioned. Use the verb cue in parentheses. Make all necessary changes. Follow the *modelo*.

MODELO Eugenio *está sentado* en el banquillo (*bench*). (sentarse)

1. Pedro ________________ en la hamaca. (tumbarse)
2. La flautista y el pianista ________________ ante el público. (inclinarse (*to bow*))
3. El bebé ________________ en su cuna (*crib*). (dormir)
4. El receptor (*catcher*) ________________ detrás del plato (*home plate*). (agacharse (*to crouch*))
5. Nosotros ________________ en el autobús. (parar)
6. Camila ________________ a caballo. (montar)
7. Los niños ya ________________ de la cama. (levantarse)
8. El abuelo ________________ en el sofá. (echarse)

DIÁLOGO 11 · ¡Cómo ha cambiado la ciudad!

Study the dialogue, then listen to the recording and repeat each line.

MARÍA	¡Cómo ha cambiado la ciudad!
FELIPE	No cabe duda. Han construido tantos rascacielos en los últimos años.
MARÍA	Han convertido muchas fábricas en apartamentos de lujo.
FELIPE	Y han hecho maravillas con los barrios bajos también.

Análisis

Check that you understand the linguistic breakdown of each speech from *Diálogo 11*.

¡Cómo ha cambiado la ciudad!	*How the city has changed!*
ha	*it has*
cambiar	*to change*
cambiado	*changed*
ha cambiado	*it has changed*
la ciudad	*the city*
No cabe duda. Han construido tantos rascacielos en los últimos años.	*That's for sure. They have built so many skyscrapers in the last few years.*
no cabe duda	*that's for sure, there is no doubt*
han	*they have*
construir	*to build*
construido	*built*
han construido	*they have built*
el rascacielos	*skyscraper*
los rascacielos	*skyscrapers*
tantos rascacielos	*so many skyscrapers*
último	*last*
en los últimos años	*in the last few years*
Han convertido muchas fábricas en apartamentos de lujo.	*They have converted many factories into luxury apartments.*
han	*they have*
convertir (**e** > **ie**)	*to convert*
convertir algo en otra cosa	*to convert something into something else*
convertido	*converted*
han convertido	*they have converted*
la fábrica	*factory*
el apartamento	*apartment*
el lujo	*luxury*
el apartamento de lujo	*luxury apartment*
Y han hecho maravillas con los barrios bajos también.	*And they've done wonders with the poor neighborhoods, too.*
han	*they have*
hacer (*irreg.*)	*to do, make*
hacer maravillas	*to do wonders*
hecho	*done, made*

han hecho	*they have done, they have made*
el barrio bajo	*poor neighborhood*

Variantes

Listen, and repeat the same structures from *Diálogo 11*, now with new vocabulary.

¡Cómo ha cambiado la ciudad!	*How the city* ***has changed****!*
ha crecido	*has grown*
La ciudad está muy cambiada.	*The city is very changed.*

DIÁLOGO 12 · El costo de la vida

Study the dialogue, then listen to the recording and repeat each line.

FELIPE Nuestra ciudad se ha convertido en una metrópoli muy importante.

MARÍA Sí, la población ha aumentado muchísimo. Actualmente hay casi siete millones de habitantes.

FELIPE El precio de las viviendas ha subido muchísimo. El costo de la vida ha subido tanto.

MARÍA A veces tengo ganas de mudarme a una ciudad menos costosa.

Análisis

Check that you understand the linguistic breakdown of each speech from *Diálogo 12*.

Nuestra ciudad se ha convertido en una metrópoli muy importante.	*Our city has become a very important metropolis.*
ha	*it has*
convertirse en (**e** > **ie**)	*to become*
convertido	*become*
se ha convertido	*it has become*
la metrópoli	*metropolis, capital (city), major city*
importante	*important*
Sí, la población ha aumentado muchísimo. Actualmente hay casi siete millones de habitantes.	*Yes, the population has increased a great deal. At present, there are nearly seven million inhabitants.*
la población	*population*
ha	*it has*
aumentar	*to increase*
aumentado	*increased*
ha aumentado	*it has increased*
muchísimo	*greatly, a great deal*
actualmente	*at present*
un millón de + *noun*	*a million* + noun
siete millones de + *noun*	*seven million* + noun
el habitante	*inhabitant*
siete millones de habitantes	*seven million inhabitants*

El precio de las viviendas ha subido muchísimo. El costo de la vida ha subido tanto.	*The price of housing has gone up tremendously. The cost of living has gone up so much.*
el precio	*price*
la vivienda	*housing, housing unit*
ha	*it has*
subir	*to go up, rise*
subido	*gone up, risen*
ha subido	*it has gone up, it has risen*
el costo	*cost*
el costo de la vida	*cost of living*
A veces tengo ganas de mudarme a una ciudad menos costosa.	*Sometimes I feel like moving to a less expensive city.*
a veces	*sometimes*
tener ganas de + *infinitive*	*to feel like (doing something)*
mudarse	*to move (change residence)*
costoso	*costly, expensive*
menos costoso	*less expensive*

Variantes

Listen, and repeat the same structures from *Diálogo 12*, now with new vocabulary.

El pueblo se ha convertido en una ciudad.	*The town has become a city.*
El desempleo ha aumentado.	*Unemployment has risen.*
Los impuestos han aumentado.	*Taxes have gone up.*

Estructura y Práctica

L **Translation.** Express the following dialogue exchanges in Spanish.

1. *How much the city has grown in the last few years!*
   And the population has increased a lot. There are almost four million inhabitants.
2. *Our little town has become a big and important city.*
   Indeed. Many buildings have been built, and little by little there are fewer poor neighborhoods.
3. *They've done wonderful things! Our city is very changed.*
   It's true. But what overcrowding (la aglomeración)*! What traffic! What noise!*

DIÁLOGO 13 · ¡Cómo había cambiado la ciudad!

Study the dialogue, then listen to the recording and repeat each line.

MARÍA Cuando yo llegué a la ciudad, ya se había convertido en una metrópoli muy importante.

FELIPE Ah sí. Cuando yo me mudé aquí, el costo de la vida ya había subido muchísimo.

Análisis

Check that you understand the linguistic breakdown of each speech from *Diálogo 13*.

Cuando yo llegué a la ciudad, ya se había convertido en una metrópoli muy importante.	*When I arrived in this city, it had already become an important metropolis.*
había (< *auxiliary verb* **haber**)	*it had*
convertirse en (**e** > **ie**)	*to become*
convertido	*become*
se había convertido	*it had become*
Ah sí. Cuando yo me mudé aquí, el costo de la vida ya había subido muchísimo.	*Oh, yes. When I moved here, the cost of living had already risen tremendously.*
mudarse	*to move* (*change residence*)
había (< *auxiliary verb* **haber**)	*it had*
subir	*to go up, rise*
subido	*gone up, risen*
había subido	*it had gone up, it had risen*

Variantes

Listen, and repeat the same structures from *Diálogo 13*, now with new vocabulary.

Cuando yo regresé, ellos ya se habían ido .	*When I came back,* ***they had already left.***
ella ya había oído la noticia	*she had already heard the news*
tú ya te habías acostado	*you had already gone to bed*

Estructura y Práctica

Past Perfect (Pluperfect)

The past perfect tense (also known as the pluperfect) in Spanish consists of the imperfect tense of the auxiliary verb **haber** + the past participle. In the perfect tenses, the past participle is invariable—it does not agree in gender or number. The Spanish past perfect corresponds to the English past perfect *had* + past participle.

SINGULAR	había comido	*I had eaten*
	habías comido	*you had eaten*
	había comido	*he, she, you* (Ud.) *had eaten*
PLURAL	habíamos comido	*we had eaten*
	habíais comido	*you had eaten*
	habían comido	*they, you* (Uds.) *had eaten*

No habían regresado cuando yo llegué.	*They hadn't returned when I arrived.*
¿No había llamado todavía?	*Hadn't she called yet?*

Object pronouns, including reflexive pronouns, precede the form of **haber** in the perfect tenses. The negative word **no** precedes the object pronouns.

¿La cámara? **Se la hemos** devuelto.	*The camera? We've returned it to them.*
No me había probado el traje.	*I hadn't tried on the suit.*

M ***Ya había pasado.*** Write sentences from the strings of elements to say that certain things had already happened by the time something else occurred. Use the preterit in the dependent **cuando** clause and the past perfect in the main clause. Follow the *modelo.*

MODELO nosotros / volver del teatro : Uds. / salir
→ Cuando nosotros volvimos del teatro, Uds. ya habían salido.

1. Ud. / comprar los cartuchos de tinta : Jorge / imprimir las invitaciones
2. los invitados / llegar para cenar : Pepita y Tomás / poner la mesa
3. despegar el avión : los pasajeros / abrocharse el cinturón de seguridad
4. nosotros / conocer a Nora : ella / hacerse ingeniera
5. Eduardo / comenzar a trabajar : sus colegas / leer los documentos
6. tú / llegar al cementerio : el entierro / tener lugar
7. sonar el teléfono : tú / despertarte
8. yo / ver a Antonio : su empresa / trasladarlo a otra sucursal
9. Uds. / darnos la noticia : nosotros / oírla del vecino
10. Nora / regresar a su pueblo natal (*hometown*) : el pueblo / ya convertirse en una ciudad grande

DIÁLOGO 14 · No habían hecho nada.

Study the dialogue, then listen to the recording and repeat each line.

MARÍA Los analistas ya habían analizado los datos cuando yo llegué a la oficina.
FELIPE No me digas. Cuando yo los vi, todavía no habían hecho nada.

Análisis

Check that you understand the linguistic breakdown of each speech from *Diálogo 14.*

Los analistas ya habían analizado los datos cuando yo llegué a la oficina.	*The analysts had already analyzed the data when I arrived at the office.*
habían (< *auxiliary verb* **haber**)	*they had*
analizar	*to analyze*
analizado	*analyzed*
habían analizado	*they had analyzed*

No me digas. Cuando yo los vi, todavía no habían hecho nada.	*You don't say. When I saw them, they still hadn't done anything.*
No me digas.	*You don't say.*
habían (< *auxiliary verb* **haber**)	*they had*
hacer (*irreg.*)	*to do, make*
hecho	*done, made* (past participle of **hacer**)
habían hecho	*they had done, they had made*
no habían hecho nada	*they hadn't done anything*

Variantes

Listen, and repeat the same structures from *Diálogo 14*, now with new vocabulary.

Él ya había elaborado el presupuesto cuando yo llamé.	***He had already drawn up the budget*** *when I called.*
Uds. ya habían resuelto el problema	*You had already solved the problem*
Ella ya había contestado el email	*She had already answered the email*
Cuando Esteban volvió, Pablo y Lidia ya se habían casado .	*When Esteban returned,* ***Pablo and Lidia had already gotten married****.*
su familia ya se había instalado en su nueva casa	*his family had already moved into their new house*
nosotros ya habíamos visto la película	*we had already seen the film*

Estructura y Práctica

N **Translation.** Express the following dialogue exchanges in Spanish.

1. *Have you* (Ud.) *drawn up the budget already?*
   Yes, I've included income and expenses.
2. *Is the table set?*
   Yes, and dinner is served.
3. *It has been a very difficult day.*
   Why is that? (literally, *Why do you say it?*) *Have you* (tú) *had to do a lot of work?*
4. *Was it snowing when you* (Uds.) *were returning home?*
   No, we had already returned home when it began to snow.
5. *When the airplane landed, the passengers had already turned on their cell phones.*
   I suppose they had also taken down their carry-on luggage.
6. *When we got to Mario's house, the party had already ended.*
   And nobody had told you (it) before? How outrageous!

The Progressive Tenses

The progressive tenses consist of the present, imperfect, preterit, future, and conditional forms of the verb **estar**, followed by the gerund. In this chapter, the progressive tenses are presented for recognition purposes only.

PRESENT PROGRESSIVE	**Estoy elaborando** el presupuesto. *I'm drawing up the budget.*
IMPERFECT PROGRESSIVE	**Estaba elaborando** el presupuesto. *I was drawing up the budget.*
PRETERIT PROGRESSIVE	**Estuve elaborando** el presupuesto hasta que llegaron. *I was drawing up the budget until they arrived.*
FUTURE PROGRESSIVE	**Estaré elaborando** el presupuesto todo el día. *I'll be drawing up the budget all day.*
CONDITIONAL PROGRESSIVE	**Estaría elaborando** el presupuesto. *I'd be drawing up the budget.*

(For a presentation of the future and conditional tenses, see Chapter 15.)

The gerund or **-ndo** form in Spanish corresponds to the *-ing* form in English. For **-ar** verbs, the ending of the gerund is **-ando**; for **-er** and **-ir** verbs, the ending is **-iendo**.

hablar	habl**ando**
esperar	esper**ando**
comer	com**iendo**
aprender	aprend**iendo**
escribir	escrib**iendo**
abrir	abr**iendo**

-Er and **-ir** verbs whose stems end in a vowel use **-yendo** and not **-iendo** to form the gerund.

caer	ca**yendo**
creer	cre**yendo**
leer	le**yendo**
oír	o**yendo**
traer	tra**yendo**

-Ir verbs whose preterit form has a change in the vowel of the stem in the third person show the same change in the gerund.

INFINITIVE	PRETERIT	GERUND
decir	dijo	**diciendo**
dormir	durmió	**durmiendo**
morir	murió	**muriendo**
pedir	pidió	**pidiendo**
repetir	repitió	**repitiendo**
sentir	sintió	**sintiendo**
servir	sirvió	**sirviendo**
venir	vino	**viniendo**

Poder and **ir** have irregular gerunds.

poder	**pudiendo**
ir	**yendo**

The gerunds of **estar**, **ir**, and **venir** are not commonly used.

For now, we will focus only on the present progressive. In Spanish, the present progressive is different from the corresponding simple present tense in that it emphasizes that the action is in progress. It may also suggest that the action is temporary, not habitual. The present progressive in Spanish can never refer to the future, as the present progressive in English does. To express future time, Spanish uses the simple present, the **ir a** + infinitive construction, or the future tense.

Salimos para el campo mañana.	*We are leaving for the country tomorrow.*
Vamos a salir para el campo mañana.	*We are going to leave for the country tomorrow.*
Saldremos para el campo mañana.	*We will leave for the country tomorrow.*

In the progressive tenses, object and reflexive pronouns may either precede the form of **estar** or be attached to the gerund in writing. In the latter case, a written accent is added over the vowel before the **-ndo** ending.

Nos estamos divirtiendo mucho. Estamos divirtiéndo**nos** mucho.	*We're having a great time.*
Se lo están explicando. Están explicándo**selo**.	*They're explaining it to them.*

NOTE Be aware that English-speaking learners of Spanish tend to overuse the present progressive.

Un paso más

Are you ready to take your Spanish a step further? Here are exercises that will enhance your knowledge of the language and allow you to express yourself freely.

O ***Preguntas personales.*** Answer each question with a complete Spanish sentence.

1. ¿Ud. elabora un presupuesto personal para los gastos de la casa? Haga (*Make*) una lista de todos los puntos que incluye en el presupuesto. (Repase (*Review*) el vocabulario del capítulo.)
2. ¿Trabaja con las bases de datos empresariales (de una empresa)? ¿Cómo las organiza?
3. ¿Qué hace para asegurar la protección y la seguridad de los datos?
4. ¿Vive en una ciudad? ¿Qué cosas le agradan de la vida urbana? ¿Qué cosas encuentra desagradables?
5. ¿Se celebran ritos y tradiciones religiosos en su familia? ¿Cuáles son? (Repase los Diálogos 3 y 6 de este capítulo.)

P ***¡Una cena fantástica!*** Write a brief description of the dinner party you gave last night. Review the vocabulary used in *Diálogo 7* to describe your table setting. Additional vocabulary is provided below. Tell what you served, who the guests were, and other details.

el azucarero (la azucarera) *sugar bowl*
la copa *wine glass*
el cubierto *cutlery, utensils; place setting*
el mantel *tablecloth*
el mantelito *place mat*
el pimentero *pepper mill*
el sopero *soup plate*
el salero *saltshaker*
la vajilla *set of dishes*
la vela *candle*

Q ***La gentrificación.*** Write a paragraph expressing your thoughts on gentrification, using the words and phrases you learned in this chapter. (Review *Diálogos 11, 12,* and *13* in this chapter.) Use these questions as a guide.

1. ¿Cuáles son los objetivos de la gentrificación?
2. ¿Cuáles son sus ventajas (*advantages*) y sus desventajas (*disadvantages*)?
3. ¿Cómo transforma la gentrificación a los espacios urbanos deteriorados?
4. ¿Hay barrios bajos donde Ud. vive? ¿Cómo son?
5. ¿Ud. conoce sectores de su comunidad que han sido gentrificados? ¿Cómo son?
6. ¿Cree que el urbanismo (*urban planning, city planning*) mejora la vida de los habitantes de las ciudades? ¿Cómo?

14

Directions, Air Travel, Recipes

Communication Goals

- Telling someone to do or not to do something
- Asking for and giving directions
- Giving instructions for a recipe
- Vocabulary: traffic signs and signals, at the airport, a doctor's advice, cooking, a hotel emergency

Grammar Topics

- The Imperative
- Imperative: Command Forms for **Ud.** and **Uds.**
- Imperative: Command Forms for **tú** and **vosotros**
- Irregular Command Forms: **tú**
- Object Pronouns in the Imperative: **tú**, **Ud.**, **Uds.**
- Imperative: Command Forms for **nosotros**
- Object Pronouns in the Imperative: **nosotros**
- Irregular Command Forms: **Ud.**, **Uds.**, **nosotros**
- Other Ways of Giving Commands

DIÁLOGO 1 · Cómo se llega al museo

Study the dialogue, then listen to the recording and repeat each line.

INÉS Perdone, señor, ¿cómo llego al museo de arte?

JAIME Pues mire Ud., siga por esta avenida. Al llegar a la calle Castaño, doble a la derecha. Camine tres cuadras hasta llegar a una plaza. Cruce la plaza. Allí queda el museo.

INÉS Muchas gracias, señor.

JAIME De nada, señorita.

Análisis

Check that you understand the linguistic breakdown of each speech from *Diálogo 1.*

Perdone, señor, ¿cómo llego al museo de arte?	*Excuse me, sir. How can I get to the art museum?*
perdonar	*to forgive, pardon*
perdone	*excuse me*
¿cómo llego?	*how do I get to?*
el museo de arte	*art museum*
Pues mire Ud., siga por esta avenida. Al llegar a la calle Castaño, doble a la derecha. Camine tres cuadras hasta llegar a una plaza. Cruce la plaza. Allí queda el museo.	*Well, look, continue along this avenue. When you get to Castaño street, turn right. Walk three blocks until you get to a square. Cross the square. That's where the museum is.*
mirar	*to look at*
mire	*look*
seguir (**e** > **i**) por	*to continue along*
siga	*continue*
al llegar	*when you arrive*
la calle	*street*
doblar	*to turn*
doble	*turn*
a la derecha	*to the right*
caminar	*to walk*
camine	*walk*
la cuadra	*(city) block*
hasta	*until*
hasta llegar	*until you get to*
la plaza	*square (in a city)*
cruzar	*to cross*
cruce	*cross*
quedar	*to be (for location of inanimate nouns)*
allí queda	*that's where it is*
Muchas gracias, señor.	*Thank you very much, sir.*
De nada, señorita.	*You're welcome, miss.*

Variantes

Listen, and repeat the same structures from *Diálogo 1,* now with new vocabulary.

Perdone, señor.	***Excuse me**, sir.*
Dispense	*Excuse me*
Disculpe	*Excuse me*
Doble a la derecha.	*Turn **right**.*
a la izquierda	*left*

Camine rápidamente.	***Walk** quickly.*
Corra	*Run*
Ande	*Walk*
Maneje con cuidado.	***Drive** carefully.*
Conduzca	*Drive*
Cruce la plaza.	*Cross **the square**.*
la calle	*the street*
el puente	*the bridge*
el río	*the river*

Estructura y Práctica

THE IMPERATIVE

The imperative is used to tell someone to do something or not to do something. There are imperative forms in Spanish for **tú**, **Ud.**, **nosotros**, **vosotros**, and **Uds.** (The imperative forms for **vosotros** (the plural form of **tú** in Spain) appear in some of the charts in this chapter, but they will not be practiced actively.)

Imperative: Command Forms for Ud. and Uds.

Most imperative forms involve a change in the vowel of the ending. In other words, the **a** in the endings of **-ar** verbs changes to **e**, and the **e** or **i** in the endings of **-er** and **-ir** verbs changes to **a**.

comprar	**Compre** (Ud.) esta calculadora.	***Buy** this calculator.*
	Compren (Uds.) esta calculadora.	***Buy** this calculator.*
leer	**Lea** (Ud.) la propuesta.	***Read** the proposal.*
	Lean (Uds.) la propuesta.	***Read** the proposal.*
añadir	**Añada** (Ud.) un comentario.	***Add** a comment.*
	Añadan (Uds.) un comentario.	***Add** a comment.*

The addition of the pronoun **Ud.** or **Uds.** to an imperative adds a polite tone to the command, much as *please* does in English.

To form the negative imperative for **Ud.** and **Uds.**, add **no** before the command form.

No compre (Ud.) esta calculadora.	***Don't buy** this calculator.*
No compren (Uds.) esta calculadora.	***Don't buy** this calculator.*
No lea (Ud.) la propuesta.	***Don't read** the proposal.*
No lean (Uds.) la propuesta.	***Don't read** the proposal.*
No añada (Ud.) un comentario.	***Don't add** a comment.*
No añadan (Uds.) un comentario.	***Don't add** a comment.*

Verbs whose present tense has an irregularity in the stem of the first person singular have the same irregular stem in the **Ud.** and **Uds.** forms of the imperative.

INFINITIVE	**yo** FORM	**Ud.** COMMAND	**Uds.** COMMAND
decir	digo	**diga**	**digan**
hacer	hago	**haga**	**hagan**
poner	pongo	**ponga**	**pongan**
tener	tengo	**tenga**	**tengan**
venir	vengo	**venga**	**vengan**
conocer	conozco	**conozca**	**conozcan**
ver	veo	**vea**	**vean**

If the present tense form of a verb has a change in the vowel of the stem, the command forms for **Ud.** and **Uds.** show that change as well. (For more on stem-changing verbs, see Chapter 6.)

INFINITIVE	**Ud., Uds.** FORMS	**Ud.** COMMAND	**Uds.** COMMAND
cerrar	cierra, cierran	**cierre**	**cierren**
mostrar	muestra, muestran	**muestre**	**muestren**
encender	enciende, encienden	**encienda**	**enciendan**
volver	vuelve, vuelven	**vuelva**	**vuelvan**
convertir	convierte, convierten	**convierta**	**conviertan**
pedir	pide, piden	**pida**	**pidan**
dormir	duerme, duermen	**duerma**	**duerman**

A Write an affirmative **Ud.** command for each item. Follow the *modelo.*

MODELO doblar a la derecha
→ Doble a la derecha.

1. correr el maratón
2. manejar con cuidado
3. abrir las ventanas
4. asistir al concierto
5. cruzar la calle
6. subir al avión
7. comer con nosotros
8. seguir por el río
9. elaborar un presupuesto
10. leer este libro
11. diseñar el sitio web
12. volver para el viernes
13. pedir una disculpa (*to apologize*)
14. hacer un plan de negocios

B Write an affirmative **Uds.** command for each item. Follow the *modelo.*

MODELO caminar rápidamente
→ Caminen rápidamente.

1. beber mucha agua
2. trabajar con el equipo
3. vivir felizmente
4. escribir el email
5. conducir con cuidado
6. aprender las fechas de memoria
7. tomar el tren
8. vestir a los niños
9. prender la televisión
10. analizar los datos
11. cobrar el cheque
12. compartir sus ideas
13. dormir la siesta
14. servir la comida

C **Please.** Express the following commands in Spanish, adding the pronoun **Ud.** or **Uds.** to add a polite tone. Follow the *modelos.*

MODELOS *Please come back soon.* (Ud.)
→ Regrese Ud. pronto.

Please come back soon. (Uds.)
→ Regresen Uds. pronto.

1. *Please arrive early.* (Uds.)
2. *Please serve dinner.* (Ud.)
3. *Please open the window.* (Ud.)
4. *Please cross the street carefully.* (Uds.)
5. *Please look at the traffic sign.* (Ud.)
6. *Please go up in the elevator.* (Uds.)
7. *Please store the data.* (Ud.)
8. *Please draw up a budget.* (Uds.)

Spelling Changes in the Imperative: Ud. and Uds.

In the command forms for **Ud.** and **Uds.**, the following spelling changes take place.

In -**ar** verbs ending in -**car**, -**gar**, -**zar**, the final consonants of the stem **c**, **g**, **z** change respectively to **qu**, **gu**, **c** before an ending beginning with -**e**.

INFINITIVE	**Ud.** COMMAND	**Uds.** COMMAND
sacar	sa**que**	sa**qu**en
pagar	pa**gue**	pa**gu**en
almorzar	almuerce	almuer**c**en

-**Er** and -**ir** verbs whose stem ends in -**g**- change the **g** to **j** before an ending beginning with -**a**.

INFINITIVE	**Ud.** COMMAND	**Uds.** COMMAND
escoger	escoja	esco**j**an
elegir	elija	eli**j**an

DIÁLOGO 2 · No estacione en esta calle.

Study the dialogue, then listen to the recording and repeat each line.

JAIME Dispense, señorita, ¿se permite estacionar en esta calle?
INÉS No, señor, se prohíbe. Mire la señal. Le pueden poner una multa.
JAIME Entonces dígame, por favor, ¿hay un estacionamiento por aquí?
INÉS Bueno, siga derecho hasta el semáforo. En la esquina hay uno.

Análisis

Check that you understand the linguistic breakdown of each speech from *Diálogo 2.*

Dispense, señorita, ¿se permite estacionar en esta calle?	*Excuse me, miss, is parking allowed on this street?*
dispensar	*to excuse*
dispense	*excuse me*
permitir	*to permit, allow*
se permite	*it is allowed*
¿se permite estacionar?	*is parking allowed?*

No, señor, se prohíbe. Mire la señal. Le pueden poner una multa.	*No, sir, it's forbidden. Look at the sign. They can fine you.*
se prohíbe	*it is forbidden*
mirar	*to look at*
mire	*look at*
la señal	*sign, road sign, traffic sign*
la multa	*fine*
ponerle una multa a uno	*to fine someone*
Le pueden poner una multa.	*They can fine you.*
Entonces dígame, por favor, ¿hay un estacionamiento por aquí?	*Then tell me, please, is there a parking garage around here?*
decir	*to say, tell*
diga	*tell*
dígame	*tell me*
el estacionamiento	*parking lot, parking garage*
por aquí	*around here*
Bueno, siga derecho hasta el semáforo. En la esquina hay uno.	*Well, keep going straight ahead until the traffic light. There's one on the corner.*
seguir (**e** > **i**) por	*to continue along*
siga	*continue*
siga derecho	*keep going straight ahead*
hasta	*until, up to*
el semáforo	*traffic light*
la esquina	*street corner*

Variantes

Listen, and repeat the same structures from *Diálogo 2*, now with new vocabulary.

No estacione en esta calle.	***Don't park** on this street.*
No aparque	*Don't park*
Mire la señal de tráfico.	*Look at **the traffic sign**.*
la placa	*the license plate*
Dígame, por favor.	***Tell me**, please.*
Míreme	*Look at me*
Cuénteme	*Tell me*
Óigame	*Listen to me*
El semáforo está en verde.	*The light is **green**.*
en rojo	*red*
en amarillo	*yellow*
en naranja	*yellow*

Estructura y Práctica

Negative Commands: Ud. and Uds.

To form the negative imperative for **Ud.** and **Uds.**, add **no** before the command form.

No firme (Ud.) el contrato.	***Don't sign*** *the contract.*
No firmen (Uds.) el contrato.	***Don't sign*** *the contract.*
No lo **crea** (Ud.).	***Don't believe*** *it.*
No lo **crean** (Uds.).	***Don't believe*** *it.*
No escriba (Ud.) otra carta.	***Don't write*** *another letter.*
No escriban (Uds.) otra carta.	***Don't write*** *another letter.*
No salga (Ud.) todavía.	***Don't leave*** *yet.*
No salgan (Uds.) todavía.	***Don't leave*** *yet.*

D Write an affirmative and a negative **Ud.** command for each item. Follow the *modelo.*

MODELO asistir al evento
→ Asista al evento.
→ No asista al evento.

1. guardar los suéteres
2. ver el programa
3. estacionar en la plaza
4. añadir más sal
5. cerrar la puerta
6. imprimir los contratos
7. poner la mesa
8. probar ese plato
9. descargar el archivo
10. repetir las palabras

E Write an affirmative and a negative **Uds.** command for each item. Follow the *modelo.*

MODELO asistir al evento
→ Asistan al evento.
→ No asistan al evento.

1. guardar los suéteres
2. ver el programa
3. estacionar en la plaza
4. añadir más sal
5. cerrar la puerta
6. imprimir los contratos
7. poner la mesa
8. probar ese plato
9. descargar el archivo
10. repetir las palabras

DIÁLOGO 3 · En el aeropuerto

Study the dialogue, then listen to the recording and repeat each line.

INÉS Aquí hay un quiosco. Vamos a registrarnos.
JAIME Sí, saquemos las tarjetas de embarque y facturemos el equipaje.
INÉS Luego, vamos a ir a la puerta de embarque.
JAIME Espera. Primero comamos algo. Yo me muero de hambre.

Análisis

Check that you understand the linguistic breakdown of each speech from *Diálogo 3.*

Aquí hay un quiosco. Vamos a registrarnos.	*There's a kiosk here. Let's check in.*
el quiosco	*automatic check-in kiosk*
vamos a + *infinitive*	*let's (do something)*
registrarse	*to check in, register*
vamos a registrarnos	*let's check in*
Sí, saquemos las tarjetas de embarque y facturemos el equipaje.	*Yes, let's get the boarding passes and check the luggage.*
sacar	*to take out, get*
sacamos	*we get*
saquemos	*let's get*
la tarjeta	*card*
el embarque	*boarding*
la tarjeta de embarque	*boarding pass*
facturar	*to check* (*luggage*)
facturamos	*we check*
facturemos	*let's check*
el equipaje	*luggage*
Luego, vamos a ir a la puerta de embarque.	*Then let's go to the departure gate.*
luego	*then*
vamos a + *infinitive*	*let's (do something)*
vamos a ir	*let's go*
la puerta	*gate*
la puerta de embarque	*departure gate*
Espera. Primero comamos algo. Yo me muero de hambre.	*Wait. Let's eat something first. I'm dying of hunger.*
espera	*wait* (**tú** command)
primero	*first*
comemos	*we eat*
comamos	*let's eat*
comamos algo	*let's eat something*
morirse (**o** > **ue**) de	*to be dying of* (often figurative)
me muero de hambre	*I'm dying of hunger. / I'm starving.*

Variantes

Listen, and repeat the same structures from *Diálogo 3*, now with new vocabulary.

Vamos a registrarnos .	*Let's* ***check in.***
irnos	*go, leave*
sacar las tarjetas de embarque	*get our boarding passes*
facturar el equipaje	*check the luggage*
comer algo	*eat something*

Registrémonos.	*Let's check in.*
Vámonos.	*Let's go.*
Sentémonos.	*Let's sit down.*
Reunámonos.	*Let's get together.*
Vistámonos.	*Let's get dressed.*
No comamos ahora.	***Let's not eat** now.*
No nos vayamos	*Let's not go*
No nos registremos	*Let's not check in*
No nos sentemos	*Let's not sit down*
No nos reunamos	*Let's not get together*
No nos vistamos	*Let's not get dressed*
Espera.	*Wait.*
Come.	*Eat.*
Sube.	*Go up.*
Vuelve.	*Come back.*
No esperes.	*Don't wait.*
No comas.	*Don't eat.*
No subas.	*Don't go up.*
No vuelvas.	*Don't come back.*
Ve.	*Go.*
Sal.	*Go out.*
Ven.	*Come.*
No vayas.	*Don't go.*
No salgas.	*Don't go out.*
No vengas.	*Don't come.*
Haz las maletas.	*Pack.* (literally, *Do the suitcases.*)
Hazlas.	*Pack them* (*the suitcases*).
No hagas las maletas.	*Don't pack.* (literally, *Don't do the suitcases.*)
No las hagas.	*Don't pack them* (*the suitcases*).
Saca la tarjeta de embarque.	*Get (out) your boarding pass.*
No saques la tarjeta de embarque.	*Don't get (out) your boarding pass.*
Sácala.	*Get it.*
No la saques.	*Don't get it.*

Estructura y Práctica

Imperative: Command Forms for tú and vosotros

Negative commands for **tú** and **vosotros** are formed just like the **Ud.** and **Uds.** commands—by switching the vowel of the ending. These negative **tú** and **vosotros** commands, as well as the command forms for **Ud.** and **Uds.**, all derive from the present subjunctive. (For a full presentation of the present subjunctive, see Chapter 16.)

INFINITIVE	**tú** PRESENT TENSE	**tú** COMMAND	**vosotros** PRESENT TENSE	**vosotros** COMMAND
comprar	no compras	**no compres**	no compráis	**no compréis**
leer	no lees	**no leas**	no leéis	**no leáis**
añadir	no añades	**no añadas**	no añadís	**no añadáis**
cerrar	no cierras	**no cierres**	no cerráis	**no cerréis**
mostrar	no muestras	**no muestres**	no mostráis	**no mostréis**
encender	no enciendes	**no enciendas**	no encendéis	**no encendáis**
volver	no vuelves	**no vuelvas**	no volvéis	**no volváis**

Irregularities that appear in the **Ud.** and **Uds.** commands also appear in the negative **tú** and **vosotros** commands.

INFINITIVE	NEGATIVE **tú** COMMAND	NEGATIVE **vosotros** COMMAND
decir	**no digas**	**no digáis**
hacer	**no hagas**	**no hagáis**
poner	**no pongas**	**no pongáis**
tener	**no tengas**	**no tengáis**
venir	**no vengas**	**no vengáis**
conocer	**no conozcas**	**no conozcáis**
ver	**no veas**	**no veáis**
ir	**no vayas**	**no vayáis**
saber	**no sepas**	**no sepáis**
ser	**no seas**	**no seáis**
dar	**no des**	**no deis**
estar	**no estés**	**no estéis**

Affirmative commands for **tú** and **vosotros** do not show a change in the vowel of the ending of the imperative. Affirmative commands for **tú** are formed by dropping the final **-s** of the **tú** form of the present tense. Affirmative commands for **vosotros** are formed by replacing the **-r** of the infinitive with **-d**.

INFINITIVE	**tú** PRESENT TENSE	**tú** COMMAND	**vosotros** PRESENT TENSE	**vosotros** COMMAND
comprar	compras	**compra**	compráis	**comprad**
comer	comes	**come**	coméis	**comed**
añadir	añades	**añade**	añadís	**añadid**
cerrar	cierras	**cierra**	cerráis	**cerrad**
encender	enciendes	**enciende**	encendéis	**encended**
convertir	conviertes	**convierte**	convertís	**convertid**
pedir	pides	**pide**	pedís	**pedid**
dormir	duermes	**duerme**	dormís	**dormid**
dar	das	**da**	dais	**dad**
estar	estás	**está**	estáis	**estad**

Irregular Command Forms: tú

Eight affirmative **tú** commands have irregular one-syllable forms. The corresponding **vosotros** commands are regular.

INFINITIVE	**tú** PRESENT TENSE	**tú** COMMAND	**vosotros** PRESENT TENSE	**vosotros** COMMAND
decir	dices	**di**	decís	decid
hacer	haces	**haz**	hacéis	haced
ir	vas	**ve**	vais	id
poner	pones	**pon**	ponéis	poned
salir	sales	**sal**	salís	salid
ser	eres	**sé**	sois	sed
tener	tienes	**ten**	tenéis	tened
venir	vienes	**ven**	venís	venid

Spelling Changes in the Imperative: Negative tú and vosotros Commands

In the command forms for the negative **tú** and **vosotros** commands, the following spelling changes take place.

In **-ar** verbs ending in **-car**, **-gar**, **-zar**, the final consonants of the stem **c**, **g**, **z** change respectively to **qu**, **gu**, **c** before an ending beginning with **-e**.

INFINITIVE	NEGATIVE **tú** COMMAND	NEGATIVE **vosotros** COMMAND
sacar	no sa**qu**es	no sa**qu**éis
pagar	no pa**gu**es	no pa**gu**éis
almorzar	no almuer**c**es	no almor**c**éis

-Er and **-ir** verbs whose stem ends in **-g-** change the **g** to **j** before an ending beginning with **-a**.

INFINITIVE	NEGATIVE **tú** COMMAND	NEGATIVE **vosotros** COMMAND
escoger	no esco**j**as	no esco**j**áis
elegir	no eli**j**as	no eli**j**áis

F Write an affirmative and a negative **tú** command for each item. Follow the *modelo*.

MODELO doblar a la izquierda
→ Dobla a la izquierda.
→ No dobles a la izquierda.

1. vender el carro
2. navegar en la web
3. subir en el ascensor
4. seguir por esta calle
5. hacer la maleta
6. pensar en eso
7. venir el sábado
8. salir antes de las cuatro
9. tener prisa
10. jugar al golf

Object Pronouns in the Imperative: tú, Ud., Uds.

In all negative imperative forms, object pronouns are placed in their usual position before the verb. This includes reflexive pronouns.

No **te** metas en estos asuntos.	*Don't butt into these matters.*
Esta camisa está rota. No **te la** pongas.	*This shirt is torn. Don't put it on.*
No **me** diga que no puede venir.	*Don't tell me that you can't come.*
Él quiere dinero. No **se lo** preste Ud.	*He wants money. Don't lend it to him.*
No **se** vayan Uds.	*Don't go away.*
¿Las maletas? No **las** facturen.	*The suitcases? Don't check them.*

For affirmative command forms, object pronouns follow the verbs and are attached to them in writing. For **tú**, **Ud.**, and **Uds.** commands, an accent mark is added to the stem vowel when an object pronoun (or reflexive pronoun) is added, if the command form has more than one syllable.

Cuídate.	***Take care.***
Aquí tienes el informe. **Léelo.**	*Here's the report.* ***Read it.***
Ana tiene la calculadora. **Pídesela.**	*Ana has the calculator.* ***Ask her for it.***
Él quiere dinero. **Présteselo Ud.**	*He wants money.* ***Lend it to him.***
Necesito los documentos. **Tráigamelos Ud.**	*I need the documents.* ***Bring them to me.***
Váyanse Uds.	***Go away.***
Escúchenme bien.	***Listen to me*** *carefully.*

No accent mark is added to a one-syllable command form when a single object pronoun is added.

Esto es tu trabajo. **Hazlo.**	*This is your work.* ***Do it.***
Ponte el abrigo. Hace frío.	***Put on*** *your coat. It's cold outside.*
Dime si necesitas algo.	***Tell me*** *if you need anything.*

However, the command forms **dé**, **esté**, and **está** may keep their accents when a pronoun is added.

Déme un consejo.	***Give me*** *some advice.*
¡**Estáte** quieto!	***Stay*** *still! / Stop fidgeting! / Behave yourself!*

All command forms require a written accent when two object pronouns are added.

Busca tus guantes y **póntelos**.	*Get your gloves and* ***put them on***.
No entiendo su idea. **Explíquemela.**	*I don't understand your idea.* ***Explain it to me.***
Si terminaron el mensaje, **envíenselo**.	*If you finished the message,* ***send it to them***.

IMPERATIVE: VOSOTROS + OBJECT PRONOUNS

No accent mark is added to **vosotros** command forms when a single object pronoun is added.

¡Niños, **hacedme** caso!	*Children, pay attention to what I say!*
Mandadle un email.	*Send her an email.*

Vosotros command forms drop the final **-d** before the reflexive pronoun **os.**

Acostaos ahora mismo.	*Go to bed right now.*
Poneos en contacto con ella.	*Get in touch with her.*
¡**Divertíos** muchísimo!	*Have a great time!*

However, the **-d** is retained in **idos** (*go away*).

G Express each of the following affirmative and negative commands for **tú** in Spanish.

1. *Don't worry.*
2. *Go away.*
3. *The truth. Tell it to them.*
4. *You owe her money. Return it to her.*
5. *Don't be like that.*
6. *This tie is ugly. Don't put it on.*
7. *Don't be angry with me.*
8. *Dinner, please. Make it for us.*
9. *He needs the headphones. Give them to him.*
10. *Be patient.*

H Express each of the following affirmative and negative commands for **Ud.** and **Uds.** in Spanish. Pay special attention to all required spelling changes.

1. *The dog? Look at him. / Don't look at him.* (Uds.)
2. *The piano? Play it. / Don't play it.* (Ud.)
3. *The magazines? Hand them to me. / Don't hand them to me.* (Ud.)
4. *The gifts? / Choose them for her. / Don't choose them for her.* (Ud.)
5. *The keys? Look for them. / Don't look for them.* (Uds.)
6. *The news (item)? Tell* (contar) *it to them. / Don't tell it to them.* (Ud.)
7. *The idea? Explain it to him. / Don't explain it to him.* (Uds.)
8. *The orchestra* (la orquesta)*? Conduct* (dirigir) *it for us. / Don't conduct it for us.* (Ud.)
9. *The bill? Pay it for him. / Don't pay it for him.* (Uds.)
10. *The game? Start it. / Don't start it.* (Uds.)

I **Object pronouns with *Ud.* and *Uds.* commands.** Write both **Ud.** and **Uds.** commands for each of the following items, adding object pronouns (including reflexive pronouns) based on the English cues. Follow the *modelo.*

MODELO mandar el paquete

Send it.	→	Mándelo.	Mándenlo.
Send it to me.	→	Mándemelo.	Mándenmelo.

1. leer el cuento
   Read it.
   Read it to them.
2. traer las cucharitas
   Bring them.
   Bring them to him.
3. explicar su punto de vista (*point of view*)
   Explain it.
   Explain it to her.
4. decir el chisme
   Tell it.
   Tell it to us.

5. mostrar las pinturas
   Show them.
   Show them to them.

6. servir el postre
   Serve it.
   Serve it to us.

7. lavarse
   Wash up.
   Wash your hands.
   Wash them.

8. pedir los datos
   Ask for it (them).
   Ask her for it (them).

9. ponerse
   Put your jacket on.
   Put it on.

10. secarse
   Dry your hair.
   Dry it.

Imperative: Command Forms for **nosotros**

As you learned in *Diálogo 1*, most imperative forms involve a change in the vowel of the ending. In other words, the **a** in the endings of **-ar** verbs changes to **e**, and the **e** or **i** in the endings of **-er** and **-ir** verbs changes to **a**. Those vowel changes for **-ar**, **-er**, and **-ir** verbs occur in the command forms for **nosotros**.

Tomemos fotos.	***Let's take*** *pictures.*
No tomemos fotos.	***Let's not take*** *pictures.*
Comamos en este restaurante.	***Let's eat*** *at this restaurant.*
No comamos en este restaurante.	***Let's not eat*** *at this restaurant.*
Escribamos una propuesta.	***Let's write*** *a proposal.*
No escribamos una propuesta.	***Let's not write*** *a proposal.*

Note that since the present indicative **nosotros** forms of **-ar** and **-er** verbs have no stem change, the **nosotros** form of the imperative does not have a stem change either.

INFINITIVE	PRESENT TENSE	**nosotros** COMMAND
cerrar (**e** > **ie**)	cerramos	cerremos
mostrar (**o** > **ue**)	mostramos	mostremos
encender (**e** > **ie**)	encendemos	encendamos
volver (**o** > **ue**)	volvemos	volvamos

Verbs whose present tense has an irregularity in the stem of the first person singular have the same irregular stem in the **nosotros** forms of the imperative.

INFINITIVE	**yo** FORM	**nosotros** COMMAND
decir	digo	**digamos**
hacer	hago	**hagamos**
poner	pongo	**pongamos**
tener	tengo	**tengamos**
venir	vengo	**vengamos**
conocer	conozco	**conozcamos**
ver	**veo**	**veamos**

However, **-ir** verbs whose preterit form has a change in the vowel of the stem in the third person show the same change in the stem vowel in the **nosotros** form of the imperative. Thus, in the **nosotros** form of the imperative, the verb **pedir** has **i** as the stem vowel and the verb **dormir** has **u** as the stem vowel. Note that the **nosotros** forms of the present tense of these verbs do not have a stem change.

INFINITIVE	**él/ella/Ud.** PRETERIT	**nosotros** PRESENT TENSE	**nosotros** COMMAND
convertir	conv**i**rtió	convertimos	conv**i**rtamos
pedir	p**i**dió	pedimos	p**i**damos
dormir	d**u**rmió	dormimos	d**u**rmamos

The **nosotros** imperative of the verb **ir** is most commonly **vamos** (*let's go*). The negative imperative, *let's not go*, is **no vayamos**.

Vamos al cine, ¿quieres?	***Let's go*** *to the movies, would you like to?*
No, **no vayamos** al cine. **Vamos** al concierto.	*No,* ***let's not go*** *to the movies.* ***Let's go*** *to the concert.*

Spelling Changes in the Imperative: nosotros

In **nosotros** command forms, the following spelling changes take place.

In **-ar** verbs ending in **-car**, **-gar**, **-zar**, the final consonants of the stem **c**, **g**, **z** change respectively to **qu**, **gu**, **c** before an ending beginning with **-e**.

INFINITIVE	**nosotros** COMMAND
sacar	sa**qu**emos
pagar	pa**gu**emos
almorzar	almor**c**emos

-Er and **-ir** verbs whose stem ends in **-g-** change the **g** to **j** before an ending beginning with **-a**.

INFINITIVE	**nosotros** COMMAND
escoger	esco**j**amos
elegir	eli**j**amos

Object Pronouns in the Imperative: nosotros

In negative **nosotros** command forms, object pronouns, including reflexive pronouns, are placed in their usual position before the verb.

No **nos** mudemos a aquella ciudad.	*Let's not move to that city.*
¿El almuerzo? No **se lo** sirvamos todavía.	*Lunch? Let's not serve it to them yet.*

However, in affirmative command forms, object pronouns follow the verb and are attached to it in writing. When an object pronoun is added to the **nosotros** command form, a written accent is placed on the **a** or **e** of the ending.

Tenemos el informe. **Traigámoselo.**	*We have the report.* ***Let's bring it to her.***
Ellos están enfermos. **Ayudémoslos.**	*They're sick.* ***Let's help them.***

Nosotros command forms lose their final **-s** before the reflexive pronoun **nos** and before the pronoun **se**.

Levantémonos. (Levantemos + nos)	***Let's get up.***
Divirtámonos. (Divirtamos + nos)	***Let's have a good time.***

Vámonos. (**Vamos** + **nos**)	***Let's go.***
Pongámonoslo. (**Pongamos** + **nos** + **lo**)	***Let's put it on.***
Expliquémoselos. (**Expliquemos** + **se** + **los**)	***Let's explain them to him.***
Digámoselo. (**Digamos** + **se** + **lo**)	***Let's tell it to them.***

J Write an affirmative and a negative **nosotros** command for each item. Follow the *modelo.*

MODELO leer este artículo
→ Leamos este artículo.
→ No leamos este artículo.

1. llegar el domingo
2. hacer turismo
3. sacar el pasaporte
4. dar consejos
5. ir al teatro
6. dormir la siesta
7. salir esta noche
8. venir en tren
9. pensar en el futuro
10. pedir un café
11. sentarse en el sofá
12. quedarse unos días más

Vamos a + Infinitive

In everyday speech, the affirmative **nosotros** command is often replaced by **vamos a** + infinitive.

Compremos flores. → **Vamos a comprar** flores.
Hagamos turismo. → **Vamos a hacer** turismo.
Sirvamos la cena. → **Vamos a servir** la cena.

However, the negative **nosotros** commands cannot be replaced by **vamos a** + infinitive. Thus, **vamos a salir** can mean *let's go out* or *we're going to go out.* **No vamos a salir**, however, means only *we are not going to go out.* The phrase *let's not go out* has to be rendered as **no salgamos**.

K Write the affirmative **nosotros** command in response to each question. Express each command in two ways, as the **nosotros** command and as the **ir a** + infinitive construction. Change direct object nouns to pronouns in your answers. Follow the *modelo.*

MODELO ¿Quieres entrar los datos?
→ Sí, entrémoslos.
→ Sí, vamos a entrarlos.

1. ¿Quieres ver la telenovela?
2. ¿Quieres discutir estas ideas?
3. ¿Quieres conseguir los boletos?
4. ¿Quieres compartir los gastos?
5. ¿Quieres pedir vino tinto?
6. ¿Quieres visitar a la tía?
7. ¿Quieres aparcar el carro?
8. ¿Quieres traducir estas palabras?
9. ¿Quieres probarte estos abrigos?
10. ¿Quieres cortarte el pelo?

L Write a negative **nosotros** command in response to each question. Change direct object nouns to pronouns in your answers. Follow the *modelo.*

MODELO ¿Quieres entrar los datos?
→ No, no los entremos.

1. ¿Quieres ver la telenovela?
2. ¿Quieres discutir estas ideas?
3. ¿Quieres conseguir los boletos?
4. ¿Quieres compartir los gastos?
5. ¿Quieres pedir vino tinto?
6. ¿Quieres visitar a la tía?
7. ¿Quieres aparcar el carro?
8. ¿Quieres traducir estas palabras al español?
9. ¿Quieres probarte estos abrigos?
10. ¿Quieres cortarte el pelo?

M ***Nosotros* commands with reflexive verbs.** Express the following pairs of sentences in Spanish. First, write an affirmative **nosotros** command, then write a negative **nosotros** command. Change direct object nouns to pronouns in your answers.

1. *Let's take a stroll in the park. / Let's not take a stroll in the park.*
2. *Let's get married in December. / Let's not get married in December.*
3. *Let's put them* (*our gloves*) *on. / Let's not put them on.*
4. *Let's get together on Sunday. / Let's not get together on Sunday.*
5. *Let's fasten them* (*our seatbelts; one per person*). */ Let's not fasten them.*
6. *Let's wake up early. / Let's not wake up early.*
7. *Let's wash them* (*our hands*). */ Let's not wash them.*
8. *Let's go now. / Let's not go now.*
9. *Let's dry it for them* (*the children's hair*). */ Let's not dry it for them.*
10. *Let's say goodbye to them. / Let's not say goodbye to them.*

DIÁLOGO 4 · A bordo del avión

Study the dialogue, then listen to the recording and repeat each line.

JAIME Por favor, señora, coloque Ud. su equipaje de mano arriba.
INÉS Es que no hay lugar.
JAIME Entonces colóquelo debajo de su asiento. Si no cabe, démelo y lo coloco en otra parte. Y abróchese Ud. el cinturón de seguridad, por favor.

Análisis

Check that you understand the linguistic breakdown of each speech from *Diálogo 4.*

Por favor, señora, coloque Ud. su equipaje de mano arriba.	*Please, ma'am, place your hand luggage above.*
colocar	*to place, put*
coloque	*place*
el equipaje de mano	*carry-on luggage, hand luggage*
arriba	*above*

Es que no hay lugar.	*But there's no room.*
es que	*the fact is that*
lugar	*place, room*
no hay lugar	*there's no room*
Entonces colóquelo debajo de su asiento. Si no cabe, démelo y lo coloco en otra parte. Y abróchese Ud. el cinturón de seguridad, por favor.	*Then place it under your seat. If it doesn't fit, give it to me and I will place it somewhere else. And fasten your seatbelt, please.*
colóquelo	*place it*
debajo de	*under*
el asiento	*seat*
debajo de su asiento	*under your seat*
caber (*irreg.*)	*to fit*
dar	*to give*
dé	*give*
démelo	*give it to me*
y lo coloco	*and I'll put it*
en otra parte	*somewhere else*
abrocharse	*to fasten*
abróchese	*fasten*
el cinturón	*belt*
la seguridad	*security, safety*
el cinturón de seguridad	*seatbelt*

Variantes

Listen, and repeat the same structures from *Diálogo 4*, now with new vocabulary.

Búsquelo.	*Look for it.*
Sáquelo.	*Take it out.*
Entréguelo.	*Hand it in.*
Páguelo.	*Pay it.*
Comiéncelo.	*Begin it.*
Analícelo.	*Analyze it.*
No lo busque.	*Don't look for it.*
No lo saque.	*Don't take it out.*
No lo entregue.	*Don't hand it in.*
No lo pague.	*Don't pay it.*
No lo comience.	*Don't begin it.*
No lo analice.	*Don't analyze it.*
Démelo.	*Give it to me.*
Hágamelo.	*Do it for me.*
Dígamelo.	*Tell it to me.*
No me lo dé.	*Don't give it to me.*
No me lo haga.	*Don't do it for me.*
No me lo diga.	*Don't tell it to me.*

Abróchese el cinturón de seguridad.	***Fasten*** *your seat belt.*
Desabróchese	*Unfasten*
Póngase el abrigo.	***Put on*** *your coat.*
Quítese	*Take off*
¿El abrigo? Póngaselo.	*Your coat?* ***Put it on.***
Quíteselo.	*Take it off.*
¿El abrigo? Póngaselo.	*Her coat?* ***Help her on with it.***
Quíteselo.	*Help her off with it.*

Estructura y Práctica

Irregular Command Forms: *Ud., Uds., nosotros*

Several verbs have irregular command forms.

INFINITIVE	**Ud.** COMMAND	**Uds.** COMMAND	**nosotros** COMMAND
ir	**vaya**	**vayan**	**vamos / no vayamos**
saber	**sepa**	**sepan**	**sepamos**
ser	**sea**	**sean**	**seamos**

The verbs **dar** and **estar** have an accent mark in the **Ud.** command form. **Estar** also has an accent mark in the **Uds.** command form. The **nosotros** command forms of **dar** and **estar** are regular.

INFINITIVE	**Ud.** COMMAND	**Uds.** COMMAND	**nosotros** COMMAND
dar	**dé**	**den**	**demos**
estar	**esté**	**estén**	**estemos**

N ***En la oficina.*** Write an affirmative and a negative **Ud.** command in response to each of the following questions. Change direct object nouns to pronouns (**le** = *to him, to her*; **les** = *to them*). Make all necessary changes. Follow the *modelos*.

MODELOS ¿Debo escribirle el email? (sí)
→ Sí, escríbaselo.

¿Debo escribirle el email? (no)
→ No, no se lo escriba.

1. ¿Debo entregarles los papeles? (sí)
   ¿Debo entregarles los papeles? (no)
2. ¿Debo mostrarles las diapositivas (*slides*)? (sí)
   ¿Debo mostrarles las diapositivas? (no)
3. ¿Debo pedirle el contrato? (sí)
   ¿Debo pedirle el contrato? (no)
4. ¿Debo darle el informe? (sí)
   ¿Debo darle el informe? (no)
5. ¿Debo calcularle los ingresos y gastos? (sí)
   ¿Debo calcularle los ingresos y gastos? (no)
6. ¿Debo hacerles la base de datos? (sí)
   ¿Debo hacerles la base de datos? (no)

7. ¿Debo describirles el plan de mercadeo? (sí)
   ¿Debo describirles el plan de mercadeo? (no)

8. ¿Debo traerles el correo (*mail*)? (sí)
   ¿Debo traerles el correo? (no)

DIÁLOGO 5 · Durante el vuelo

Study the dialogue, then listen to the recording and repeat each line.

INÉS Quiero oír música pero no tengo auriculares.
JAIME Pídeselos al auxiliar de vuelo. Oye, ¿tú ves mi almohada?
INÉS No. Pídesela al auxiliar de vuelo.

Análisis

Check that you understand the linguistic breakdown of each speech from *Diálogo 5*.

Quiero oír música pero no tengo auriculares.	*I want to listen to music, but I don't have headphones.*
oír (*irreg.*)	*to hear, listen to*
oír música	*to listen to music*
los auriculares	*headphones, headset*
Pídeselos al auxiliar de vuelo.	*Ask the flight attendant for them.*
Oye, ¿tú ves mi almohada?	*Say, do you see my pillow?*
pedir (**e** > **i**)	*to ask for*
pedirle algo a uno	*to ask someone for something*
pide	*ask*
pídeselos	*ask him for them*
el auxiliar de vuelo	*flight attendant*
Pídeselos al auxiliar de vuelo.	*Ask the flight attendant for them.*
la almohada	*pillow*
No. Pídesela al auxiliar de vuelo.	*No, ask the flight attendant for it.*
pídesela	*ask him for it*

Variantes

Listen, and repeat the same structures from *Diálogo 5*, now with new vocabulary.

¿Los auriculares? Pídeselos.	*The headphones? Ask her for them.*
¿Las galletas? Pídeselas.	*The cookies? Ask her for them.*
¿El periódico? Pídeselo.	*The newspaper? Ask him for it.*
¿La revista? Pídesela.	*The magazine? Ask him for it.*
¿Debo pedírselo?	*Should I ask him for it?*
No, no se lo pidas.	*No, don't ask him for it.*

DIÁLOGO 6 · Niños, a la cama.

Study the dialogue, then listen to the recording and repeat each line.

INÉS Niños, acuéstense. Ya son las nueve.
JAIME Pero mamá, por favor, queremos terminar este videojuego. Falta poco.
INÉS Bueno, termínenlo y apaguen la computadora. Luego pónganse el pijama, cepíllense los dientes y a la cama.

Análisis

Check that you understand the linguistic breakdown of each speech from *Diálogo 6*.

Niños, acuéstense. Ya son las nueve.	*Children, go to bed. It's already nine o'clock.*
acostarse (**o** > **ue**)	*to go to bed*
acuéstense	*go to bed*
son las nueve	*it's nine o'clock*
Pero mamá, por favor, queremos terminar este videojuego. Falta poco.	*Please, mom. We want to finish this video game. It's almost over.*
terminar	*to finish*
queremos terminar	*we want to finish*
el videojuego	*video game*
faltar	*to be missing*
falta poco	*there is little (time) remaining, it's almost over*
Bueno, termínenlo y apaguen la computadora. Luego pónganse el pijama, cepíllense los dientes y a la cama.	*All right, finish it and shut off the computer. Then put on your pajamas, brush your teeth, and off to bed.*
terminar	*to finish*
terminen	*finish*
termínenlo	*finish it*
apagar	*to turn off, shut off, extinguish*
apaguen	*shut off*
ponerse (*irreg.*)	*to put on* (*article of clothing*)
pónganse	*put on*
pónganse el pijama	*put on your pajamas*
cepillarse (**o** > **ue**)	*to brush*
cepíllense	*brush*
cepíllense los dientes	*brush your teeth*
la cama	*bed*
a la cama	*(off) to bed*

Variantes

Listen, and repeat the same structures from *Diálogo 6*, now with new vocabulary.

Niños, acuéstense.	*Children,* ***go to bed.***
duérmanse	*go to sleep, fall asleep*
despiértense	*wake up*
levántense	*get up, get out of bed*
vístanse	*get dressed*

No se acuesten.	*Don't go to bed.*
No se duerman.	*Don't fall asleep.*
¿El pijama? Pónganselo.	*Your pajamas?* ***Put them on.***
Quítenselo.	*Take them off.*
¿El pijama? No se lo pongan.	*Your pajamas?* ***Don't put them on.***
No se lo quiten.	*Don't take them off.*
Límpiense los dientes.	*Brush your teeth.*
Lávense la cara.	*Wash your faces.*
Córtense el pelo.	*Cut your hair.*
¿La computadora? Apáguenla.	*The computer?* ***Shut it off.***
Préndanla.	*Turn it on.*

DIÁLOGO 7 · En la consulta de médico

Study the dialogue, then listen to the recording and repeat each line.

JAIME	Doctora, ¿qué hago para perder peso?
DOCTORA REYES	Bueno, señor Díaz, póngase a dieta. Coma granos integrales y deje de comer tanta grasa.
JAIME	¿Ud. me va a recetar unas pastillas para adelgazar?
DOCTORA REYES	De ningún modo. Haga Ud. ejercicio y cambie su manera de comer.

Análisis

Check that you understand the linguistic breakdown of each speech from *Diálogo 7.*

Doctora, ¿qué hago para perder peso?	*Doctor, what shall I do to lose weight?*
¿qué hago?	*what shall I do?*
el peso	*weight*
perder (**e** > **ie**)	*to lose*
perder peso	*to lose weight*
Bueno, señor Díaz, póngase a dieta. Coma granos integrales y deje de comer tanta grasa.	*Well, Mr. Díaz, go on a diet. Eat whole grains and stop eating so much fat.*
ponerse	*to put on (article of clothing)*
póngase	*put yourself on*
póngase a dieta	*put yourself on a diet, go on a diet*
comer	*to eat*
coma	*eat*
el grano	*grain*
el grano integral	*whole grain*

dejar	*to leave, let*
dejar de + *infinitive*	*to stop (doing something)*
deje de comer	*stop eating*
la grasa	*fat*
tanta grasa	*so much fat*
¿Ud. me va a recetar unas pastillas para adelgazar?	*Are you going to prescribe some pills for me to lose weight?*
recetarle algo a uno	*to prescribe something for someone*
recetarle pastillas a uno	*to prescribe pills for someone*
adelgazar	*to get thinner, lose weight*
para adelgazar	*in order to lose weight*
De ningún modo. Haga Ud. ejercicio y cambie su manera de comer.	*Absolutely not. Start exercising and change your way of eating.*
de ningún modo	*absolutely not, no way*
hacer	*to do, make*
haga	*do*
haga ejercicio	*do exercise, start exercising*
cambiar	*to change*
cambie	*change*
la manera	*way*
la manera de comer	*way of eating*

Variantes

Listen, and repeat the same structures from *Diálogo 7*, now with new vocabulary.

Beba mucha agua.	*Drink a lot of water.*
No beba refrescos.	*Don't drink soft drinks.*
Viva la vida plenamente.	*Live life to its fullest.*
Baje de peso.	*Lose weight.*
Pierda peso.	*Lose weight.*
Adelgace.	*Lose weight.*
Aumente de peso.	*Gain weight.*
Engorde.	*Gain weight.*
Ponte a dieta.	*Go on a diet.*
Pierde peso.	*Lose weight.*
Cambia tu manera de comer.	*Change your way of eating.*
Haz ejercicio.	*Exercise.*
No seas comilón.	*Don't overeat. / Don't be a glutton.*
No comas comida basura.	*Don't eat junk food.*
No tomes refrescos.	*Don't drink soft drinks.*

EATING AND DRINKING

Diálogo 7 deals with diet and the food we eat. Here are some expressions that are related to how and what we eat.

comer como un rey	*to eat like a king*
comer como un pajarito	*to eat like a bird*
tener afición a los dulces, ser goloso	*to have a sweet tooth*
repetir (**e** > **i**)	*to have a second helping*
Come y bebe que la vida es breve.	*Eat and drink, because life is short.*
La vida es demasiado corta para beber mal vino.	*Life is too short to drink bad wine.*
Todo lo bueno o es pecado o engorda.	*Everything that's good is either a sin or makes you fat.*
Uvas y queso, saben a beso.	*Grapes and cheese, they taste like a kiss.*

Estructura y Práctica

O ***¿Ud. o tú?* Affirmative commands.** Answer each question with an affirmative command for **Ud.** or **tú**, based on the question. Change direct object nouns to pronouns and make all necessary changes. Follow the *modelos.*

MODELOS ¿Le enseño las fotos? → Sí, enséñemelas.
¿Te enseño las fotos? → Sí, enséñamelas.

1. ¿Le muestro los cuadros?
2. ¿Le explico mi idea?
3. ¿Te pongo el abrigo?
4. ¿Te hago la merienda?
5. ¿Le entrego los cartuchos de tinta?
6. ¿Le doy las tarjetas de crédito?
7. ¿Te presto el paraguas?
8. ¿Le envío la copia de seguridad?
9. ¿Te digo lo que pasó?
10. ¿Te sirvo las tapas?

P ***¿Ud. o tú?* Negative commands.** Answer each question with a negative command for **Ud.** or **tú**, based on the question. Change direct object nouns to pronouns and make all necessary changes. Follow the *modelos.*

MODELOS ¿Le enseño las fotos? → No, no me las enseñe.
¿Te enseño las fotos? → No, no me las enseñes.

1. ¿Le muestro los cuadros?
2. ¿Le explico mi idea?
3. ¿Te pongo el abrigo?
4. ¿Te hago la merienda?
5. ¿Le entrego los cartuchos de tinta?
6. ¿Le doy las tarjetas de crédito?
7. ¿Te presto el paraguas?
8. ¿Le envío la copia de seguridad?
9. ¿Te digo lo que pasó?
10. ¿Te sirvo las tapas?

DIÁLOGO 8 · En la playa

Study the dialogue, then listen to the recording and repeat each line.

JAIME	Oye chica, te vas a quemar. Ponte más filtro solar.
INÉS	Mírame, ya estoy bronceada. No me hace falta.
JAIME	No seas tonta. El sol daña la piel. Cuídate de él.

Análisis

Check that you understand the linguistic breakdown of each speech from *Diálogo 8*.

Oye chica, te vas a quemar. Ponte más filtro solar.	*Listen, you're going to get burned. Put on more sunscreen.*
quemarse	*to get burned, get sunburned*
poner (*irreg.*)	*to put*
pon	*put*
ponerse	*to put on oneself*
ponte	*put on*
el filtro solar	*sunscreen*
ponte más filtro solar	*put on more sunscreen*
Mírame, ya estoy bronceada. No me hace falta.	*Look at me, I'm already tan. I don't need it.*
mirar	*to look at*
mira	*look*
mírame	*look at me*
bronceado	*tanned, suntanned*
estar bronceado	*to be tanned*
hacerle falta a uno	*to need*
no me hace falta	*I don't need it*
No seas tonta. El sol daña la piel. Cuídate de él.	*Don't be silly. The sun damages the skin. Protect yourself from it.*
ser	*to be*
no seas	*don't be*
tonto	*silly, stupid*
no seas tonta	*don't be silly, don't be stupid*
el sol	*the sun*
dañar	*to harm, damage*
la piel	*skin*
cuidarse de	*to take care of, protect/guard oneself from*
cuídate	*protect yourself, take care*
cuídate de él	*protect yourself from it*

Variantes

Listen, and repeat the same structures from *Diálogo 8*, now with new vocabulary.

Ponte el filtro solar.	*Put on sunscreen.*
Póntelo.	*Put it on.*
No te lo pongas.	*Don't put it on.*

Cuídate.	*Take care of yourself.*
No te quemes.	*Don't burn.*

DIÁLOGO 9 · Una receta de cocina

Study the dialogue, then listen to the recording and repeat each line.

INÉS Y ahora, ¿qué hago? ¿Bato los huevos?
JAIME Primero calienta un poco de aceite de oliva en la sartén. Luego, bate los huevos y añádelos a la sartén. Fríelos a fuego lento.
INÉS ¿Echo sal a los huevos?
JAIME Sí, pero no les pongas demasiada sal.

Análisis

Check that you understand the linguistic breakdown of each speech from *Diálogo 9*.

Y ahora, ¿qué hago? ¿Bato los huevos?	*And now what shall I do? Should I beat the eggs?*
¿qué hago?	*what shall I do?*
el huevo	*egg*
batir	*to beat*
batir los huevos	*to beat the eggs*
¿Bato los huevos?	*Do I beat the eggs?*
Primero calienta un poco de aceite de oliva en la sartén. Luego, bate los huevos y añádelos a la sartén. Fríelos a fuego lento.	*First, heat a little olive oil in the frying pan. Then beat the eggs and add them to the frying pan. Fry them over low heat.*
calentar (**e** > **ie**)	*to heat, warm up*
calienta	*heat*
el aceite	*oil*
el aceite de oliva	*olive oil*
la sartén (also, **el sartén**)	*frying pan*
batir	*to beat*
bate	*beat*
añadir	*to add*
añade	*add*
añádelos	*add them*
freír (**e** > **i**)	*to fry*
fríe	*fry*
fríelos	*fry them*
el fuego	*fire*
lento	*slow*
a fuego lento	*on a low flame, over low heat*
¿Echo sal a los huevos?	*Should I put salt on the eggs?*
la sal	*salt*
echar	*to throw*
echar sal	*to salt*
¿echo sal?	*shall I put salt?*

Sí, pero no les pongas demasiada sal. — *Yes, but don't put too much salt on them.*
poner — *to put*
no pongas — *don't put*
no les pongas — *don't put (on them)*
demasiada sal — *too much salt*

Variantes

Listen, and repeat the same structures from *Diálogo 9*, now with new vocabulary.

No batas los huevos. — ***Don't beat** the eggs.*
No calientes — *Don't warm*
No añadas — *Don't add*
No frías — *Don't fry*
No sirvas — *Don't serve*
No cocines — *Don't cook*
No hagas — *Don't make*

Estructura y Práctica

LA COCINA: SABORES (*TASTES*) Y OLORES (*SMELLS*)

saber *to taste*
Este plato **sabe** bien/mal. — *This dish tastes good/bad.*
Sabe un poco dulce/amargo. — *It tastes rather sweet/bitter.*

saber a *to taste of*
¿**A** qué **sabe** el guacamole? — *What does the guacamole taste of?*
El guacamole **sabe a** ajo. — *The guacamole tastes of garlic.*

saborear *to taste, savor, relish, enjoy* (also figuratively)
¡**Saborea** este chocolate negro artesanal! — *Taste this dark artisanal chocolate!*
¡**Saboreemos** el éxito de nuestro libro! — *Let's enjoy the success of our book!*

el sabor *taste*
Me gusta **el sabor** de la miel. — *I love the taste of honey.*
Tiene buen/mal **sabor**. — *It tastes good/bad.*

oler (huele) *to smell*
El arroz con pollo **huele** bien/mal. — *The chicken and rice smells good/bad.*

oler a *to smell of*
La torta **huele a** canela. — *The cake smells of cinnamon.*
El vino **huele a** cerezas. — *The wine smells of cherries.*

el olor *smell*
El pan tiene **un olor** a quemado. — *The bread smells burned.*
Tiene buen/mal **olor**. — *It smells good/bad.*

Q ***¡Casi listos para la cena!*** Write a response to each of the following questions about how to prepare for your dinner party. Use affirmative and negative **tú** commands, based on the cue in parentheses. Change direct object nouns to pronouns in your answers. Follow the *modelos.*

MODELOS ¿Tengo que lavar las uvas? (sí)
→ Sí, lávalas.

¿Tengo que lavar las uvas? (no)
→ No, no las laves todavía.

1. ¿Necesito leer la receta de cocina? (sí)
2. ¿Debo poner la mesa ahora? (no)
3. ¿Tengo que sacar los tenedores de la gaveta? (sí)
4. ¿Debo calentar el aceite de oliva? (no)
5. ¿Necesito batir las yemas de huevo (*egg yolks*)? (sí)
6. ¿Tengo que echar sal y pimienta? (sí)
7. ¿Debo añadir este queso? (no)
8. ¿Necesito freír las papas? (sí)
9. ¿Debo servir los espárragos? (no)
10. ¿Tengo que preparar el postre? (sí)

R ***¡Cálmate!*** Write an affirmative or negative **tú** command for each item to tell your excited and nervous friend to relax and enjoy the party. Follow the *modelos.*

MODELOS calmarse
→ Cálmate.

angustiarse
→ No te angusties.

1. tranquilizarse
2. no preocuparse
3. volverse loca (*to go crazy*)
4. no morderse (**o** > **ue**) las uñas (morderse las uñas (*to bite one's nails*))
5. no ser tonta
6. ir a la fiesta sin cuidado
7. no ponerse nerviosa
8. no alterarse (*to be upset*)
9. ser feliz
10. relajarse
11. disfrutar de las festividades
12. divertirse mucho

DIÁLOGO 10 · ¡Suena la alarma!

Study the dialogue, then listen to the recording and repeat each line.

JAIME ¡Suena la alarma! Salgan Uds. del hotel inmediatamente.
INÉS Sí, señor, pero primero vamos por nuestras cosas. Bajamos en seguida.
JAIME Señores, no suban a su habitación por nada. Puede haber un incendio.

Análisis

Check that you understand the linguistic breakdown of each speech from *Diálogo 10*.

¡Suena la alarma! Salgan Uds. del hotel inmediatamente.	*The alarm is sounding! Please leave the hotel immediately.*
sonar (**o** > **ue**)	*to sound*
la alarma	*alarm*
salir	*to go out*
salgan	*leave, go out*
salgan Uds.	*please leave*
salir de + *place*	*to leave* + place
salir del hotel	*to leave the hotel*
salgan Uds. del hotel	*please leave the hotel*
inmediatamente	*immediately*
Sí, señor, pero primero vamos por nuestras cosas. Bajamos en seguida.	*Yes, sir, but first we'll go get our things. We'll come down right away.*
ir por algo	*to go to get something*
vamos por nuestras cosas	*we'll go to get our things*
bajar	*to come down*
en seguida	*immediately, right away*
Señores, no suban a su habitación por nada. Puede haber un incendio.	*Excuse me, don't go up to your room for any reason. There may be a fire.*
subir	*to go up, go upstairs*
no suban	*don't go up*
la habitación	*room (especially in a hotel, dormitory,* etc.)
por nada	*for any reason*
puede haber	*there may be*
el incendio	*fire (accidental)*

Variantes

Listen, and repeat the same structures from *Diálogo 10*, now with new vocabulary.

Vayan Uds. al hotel.	***Go*** *to the hotel.*
Vuelvan	*Go back*
Vengan	*Come*
Caminen	*Walk*
Regresen	*Go back*
Puede haber un encendio.	*There may be* ***a fire****.*
un huracán	*a hurricane*
un terremoto	*an earthquake*
un sismo	*an earthquake*
un atentado terrorista	*a terrorist attack*
un ataque terrorista	*a terrorist attack*
una emergencia	*an emergency*

Estructura y Práctica

Other Ways of Giving Commands

Commands Using the Infinitive

Another way of giving commands is to use the infinitive instead of the command form. This type of command is mostly used in formal written language. Examples are newspaper ads for employment, recipes, instructions on product labels, and public service announcements. They are depersonalized commands, that is, not directed at a specific person.

Interesados **mandar** curriculum vitae.	*Interested persons,* ***send*** *your curriculum vitae.*
Interesados **llamar** al teléfono...	*Interested persons,* ***call*** *. . .*
Pelar y **cortar** las zanahorias.	***Peel*** *and* ***cut*** *the carrots.*
Masajear suavemente el cuero cabelludo.	***Massage*** *the scalp gently.*
Hacer clic en el enlace.	***Click*** *on the link.*
No fumar.	***No smoking.***

S Change the **Uds.** commands to commands with infinitives. Follow the *modelo.*

MODELO Conecten la cámara a la computadora.
→ Conectar la cámara a la computadora.

1. Sigan las instrucciones.
2. No pisen el césped (*grass, lawn*).
3. ¡Pintura fresca, no toquen!
4. Agreguen una pizca (*pinch*) de sal.
5. Laven y sequen las hojas de lechuga.
6. Pulsen (*Press*) el botón.
7. Enjuaguen (*Rinse*) bien el pelo.
8. Introduzcan la contraseña (*password*).

DIÁLOGO 11 · Trabajen en el proyecto.

Study the dialogue, then listen to the recording and repeat each line.

JAIME Hemos recogido y guardado los datos. ¿Qué hacemos ahora?
INÉS Por favor, analicen los datos y entréguenme su análisis.
JAIME También hemos elaborado el presupuesto. ¿Quiere Ud. verlo?
INÉS Sí, por favor. Enséñenmelo lo antes posible.

Análisis

Check that you understand the linguistic breakdown of each speech from *Diálogo 11.*

Hemos recogido y guardado los datos.	*We have collected and stored the data.*
¿Qué hacemos ahora?	*What shall we do now?*
recoger	*to collect, gather*
hemos recogido	*we have collected, we have gathered*
guardar	*to store*
los datos	*the data*
¿Qué hacemos ahora?	*What shall we do now?*

Por favor, analicen los datos y entréguenme su análisis.	*Analyze the data, please, and submit your analysis to me.*
analizar	*to analyze*
analicen	*analyze*
entregar	*to submit, hand in*
entreguen	*submit*
entréguenme	*hand in to me, submit to me*
el análisis	*analysis*
También hemos elaborado el presupuesto. ¿Quiere Ud. verlo?	*We have also drawn up the budget. Do you want to see it?*
hemos elaborado	*we have drawn up*
el presupuesto	*budget*
Sí, por favor. Enséñenmelo lo antes posible.	*Yes, please. Show it to me as soon as possible.*
enseñar	*to show*
enseñen	*show*
enséñenmelo	*show it to me*
antes	*before*
lo antes posible	*as soon as possible*

Variantes

Listen, and repeat the same structures from *Diálogo 11*, now with new vocabulary.

Enséñenmelo.	*Show it to me.*
Tráiganmelo.	*Bring it to me.*
Dénmelo.	*Give it to me.*
Muéstrenmelo.	*Show it to me.*
Entréguenmelo.	*Hand it to me.*
Explíquenmelo.	*Explain it to me.*
Háganmelo.	*Do it for me.*
No me lo enseñen.	*Don't show it to me.*
No me lo traigan.	*Don't bring it to me.*
No me lo den.	*Don't give it to me.*
No me lo muestren.	*Don't show it to me.*
No me lo entreguen.	*Don't hand it to me.*
No me lo expliquen.	*Don't explain it to me.*
No me lo hagan.	*Don't do it for me.*
Favor de enseñármelas.	***Please** show them to me.*
Haga el favor de	*Please*
Tenga la bondad de	*Please*
Favor de firmar los papeles.	***Please** sign the papers.*
Hagan el favor de	*Please*
Tengan la bondad de	*Please*

Commands Using the Infinitive + Expressions of Formality

The infinitive rather than the command form is also used with expressions that convey formality and politeness. They are the English equivalent of asking something with *please* and may be used in written or spoken language.

Favor de entrar.	***Please** come in.*
Haga el favor de sentarse.	***Please** sit down.*
Hágame el favor de llegar a las siete en punto.	***Please** arrive at seven o'clock sharp.*
Tenga la bondad de pasar al comedor.	***Please** go into the dining room.*

You will remember that in *Diálogo 1* of this chapter, you learned that the addition of the pronoun **Ud.** or **Uds.** to an imperative adds a polite tone to the command, much as *please* does in English.

Siéntese Ud.	*Please sit down.*
Pasen Uds. a la sala de reuniones.	*Please go into the meeting room.*

T **Polite commands.** For each of the following sentences, change the command form for **Ud.** to the infinitive, and add the expression in parentheses. Follow the *modelo.*

MODELO Mándeme el informe. (favor de)
→ Favor de mandarme el informe.

1. Présteme los auriculares. (tenga la bondad de)
2. Cuénteme lo ocurrido (*what happened*). (haga el favor de)
3. Explíquenoslo. (favor de)
4. Haga una copia de seguridad (*backup*). (favor de)
5. Dígamelo. (tenga la bondad de)
6. Ayúdeme con el abrigo. (favor de)
7. Llámeme lo antes posible. (haga el favor de)
8. Envíemelas para la semana entrante. (tenga la bondad de)

Un paso más

Are you ready to take your Spanish a step further? Here are exercises that will enhance your knowledge of the language and allow you to express yourself freely.

U ***Preguntas personales.*** Answer each question with a complete Spanish sentence.

1. ¿Cómo llega Ud. de su casa a su lugar de trabajo? (*Give a friend directions.*)
2. ¿Cómo es el tráfico donde vive? ¿Se permite o se prohíbe estacionar en su calle?
3. Cuando viaja en avión, ¿qué le pide al auxiliar de vuelo?

V *Miguel de Cervantes Saavedra (1547–1616) fue un gran novelista, poeta y dramaturgo. Es el escritor más famoso de la literatura española y universalmente conocido por ser el autor de* El Ingenioso Hidalgo Don Quijote de la Mancha, *una de las obras más importantes de la literatura universal. La primera parte de* El Quijote *fue publicada en 1605 y la segunda en 1615.*

Escriba una explicación en español de lo que significa la siguiente cita de El Quijote. *Se trata de un consejo que le da don Quijote a su escudero Sancho Panza.*

"Come poco y cena más poco que la salud de todo el cuerpo se fragua en la oficina del estómago."

la cita *quote*
comer *to have a heavy lunch* (la comida) (Spain)
el dramaturgo *playwright*
el escudero *squire*
se fragua *is forged*
el hidalgo *nobleman* (*lower nobility*) (Spain)
ingenioso *ingenious, clever*
más poco *even less* (archaic)
la oficina *workshop*
se trata de *it's about, it deals with*
significar *to mean*

W ***¡Buen provecho!*** **(Enjoy your meal!)** Express the cooking instructions below in Spanish, using the **Ud.** command form of these verbs. Use the vocabulary terms below as a resource.

agregar *to add*
asar *to roast*
asar a la parrilla *to grill, broil*
condimentar *to season*
cortar *to cut*
cortar en trocitos (el trozo) *to cut in small pieces*
descongelar *to defrost*
enfriar *to chill*
guisar *to stew*
hervir (**e** > **ie**, **e** > **i**) *to boil*
hornear *to bake*
mezclar *to mix*
pelar *to peel*
picar *to chop, dice*
remover (**o** > **ue**) *to stir*
sazonar *to season*

1. *Grill the meat.*
2. *Stir the soup.*
3. *Mix the fruits and chocolate chips* (las chispas de chocolate).
4. *Add lemon juice to the fish.*
5. *Chill the wine.*
6. *Season with salt and pepper.*
7. *Bake the bread.*
8. *Chop the onions.*

X ***Conversaciones.*** Write short conversations in Spanish about the following situations, using the appropriate command forms (**Ud.**, **Uds.**, **tú**, **nosotros**) in your exchanges. Draw upon the theme-related vocabulary you learned in this chapter.

1. En la ciudad: *A tourist stops you on the street to ask directions to* ________________.
2. En la oficina: *You are a project manager addressing your team about the tasks they must carry out.*
3. En la playa: *You and your children are having a conversation while at the beach.*
4. En el avión: *You and your husband (wife, friend), passengers on an airplane, are speaking with a flight attendant.*
5. En la consulta del médico: *You are a doctor giving advice to a patient about how to treat his/her medical problem.*

15

Holidays and Celebrations, Planning for the Future

Communication Goals

- Telling what you will do
- Telling what you would do
- Expressing probability and conjecture
- Vocabulary: holidays, planning a wedding, post-graduation plans, vacations

Grammar Topics

- The Future Tense
- The Future Tense: Verbs with a Modified Infinitive
- The Future Used to Express Probability or Conjecture
- The Conditional Tense
- The Conditional Used to Express Probability or Conjecture
- Review: Reverse Construction Verbs
- The Future Tense: Usage
- The Future Tense in Conditional Sentences
- The Future Tense in Subordinate Clauses
- The Conditional Tense in Subordinate Clauses

DIÁLOGO 1 · Planes para el futuro

Study the dialogue, then listen to the recording and repeat each line.

PEDRO Bueno chica, nos graduaremos en junio. ¿Sabes qué harás después?

EVA Haré un viaje a Israel con mi familia. Luego trabajaré en la empresa de mi papá. ¿Y tú?

PEDRO Comenzaré mis estudios de administración de empresas. Tendré la maestría en dos años.

EVA Yo también cursaré el MBA. Solicitaré una beca el año que viene.

Análisis

Check that you understand the linguistic breakdown of each speech from *Diálogo 1.*

Bueno chica, nos graduaremos en junio. ¿Sabes qué harás después?	*Well, my friend, we'll graduate in June. Do you know what you'll do afterwards?*
graduarse	*to graduate*
nos graduaremos	*we'll graduate*
harás	*you'll do*
después	*after, afterwards*
Haré un viaje a Israel con mi familia. Luego trabajaré en la empresa de mi papá. ¿Y tú?	*I'll take a trip to Israel with my family. Then I'll work in my father's company. How about you?*
haré	*I will do, I will make*
haré un viaje	*I'll take a trip*
Israel	*Israel*
trabajaré	*I'll work*
la empresa	*firm, company*
Comenzaré mis estudios de administración de empresas. Tendré la maestría en dos años.	*I'll begin studying business administration. I'll have a master's degree in two years.*
comenzaré	*I'll begin*
comenzar sus estudios de + *subject*	*to begin studying* + subject
tendré	*I will have*
la maestría	*master's degree*
Yo también cursaré el MBA. Solicitaré una beca el año que viene.	*I'll also study for the MBA. I'll apply for a scholarship next year.*
cursar + *subject*	*to study* + subject
cursaré	*I'll study for*
el MBA	*MBA*
solicitar algo	*to apply for something*
solicitaré	*I'll apply for*
una beca	*a scholarship*

Variantes

Listen, and repeat the same structures from *Diálogo 1,* now with new vocabulary.

Nos graduaremos en junio.	***We will graduate** in June.*
Nos matricularemos	*We will register*
Nos mudaremos	*We will move*
Nos instalaremos	*We will move in*
Nos comprometeremos	*We will get engaged*
Nos casaremos	*We will get married*
¿Qué harás?	*What **will you do**?*
dirás	*will you say*
querrás	*will you want*

Trabajaré.	*I will work.*
Comeré.	*I will eat.*
Leeré.	*I will read.*
Escribiré.	*I will write.*
Subiré.	*I will go up.*

Tendré una beca el año que viene.	***I will have** a scholarship next year.*
Solicitaré	*I will apply for*
Recibiré	*I will receive*
Necesitaré	*I will need*

Estructura y Práctica

The Future Tense

The future tense in Spanish, used to express future time, is formed by adding a specific set of endings to the infinitive of the verb. All verbs, regular, irregular, and stem-changing, form the future tense in this way.

Estudiaré español en Madrid.	***I'll study** Spanish in Madrid.*
Comeremos al aire libre.	***We'll eat** outside.*
Subirán a la azotea.	***They'll go up** to the rooftop terrace.*
¿**Harás** un descanso pronto?	***Will you take** a break soon?*
Uds. **vendrán** a vernos, ¿no?	***You'll come** to see us, won't you?*

trabajar *to work*

Trabajar**é** con el equipo.	*I'll work with the team.*
Trabajar**ás** con el equipo.	*You'll work with the team.*
Trabajar**á** con el equipo.	*He'll/She'll/You'll work with the team.*
Trabajar**emos** con el equipo.	*We'll work with the team.*
Trabajar**éis** con el equipo.	*You'll work with the team.*
Trabajar**án** con el equipo.	*They'll/You'll work with the team.*

comer *to eat*

Comer**é** al aire libre.	*I'll eat outside.*
Comer**ás** al aire libre.	*You'll eat outside.*
Comer**á** al aire libre.	*He'll/She'll/You'll eat outside.*
Comer**emos** al aire libre.	*We'll eat outside.*
Comer**éis** al aire libre.	*You'll eat outside.*
Comer**án** al aire libre.	*They'll/You'll eat outside.*

discutir *to discuss*

Discutir**é** el asunto.	*I'll discuss the matter.*
Discutir**ás** el asunto.	*You'll discuss the matter.*
Discutir**á** el asunto.	*He'll/She'll/You'll discuss the matter.*
Discutir**emos** el asunto.	*We'll discuss the matter.*
Discutir**éis** el asunto.	*You'll discuss the matter.*
Discutir**án** el asunto.	*They'll/You'll discuss the matter.*

A ***Del presente al futuro.*** Rewrite each of the following sentences, changing the verb from the present tense to the future tense. Follow the *modelo.*

MODELO Viaja la semana entrante.
→ Viajará la semana entrante.

1. Entrego el informe.
2. Vende su casa.
3. No discuten ese asunto.
4. Te diviertes mucho.
5. Duerme la siesta.
6. Juego al tenis.
7. Diseñamos el sitio web.
8. Elijo un nuevo celular.
9. ¿No comes nada más?
10. Se reúnen en la sala de conferencias.
11. Consigo una beca.
12. Hace ochenta grados.

DIÁLOGO 2 · Estarán muy contentos.

Study the dialogue, then listen to the recording and repeat each line.

PEDRO ¿Sabes que Rodrigo ganó una beca? Ahora podrá terminar su maestría en computación.
EVA Estará contentísimo.
PEDRO ¡Y sus papás aún más, porque no tendrán que pagar la matrícula!

Análisis

Check that you understand the linguistic breakdown of each speech from *Diálogo 2.*

¿Sabes que Rodrigo ganó una beca? Ahora podrá terminar su maestría en computación.	*Do you know that Rodrigo won a scholarship? Now he will be able to finish his master's in computer science.*
ganar una beca	*to win a scholarship*
podrá	*he will be able to*
la maestría	*master's degree*
terminar la maestría	*finish one's master's degree*
la computación	*computer science*
Estará contentísimo.	*He must be very happy.*
estará	*he must be, he is probably*
contentísimo	*very happy*
¡Y sus papás aún más, porque no tendrán que pagar la matrícula!	*And his parents even more so, because they won't have to pay the tuition!*
aún	*even*
aún más	*even more*
tendrán	*they will have*
no tendrán que	*they won't have to*
la matrícula	*tuition*

Variantes

Listen, and repeat the same structures from *Diálogo 2*, now with new vocabulary.

Podrá terminar su maestría.	***He will be able to*** *finish his master's degree.*
Querrá	*He will want to*
Tendrá que	*He will have to*
Estará contentísimo.	*He must be* ***very happy****.*
ocupadísimo	*very busy*
aburridísimo	*very bored*
No tendrán que pagar la matrícula.	***They won't have*** *to pay the tuition.*
No podrán	*They won't be able*
No querrán	*They won't want*

Estructura y Práctica

The Future Tense: Verbs with a Modified Infinitive

There are 12 verbs that have modified infinitive forms in the future. These verbs have the same endings as the verbs in the charts that appear after *Diálogo 1.* The **yo** form is shown as a model for the entire conjugation.

INFINITIVE	FUTURE
poner	**pondré**
salir	**saldré**
tener	**tendré**
valer	**valdré**
venir	**vendré**
caber	**cabré**
poder	**podré**
querer	**querré**
saber	**sabré**
decir	**diré**
hacer	**haré**
haber	**habré**

Compounds of verbs that have modified infinitives in the future have the same shortened infinitives when conjugated in the future: **componer** → **compondré**, **mantener** → **mantendré**, **convenir** → **convendré**, **rehacer** → **reharé**.

The future of **hay**, derived from **haber**, is **habrá** (*there will be*).

-**Ir** verbs that have an accent mark in the infinitive, such as **oír** (*to hear*), **freír** (*to fry*), and **reír** (*to laugh*), lose that accent mark in the future tense: **freiré**, **oiré**, **reiré**.

B **The future: verbs with modified infinitives.** Write the future form of the verb in parentheses that correctly completes each of the following sentences. Follow the *modelo.*

MODELO No _cabrá_ nadie más en el taxi. (caber)

1. Yo les ____________ lo que pasó. (decir)
2. El libro ____________ a fines del mes. (salir)
3. Tú ____________ solicitar una beca, ¿verdad? (querer)
4. Camila y yo ____________ en contacto. (ponerse)
5. ¿A qué hora ____________ los invitados? (venir)
6. Las reuniones ____________ lugar en esa oficina. (tener)
7. ____________ mucho frío esta noche. (hacer)
8. Nosotros no ____________ nada hasta la semana próxima. (saber)
9. ¿Ud. no ____________ acompañarnos? (poder)
10. ____________ gangas en las tiendas por departamentos en enero. (haber)

The Future Used to Express Probability or Conjecture

One of the most common uses of the future tense is to express probability or conjecture about the present. Speakers use the future of probability when wondering about things that are going on in the present. The English equivalents of the future of probability (*I wonder, it's probably, it might,* etc.) are usually unlike the Spanish structures. The verbs most commonly used to express this are **estar**, **haber**, **ser**, and **tener**.

¿Qué hora **será**?	***I wonder*** *what time* ***it is.***
Serán las nueve.	***It's probably*** *nine o'clock.*
Habrá un atasco de tráfico.	***There's probably*** *a traffic jam.*
¿Cuántos años **tendrá** Carlitos?	***I wonder*** *how old Carlitos* ***is.***
Tendrá cinco años.	***He must be*** *five years old.*
¿Qué **querrá** para su cumpleaños?	***I wonder*** *what* ***she wants*** *for her birthday.*
Estarán de vacaciones todavía.	***They're probably*** *still on vacation.*

Context will determine whether a verb in the future tense refers to a future time or to probability or conjecture in present time. For example, **¿Qué pasará?** means *What will happen?* as well as *I wonder what's happening.*

C ***Probabilidad en el presente.*** Rewrite each sentence using the future tense to express probability in present time. Remove the word or words that express probability or conjecture in the original sentence. Follow the *modelo.*

MODELO Probablemente no entiende nada.
→ No entenderá nada.

1. Supongo que los gemelos tienen siete u ocho años.
2. Me imagino que sabes su número de teléfono.
3. Probablemente son las once.

4. Supongo que Camila quiere ver esta obra de teatro.
5. Me imagino que su casa cuesta una fortuna.
6. Probablemente están acatarrados.
7. Me imagino que Cristóbal se hace ingeniero.
8. Supongo que este anillo vale miles de dólares.
9. Probablemente hay muchos documentos sobre este tema.
10. Probablemente cabe el equipaje en el maletero del coche.

D **Translation.** Express the following sentences in Spanish, using the future of probability.

1. *I wonder how old Mr. Durán is.*
2. *He must be fifty years old.*
3. *I wonder what time it is.*
4. *It's probably four o'clock.*
5. *What an elegant suit! It must cost a lot of money.*
6. *I can't find my credit card. I wonder where it is.*
7. *I imagine it will snow tomorrow.*
8. *They probably know what happened.*

DIÁLOGO 3 · El organizador de bodas

Study the dialogue, then listen to the recording and repeat each line.

JORGE Como organizador de bodas, yo me encargaré de todo—las invitaciones, la ceremonia, la música, la comida, el pastel, las flores, la fotografía.

LUCÍA ¡Magnífico! Felipe y yo no podríamos hacer todo esto sin ti. Ni sabemos dónde será la ceremonia.

JORGE Bueno, mañana los llevaré a conocer el jardín de una hermosa hacienda y unos elegantes salones de hotel. Uds. escogerán el lugar.

Análisis

Check that you understand the linguistic breakdown of each speech from *Diálogo 3*.

Como organizador de bodas, yo me encargaré de todo—las invitaciones, la ceremonia, la música, la comida, el pastel, las flores, la fotografía.	*As a wedding planner, I'll take care of everything—the invitations, the ceremony, the music, the food, the cake, the flowers, the photography.*
encargarse de	*to take care of*
yo me encargaré de	*I'll take care of*
yo me encargaré de todo	*I'll take care of everything*
la invitación	*invitation*
la ceremonia	*ceremony*
la música	*music*
la comida	*food*

el pastel	*cake, pie*
la flor	*flower*
la fotografía	*photography*
¡Magnífico! Felipe y yo no podríamos hacer todo esto sin ti. Ni sabemos dónde será la ceremonia.	*Terrific! Felipe and I wouldn't be able to do all of this without you. We don't even know where the ceremony will be.*
podríamos	*we would be able to*
ni	*not even*
ni sabemos	*we don't even know*
será	*it will be*
dónde será la ceremonia	*where the ceremony will be*
Bueno, mañana los llevaré a conocer el jardín de una hermosa hacienda y unos elegantes salones de hotel. Uds. escogerán el lugar.	*Well, tomorrow I will take you to see the garden of a lovely estate and some elegant hotel ballrooms. You will pick the place.*
llevaré	*I will take*
los llevaré	*I will take you*
conocer	*to get to know, see*
el jardín	*garden*
hermoso	*beautiful*
la hacienda	*estate; farm, ranch*
el salón	*large public room*
escoger	*to choose*
escogerán	*you will choose*
el lugar	*the place*

Variantes

Listen, and repeat the same structures from *Diálogo 3*, now with new vocabulary.

La ceremonia será en una hacienda.	*The wedding **will be** at an estate.*
tendrá lugar	*will take place*
se realizará	*will take place*
Los novios llegarán a las cuatro.	*The bride and groom **will arrive** at four o'clock.*
vendrán	*will come*
saldrán	*will leave*
No podríamos hacerlo.	***We wouldn't be able** to do it.*
No tendríamos que	*We wouldn't have*
No querríamos	*We wouldn't want*
No necesitaríamos	*We wouldn't need*
Los llevaré .	***I'll take** you.*
llamaré	*I'll call*
veré	*I'll see*
comprenderé	*I'll understand*
ayudaré	*I'll help*
buscaré	*I'll look for*

Uds. escogerán el lugar. — ***You'll choose** the place.*
- elegirán — *You'll choose*
- encontrarán — *You'll find*
- conocerán — *You'll be familiar with*

Estructura y Práctica

The Conditional Tense

The conditional tense is formed by adding the imperfect tense endings of **-er** and **-ir** verbs to the infinitive. All verbs, including **-ar** verbs, use these endings in the conditional.

¿Qué **haría** Ud.?	*What **would** you **do**?*
Yo no **diría** nada.	*I **wouldn't say** anything.*
¡Con una prometida como la tuya, yo no **me casaría** nunca!	*With a fiancée like yours, I **would** never **get married**!*

trabajar *to work*

Trabajar**ía** con el equipo.	*I'd work with the team.*
Trabajar**ías** con el equipo.	*You'd work with the team.*
Trabajar**ía** con el equipo.	*He'd/She'd/You'd work with the team.*
Trabajar**íamos** con el equipo.	*We'd work with the team.*
Trabajar**íais** con el equipo.	*You'd work with the team.*
Trabajar**ían** con el equipo.	*They'd/You'd work with the team.*

comer *to eat*

Comer**ía** al aire libre.	*I'd eat outside.*
Comer**ías** al aire libre.	*You'd eat outside.*
Comer**ía** al aire libre.	*He'd/She'd/You'd eat outside.*
Comer**íamos** al aire libre.	*We'd eat outside.*
Comer**íais** al aire libre.	*You'd eat outside.*
Comer**ían** al aire libre.	*They'd/You'd eat outside.*

discutir *to discuss*

Discutir**ía** el asunto.	*I'd discuss the matter.*
Discutir**ías** el asunto.	*You'd discuss the matter.*
Discutir**ía** el asunto.	*He'd/She'd/You'd discuss the matter.*
Discutir**íamos** el asunto.	*We'd discuss the matter.*
Discutir**íais** el asunto.	*You'd discuss the matter.*
Discutir**ían** el asunto.	*They'd/You'd discuss the matter.*

The same 12 verbs that have modified infinitive forms in the future have them in the conditional. These verbs have the same endings as the verbs in the charts above. The **yo** form is shown as a model for the entire conjugation.

INFINITIVE	CONDITIONAL
poner	**pondría**
salir	**saldría**
tener	**tendría**

INFINITIVE	CONDITIONAL
valer	**valdría**
venir	**vendría**
caber	**cabría**
poder	**podría**
querer	**querría**
saber	**sabría**
decir	**diría**
hacer	**haría**
haber	**habría**

Compounds of verbs that have modified infinitives in the conditional have the same shortened infinitives when conjugated in the conditional: **componer** → **compondría, mantener** → **mantendría, convenir** → **convendría, rehacer** → **reharía.**

The conditional of **hay**, derived from **haber**, is **habría** (*there would be*).

-Ir verbs that have an accent mark in the infinitive, such as **oír** (*to hear*), **freír** (*to fry*), and **reír** (*to laugh*), lose that accent mark in the conditional tense: **freiría, oiría, reiría.**

E ***¿Qué harían?*** Write sentences using the strings of elements given to tell what would or would not happen. Use the correct conditional form of the verb. Follow the *modelo.*

MODELO los empleados / llegar / a las nueve
→ Los empleados llegarían a las nueve.

1. Daniel y yo / elaborar / el presupuesto
2. Uds. / aprender / español / en Bogotá
3. tú / tener / suerte
4. yo / no / decírselo / a nadie
5. la cocinera / querer / añadir / más sal
6. nosotros / hacer escala / en Miami
7. mis colegas / compartir / los gastos
8. sus suegros / no poder / visitarlos
9. tú / salir / más tarde
10. Ud. / mudarse / a ese barrio

The Conditional Used to Express Probability or Conjecture

The conditional in Spanish is also used to express probability or conjecture in past time. The verbs most commonly used to express this are **estar**, **haber**, **ser**, and **tener**. Context will determine whether a verb in the conditional refers to the conditional or to probability in past time.

¿Dónde **estaría** Blanca?	***I wonder** where Blanca **was.***
Habría un atasco de tráfico.	***There was probably** a traffic jam.*
Serían las seis.	***It was probably** six o'clock.*
Tendrían mucho éxito.	***I imagine they were** very successful.*

F ***Probabilidad en el pasado.*** Express the following short dialogues in Spanish, using the conditional to express probability.

1. *I wonder how old María Elena was when she finished her master's.*
2. *She was probably twenty-three when she finished it.*

3. *I wonder what time it was when Mr. and Mrs. Fernández arrived at the seaside resort* (el balneario).
4. *It was probably noon.*
5. *I wonder who was to blame for the crime.*
6. *I suppose it was the butler* (el mayordomo).
7. *I wonder where you* (Uds.) *were when we called you.*
8. *We were probably still at the office.*
9. *I wonder what (there) was in the package.*
10. *I suppose there were toys for the children.*

REVIEW: USE OF SER

As you learned in Chapter 4, the verb **ser** is used to indicate where an event takes place.

Note this sentence from *Diálogo 3* of this chapter:

Ni sabemos dónde **será** la ceremonia.	*We don't even know where the ceremony* ***will be.***

Estar cannot be used for this purpose.

DIÁLOGO 4 · Celebraremos la Pascua.

Study the dialogue, then listen to the recording and repeat each line.

LUIS ¿Cómo celebrarán Uds. la Pascua?
BLANCA Habrá una comida grande con todos nuestros parientes, como de costumbre.
LUIS ¿Tú harás la comida o será en casa de tus papás?
BLANCA Nos tocará a nosotros tenerla en nuestra casa. Mi esposo, mis hijos y yo prepararemos la comida y usaremos las recetas de las abuelas.

Análisis

Check that you understand the linguistic breakdown of each speech from *Diálogo 4*.

¿Cómo celebrarán Uds. la Pascua?	*How will you celebrate Easter?*
celebrar	*to celebrate*
celebrarán	*you will celebrate*
la Pascua	*Easter*
Habrá una comida grande con todos nuestros parientes, como de costumbre.	*There will be a big dinner with all our relatives, as usual.*
habrá	*there will be*
una comida	*dinner*
los parientes	*relatives*
de costumbre	*as usual*
como de costumbre	*as usual, as we usually do*

¿Tú harás la comida o será en casa de tus papás?	*Will you make the meal or will it be at your parents' house?*
harás	*you will do, you will make*
será	*it will be*
tus papás	*your parents* (especially in Spanish America)
Nos tocará a nosotros tenerla en nuestra casa. Mi esposo, mis hijos y yo prepararemos la comida y usaremos las recetas de las abuelas.	*It will be our turn to have it at our house. My husband, my children, and I will prepare the meal, and we will use our grandmothers' recipes.*
tocarle a uno (*rev. constr.*)	*to be someone's turn*
nos tocará a nosotros	*it will be our turn*
prepararemos	*we will prepare*
usaremos	*we will use*
la receta	*recipe*

Variantes

Listen, and repeat the same structures from *Diálogo 4*, now with new vocabulary.

¿Cómo celebrarán Uds. la Pascua?	*How will you celebrate* ***Easter****?*
la Pascua judía	*Passover*
la Navidad	*Christmas*
Jánuca	*Hanukkah*
el Año Nuevo	*New Year's*
la Noche Vieja	*New Year's Eve*
el Día de la Independencia	*Independence Day*
el Día de los Enamorados	*Valentine's Day*
su aniversario	*your anniversary*
el Ramadán	*Ramadan*
Habrá una comida grande.	*There will be* ***a big dinner****.*
mucha gente	*many people*
una orquesta	*an orchestra*
un desfile	*a parade*
champaña	*champagne*
un brindis	*a toast*
Nos tocará a nosotros.	*It will be our turn.*
Me tocará a mí.	*It will be my turn.*
Te tocará a ti.	*It will be your turn.*
Le tocara a él.	*It will be his turn.*
Le tocará a ella.	*It will be her turn.*
Les tocará a Uds.	*It will be your turn.*
Les tocará a ellos.	*It will be their turn.*
Les tocará a ellas.	*It will be their turn.*

Prepararemos la comida.	***We will prepare** the meal.*
Cocinaremos	*We will cook*
Haremos	*We will make*
Pediremos	*We will order*
Serviremos	*We will serve*
Disfrutaremos (de)	*We will enjoy*

Estructura y Práctica

FIESTAS Y CELEBRACIONES

Many of the holidays celebrated in the United States are also celebrated in Spanish-speaking countries, for example, Independence Day—**el Día de la Independencia** (a different date in each country), Mother's Day—**el Día de la Madre**, Father's Day—**el Día del Padre**, and New Year's Eve—**la Noche Vieja** (**el Fin de Año**). Columbus Day is celebrated in Spain as **el Día de la Hispanidad** and in many Spanish American countries as **el Día de la Raza**.

Christmas holidays are also celebrated in some countries, such as Mexico, where the **Posadas** (**posada** (*room at the inn*)) last for nine days leading up to Christmas Eve. In most Spanish-speaking countries, children traditionally receive holiday gifts on January 6, **El Día de los Reyes Magos** (**la Epifanía**)—Three Kings' Day (Epiphany).

In many countries of Spanish America, a young woman's fifteenth birthday is celebrated with a special event known as the **Fiesta de quinceañera** (**Fiesta de quince**). The young woman is the **quinceañera**. This event, ranging from informal festivities at home, sometimes of a religious nature, to an extravagant party in a hotel, is also widely celebrated in the Spanish-speaking community of the United States and is reminiscent of the traditional sweet sixteen coming-of-age party.

Review: Reverse Construction Verbs

You learned about reverse construction verbs in Chapter 9. These are verbs that pattern like **gustar**: **Me gusta el libro.** (*I like the book.*)

Note the use of **tocar** as a reverse construction verb in this sentence from *Diálogo 4*:

Nos tocará a nosotros tenerla en nuestra casa.	***It will be our turn** to have it (the dinner) at our house.*

The infinitive **tener** is the subject of **tocar**, which is therefore in third person singular: **tocará**. To focus on the person involved in sentences with reverse construction verbs, a phrase consisting of the preposition **a** + a prepositional pronoun is used. In this sentence, **a nosotros** focuses on the people whose turn it is to have the dinner.

G Express the following sentences in Spanish, using reverse construction verbs in the future tense. Use the correct **a** + prepositional pronoun with each reverse construction verb.

1. *You* (Uds.) *will like this Mexican food.*
2. *She'll be excited to meet our friends.*
3. *You* (tú) *will be interested in this project.*
4. *I'll still have two exams left.*
5. *They'll be short of money.*
6. *We'll need more information.*
7. *It will be good for you* (Ud.) *to be in charge of the office.*
8. *Nothing will matter to him.* (*He won't care about anything.*)

DIÁLOGO 5 · El fin de semana

Study the dialogue, then listen to the recording and repeat each line.

ANTONIO	Mis primos estarán de visita este fin de semana. ¿Adónde los llevaremos?
VICTORIA	Dicen que el sábado hará buen tiempo así que podremos enseñarles la ciudad.
ANTONIO	Creo que el domingo lloverá así que podremos ir a un museo.
VICTORIA	Y querremos llevarlos a cenar a nuestros restaurantes favoritos.

Análisis

Check that you understand the linguistic breakdown of each speech from *Diálogo 5.*

Mis primos estarán de visita este fin de semana. ¿Adónde los llevaremos?	*My cousins will be visiting (us) this weekend. Where shall we take them?*
los primos	*cousins*
estarán	*they will be*
estar de visita	*to be visiting*
el fin de semana	*weekend*
llevaremos	*we will take*
Dicen que el sábado hará buen tiempo así que podremos enseñarles la ciudad.	*They say that Saturday the weather will be nice, so we can show them the city.*
el sábado	*Saturday, on Saturday*
hará	*it will do, it will make*
hará buen tiempo	*the weather will be nice*
así que	*so*
podremos	*we will be able to*
enseñarles	*to show them*
Creo que el domingo lloverá así que podremos ir a un museo.	*I think that it will rain on Sunday, so we will be able to go to a museum.*
el domingo	*Sunday, on Sunday*
lloverá	*it will rain*
podremos	*we will be able to*
el museo	*museum*

Y querremos llevarlos a cenar a nuestros restaurantes favoritos. — *And we'll want to take them to have dinner at our favorite restaurants.*
- querremos — *we will want to*
- llevarlos a cenar — *to take them to have dinner*

Variantes

Listen, and repeat the same structures from *Diálogo 5*, now with new vocabulary.

Dicen que hará buen tiempo. — *They say* ***the weather will be nice.***
- lloverá — *it will rain*
- nevará — *it will snow*
- estará nublado — *it will be cloudy*
- hará ochenta grados — *it will be eighty degrees*
- hará sol — *it will be sunny*
- habrá sol — *it will be sunny*

Podremos enseñarles la ciudad. — ***We will be able*** *to show them the city.*
- Querremos — *We will want*
- Preferiremos — *We will prefer*
- Tendremos que — *We will have*

Si ellos salen a cenar, nosotros saldremos a cenar también. — *If they go out for dinner, we will go out for dinner, too.*

Nosotros saldremos a cenar si ellos salen a cenar. — *We will go out for dinner if they go out for dinner.*

Estructura y Práctica

The Future Tense: Usage

In spoken Spanish, the **ir a** + infinitive construction and the present tense are used more frequently than the future tense to express future events.

Los **veremos** el sábado. — ***We'll see*** *them on Saturday.*
Vamos a verlos el sábado. — ***We're going to see*** *them on Saturday.*
Los **vemos** el sábado. — ***We're seeing*** *them on Saturday.*

H ***Ir a*** **+ infinitive.** Rewrite each sentence, changing the future tense of the verb to the **ir a** + infinitive construction to tell what's going to happen. Follow the *modelo.*

MODELO Comerán comida japonesa.
→ Van a comer comida japonesa.

1. Asistiremos al concierto.
2. Saldré para la hacienda.
3. Uds. se irán pasado mañana.
4. ¿Podrás acompañarme a la boda?
5. Habrá una fiesta de quinceañera para Inés.
6. La fiesta será en el Hotel Palacio.
7. Ellos tendrán que trabajar.
8. Manuel querrá esquiar.

The Future Tense in Conditional Sentences

The future tense is commonly used in the main clause of a conditional sentence when the **si**-clause (*if*-clause) has the verb in the present tense. Note that the order of the clauses can be reversed, with the **si**-clause following the main clause.

Si tú **vas** al concierto, yo **iré** también.	*If **you go** to the concert, **I'll go**, too.*
Yo **iré** al concierto si **vas** tú.	***I'll go** to the concert if **you go**.*

I **Future tense in sentences with a *si*-clause.** Write the forms of each verb in parentheses that correctly complete each of the following sentences. The main clause has the verb in future tense, and the **si**-clause has the verb in present tense. Follow the *modelos.*

MODELOS Si tú *pruebas* este plato, yo lo *probaré* también. (probar)

Yo *probaré* este plato si lo *pruebas* tú.

1. Si Uds. ________________ a la fiesta, nosotros ________________ a la fiesta también. (ir)
2. Ella ________________ ejercicio si sus amigas ________________ ejercicio también. (hacer)
3. Si él ________________ postre, yo lo ________________ también. (pedir)
4. Si nosotros ________________ el lunes, Ud. ________________ el lunes también. (volver)
5. Ud. ________________ el tren si ella ________________ el tren también. (tomar)
6. Si yo ________________ por la mañana, tú ________________ por la mañana también. (pasearse)
7. Nosotros ________________ en el centro si Uds. ________________ en el centro también. (almorzar)
8. Si tú ________________ con el gerente, yo ________________ con el gerente también. (reunirse)

The Future Tense in Subordinate Clauses

The future is used commonly in subordinate (dependent) clauses after main verbs of communication (**decir**) and verbs of knowledge or belief (**saber, creer**).

Osvaldo **dice** que **saldrá**.	*Osvaldo **says he'll go out**.*
Creo que **hará** mucho calor.	***I think it will be** very hot.*

J ***Creen que...*** Write the future tense form of the verb in parentheses that correctly completes each of the following sentences to find out what people say, know, or believe will happen. Follow the *modelo.*

MODELO Pablo dice que nos *llamará*. (llamar)

1. Ana dice que ________________ toda la semana. (llover)
2. Miguel sabe que nosotros ________________ tarde. (llegar)
3. Laura está segura de que ________________ en contacto con nosotros. (ponerse)

4. Juan Carlos nos escribe que ______________ en la universidad estatal. (matricularse)
5. Me aseguran que ______________ el informe para la semana próxima. (entregar)
6. Alicia cree que sus papás ______________ su condominio. (vender)
7. Sé que tú ______________ instalarte en el apartamento lo antes posible. (querer)
8. Parece que Uds. ______________ de hacer los trámites. (encargarse)

DIÁLOGO 6 · ¿Adónde irán Uds.?

Study the dialogue, then listen to the recording and repeat each line.

DIEGO ¿Cómo pasarán tú y Jaime las vacaciones?
ALICIA Creo que iremos a la sierra para esquiar. ¿Y tú y Carlota? ¿Viajarán o se quedarán en casa?
DIEGO Vendrán mis suegros. Nos dijeron que les gustaría pasar unos días en la playa.

Análisis

Check that you understand the linguistic breakdown of each speech from *Diálogo 6*.

¿Cómo pasarán tú y Jaime las vacaciones?	*How will you and Jaime spend your vacation?*
pasarán	*you will spend*
las vacaciones	*vacation, your vacation*
Creo que iremos a la sierra para esquiar. ¿Y tú y Carlota? ¿Viajarán o se quedarán en casa?	*I think we'll go to the mountains to ski. How about you and Carlota? Will you travel, or will you stay home?*
iremos	*we will go*
la sierra	*the mountains*
para	*in order to*
esquiar	*to ski*
viajarán	*you will travel*
se quedarán	*you will stay*
se quedarán en casa	*you will stay home*
Vendrán mis suegros. Nos dijeron que les gustaría pasar unos días en la playa.	*My in-laws will come. They told us that they would like to spend a few days at the beach.*
vendrán	*they will come*
los suegros	*in-laws (mother-in-law and father-in-law)*
les gustaría	*they would like*

Variantes

Listen, and repeat the same structures from *Diálogo 6*, now with new vocabulary.

Vendrán mis suegros.	*My in-laws* ***will come****.*
Se irán	*will leave*
Se quedarán	*will stay*

Llegarán	*will arrive*
Volverán	*will come back*
Regresarán	*will come back*
Se pasearán	*will go for a walk*
Dijeron que haría buen tiempo.	*They said* ***the weather would be nice.***
llovería	*it would rain*
nevaría	*it would snow*
estaría nublado	*it would be cloudy*
haría ochenta grados	*it would be eighty degrees*
haría sol	*it would be sunny*
habría sol	*it would be sunny*
¿A Uds. les gustaría ir a la playa?	*Would you like to go to the beach?*
Sí, nos encantaría.	*Yes, we'd love to.*
¿Te gustaría reunirte con nosotros mañana?	*Would you like to meet with us tomorrow?*
En realidad, no me convendría esta semana.	*Actually, it wouldn't work for me this week.*
¿Le interesaría jugar al ajedrez?	*Would you be interested in playing chess?*
Me interesaría mucho.	*I'd be very interested.*

Estructura y Práctica

The Conditional Tense in Subordinate Clauses

The conditional tense is used commonly in subordinate (dependent) clauses after main verbs of communication (**decir**) and verbs of knowledge or belief (**saber**, **creer**) when the main verb is in one of the past tenses.

This correspondence of tenses occurs in both Spanish and English: The present tense in the main clause is used with the future tense in a subordinate clause; a past tense in the main clause is used with the conditional tense in a subordinate clause.

Consuelo **dice** que **volverá** el viernes.	*Consuelo* ***says she'll be back*** *on Friday.*
Consuelo **dijo** que **volvería** el viernes.	*Consuelo* ***said she would be back*** *on Friday.*
Sabemos que nos **visitarán.**	*We* ***know they'll visit*** *us.*
Sabíamos que nos **visitarían.**	*We* ***knew they'd visit*** *us.*

K ***Dijeron que...*** Write the conditional form of the verb in parentheses that correctly completes each of the following sentences to find out what people said, knew, or believed would happen. Follow the *modelo.*

MODELO Marta me dijo que *estaría* en casa toda la tarde. (estar)

1. Eugenia me escribió que ________________ el miércoles. (regresar)
2. Rafael y María anunciaron que ________________ en la primavera. (casarse)
3. ¿Sabías lo que ________________? (pasar)

4. Creíamos que el asesor nos ______________ buenos consejos. (dar)
5. Yo les pregunté si ______________ pasar por mí. (poder)
6. Te aseguraron que no ______________ ninguna dificultad. (haber)
7. Me dijeron que a sus hijos les ______________ los regalos. (encantar)
8. Creías que nosotros nos ______________ más a menudo. (ver)

L Express the following sentences in Spanish, using reverse construction verbs in the conditional tense.

1. *I would like to learn to ski.*
2. *The children would be excited to open their presents.*
3. *You* (tú) *would be very interested in these museums.*
4. *We'd love to have a glass* (una copa) *of champagne!*
5. *Carlos wouldn't care about anything.*
6. *You* (Ud.) *would need your passport.*
7. *It would be Julia's turn in the board game* (el juego de mesa).
8. *It would be best* (*most convenient*) *for you* (Uds.) *to take a nonstop flight.*

DIÁLOGO 7 · Buscaremos un regalo.

Study the dialogue, then listen to the recording and repeat each line.

PEDRO Susana cumplirá veintiocho años el sábado. Tendré que comprarle un regalo.
EVA ¡Caramba! Me olvidé de su cumpleaños. ¿Qué le regalarás?
PEDRO No tengo la menor idea. ¿Qué querrá?
EVA No sabría decirte. Vamos al centro comercial. Estoy segura de que encontraremos algo.

Análisis

Check that you understand the linguistic breakdown of each speech from *Diálogo 7*.

Susana cumplirá veintiocho años el sábado. Tendré que comprarle un regalo.	*Susana will be twenty-eight on Saturday. I'll have to buy her a gift.*
cumplir años	*to have a birthday, get to be* ____ *years old*
cumplirá	*she will be/turn*
cumplirá veintiocho años	*she will be twenty-eight*
tendré	*I will have*
Tendré que comprarle un regalo.	*I'll have to buy her a gift.*

¡Caramba! Me olvidé de su cumpleaños. ¿Qué le regalarás?	*Gosh! I forgot her birthday. What will you give her?*
¡Caramba!	*Gosh!*
olvidarse de algo	*to forget something*
el cumpleaños	*birthday*
Me olvidé de su cumpleaños.	*I forgot her birthday.*
regalarle algo a uno	*to give someone something (as a gift)*
regalarás	*you will give (as a gift)*
No tengo la menor idea. ¿Qué querrá?	*I haven't the slightest idea. What might she want?*
la idea	*idea*
menor	*least*
la menor idea	*the slightest idea*
querrá	*she might want*
No sabría decirte. Vamos al centro comercial. Estoy segura de que encontraremos algo.	*I couldn't tell you. Let's go to the shopping center. I'm sure that we will find something (there).*
sabría	*I would know*
No sabría decirte.	*I couldn't tell you. / I wouldn't know what to tell you.*
estar seguro de que	*to be sure that*
encontraremos	*we will find*

Variantes

Listen, and repeat the same structures from *Diálogo 7*, now with new vocabulary.

¿Qué le regalarás ?	*What **will you give** her?*
darás	*will you give*
ofrecerás	*will you offer*
traerás	*will you bring*
prestarás	*will you lend*
entregarás	*will you hand*
¿Qué querrá para su cumpleaños?	*I wonder what she wants for her birthday.*
Querrá unos aretes.	*She probably wants earrings.*
Probablemente quiere unos aretes.	*She probably wants earrings.*
Isaac y Valeria estarán cansados después de su vuelo.	*Isaac and Valeria must be tired after their flight.*
Y tendrán mucha hambre también.	*And they must be very hungry, too.*
Supongo que tienen mucha hambre también.	*I suppose they're very hungry, too.*
¿ Lloverá mañana?	***Do you think it may rain** tomorrow?*
Nevará	*Do you think it may snow*
Hará frío	*Do you think it will be cold*
Estará nublado	*Do you think it will be cloudy*
Habrá sol	*Do you think it will be sunny*

Estructura y Práctica

M ***Conjeturas.*** **Nobody understands María Dolores!** Express the following questions in Spanish, using the future of probability, to ask what María Dolores might be thinking. Follow the *modelo*.

MODELO *What might María Dolores want?*
→ ¿Qué querrá?

1. *What might she say?*
2. *What might she know?*
3. *What might she think?*
4. *What might she understand?*
5. *What might she imagine?*
6. *What might she suppose?*
7. *What might she wonder* (preguntarse)*?*
8. *What might she conjecture* (conjeturar)*?*

DIÁLOGO 8 · En la sala de recepción

Study the dialogue, then listen to the recording and repeat each line.

ELADIO Buenas tardes, señorita. Me gustaría ver al señor Torres. Soy Eladio Díaz. Tengo cita con él a las tres.

MARTA Mucho gusto, señor. Yo le diré al director que Ud. está. Él no tardará en llegar. Siéntese, por favor.

Análisis

Check that you understand the linguistic breakdown of each speech from *Diálogo 8*.

Buenas tardes, señorita. Me gustaría ver al señor Torres. Soy Eladio Díaz. Tengo cita con él a las tres. — *Good afternoon, miss. I would like to see Mr. Torres. I'm Eladio Díaz. I have an appointment with him at three.*

me gustaría — *I'd like*
la cita — *appointment*
tener cita con — *to have an appointment with*

Mucho gusto, señor. Yo le diré al director que Ud. está. Él no tardará en llegar. Siéntese, por favor. — *Pleased to meet you, sir. I'll tell the director you are here. He won't be long (in arriving). Please sit down.*

diré — *I will tell*
le diré al director — *I'll tell the director*
Ud. está — *you are here*
tardar en + *infinitive* — *to be long in (doing something)*
tardará — *he will be long*
no tardará en llegar — *he won't be long in arriving*
siéntese — *sit down*

Variantes

Listen, and repeat the same structures from *Diálogo 8*, now with new vocabulary.

Me gustaría verlos.	***I would like*** *to see them.*
Me encantaría	*I would love*
¿No te importaría su actitud?	*Wouldn't you care about his attitude?*
Sí, pero me importarían más sus valores.	*Yes, but I would care more about his values.*

Estructura y Práctica

N ***Eladio Díaz y la entrevista de trabajo.*** Imagine that Eladio Díaz has an appointment with Mr. Torres for a job interview. Express the following dialogue between Eladio Díaz and Mr. Torres in Spanish. Helpful vocabulary is included below. Pay special attention to the use of the future and conditional tenses.

La entrevista de trabajo

el/la aspirante *applicant*
la autoconfianza *self-confidence*
el candidato / la candidata *applicant*
la carta de motivación *cover letter*
la confianza en sí mismo/a *self-confidence*
los conocimientos de informática *computer skills*
cumplir con fechas límites / con los plazos establecidos *to meet deadlines*
el currículum vitae *curriculum vitae, CV*
la entrevista de trabajo/empleo *job interview*
entrevistar *to interview*
la experiencia profesional *professional experience*
la fecha límite *deadline*
la formación *background*
las habilidades comunicativas *communication skills*
las habilidades requeridas *skill set*
llevar a cabo múltiples tareas *to multitask*
mostrar (**o** > **ue**) iniciativa *to show initiative*
el nivel educativo / de formación *level of education*
la oferta de trabajo/empleo *job offer*
el plazo establecido *deadline*
el puesto disponible *available position*
resolver (**o** > **ue**) problemas *to solve problems*
el/la solicitante *applicant*
solicitar un empleo *to apply for a job*
la solicitud *application*
solucionar problemas *to solve problems*
el trabajo en equipo *teamwork*

1. SEÑOR TORRES *Good afternoon, Mr. Díaz. You are one of the few candidates for this position.*
2. ELADIO DÍAZ *Pleased to meet you, sir. Thank you very much.*
3. SEÑOR TORRES *We liked your cover letter, and your CV is impressive. Please tell me more about your professional experience.*
4. ELADIO DÍAZ *I had been working for my former company for fifteen years. I have the skill set and very good communication skills. And I always meet deadlines.*
5. SEÑOR TORRES *You would have to solve difficult problems and show initiative.*
6. ELADIO DÍAZ *I'm sure I would be able to. As manager and project manager, I was successful in all my projects and got along very well with my team.*
7. SEÑOR TORRES *I'm glad to know it. Teamwork is very important for our company. Thank you, Mr. Díaz. We'll be in touch with you.*
8. ELADIO DÍAZ *Thank you very much, Mr. Torres. I would be very glad to work with you.*

DIÁLOGO 9 · Habrá reunión a las dos.

Study the dialogue, then listen to the recording and repeat each line.

EVA — Acaban de anunciar que habrá reunión a las dos. Podrás asistir, ¿no?

ELADIO — Yo sí, pero es una reunión imprevista. No sé si los otros miembros del equipo podrán.

Análisis

Check that you understand the linguistic breakdown of each speech from *Diálogo 9*.

Acaban de anunciar que habrá reunión a las dos. Podrás asistir, ¿no? — *They've just announced that there will be a meeting at two. You'll be able to attend, won't you?*

- acabar de + *infinitive* — *to have just (done something)*
- habrá — *there will be*
- la reunión — *meeting*
- podrás — *you will be able to*
- asistir a + *event* — *to attend +* event

Yo sí, pero es una reunión imprevista. No sé si los otros miembros del equipo podrán. — *I will, but it's an unexpected meeting. I don't know if the other members of the team will be able to.*

- yo sí — *I will (be able to)*
- imprevisto — *unexpected, unscheduled, unforeseen*
- el miembro — *member*
- el equipo — *team*
- podrán — *they will be able to*

Variantes

Listen, and repeat the same structures from *Diálogo 9*, now with new vocabulary.

Acaban de anunciar que habrá reunión hoy. — ***They have just announced that*** *there will be a meeting today.*

- Dicen que — *They say that*
- Creen que — *They think that*
- Saben que — *They know that*
- Escriben que — *They write that*
- Están seguros de que — *They are sure that*

Yo no sé si estarán en la oficina. — *I don't know* ***if they will be in the office****.*

- si habrá reunión — *if there will be a meeting*
- si podré asistir — *if I will be able to attend*
- si nuestros colegas tendrán otra cita — *if our colleagues will have another appointment*
- si la reunión será a las dos — *if the meeting will be at 2:00*
- si nos reuniremos en la sala de conferencias — *if we'll meet in the conference room*

Si mis colegas van, yo iré también. — *If my colleagues go, I'll go too.*
Yo iré si mis colegas van. — *I will go if my colleagues go.*

Estructura y Práctica

O ***Eladio Díaz consiguió el puesto.*** Eladio has joined the company and is talking with a team member about what they'll discuss at the meeting. Express the following dialogue between Eladio and Eva in Spanish, using additional vocabulary included below. Pay special attention to the use of the future and conditional tenses.

El marketing

la agencia de publicidad / publicitaria *advertising agency*
el anuncio *ad*
la campaña publicitaria *publicity campaign*
fomentar *to promote*
lanzar un nuevo producto *to launch a new product*
el lema *motto, slogan*
el logo *logo*
la marca *brand*
los medios sociales *social media*
el mercadeo de redes *network marketing*
el mercado *market*
la muestra *sample*
poner a prueba *to test*
el producto *product*
la promoción *advertising*
promocionar *to promote*
promover (**o** > **ue**) *to promote*
la publicidad *advertising*

1. ELADIO *Eva, do you know if Carmen, Daniel, and Federico will attend the meeting?*
2. EVA *Carmen and Federico will certainly be here, but Daniel told me he would have to see a client in the afternoon. He didn't know there would be a meeting today.*
3. ELADIO *Mr. Torres wants to launch a publicity campaign to announce the new product, so we'll have a lot to do.*
4. EVA *Eladio, you and I will draw up the budget. Federico will discuss network marketing, and Carmen will explain her ideas about social media.*
5. ELADIO *Mr. Torres will have samples of the product and will want to create a logo and a slogan.*
6. EVA *I think the designers will be in charge of graphic design. Look. Mr. Torres has just come in. The meeting will begin.*

DIÁLOGO 10 · Serán las cuatro.

Study the dialogue, then listen to the recording and repeat each line.

PEDRO ¿Qué hora es? No tengo mi reloj.
EVA Serán las cuatro.

Análisis

Check that you understand the linguistic breakdown of each speech from *Diálogo 10.*

¿Qué hora es? No tengo mi reloj. — *What time is it? I don't have my watch.*
el reloj — *watch*

Serán las cuatro.	*It's probably about four.*
serán	*it must be, it's probably*
serán las cuatro	*it must be four, I guess it's four, it's probably four*

Variantes

Listen, and repeat the same structures from *Diálogo 10,* now with new vocabulary.

¿Qué hora será?	*I wonder what time it is.*
Serán las diez.	*It's probably ten o'clock.*
Probablemente son las diez.	*It's probably ten o'clock.*
¿Tomaremos el tren de las ocho?	*Will we take the eight o'clock train?*
Será demasiado tarde ya.	*It's probably too late already.*
Me imagino que es demasiado tarde ya.	*I imagine it's too late already.*

DIÁLOGO 11 · ¿Dónde estará el anillo?

Study the dialogue, then listen to the recording and repeat each line.

LUCÍA ¡Qué horror! No puedo encontrar mi anillo de boda. ¿Dónde estará?
JORGE Me imagino que lo encontrarás. Valdrá mucho dinero.
LUCÍA Muchísimo. Pero yo no podría calcular su valor sentimental.

Análisis

Check that you understand the linguistic breakdown of each speech from *Diálogo 11.*

¡Qué horror! No puedo encontrar mi anillo de boda. ¿Dónde estará?	*How awful! I can't find my wedding ring. Where could it be?*
el horror	*horror*
¡Qué horror!	*How awful!*
el anillo	*ring*
la boda	*wedding*
el anillo de boda	*wedding ring*
estará	*it will be*
¿Dónde estará?	*Where could it be?*
Me imagino que lo encontrarás. Valdrá mucho dinero.	*I imagine that you will find it. It must be worth a lot of money.*
imaginarse	*to imagine*
me imagino que	*I imagine that*
encontrarás	*you will find*
valer	*to be worth*
valdrá	*it will be worth, it's probably worth*
Valdrá mucho dinero.	*It must be worth a lot of money.*

Muchísimo. Pero yo no podría calcular su valor sentimental.	*An awful lot. But I couldn't calculate its sentimental value.*
muchísimo	*very much*
podría	*I would be able to*
calcular	*to calculate, figure out*
el valor	*value*
sentimental	*sentimental*

Variantes

Listen, and repeat the same structures from *Diálogo 11*, now with new vocabulary.

¿**Dónde** estará Mauricio?	*I wonder* ***where*** *Mauricio is.*
Cómo	*how*
Con quién	*with whom*
Tendrá gran valor sentimental.	*It probably has great sentimental value.*
Probablemente tiene gran valor sentimental.	*It probably has great sentimental value.*

DIÁLOGO 12 · ¿Cuántos años tendrá?

Study the dialogue, then listen to the recording and repeat each line.

ANTONIO Juan Carlos está muy grande. ¿Cuántos años tendrá?

VICTORIA No sé exactamente. Tendrá catorce o quince. Preguntémoselo a su mamá. ¡Ella sí lo sabrá!

Análisis

Check that you understand the linguistic breakdown of each speech from *Diálogo 12*.

Juan Carlos está muy grande. ¿Cuántos años tendrá?	*Juan Carlos has gotten very big. I wonder how old he is.*
está muy grande	*has gotten very big*
tendrá	*he must have, I wonder if he has*
¿Cuántos años tendrá?	*I wonder how old he is.*
No sé exactamente. Tendrá catorce o quince. Preguntémoselo a su mamá. ¡Ella sí lo sabrá!	*I don't know exactly. He must be fourteen or fifteen. Let's ask his mother. She will certainly know!*
exactamente	*exactly*
tendrá	*he must have, he probably has*
preguntémoselo	*let's ask her (it)*
sabrá	*she will know, she probably knows*
sí	(emphatic particle)
sí lo sabrá	*she will certainly know*

Variantes

Listen, and repeat the same structures from *Diálogo 12*, now with new vocabulary.

¿Cuántos meses tendrán los gemelos?	*How many months old are the twins?*
Tendrán casi tres meses.	*They must be almost three months old.*
Probablemente tienen casi tres meses.	*They're probably almost three months old.*
¡Ella sí lo sabrá !	*She'll certainly **know**!*
dirá	*tell*

Estructura y Práctica

P ***¡Sí reaccionarán así!*** Express the following sentences in Spanish, using the future tense and the emphatic particle **sí** to stress that people will certainly react in a certain way when they hear the gossip. Follow the *modelo.*

MODELO *Juan will certainly be annoyed!*
→ ¡Juan sí se molestará!

1. *Isabel will certainly worry!*
2. *My parents will certainly understand!*
3. *You* (tú) *will certainly complain!*
4. *I will certainly tell everyone (it)!*
5. *You* (Ud.) *will certainly get offended!*
6. *Rodrigo and I will certainly be surprised* (sorprenderse)*!*
7. *You* (Uds.) *will certainly get angry!*
8. *Alfredo will certainly be to blame!*

DIÁLOGO 13 · No se podrá hacer la ensalada.

Study the dialogue, then listen to the recording and repeat each line.

VICTORIA Me dice Ester que no podrá hacer la ensalada de frutas porque no tiene duraznos.

ANTONIO Dile que yo iré al supermercado para comprarlos. ¿Qué más necesitará?

VICTORIA Bueno, querrá añadir manzanas y fresas, que tampoco tiene.

Análisis

Check that you understand the linguistic breakdown of each speech from *Diálogo 13.*

Me dice Ester que no podrá hacer la ensalada de frutas porque no tiene duraznos.	*Ester tells me that she won't be able to make the fruit salad because she doesn't have any peaches.*
no podrá	*she won't be able to*
la fruta	*fruit*
la ensalada de frutas	*fruit salad*
el durazno	*peach*

Dile que yo iré al supermercado para comprarlos. ¿Qué más necesitará?	*Tell her that I will go to the supermarket to buy them. What else might she need?*
dile	*tell her*
necesitará	*she might need, she must need*
Bueno, querrá añadir manzanas y fresas, que tampoco tiene.	*Well, she will probably want to add apples and strawberries, which she also doesn't have.*
querrá	*she may want*
añadir	*to add*
la manzana	*apple*
la fresa	*strawberry*
tampoco	*neither*

Variantes

Listen, and repeat the same structures from *Diálogo 13*, now with new vocabulary.

Querrá comprar uvas.	*She probably wants to buy* ***grapes***.
cerezas	*cherries*
peras	*pears*
mangos	*mangos*
papayas	*papayas*
cebollas	*onions*
aceitunas	*olives*
aguacates	*avocados*
tomates	*tomatoes*
ajo	*garlic*
azúcar	*sugar*

DIÁLOGO 14 · ¿Te interesaría ver el partido de béisbol?

Study the dialogue, then listen to the recording and repeat each line.

ANTONIO ¿Te interesaría ver el partido de béisbol hoy?

VICTORIA Me encantaría. ¿Cómo podríamos sacar boletos una hora antes del partido?

ANTONIO Andrés me dijo que él nos vendería los suyos. Parece que él y su hermano no pueden ir.

Análisis

Check that you understand the linguistic breakdown of each speech from *Diálogo 14*.

¿Te interesaría ver el partido de béisbol hoy?	*Would you be interested in seeing the baseball game today?*
te interesaría	*would you be interested in*
el partido	*game*

Me encantaría. ¿Cómo podríamos sacar boletos una hora antes del partido? — *I would love to. How could we get tickets an hour before the game?*
- me encantaría — *I'd love to*
- podríamos — *we'd be able to*
- sacar boletos — *to get tickets, buy tickets*
- antes de — *before*

Andrés me dijo que él nos vendería los suyos. Parece que él y su hermano no pueden ir. — *Andrés told me that he would sell us his. It seems that he and his brother can't go.*
- vender — *to sell*
- vendería — *he would sell*
- los suyos — *his*

Variantes

Listen, and repeat the same structures from *Diálogo 14*, now with new vocabulary.

¿Les interesaría asistir a este concierto? — *Would you be interested in attending this concert?*

Claro, nos encantaría. — *Of course, we'd love to.*

¿Cómo podríamos llegar a tiempo? — *How would we be able to arrive on time?*
Ya te dije que no podríamos. — *I told you that we wouldn't be able to.*

Él me dijo que iría. — *He told me that **he would go**.*
- saldría — *he would go out*
- vendría — *he would come*
- regresaría — *he would come back*

DIÁLOGO 15 · A la comisaría

Study the dialogue, then listen to the recording and repeat each line.

POLICÍA Señorita, Ud. rebasó la velocidad de sesenta y cinco millas. Su licencia de manejar, por favor.
MARTA ¿Dónde estará? Señor policía, lo siento. Creo que la dejé en casa.
POLICÍA Bueno, Ud. tendrá que acompañarme a la comisaría. Tendrán que chequear su licencia de manejar en la base de datos.

Análisis

Check that you understand the linguistic breakdown of each speech from *Diálogo 15*.

Señorita, Ud. rebasó la velocidad de sesenta y cinco millas. Su licencia de manejar, por favor. — *Miss, you went above the sixty-five mile an hour speed limit. Your driver's license, please.*
- rebasar — *to pass, exceed*
- la velocidad — *speed*
- la milla — *mile*
- la licencia de manejar — *driver's license*

¿Dónde estará? Señor policía, lo siento. Creo que la dejé en casa.	*Where could it be? Officer, I'm sorry. I think I left it at home.*
estará	*it will be, it may be*
creer	*to believe*
creo que	*I think that*
dejar	*to leave (something somewhere)*
Bueno, Ud. tendrá que acompañarme a la comisaría. Tendrán que chequear su licencia de manejar en la base de datos.	*Well, you'll have to come with me to the police station. They will have to check your driver's license in the database.*
tendrá	*you will have*
tendrá que	*you will have to*
acompañar	*to accompany*
la comisaría	*police station*
tendrán	*they will have*
tendrán que	*they will have to*
chequear	*to check*
la base de datos	*database*

Variantes

Listen, and repeat the same structures from *Diálogo 15*, now with new vocabulary.

Mi pasaporte . ¿Dónde estará?	***My passport**. I wonder where it is.*
Mi tarjeta de embarque	*My boarding pass*
Mi cartera	*My wallet*
Mis llaves . ¿Dónde estarán?	***My keys**. Where can they be?*
Mis papeles	*My papers*
Mis tarjetas de crédito	*My credit cards*

Un paso más

Are you ready to take your Spanish a step further? Here are exercises that will enhance your knowledge of the language and allow you to express yourself freely.

Q ***Preguntas personales.*** *Contesta las siguientes preguntas con oraciones completas en español.*

1. Si estudias en la universidad, ¿cuándo te graduarás? ¿Cuál es tu especialidad?
2. ¿Harás estudios de posgrado? ¿Querrás obtener la maestría o el doctorado? ¿En qué te especializarás?
3. ¿Cuándo irás de vacaciones? ¿Adónde irás? ¿Qué países y ciudades te gustaría conocer?
4. ¿Rebasaste la velocidad máxima en la carretera alguna vez? ¿Un(a) policía te paró? Explica qué pasó.
5. ¿Contrataste un organizador / una organizadora para tu boda u otra celebración? ¿De qué se encargó? ¿Estuviste contento/a con su trabajo?
6. ¿Se te perdió algo de valor alguna vez? ¿Qué fue? ¿Lograste encontrarlo? ¿Dónde y cómo lo encontraste?

R ***En mis ratos libres.*** **(In my free time.)** *Expresa en español lo que te gustaría hacer en tus ratos libres.*

1. Me gustaría...
2. Me interesaría...
3. Me encantaría...

S ***Fiestas y celebraciones.*** *En este capítulo aprendiste los nombres de unas fiestas en español, por ejemplo,* **la Pascua, la Pascua judía, la Navidad, el Día de la Independencia, la Fiesta de Quinceañera, el Día de la Madre,** *y* **el Día del Padre.** *Escribe un párrafo* (paragraph) *en español en el que hablas de las fiestas más importantes que celebras y de su significado* (meaning) *para ti.*

T **Translation.** *Lee las siguientes citas* (quotes) *y tradúcelas al inglés. Fíjate en el uso del tiempo futuro y el imperativo. Después, explica lo que significan* (they mean) *en español. Una pista* (hint): *Tienen que ver con* (they have to do with) *el matrimonio.* (See the Answer Key for translations.)

1. "Ten tus ojos bien abiertos antes del matrimonio y medio cerrados después de él."
   — *Benjamin Franklin*
2. "Cásate con un arqueólogo. Cuánto más vieja te hagas, más encantadora te encontrará."
   — *Agatha Christie*
3. "Casarse por segunda vez es el triunfo de la esperanza sobre la experiencia."
   — *Samuel Johnson*

16

Family Relations and Careers

Communication Goals

- Expressing emotions, doubt, value judgments, imposition of will, and denial
- Vocabulary: the classroom, family relations, choosing a career

Grammar Topics

- The Present Subjunctive
- Use of the Present Subjunctive in Noun Clauses
- Formation of the Present Subjunctive of Regular Verbs
- Formation of the Present Subjunctive of Irregular Verbs
- Spelling Changes in the Present Subjunctive

DIÁLOGO 1 · La maestra y sus alumnos

Study the dialogue, then listen to the recording and repeat each line.

SEÑORITA RIVERA	Chicos, quiero que estudien los capítulos siete y ocho para mañana. Será útil que tomen apuntes porque habrá una prueba el viernes.
RAFAEL	Señorita Rivera, ¿es necesario que aprendamos las fechas de memoria?
SEÑORITA RIVERA	Claro que sí, Rafael. Es muy importante que sepas las fechas de los acontecimientos históricos más importantes.

Análisis

Check that you understand the linguistic breakdown of each speech from *Diálogo 1.*

Chicos, quiero que estudien los capítulos siete y ocho para mañana. Será útil que tomen apuntes porque habrá una prueba el viernes.	*Kids, I want you to study chapters seven and eight for tomorrow. It will be useful for you to take notes, since there will be a test on Friday.*
estudian	*you study*
que estudien (*subjunctive*)	*you study*
quiero que + *subjunctive*	*I want (someone to do something)*
quiero que estudien	*I want you to study*
el capítulo	*chapter*
será útil	*it will be useful*
tomar apuntes	*to take notes*
toman	*you take*
que tomen (*subjunctive*)	*you take*
es útil que + *subjunctive*	*it's useful for (someone to do something)*
será útil que tomen apuntes	*it will be useful for you to take notes*
habrá	*there will be*
la prueba	*quiz, test*
Señorita Rivera, ¿es necesario que aprendamos las fechas de memoria?	*Miss Rivera, is it necessary for us to memorize the dates?*
aprender	*to learn*
aprendemos	*we learn*
que aprendamos (*subjunctive*)	*we learn*
es necesario que + *subjunctive*	*it is necessary for (someone to do something)*
es necesario que aprendamos	*it is necessary for us to learn*
aprender de memoria	*to memorize*
aprender las fechas de memoria	*to memorize the dates*
Claro que sí, Rafael. Es muy importante que sepas las fechas de los acontecimientos históricos más importantes.	*Yes, of course, Rafael. It's very important for you to know the dates of the most important historical events.*
Claro que sí.	*Yes, of course.*
sabes	*you know*
que sepas (*subjunctive*)	*you know*
es muy importante que + *subjunctive*	*it's very important for (someone to do something)*
es muy importante que sepas	*it's very important for you to know*
el acontecimiento	*event*
el acontecimiento histórico	*historical event*

Variantes

Listen, and repeat the same structures from *Diálogo 1*, now with new vocabulary.

Quiero que estudien el libro.	***I want you to study*** *the book.*
Quiero que lean	*I want you to read*
Quiero que abran	*I want you to open*
Quiero que compren	*I want you to buy*
Quiero estudiar el libro.	***I want to study*** *the book.*
Quiero leer	*I want to read*
Quiero abrir	*I want to open*
Quiero comprar	*I want to buy*
Es útil que tomen apuntes.	*It's useful* ***for you to take notes.***
que lean este capítulo	*for you to read this chapter*
que miren el mapa	*for you to look at the map*
que escriban una composición	*for you to write a composition*
Es útil tomar apuntes.	*It's useful* ***to take notes.***
leer este capítulo	*to read this chapter*
mirar el mapa	*to look at the map*
escribir una composición	*to write a composition*
Es necesario que aprendamos las fechas de memoria.	***It's necessary*** *for us to memorize the dates.*
Es imprescindible	*It's crucial*
Es bueno	*It's good*
Es preciso	*It's necessary*
Es necesario aprender las fechas de memoria.	***It's necessary*** *to memorize the dates.*
Es imprescindible	*It's crucial*
Es bueno	*It's good*
Es preciso	*It's necessary*
Es importante que sepas las fechas.	*It's important* ***that you know the dates.***
que saques buenas notas	*that you get good grades*
que vayas a la sala de clase	*that you go to the classroom*
que seas aplicado	*that you be studious*
que te prepares para la prueba	*that you prepare for the test*
que traigas la calculadora de bolsillo	*that you bring your pocket calculator*
que hagas la tarea	*that you do the homework*
Es importante saber las fechas.	*It's important* ***to know the dates.***
sacar buenas notas	*to get good grades*
ir a la sala de clase	*to go to the classroom*
ser aplicado	*to be studious*
prepararse para la prueba	*to prepare for the test*
traer la calculadora de bolsillo	*to bring your pocket calculator*
hacer la tarea	*to do the homework*

Estructura y Práctica

THE PRESENT SUBJUNCTIVE

The Spanish tenses studied in previous chapters belong to the indicative mood. Verbs in the indicative mood express events or states that are considered factual, definite, or part of the speaker's experienced reality. Verbs that are in the subjunctive mood express an action that is not yet part of reality and/or the speaker's experience.

Use of the Present Subjunctive in Noun Clauses

The following examples have subordinate (dependent) noun clauses in the indicative. They show events perceived as part of reality, because they are the objects of verbs in the main clause: **saber**, **ver**, **oír**, **parecer**.

Sé que **llegan** mañana.	***I know*** *that* ***they're arriving*** *tomorrow.*
¿No **ves** que **llueve**?	*Don't* ***you see it's raining?***
Oímos que **tienen** problemas todavía.	***We hear they're*** *still* ***having*** *problems.*
Parece que no **hay** vuelo directo.	***It seems there's*** *no direct flight.*

There are verbs that appear in the main clause that require the use of the subjunctive in the subordinate (dependent) clause. These can be in the present, present perfect, or future tenses, or the imperative. Here is a list of such verbs categorized by meaning.

1 · Imposition of will: **querer que**, **desear que**, **esperar que**, **necesitar que**, **preferir que**. The negative of these verbs is also followed by a clause in the present subjunctive.

Queremos que **te quedes** un poco más.	*We want you to stay a little longer.*
Espero que **puedan** venir.	*I hope they'll be able to come.*
No necesitamos que nos **ayudes**.	*We don't need you to help us.*

2 · Getting someone to do something: **aconsejarle a uno que**, **exigirle a uno que**, **pedirle a uno que**, **mandarle a uno que**, **proponerle a uno que**, **recomendarle a uno que**, **insistir en que**. The indirect object may be omitted when a subjunctive clause follows.

Te aconsejo que le **hagas** caso.	*I advise you to pay attention to what he says.*
Me exigen que **trabaje** los fines de semana.	*They demand that I work on weekends.*
Siempre nos pide que le **prestemos** dinero.	*He always asks us to lend him money.*
Les propongo que **salgan** antes de la una.	*I suggest they leave before one o'clock.*
Insisto en que Ud. **coma** con nosotros.	*I insist that you eat with us.*

An infinitive clause is also possible with **aconsejar**, **exigir**, **pedir**, **mandar**, **proponer**, **recomendar** (**e** > **ie**), **permitir**, **prohibir** (**prohíbo** (*to forbid*)).

Te aconsejo **hacerle** caso.	*I advise you to pay attention to what he says.*

3 · Doubt, uncertainty: **dudar que, no creer que, no pensar que**

Dudo que ella lo **sepa**.	*I doubt she knows it.*
No creen que **seamos** capaces de hacerlo.	*They don't think we're capable of doing it.*

Note that the negative of **dudar** and the affirmative of **creer** and **pensar** are followed by the indicative, not the subjunctive.

No dudamos que te **ama**.	*We don't doubt that he loves you.*
Pienso que **es** una tienda muy cara.	*I think it's a very expensive store.*

4 · Emotions and subjective value judgments: **alegrarse (de) que, sentir que, (no) gustarle a uno que, (no) parecerle a uno bien/mal que, es una lástima que**

Me alegro de que me **comprendas**.	*I'm glad you understand me.*
Sentimos que él **esté** enojado.	*We're sorry that he's angry.*
No les gusta que su hija **salga** con Álvaro.	*They don't like that their daughter is going out with Álvaro.*
Me parece bien que **tengamos** vacaciones.	*I think it's good that we'll have a vacation.*
Es una lástima que no **se lleven** bien.	*It's a pity they don't get along well.*

Expressions consisting of **es** + adjective + **que** (impersonal expressions) that have meanings similar to the verbs listed in these categories (imposition of will, getting someone to do something, doubt, emotions and subjective value judgments) are also followed by the subjunctive.

Es necesario que **vengas**.	*It's necessary for you to come.*
Es importante que ella **hable** con su esposo.	*It's important for her to talk with her husband.*
Es poco probable que me **conozcan**.	*It's unlikely that they will know me.*
Es triste que no **encuentren** empleo.	*It's sad that they can't find work.*
Es mejor que las **llamemos** mañana.	*It's better for us to call them tomorrow.*

The following impersonal expressions are followed by the subjunctive only when negative: **no es cierto que, no es verdad que, no es evidente que, no estoy seguro (de) que**.

No es verdad que él **sea** médico.	*It's not true that he's a doctor.*
No estoy seguro de que **quieran** salir.	*I'm not sure they want to go out.*

When these expressions are affirmative, they are followed by the indicative.

Es verdad que él **es** médico.	*It's true that he's a doctor.*
Es evidente que tú la **amas**.	*It's evident that you love her.*

The expression **es dudoso que** is followed by the subjunctive when affirmative, but by the indicative when negative.

Es dudoso que se **pueda** terminar este proyecto.	*It's doubtful that this project can be completed.*
No es dudoso que se **puede** terminar este proyecto.	*It's not doubtful that this project can be completed.*

The English equivalent of a subjunctive clause is often an infinitive clause rather than a subordinate clause beginning with *that*.

Quiero **que ellos vayan**.	*I want **them to go**.*

If, however, there is no change of subject, the subjunctive is not used in Spanish. The infinitive, not the subjunctive, is used in Spanish when the subject is the same in both clauses of the sentence.

Verb in Main Clause + Subordinate Clause in Subjunctive
(two clauses: two different subjects)

Quiero que Uds. **estudien** español.	*I want you to study Spanish.*
Esperamos que **regreses** pronto.	*We hope you'll come back soon.*
Prefieren que **vivamos** en el centro.	*They prefer that we live downtown.*

Verb in Main Clause + Infinitive
(both clauses of the sentence have the same subject)

Quiero estudiar español.	*I want to study Spanish.*
Esperamos regresar pronto.	*We hope to come back soon.*
Prefieren vivir en el centro.	*They prefer to live downtown.*

The expressions **tal vez** (*perhaps*) and **quizás** (*perhaps*) can be followed either by the indicative or the subjunctive.

Tal vez nieve esta noche.	*Perhaps it will snow tonight.*
Quizás juegan al golf mañana.	*Perhaps they'll play golf tomorrow.*

Formation of the Present Subjunctive of Regular Verbs

The present subjunctive is formed by switching the characteristic vowels of the conjugations. -**Ar** verbs change the **a** of the present indicative to **e**, while -**er** and -**ir** verbs change the vowels **e** and **i** of the present indicative to **a** in the subjunctive. Regular -**er** and -**ir** verbs have identical endings in all persons of the subjunctive.

trabajar *to work*

Quiere que trabaj**e** con él.	*He wants me to work with him.*
Quiere que trabaj**es** con él.	*He wants you to work with him.*
Quiere que trabaj**e** con él.	*He wants her to work with him.*
Quiere que trabaj**emos** con él.	*He wants us to work with him.*
Quiere que trabaj**éis** con él.	*He wants you to work with him.*
Quiere que trabaj**en** con él.	*He wants them to work with him.*

aprender *to learn*

Espera que aprend**a** español.	*She hopes I'll learn Spanish.*
Espera que aprend**as** español.	*She hopes you'll learn Spanish.*
Espera que aprend**a** español.	*She hopes he'll learn Spanish.*
Espera que aprend**amos** español.	*She hopes we'll learn Spanish.*
Espera que aprend**áis** español.	*She hopes you'll learn Spanish.*
Espera que aprend**an** español.	*She hopes they'll learn Spanish.*

escribir *to write*

Prefieren que les escrib**a** un email.	*They prefer that I write them an email.*
Prefieren que les escrib**as** un email.	*They prefer that you write them an email.*
Prefieren que les escrib**a** un email.	*They prefer that he write them an email.*
Prefieren que les escrib**amos** un email.	*They prefer that we write them an email.*
Prefieren que les escrib**áis** un email.	*They prefer that you write them an email.*
Prefieren que les escrib**an** un email.	*They prefer that they write them an email.*

NOTE In the present subjunctive, the **yo** form and the **él/ella/Ud.** form are identical.

-**Ar** and -**er** verbs that have changes in the vowel of the stem in the present indicative have these same changes in the present subjunctive.

Quiero que c**ie**rres la puerta.	*I want you to close the door.*
Quieren que c**e**rremos la puerta.	*They want us to close the door.*
Prefiero que Uds. no v**ue**lvan muy tarde.	*I prefer that you don't come back very late.*
¿A qué hora quieres que v**o**lvamos?	*What time do you want us to come back?*

-**Ir** verbs that have the change **e** > **ie** or **e** > **i** in the present indicative also have these changes in the present subjunctive. These verbs also change the **e** of the stem to **i** in the **nosotros** and **vosotros** forms of the present subjunctive.

sentir (i > ie) *to feel*	
s**ie**nta	s**i**ntamos
s**ie**ntas	s**i**ntáis
s**ie**nta	s**ie**ntan

pedir (e > i) *to ask for*	
p**i**da	p**i**damos
p**i**das	p**i**dáis
p**i**da	p**i**dan

Dormir and **morir** change **o** to **u** in the stem of the **nosotros** and **vosotros** forms.

dormir (o > ue) *to sleep*	
d**ue**rma	d**u**rmamos
d**ue**rmas	d**u**rmáis
d**ue**rma	d**ue**rman

morir (o > ue) *to die*	
m**ue**ra	m**u**ramos
m**ue**ras	m**u**ráis
m**ue**ra	m**ue**ran

Verbs ending in -**iar** or -**uar** that have an accent mark on the **i** (í) or the **u** (ú) in the singular and third person plural of the present tense also have the accent mark in the same four persons of the present subjunctive. The **nosotros** and **vosotros** forms do not have an accent over the **i** or the **u** of the stem.

enviar	envíe, envíes, envíe, enviemos, enviéis, envíen
continuar	contin**ú**e, contin**ú**es, contin**ú**e, continuemos, continuéis, contin**ú**en

Formation of the Present Subjunctive of Irregular Verbs

Verbs that have an irregularity such as -**g**- or -**zc**- in the **yo** form of the present indicative have that irregularity in all persons of the present subjunctive. These irregularities occur only in -**er** and -**ir** verbs; therefore, all of these verbs have present subjunctive endings with -**a**-.

PRESENT INDICATIVE	SUBJUNCTIVE yo	tú	él, ella, Ud.	nosotros	vosotros	ellos, ellas, Uds.
caber						
quepo	quepa	quepas	quepa	quepamos	quepáis	quepan
caer						
caigo	caiga	caigas	caiga	caigamos	caigáis	caigan
conocer						
conozco	conozca	conozcas	conozca	conozcamos	conozcáis	conozcan
construir						
construyo	construya	construyas	construya	construyamos	construyáis	construyan
decir						
digo	diga	digas	diga	digamos	digáis	digan
hacer						
hago	haga	hagas	haga	hagamos	hagáis	hagan
oír						
oigo	oiga	oigas	oiga	oigamos	oigáis	oigan
poner						
pongo	ponga	pongas	ponga	pongamos	pongáis	pongan
salir						
salgo	salga	salgas	salga	salgamos	salgáis	salgan
tener						
tengo	tenga	tengas	tenga	tengamos	tengáis	tengan
traer						
traigo	traiga	traigas	traiga	traigamos	traigáis	traigan
venir						
vengo	venga	vengas	venga	vengamos	vengáis	vengan
ver						
veo	vea	veas	vea	veamos	veáis	vean

Other irregular verbs in the present subjunctive are some of the most commonly used verbs.

	yo	tú	él, ella, Ud.	nosotros	vosotros	ellos, ellas, Uds.
dar	dé	des	dé	demos	deis	den
estar	esté	estés	esté	estemos	estéis	estén
haber	haya	hayas	haya	hayamos	hayáis	hayan
ir	vaya	vayas	vaya	vayamos	vayáis	vayan
saber	sepa	sepas	sepa	sepamos	sepáis	sepan
ser	sea	seas	sea	seamos	seáis	sean

Spelling Changes in the Present Subjunctive

Spelling changes in the present subjunctive are similar to those that you learned for the **yo** form of the preterit. (For a review of the preterit, see Chapter 9).

Verbs with stems ending in the letters **c**, **g**, **z**, and **j** have spelling changes in the present subjunctive.

According to Spanish spelling conventions, the sounds /k/, /g/, /s/ (written **z**, not **s**), and /x/ are written differently before **e** and **i** than before **a**, **o**, and **u**.

/k/	/g/	/s/	/x/
ca	ga	za	ja
que	**gue**	**ce**	**ge**
qui	**gui**	**ci**	**gi**
co	go	zo	jo
cu	gu	zu	ju

PRESENT TENSE	SUBJUNCTIVE
Lo bus**co**.	Quieren que lo bus**que**.
Lle**gan** en tren.	Prefiero que lle**gue**n en tren.
Empie**za** a llorar.	Tememos que empie**ce** a llorar.
Esco**ges** algo.	Desean que esco**jas** algo.
Si**gue** esta ruta.	Esperas que si**ga** esta ruta.

The spelling change **g** > **j** also occurs in the **yo** form of the present tense of verbs with infinitives that end in **-ger** and **-gir**: **escojo, finjo**. It occurs in all persons of the present subjunctive: **que yo escoja/finja, que tú escojas/finjas, que él escoja/finja, que nosotros escojamos/finjamos, que vosotros escojáis/finjáis, que ellos escojan/finjan**.

A **Present subjunctive.** Write the present subjunctive form of the verb in parentheses that correctly completes each of the following sentences. Follow the *modelo.*

MODELO Quieren que Ud. *imprima* los documentos. (imprimir)

1. Prefiero que ellos ____________________ para las ocho. (llegar)
2. Es necesario que tú ____________________ el cinturón de seguridad. (abrocharse)
3. Siente que ellos no le ____________________ una beca. (dar)
4. Es muy importante que ____________________ reunión hoy. (haber)
5. Esperamos que nuestros hijos ____________________ sanos y felices. (ser)
6. Es preciso que Ud. nos ____________________ toda la verdad. (decir)
7. Es bueno que nadie ____________________. (enfermarse)
8. Desean que nosotros ____________________ los gastos. (compartir)

B **Present subjunctive or present indicative?** Write either the present subjunctive or the present indicative of the verb in parentheses to correctly complete each of the following sentences. Follow the *modelos*.

MODELOS Creo que él *manda* un email. (mandar)

Necesito que él *mande* un email. (mandar)

1. Sabemos que ellos ________________ la semana entrante. (volver)
2. Espero que tú ________________ buenas notas. (sacar)
3. Prefieren que ella ________________ la tarea ahora mismo. (hacer)
4. Han oído que ________________ un buen club de jazz. (ser)
5. Desean que nosotros ________________ la cuenta. (pagar)
6. Vemos que tú ________________ muy estresado. (estar)
7. Quieren que yo ________________ un rato más. (quedarse)
8. Me parece que ella no ________________ pelos en la lengua. (tener)
9. Siento que no les ________________ mi regalo. (gustar)
10. Tememos que Uds. ________________ el tren. (perder)

C ***En la sala de clase.*** Write sentences that express how Mr. Arenas responds to his students when he insists that they do what they don't want to do. Use the cue in parentheses in the main clause of your answer; use the present subjunctive of the verb (from the student's statement) in the subordinate clause. Change direct object nouns to pronouns. Follow the *modelo*.

MODELO MARCOS Yo no quiero mirar el mapa. (insistir en)
→ SEÑOR ARENAS Marcos, yo insisto en que lo mires.

1. PILAR Yo no quiero sacar mi computadora. (es necesario)
2. ALONSO Yo no quiero tomar apuntes. (es importante)
3. ANDRÉS Yo no quiero traer mi libro de texto. (es útil)
4. SILVIA Yo no quiero aprender las fechas de memoria. (insistir en)
5. GILBERTO Yo no quiero hacer la tarea. (es imprescindible)
6. FLOR Yo no quiero empezar a escribir la composición. (es preciso)

D **Translation.** Express the following sentences in Spanish. Write either a sentence with two clauses and two different subjects (which will require a verb in present subjunctive) or a sentence with a verb in the main clause + an infinitive.

1. *I want to go out.*
2. *We hope she'll be studious.*
3. *It's necessary to take notes.*
4. *It's important that they read a lot.*
5. *Do you* (tú) *prefer to buy the tickets online?*
6. *It will be crucial for us to learn all the dates.*
7. *They want to have a great time!*
8. *It's good that you* (Uds.) *are graduating this year.*

DIÁLOGO 2 · Relaciones familiares: Rosario y su papá

Study the dialogue, then listen to the recording and repeat each line.

ROSARIO	Papá, quiero que conozcas a mi novio. Jaime es muy buena gente.
PAPÁ	Hija, tu mamá y yo preferimos que salgas con Antonio Maldonado. Es que nosotros somos íntimos amigos de sus papás.
ROSARIO	Ay papi, no creo que eso tenga importancia. Es más importante que Jaime y yo nos queramos.
PAPÁ	Bueno, Rosario, te aconsejo que pienses mucho en lo que haces. Antes que te cases mira lo que haces.

Análisis

Check that you understand the linguistic breakdown of each speech from *Diálogo 2*.

Papá, quiero que conozcas a mi novio. Jaime es muy buena gente.	*Dad, I want you to meet my boyfriend. Jaime is a wonderful person.*
conoces	*you know, get to know*
que conozcas (*subjunctive*)	*you know*
quiero que conozcas	*I want you to meet*
ser buena gente	*to be a nice person*
Hija, tu mamá y yo preferimos que salgas con Antonio Maldonado. Es que nosotros somos íntimos amigos de sus papás.	*Well, your mother and I prefer that you go out with Antonio Maldonado. The fact is that we are close friends of his parents.*
sales	*you go out*
que salgas (*subjunctive*)	*you go out*
preferir que + *subjunctive*	*to prefer that (someone do something)*
preferimos que salgas	*we prefer that you go out*
es que	*the fact is that, because*
íntimo	*intimate, close*
íntimos amigos	*close friends*
Ay papi, no creo que eso tenga importancia. Es más importante que Jaime y yo nos queramos.	*Oh, Dad, I don't think that that is important. It's more important that Jaime and I love each other.*
tiene importancia	*it's important*
que tenga (*subjunctive*)	*it has*
que tenga importancia	*it's important*
no creo que + *subjunctive*	*I don't think that . . .*
no creo que eso tenga importancia	*I don't think that that's important*
quererse	*to love each other*
nos queremos	*we love each other*
que nos queramos (*subjunctive*)	*we love each other*
es más importante que + *subjunctive*	*it's more important that . . .*
es más importante que nos queramos	*it's more important that we love each other*

Bueno, Rosario, te aconsejo que pienses mucho en lo que haces. Antes que te cases mira lo que haces.	*Well, Rosario, I advise you to think carefully about what you are doing. Look before you leap.*
pensar en	*to think about*
piensas	*you think*
que pienses (*subjunctive*)	*you think*
aconsejarle a uno que + *subjunctive*	*to advise someone to (do something)*
te aconsejo que pienses mucho	*I advise you to think carefully*
lo que	*what*
antes que + *subjunctive*	*before (doing something)*
antes que te cases	*before you get married*
mira	*look; examine*
mira lo que haces	*look at what you are doing*
Antes que te cases mira lo que haces.	*Look before you leap.* (literally, *before you get married, look at what you're doing*)

Variantes

Listen, and repeat the same structures from *Diálogo 2*, now with new vocabulary.

Quiero que lo conozcas.	*I want **you to meet** him.*
conozcan	*them to meet*
conozca	*her to meet*
conozcamos	*us to meet*
conozca	*you* (Ud.) *to meet*
conozcan	*you* (Uds.) *to meet*
conozca	*him to meet*
Quiero conocerlo.	***I want** to know him.*
Quiere	*She wants*
Queremos	*We want*
Quieren	*They want*
Preferimos que salgas con él.	***We prefer you go out** with him.*
Queremos que salgas	*We want you to go out*
Esperamos que salgas	*We hope you'll go out*
Deseamos que salgas	*We want you to go out*
Insistimos en que salgas	*We insist that you go out*
Queremos salir con él.	***We want to go out** with him.*
Esperamos salir	*We hope to go out*
Deseamos salir	*We want to go out*
Insistimos en salir	*We insist on going out*
No creo que tenga importancia.	***I don't think** it's important.*
No pienso que	*I don't think*
No me parece que	*I don't think*
Dudo que	*I doubt*

Es importante que se lleven bien.	***It's important that** they get along well.*
Es necesario que	*It's necessary that*
Es bueno que	*It's good that*
Es imprescindible que	*It's crucial that*
Es posible que	*It's possible that*
Es probable que	*It's probable that*
Es dudoso que	*It's doubtful that*
Te aconsejo que pienses mucho.	***I advise you** to think hard.*
Te digo que	*I'm telling you*
Les recomiendo que esperen.	***I recommend that** they wait.*
Les pido que	*I ask that*
Les exijo que	*I demand that*
Les ruego que	*I request that*
Les propongo que	*I propose that*

Estructura y Práctica

E ***Les aconsejo que...*** Write a sentence from the elements given to advise people how they can live healthier lives. Use the present subjunctive. Follow the *modelo.*

MODELO Le aconsejo a Bernardo... / comer sano
→ Le aconsejo a Bernardo que coma sano.

1. Le aconsejo a Marta... / beber mucha agua
2. Les recomiendo a mis amigos... / dormir ocho horas diarias (*daily*)
3. Le propongo a Pablo... / ponerse a dieta
4. Le digo a Inés... / tomar vitaminas
5. Le exijo a mi primo... / perder peso
6. Les pido a mis papás... / hacer ejercicio
7. Le ruego a mi abuelito... / dejar de comer comida basura
8. Insisto en que mis colegas... / alimentarse bien

F ***Problemas de familia.*** Express the following sentences in Spanish to find out some of this family's problems. Use the present subjunctive.

1. *Dad, I don't think that you* (tú) *understand the problem.*
2. *We hope that Marta succeeds in catching a husband* (pescar un marido; pescar (*to fish*)).
3. *It's doubtful that Antonio and Victoria love each other.*
4. *Blanca doesn't think her parents know her boyfriend.*
5. *It's bad that the relatives don't get along well.*
6. *The grandparents tell their grandchildren to visit them.*
7. *Mario demands that his brother-in-law return the money to him.*
8. *Cristina insists that her father-in-law pay for the wedding.*

DIÁLOGO 3 · Relaciones familiares: Jaime y su mamá

Study the dialogue, then listen to the recording and repeat each line.

MAMÁ Jaime, me alegro de que estés contento pero te aconsejo que pienses mucho antes de comprometerte.

JAIME Mamá, a ti y a papá les cae bien Rosario, ¿verdad? Entonces, ¿por qué no quieren que yo me case con ella?

MAMÁ Es que nosotros no conocemos a los padres de Rosario. Preferimos que te comprometas con Aurora Elizondo porque somos íntimos amigos de sus papás.

JAIME Pero mamá, yo no quiero a Aurora. Y no dudo que te van a caer muy bien los papás de Rosario.

Análisis

Check that you understand the linguistic breakdown of each speech from *Diálogo 3.*

Jaime, me alegro de que estés contento pero te aconsejo que pienses mucho antes de comprometerte.	*Jaime, I'm glad you are happy, but I advise you to think carefully before getting engaged.*
alegrarse (de) que + *subjunctive*	*to be glad about (something)*
que estés (*subjunctive*)	*you are*
me alegro de que estés contento	*I'm glad you are happy*
aconsejarle a uno que + *subjunctive*	*to advise someone to (do something)*
te aconsejo que pienses mucho	*I advise you to think carefully*
antes de + *infinitive*	*before (doing something)*
comprometerse	*to get engaged*
antes de comprometerte	*before getting engaged*
Mamá, a ti y a papá les cae bien Rosario, ¿verdad? Entonces, ¿por qué no quieren que yo me case con ella?	*Mom, you and Dad like Rosario, don't you? So then why don't you want me to marry her?*
caerle bien a uno	*to like someone*
les cae bien Rosario	*you like Rosario*
no quieren que + *subjunctive*	*you don't want (someone to do something)*
casarse con uno	*to marry someone*
no quieren que yo me case	*you don't want me to marry*
Es que nosotros no conocemos a los padres de Rosario. Preferimos que te comprometas con Aurora Elizondo porque somos íntimos amigos de sus papás.	*Because we don't know Rosario's parents. We prefer that you get engaged to Aurora Elizondo, because we are close friends of her parents.*
comprometerse con	*to get engaged to*
te comprometes	*you get engaged*
que te comprometas (*subjunctive*)	*you get engaged*
preferir que + *subjunctive*	*to prefer that (someone do something)*
preferimos que te comprometas	*we prefer that you get engaged*

Pero mamá, yo no quiero a Aurora. Y no dudo que te van a caer muy bien los papás de Rosario.	*But Mom, I don't love Aurora. And I don't doubt that you are going to like Rosario's parents very much.*
querer a uno	*to love someone*
yo no quiero a Aurora	*I don't love Aurora*
no dudar que + *indicative*	*not to doubt that . . .*
no dudo que te van a caer muy bien	*I don't doubt that you are going to like them very much*

Variantes

Listen, and repeat the same structures from *Diálogo 3*, now with new vocabulary.

Se alegra de que se vayan.	***She's glad** they're leaving.*
Siente que	*She's sorry*
Tiene miedo de que	*She's afraid*
Teme que	*She fears*
Le sorprende que	*She's surprised*
¿No quieren que me case?	*Don't you want **me to get married?***
se case	*him to get married*
nos casemos	*us to get married*
se case	*her to get married*
se casen	*them to get married*
Es que somos íntimos amigos.	***The fact is that** we're close friends.*
Es verdad que	*It's true that*
Es cierto que	*It's true that*
Está seguro que	*He's sure that*
No es que seamos íntimos amigos.	***It's not that** we're close friends.*
No es verdad que	*It's not true that*
No es cierto que	*It's not true that*
No está seguro que	*He's not sure that*
Prefieren que vengamos en taxi.	***They prefer that we come** by taxi.*
Les gusta que vengamos	*They like us to come*
Les sorprende que vengamos	*They're surprised that we come*
No dudo que te van a caer bien.	***I don't doubt that** you'll like them.*
No es dudoso que	*It's not doubtful that*

Estructura y Práctica

G **Impersonal expressions.** Write a sentence from the elements given, using the correct present subjunctive or present indicative form of the verb in parentheses. Follow the *modelos.*

MODELOS es verdad / ellos / casarse en tres meses
→ Es verdad que ellos se casan en tres meses.

no es verdad / ellos / casarse en tres meses
→ No es verdad que ellos se casen en tres meses.

1. es que / nosotros / ser íntimos amigos
2. no estoy seguro / ella / ir a la fiesta
3. es dudoso / hacer buen tiempo mañana
4. es cierto / mis primos / estar de vacaciones
5. no es evidente / la empresa / tener problemas económicos
6. no es que / tú y yo / verse todos los días
7. es evidente / Uds. / no ponerse de acuerdo
8. estamos seguros / él / poder diseñar el sitio web

H **Translation.** Express the following sentences in Spanish, using the correct present subjunctive form of the verb.

1. *They're glad we're staying with them.*
2. *She's surprised the museum is closed.*
3. *We're afraid that they spend too much money.*
4. *I'm sorry you're* (tú) *feeling sick.*
5. *We fear the airplane is not taking off now.*
6. *They like us to stay in touch with them.*

DIÁLOGO 4 · Quieren que me haga médico.

Study the dialogue, then listen to the recording and repeat each line.

RICARDO Sara, me dicen que te has inscrito en la facultad de bellas artes.
SARA Sí, pero mis padres se oponen. Ellos prefieren que yo curse medicina.
RICARDO Los míos también quieren que yo me haga médico. Pero yo sé que me van a apoyar de todas formas.

Análisis

Check that you understand the linguistic breakdown of each speech from *Diálogo 4*.

Sara, me dicen que te has inscrito en la facultad de bellas artes.	*Sara, I'm told you have registered in the School of Fine Arts.*
inscribirse en	*to register in, register at, register for*
te has inscrito	*you have registered*
el arte	*art* (masculine in the singular)
las artes	*arts* (feminine in the plural)
las bellas artes	*fine arts*
la facultad	*school within a university*
la facultad de bellas artes	*School of Fine Arts*
Sí, pero mis padres se oponen. Ellos prefieren que yo curse medicina.	*Yes, but my parents are against it. They prefer that I study medicine.*
oponerse	*to oppose* (*it*), *be against* (*it*) (conjugated like **poner**)
cursar	*to take* (*courses, a major*)
que curse (*subjunctive*)	*I take*
preferir que + *subjunctive*	*to prefer (someone do something)*
prefieren que curse	*they prefer that I study*
Los míos también quieren que yo me haga médico. Pero yo sé que me van a apoyar de todas formas.	*My parents also want me to become a doctor. But I know that they will support me in any case.*
hacerse + *profession*	*to become* + profession
me hago médico	*I become a doctor*
que me haga médico (*subjunctive*)	*I become a doctor*
quieren que + *subjunctive*	*they want (someone to do something)*
quieren que yo me haga médico	*they want me to become a doctor*
apoyar a uno	*to support someone* (*morally*, etc.), *support someone's choice*
de todas formas	*anyway, in any case*

Variantes

Listen, and repeat the same structures from *Diálogo 4*, now with new vocabulary.

Él me dice que se ha inscrito al curso.	*He tells me he has signed up for the course.*
Él me dice que me inscriba al curso.	*He tells me to sign up for the course.*
Les digo que se van pronto.	*I'm telling them that they're leaving soon.*
Les digo que se vayan pronto.	*I'm telling them to leave soon.*
Le digo que curso medicina.	*I tell her I'm studying medicine.*
Le digo que curse medicina.	*I tell her to study medicine.*

Prefieren que yo me haga médico.	***They prefer that I*** *become a doctor.*
Esperan que yo	*They hope that I*
Quieren que yo	*They want me to*
Exigen que yo	*They demand that I*
Me aconsejan que	*They advise me to*
Insisten en que yo	*They insist that I*
Me piden que	*They ask that I*
Me recomiendan que	*They recommend that I*
Me proponen que	*They propose that I*
Saben que me hago médico.	***They know that*** *I'm becoming a doctor.*
Piensan que	*They think that*
Dicen que	*They say that*
Comprenden que	*They understand that*
Han oído que	*They've heard that*
Les parece que	*They think that*
Ven que	*They see that*

Estructura y Práctica

I **Getting someone to do something.** Write a sentence from the elements given, using the correct present subjunctive form of the verb. Follow the *modelo.*

MODELO le aconsejo a Roberto / terminar el plan de negocios
→ Le aconsejo a Roberto que termine el plan de negocios.

1. le pido a Juan / elaborar el presupuesto
2. le exijo a Enrique / crear una base de datos
3. les digo a mis asistentes / trabajar en equipo
4. le mando a Nora / dedicarse a los medios sociales
5. insisto en que Catalina / encargarse de lanzar el nuevo producto
6. les digo a los asesores / resolver el problema del servicio al cliente
7. le aconsejo a Lorena / comenzar la campaña publicitaria
8. les propongo a mis colegas / realizar un plan de investigación global de mercado

J Write the present subjunctive or present indicative form of the verb in parentheses to correctly complete each of the following sentences. Follow the *modelo.*

MODELO Sé que Octavio _quiere_ estudiar medicina. (querer)

1. He oído que Vicente ________________ de vuelta. (estar)
2. Nos piden que los ________________. (apoyar)
3. Creo que Uds. ________________ una prueba de matemáticas hoy. (tener)
4. Te recomiendo que ________________ al perro en el jardín. (buscar)

5. Veo que estos alumnos ________________ muy aplicados. (ser)
6. Los jugadores me proponen que ________________ al béisbol con ellos. (jugar)
7. Le aconsejamos a Raquel que ________________ con su novio. (romper)
8. Les exijo a los maestros que ________________ más paciencia. (tener)

K **Translation.** Express each of the following sentences in Spanish. Write sentences in two ways where indicated by (2).

1. *The teacher tells us to read chapter seven.*
2. *I advise you* (Ud.) *to write the report.* (2)
3. *They recommend that I bring my pocket calculator.* (2)
4. *Eduardo tells me that he and Lorenzo don't get along well.*
5. *I insist that you* (tú) *stop smoking.*
6. *I ask them to come to our house.* (2)
7. *The boss demands that I hand in the report by Tuesday.* (2)
8. *I suggest that you* (Uds.) *attend the meeting.* (2)

DIÁLOGO 5 · Ojalá que ella cambie de idea.

Study the dialogue, then listen to the recording and repeat each line.

JUDITH Ay Lorenzo, siento que Sara no nos haga caso. Ya se ha inscrito en la facultad de bellas artes.

LORENZO Judith, no podemos permitir que estudie arte. ¿Cómo se ganará la vida?

JUDITH Ojalá que ella cambie de idea. Pero si no, de todas formas la vamos a apoyar.

Análisis

Check that you understand the linguistic breakdown of each speech from *Diálogo 5.*

Ay Lorenzo, siento que Sara no nos haga caso. Ya se ha inscrito en la facultad de bellas artes.	*Oh, Lorenzo, I regret that Sara is not listening to us. She has already registered at the School of Fine Arts.*
hacerle caso a uno	*to pay attention to someone, listen to someone*
no nos hace caso	*she doesn't listen to us, she doesn't pay attention to us*
que no nos haga caso (*subjunctive*)	*she doesn't listen to us, she doesn't pay attention to us*
sentir (**e** > **ie**)	*to regret, be sorry*
siento que + *subjunctive*	*to be sorry that (something is happening)*
siento que no nos haga caso	*I'm sorry that she doesn't listen to us*

Judith, no podemos permitir que estudie arte. ¿Cómo se ganará la vida?	*Judith, we can't allow her to study art. How will she make a living?*
permitir que + *subjunctive*	*to permit (someone to do something), allow (someone to do something)*
permitir que estudie arte	*to allow her to study art*
ganarse la vida	*to earn one's living*
Ojalá que ella cambie de idea. Pero si no, de todas formas la vamos a apoyar.	*I hope that she changes her mind. But if she doesn't, we'll support her anyway.*
ojalá que + *subjunctive*	*I hope that . . .*
cambiar de idea	*to change one's mind*
que cambie de idea (*subjunctive*)	*she changes her mind*
ojalá que cambie de idea	*I hope she changes her mind*
si no	*if she doesn't*
la vamos a apoyar	*we'll support her (choice)*

Variantes

Listen, and repeat the same structures from *Diálogo 5*, now with new vocabulary.

Siento que ella estudie arte.	***I'm sorry that** she's studying art.*
Dudo que	*I doubt that*
Me alegro de que	*I'm glad that*
Me gusta que	*I like that*
Me sorprende que	*I'm surprised that*
No permitimos que estudie arte.	***We don't allow her** to study art.*
No le mandamos que	*We don't order her*
No le prohibimos que	*We don't forbid her*
No le permitimos estudiar arte.	***We don't allow her** to study art.*
No le mandamos	*We don't order her*
No le prohibimos	*We don't forbid her*
Dejamos que él estudie arte.	***We let him** study art.*
Hacemos que él	*We make him*
La dejamos estudiar arte.	***We let her** study art.*
La hacemos	*We make her*
Ojalá que tenga éxito.	*I hope he'll be successful.*
Ojalá no se pierdan.	*I hope they don't get lost.*

Estructura y Práctica

L ***La familia Gómez.*** Write sentences from the elements given to find out about the Gómez family. Use the correct present subjunctive form of the verb. Follow the *modelo.*

MODELO ojalá / todos los miembros de la familia Gómez / salir adelante
→ Ojalá que todos los miembros de la familia Gómez salgan adelante.

1. a sus papás les gusta / Leonor / hacerse actriz
2. el abuelo se alegra de que / Ramón / seguir la carrera de ingeniería

3. la abuela prohíbe / su nieta / salir con ese tipo
4. los tíos / dejan / su hija / ir al extranjero para estudiar inglés
5. Miguel le aconseja / a su hermano / no comprometerse con Lola
6. los papás les dicen / a sus hijos / ser corteses y amables
7. los cuñados hacen / sus hijos / inscribirse en la universidad
8. la familia Gómez espera / que todos ellos / lograr tener salud, felicidad y éxito

EXPRESSIONS WITH HACER

hacerle caso a uno	*to pay attention to someone, listen to someone*
hacerse + *profession*	*to become* + profession
hacer las paces	*to make up* (la paz (*peace*))
hacerse tarde	*to become late, get late*
hacer juego (con)	*to match*
hacer el ridículo	*to make a fool of oneself; to look foolish*
hacer un alto	*to take a break*
hacer un papel	*to play a role, play a part*

M ***Expresiones con hacer.*** Express the following sentences in Spanish, using idioms and expressions with **hacer** from the box above. All answers require the present subjunctive.

1. *It's bad that Luisito doesn't pay attention to his parents.*
2. *It's possible Fernanda will become an archaeologist.*
3. *Aunt Sara wants Juan and Blanca to make up once and for all* (de una vez).
4. *Let's leave before it gets late* (antes (de) que + *subjunctive*).
5. *I don't think this blouse matches the skirt.*
6. *They tell Arturo to stop making a fool of himself.*
7. *We advise you* (tú) *to take a break.*
8. *We hope Lorenzo Olivo will play the role of Hamlet in this production* (la producción).

DIÁLOGO 6 · Es necesario ahorrar más.

Study the dialogue, then listen to the recording and repeat each line.

ÁLVARO Es una lástima que no podamos salir de vacaciones este año.
JIMENA ¿Por qué? ¿Problemas de dinero?
ÁLVARO Pues sí. Con los tiempos que corren es mejor que no gastemos tanto dinero en un viaje a Europa.
JIMENA Yo le entiendo. Es necesario que todos tratemos de ahorrar más y gastar menos.

Análisis

Check that you understand the linguistic breakdown of each speech from *Diálogo 6.*

Es una lástima que no podamos salir de vacaciones este año.	*It's a shame that we can't go on vacation this year.*
la lástima	*pity, shame*
es una lástima que + *subjunctive*	*it's a shame that . . .*
podemos	*we can*
que podamos (*subjunctive*)	*we can*
es una lástima que no podamos	*it's a shame that we can't*
salir de vacaciones	*go on vacation, leave on vacation*
¿Por qué? ¿Problemas de dinero?	*Why? Money problems?*
Pues sí. Con los tiempos que corren es mejor que no gastemos tanto dinero en un viaje a Europa.	*Well, yes. In these times, it's better that we don't spend so much money on a trip to Europe.*
correr	*to run*
los tiempos que corren	*these times*
gastamos	*we spend*
que gastemos (*subjunctive*)	*we spend*
es mejor que + *subjunctive*	*it's better that . . .*
es mejor que no gastemos tanto dinero	*it's better that we don't spend so much money*
Yo le entiendo. Es necesario que todos tratemos de ahorrar más y gastar menos.	*I understand you. It's necessary for all of us to try to save more and spend less.*
entender (**e** > **ie**)	*to understand*
es necesario que + *subjunctive*	*it's necessary for (someone to do something)*
tratar de + *infinitive*	*to try to (do something)*
tratamos de	*we try to*
que tratemos de (*subjunctive*)	*we try to*
es necesario que tratemos	*it's necessary for us to try*
ahorrar	*to save*
gastar	*to spend*

Variantes

Listen, and repeat the same structures from *Diálogo 6,* now with new vocabulary.

Es una lástima que Uds. se vayan .	*It's a pity **that you're going away**.*
que Uds. salgan	*that you're going out*
que Uds. vuelvan	*that you're going back*
que Uds. se muden	*that you're moving away*

Es mejor que gastemos menos dinero.	***It's better*** *that we spend less money.*
Es necesario	*It's necessary*
Es importante	*It's important*
Es imprescindible	*It's crucial*
Es preciso	*It's necessary*
Es bueno	*It's good*
Es urgente	*It's urgent*
Es mejor gastar menos.	***It's better*** *to spend less.*
Es necesario	*It's necessary*
Es importante	*It's important*
Es imprescindible	*It's crucial*
Es preciso	*It's necessary*
Es bueno	*It's good*
Es urgente	*It's urgent*
Hace falta que ahorremos más.	***It's necessary that*** *we save more.*
Más vale que	*It's better that*
Urge que	*It's urgent that*
Hace falta ahorrar más.	***It's necessary*** *to save more.*
Más vale	*It's better*
Urge	*It's urgent*

Estructura y Práctica

N ***Expresiones impersonales.*** Rewrite each of the following sentences, conjugating the verb in the subordinate clause with the subject shown in parentheses. Follow the *modelo.*

MODELO Es necesario ganarse la vida. (tú)
→ Es necesario que tú te ganes la vida.

1. Es bueno ahorrar dinero. (Ud.)
2. Es imprescindible ponerse el repelente contra mosquitos. (ellos)
3. Es urgente salir para el aeropuerto. (yo)
4. Es preciso promocionar la marca. (Uds.)
5. Es mejor jugar al tenis por la mañana. (tú)
6. Es importante comer granos integrales. (todos nosotros)
7. Urge ir al medico. (él)
8. Más vale viajar en tren. (Ud.)
9. Hace falta aprender las fechas de memoria. (ella)
10. Es útil actualizar los datos. (yo)

DIÁLOGO 7 · Es poco probable que yo pueda ir.

Study the dialogue, then listen to the recording and repeat each line.

JIMENA Mañana vamos a reunirnos en mi casa para ver una película. Vienes, ¿no?
RICARDO Es poco probable que yo pueda ir.
JIMENA ¿Por qué? ¿Tienes un compromiso?
RICARDO Sí, mi hermana se muda y me ha pedido que la ayude.

Análisis

Check that you understand the linguistic breakdown of each speech from *Diálogo 7*.

Mañana vamos a reunirnos en mi casa para ver una película. Viene s, ¿no?	*Tomorrow we are going to get together at my house to see a movie. You'll come, won't you?*
reunirse	*to get together*
vamos a reunirnos	*we're going to get together*
Es poco probable que yo pueda ir.	*It's improbable that I'll be able to come.*
probable	*probable*
poco probable	*improbable, not likely, unlikely*
es poco probable que + *subjunctive*	*it's improbable that . . .*
es poco probable que yo pueda ir	*it's improbable that I can come*
¿Por qué? ¿Tienes un compromiso?	*Why? Do you have an appointment?*
el compromiso	*appointment, engagement, commitment*
Sí, mi hermana se muda y me ha pedido que la ayude.	*Yes, my sister is moving and has asked me to help her.*
mudarse	*to move (change residence)*
pedirle a uno que + *subjunctive*	*to ask someone to (do something)*
la ayudo	*I help her*
que la ayude (*subjunctive*)	*I help her*
me ha pedido que la ayude	*she has asked me to help her*

Variantes

Listen, and repeat the same structures from *Diálogo 7*, now with new vocabulary.

Es poco probable que yo vaya.	***It's improbable** that I'll go.*
Es posible	*It's possible*
Es dudoso	*It's doubtful*
Tal vez haya una prueba esta semana.	***Perhaps** there will be a quiz this week.*
Quizás	*Perhaps*
Tal vez hay una prueba esta semana.	***Perhaps** there will be a quiz this week.*
Quizás	*Perhaps*
Me ha pedido que la ayude.	***She has asked me** to help her.*
Me ha dicho	*She has told me*
Me ha mandado	*She has ordered me*

Él niega que hable mal de Uds.	*He denies that he speaks badly about you.*
Él no niega que habla mal de Uds.	*He doesn't deny that he speaks badly about you.*
No me parece que entiendan el asunto.	*I don't think they understand the issue.*
Me parece que entienden el asunto.	*I think they understand the issue.*

Estructura y Práctica

O ***Imperativo y presente de subjuntivo.*** Express each of the following **tú** commands as a sentence using the present subjunctive. Use the cues in parentheses. (To review the imperative, see Chapter 14.) Follow the *modelo*.

MODELO Vive la vida plenamente. (Espero que)
→ Espero que vivas la vida plenamente.

1. Cuídate mucho. (Te aconsejo que)
2. Sal con nosotros al teatro. (Quiero que)
3. Córtate el pelo. (Es necesario que)
4. Apaga la computadora. (Hace falta que)
5. Ven a vernos hoy. (Es mejor que)
6. Hazme caso. (Insisto en que)
7. Ten paciencia. (Más vale que)
8. Diviértete mucho. (Me alegro de que)
9. Pruébate el abrigo azul marino. (Te recomiendo que)
10. Aprovéchate de las ofertas de enero. (Urge que)

P Express the following sentences in Spanish, using the present subjunctive form of the verb.

1. *It's improbable that Pedro will get the position.*
2. *It's crucial that we support our friends.*
3. *Perhaps these foreign students* [masc.] *are of English descent.*
4. *It's a pity that Lupe can't find her earrings.*
5. *Laura and Sergio deny they're getting a divorce.*
6. *I've told the children to wash their hands.*
7. *It's better that you* (tú) *do your homework now.*
8. *It's bad that they don't get in touch with us more often.*

Un paso más

Are you ready to take your Spanish a step further? Here are exercises that will enhance your knowledge of the language and allow you to express yourself freely.

Q ***Más vale...*** The impersonal expression **más vale** appears in many Spanish sayings and aphorisms. Express the following sayings in English, then write an explanation of the meaning in Spanish. Note that in these sayings, **más vale** is not followed by a verb in present subjunctive, but rather by an infinitive, a noun, or an adverb. (See the Answer Key for meanings.)

1. Más vale tarde que nunca.
2. Más vale estar solo que mal acompañado.
3. Más vale dar que recibir.
4. Más vale pájaro en mano que ciento volando. (volar (**o** > **ue**) (*to fly*))
5. Más vale arrepentirse de lo que se hizo que de lo que no se hizo.
6. Más vale prevenir que curar.
7. Más vale lo malo conocido que lo bueno por conocer.
8. Más vale la salud que el dinero.

R ***Preguntas personales.*** *Contesta las siguientes preguntas con oraciones completas en español.*

1. ¿Qué esperas lograr en tu vida personal y profesional?
2. ¿Qué quieres que tus hijos logren en su vida personal y profesional?
3. ¿Qué les aconsejas a tus amigos? ¿A tus padres e hijos?
4. ¿Qué te aconsejan tus amigos? ¿Tus familiares?
5. ¿Tienes una alma gemela (una media naranja) (*soulmate*)? ¿Quién es? ¿Cómo es?
6. ¿Crees que es importante tener una alma gemela? ¿Por qué?
7. ¿Te caen bien tus familiares políticos (*relatives by marriage*)? ¿Quiénes son?
8. En los diálogos 2 y 3 del capítulo 16, leíste conversaciones sobre las relaciones familiares. ¿Qué te parecen las ideas de los papás y las de sus hijos, Rosario y Jaime, con respecto al matrimonio? Compara sus ideas con las tuyas y con las de la sociedad norteamericana.

S ***Mis sentimientos y pensamientos.*** Complete each of the following phrases, using the present subjunctive to express your feelings and thoughts in Spanish.

1. Yo quiero que...
2. Yo espero que...
3. Yo necesito que...
4. Me alegro de que...
5. Siento que...
6. Dudo que...
7. Es importante que...
8. Es posible que...
9. Es bueno que...
10. Es imprescindible que...
11. Es una lástima que...
12. Ojalá...

Verb Charts

Regular Verbs

-ar verbs

cantar *to sing*

INDICATIVE MOOD

PRESENT	canto, cantas, canta · cantamos, cantáis, cantan
IMPERFECT	cantaba, cantabas, cantaba · cantábamos, cantabais, cantaban
PRETERIT	canté, cantaste, cantó · cantamos, cantasteis, cantaron
FUTURE	cantaré, cantarás, cantará · cantaremos, cantaréis, cantarán
CONDITIONAL	cantaría, cantarías, cantaría · cantaríamos, cantaríais, cantarían
PRESENT PERFECT	he cantado, has cantado, ha cantado · hemos cantado, habéis cantado, han cantado
PLUPERFECT	había cantado, habías cantado, había cantado · habíamos cantado, habíais cantado, habían cantado
PRETERIT PERFECT	hube cantado, hubiste cantado, hubo cantado · hubimos cantado, hubisteis cantado, hubieron cantado
FUTURE PERFECT	habré cantado, habrás cantado, habrá cantado · habremos cantado, habréis cantado, habrán cantado
CONDITIONAL PERFECT	habría cantado, habrías cantado, habría cantado · habríamos cantado, habríais cantado, habrían cantado

SUBJUNCTIVE MOOD

PRESENT	cante, cantes, cante · cantemos, cantéis, canten
IMPERFECT	cantara, cantaras, cantara · cantáramos, cantarais, cantaran cantase, cantases, cantase · cantásemos, cantaseis, cantasen
PRESENT PERFECT	haya cantado, hayas cantado, haya cantado · hayamos cantado, hayáis cantado, hayan cantado
PLUPERFECT	hubiera/hubiese cantado, hubieras/hubieses cantado, hubiera/hubiese cantado · hubiéramos/hubiésemos cantado, hubierais/hubieseis cantado, hubieran/hubiesen cantado

IMPERATIVE MOOD

canta / no cantes (tú), cante (Ud.) · cantemos (nosotros), cantad / no cantéis (vosotros), canten (Uds.)

-er verbs

comer *to eat*

INDICATIVE MOOD

PRESENT	como, comes, come · comemos, coméis, comen
IMPERFECT	comía, comías, comía · comíamos, comíais, comían
PRETERIT	comí, comiste, comió · comimos, comisteis, comieron
FUTURE	comeré, comerás, comerá · comeremos, comeréis, comerán
CONDITIONAL	comería, comerías, comería · comeríamos, comeríais, comerían
PRESENT PERFECT	he comido, has comido, ha comido · hemos comido, habéis comido, han comido
PLUPERFECT	había comido, habías comido, había comido · habíamos comido, habíais comido, habían comido
PRETERIT PERFECT	hube comido, hubiste comido, hubo comido · hubimos comido, hubisteis comido, hubieron comido
FUTURE PERFECT	habré comido, habrás comido, habrá comido · habremos comido, habréis comido, habrán comido
CONDITIONAL PERFECT	habría comido, habrías comido, habría comido · habríamos comido, habríais comido, habrían comido

SUBJUNCTIVE MOOD

PRESENT	coma, comas, coma · comamos, comáis, coman
IMPERFECT	comiera, comieras, comiera · comiéramos, comierais, comieran comiese, comieses, comiese · comiésemos, comieseis, comiesen
PRESENT PERFECT	haya comido, hayas comido, haya comido · hayamos comido, hayáis comido, hayan comido
PLUPERFECT	hubiera/hubiese comido, hubieras/hubieses comido, hubiera/hubiese comido · hubiéramos/hubiésemos comido, hubierais/hubieseis comido, hubieran/hubiesen comido

IMPERATIVE MOOD

come / no comas (tú), coma (Ud.) ·
comamos (nosotros), comed / no comáis (vosotros), coman (Uds.)

-ir verbs

vivir *to live*

INDICATIVE MOOD

PRESENT	vivo, vives, vive · vivimos, vivís, viven
IMPERFECT	vivía, vivías, vivía · vivíamos, vivíais, vivían
PRETERIT	viví, viviste, vivió · vivimos, vivisteis, vivieron
FUTURE	viviré, vivirás, vivirá · viviremos, viviréis, vivirán
CONDITIONAL	viviría, vivirías, viviría · viviríamos, viviríais, vivirían
PRESENT PERFECT	he vivido, has vivido, ha vivido · hemos vivido, habéis vivido, han vivido
PLUPERFECT	había vivido, habías vivido, había vivido · habíamos vivido, habíais vivido, habían vivido
PRETERIT PERFECT	hube vivido, hubiste vivido, hubo vivido · hubimos vivido, hubisteis vivido, hubieron vivido
FUTURE PERFECT	habré vivido, habrás vivido, habrá vivido · habremos vivido, habréis vivido, habrán vivido
CONDITIONAL PERFECT	habría vivido, habrías vivido, habría vivido · habríamos vivido, habríais vivido, habrían vivido

SUBJUNCTIVE MOOD

PRESENT	viva, vivas, viva · vivamos, viváis, vivan
IMPERFECT	viviera, vivieras, viviera · viviéramos, vivierais, vivieran viviese, vivieses, viviese · viviésemos, vivieseis, viviesen
PRESENT PERFECT	haya vivido, hayas vivido, haya vivido · hayamos vivido, hayáis vivido, hayan vivido
PLUPERFECT	hubiera/hubiese vivido, hubieras/hubieses vivido, hubiera/hubiese vivido · hubiéramos/hubiésemos vivido, hubierais/hubieseis vivido, hubieran/hubiesen vivido

IMPERATIVE MOOD

vive / no vivas (tú), viva (Ud.) ·
vivamos (nosotros), vivid / no viváis (vosotros), vivan (Uds.)

Verbs with Changes in the Vowel of the Stem

pensar (**e** > **ie**) *to think*

PRESENT INDICATIVE	p**ie**nso, p**ie**nsas, p**ie**nsa · pensamos, pensáis, p**ie**nsan
PRESENT SUBJUNCTIVE	p**ie**nse, p**ie**nses, p**ie**nse · pensemos, penséis, p**ie**nsen
IMPERATIVE	p**ie**nsa / no p**ie**nses, p**ie**nse · pensemos, pensad / no penséis, p**ie**nsen

Other tenses and forms have no changes in the vowel of the stem.

entender (**e** > **ie**) *to understand*

PRESENT INDICATIVE	ent**ie**ndo, ent**ie**ndes, ent**ie**nde · entendemos, entendéis, ent**ie**nden
PRESENT SUBJUNCTIVE	ent**ie**nda, ent**ie**ndas, ent**ie**nda · entendamos, entendáis, ent**ie**ndan
IMPERATIVE	ent**ie**nde / no ent**ie**ndas, ent**ie**nda · entendamos, entended / no entendáis, ent**ie**ndan

Other tenses and forms have no changes in the vowel of the stem.

recordar (**o** > **ue**) *to remember*

PRESENT INDICATIVE	rec**ue**rdo, rec**ue**rdas, rec**ue**rda · recordamos, recordáis, rec**ue**rdan
PRESENT SUBJUNCTIVE	rec**ue**rde, rec**ue**rdes, rec**ue**rde · recordemos, recordéis, rec**ue**rden
IMPERATIVE	rec**ue**rda / no rec**ue**rdes, rec**ue**rde · recordemos, recordad / no recordéis, rec**ue**rden

Other tenses and forms have no changes in the vowel of the stem.

volver (**o** > **ue**) *to return*

PRESENT INDICATIVE	v**ue**lvo, v**ue**lves, v**ue**lve · volvemos, volvéis, v**ue**lven
PRESENT SUBJUNCTIVE	v**ue**lva, v**ue**lvas, v**ue**lva · volvamos, volváis, v**ue**lvan
IMPERATIVE	v**ue**lve / no v**ue**lvas, v**ue**lva · volvamos, volved / no volváis, v**ue**lvan

Other tenses and forms have no changes in the vowel of the stem.

Stem-changing **-ir** verbs have three types of possible changes in the vowel of the stem: **e** > **ie**, **e** > **i**, **o** > **ue**. In addition to the expected changes in the present subjunctive and imperative, verbs having the change **e** > **ie** and **e** > **i** have **i** as the stem vowel and verbs having the change **o** > **ue** have **u** as the stem vowel in the following forms:

- The **nosotros** and **vosotros** forms of the present subjunctive
- The **nosotros** command and the negative **vosotros** commands
- The third person singular and third person plural forms of the preterit
- All persons of the imperfect subjunctive (both **-ra** and **-se** forms)
- The present participle

Sample Conjugations

sentir (e > ie) *to feel, regret*

PRESENT INDICATIVE	siento, sientes, siente · sentimos, sentís, sienten
PRESENT SUBJUNCTIVE	sienta, sientas, sienta · sintamos, sintáis, sientan
IMPERATIVE	siente / no sientas, sienta · sintamos, sentid / no sintáis, sientan
PRETERIT	sentí, sentiste, sintió · sentimos, sentisteis, sintieron
IMPERFECT SUBJUNCTIVE	sintiera, sintieras, sintiera · sintiéramos, sintierais, sintieran sintiese, sintieses, sintiese · sintiésemos, sintieseis, sintiesen
PRESENT PARTICIPLE	sintiendo

Other tenses and forms have no changes in the vowel of the stem.

pedir (e > i) *to ask for*

PRESENT INDICATIVE	pido, pides, pide · pedimos, pedís, piden
PRESENT SUBJUNCTIVE	pida, pidas, pida · pidamos, pidáis, pidan
IMPERATIVE	pide / no pidas, pida · pidamos, pedid / no pidáis, pidan
PRETERIT	pedí, pediste, pidió · pedimos, pedisteis, pidieron
IMPERFECT SUBJUNCTIVE	pidiera, pidieras, pidiera · pidiéramos, pidierais, pidieran pidiese, pidieses, pidiese · pidiésemos, pidieseis, pidiesen
PRESENT PARTICIPLE	pidiendo

Other tenses and forms have no changes in the vowel of the stem.

dormir (o > ue) *to sleep*

PRESENT INDICATIVE	duermo, duermes, duerme · dormimos, dormís, duermen
PRESENT SUBJUNCTIVE	duerma, duermas, duerma · durmamos, durmáis, duerman
IMPERATIVE	duerme / no duermas, duerma · durmamos, dormid / no durmáis, duerman
PRETERIT	dormí, dormiste, durmió · dormimos, dormisteis, durmieron
IMPERFECT SUBJUNCTIVE	durmiera, durmieras, durmiera · durmiéramos, durmierais, durmieran durmiese, durmieses, durmiese · durmiésemos, durmieseis, durmiesen
PRESENT PARTICIPLE	durmiendo

Other tenses and forms have no changes in the vowel of the stem.

Verbs with Spelling Changes

These changes occur in the first person singular of the preterit, in all persons of the present subjunctive, and in imperative forms derived from the present subjunctive.

Verbs Ending in -car (c > qu before -e)

tocar *to play an instrument; to touch*

PRETERIT	toqué, tocaste, tocó · tocamos, tocasteis, tocaron
PRESENT SUBJUNCTIVE	toque, toques, toque · toquemos, toquéis, toquen
IMPERATIVE	toca / no toques, toque · toquemos, tocad / no toquéis, toquen

Verbs Ending in **-gar** (**g** > **gu** before **-e**)

llegar *to arrive*

PRETERIT	**llegué**, llegaste, llegó · llegamos, llegasteis, llegaron
PRESENT SUBJUNCTIVE	**llegue**, **llegues**, **llegue** · **lleguemos**, **lleguéis**, **lleguen**
IMPERATIVE	llega / no **llegues**, **llegue** · **lleguemos**, llegad / no **lleguéis**, **lleguen**

Verbs Ending in **-zar** (**z** > **c** before **-e**)

cruzar *to cross*

PRETERIT	**crucé**, cruzaste, cruzó · cruzamos, cruzasteis, cruzaron
PRESENT SUBJUNCTIVE	**cruce**, **cruces**, **cruce** · **crucemos**, **crucéis**, **crucen**
IMPERATIVE	cruza / no **cruces**, **cruce** · **crucemos**, cruzad / no **crucéis**, **crucen**

Verbs Ending in **-ger** and **-gir** (**g** > **j** before **-a** and **-o**)

recoger *to pick up*

PRESENT INDICATIVE	**recojo**, recoges, recoge · recogemos, recogéis, recogen
PRESENT SUBJUNCTIVE	**recoja**, **recojas**, **recoja** · **recojamos**, **recojáis**, **recojan**
IMPERATIVE	recoge / no **recojas**, **recoja** · **recojamos**, recoged / no **recojáis**, **recojan**

exigir *to demand*

PRESENT INDICATIVE	**exijo**, exiges, exige · exigimos, exigís, exigen
PRESENT SUBJUNCTIVE	**exija**, **exijas**, **exija** · **exijamos**, **exijáis**, **exijan**
IMPERATIVE	exige / no **exijas**, **exija** · **exijamos**, exegid / no **exijáis**, **exijan**

Verbs Ending in **-guir** (**gu** > **g** before **-a** and **-o**)

seguir *to follow*

PRESENT INDICATIVE	**sigo**, sigues, sigue · seguimos, seguís, siguen
PRESENT SUBJUNCTIVE	**siga**, **sigas**, **siga** · **sigamos**, **sigáis**, **sigan**
IMPERATIVE	sigue / no **sigas**, **siga** · **sigamos**, seguid / no **sigáis**, **sigan**

Verbs Ending in a Consonant + **-cer**, **-cir** (**c** > **z** before **-a** and **-o**)

convencer *to convince*

PRESENT INDICATIVE	**convenzo**, convences, convence · convencemos, convencéis, convencen
PRESENT SUBJUNCTIVE	**convenza**, **convenzas**, **convenza** · **convenzamos**, **convenzáis**, **convenzan**
IMPERATIVE	convence / no **convenzas**, **convenza** · **convenzamos**, convenced / no **convenzáis**, **convenzan**

-Er Verbs Having Stems Ending in a Vowel

These verbs change the **i** of the preterit endings **-ió** and **-ieron** and the **i** of the present participle ending **-iendo** to **y**. The **y** appears in all persons of the imperfect subjunctive. These verbs also add written accents to the endings of the second person singular and the first and second person plural forms of the preterit and the past participle.

creer *to believe*

PRETERIT	creí, creíste, creyó · creímos, creísteis, creyeron
IMPERFECT SUBJUNCTIVE	creyera (creyese), creyeras, creyera · creyéramos, creyerais, creyeran
PRESENT PARTICIPLE	creyendo
PAST PARTICIPLE	creído

-Ar Verbs Having Stems Ending in Syllabic -i or -u (Not as Part of a Diphthong)

These verbs have an accent mark over the **i** or **u** in all persons of the singular and in the third person plural of the present indicative and present subjunctive, and in all imperative forms except **nosotros** and **vosotros**.

enviar *to send*

PRESENT	envío, envías, envía · enviamos, enviáis, envían
PRESENT SUBJUNCTIVE	envíe, envíes, envíe · enviemos, enviéis, envíen
IMPERATIVE	envía / no envíes, envíe · enviemos, enviad / no enviéis, envíen

continuar *to continue*

PRESENT	contin**ú**o, contin**ú**as, contin**ú**a · continuamos, continuáis, contin**ú**an
PRESENT SUBJUNCTIVE	contin**ú**e, contin**ú**es, contin**ú**e · continuemos, continuéis, contin**ú**en
IMPERATIVE	contin**ú**a / no contin**ú**es, contin**ú**e · continuemos, continuad / no continuéis, contin**ú**en

Irregular Verbs

Only tenses with irregular forms are shown.

Verbs Ending in a Vowel + -cer or -ucir

These verbs change the final **-c** of the stem to **-zc** before **-a** and **-o**. The **-zc** appears in the first person singular of the present indicative, in all persons of the present subjunctive, and in imperative forms derived from the present subjunctive.

The verb **mecer** (*to rock a child/cradle*) is conjugated like **convencer**, and not like **conocer**: present **mezo**, **meces**, etc.; present subjunctive **meza**, **mezas**, etc. The verb **cocer** is also conjugated like **convencer** and, in addition, has the stem change **o** > **ue**: present **cuezo**, **cueces**, etc.; present subjunctive **cueza**, **cuezas**, etc.

conocer *to know*

PRESENT INDICATIVE	cono**zc**o, conoces, conoce · conocemos, conocéis, conocen
PRESENT SUBJUNCTIVE	cono**zc**a, cono**zc**as, cono**zc**a · cono**zc**amos, cono**zc**áis, cono**zc**an
IMPERATIVE	conoce / no cono**zc**as, cono**zc**a · cono**zc**amos, conoced / no cono**zc**áis, cono**zc**an

conducir *to drive*

PRESENT INDICATIVE	condu**zc**o, conduces, conduce · conducimos, conducís, conducen
PRESENT SUBJUNCTIVE	condu**zc**a, condu**zc**as, condu**zc**a · condu**zc**amos, condu**zc**áis, condu**zc**an
IMPERATIVE	conduce / no condu**zc**as, condu**zc**a · condu**zc**amos, conducid / no condu**zc**áis, condu**zc**an

Verbs Ending in -uir (Not Including Those Ending in -guir)

These verbs add **y** before a vowel other than **i** and change the unaccented **i** between vowels to **y**. The **y** appears in all singular forms and in the third person plural of the present, in the third person singular and plural of the preterit, in all persons of the present and imperfect subjunctive, and in all imperative forms except the affirmative **vosotros** command.

construir *to build*

PRESENT INDICATIVE	constru**y**o, constru**y**es, constru**y**e · construimos, construís, constru**y**en
PRETERIT	construí, construiste, constru**y**ó · construimos, construisteis, constru**y**eron
IMPERATIVE	constru**y**e / no constru**y**as, constru**y**a · constru**y**amos, construid / no constru**y**áis, constru**y**an
PRESENT SUBJUNCTIVE	constru**y**a, constru**y**as, constru**y**a · constru**y**amos, constru**y**áis, constru**y**an
IMPERFECT SUBJUNCTIVE	constru**y**era (constru**y**ese), constru**y**eras, constru**y**era · constru**y**éramos, constru**y**erais, constru**y**eran

Other Irregular Verbs

Only tenses with irregular forms are shown.

andar *to walk*

PRETERIT	anduve, anduviste, anduvo · anduvimos, anduvisteis, anduvieron
IMPERFECT SUBJUNCTIVE	anduviera (anduviese), anduvieras, anduviera · anduviéramos, anduvierais, anduvieran

caber *to fit*

PRESENT INDICATIVE	quepo, cabes, cabe · cabemos, cabéis, caben
PRETERIT	cupe, cupiste, cupo · cupimos, cupisteis, cupieron
FUTURE	cabré, cabrás, cabrá · cabremos, cabréis, cabrán
CONDITIONAL	cabría, cabrías, cabría · cabríamos, cabríais, cabrían
IMPERATIVE	cabe / no quepas, quepa · quepamos, cabed / no quepáis, quepan
PRESENT SUBJUNCTIVE	quepa, quepas, quepa · quepamos, quepáis, quepan
IMPERFECT SUBJUNCTIVE	cupiera (cupiese), cupieras, cupiera · cupiéramos, cupierais, cupieran

caer *to fall*

PRESENT INDICATIVE	caigo, caes, cae · caemos, caéis, caen
PRETERIT	caí, caíste, cayó · caímos, caísteis, cayeron
IMPERATIVE	cae / no caigas, caiga · caigamos, caed / no caigáis, caigan
PRESENT SUBJUNCTIVE	caiga, caigas, caiga · caigamos, caigáis, caigan
IMPERFECT SUBJUNCTIVE	cayera (cayese), cayeras, cayera · cayéramos, cayerais, cayeran
PRESENT PARTICIPLE	cayendo
PAST PARTICIPLE	caído

dar *to give*

PRESENT INDICATIVE	doy, das, da · damos, dais, dan
PRETERIT	di, diste, dio · dimos, disteis, dieron
IMPERATIVE	da / no des, dé · demos, dad / no deis, den
PRESENT SUBJUNCTIVE	dé, des, dé · demos, deis, den
IMPERFECT SUBJUNCTIVE	diera (diese), dieras, diera · diéramos, dierais, dieran

decir *to say, tell*

PRESENT INDICATIVE	digo, dices, dice · decimos, decís, dicen
PRETERIT	dije, dijiste, dijo · dijimos, dijisteis, dijeron
FUTURE	diré, dirás, dirá · diremos, diréis, dirán
CONDITIONAL	diría, dirías, diría · diríamos, diríais, dirían
IMPERATIVE	di / no digas, diga · digamos, decid / no digáis, digan
PRESENT SUBJUNCTIVE	diga, digas, diga · digamos, digáis, digan
IMPERFECT SUBJUNCTIVE	dijera (dijese), dijeras, dijera · dijéramos, dijerais, dijeran
PRESENT PARTICIPLE	diciendo
PAST PARTICIPLE	dicho

estar *to be*

PRESENT INDICATIVE	estoy, estás, está · estamos, estáis, están
PRETERIT	estuve, estuviste, estuvo · estuvimos, estuvisteis, estuvieron
IMPERATIVE	está / no estés, esté · estemos, estad / no estéis, estén
PRESENT SUBJUNCTIVE	esté, estés, esté · estemos, estéis, estén
IMPERFECT SUBJUNCTIVE	estuviera (estuviese), estuvieras, estuviera · estuviéramos, estuvierais, estuvieran

haber *to have* (auxiliary verb)

PRESENT INDICATIVE	he, has, ha · hemos, habéis, han
PRETERIT	hube, hubiste, hubo · hubimos, hubisteis, hubieron
FUTURE	habré, habrás, habrá · habremos, habréis, habrán
CONDITIONAL	habría, habrías, habría · habríamos, habríais, habrían
PRESENT SUBJUNCTIVE	haya, hayas, haya · hayamos, hayáis, hayan
IMPERFECT SUBJUNCTIVE	hubiera (hubiese), hubieras, hubiera · hubiéramos, hubierais, hubieran

hacer *to do, make*

PRESENT INDICATIVE	hago, haces, hace · hacemos, hacéis, hacen
PRETERIT	hice, hiciste, hizo · hicimos, hiciste, hicieron
FUTURE	haré, harás, hará · haremos, haréis, harán
CONDITIONAL	haría, harías, haría · haríamos, haríais, harían
IMPERATIVE	haz / no hagas, haga · hagamos, haced / no hagáis, hagan
PRESENT SUBJUNCTIVE	haga, hagas, haga · hagamos, hagáis, hagan
IMPERFECT SUBJUNCTIVE	hiciera (hiciese), hicieras, hiciera · hiciéramos, hicierais, hicieran
PAST PARTICIPLE	hecho

ir *to go*

PRESENT INDICATIVE	voy, vas, va · vamos, vais, van
IMPERFECT	iba, ibas, iba · íbamos, ibais, iban
PRETERIT	fui, fuiste, fue · fuimos, fuisteis, fueron
IMPERATIVE	ve / no vayas, vaya · vamos / no vayamos, id / no vayáis, vayan
PRESENT SUBJUNCTIVE	vaya, vayas, vaya · vayamos, vayáis, vayan
IMPERFECT SUBJUNCTIVE	fuera (fuese), fueras, fuera · fuéramos, fuerais, fueran
PRESENT PARTICIPLE	yendo

oír *to hear*

PRESENT INDICATIVE	oigo, oyes, oye · oímos, oís, oyen
PRETERIT	oí, oíste, oyó · oímos, oísteis, oyeron
IMPERATIVE	oye / no oigas, oiga · oigamos, oíd / no oigáis, oigan
PRESENT SUBJUNCTIVE	oiga, oigas, oiga · oigamos, oigáis, oigan
IMPERFECT SUBJUNCTIVE	oyera (oyese), oyeras, oyera · oyéramos, oyerais, oyeran
PRESENT PARTICIPLE	oyendo
PAST PARTICIPLE	oído

poder *to be able, can*

PRESENT INDICATIVE	puedo, puedes, puede · podemos, podéis, pueden
PRETERIT	pude, pudiste, pudo · pudimos, pudisteis, pudieron
FUTURE	podré, podrás, podrá · podremos, podréis, podrán
CONDITIONAL	podría, podrías, podría · podríamos, podríais, podrían
PRESENT SUBJUNCTIVE	pueda, puedas, pueda · podamos, podáis, puedan
IMPERFECT SUBJUNCTIVE	pudiera (pudiese), pudieras, pudiera · pudiéramos, pudierais, pudieran
PRESENT PARTICIPLE	pudiendo

poner *to put*

PRESENT INDICATIVE	pongo, pones, pone · ponemos, ponéis, ponen
PRETERIT	puse, pusiste, puso · pusimos, pusisteis, pusieron
FUTURE	pondré, pondrás, pondrá · pondremos, pondréis, pondrán
CONDITIONAL	pondría, pondrías, pondría · pondríamos, pondríais, pondrían
IMPERATIVE	pon / no pongas, ponga · pongamos, poned / no pongáis, pongan
PRESENT SUBJUNCTIVE	ponga, pongas, ponga · pongamos, pongáis, pongan
IMPERFECT SUBJUNCTIVE	pusiera (pusiese), pusieras, pusiera · pusiéramos, pusierais, pusieran
PAST PARTICIPLE	puesto

producir *to produce*

PRESENT INDICATIVE	produzco, produces, produce · producimos, producís, producen
PRETERIT	produje, produjiste, produjo · produjimos, produjisteis, produjeron
IMPERATIVE	produce / no produzcas, produzca · produzcamos, producid / no produzcáis, produzcan
PRESENT SUBJUNCTIVE	produzca, produzcas, produzca · produzcamos, produzcáis, produzcan
IMPERFECT SUBJUNCTIVE	produjera (produjese), produjeras, produjera · produjéramos, produjerais, produjeran

querer *to want*

PRESENT INDICATIVE	quiero, quieres, quiere · queremos, queréis, quieren
PRETERIT	quise, quisiste, quiso · quisimos, quisisteis, quisieron
FUTURE	querré, querrás, querrá · querremos, querréis, querrán
CONDITIONAL	querría, querrías, querría · querríamos, querríais, querrían
IMPERATIVE	quiere / no quieras, quiera · queramos, quered / no queráis, quieran
PRESENT SUBJUNCTIVE	quiera, quieras, quiera · queramos, queráis, quieran
IMPERFECT SUBJUNCTIVE	quisiera (quisiese), quisieras, quisiera · quisiéramos, quisierais, quisieran

saber *to know*

PRESENT INDICATIVE	sé, sabes, sabe · sabemos, sabéis, saben
PRETERIT	supe, supiste, supo · supimos, supisteis, supieron
FUTURE	sabré, sabrás, sabrá · sabremos, sabréis, sabrán
CONDITIONAL	sabría, sabrías, sabría · sabríamos, sabríais, sabrían
IMPERATIVE	sabe / no sepas, sepa · sepamos, sabed / no sepáis, sepan
PRESENT SUBJUNCTIVE	sepa, sepas, sepa · sepamos, sepáis, sepan
IMPERFECT SUBJUNCTIVE	supiera (supiese), supieras, supiera · supiéramos, supierais, supieran

salir *to go out*

PRESENT INDICATIVE	salgo, sales, sale · salimos, salís, salen
FUTURE	saldré, saldrás, saldrá · saldremos, saldréis, saldrán
CONDITIONAL	saldría, saldrías, saldría · saldríamos, saldríais, saldrían
IMPERATIVE	sal / no salgas, salga · salgamos, salid / no salgáis, salgan
PRESENT SUBJUNCTIVE	salga, salgas, salga · salgamos, salgáis, salgan

ser *to be*

PRESENT INDICATIVE	soy, eres, es · somos, sois, son
IMPERFECT	era, eras, era · éramos, erais, eran
PRETERIT	fui, fuiste, fue · fuimos, fuisteis, fueron
IMPERATIVE	sé / no seas, sea · seamos, sed / no seáis, sean
PRESENT SUBJUNCTIVE	sea, seas, sea · seamos, seáis, sean
IMPERFECT SUBJUNCTIVE	fuera (fuese), fueras, fuera · fuéramos, fuerais, fueran

tener *to have*

PRESENT INDICATIVE	tengo, tienes, tiene · tenemos, tenéis, tienen
PRETERIT	tuve, tuviste, tuvo · tuvimos, tuvisteis, tuvieron
FUTURE	tendré, tendrás, tendrá · tendremos, tendréis, tendrán
CONDITIONAL	tendría, tendrías, tendría · tendríamos, tendríais, tendrían
IMPERATIVE	ten / no tengas, tenga · tengamos, tened / no tengáis, tengan
PRESENT SUBJUNCTIVE	tenga, tengas, tenga · tengamos, tengáis, tengan
IMPERFECT SUBJUNCTIVE	tuviera (tuviese), tuvieras, tuviera · tuviéramos, tuvierais, tuvieran

traer *to bring*

PRESENT INDICATIVE	traigo, traes, trae · traemos, traéis, traen
PRETERIT	traje, trajiste, trajo · trajimos, trajisteis, trajeron
IMPERATIVE	trae / no traigas, traiga · traigamos, traed / no traigáis, traigan
PRESENT SUBJUNCTIVE	traiga, traigas, traiga · traigamos, traigáis, traigan
IMPERFECT SUBJUNCTIVE	trajera (trajese), trajeras, trajera · trajéramos, trajerais, trajeran
PRESENT PARTICIPLE	trayendo
PAST PARTICIPLE	traído

valer *to be worth*

PRESENT INDICATIVE	valgo, vales, vale · valemos, valéis, valen
FUTURE	valdré, valdrás, valdrá · valdremos, valdréis, valdrán
CONDITIONAL	valdría, valdrías, valdría · valdríamos, valdríais, valdrían
IMPERATIVE	vale / no valgas, valga · valgamos, valed / no valgáis, valgan
PRESENT SUBJUNCTIVE	valga, valgas, valga · valgamos, valgáis, valgan

venir *to come*

PRESENT INDICATIVE	vengo, vienes, viene · venimos, venís, vienen
PRETERIT	vine, viniste, vino · vinimos, vinisteis, vinieron
FUTURE	vendré, vendrás, vendrá · vendremos, vendréis, vendrán
CONDITIONAL	vendría, vendrías, vendría · vendríamos, vendríais, vendrían
IMPERATIVE	ven / no vengas, venga · vengamos, venid / no vengáis, vengan
PRESENT SUBJUNCTIVE	venga, vengas, venga · vengamos, vengáis, vengan
IMPERFECT SUBJUNCTIVE	viniera (viniese), vinieras, viniera · viniéramos, vinierais, vinieran
PRESENT PARTICIPLE	viniendo

ver *to see*

PRESENT INDICATIVE	veo, ves, ve · vemos, veis, ven
IMPERFECT	veía, veías, veía · veíamos, veíais, veían
PRETERIT	vi, viste, vio · vimos, visteis, vieron
IMPERATIVE	ve / no veas, vea · veamos, ved / no veáis, vean
PRESENT SUBJUNCTIVE	vea, veas, vea · veamos, veáis, vean
IMPERFECT SUBJUNCTIVE	viera (viese), vieras, viera · viéramos, vierais, vieran
PAST PARTICIPLE	visto

Answer Key

1 Getting Around Town—Where Is It?

A

1. ¿Qué hay en el cartapacio? / Hay un teléfono celular en el cartapacio. 2. ¿Hay carpetas en la gaveta? / Sí, las hay. 3. ¿Qué hay en el estante? / Hay libros en el estante. 4. ¿Hay CDs (cedés) en el paquete? / Sí, los hay. 5. ¿Hay una computadora en la mochila? / No, hay una cámara.

B

1. Es un billetero. 2. Es una cartera. 3. Es un reloj. 4. Es una agenda electrónica. 5. Es un bolso. 6. Es una cámara. 7. Es un iPod. 8. Es un cartapacio.

C

1. El billetero no es para José. Es para Juan. 2. La cartera no es para Matilde. Es para Julia. 3. El reloj no es para Jorge. Es para Alberto. 4. La agenda electrónica no es para Lorenzo. Es para Nora. 5. El bolso no es para Rosa. Es para Margarita. 6. La cámara no es para Luz. Es para Daniel. 7. El iPod no es para Susana. Es para Guillermo. 8. El cartapacio no es para Carlos. Es para Roberto.

D

1. la / una 2. el / un 3. el / un 4. la / una 5. el / un 6. la / una 7. la / una 8. la / una 9. la / una 10. el / un 11. el / un 12. la / una 13. el / un 14. la / una 15. el / un 16. el / un

E

1. el mes 2. la gente 3. la mochila 4. el carro 5. el regalo 6. la maleta 7. la clase 8. la computadora 9. el libro 10. el reloj

F

1. teléfono 2. cartera 3. el cibercafé 4. hay 5. en 6. pulsera 7. las 8. cartapacio

G

1. ¿Qué hay en el armario? 2. ¿Es un regalo? 3. ¿Es cómodo el hotel? 4. ¿Qué flores hay? 5. ¿Qué cafés hay en la ciudad? 6. ¿Hay unos papeles en la mochila? 7. ¿Que libros hay en los estantes? 8. ¿El juguete es para Juanito?

H

1. La cámara no es un regalo. 2. No hay una computadora en el armario. 3. No es un iPod. 4. El paquete no es para Miguel. 5. No hay un cibercafé por aquí. 6. No hay maletas en el carro. 7. No es una oficina cómoda. 8. No hay dinero en el billetero.

I

1. No, no es una agenda electrónica. 2. No, no hay libros en el estante. 3. No, el reloj no es para Carlos. 4. No, no hay un supermercado por aquí. 5. No, no es un regalo para Julieta. 6. No, no hay ropa en la maleta. 7. No, no hay un cartapacio en la oficina. 8. No, no es un problema.

J

1. las maletas / unas maletas 2. los cines / unos cines 3. los relojes / unos relojes 4. las librerías / unas librerías 5. los problemas / unos problemas 6. las oficinas / unas oficinas 7. los teatros / unos teatros 8. los restaurantes / unos restaurantes 9. los papeles / unos papeles 10. las ciudades / unas ciudades 11. los teléfonos / unos teléfonos 12. las flores / unas flores 13. los meses / unos meses 14. las calles / unas calles 15. los maletines / unos maletines 16. las luces / unas luces

K

1. el libro / un libro 2. la bolsa / una bolsa 3. la clase / una clase 4. el lugar / un lugar 5. el hotel / un hotel 6. la llave / una llave 7. el tren / un tren 8. el animal / un animal 9. la cosa / una cosa 10. la vez / una vez 11. la pulsera / una pulsera 12. la cámara / una cámara 13. el mapa / un mapa 14. el tema / un tema 15. el café / un café 16. el hospital / un hospital

L
1. —Perdón, señor. ¿Hay un banco por aquí?
—Sí, señorita, hay uno en la esquina.
—Gracias, señor. —De nada. Adiós.
2. —Por favor, señorita. ¿Dónde hay una peluquería? —Hay una en la esquina, señora.
—Muchas gracias, señorita. —De nada, señora.

M
1. la tienda de ropa / las tiendas de ropa
2. la tienda de cómputo / las tiendas de cómputo
3. la tienda de zapatos / las tiendas de zapatos
4. la tienda de electrodomésticos / las tiendas de electrodomésticos 5. la tienda de deportes / las tiendas de deportes 6. la tienda por departamentos / las tiendas por departamentos

N
1. el libro de texto / los libros de texto 2. la base de datos / las bases de datos 3. el museo de arte / los museos de arte 4. la tarjeta de crédito / las tarjetas de crédito 5. la oficina de turismo / las oficinas de turismo 6. el salón de belleza / los salones de belleza

O
1. una computadora 2. dos ciudades
3. tres relojes 4. cuatro cosas 5. cinco cines
6. seis tiendas de ropa 7. siete hoteles 8. ocho regalos 9. nueve cámaras 10. diez heladerías
11. once cajas 12. doce cibercafés 13. trece mochilas 14. catorce teléfonos 15. quince días
16. dieciséis supermercados 17. diecisiete fotos
18. dieciocho tiendas por departamentos
19. diecinueve paquetes 20. veinte deportes

P
1. ¿Cómo? ¿Cuántos? 2. ¿Cómo? ¿Cuántos?
3. ¿Cómo? ¿Cuántas? 4. ¿Cómo? ¿Cuántos?
5. ¿Cómo? ¿Cuántas? 6. ¿Cómo? ¿Cuántos?
7. ¿Cómo? ¿Cuántas? 8. ¿Cómo? ¿Cuántas?
9. ¿Cómo? ¿Cuántos? 10. ¿Cómo? ¿Cuántas?

Q
1. un museo de arte 2. seis meses 3. la tienda por departamentos 4. una tarjeta de crédito
5. el centro comercial 6. once tiendas de cómputo
7. veinte paquetes 8. unas ciudades

R
1. la cámara 2. el documento 3. el sistema
4. el teléfono 5. la computadora 6. el análisis
7. el turismo 8. el arte 9. el teatro 10. el crédito
11. la farmacia 12. el museo 13. el texto
14. el supermercado 15. el problema
16. el departamento 17. el mapa 18. el banco

S
Answers will vary.

2 Describing Places and Things

A
1. El condominio es nuevo también. 2. La zona es comercial también. 3. La catedral es maravillosa también. 4. El café es animado también.
5. La tienda por departamentos es grande también.
6. El cartapacio es pequeño también. 7. El celular es útil también. 8. La habitación es oscura también. 9. La cámara es vieja también.
10. La calle es bonita también.

B
1. Los exámenes son difíciles también.
2. Las cajas son chiquitas también. 3. Los relojes son hermosos también. 4. Las tiendas de deportes son modernas también. 5. Las películas son interesantes también. 6. Las joyas son caras también. 7. Las farmacias son grandes también.
8. Los cartapacios son buenos también.
9. Las computadoras son útiles también.
10. Los restaurantes son malos también.

C
1. buen 2. tercera 3. algunos 4. primer
5. malas 6. gran 7. ningún 8. algún

D
1. la primera semana 2. algunas avenidas animadas 3. ciertas calles transitadas 4. bastantes zonas peatonales 5. cualquier periódico importante 6. varias revistas pesadas 7. ninguna computadora vieja 8. muchos problemas difíciles
9. ningún coche ruidoso 10. poca ropa barata

E
1. Son unas niñas grandes. 2. Es el mismo perro.
3. Hay algunas personas pobres. 4. Es su única oportunidad. 5. Es una civilización antigua.
6. Es medio americano. 7. Es un gran científico.
8. Hay ciertas cosas.

F
1. La avenida es animada y muy transitada.
2. Las casas son hermosas y muy caras.
3. Las calles son comerciales y muy ruidosas.
4. La biblioteca es vieja y muy importante.
5. La tienda por departamentos es nueva y muy grande. 6. Los condominios son pequeños y muy baratos. 7. La zona es tranquila y muy bonita.
8. Los garajes son oscuros y muy feos. 9. El salón de belleza es lindo y muy bueno. 10. Los jardines son peatonales y muy interesantes.

G

1. ¿Hay mucho ruido en el barrio? / No, la zona no es muy ruidosa. 2. ¿Cómo es la casa? / Es moderna y hermosa. / Y los cuartos, ¿cómo son? / Son claros y pequeños. 3. Los regalos son para Raquel. / ¿Qué hay en esta caja bonita? / Es una pulsera. 4. ¿Hay un centro comercial por aquí? / Sí, hay veinte tiendas. / No es muy grande. / No, pero las tiendas son muy buenas. 5. El jardín es lindo y hay muchas flores. / ¿No son hermosas? / El jardín es muy tranquilo. / Sí, es un lugar maravilloso.

H

1. los estantes de la librería 2. el maletín del director 3. el cibercafé de la esquina 4. los temas del documento 5. el supermercado del barrio 6. el condominio de la señorita 7. los teatros del centro 8. las computadoras de la oficina 9. el mapa de la ciudad 10. la luz del día 11. los coches de los garajes 12. los electrodomésticos de las casas 13. los datos del libro 14. el ruido del carro 15. los problemas de los museos 16. las cámaras del banco

I

1. la farmacia de la esquina 2. la oficina del director 3. las llaves del apartamento 4. los juguetes de la juguetería 5. las flores del jardín 6. los armarios de la habitación 7. los relojes de la joyería 8. el cine del barrio 9. las tiendas de la zona comercial 10. los datos de la agenda electrónica

J

1. su clase 2. mis libros 3. nuestro barrio 4. su dinero 5. sus perros 6. sus maletas 7. tu billetero (cartera) 8. mi teléfono celular 9. sus problemas 10. sus tarjetas de crédito 11. nuestras carpetas 12. su calle 13. tus zapatos 14. nuestra ciudad 15. su hotel 16. nuestros juguetes 17. sus tiendas de cómputo 18. sus tarjetas de embarque

K

1. su / Su 2. su / su 3. su / nuestra 4. sus / sus 5. sus / Sus 6. su / mi 7. sus / Mis 8. sus / nuestros

L

1. la ropa negra y blanca 2. unos carros azules 3. mi cuarto verde 4. muchas flores rojas y amarillas 5. sus maletas grises 6. tu mochila morada (violeta) 7. unas carteras marrones 8. su camiseta azul claro 9. los abrigos azul oscuro 10. unos bolsos beige

M

1. ¿Cómo es su casa? 2. ¿Cuántas tarjetas de crédito hay en su billetero? / ¿Qué hay en su billetero? 3. ¿De qué color es tu (su) carro? 4. ¿Qué hay en la caja? 5. ¿Dónde queda el restaurante mexicano? / ¿Qué queda en la esquina? 6. ¿Cómo son las revistas? 7. ¿Para quién son los regalos? 8. ¿Dónde queda el museo de arte? 9. ¿Cuántos estudiantes hay en la clase? 10. ¿Qué es? 11. ¿Qué son? 12. ¿De qué color es el interior de su casa? 13. ¿Qué tiendas hay en esta avenida? 14. ¿Cómo es su jardín?

N

1. ¿Son útiles los teléfonos celulares? 2. ¿Es caro su reloj? 3. ¿Son muy transitados los paseos? 4. ¿Es vieja la catedral? 5. ¿Son difíciles las preguntas? 6. ¿Son inteligentes Ana y Fernando? 7. ¿Es bueno el hotel? 8. ¿Es muy ruidosa esta calle? 9. ¿Son hermosas las flores? 10. ¿Es aburrido el profesor?

O

1. Mi clase de historia es muy interesante. 2. Las casas son tan hermosas. 3. El libro de arte es realmente maravilloso. 4. Es una ciudad bastante grande. 5. ¿Son demasiado largos los informes? 6. Nuestra empresa es relativamente nueva. 7. Unas calles son poco transitadas. 8. Sus hijos son sumamente inteligentes. 9. ¿Es verdaderamente tranquilo tu barrio? 10. ¿No son suficientemente modernas las oficinas?

P

1. quince folletos largos 2. unas avenidas animadas 3. en el maletín 4. mi examen de química 5. muchas flores amarillas 6. veinte habitaciones modernas 7. para nuestros amigos 8. el carro rojo 9. sus clases de matemáticas. 10. en los paseos transitados

Q

1. ¿Es animado tu barrio? / No, mi barrio es bastante tranquilo. 2. ¿Son interesantes sus libros de biología? / No, nuestros libros de biología son aburridos. 3. ¿Es nueva su empresa? / Sí, su empresa es nueva y muy importante. 4. ¿Son negras sus maletas? / No, sus maletas son marrones. 5. ¿Son difíciles sus artículos? / No, sus artículos son fáciles.

R

1. importante 2. difícil 3. ruidoso 4. tranquilo 5. comercial 6. nuevo 7. claro 8. interesante 9. hermoso 10. fácil 11. anaranjado 12. grande 13. transitado 14. oscuro 15. bueno 16. útil 17. cómodo 18. moderno 19. peatonal 20. animado 21. viejo 22. malo 23. verdadero

S

Answers will vary.

3 Nationalities, Professions, Food, and Films

A

1. Ud., él 2. nosotros 3. Uds., ellas 4. yo 5. Ud., ella 6. Uds., ellos, ellas 7. tú 8. nosotras

B

1. Eres de México. 2. Son de México. 3. Soy de México. 4. Son de México. 5. Es de México. 6. Somos de México. 7. Es de México. 8. Son de México.

C

1. De España, no. Son de los Estados Unidos.
2. De China, no. Es de los Estados Unidos.
3. De Australia, no. Soy de los Estados Unidos.
4. De Colombia, no. Es de los Estados Unidos.
5. De Alemania, no. Somos de los Estados Unidos.
6. De Irlanda, no. Son de los Estados Unidos.
7. De Corea del Sur, no. Soy de los Estados Unidos.
8. De Perú, no. Son de los Estados Unidos.

D

1. Sí, es escocés. 2. Sí, son tailandeses. 3. Sí, es vietnamita. 4. Sí, somos costarricenses. 5. Sí, son israelíes. 6. Sí, es sueca. 7. Sí, es belga. 8. Sí, son taiwanesas. 9. Sí, es iraní. 10. Sí, son egipcios.

E

Raquel es ecuatoriana, pero de origen alemán. 2. Los señores Fuentes son brasileños, pero de origen danés. 3. Yo soy escocés, pero de origen austríaco. 4. María y Catalina son salvadoreñas, pero de origen libanés. 5. Tú eres belga, pero de origen iraní. 6. Regina y Mauricio son uruguayos, pero de origen ucranio (ucraniano). 7. Uds. son francesas, pero de origen paquistaní. 8. La señorita Rivas es israelí, pero de origen polaco. 9. Victoria y yo somos ingleses, pero de origen marroquí. 10. Ignacio y Alberto son nicaragüenses, pero de origen vietnamita.

F

1. el sueco 2. el portugués 3. el ruso 4. el finlandés 5. el francés 6. el alemán 7. el japonés 8. el italiano 9. el vietnamita 10. el holandés 11. el chino 12. el árabe 13. el alemán 14. el español 15. el coreano 16. el tailandés

G

1. ¡Qué hoteles más modernos! 2. ¡Qué comida tan sabrosa! 3. ¡Qué libro más interesante! 4. ¡Qué señoras tan simpáticas! 5. ¡Qué ciudad más animada! 6. ¡Qué temas tan importantes! 7. ¡Qué informe más aburrido! 8. ¡Qué calles tan ruidosas! 9. ¡Qué jardín más tranquilo! 10. ¡Qué estudiantes tan inteligentes!

H

1. ¡Qué día! 2. ¡Qué maravilloso! 3. ¡Qué postre! 4. ¡Qué feo! 5. ¡Qué fácil! 6. ¡Qué músico! 7. ¡Qué auténtico! 8. ¡Qué pintora!

I

1. ¿De dónde es Ud.? / Soy norteamericano, de Los Ángeles. / ¡Qué casualidad! Yo también soy de California, de San Francisco. 2. Mi esposo (marido) y yo somos ingleses, de Londres. / ¿De veras? Mi esposa (mujer) y yo también somos de Londres. ¿De qué parte de la ciudad? 3. ¿De qué origen eres? / Soy de origen irlandés. ¿Y tú? / Mi familia es de origen escocés. 4. ¿De quién es la tarjeta de embarque? / Es del señor Aguilar. 5. ¿Para quién es el regalo? / Es para mi novia.

J

1. ¿Es peruano el marido de Anita? 2. ¿Es hondureña Pilar? 3. ¿Son guatemaltecos los esposos? 4. ¿Es chilena su (tu) mujer? 5. ¿Es ecuatoriano Rafael? 6. ¿Son costarricenses los novios? 7. ¿Son brasileños su marido y Ud.? (¿Son brasileños tu marido y tú?) 8. ¿Son panameñas Blanca y Consuelo?

K

1. No, Jaime no es de Venezuela. 2. No, no soy de origen europeo. 3. No, Manuel no es el esposo de Carolina. 4. No, sus estudiantes no son hindúes. 5. No, la profesora Arriaga no es griega. 6. No, Santiago y Emilia no son novios. 7. No, no somos de la capital. 8. No, nuestra familia no es de Marruecos.

L
1. ningún queso suizo 2. varios jamones ingleses 3. bastante torta italiana 4. pocas uvas chilenas 5. algunas nueces españolas 6. suficiente aceite de oliva griego 7. algún pescado japonés 8. varias manzanas estadounidenses

M
1. carnes y aves 2. lácteos 3. frutas 4. postres 5. legumbres 6. carnes y aves 7. legumbres 8. postres 9. lácteos 10. frutas 11. lácteos 12. carnes y aves 13. frutas 14. postres 15. legumbres 16. frutas 17. legumbres 18. postres 19. carnes y aves 20. lácteos

N
1. en 2. Para / de / para / con / para 3. de / de 4. en 5. de 6. de / en 7. con / en / por 8. De 9. con OR en 10. de / para 11. Por / por / en 12. del 13. De / de / en 14. De 15. con / en 16. de / con / en

O
1. esta / esa / aquella 2. este / ese / aquel 3. estos / esos / aquellos 4. estas / esas / aquellas 5. esta / esa / aquella 6. este / ese / aquel 7. estas / esas / aquellas 8. estos / esos / aquellos 9. este / ese / aquel 10. esta / esa / aquella

P
1. Estas programadoras son buenas. 2. Este asesor es muy inteligente. 3. Estos dentistas son viejos. 4. Esta cocinera es italiana. 5. Este escritor es famoso. 6. Estos músicos son de Cuba. 7. Este cantante es brasileño. 8. Esta abogada es trabajadora. 9. Estas bailarinas son maravillosas. 10. Estos médicos son hindúes.

Q
1. toda la ciudad 2. todas las películas 3. todos los vinos 4. todo el centro 5. todo el país 6. todo el mes 7. toda la semana 8. todas las comidas 9. todo el barrio 10. todas las actrices

R
1. la desarrolladora de programas 2. la desarrolladora de web 3. la administradora de bases de datos 4. la arquitecta de red 5. la analista de seguridad de (la) información 6. la enfermera practicante 7. la médico (médica) asistente 8. la gerente (gerenta) de marketing (mercadeo) 9. la gerente (gerenta) de ventas 10. la diseñadora de videojuegos

S
1. hotel manager / la hotelera 2. electrician / la electricista 3. policeman / la policía 4. taxi driver / la taxista 5. Uber driver / la uberista 6. waiter / la mesera 7. florist / la florista 8. gardener / la jardinera 9. baker / la panadera 10. mechanic / la mecánico (mecánica) 11. carpenter / la carpintera 12. plumber / la plomera 13. journalist / la periodista 14. bookseller / la librera 15. secretary / la secretaria 16. receptionist / la recepcionista 17. banker / la banquera 18. hairstylist / la estilista 19. office worker / la oficinista 20. butcher / la carnicera 21. pharmacist / la farmacéutica 22. jeweler / la joyera

T
Answers will vary.

4 Describing People, Emotions, and Health

A
1. está 2. están 3. estoy 4. estás 5. está 6. estamos 7. están 8. están

B
1. Mi mamá está entusiasmada. 2. Mis hijos están emocionados. 3. Yo estoy contenta. 4. Los tíos están tristes. 5. La cuñada está estresada. 6. Tú estás preocupada. 7. La tía está deprimida. 8. Mis hermanos y yo estamos molestos. 9. Los abuelos están inquietos. 10. Mi papá está nervioso. 11. Mis nietas están alegres. 12. Las sobrinas están angustiadas.

C
1. está 2. es 3. está 4. es 5. está 6. está 7. está 8. es 9. está 10. está 11. es 12. está

D
1. Está a nueve millas del centro. 2. Queda detrás de la iglesia. 3. Está debajo de la mesa. 4. Están cerca de la zona comercial. 5. Está en la esquina. 6. Están encima del estante. 7. Queda a una cuadra del cibercafé. 8. Queda lejos de la ciudad. 9. Están por aquí. 10. Está a la derecha de nuestra oficina. 11. Queda al lado de un restaurante italiano. 12. Está delante de mi casa. 13. Queda enfrente del hospital. 14. Están detrás del sofá. 15. Están al fondo del armario. 16. Queda a la izquierda de la plaza.

E
1. son 2. soy 3. eres 4. es 5. somos 6. es 7. son 8. es 9. son 10. es

F

1. Son las siete. 2. Es la una. 3. Son las nueve y media. / Son las nueve y treinta. 4. Son las dos y cuarto. / Son las dos y quince. 5. Son las cinco menos cuarto. / Son las cuatro (y) cuarenta y cinco. / Faltan quince para las cinco. 6. Son las diez y veinte. 7. Son las cuatro menos diez. / Son las tres (y) cincuenta. / Faltan diez para las cuatro. 8. Son las seis de la mañana. 9. Son las cinco y veinticinco de la tarde. 10. Son las once y diez de la noche. 11. Son las ocho y cinco de la mañana. 12. Son las doce del día. (Es mediodía.) / Son las doce de la noche. (Es medianoche.)

G

1. ¿Dónde es la reunión? / Es en la sala de conferencias. / ¿A qué hora? / Es a las once y media de la mañana. 2. ¿Dónde es la fiesta de cumpleaños? / Es en la casa de Bernardo y Josefa. / ¿A qué hora? / Es a las siete de la tarde. 3. ¿Dónde es el partido de fútbol? / Es en el campo de fútbol. / ¿A qué hora? / Es a la una y media de la tarde. 4. ¿Dónde es la boda? / Es en la iglesia. / ¿A qué hora? / Es a las cuatro de la tarde. 5. ¿Dónde es la comida? / Es en el hotel. ¿A qué hora? / Es a las diez de la noche. / 6. ¿Dónde es el examen de historia? / Es en el salón de clase. / ¿A qué hora? / Es a las nueve y cuarto de la mañana.

H

1. Hay un partido de fútbol el sábado. 2. ¿Qué día es hoy? 3. Los museos están cerrados los lunes. 4. Su boda es el domingo. 5. Esta tienda por departamentos está abierta todos los días. 6. El señor Paz está en la oficina de lunes a jueves. 7. Hay conferencias en la universidad los miércoles. 8. Estamos reunidos todo el día.

I

1. es 2. es 3. están 4. Es / estoy 5. es 6. está 7. es / está 8. están 9. es 10. está 11. son 12. está 13. es 14. está

J

1. Tu impresora está descompuesta, ¿no? 2. Esta salsa está muy picante, ¿verdad? 3. Esos hombres de negocios son costarricenses, ¿no es cierto? 4. La carretera no queda lejos de aquí, ¿verdad? 5. La clase de economía es a las tres, ¿no es verdad? 6. El partido de béisbol es el sábado, ¿no? 7. No estás de mal humor, ¿verdad? 8. El domingo es tu día libre, ¿no es cierto?

K

1. Julio y Laura están sentados en la sala de conferencias. 2. Las hermanas están tumbadas en la cama. 3. El bebé está dormido. 4. Los jardineros están arrodillados. 5. Algunos pasajeros están parados en el autobús. 6. Virginia está echada en el sofá. 7. El receptor está agachado.

L

1. Estoy seguro que Marta está ocupada con su sitio web. 2. Estoy seguro que los señores Martínez están de vacaciones. 3. Estoy seguro que Paco está tumbado en la playa como de costumbre. 4. Estoy seguro que mis amigas están sentadas frente a la televisión. 5. Estoy seguro que los chicos están de viaje. 6. Estoy seguro que Lorenzo está acostado. 7. Estoy seguro que tu computadora está descompuesta. 8. Estoy seguro que están en la oficina todo el día.

M

1. Mis sobrinos son rubios y bajos. 2. Mis papás son inteligentes y simpáticos. 3. Mi hermano es alto y moreno. 4. Mis hijos son guapos y encantadores. 5. Mis cuñadas son antipáticas y arrogantes. 6. Mi hermana es emprendedora y rica. 7. Mis nietos son morenos y delgados. 8. Mi tía es flaca y linda. 9. Mi esposa es honrada y amable. 10. Mis primas son alegres y atentas. 11. Mis abuelos son trabajadores y divertidos. 12. Mi cuñado es gordo y feo.

N

1. ¿De quién es este libro? / Es del profesor. 2. Estos zapatos. ¿De quién son? / Son de ella. 3. ¿De quién es esa cartera (ese billetero)? / Es del doctor Lara. 4. Estas medias. ¿De quién son? / Son de ella. 5. ¿De quiénes es el coche (carro)? / Es de ellos.

O

1. Es de seda. 2. Son de cuero. 3. Son de poliéster. 4. Es de lino. 5. Son de pana. 6. Es de algodón.

P

1. ¿De quién es esta maleta? / Es de él. 2. ¿De qué son esos trajes? / Son de lana. 3. ¿Por favor, señorita, ¿dónde están las corbatas de seda? / Están al lado de las camisas. 4. ¿De quiénes son esos abrigos? / Son de ellos. 5. ¿Cuál es su nacionalidad? / Somos peruanos. 6. ¿Cuál es su profesión? / Soy abogada. / ¿Cuál es su nacionalidad? / Soy panameña. / ¿Y su origen? / Soy de origen inglés.

Q

1. ¿Dónde están los señores Arriaga? 2. ¿Cuál es su profesión? 3. ¿Cómo están las chicas? 4. ¿Qué hora es? 5. ¿De qué son las camisetas? 6. ¿Cuál es la capital de Chile? 7. ¿Cómo es la novia de Arturo? 8. ¿Qué día es hoy? 9. ¿Dónde es la reunión? 10. ¿A qué hora es la fiesta? 11. ¿De quién son los zapatos? 12. ¿Para quién es la pulsera? 13. ¿Cómo están estos platos? 14. ¿Cuál es tu (su) estado civil? 15. ¿Cuál es la dirección? 16. ¿Cuál es su religión?

R

1. ¿Están abiertas las tiendas por departamentos? 2. ¿Es aburrido su trabajo? 3. ¿Están emocionados sus hijos? 4. ¿Es atenta la novia de Juan Antonio? 5. ¿Están asustados los niños? 6. ¿Está muy ocupado este contador? 7. ¿Son simpáticos sus papás? 8. ¿Está descompuesto tu coche? 9. ¿Son impresionantes esos museos? 10. ¿Son casados Lola y Diego? 11. ¿Es emprendedor su hermano? 12. ¿Están muy adelantados estos países?

S

1. aburrido 2. acatarrado 3. adelantado 4. alegre 5. angustiado 6. asustado 7. reunido 8. cansado 9. emocionado 10. enfermo 11. entusiasmado 12. estresado 13. inquieto 14. molesto 15. nervioso 16. preocupado 17. atrasado 18. triste 19. divorciado 20. gracioso

T

Answers will vary.

U

Answers will vary.

5 Work and Leisure

A

1. Tú montas en bicicleta. 2. Uds. nadan. 3. Yo patino sobre hielo. 4. Mis amigos y yo montamos a caballo. 5. Ud. camina ocho millas diarias. 6. Marta y Simón trotan. 7. Nicolás levanta pesas. 8. Diana patina sobre ruedas.

B

1. hacen 2. hago 3. hace 4. hacen 5. hace 6. haces 7. hacemos 8. hace

C

1. Yo nado dos veces por semana. 2. ¿Montamos en bicicleta hoy? 3. Yo hago ejercicio mañana. 4. ¿Por qué no vamos al gimnasio juntos? 5. Mis amigos no hacen deportes. 6. Vamos a caminar a la cancha de baloncesto.

D

1. Felipe y yo vamos al campo. 2. Uds. van a la cancha de tenis. 3. Mercedes va a la piscina. 4. Los señores Vargas van a la playa. 5. Yo voy al concierto. 6. Tú vas al bar. 7. Mauricio va al bosque nacional. 8. Ud. va a la galería de arte.

E

1. Uds. van a tomar una copa. 2. Mario va a descargar música brasileña. 3. Yo voy a hacer las tapas. 4. Manuel y Leticia van a bailar el tango. 5. Tú vas a hablar con los invitados. 6. Alicia y yo vamos a tocar el piano. 7. Clara va a grabar un video. 8. ¡Nosotros vamos a disfrutar de una fiesta muy divertida!

F

1. ¿Uds. van a ir al mar mañana? / Sí, vamos a ir a la playa mañana en la tarde. 2. ¿Vas al gimnasio? / No, voy al club. 3. ¿Ud. camina a la tienda de cómputo? / Sí, pero primero voy a la heladería. 4. ¿Tus amigos van a la universidad? / No, van al campo de fútbol. 5. La reunión es a las dos, ¿verdad? / No, es a la una. 6. El teatro está a una cuadra de aquí, ¿no? / Ah sí. Queda al lado de una galería de arte.

G

1. Voy a tomar el almuerzo. 2. Vamos al museo. 3. ¿De qué hablan Uds.? 4. Hablamos del espectáculo. 5. ¿Qué escuchas? 6. Descargo música española. 7. ¿Por qué no patinamos sobre hielo?

H

1. X 2. ¿Vas a visitar a tus primos? 3. X 4. Voy a llamar a mis suegros. 5. X 6. ¿A quién miras? 7. Vamos a ayudar al asesor. 8. X 9. Buscan a su perro. 10. Armando lleva a su esposa al centro. 11. X 12. ¿Esperas a alguien?

I

1. Pedro es mi amigo que toca el saxofón. 2. Rebeca y Nora son mis amigas que estudian física. 3. Lorenzo es mi amigo que diseña sitios web. 4. Elena es mi amiga que cocina muy bien. 5. Antonio y Matilde son mis amigos que trabajan en mi oficina. 6. Ricardo es mi amigo que hace programación.

J

1. El museo que está abierto los lunes. 2. Las mujeres de negocios que ganan mucho dinero. 3. El asesor que habla tres idiomas. 4. El coche negro que está descompuesto. 5. Los estudiantes que hacen deportes. 6. La cancha de tenis que queda enfrente de la piscina. 7. Los profesores que

enseñan administración de empresas. 8. Los trajes que son de lana.

K

1. No, no esperamos a nadie. 2. No, Roberto no va a bailar salsa nunca. 3. No, los cocineros no preparan ningún plato de pollo (ninguno de pollo). 4. No, Leonor no habla ruso tampoco. 5. No, no estudio en la biblioteca nunca. 6. No, ya no patino sobre hielo. 7. No, Julio no busca ni a su perro ni a su gato. 8. No, ninguna abogada trabaja los sábados.

L

1. el lavaplatos / dishwasher 2. el rascacielos / skyscraper 3. el cortaúñas / nail clippers 4. el cubrecama / bedcover 5. el paracaídas / parachute 6. el abrelatas / can opener 7. el cortacésped / lawn mower 8. el sacacorchos / corkscrew

M

1. preparan las maletas 2. viajan en avión 3. visitan varios museos 4. llegan al aeropuerto 5. sacan las tarjetas de embarque 6. hacen turismo 7. bailan salsa 8. nadan en la piscina

N

1. Vamos a hacer turismo mañana. 2. Hago las maletas ahora mismo. 3. Siempre ayudo a mis papás. 4. ¿Hacemos un viaje en el verano? 5. ¿Por qué no cenamos fuera el viernes? 6. ¿Uds. van al bosque nacional temprano? 7. Sí, vamos a ir a las siete de la mañana. 8. Emilia visita a su hermano pasado mañana. 9. Los diseñadores de web van a trabajar juntos muy pronto. 10. Vamos a llevar a los niños a la tienda de zapatos más tarde.

O

1. navega 2. escucho 3. tomas 4. hacen 5. observa 6. montan 7. diseña 8. disfrutamos

P

1. work / trabajar 2. song / cantar 3. wait / esperar 4. invitation / invitar 5. look / mirar 6. help / ayudar 7. visit / visitar 8. development / desarrollar 9. practice / practicar 10. celebration / celebrar 11. drawing, sketch / dibujar 12. arrival / llegar 13. preparation / preparar 14. purchase / comprar 15. cuisine, kitchen / cocinar 16. saving / ahorrar 17. expense / gastar 18. surfing / navegar 19. payment / pagar 20. recording / grabar 21. call / llamar 22. design / diseñar

Q

Answers will vary.

6 Weather, Foreign Languages, and Sports

A

1. corren 2. vivimos 3. rompe 4. creo 5. subes 6. comparte 7. venden 8. resiste

B

1. Mario escribe un informe. 2. Nosotros leemos en la biblioteca. 3. Yo asisto a una conferencia. 4. Uds. abren los libros de texto. 5. Tú comprendes las teorías de la física. 6. María Elena imprime un artículo. 7. Rodrigo y Mateo suben unos archivos. 8. Ud. sale para el laboratorio.

C

1. ¿Cuánto tiempo hace que esperas a tus amigos? / Hace quince minutos que espero a mis amigos. / Espero a mis amigos hace quince minutos. 2. ¿Cuánto tiempo hace que los niños buscan a su perro? / Hace dos días que buscan a su perro. / Buscan a su perro hace dos días. 3. ¿Cuánto tiempo hace que Uds. viven en este barrio? / Hace dieciséis años que vivimos en este barrio. / Vivimos en este barrio hace dieciséis años. 4. ¿Cuánto tiempo hace que Pedro toma clases a distancia? / Hace un año que toma clases a distancia. / Toma clases a distancia hace un año. 5. ¿Cuánto tiempo hace que Uds. hacen deportes? / Hace cuatro meses que hacemos deportes. / Hacemos deportes hace cuatro meses. 6. ¿Cuánto tiempo hace que Susana y Fernando buscan casa? / Hace varios meses que buscan casa. / Buscan casa hace varios meses. 7. ¿Cuánto tiempo hace que nosotros asistimos a estos conciertos? / Hace mucho tiempo que asistimos a estos conciertos. / Asistimos a estos conciertos hace mucho tiempo. 8. ¿Cuánto tiempo hace que Ud. manda emails? / Hace una hora que mando emails. / Mando emails hace una hora.

D

1. comienza 2. vuelven 3. quiero 4. encuentras 5. piden 6. piensa 7. cuestan 8. prefiere 9. prueba 10. duerme 11. empiezan 12. entendemos 13. almuerzo 14. sirven 15. juegas 16. merendamos

E

1. Hace calor en Miami. 2. Llueve en Seattle. 3. Hace fresco en Philadelphia. 4. Hace buen tiempo en San Diego. 5. Hace mucho viento en Chicago. 6. Nieva en Boston. 7. Hace mucho frío en Anchorage. 8. Hace setenta y cinco grados en Washington, D.C. 9. Truena en Nueva York. 10. Hace sol en Dallas. 11. Hace mal tiempo en Baton Rouge.

F

1. X 2. a 3. X 4. a 5. X 6. que 7. de 8. X 9. de 10. a 11. X 12. a 13. que 14. X 15. X 16. de 17. X 18. X

G

1. Quiere ser experto en su campo. 2. ¿No puedes encontrar tus gafas? 3. ¿Tienes que escribir el informe en español? 4. Acabo de conocer a los asesores chilenos. 5. Empieza a entender el inglés muy bien. 6. Sé hacer programación. 7. El niño aprende a contar hasta cien. 8. Esperan tener mucho éxito con su empresa. 9. Piensan volver de México la semana entrante. 10. Va a probar las tapas, ¿no? 11. Prefieren jugar al fútbol. 12. Tratan de resistir a la tentación.

H

1. para 2. por 3. para 4. por 5. para 6. para 7. por 8. por 9. para 10. para / para 11. por / por

I

1. sabe 2. sabes 3. conozco 4. saben 5. conoce 6. sé / conoces 7. sabe OR conoce 8. conocemos / sabemos 9. sabe 10. conocen 11. sabes 12. conozco

J

1. Sí, lo leen. 2. No, no lo conozco. 3. Sí, lo llamo. 4. No, no lo servimos. 5. Sí, lo visita. 6. No, no lo busca. 7. Sí, lo ayudo. 8. Sí, lo empezamos. 9. No, no lo cuenta. 10. No, no lo encontramos.

K

1. sirve 2. pedimos 3. sirven 4. pides 5. pido 6. servimos 7. sirves 8. pide 9. sirvo 10. piden

L

1. para ella 2. contigo 3. de él 4. para mí 5. con nosotros 6. de Uds. 7. por mí 8. conmigo 9. a ti 10. para ti 11. por Ud. 12. a mí 13. por ti 14. en él 15. de ti 16. en ellos

M

1. cuarenta y un 2. ochenta y cuatro 3. cien 4. setecientas treinta y una 5. novecientos setenta y seis 6. mil 7. mil cuatrocientas noventa y cinco 8. tres mil quinientos ochenta y un 9. diez mil setecientas veintinueve 10. doscientos sesenta y cinco mil 11. un millón de 12. noventa y dos millones de

N

1. Uds. siguen por la autopista. 2. Sigues la conversación. 3. El perro sigue a los niños. 4. ¿Ud. sigue un curso de inglés a distancia? 5. Sigo los consejos de mis padres. 6. Seguimos por una avenida bajo construcción. 7. Sigue las órdenes del médico. 8. Siguen el ejemplo de su abuelo.

O

1. Joaquín y yo jugamos al ajedrez. 2. Estos dos equipos juegan en la Serie Mundial. 3. Nunca juego al tenis de mesa. 4. Carlitos juega a los videojuegos. 5. ¿Juegas a las cartas? 6. Ud. juega al vólibol, ¿no? 7. Uds. juegan al dominó. 8. Blanca juega un juego de sociedad.

P

Synonyms 1. comenzar 2. regresar 3. descargar 4. beber 5. cargar 6. desear 7. comprender
Antonyms 1. triste 2. atrasado 3. cerrado 4. tranquilo 5. gordo 6. barato 7. aburrido 8. viejo 9. hermoso 10. pobre 11. claro 12. antipático

Q

1. Hace mal tiempo. Hace frío y viento. 2. Y empieza a llover. 3. Hace veintiún años que Benjamín trabaja en este campo. 4. Él conoce el mercado muy bien. 5. Los estudiantes piensan tomar un curso de español por internet. 6. Saben que tienen que practicar mucho para dominar el idioma hablado. 7. Este restaurante sirve los mejores postres de la ciudad. 8. Por eso pido dos. ¡No puedo resistir a la tentación! 9. ¿Sabes jugar al tenis? 10. No, pero quiero aprender a jugar. 11. Tengo ganas de ir a la playa. ¿Quieres ir conmigo? 12. Acabo de volver del mar. Prefiero ir al campo.

R

Answers will vary.

7 Entertaining at Home

A

1. Hace / cae 2. trae / traigo 3. es / salgo 4. oyen / oímos 5. vienes / vengo 6. ponen / dice 7. ves / veo 8. hago / voy 9. cabemos / quepo 10. dice / decimos 11. eres / Soy 12. están / estoy / está

B

1. Tienen mucha hambre. 2. ¿Tienes poca sed? 3. Tenemos razón. 4. Tiene mucha suerte. 5. ¿Por qué tiene tanta vergüenza? 6. No tengo prisa. 7. ¿Tienen demasiado frío? 8. Tiene demasiado cuidado. 9. ¿Por qué tienen tanto sueño? 10. Tenemos muchas ganas de verlo. 11. Espero tener éxito. 12. ¿No tienes mucho calor?

C

1. el agua potable 2. las aguas destiladas 3. el hambre extrema 4. el ave negra 5. las aves rapaces 6. el alma divina 7. las almas humanas 8. el área grande 9. las áreas protegidas 10. el haba blanca 11. las habas frescas 12. el hacha afilada

D

1. veo 2. ve 3. ven 4. ve 5. ves 6. ve 7. vemos 8. ven

E

1. Sí, la pone. 2. No, no la venden. 3. Sí, las servimos. 4. No, no los sube. 5. No, no la comprendo. 6. Sí, los conozco. 7. Sí los preferimos. 8. No, no la sé. 9. Sí, lo oímos. 10. Sí, lo entiendo. 11. No, no las llevo. 12. Sí, la comienza.

F

1. pone 2. ponen 3. pongo 4. pone 5. pone 6. pones 7. ponen 8. ponemos

G

1. No, señora, no la conozco. 2. No, señores, no los busco. 3. No, señoras, no las llamo. 4. No, señorita, no la comprendo. 5. No, señor, no lo ayudo. 6. No, señoritas, no las conozco. 7. No, señor, no lo quiero visitar. / No, señor, no quiero visitarlo. 8. No, señores, no los pienso invitar. / No, señores, no pienso invitarlos. 9. No, señora, no la voy a llevar. / No señora, no voy a llevarla. 10. No, señor, no los necesito ver. / No, señor, no necesito verlos.

H

1. Yo la veo. 2. Él me llama. 3. Nosotros vamos a llevarlas. / Nosotros las vamos a llevar. 4. ¿Tú lo buscas? 5. ¿Uds. quieren esperarnos? /¿Uds. nos quieren esperar? 6. Ella espera conocerte. / Ella te espera conocer. 7. ¿Ud. piensa ayudarlos? /¿Ud. los piensa ayudar? 8. Ellas no pueden comprenderla. / Ellas no la pueden comprender. 9. Yo deseo invitarlos. / Yo los deseo invitar. 10. Yo no la voy a visitar. / Yo no voy a visitarla.

I

1. Antonio y yo nunca damos consejos. 2. Juan nunca da consejos. 3. María y Susana nunca dan consejos. 4. Yo nunca doy consejos. 5. Tú nunca das consejos. 6. La hermana de Pablo nunca da consejos. 7. Uds. nunca dan consejos.

J

1. Tú no dices nada. 2. Nuestros amigos no dicen nada. 3. Raúl no dice nada. 4. Ud. no dice nada. 5. Yo no digo nada. 6. Camila no dice nada. 7. Uds. no dicen nada. 8. Ana María y yo no decimos nada.

K

1. Nosotros salimos a las seis y media. 2. Roberto sale dentro de unos minutos. 3. Yo salgo en veinte minutos. 4. Ud. sale muy pronto. 5. Los empleados salen ahora mismo. 6. Tú sales un poco tarde. 7. Uds. salen a la hora de cenar. 8. Timoteo y Rebeca salen temprano.

L

1. Más vale salir al mediodía. 2. Más vale discutir los problemas. 3. Más vale no ir. 4. Más vale compartir la información.

M

1. Hay que dominar un idioma. 2. Hay que tener suerte. 3. A veces hay que resistir a la tentación. 4. Hay que tener paciencia.

N

1. Debes devolverla. / La debes devolver. 2. ¿Uds. no quieren probarlas? / ¿Uds. no las quieren probar? 3. Empiezan a tenerlo. / Lo empiezan a tener. 4. No puedo traducirlos. / No los puedo traducir. 5. Esperamos verlos. / Los esperamos ver. 6. Voy a traerlas. / Las voy a traer. 7. Tenemos que ayudarlos. / Los tenemos que ayudar. 8. Ud. logra dominarlo. / Ud. lo logra dominar. 9. Alicia sabe diseñarlas. / Alicia las sabe diseñar. 10. ¿Ud. piensa llamarla? / ¿Ud. la piensa llamar? 11. Trato de entenderlo. / Lo trato de entender. 12. Acaba de encontrarla. / La acaba de encontrar.

O

1. Marta y yo oímos el timbre. 2. Ud. oye música. 3. Ellos oyen unos sonidos. 4. Yo oigo voces. 5. Tú oyes gritos. 6. Uds. oyen el teléfono. 7. Leonor oye una conversación.

P

1. Los chicos vienen en la tarde. 2. Ud. viene el jueves. 3. Yo vengo a las ocho. 4. Uds. vienen por la mañana. 5. Anita y yo venimos esta noche. 6. Tú vienes el miércoles. 7. Javier viene a la una y media.

Q

1. No, los traen Lucas y Laura. 2. No, lo traigo yo. 3. No, las traen Uds. 4. No, la trae Guillermo. 5. No, los traes tú. 6. No, la traemos nosotros. 7. No, las traen Uds.

R

1. La reunión tiene lugar en la oficina del director. 2. Hay que poner las cartas sobre la mesa. 3. Clara ya no tiene novio. Ojos que no ven, corazón que no siente. 4. ¿Un trabajo excelente? Vale la pena esperarlo. 5. Juanito siempre da guerra. Y su hermana da lata. 6. Su plan no tiene pies ni cabeza. 7. No debemos decir nada. Las paredes oyen. 8. Nadie tiene la culpa de eso. 9. Diego, ¿estás enfermo? Tienes mala cara. 10. Doy una vuelta en el parque. ¿Vienes conmigo?

S

Answers will vary.

T

1. Es hora de almorzar. ¿Tienes hambre? / No, no tengo hambre pero tengo mucha sed. 2. Señor, por favor, ¿me puede ayudar con mi computadora? / Claro que sí, señora, la ayudo en seguida.
3. Nuestros amigos dicen que la película que dan en ese cine es estupenda. Tengo muchas ganas de verla. / Tienen razón. Acabo de verla. 4. Hace veinticinco grados y hace mucho viento. Tengo frío. / Sí, hace frío y la nieve cae pero no tengo mucho frío. 5. Quiero ver el programa de detectives. / Yo lo quiero ver también. 6. ¿Ud. conoce a los hombres de negocios que vienen esta tarde? / No, no los conozco pero pienso conocerlos. 7. Va a haber mucha gente en el teatro. / Yo sé. Vamos a tener que hacer cola. ¡Y yo no tengo paciencia! 8. ¿Cómo se dice *advice* en español? / Se dice "consejos".

8 The Daily Routine

A

1. Julio se molesta. 2. Uds. se aburren.
3. Victoria y yo nos entusiasmamos. 4. Tú te ríes.
5. Alfonso y Edit se asustan. 6. Ud. se emociona.
7. Yo me divierto. 8. Consuelo y Javier se ofenden.
9. María Elena se enoja. 10. Juan Carlos y yo nos animamos.

B

1. Yo me aburro. ¿Y tú? / ¡Qué va! Me divierto mucho. 2. ¿Él se ofende fácilmente? / Sí, y se molesta a menudo. 3. Los niños se entusiasman. / Sí, se ríen mucho. 4. ¿Por qué se enojan (se enfadan)? / No nos enojamos (nos enfadamos) pero sí nos exasperamos.

C

1. aburre 2. se enojan 3. nos emocionamos
4. exaspera 5. asustan 6. me divierto
7. se preocupa 8. anima 9. sorprende
10. se sientan

D

1. Nos asustas. 2. La tranquilizamos (calmamos).
3. Levanta la mano. 4. Lo animo. 5. Me molestan.
6. Aburren a sus amigos.

E

1. Yo me jacto de mis hijos. 2. Tú te quejas de todo. 3. Nosotros no nos atrevemos a hablar de eso. 4. Pedro y Elena se divorcian por falta de comunicación. 5. Maite y su hermano se desmayan por tener la tensión baja.

F

1. Dicen que Lucía se compromete con Benjamín. / Y parece que Margarita se casa con Leonardo.
2. ¿Se acuerda de la dirección de Armando? / Lo siento. ¡Me olvido de todo! 3. ¿No sabes? Nos instalamos en nuestra casa nueva hoy. / Me alegro de saberlo. 4. ¿Quién se ocupa de los detalles de la reunión? / Yo me ocupo de los informes y Diego se ocupa de los otros documentos. 5. ¿Por qué te despides de todos los invitados? / Es que la fiesta me aburre mucho. ¡Me voy!

G

1. Ud. y Jorge se entienden (se comprenden) muy bien. 2. Micaela y yo nos vemos todos los días.
3. ¿Por qué no nos tuteamos? 4. Los niños se abrazan. 5. ¿Nos ayudamos con el proyecto?
6. Roberto y Alejandra se quieren mucho.
7. Nos conocemos bastante bien. 8. Eunice y su prima (primo) se escriben una vez al año.

H

1. Me pruebo la blusa y la falda. 2. Los niños se quitan los zapatos. 3. María Elena se peina.
4. ¿Te vistes ahora mismo? 5. Nos levantamos a las siete de la mañana todos los días. 6. Se hace tarde. ¡Tienen que apresurarse! 7. Cada vez que Samuel juega al fútbol se lastima el pie. 8. Nos arreglamos y nos vamos.

I

1. Deben darse prisa. 2. ¿Vas a despertarte temprano? 3. Manolo acaba de probarse el traje.
4. Ud. comienza a alimentarse bien. 5. Tratamos de cuidarnos lo más posible. 6. Quieren divertirse mucho en la playa. 7. Tengo que mantenerme en forma. 8. ¿Arturo no puede ponerse en forma? 9. Las chicas empiezan a acatarrarse.
10. Necesitamos relajarnos un poco.
11. ¿Prefieres ducharte por la mañana?
12. Logran instalarse en el condominio.

J

1. Me voy a graduar en junio. 2. Se quieren sentar cerca de nosotros. 3. El niñito se sabe vestir solo. 4. No se deben meter en todo. 5. Me prefiero reunir con Uds. la semana próxima. 6. Nos tenemos que apresurar o perdemos el avión. 7. Se empiezan a reír. 8. ¿Te piensas casar con Federico? 9. Nos esperamos ver pronto. 10. ¿Catalina se vuelve a enamorar? 11. Se acaba de acordar de la fecha. 12. Pablo se logra colocar en una empresa importante.

K

1. hermosamente 2. estupendamente 3. inteligentemente 4. honradamente 5. regularmente 6. alegremente 7. nerviosamente 8. compulsivamente 9. comercialmente 10. tristemente 11. cómodamente 12. fácilmente 13. atentamente 14. arrogantemente 15. asustadamente

L

1. perfecto 2. general 3. cuidadoso 4. reciente 5. último 6. difícil 7. frecuente 8. rotundo 9. pesado 10. frío 11. normal 12. gracioso 13. pobre 14. amable 15. tranquilo

M

1. frecuentemente 2. claramente 3. inteligentemente 4. difícilmente 5. alegremente 6. tranquilamente 7. atentamente 8. cómodamente 9. tristemente 10. amablemente 11. arrogantemente 12. felizmente 13. sinceramente 14. oscuramente 15. ruidosamente

N

1. Tú te cepillas los dientes. 2. Pilar y yo nos lavamos la cabeza. 3. Roberto se afeita. 4. Uds. se secan el pelo. 5. Ignacio se pone la ropa. 6. Yo me paso el hilo dental. 7. Marisol y Julieta se pintan los labios. 8. Ud. se ducha.

O

1. Me emociono mucho al oír música. / Al oír música, me emociono mucho. 2. Mario va a casa al salir de la oficina. / Al salir de la oficina, Mario va a casa. 3. ¿Te duermes en seguida al acostarte? / Al acostarte, ¿te duermes en seguida? 4. Eva se enoja al saber qué pasa. / Al saber qué pasa, Eva se enoja. 5. Uds. se visten al terminar de ducharse. / Al terminar de ducharse, Uds. se visten. 6. Te limpias los dientes al despertarte. / Al despertarte, te limpias los dientes. 7. Los niños se bañan al llegar del parque. / Al llegar del parque, los niños se bañan. 8. ¿Ud. se lava el pelo al levantarse? / Al levantarse, ¿Ud. se lava el pelo? 9. Me divierto mucho al reunirme con mis amigos. / Al reunirme con mis amigos, me divierto mucho. 10. Nos tranquilizamos al ver que todo está bien. / Al ver que todo está bien, nos tranquilizamos.

P

1. de 2. de 3. a 4. en 5. con 6. a 7. En 8. de 9. con 10. de 11. de 12. de 13. de 14. de

Q

1. Leemos el quinto libro. 2. Juego en el octavo partido. 3. Escribo el sexto correo electrónico. 4. Siguen el tercer plan. 5. Es la séptima semana del viaje. 6. Hacen la segunda práctica. 7. Tomas la novena clase a distancia. 8. Se reúnen el primer miércoles del mes. 9. Es la cuarta vez que los visitamos. 10. Es la primera conferencia de la serie. 11. Es el décimo año de la empresa. 12. ¿Conoces a su tercera hija?

R

1. Señora, ¿cómo se llama Ud.? / Me llamo Isabel Ortega Castellanos. 2. ¿Cómo se llama él? / Se llama Antonio Herrera Calderón. 3. Niño, ¿cómo te llamas? / Me llamo Juan Manuel Echevarría. 4. ¿Cómo se llama ella? / Se llama Alicia Marqués Goya.

S

1. se callan 2. se equivoca 3. se mejora 4. aprovecharnos 5. se hace 6. se muere 7. se portan 8. burlarse

T

1. Me llamo Gabriela Torres Ribera. Al despertarme, me cepillo los dientes, me ducho y me lavo el pelo. Después de vestirme, me maquillo (me pinto la cara) y me peino. Mi esposo Fernando se ducha, se afeita y se viste. Después de desayunar, visto a los niños y Fernando los lleva al colegio. Mi esposo y yo nos vamos para la oficina.
2. Me llamo Antonio Lapesa Mondragón. Acabo de graduarme en la universidad y busco trabajo. Soy contador. Espero colocarme en una empresa grande. También acabo de comprometerme. Mi prometida Pilar, que es diseñadora de páginas web, quiere casarse este año pero yo creo que no debemos apresurarnos. Tenemos que trabajar unos años para poder comprar una casa. No nos preocupamos porque nos queremos, nos entendemos y siempre nos ayudamos. Sabemos que vamos a tener éxito.

3. Me llamo Mario Sánchez Vargas. Me acatarro frecuentemente. Hace seis semanas que me siento mal. El médico me dice que estoy bien pero que debo cuidarme mejor. Por eso voy a comenzar a hacer ejercicio. Quiero ponerme en forma. Voy a trotar y levantar pesas. Tengo que dejar de comer comida basura y empezar a alimentarme bien. Sé que debo relajarme más, acostarme más temprano y vivir más tranquilamente. ¡Voy a aburrirme pero voy a sentirme muy bien!

U

Answers will vary.

9 Travel, Likes and Dislikes

A

1. trabajó 2. esperaste 3. comprendimos 4. miré 5. imprimieron 6. llevaron 7. compró 8. comieron 9. viajé 10. debiste 11. corriste 12. aprendí 13. bebió 14. abrimos 15. vendió 16. manejé 17. escribió 18. regresamos 19. viviste 20. tomaron

B

1. Subiste al avión. 2. Prefirió un vuelo directo. 3. Viajamos a Ciudad de Panamá. 4. Fui al aeropuerto en taxi. 5. Hicieron escala en Miami. 6. Saqué mi tarjeta de embarque. 7. Facturaron el equipaje. 8. Volvió de Panamá el domingo. 9. Pagué los billetes en línea. 10. ¿No pudiste encontrar tu maleta? 11. Se abrocharon el cinturón de seguridad. 12. Perdió el vuelo. 13. Llegué a la terminal A. 14. ¡Fue un viaje maravilloso!

C

1. Me mandó un email. 2. Le expliqué mi idea. 3. Nos recordaron la fecha. 4. Les entregó los documentos. 5. Le vendiste tu carro. 6. Te devolvimos el dinero. 7. Le contó la historia. 8. Les enseñaron la casa.

D

1. Ellos nos pidieron un favor. 2. Tú le leíste un libro. 3. Yo les traje el periódico. 4. Nosotros te dijimos lo que pasó. 5. Ud. le explicó el plan. 6. Él me regaló unas flores. 7. Ellas le hicieron una comida muy rica. 8. Uds. les dieron un regalo.

E

1. Tú le entregaste el informe al director. 2. Manolo les mostró su nuevo apartamento a sus amigos. 3. Yo le hice unas preguntas al asesor. 4. Ellos le pidieron la cuenta a la mesera. 5. Daniela les sirvió unas tapas a los invitados. 6. Uds. le dieron el software al programador. 7. Ella le dijo la verdad a su abogada. 8. Tú les escribiste un email a tus abuelos. 9. Nosotros le vendimos el coche a nuestra vecina. 10. Los profesores les explicaron los problemas a sus estudiantes.

F

1. Me interesan tus ideas. 2. Les encantan estas novelas. 3. Le faltan unas reservaciones. 4. Nos entusiasman los partidos de béisbol. 5. Me gustan estos conciertos. 6. ¿Te caen bien los gerentes? 7. Le quedan unos proyectos. 8. Nos hacen falta otras computadoras. 9. Les fascinan aquellas tiendas de ropa. 10. ¿No te importan sus problemas?

G

1. Nos interesó esa película. 2. Le gustaron los programas. 3. ¿Te cayó mal este tipo? 4. Les hizo falta más dinero. 5. Me encantó la obra de teatro. 6. Nos faltó tiempo para terminar el proyecto. 7. Le quedó el examen de química. 8. Les entusiasmaron las conferencias.

H

1. Me gustó. 2. No le importaron. 3. Les encantó. 4. ¿Te hicieron falta? 5. Les convino. 6. Nos interesó mucho. 7. Les sobraron. 8. Me entusiasmó verlos. 9. Les cayó mal. 10. ¿Le interesó trabajar en Europa? 11. Nos encantó manejar por el desierto. 12. ¿Te importó pasar por el control de seguridad?

I

1. Nos van a interesar esos libros. 2. Le va a hacer falta un mapa. 3. Les va a sobrar comida. 4. Te van a caer bien nuestros amigos. 5. Me va a encantar viajar en tren. 6. No les va a importar llegar tarde. 7. Te va a convenir conocer al director de mercadeo. 8. Le va a tocar jugar pronto.

J

1. creyó 2. construí 3. leyeron 4. distribuimos 5. contó 6. volvieron 7. quise 8. entendimos 9. comenzamos 10. llovió 11. pensaste 12. dije 13. pudieron 14. supe 15. trajimos 16. vino 17. seguiste 18. durmieron 19. estuve 20. dio 21. puse 22. fuimos 23. hiciste 24. fueron 25. pidió 26. hubo 27. conduje 28. tuvieron 29. viste 30. prefirió

K

1. Ya los vio. 2. Ya nos reunimos. 3. Ya lo pidieron. 4. Ya me matriculé. 5. Ya se casó con él. 6. Ya los trajimos. 7. Ya lo comencé. 8. Ya la construyeron. 9. Ya los hice. 10. Ya se puso en contacto conmigo. 11. Ya las siguieron. 12. Ya almorcé. 13. Ya fuimos. 14. Ya lo busqué. 15. Ya lo recogió.

L
1. sonó 2. se asustó 3. se levantó 4. se afeitó 5. se duchó 6. se vistió 7. Se dio 8. Llegó 9. Corrió 10. tuvo

M
1. hice 2. viajamos 3. pasamos 4. tomamos 5. nos quedamos 6. llegamos 7. tuvimos 8. pudimos 9. Fue

N
1. estudiaron 2. se graduaron 3. se colocó 4. empezó 5. se comprometieron 6. se casaron 7. compraron 8. tuvieron

O
1. Les falta un asiento de pasillo. 2. Les quedan tres asientos de ventana. 3. Le toca a Ud. pasar por la aduana. 4. No nos conviene hacer escala. 5. Me caen bien estos auxiliares de vuelo. 6. ¿Le hace falta sacar su tarjeta de embarque? 7. ¡A ti te gusta viajar en avión pero a mí me encanta tomar el tren de alta velocidad!

P
1. cumplió 2. asistí 3. comimos 4. bebimos 5. se alegró 6. traje 7. tuvo 8. se entusiasmó 9. fuimos 10. oímos 11. bailamos 12. nos divertimos

Q
1. Pudimos recorrer seis países. 2. Por fin supe su dirección. 3. Tuvo una idea maravillosa. 4. La pasajera no quiso apagar su celular. 5. ¿Pudiste facturar tu equipaje? 6. ¿Cuándo conociste a los señores Díaz?

R
1. el viaje de negocios 2. el asiento de ventana 3. el auxiliar de vuelo 4. la puerta de embarque 5. el equipaje de mano 6. el control de seguridad 7. el vuelo de conexión 8. el tren de alta velocidad 9. el plan de mercadeo

S
1. Hace cinco años que hicimos un viaje a Chile. / Fue un vuelo agotador, ¿verdad? 2. El avión despegó y veinte minutos después me desabroché el cinturón de seguridad. / Y yo me acomodé en mi asiento y me dormí inmediatamente. 3. ¿Te gustó el paisaje del sudoeste? / Sí, me encantó. Manejamos por el desierto y vimos cactos impresionantes. 4. ¿Tuvieron que hacer escala? / No, fue un vuelo directo. 5. ¿Qué hizo cuando bajó (al bajar) del avión? / Recogí mi equipaje y pasé por la aduana. 6. ¿Mostraste tu pasaporte en la puerta de embarque? / No, pero le entregué la tarjeta de embarque a la señorita. 7. ¿Facturó su maleta? / No, el auxiliar de vuelo la colocó en el compartimiento de arriba. 8. ¡Qué embotellamiento! Vamos a perder nuestro vuelo. / ¡Qué va! Conozco un atajo.

T
Answers will vary.

U
Answers will vary.

10 Childhood, Family History, University

A
1. hablaba 2. comían 3. escribíamos 4. eran 5. creías 6. tenía 7. volvían 8. sabía 9. decías 10. veía 11. venían 12. había 13. tomábamos 14. hacía 15. vivías 16. podía 17. querían 18. pedía 19. iba 20. jugabas 21. subían 22. entendía 23. leíamos 24. dábamos 25. estaba 26. ponía 27. pensaban 28. almorzabas 29. seguía 30. construía

B
1. trabajaban 2. recorrías 3. iba 4. nos reuníamos 5. Hacía 6. veía 7. eran 8. servían 9. enseñaba 10. había 11. encantaba 12. dábamos 13. querían 14. tomaba 15. pensabas 16. sabía 17. gustaba 18. vestía 19. vivían 20. estábamos

C
1. Yo me reunía con mis amigos todos los domingos. 2. ¿Uds. iban a la sierra todos los inviernos? 3. María Elena almorzaba con nosotros cada semana. 4. Rodrigo y yo asistíamos a un concierto todas las semanas. 5. ¿No podías hacer un viaje cada año? 6. Les daba muchos regalos todos los años. 7. Siempre se divertían mucho en las fiestas. 8. Los chicos veían ese programa a menudo.

D
1. los maletines nuestros 2. el cartapacio mío 3. las cámaras suyas 4. el gorro suyo 5. el celular tuyo 6. el abrigo suyo 7. las tarjetas de crédito suyas 8. el coche suyo 9. la cartera mía 10. la pintura nuestra 11. los aretes tuyos 12. la casa de campo suya

E
1. estos informes tuyos 2. tres amigas suyas 3. un apartamento suyo 4. una idea mía 5. estos problemas suyos 6. ese coche suyo 7. una empresa nuestra 8. unos planes suyos 9. este reloj mío 10. esa cuñada suya

F

1. era 2. íbamos 3. quedaba 4. gustaba 5. preferían 6. encantaban 7. hacía 8. nadábamos 9. nevaba 10. esquiábamos 11. montaba 12. se llamaba 13. fascinaba

G

1. fueron pintados 2. fue prendida 3. fueron entregadas 4. fue vendido 5. fueron acostados 6. fue servido 7. fueron cultivadas 8. fue fundada 9. fueron discutidos 10. fue subido 11. fueron despedidos 12. fue cantada

H

1. Los papeles fueron firmados por el director. 2. La teoría fue explicada por la doctora Vega. 3. El informe fue terminado por los asesores. 4. Las fotos fueron tomadas por los turistas italianos. 5. Mi sitio web fue diseñado por un amigo mío. 6. El botón fue cosido por Consuelo. 7. Todas las fechas fueron aprendidas por los estudiantes. 8. Los datos fueron entrados por el desarrollador de programas. 9. El partido fue ganado por el equipo peruano. 10. La tele fue prendida por Guillermo.

I

1. Se visita la zona histórica. 2. Se sacan fotos. 3. Se cultivan verduras. 4. Se hace turismo. 5. Se resuelve el problema. 6. Se oye música. 7. Se realiza el proyecto. 8. Se producen vinos. 9. Se sirven platos vegetarianos. 10. Se ven mariposas.

J

1. Se navega en la red. 2. Se abre a las nueve y media. 3. Se vive muy bien en nuestro país. 4. Se habla por celular. 5. Se trabaja de lunes a jueves. 6. Se sale para el centro. 7. Se sube en el ascensor. 8. Se llega a la puerta de embarque. 9. Se maneja con cuidado. 10. Se baja en la escalera mecánica.

K

1. Se puede cambiar el vuelo. 2. Se permite subir a la pirámide. 3. No se debe comer comida basura. 4. Se necesita apagar el celular. 5. No se puede ver nada por la niebla. 6. No se permite fumar en este edificio. 7. Se debe dejar una propina. 8. Se necesita pasar por el control de seguridad.

L

1. Se lo enseñábamos. 2. Te los consigo. 3. Se la cuenta. 4. Me las trajeron. 5. Se lo entregué. 6. Nos las mostraban. 7. Se los mandabas. 8. Se la sirvió. 9. No se lo presta. 10. Me las enviaba.

M

1. Sí, me la puse. 2. Sí, se las prueba. 3. Sí, se lo abrocharon. 4. Sí, se lo corta. 5. Sí, nos los cepillábamos. 6. Sí, se la maquillan. 7. Sí, se lo rompió. 8. Sí, me lo sequé.

N

1. conocía / llegaron 2. tenías / te casaste 3. recorríamos / empezó 4. fue / dolía 5. se durmió / escuchaba 6. buscábamos / vimos 7. Eran / regresaron 8. era / llevaron 9. Hacía / salieron 10. estaban / fundaron 11. comprendía / explicó 12. dijeron / pensaban 13. hacíamos / pidieron 14. podía / se rompió 15. nadabas / sirvieron

O

1. Vamos a vendérsela. / Se la vamos a vender. 2. Acaba de regalárnoslos. / Nos los acaba de regalar. 3. Voy a decírselo. / Se lo voy a decir. 4. Acabamos de escribírtelo. / Te lo acabamos de escribir. 5. Van a llevármelas. / Me las van a llevar. 6. Acabas de devolvérsela. / Se la acabas de devolver. 7. Voy a hacérselos. / Se los voy a hacer. 8. Acaban de dárnoslo. / Nos lo acaban de dar.

P

1. No, pero se lo voy a abrochar pronto. / No, pero voy a abrochárselo pronto. 2. No, pero se los voy a limpiar pronto. / No, pero voy a limpiárselos pronto. 3. No, pero se las voy a poner pronto. / No, pero voy a ponérselas pronto. 4. No, pero se los voy a atar pronto. / No, pero voy a atárselos pronto. 5. No, pero se lo voy a secar pronto. / No, pero voy a secárselo pronto. 6. No, pero se lo voy a quitar pronto. / No, pero voy a quitárselo pronto. 7. No, pero se lo voy a cepillar pronto. / No, pero voy a cepillárselo pronto. 8. No, pero se lo voy a cortar pronto. / No, pero voy a cortárselo pronto.

Q

1. Quisimos hacer turismo. 2. Supieron su nacionalidad. 3. ¿El contrato? No quiso dárselo. 4. Yo tenía un plan. 5. ¿Conociste a esos amigos suyos? 6. No pudo reunirse conmigo.

R

1. Estaba muy nublado cuando llegamos a la playa. 2. Cuando los turistas fueron a ver las pirámides, hacía mucho calor. 3. Hacía noventa grados cuando volvió al cafetal. 4. Cuando el avión despegó, hacía mucho viento. 5. Estaba despejado cuando empezó la merienda campestre. 6. ¿Llovía cuando saliste del teatro? 7. Nevaba cuando ella pasó por la casa. 8. Hacía frío cuando se despertaron.

S

1. Nos dio hambre. 2. Les dio miedo. 3. Te dio sueño. 4. Le dio vergüenza. 5. Me dio confianza. 6. Le dio calor. 7. Les dio celos. 8. Le dio dolor. 9. Les dio envidia. 10. Nos dio frío.

T

1. La película aburrida le daba sueño. 2. Las canciones nos daban ganas de bailar. 3. Nuestro apoyo les daba confianza. 4. Su amigo guapo le daba celos a su novio. 5. El buen aroma de la sopa me daba hambre. 6. El comportamiento de su niño les daba vergüenza a sus padres. 7. ¿Qué te daba envidia? 8. La lluvia nos daba frío.

U

1. me despertaba 2. me cepillaba 3. me duchaba 4. me maquillaba 5. me vestía 6. desayunaba 7. salía 8. asistía 9. hacía 10. esperaba 11. tenía 12. faltaba 13. trabajaba

V

1. Eran las nueve de la noche cuando ellos volvieron de las pirámides. 2. Eran las siete y media de la mañana cuando tú te levantaste. 3. Era la una de la tarde cuando nosotros fuimos a la merienda campestre. 4. Eran las tres cuarenta y cinco de la tarde cuando los directores de la empresa se reunieron. 5. Eran las cinco de la tarde cuando yo empecé a jugar al tenis. 6. Eran las ocho menos veinte de la noche cuando Uds. llegaron a la finca. 7. Eran casi las once de la noche cuando Ud. terminó de escribir su informe. 8. Eran las diez de la mañana cuando él salió para el cafetal.

W

1. llegaba 2. eran 3. esperaban 4. soñaban 5. tenían 6. trabajaban 7. era 8. sabían 9. vivían 10. daba

X

1. ¿Cuánto tiempo hacía que tú tocabas el piano cuando te dieron una beca? / Hacía ocho años que tocaba el piano. 2. ¿Cuánto tiempo hacía que ella jugaba al golf cuando comenzó a llover? / Hacía dos horas que jugaba al golf. 3. ¿Cuánto tiempo hacía que Uds. esperaban a sus primos cuando llegaron? / Hacía media hora que esperábamos a nuestros primos. 4. ¿Cuánto tiempo hacía que él trabajaba en Chile cuando su empresa lo mandó al Perú? / Hacía cinco meses que trabajaba en Chile.

Y

1. Hacía una hora que yo buscaba al perro. (Yo buscaba al perro hacía una hora.) 2. ¿Desde cuándo cultivaban los agricultores el maíz? 3. ¿Cuánto (tiempo) hacía que te interesaba el arte moderno? 4. Hacía cincuenta años que se producían carros en esta planta. (Se producían carros en esta planta hacía cincuenta años.) 5. Hacíamos ecoturismo desde junio. 6. Hacía muchos años que servían comida sana. (Servían comida sana hacía muchos años.) 7. ¿Cuánto (tiempo) hacía que nevaba? 8. Él asistía a una universidad estatal desde el año pasado.

Z

1. Me dijeron que mi primo se casaba. 2. Nos escribió que iba al extranjero. 3. Me escribieron que disfrutaban de sus vacaciones. 4. Me texteó que estaba en camino. 5. Le dije que la quería mucho. 6. Le pregunté si trabajaba todavía en la base de datos. 7. Me contó que le interesaba estudiar administración de empresas. 8. Nos informó que hacía un estudio de mercado.

AA

1. ¿Las carpetas? Se las devolvimos a ella ayer. 2. ¿El contrato? Se lo mandó a los abogados ayer. 3. ¿El billete? Me lo dieron ayer. 4. ¿Los jardines? Nos los mostró ayer. 5. ¿El paquete? Se lo envolvieron ayer. 6. ¿El dinero? Me lo pidió ayer. 7. ¿Los aretes? Se los regalamos ayer. 8. ¿La cartera? Te la traje ayer. 9. ¿Los documentos? Se los entregué ayer. 10. ¿Las galletas? Se las hice ayer.

BB

Answers will vary.

CC

Answers will vary.

11 Health and Accidents

A

1. iba / pudo 2. pensaban / cambiaron 3. bajaba / subía 4. entró / saludó 5. dijo / quería 6. almorcé / seguí 7. visitábamos / montábamos 8. se levantaron / se arreglaron 9. me desperté / tenía

B

1. Llovía / tuvieron 2. esperábamos / dejó 3. comía / tomaba 4. Estaba / hubo 5. pegó / se pusieron

C

1. Yo era secretario del director ejecutivo hasta que se enfermó. 2. Elena y Mercedes dejaron de trabajar en esa sucursal. 3. El número de teléfono fue cambiado así que no pudimos llamarlos.
4. ¿El gerente trasladó o despidió a Joaquín?
5. Víctor no terminó el informe porque no había suficientes datos.

D

1. ¿Cuánto tiempo hacía que se conocían cuando se comprometieron? 2. Hacía una semana que nos veíamos cuando empezamos a tutearnos.
3. ¿Cuánto tiempo hacía que nos ayudábamos con el proyecto cuando Ud. se mudó? 4. Mientras Lola y Juan se abrazaban y se besaban, el hermanito de Lola empezó a reírse. 5. Se comprendían muy bien hasta que algo pasó. 6. Nos conocimos cuando trabajábamos en una compañía de alta tecnología.

E

1. imprimíamos / dejó 2. leía / oyó 3. veía / vinieron 4. preparaba / tocó 5. jugaban / comenzó

F

1. Me dijeron que su hija iba a graduarse en la universidad. 2. Alonso era solterón hasta que conoció a y se casó con Sofía. 3. Victoria se hizo abogada cuando tenía veintisiete años.
4. Eras muy joven cuando te recibiste de médico.
5. Los gemelos eran superdotados y simpáticos pero también algo presumidos.

G

1. la casona 2. contestón 3. facilón 4. llorón 5. mirón 6. la muchachona 7. matón 8. el martillazo 9. el perrazo 10. el puñetazo 11. los ojazos 12. el catarrazo

H

1. la ropita 2. el dedito 3. la niñita 4. el pajarito 5. la vocecita 6. el chiquito 7. fresquito 8. el jovencito 9. la botellita 10. el calorcito 11. la fiestecita 12. Miguelito 13. poquito 14. la nietecita 15. el abuelito 16. cerquita 17. la cabecita 18. Rodriguito 19. mismito 20. el choquecito 21. el pececito 22. la lucecita 23. la tosecita

I

1. A Juanita le duele el estómago. 2. A Pedro le dolía la espalda. 3. Les duelen las rodillas.
4. A nuestra sobrinita le duele la garganta.
5. Te dolía la cabeza. 6. Al jugador le duelen los tobillos. 7. Al nietecito de Paco le dolía el oído.
8. Les dolían los ojos.

J

1. Se le acabó el filtro solar. 2. Se nos olvidaron las toallas de playa. 3. ¿Se les quedó el repelente contra mosquitos en casa? 4. Se me cayeron los lentes de sol. 5. Se les descompuso el carro.
6. Se te perdieron las gafas oscuras. 7. Se le quebraron los platos.

K

1. Los mosquitos nos comían vivos. 2. ¡Qué picadura! No debes rascártela. 3. Catalina tomaba el sol hasta que una abeja le picó. 4. A Pedro se le perdieron las gafas oscuras (los lentes de sol) en la arena. 5. Se les quedó la tienda de campaña en el campamento. 6. ¡Pobrecita! El champú le entró en los ojos.

L

1. supe / estaba 2. dijeron / iba 3. esperábamos / dio 4. estaba / hizo 5. llevaron / dolía / tenía

M

1. bajábamos / vimos 2. estaba / sonó 3. ardía / apagaron 4. era / estalló

N

1. iba 2. llegó 3. quedaba 4. se acercó 5. oyó 6. vio 7. preguntó 8. pasaba (pasó) 9. dijo 10. cruzaba 11. atropelló 12. atendían 13. tenía

O

Answers will vary.

P

Answers will vary.

Q

Answers will vary.

R

Answers will vary.

12 People: Character and Personality, Societal Problems

A

1. Consuelo es más presumida que Aurora. / Aurora es menos presumida que Consuelo.
2. Nosotros estamos más entusiasmados que Jaime y Federico. / Jaime y Federico están menos entusiasmados que nosotros. 3. La profesora de química es más exigente que el profesor de física. / El profesor de física es menos exigente que la profesora de química. 4. La chaqueta es más cara que los pantalones. / Los pantalones son menos caros que la chaqueta. 5. Yo soy más optimista que tú. / Tú eres menos optimista que yo.
6. El condominio es más moderno que la casa. / La casa es menos moderna que el condominio.

7. Uds. son más corteses que Juan Manuel. / Juan Manuel es menos cortés que Uds.
8. Los tacos están más ricos que los tamales. / Los tamales están menos ricos que los tacos.

B

1. Elena es tan caprichosa como Victoria. 2. Pedro es tan ingenuo como tú. 3. Ellos son tan egoístas como Rodrigo. 4. Paquita es tan coqueta como su prima. 5. Los empleados son tan trabajadores como el director. 6. Uds. están tan estresados como sus amigos. 7. Ana María es tan calculadora como su cuñada. 8. Bernardo está tan emocionado como Beatriz. 9. Nuestros hijos están tan ocupados como nosotros. 10. Tú eres tan comprensiva como tus papás.

C

1. Guillermo escuchó más atentamente que Josefa. / Josefa escuchó menos atentamente que Guillermo. / Guillermo escuchó tan atentamente como Josefa. 2. Alberto trabajó más ambiciosamente que Santiago. / Santiago trabajó menos ambiciosamente que Alberto. / Alberto trabajó tan ambiciosamente como Santiago.
3. Uds. fueron de compras más frecuentemente que nosotros. / Nosotros fuimos de compras menos frecuentemente que Uds. / Uds. fueron de compras tan frecuentemente como nosotros. 4. La familia Suárez vivió más cómodamente que la familia Morales. / La familia Morales vivió menos cómodamente que la familia Suárez. / La familia Suárez vivió tan cómodamente como la familia Morales. 5. Nosotros manejamos más lentamente que tú. / Tú manejaste menos lentamente que nosotros. / Nosotros manejamos tan lentamente como tú. 6. Antonio se ofendió más fácilmente que su hermano. / Su hermano se ofendió menos fácilmente que Antonio. / Antonio se ofendió tan fácilmente como su hermano. 7. Damián corrió más rápidamente que Uds. / Uds. corrieron menos rápidamente que Damián. / Damián corrió tan rápidamente como Uds. 8. Tú pensaste más profundamente que yo. / Yo pensé menos profundamente que tú. / Tú pensaste tan profundamente como yo. 9. Blanca contestó más amablemente que Pepe. / Pepe contestó menos amablemente que Blanca. / Blanca contestó tan amablemente como Pepe. 10. Ud. reaccionó más sensiblemente que Daniela. / Daniela reaccionó menos sensiblemente que Ud. / Ud. reaccionó tan sensiblemente como Daniela.

D

1. Yo cursaba más materias que tú. / Tú cursabas menos materias que yo. / Yo cursaba tantas materias como tú. 2. El niño tenía más hambre que su hermanita. / Su hermanita tenía menos hambre que el niño. / El niño tenía tanta hambre como su hermanita. 3. Uds. compraban más libros de texto que los otros estudiantes. / Los otros estudiantes compraban menos libros de texto que Uds. / Uds. compraban tantos libros de texto como los otros estudiantes. 4. Eva veía más películas que María Elena. / María Elena veía menos películas que Eva. / Eva veía tantas películas como María Elena. 5. Tú comías más comida chatarra que tus amigos. / Tus amigos comían menos comida chatarra que tú. / Tú comías tanta comida chatarra como tus amigos. 6. Nosotros leíamos más obras maestras que ellos. / Ellos leían menos obras maestras que nosotros. / Nosotros leíamos tantas obras maestras como ellos. 7. Sofía recorría más países que su marido. / Su marido recorría menos países que Sofía. / Sofía recorría tantos países como su marido. 8. Ignacio hacía más ejercicio que Mateo. / Mateo hacía menos ejercicio que Ignacio. / Ignacio hacía tanto ejercicio como Mateo.

E

1. La abuela Raquel es la más sensata. 2. El tío Rodrigo es el más cascarrabias. 3. Los primos Laura y Martín son los más calculadores.
4. Las nietas Teresita y Paquita son las más coquetas. 5. La cuñada Lucía es la más entrometida. 6. Los sobrinos Ramón y Eugenia son los más tercos. 7. El yerno Manolo es el más realista. 8. La nuera Montserrat es la más pesada.

F

1. Anita es más presumida que su hermana.
2. Jorge es menos maleducado que sus amigos.
3. Cristóbal estaba tan estresado como tú.
4. Mis hermanos son tan considerados como yo.
5. Matilde es la persona más tímida de su familia.
6. Juanito es el alumno más raro de su clase.

G

1. elegantísima 2. riquísimos 3. larguísimos
4. interesantísimo 5. buenísimas 6. hermosísimos
7. simpatiquísimas 8. facilísimos 9. clarísima
10. ocupadísimos

H

1. Es el mejor libro de nuestra biblioteca.
2. Es la marca más famosa del mercado.
3. Trabajábamos más que nunca. 4. Enrique viajaba tan frecuentemente como nosotros.

5. El año pasado Perla ganó más de doscientos mil dólares. 6. A Pablo no le quedan más que mil setecientos dólares en su cuenta de ahorros. 7. Nuestro equipo le ganó al otro equipo y con mucho. 8. Ellos compraron tantos bolígrafos y lápices como nosotros. 9. ¿Cree que este gerente es más exigente que el antiguo (el anterior)? 10. ¡Qué va! Es el gerente más indulgente de la empresa. 11. La salud es más importante que nada. 12. Raquel se queja más que nadie.

I

1. Prefiero el marrón, pero me gusta el negro también. 2. Prefiero los de cuentos, pero me gustan los de poesía también. 3. Prefiero la de enfrente, pero me gusta la de al lado también. 4. Prefiero los de arte, pero me gustan los de ciencias también. 5. Prefiero el italiano, pero me gusta el mexicano también. 6. Prefiero los fabricados en los Estados Unidos, pero me gustan los fabricados en el extranjero también. 7. Prefiero la grande, pero me gusta la pequeña también. 8. Prefiero las obligatorias, pero me gustan las optativas también. 9. Prefiero los vegetarianos, pero me gustan los de carne también. 10. Prefiero el de lana, pero me gusta el de algodón también.

J

1. Nuestra calle es más tranquila que la suya (la de ellos). 2. Tu proyecto era tan interesante como el mío. 3. Sus cursos son menos difíciles que los nuestros. 4. Nuestras empresas ganaron tanto dinero como las suyas (las de Ud.). 5. Su equipo juega tan bien como el tuyo. 6. La novia de Ricardo es tan alegre como la suya (la de su hermano). 7. Este celular funcionaba mejor que el suyo (el de Susana). 8. Tus profesores son tan exigentes como los míos.

K

1. Me gusta ésta (esta) más que aquélla (aquella). 2. Me gusta aquél (aquel) más que éste (este). 3. Me gustan ésos (esos) más que éstos (estos). 4. Me gustan éstas (estas) más que aquéllas (aquellas). 5. Me gusta éste (este) más que aquél (aquel). 6. Me gustan éstos (estos) más que ésos (esos).

L

1. Estos cartuchos de tinta cuestan más que esos (ésos/aquellos/aquéllos). 2. Los guantes de seda son más finos que los de cuero. 3. Este abrigo rojo es más largo que ese (ése/aquel/aquél) azul marino. 4. Creo que (Me parece que) conociste tantas ciudades latinoamericanas como nosotros.

M

1. Hay más ruido ambiental que nunca en nuestra sociedad. 2. Esta es la región más contaminada del estado. 3. Hay gente que cree que el reciclaje es más importante que nada. 4. Hay menos crimen en nuestra ciudad que en la suya. 5. Había muchísimo espíritu cívico en el país durante los años cincuenta. 6. Hay más drogadicción que nunca.

N

1. Este apartamento es más amplio que los que vio anteriormente. 2. Aquel condominio es más grande y menos caro que el mío. 3. Esta casa tiene tantos dormitorios como la suya pero tiene menos cuartos de baño que la nuestra. 4. Esta computadora es más potente que la que tenía. 5. La computadora anterior era más fácil de usar que la que tengo ahora.

O

1. lingüística e idiomas 2. Costa Rica u Honduras 3. sensible e ingenua 4. mujeres u hombres 5. pesimista u optimista 6. franceses e italianos 7. este u oeste 8. sinagogas e iglesias 9. oxígeno e hidrógeno 10. libertad e igualdad 11. rinocerontes e hipopótamos 12. escocés u holandés

P

1. No, para ellos, no. 2. No, por Uds., no. 3. No, con ellas, no. 4. No, para ti, no. 5. No, con él, no. 6. No, por ella, no. 7. No, contigo, no. 8. No, contigo, no.

Q

Answers will vary.

R

Answers will vary.

13 Business and the Growth of the Cities

A

1. descompuesto 2. escrita 3. caídos 4. roto 5. aumentado 6. hecha 7. vistos 8. leídas 9. muertas 10. llevados

B

1. Carmen está angustiada. 2. Rodrigo y Diego están aburridos. 3. Nosotras estamos emocionadas. 4. Tú estás estresada. 5. Juanita está deprimida. 6. Carlos y Mateo están entusiasmados. 7. Yo estoy preocupado. 8. Esteban y Vera están acatarrados. 9. Ud. está cansada. 10. Fernando está confundido.

C

1. he 2. vuelto 3. oído 4. ha 5. dicho 6. han 7. visto 8. hemos 9. has 10. dado

D

1. Ha cursado dos asignaturas optativas. 2. Han querido visitarnos. 3. Hemos puesto la mesa. 4. Ha llovido todo el día. 5. Ha sido difícil adelgazar. 6. Se han incluido los ingresos y los gastos. 7. He abierto las ventanas. 8. No has visto a nadie, ¿verdad? 9. Ha habido mucho ajetreo hoy. 10. Hemos estado tan emocionados como Uds. 11. Han tenido que pagar el seguro de salud. 12. ¿Has pedido más vino?

E

1. Yo he escrito los documentos. / Los documentos están escritos. 2. Nosotros hemos hecho el plan de negocios. / El plan de negocios está hecho. 3. Ella ha pagado la hipoteca. / La hipoteca está pagada. 4. Uds. han recibido la invitación. / La invitación está recibida. 5. Ellos han abierto las fábricas. / Las fábricas están abiertas. 6. Tú has facturado el equipaje. / El equipaje está facturado. 7. Él ha alquilado el apartamento. / El apartamento está alquilado. 8. Ellas han puesto la mesa. / La mesa está puesta. 9. Ud. ha descargado su canción favorita. / Su canción favorita está descargada. 10. Ellos han construido los rascacielos. / Los rascacielos están construidos.

F

1. El equipo ha hecho el plan de negocios. 2. Alejo y yo hemos elaborado el presupuesto. 3. Los asesores han recogido los datos. 4. El artista gráfico ha dibujado el logo. 5. Yo he creado diapositivas en PowerPoint. 6. Tú has mandado los emails. 7. Uds. se han reunido en la sala de conferencias. 8. Leonardo ha diseñado el folleto. 9. Claudia y su asistente han leído todos los documentos. 10. Ud. ha impreso el volante.

G

1. Ya se las he regalado. 2. Ya se lo hemos pedido. 3. Ya se lo ha leído. 4. Ya se lo he dado. 5. Ya las he llevado. 6. Ya nos lo han dicho. 7. Ya me la ha prestado. 8. Ya lo hemos hecho.

H

1. Ya les ha dicho lo que oyó. 2. ¿Ya le has dado el pésame a la viuda de Daniel? 3. ¿El presupuesto? Se lo hemos elaborado. 4. ¿El contrato? No nos lo han explicado todavía. 5. ¿La cafetera? No he tenido tiempo de devolvérsela. 6. ¿Los ingresos y los gastos? ¿Se los ha mostrado a la contadora? 7. Ha habido mucho ajetreo en la empresa.

I

1. Nos hemos matriculado ya. 2. Se ha graduado ya. 3. Me la he lavado ya. 4. Se han reunido ya. 5. Me las he probado ya. 6. Se han casado ya. 7. Me he comprometido con él ya. 8. Nos hemos mudado ya. 9. Se los han cepillado ya. 10. Se la ha maquillado ya.

J

1. Ya está levantado. 2. Ya estoy enamorada. 3. Ya están acostados. 4. Ya estamos vestidas. 5. Ya estamos bañados. 6. Ya estoy arreglada. 7. Ya están instalados. 8. Ya están divorciados.

K

1. está tumbado 2. están inclinados 3. está dormido 4. está agachado 5. estamos parados 6. está montada 7. están levantados 8. está echado

L

1. ¡Cuánto ha crecido la ciudad en los últimos años! / Y la población ha aumentado muchísimo. Hay casi cuatro millones de habitantes. 2. Nuestro pueblecito se ha convertido en una ciudad grande e importante. / Ya lo creo. Muchos edificios han sido construidos (se han construido) y poco a poco hay menos barrios bajos. 3. ¡Han hecho maravillas! Nuestra ciudad está muy cambiada. / Es verdad. Pero, ¡qué aglomeración! ¡Qué tráfico! ¡Qué ruido!

M

1. Cuando Ud. compró los cartuchos de tinta, Jorge ya había impreso las invitaciones. 2. Cuando los invitados llegaron para cenar, Pepita y Tomás ya habían puesto la mesa. 3. Cuando despegó el avión, los pasajeros ya se habían abrochado el cinturón de seguridad. 4. Cuando nosotros conocimos a Nora, ella ya se había hecho ingeniera. 5. Cuando Eduardo comenzó a trabajar, sus colegas ya habían leído los documentos. 6. Cuando llegaste al cementerio, el entierro ya había tenido lugar. 7. Cuando sonó el teléfono, tú ya te habías despertado. 8. Cuando vi a Antonio, su empresa ya lo había trasladado a otra sucursal. 9. Cuando Uds. nos dieron la noticia, ya la habíamos oído del vecino. 10. Cuando Nora regresó a su pueblo natal, el pueblo ya se había convertido en una ciudad grande.

N

1. ¿Ya ha elaborado el presupuesto? / Sí, he incluido ingresos y gastos. 2. ¿Está puesta la mesa? / Sí, y la cena está servida. 3. Ha sido un día muy difícil. / ¿Por qué lo dices? ¿Has tenido que hacer mucho trabajo? 4. ¿Nevaba cuando regresaban a casa? /

No, ya habíamos regresado a casa cuando empezó a nevar. 5. Cuando aterrizó el avión, los pasajeros ya habían prendido sus celulares. / Supongo que también habían bajado el equipaje de mano. 6. Cuando llegamos a casa de Mario, la fiesta ya había terminado. / ¿Y nadie se lo había dicho antes? ¡Qué barbaridad!

O

Answers will vary.

P

Answers will vary.

Q

Answers will vary.

14 Directions, Air Travel, Recipes

A

1. Corra el maratón. 2. Maneje con cuidado. 3. Abra las ventanas. 4. Asista al concierto. 5. Cruce la calle. 6. Suba al avión. 7. Coma con nosotros. 8. Siga por el río. 9. Elabore un presupuesto. 10. Lea este libro. 11. Diseñe el sitio web. 12. Vuelva para el viernes. 13. Pida una disculpa. 14. Haga un plan de negocios.

B

1. Beban mucha agua. 2. Trabajen con el equipo. 3. Vivan felizmente. 4. Escriban el email. 5. Conduzcan con cuidado. 6. Aprendan las fechas de memoria. 7. Tomen el tren. 8. Vistan a los niños. 9. Prendan la televisión. 10. Analicen los datos. 11. Cobren el cheque. 12. Compartan sus ideas. 13. Duerman la siesta. 14. Sirvan la comida.

C

1. Lleguen Uds. temprano. 2. Sirva Ud. la cena. 3. Abra Ud. la ventana. 4. Crucen Uds. la calle con cuidado. 5. Mire Ud. la señal de tráfico. 6. Suban Uds. en el ascensor. 7. Guarde Ud. los datos. 8. Elaboren Uds. un presupuesto.

D

1. Guarde los suéteres. / No guarde los suéteres. 2. Vea el programa. / No vea el programa. 3. Estacione en la plaza. / No estacione en la plaza. 4. Añada más sal. / No añada más sal. 5. Cierre la puerta. / No cierre la puerta. 6. Imprima los contratos. / No imprima los contratos. 7. Ponga la mesa. / No ponga la mesa. 8. Pruebe ese plato. / No pruebe ese plato. 9. Descargue el archivo. / No descargue el archivo. 10. Repita las palabras. / No repita las palabras.

E

1. Guarden los suéteres. / No guarden los suéteres. 2. Vean el programa. / No vean el programa. 3. Estacionen en la plaza. / No estacionen en la plaza. 4. Añadan más sal. / No añadan más sal. 5. Cierren la puerta. / No cierren la puerta. 6. Impriman los contratos. / No impriman los contratos. 7. Pongan la mesa. / No pongan la mesa. 8. Prueben ese plato. / No prueben ese plato. 9. Descarguen el archivo. / No descarguen el archivo. 10. Repitan las palabras. / No repitan las palabras.

F

1. Vende el carro. / No vendas el carro. 2. Navega en la web. / No navegues en la web. 3. Sube en el ascensor. / No subas en el ascensor. 4. Sigue por esta calle. / No sigas por esta calle. 5. Haz la maleta. / No hagas la maleta. 6. Piensa en eso. / No pienses en eso. 7. Ven el sábado. / No vengas el sábado. 8. Sal antes de las cuatro. / No salgas antes de las cuatro. 9. Ten prisa. / No tengas prisa. 10. Juega al golf. / No juegues al golf.

G

1. No te preocupes. 2. Vete. 3. La verdad. Dísela. 4. Le debes dinero. Devuélveselo. 5. No seas así. 6. Esta corbata es fea. No te la pongas. 7. No estés enojado (enojada) conmigo. (No te enojes conmigo.) 8. La cena, por favor. Háznosla. 9. Él necesita los auriculares. Dáselos. (A él le hacen falta los auriculares. Dáselos.) 10. Ten paciencia.

H

1. ¿El perro? Mírenlo. / No lo miren. 2. ¿El piano? Tóquelo. / No lo toque. 3. ¿Las revistas? Entréguemelas. / No me las entregue. 4. ¿Los regalos? Escójaselos. / No se los escoja. 5. ¿Las llaves? Búsquenlas. / No las busquen. 6. ¿La noticia? Cuéntesela. / No se la cuente. 7. ¿La idea? Explíquensela. / No se la expliquen. 8. ¿La orquesta? Diríjanosla. / No nos la dirija. 9. ¿La cuenta? Páguensela. / No se la paguen. 10. ¿El partido? Empiécenlo. / No lo empiecen.

I

1. Léalo. / Léanlo. / Léaselo. / Léanselo. 2. Tráigalas. / Tráiganlas. / Tráigaselas. / Tráiganselas. 3. Explíquelo. / Explíquenlo. / Explíqueselo. / Explíquenselo. 4. Dígalo. / Díganlo. / Díganoslo. / Digánnoslo. 5. Muéstrelas. / Muéstrenlas. / Muéstreselas. / Muéstrenselas. 6. Sírvalo. / Sírvanlo. / Sírvanoslo. / Sírvannoslo. 7. Lávese. / Lávense. / Lávese las manos. / Lávense las manos. / Láveselas. /

Lávenselas. 8. Pídalos. / Pídanlos. / Pídaselos. / Pídanselos. 9. Póngase la chaqueta. / Pónganse la chaqueta. / Póngasela. / Pónganselа. 10. Séquese el pelo. / Séquense el pelo. / Séqueselo. / Séquenselo.

J

1. Lleguemos el domingo. / No lleguemos el domingo. 2. Hagamos turismo. / No hagamos turismo. 3. Saquemos el pasaporte. / No saquemos el pasaporte. 4. Demos consejos. / No demos consejos. 5. Vamos al teatro. / No vayamos al teatro. 6. Durmamos la siesta. / No durmamos la siesta. 7. Salgamos esta noche. / No salgamos esta noche. 8. Vengamos en tren. / No vengamos en tren. 9. Pensemos en el futuro. / No pensemos en el futuro. 10. Pidamos un café. / No pidamos un café. 11. Sentémonos en el sofá. / No nos sentemos en el sofá. 12. Quedémonos unos días más. / No nos quedemos unos días más.

K

1. Sí, veámosla. / Sí, vamos a verla.
2. Sí, discutámoslas. / Sí, vamos a discutirlas.
3. Sí, consigámoslos. / Sí, vamos a conseguirlos.
4. Sí, compartámoslos. / Sí, vamos a compartirlos.
5. Sí, pidámoslo. / Sí, vamos a pedirlo.
6. Sí, visitémosla. / Sí, vamos a visitarla.
7. Sí, aparquémoslo. / Sí, vamos a aparcarlo.
8. Sí, traduzcámoslas. / Sí, vamos a traducirlas.
9. Sí, probémonoslos. / Sí, vamos a probárnoslos.
10. Sí, cortémonoslo. / Sí, vamos a cortárnoslo.

L

1. No, no la veamos. 2. No, nos las discutamos. 3. No, no los consigamos. 4. No, no los compartamos. 5. No, no lo pidamos. 6. No, no la visitemos. 7. No, lo aparquemos. 8. No, no las traduzcamos. 9. No, no nos los probemos. 10. No, no nos lo cortemos.

M

1. Paseémonos por el parque. / No nos paseemos por el parque. 2. Casémonos en diciembre. / No nos casemos en diciembre.
3. Pongámonoslos. / No nos los pongamos.
4. Reunámonos el domingo. / No nos reunamos el domingo. 5. Abrochémonoslo. / No nos lo abrochemos. 6. Despertémonos temprano. / No nos despertemos temprano. 7. Lavémonoslas. / No nos las lavemos. 8. Vámonos ahora. / No nos vayamos ahora. 9. Sequémoselo. / No se lo sequemos. 10. Despidámonos de ellos. / No nos despidamos de ellos.

N

1. Sí, entrégueselos. / No, no se los entregue.
2. Sí, muéstreselas. / No, no se las muestre.
3. Sí, pídaselo. / No, no se lo pida. 4. Sí, déselo. / No, no se lo dé. 5. Sí, calcúleselos. / No, no se los calcule. 6. Sí, hágasela. / No, no se la haga.
7. Sí, descríbaselo. / No, no se lo describa.
8. Sí, tráigaselo. / No, no se lo traiga.

O

1. Sí, muéstremelos. 2. Sí, explíquemela.
3. Sí, pónmelo. 4. Sí, házmela.
5. Sí, entréguemelos. 6. Sí, démelas.
7. Sí, préstamelo. 8. Sí, envíemela. 9. Sí, dímelo.
10. Sí, sírvemelas.

P

1. No, no me los muestre. 2. No, no me la explique. 3. No, no me lo pongas. 4. No, no me la hagas. 5. No, no me los entregue. 6. No, no me las dé. 7. No, no me lo prestes. 8. No, no me la envíe. 9. No, no me lo digas. 10. No, no me las sirvas.

Q

1. Sí, léela. 2. No, no la pongas todavía.
3. Sí, sácalos. 4. No, no lo calientes todavía.
5. Sí, bátelas. 6. Sí, échalas. 7. No, no lo añadas todavía. 8. Sí, fríelas. 9. No, no los sirvas todavía.
10. Sí, prepáralo.

R

1. Tranquilízate. 2. No te preocupes.
3. No te vuelvas loca. 4. No te muerdas las uñas.
5. No seas tonta. 6. Ve a la fiesta sin cuidado.
7. No te pongas nerviosa. 8. No te alteres.
9. Sé feliz. 10. Relájate. 11. Disfruta de las festividades. 12. Diviértete mucho.

S

1. Seguir las instrucciones. 2. No pisar el césped.
3. ¡Pintura fresca, no tocar! 4. Agregar una pizca de sal. 5. Lavar y secar las hojas de lechuga.
6. Pulsar el botón. 7. Enjuagar bien el pelo.
8. Introducir la contraseña.

T

1. Tenga la bondad de prestarme los auriculares.
2. Haga el favor de contarme lo ocurrido.
3. Favor de explicárnoslo. 4. Favor de hacer una copia de seguridad. 5. Tenga la bondad de decírmelo. 6. Favor de ayudarme con el abrigo.
7. Haga el favor de llamarme lo antes posible.
8. Tenga la bondad de enviármelas para la semana entrante.

U

Answers will vary.

V
Answers will vary.

W
1. Ase la carne a la parrilla. 2. Remueva la sopa. 3. Mezcle las frutas y las chispas de chocolate. 4. Agregue (Agréguele) jugo de limón al pescado. 5. Enfríe el vino. 6. Sazone con sal y pimienta. 7. Hornee el pan. 8. Pique las cebollas.

X
Answers will vary.

15 Holidays and Celebrations, Planning for the Future

A
1. Entregaré el informe. 2. Venderá su casa. 3. No discutirán ese asunto. 4. Te divertirás mucho. 5. Dormirá la siesta. 6. Jugaré al tenis. 7. Diseñaremos el sitio web. 8. Elegiré un nuevo celular. 9. ¿No comerás nada más? 10. Se reunirán en la sala de conferencias. 11. Conseguiré una beca. 12. Hará ochenta grados.

B
1. diré 2. saldrá 3. querrás 4. nos pondremos 5. vendrán 6. tendrán 7. Hará 8. sabremos 9. podrá 10. Habrá

C
1. Los gemelos tendrán siete u ocho años. 2. Sabrás su número de teléfono. 3. Serán las once. 4. Camila querrá ver esta obra de teatro. 5. Su casa costará una fortuna. 6. Estarán acatarrados. 7. Cristóbal se hará ingeniero. 8. Este anillo valdrá miles de dólares. 9. Habrá muchos documentos sobre este tema. 10. Cabrá el equipaje en el maletero del coche.

D
1. ¿Cuántos años tendrá el señor Durán? 2. Tendrá cincuenta años. 3. ¿Qué hora será? 4. Serán las cuatro. 5. ¡Qué traje más elegante! Costará mucho dinero. 6. No puedo encontrar mi tarjeta de crédito. ¿Dónde estará? 7. Nevará mañana. 8. Sabrán lo que pasó.

E
1. Daniel y yo elaboraríamos el presupuesto. 2. Uds. aprenderían español en Bogotá. 3. Tú tendrías suerte. 4. Yo no se lo diría a nadie. 5. La cocinera querría añadir más sal. 6. Nosotros haríamos escala en Miami. 7. Mis colegas compartirían los gastos. 8. Sus suegros no podrían visitarlos. 9. Tú saldrías más tarde. 10. Ud. se mudaría a ese barrio.

F
1. ¿Cuántos años tendría María Elena cuando terminó la maestría? 2. Tendría veintitrés años cuando la terminó. 3. ¿Qué hora sería cuando los señores Fernández llegaron al balneario? 4. Sería mediodía. 5. ¿Quién tendría la culpa del crimen? 6. Sería el mayordomo. 7. ¿Dónde estarían Uds. cuando los llamamos? 8. Estaríamos todavía en la oficina. 9. ¿Qué habría en el paquete? 10. Habría juguetes para los niños.

G
1. A Uds. les gustará esta comida mexicana. 2. A ella le entusiasmará conocer a nuestros amigos. 3. A ti te interesará este proyecto. 4. A mí me quedarán dos exámenes todavía. 5. A ellos les faltará dinero. 6. A nosotros nos harán falta más datos. 7. A Ud. le convendrá encargarse de la oficina. 8. A él no le importará nada.

H
1. Vamos a asistir al concierto. 2. Voy a salir para la hacienda. 3. Uds. van a irse pasado mañana. 4. ¿Vas a poder acompañarme a la boda? 5. Va a haber una fiesta de quinceañera para Inés. 6. La fiesta va a ser en el Hotel Palacio. 7. Ellos van a tener que trabajar. 8. Manuel va a querer esquiar.

I
1. van / iremos 2. hará / hacen 3. pide / pediré 4. volvemos / volverá 5. tomará / toma 6. me paseo / te pasearás 7. almorzaremos / almuerzan 8. te reúnes / me reuniré

J
1. lloverá 2. llegaremos 3. se pondrá 4. se matriculará 5. entregarán 6. venderán 7. querrás 8. se encargarán

K
1. regresaría 2. se casarían 3. pasaría 4. daría 5. podrían 6. habría 7. encantarían 8. veríamos

L
1. Me gustaría aprender a esquiar. 2. A los niños les entusiasmaría abrir sus regalos. 3. Te interesarían mucho estos museos. 4. ¡Nos encantaría tomar una copa de champaña! 5. A Carlos no le importaría nada. 6. A Ud. le haría falta su pasaporte. 7. Le tocaría a Julia en el juego de mesa. 8. A Uds. les convendría tomar un vuelo sin escala.

M
1. ¿Qué dirá? 2. ¿Qué sabrá? 3. ¿Qué pensará? (¿Qué creerá?) 4. ¿Qué comprenderá? (¿Qué entenderá?) 5. ¿Qué se imaginará? 6. ¿Qué supondrá? 7. ¿Qué se preguntará? 8. ¿Qué conjeturará?

N

1. Buenas tardes, señor Díaz. Ud. es uno de los pocos candidatos que hay para este puesto.
2. Mucho gusto, señor. Muchas gracias.
3. Nos gustó su carta de motivación y su currículum vitae es impresionante. Por favor, dígame más de su experiencia profesional.
4. Hacía quince años que trabajaba para mi empresa anterior. Tengo las habilidades requeridas y las habilidades comunicativas muy buenas. Y siempre cumplo con las fechas límite.
5. Ud. tendría que resolver problemas difíciles y mostrar iniciativa. 6. Estoy seguro de que podría. Como gerente y director de proyecto, tuve éxito en todos mis proyectos y me llevé muy bien con mi equipo. 7. Estoy contento de saberlo. El trabajo en equipo es muy importante para nuestra empresa. Gracias, señor Díaz. Estaremos en contacto con Ud. 8. Muchas gracias, señor Torres. Yo estaría muy contento de trabajar con Ud.

O

1. Eva, ¿sabes si Carmen, Daniel y Federico asistirán a la reunión? 2. Carmen y Federico sí estarán pero Daniel me dijo que tendría que ver a un cliente por la tarde. No sabía que habría una reunión hoy. 3. El señor Torres quiere lanzar una campaña publicitaria para anunciar el nuevo producto así que tendremos mucho que hacer.
4. Eladio, tú y yo elaboraremos el presupuesto. Federico hablará del mercadeo de redes y Carmen explicará sus ideas sobre los medios sociales.
5. El señor Torres tendrá muestras del producto y querrá crear un logo y un lema. 6. Creo que los diseñadores se encargarán del diseño gráfico. Mira. El señor Torres acaba de entrar. Empezará la reunión.

P

1. ¡Isabel sí se preocupará! 2. ¡Mis papás sí comprenderán! 3. ¡Tú sí te quejarás! 4. ¡Yo sí se lo diré a todos! 5. ¡Ud. sí se ofenderá! 6. ¡Rodrigo y yo sí nos sorprenderemos! 7. ¡Uds. sí se enojarán!
7. ¡Alfredo sí tendrá la culpa!

Q

Answers will vary.

R

Answers will vary.

S

Answers will vary.

T

1. "Keep your eyes open before marriage and half closed after it."—Benjamin Franklin 2. "Marry an archaeologist. The older you become, the lovelier he'll find you."—Agatha Christie 3. "Marrying for a second time is the triumph of hope over experience."—Samuel Johnson

16 Family Relations and Careers

A

1. lleguen 2. te abroches 3. den 4. haya 5. sean 6. diga 7. se enferme 8. compartamos

B

1. vuelven 2. saques 3. haga 4. es 5. paguemos 6. estás 7. me quede 8. tiene 9. guste
10. pierdan

C

1. Pilar, es necesario que la saques. 2. Alonso, es importante que los tomes. 3. Andrés, es útil que lo traigas. 4. Silvia, insisto en que las aprendas de memoria. 5. Gilberto, es imprescindible que la hagas. 6. Flor, es preciso que empieces a escribirla.

D

1. Quiero (Deseo) salir. 2. Esperamos que sea aplicada. 3. Es necesario (Es preciso) tomar apuntes. 4. Es importante que lean mucho.
5. ¿Prefieres comprar los boletos en línea?
6. Será imprescindible que aprendamos todas las fechas. 7. ¡Quieren (Desean) divertirse mucho!
8. Es bueno que se gradúen este año.

E

1. Le aconsejo a Marta que beba mucha agua.
2. Les recomiendo a mis amigos que duerman ocho horas diarias. 3. Le propongo a Pablo que se ponga a dieta. 4. Le digo a Inés que tome vitaminas.
5. Le exijo a mi primo que pierda peso. 6. Les pido a mis papás que hagan ejercicio. 7. Le ruego a mi abuelito que deje de comer comida basura.
8. Insisto en que mis colegas se alimenten bien.

F

1. Papá, no creo que entiendas el problema.
2. Esperamos que Marta logre pescar un marido.
3. Es dudoso que Antonio y Victoria se quieran.
4. Blanca no cree que sus padres conozcan a su novio. 5. Es malo que los familiares no se lleven bien. 6. Los abuelos les dicen a sus nietos que los visiten. 7. Mario le exige a su cuñado que le devuelva el dinero. 8. Cristina insiste en que su suegro pague la boda.

G

1. Es que nosotros somos íntimos amigos.
2. No estoy seguro que ella vaya a la fiesta.
3. Es dudoso que haga buen tiempo mañana.

4. Es cierto que mis primos están de vacaciones. 5. No es evidente que la empresa tenga problemas económicos. 6. No es que tú y yo nos veamos todos los días. 7. Es evidente que Uds. no se ponen de acuerdo. 8. Estamos seguros que él puede diseñar el sitio web.

H

1. Se alegran de que nos quedemos con ellos. 2. Le sorprende que el museo esté cerrado. 3. Tenemos miedo de que gasten demasiado dinero. 4. Siento que te sientas mal. 5. Tememos que el avión no despegue ahora. 6. Les gusta que nos mantengamos en contacto con ellos.

I

1. Le pido a Juan que elabore el presupuesto. 2. Le exijo a Enrique que cree una base de datos. 3. Les digo a mis asistentes que trabajen en equipo. 4. Le mando a Nora que se dedique a los medios sociales. 5. Insisto en que Catalina se encargue de lanzar el nuevo producto. 6. Les digo a los asesores que resuelvan el problema del servicio al cliente. 7. Le aconsejo a Lorena que comience la campaña publicitaria. 8. Les propongo a mis colegas que realicen un plan de investigación global de mercado.

J

1. está 2. apoyemos 3. tienen 4. busques 5. son 6. juegue 7. rompa 8. tengan

K

1. La maestra nos dice que leamos el capítulo siete. 2. Le aconsejo que escriba el informe. / Le aconsejo escribir el informe. 3. Me recomiendan que traiga mi calculador de bolsillo. / Me recomiendan traer mi calculador de bolsillo. 4. Eduardo me dice que él y Lorenzo no se llevan bien. 5. Insisto en que dejes de fumar. 6. Les pido que vengan a nuestra casa. / Les pido venir a nuestra casa. 7. El jefe me exige que entregue el informe para el martes. / El jefe me exige entregar el informe para el martes. 8. Les propongo que asistan a la reunión. / Les propongo asistir a la reunión.

L

1. A sus papás les gusta que Leonor se haga actriz. 2. El abuelo se alegra de que Ramón siga la carrera de ingeniería. 3. La abuela prohíbe que su nieta salga con ese tipo. 4. Los tíos dejan que su hija vaya al extranjero para estudiar inglés. 5. Miguel le aconseja a su hermano que no se comprometa con Lola. 6. Los papás les dicen a sus hijos que sean corteses y amables. 7. Los cuñados hacen que sus hijos se inscriban en la universidad. 8. La familia Gómez espera que todos ellos logren tener salud, felicidad y éxito.

M

1. Es malo que Luisito no les haga caso a sus papás. 2. Es posible que Fernanda se haga arqueóloga. 3. La tía Sara quiere que Juan y Blanca hagan las paces de una vez. 4. Vámonos antes de que se haga tarde. 5. No me parece que esta blusa haga juego con la falda. 6. Le dicen a Arturo que deje de hacer el ridículo. 7. Te aconsejamos que hagas un alto. 8. Esperamos que Lorenzo Olivo haga el papel de Hamlet en esta producción.

N

1. Es bueno que Ud. ahorre dinero. 2. Es imprescindible que ellos se pongan el repelente contra mosquitos. 3. Es urgente que yo salga para el aeropuerto. 4. Es preciso que Uds. promocionen la marca. 5. Es mejor que tú juegues al tenis por la mañana. 6. Es importante que todos nosotros comamos granos integrales. 7. Urge que él vaya al médico. 8. Más vale que Ud. viaje en tren. 9. Hace falta que ella aprenda las fechas de memoria. 10. Es útil que yo actualice los datos.

O

1. Te aconsejo que te cuides mucho. 2. Quiero que salgas con nosotros al teatro. 3. Es necesario que te cortes el pelo. 4. Hace falta que apagues la computadora. 5. Es mejor que vengas a vernos hoy. 6. Insisto en que me hagas caso. 7. Más vale que tengas paciencia. 8. Me alegro de que te diviertas mucho. 9. Te recomiendo que te pruebes el abrigo azul marino. 10. Urge que te aproveches de las ofertas de enero.

P

1. Es poco probable que Pedro consiga el puesto. 2. Es imprescindible que apoyemos a nuestros amigos. 3. Quizás (Tal vez) estos estudiantes extranjeros sean de origen inglés. 4. Es una lástima que Lupe no encuentre sus aretes. 5. Laura y Sergio niegan que se divorcien. 6. Les he dicho a los niños que se laven las manos. 7. Más vale que hagas tu tarea ahora. 8. Es malo que no se pongan en contacto con nosotros más a menudo.

Q

1. Better late than never. 2. It's better to be alone than in bad company. 3. It's better to give than to receive. 4. A bird in the hand is worth two in the bush. 5. It's better to regret what you did rather than what you didn't do. 6. Prevention is better than cure. 7. Better the devil you know than the one you don't. 8. Health is better than wealth.

R

Answers will vary.

S

Answers will vary.

Glossary

The Spanish-English glossary includes the vocabulary used in the text. Numbers after glossary entries refer to the chapter in which the item first appears. Gender is indicated by the definite articles **el**, **la**, **los**, **las**. The following abbreviations are also used.

adj.	adjective	*i.o.*	indirect object	*pl.*	plural
d.o.	direct object	*irreg.*	irregular verb	*p.p.*	past participle
fem.	feminine	*lit.*	literally	*rev. constr.*	reverse construction verb
inf.	infinitive	*masc.*	masculine	*sing.*	singular

Verbs like **ir**, marked "**ir** (*irreg.*)", have multiple irregularities and should be checked in the Verb Charts. Verbs with an irregularity only in the **yo** form of the present tense are marked as in "**conocer (yo conozco)**." Remember that irregularities in the **yo** form also appear in the subjunctive.

Verbs with changes in the vowel of the stem are marked as follows: **pensar (e > ie)**, **volver (o > ue)**, **pedir (e > i)**.

Verbs with spelling changes are marked as follows: **buscar (c > qu/e)**, **llegar (g > gu/e)**, **abrazar (z > c/e)**, **escoger (g > j/o, a)**.

Verbs with both changes in the vowel of the stem and spelling changes are marked as follows: **comenzar (e > ie, z > c/e)**, **seguir (e > i, gu > g/o, a)**.

la abeja *bee* 11
abierto *open* 4
el abogado, la abogada *lawyer* 3
abrazar (z > c/e) *to hug* 8
el abrigo *overcoat* 2; *coat* 4
abril *April* 5
abrir *to open* 6
abrocharse *to buckle/fasten* 9
  abrocharse el cinturón de seguridad *to fasten one's seatbelt* 9
la abuela *grandmother* 4
el abuelo *grandfather* 4
aburrido *bored, boring* 4
aburrir *to bore (someone)* 8
aburrirse *to get bored, be bored* 8
el abuso *abuse* 12
  abuso de drogas *drug abuse* 12
acabar *to finish* 6
  acabar de + *inf.* *to have just (done something)* 6
acabársele a uno *to run out of* 11
acampar *to camp, go camping* 11
acaso *maybe, perhaps* 13
acatarrado *sick with a cold* 4
acatarrarse *to catch a cold* 8
el accidente *accident* 11
el aceite *oil* 1
  aceite de oliva *olive oil* 3
  los aceites de baño *bath oils* 8
la aceituna *olive* 3
acercarse (a) (c > qu/e) *to come/go closer, approach* 8
acomodarse *to get comfortable, settle in* 9
acompañar *to accompany, go with* 11
el acondicionador *conditioner* 8
aconsejar *to advise* 16
el acontecimiento *event* 16
acordarse (de) (o > ue) *to remember* 8
acostado *lying down* 4
acostarse (o > ue) *to go to bed* 8
la actitud *attitude* 15
actualizar (z > c/e) *to update* 9
actualmente *at present, currently* 13
adelgazar (z > c/e) *to get thin* 11
además *besides, in addition* 6
adiós *goodbye* 1
la administración de empresas *business administration* 2
el administrador, la administradora de bases de datos *database administrator* 3
adorable *cute, adorable* 11
la aduana *customs* 9
el aduanero *customs inspector* 9
el aeropuerto *airport* 9
afeitarse *to shave* 8
afortunadamente *fortunately* 11
la agenda electrónica *electronic appointment book* 1
el/la agente *agent* 3
agosto *August* 5
agotado *exhausted, wiped out* 9
agotador *exhausting* 9
agradable *nice, pleasant* 9
el agricultor *farmer* 10
el agua (*fem.*) *water* 3
  agua de colonia *cologne* 8
  agua mineral *mineral water*

el aguacate *avocado* 3
el aguacero *downpour* 11
el aguafiestas *wet blanket, party pooper* 8
ahora *now* 4
ahora mismo *right now* 5
ahorrar *to save* 5
el aire *air* 1
en el aire *in the air, airborne* 9
el aire acondicionado *air conditioning* 7
el ajetreo *hustle and bustle* 13
el ajo *garlic* 15
al (*contraction*) *to the* 5
al contrario *on the contrary* 11
al fondo de *at the back of* 4
al lado (de) *next to* 4
al + *inf. upon, when* 8
la alarma *alarm* 9
falsa alarma *false alarm* 11
la albóndiga *meatball* 3
alegrarse (de) *to be glad, be happy* 8
alegre *cheerful* 4
alejarse (de) *to move away (from)* 8
la alergia *allergy* 11
algo *something* 5
el algodón *cotton* 4
alguien *someone, anyone* 5
alguno, alguna, algunos, algunas *some* 2
alimentarse *to feed oneself, eat* 8
el alimento *food* 3
los alimentos frescos *fresh food* 3
la almohada *pillow* 14
almorzar (o > ue, z > c/e) *to have lunch* 8
el almuerzo *lunch* 5
tomar el almuerzo *to have lunch* 5
alquilar *to rent* 5
alterado *upset, unnerved* 11
alto *tall* 4; *high* 11
amable *kind* 4
amarillo *yellow* 2
ambicioso *ambitious* 12
ambos, ambas *both* 2
la ambulancia *ambulance* 11
el amigo, la amiga *friend* 2
amplio *spacious* 12
el análisis *analysis* 1
análisis de sangre *blood test* 11
el/la analista *analyst* 3
analista de seguridad de (la) información *information security analyst* 3
analizar (z > c/e) *to analyze* 13
anaranjado *orange* 2
anda (< andar) *come on* 6
el anfitrión, la anfitriona *host* 3
angustiado *distressed* 4
el anillo *ring* 15
anillo de boda *wedding ring* 15
animado *lively, busy, bustling* 2
el animal *animal* 1
animar(se) *to cheer up, feel like doing something* 8
el aniversario *anniversary* 15
anoche *last night* 9
anteayer *the day before yesterday* 9
anterior *previous* 12
antes (de) *before* 8
lo antes posible *as soon as possible* 8
el antibiótico *antibiotic* 11
antiguo *former* 12
antipático *unpleasant* 4
anunciar *to announce* 15
el anuncio *announcement* 7
añadir *to add* 14
el año *year* 6
el año que viene *next year* 6
el año próximo *next year* 8
el Año Nuevo *New Year's* 15
apagar (g > gu/e) *to shut off* (*appliance*) 9
aparcar (c > qu/e) *to park* 14
el apartamento *apartment* 2
apartamento de lujo *luxury apartment* 13
apenas *hardly, barely* 13
aplicado *studious* 16
apoyar *to support* 16
aprender *to learn* 6
aprender de memoria *to learn by heart* 16
apresurarse (de) *to hurry* 8
aprovechar *to take advantage of* 6
aquel, aquella, aquellos, aquellas *that, those* 3
aquí *here* 1
el arete *earring* 1
el armario *closet* 1
el arquitecto *architect* 4
el arquitecto, la arquitecta de red *computer network architect* 3
arreglarse *to get ready* (*clothing, hair*) 8
arrepentirse (e > ie) (de) *to regret (something)* 8
arriba *above, upstairs, overhead* 9
arrogante *arrogant* 4
el arroz *rice* 3
arroz con pollo *chicken with rice* 3
el arte *art* 1
el artículo *article* 2
el/la artista *artist, performing artist* 3
el ascensor *elevator* 11
asegurar *to assure* 13
el aseo personal *personal grooming* 8
el asesor, la asesora *consultant* 3
asesor financiero, asesora financiera *financial advisor* 3
el asiento *seat* 9
asiento de pasillo *aisle seat* 9
asiento de ventana *window seat* 9
la asignatura *subject* (*school*), *course* 12
asignatura obligatoria *required course, requirement* 12
asignatura optativa *elective (course)* 12
el/la asistente médico *physician assistant* 3
asistir a *to attend* 6
asombroso *amazing* 4
la aspirina *aspirin* 11
asustado *scared* 4
asustar *to frighten/scare (someone)* 8
asustarse *to get frightened/scared* 8
el atajo *shortcut* 9
atender (e > ie) *to tend to, look after* 11
atento *considerate* 4
el aterrizaje *landing* (*airplane*) 9
aterrizar (z > c/e) *to land* (*airplane*) 9
el/la atleta *athlete* 3
el atraco *holdup* 11
atractivo *attractive* 12
atrapar *to catch* 11
atrasado *late, behind schedule* 4
atreverse a *to dare to* 13

atropellar *to run over* 11
el atún *tuna* 3
aumentar *to gain* 11; *to increase* 13
  aumentar de peso *to gain weight* 11
aún *even* 12
los auriculares *earphones, headset* 9
auténtico *authentic* 3
el autobús *bus* 5
el automóvil *car* 1
la autopista *turnpike* 4
el autor, la autora *author* 12
el auxiliar / la auxiliar de vuelo *flight attendant* 9
el ave *bird, chicken* 3
la avenida *avenue* 2
las aves *poultry* 3
el avión *airplane* 5
ayer *yesterday* 9
ayudar *to help* 5
el azúcar *sugar* 3
azul *blue* 2

bailar *to dance* 5
el bailarín, la bailarina *dancer* 3
el baile *dance* 4
bajar *to go down* 6
  bajar de peso *to lose weight* 11
  bajar del avión *to get off the airplane* 9
el baloncesto *basketball* 6
  jugar al baloncesto *to play basketball* 6
bañar(se) *to bathe, take a bath* 8
el banco *bank* 1
la banda *band* 5
el baño *bath* 8
el bar *bar* 1
barato *inexpensive, cheap* 2
la barbaridad *outrageousness* 13
el barco *boat* 5
el barrio *neighborhood* 2
  barrio bajo *poor neighborhood* 13
la base *base* 1
  base de datos *database* 1
bastante, bastantes *quite a lot of* (Spanish America); *enough* (Spain) 2
la basura *garbage* 12
la batata *sweet potato* 3
el batido de fruta *fruit shake* 3
batir *to beat* 14
el bautizo *baptism* 13
el bebé *baby* 13
beber *to drink* 6
la bebida *beverage* 3
  bebida sin alcohol *nonalcoholic beverage* 3
la beca *scholarship* 10
el béisbol *baseball* 6
  jugar al béisbol *to play baseball* 6
las bellas artes *fine arts* 16
  la facultad de bellas artes *School of Fine Arts* 16
la belleza *beauty* 8
besar *to kiss* 8
la biblioteca *library* 4
la bicicleta *bicycle* 5
  montar en bicicleta *to take a bicycle ride* 5
bien *well* 4
el billete *ticket, bill* (*currency*) 1
el billetero *wallet* 1
la biología *biology* 12
el bistec, el biftec *steak* 3
blanco *white* 2
el bluejean *jeans* 4
la blusa *blouse* 4
la boda *wedding* 4
el boleto *ticket* 9
el bolígrafo *ballpoint pen* 12
la bolsa *bag* 1
el bolso *handbag* 1
el bombero, la bombera *firefighter* 11
la bondad *goodness* 14
bonito *pretty* 2
bordo: a bordo *on board* 9
el bosque nacional *national forest* 5
la botella *bottle* 5
  botella de vino *bottle of wine* 5
el brazo *arm* 9
el brindis *toast* 15
bronceado *tan, suntanned* 14
el bronceador *suntan lotion* 8
bueno *good* 2
la bufanda *scarf* 4
el bufete *lawyer's office* 5
buscar (c > qu/e) *to look for, seek* 9
el buzón *mailbox, inbox* 10

el caballo *horse* 5
  montar a caballo *to go horseback riding* 5
el cabello *hair* 8
caber (*irreg.*) *to fit* 7
la cabeza *head* 8
la cabra *goat* 10
el cacto *cactus* 9
caer (*irreg.*) *to fall* 7
  caerle a uno (*rev. constr.*) *to like/dislike* (*usually a person*) 9
  caérsele a uno *to drop* 11
el café *café* 1; *coffee* 3
el cafetal *coffee plantation* 10
la cafetera *coffee pot* 13
la caja *box* 1
el cajero automático *ATM* 11
calculador *calculating* 12
la calculadora de bolsillo *pocket calculator* 16
calcular *to calculate* 15
la calefacción *heat* 7
calentar (e > ie) *to heat* 14
la calle *street* 1
calmar(se) *to calm down* 8
la cama *bed* 9
la cámara *camera* 1
cambiar *to change* 9
  cambiar de idea *to change one's mind* 11
caminar *to walk* 5
el camino *path* 9
la camisa *shirt* 2
la camiseta *T-shirt* 2
campestre *rural, country* 10
el camping *camping* 5
  hacer camping *to go camping* 5
el campo *field* 4
  campo de fútbol *soccer field* 4
  campo de fútbol americano *football field* 5
la cancha *field, court* 5
  cancha de baloncesto *basketball court* 5
  cancha de tenis *tennis court* 5
la canción *song* 7
cansado *tired* 4

el/la cantante *singer* 3
cantar *to sing* 5
la cantidad *quantity* 7
una cantidad de *a lot of* 7
una gran cantidad de *a large amount/number of* 10
la capital *capital (city)* 3
el capítulo *chapter* 16
caprichoso *unpredictable* 12
la cara *face* 8
¡caramba! *oh no!, my goodness!* 4
cargar (g > gu/e) *to upload* 5
cariñoso *loving, affectionate* 10
la carne *meat* 3
la carne de res, la carne de vaca *beef* 3
la carne roja *red meat* 3
el carnicero, la carnicera *butcher* 3
caro *expensive* 2
la carpeta *folder* 1
el carpintero, la carpintera *carpenter* 3
la carretera *highway, road* 4
el carro *car* 1
la carta *menu* 3
el cartapacio *briefcase* 1
la cartera *wallet; handbag* 1
el cartucho de tinta *ink cartridge* 12
la casa *house* 1
en casa *at home* 5
casado (con) *married (to)* 4
casarse (con) *to get married (to)* 8
cascarrabias *cantankerous* 12
el catarro *cold (health)* 11
la catedral *cathedral* 1
católico *Catholic* 4
la cazuela *pot* 13
el CD (cedé) *CD* 1
la cebolla *onion* 3
celebrar *to celebrate* 5
el celular *cell phone* 9
el cementerio *cemetery* 13
cenar *to have dinner* 5
el centro *downtown* 1
el centro comercial *shopping center, mall* 1
cepillar(se) *to brush* 8
cepillarse el pelo / los dientes *to brush one's hair/teeth* 8
el cepillo de dientes *toothbrush* 8
el cepillo para el pelo *hairbrush* 8
cerca (de) *near* 4
el cerdo *pork* 3
la cereza *cherry* 3
cerrado *closed* 4
cerrar (e > ie) *to close* 6
la cerveza *beer* 3
la champaña *champagne* 15
el champú *shampoo* 8
la chaqueta *jacket* 4
chequear *to check* 15
el chequeo *checkup* 11
la chica *girl* 4
el chico *boy, kid* 4
chiquito *small* 2
el chisme *gossip* 13
chocar (c > qu/e) *to crash* 11
el chocolate *chocolate* 3
chocolate caliente *hot chocolate* 3
el colesterol *cholesterol* 11
el choque *crash* 11
choque de carros *car crash* 11
el cibercafé *internet café* 1
el científico, la científica *scientist* 3
cierto *certain* 2
el cine *movie theater* 1
la cita *appointment* 11
tener cita con el médico *to have a doctor's appointment* 11
la ciudad *city* 1
la civilización *civilization* 10
el clarinete *clarinet* 5
claro *bright, light* 2; *of course* 1
claro que sí *of course* 1
la clase *class* 1
clase a distancia *internet course* 6
el clima *climate* 1
el club *club* 5
club de jazz *jazz club* 4
el coche *car* 1
la cocina *kitchen; cuisine* 6
cocinar *to cook* 5
el cocinero, la cocinera *cook, chef* 3
coger (g > j/o, a) *to take, grab* 9
el/la colega *colleague* 15
el colegio *high school* 4
colocar (c > qu/e) *to place, put* 9
colocarse (c > qu/e) *to get a job/position* 8
comenzar (i > ie, z > c/e) *to begin* 6
comenzar a + *inf.* *to begin to (do something)* 6
comer *to eat* 6
comer como un pajarito *to eat like a little bird* 11
comercial *commercial* 2
la comida *food, meal* 3; *dinner* 4
comida basura *junk food* 8
comida orgánica *organic food* 3
comida rápida/chatarra *fast food, junk food* 3
comida vegetariana *vegetarian food* 3
comilón (< comer) *big eater, gluttonous* 11
la comisaría de policía *police station* 15
como *as, like* 6
como de costumbre *as usual* 4
cómo no *of course* 4
¿cómo? *how?, what?* 1
cómodo *comfortable* 1
el compañero *friend* 11
compañero de clase *classmate* 11
la compañía *company* 4
el compartimiento de arriba *overhead compartment* 9
compartir *to share* 6
completamente *completely* 2
componer (*irreg.*) *to compose* 11
la composición *composition* 12
el comprador, la compradora *shopper* 6
comprar *to buy* 5
comprender *to understand* 6
comprensivo *understanding* 12
comprometerse *to get engaged* 8
el compromiso *date, appointment* 16
compulsivo *compulsive* 6
la computación *computer science* 2
la computadora *computer* 1
el cómputo *computation* 1
la tienda de cómputo *computer store* 1
con *with* 3
el concierto *concert* 4
el condominio *condominium* 2

conducir (*irreg.*) *to drive* 9
la conferencia *lecture* 4
conmigo *with me* 6
conocer (yo conozco) *to know* 6
conseguir (e > i) *to get* 9
el consejo *piece of advice* 7
dar consejos *to give advice* 7
considerado *considerate* 12
construir *to build* 10
la contabilidad *accounting* 2
el contador, la contadora *accountant* 3
la contaminación del ambiente *environmental pollution* 12
contaminado *polluted* 12
contar (o > ue) *to tell, relate, narrate* 6
contar (o > ue) (con) *to count (on)* 6
contento *happy* 4
contestar *to answer* 13
contigo *with you* 6
el contrato *contract* 2
el control de seguridad *security (check)* 9
convenirle a uno (*rev. constr.*) *to be good/suitable for someone* 9
convertir (e > ie, e > i) *to convert* 13
convertirse (en) *to become* 13
coqueta *flirtatious* 12
la corbata *necktie* 4
el cordero *lamb* 3
el correo *mail* 6
correo electrónico *email* 4
cortar *to cut* 8
cortarse el pelo *to cut one's hair* 8
el cortaúñas *nail clippers* 8
cortés *polite* 12
corto *short* 2
la cosa *thing* 8
por cualquier cosa *for every little thing* 8
coser *to sew* 6
la costa *coast, seashore* 6
costar (o > ue) *to cost* 10
costoso *costly, expensive* 13
la costumbre *custom* 15
como de costumbre *as usual* 15
crecer (yo crezco) *to grow* 13
creer *to believe, think* 6
la crema de afeitar *shaving cream* 8
la crema hidratante *moisturizing cream* 8
el crimen *crime* 12
la crisis *crisis* 1
cruzar (z > c/e) *to cross* 14
el cuaderno *notebook* 12
la cuadra *(city) block* 4
a una cuadra de *one block from* 4
el cuadro *painting, picture* 5
¿cuál? ¿cuáles? *which (one)?, which ones?* 4
cualquiera *any* 2
¿cuánto? ¿cuánta? *how much?* 2
¿cuántos? ¿cuántas? *how many?* 1
el cuarto *room* 1
cuarto de baño *bathroom* 12
la cuchara *spoon* 13
la cucharita *teaspoon* 13
el cuchillo *knife* 13
el cuello *neck* 11
el cuidado *care* 8
cuidado personal *personal care* 8
con cuidado *carefully* 8
cuidadosamente *carefully* 8
cuidarse *to take care of oneself* 8
cultivar *to grow, raise* 10
el cumpleaños *birthday* 5
cumplir *to be/turn ___ years old* 15
cumplir con *to meet (as a deadline)* 15
la cuñada *sister-in-law* 4
el cuñado *brother-in-law* 4
cursar *to take a course* 12
el curso *course (of study)* 12

dañar *to damage, harm* 14
dar (*irreg.*) *to give* 7
dar a luz *to give birth* 11
dar consejos *to give advice* 7
dar el pésame *to express one's sympathy/condolences* 13
darse prisa *to hurry, be in a hurry* 8
los datos *data* 1
de *of, from* 2
de nada *you're welcome* 1
¿de qué parte? *where?, from which part?* 3
de repente *suddenly* 11
de todas formas *anyway* 7
de veras *really* 3
debajo de *under* 4
deber *should, ought to, must* 6
decepcionado *disappointed* 12
decir (*irreg.*) *to say, tell* 7
decir que sí/no *to say yes/no* 7
¿cómo se dice? *how do you say?* 7
el dedo *finger* 11
dejar *to leave, let* 8
dejar de + *inf. to stop (doing something)* 8
del (*contraction*) *of/from the* 2
delante de *in front of* 4
deletrear *to spell* 10
delgado *thin* 4
delicioso *delicious* 3
demasiado *too much* 5
el/la dentista *dentist* 3
el departamento *department* 1
el/la dependiente *salesperson* 3
el depilatorio *depilatory, hair remover* 8
el deporte *sport* 1
hacer deportes *to do/play sports* 5
deprimido *depressed* 4
la derecha *right side* 4
a la derecha de *to the right of* 4
el derecho *law* 2
derecho *straight ahead* 14
desabrocharse *unfasten, unbuckle* 9
desabrocharse el cinturón de seguridad *to unfasten one's seatbelt* 9
el desarrollador / la desarrolladora de programas *software developer* 3
el desarrollador / la desarrolladora de web *web developer* 3
desayunar *to have breakfast* 8
el desayuno *breakfast* 5
tomar el desayuno *to have breakfast* 5
descargar (g > gu/e) *to download* 5
descomponérsele a uno *to have something break down* 11
descompuesto (*p.p.* descomponer) *broken, broken down, malfunctioning* 4
descubrir *to discover* 9

desde luego *of course* 10
desear *to want, wish* 6
el desempleo *unemployment* 13
el desfile *parade* 15
el desierto *desert* 9
la desilusión *disappointment* 10
desnudarse *to get undressed* 8
el desodorante *deodorant* 8
despedir (e > i) *to fire* 11
despedirse (e > i) (de) *to say goodbye (to)* 8
despegar (g > gu/e) *to take off (airplane)* 9
el despegue *takeoff (airplane)* 9
despejar *to clear (up)* 6
despertarse (e > ie) *to wake up* 8
despistado *absentminded* 12
después *after, afterwards* 5
después (de) *after* 8
detrás de *behind* 4
devolver (o > ue) *to return, give back* 6
el día *day* 1
  día libre *day off* 4
  al día siguiente *the next day* 9
la diapositiva *slide* 7
dibujar *to draw* 5
diciembre *December* 5
el diente *tooth* 8
la dieta *diet* 11
  ponerse a dieta *to go on a diet* 11
diferente *different* 2
difícil *difficult* 2
difícilmente *with difficulty* 8
la dificultad *difficulty* 8
  con dificultad *with difficulty* 8
el dinero *money* 1
Dios mío *my gosh, my goodness* 11
la dirección *address* 4
  dirección electrónica *email address* 6
directo *direct* 9
  el vuelo directo *direct flight* 9
el director, la directora *director* 4
el disco compacto *compact disc, CD* 4
la discoteca *discotheque* 5
disculpar *to excuse* 14
discutir *to discuss, argue* 6
el diseñador, la diseñadora de videojuegos *video game designer* 3
diseñar *to design* 5
disfrutar (de) *to enjoy* 5
dispensar *to excuse* 14
el disquete *diskette* 12
la distancia *distance* 6
divertido *amusing, entertaining, fun* 3
divertirse (e > ie, e > i) *to have a good time* 8
divorciado *divorced* 4
divorciarse *to get divorced* 8
doblar *to turn* 14
el documental *documentary* 7
el documento *document, paper* 1
doler (o > ue) (*rev. constr.*) *to hurt, ache; distress* 11
el dolor *pain, ache* 11
  dolor de cabeza/estómago/diente *headache/stomachache/toothache* 11
dominar *to master* 6
el domingo *Sunday* 4
¿dónde? *where?* 1
  ¿adónde? *(to) where?* 1
  ¿de dónde? *(from) where?* 1
dormido *sleeping* 4
dormilón (< dormir) *given to sleeping, sleepyhead* 11
dormir (o > ue) *to sleep* 6
dormirse *to go to sleep, fall asleep* 8
el dormitorio *bedroom* 12
el drama *drama* 1
la drogadicción *drug addiction* 12
ducharse *to take a shower* 8
la duda *doubt* 13
  no cabe duda *there's no doubt* 13
dudar *to doubt* 16
dudoso *doubtful* 16
los dulces *candy* 3
el durazno *peach* 3
duro *hard, difficult* 13

echar *to throw* 14
la economía *economics* 2
el ecoturismo *ecotourism* 10
el edificio *building* 4
el efecto *effect* 9
  en efecto *exactly* 9
egoísta *selfish* 12
el ejercicio *exercise* 5
  hacer ejercicio *to exercise* 5
el *the* (before a masc. noun) 1
elaborar *to make, draw up* 13
el/la electricista *electrician* 3
el electrodoméstico *household appliance* 1
elegante *elegant* 15
elegir (e > i, g > j/o, a) *to choose* 9
el elevador *elevator* 11
ellas *they* (fem.) 4
ellos *they* (masc.) 4
el email *email* 13
embarazada *pregnant* 11
  estar embarazada *to be pregnant* 11
el embotellamiento *traffic jam* 9
emocionado *excited* 4
emocionarse *to be moved, get excited* 8
empezar (e > ie, z > c/e) *to begin* 6
  empezar a + *inf. to begin to (do something)* 6
emprendedor(a) *enterprising* 4
la empresa *firm, company* 5
en *in, at, on* 1
  en absoluto *not at all* 4
  en efecto *exactly* 8
  en frente *across the street, opposite* 1
  en frente de *opposite, facing* 4
  en punto *on the dot* 4
  en realidad *really, actually* 4
  en seguida *immediately* 7
enamorado *in love* 8
  el Día de los Enamorados *Valentine's Day* 15
enamorarse (de) *to fall in love (with)* 8
encantador(a) *charming* 4
encantarle a uno (*rev. constr.*) *to love something* 9
encargar (g > gu/e) *to order* 5
encargarse (de) (g > gu/e) *to be in charge (of)* 15
la enchilada *enchilada* 3
encima de *on top of* 4
encontrar (o > ue) *to find* 6
enero *January* 5
enfadado *angry* 4
enfadar *to make (someone) angry* 8
enfadarse *to get angry* 8
enfermarse *to get sick* 8

la enfermedad *illness* 11
la enfermería *nursing* 2
el enfermero, la enfermera *nurse* 3
el enfermero practicante *nurse practitioner* 3
engañar *to deceive* 12
engordar *to get fat* 11
el enjuague *mouthwash* 8
enojado *angry* 4
enojar *to make (someone) angry* 8
enojarse *to get angry* 8
la ensalada *salad* 3
enseñar *to show* 10
entender (e > ie) *to understand* 6
entenderse *to understand each other, get along* 8
el entierro *funeral, burial* 13
entonces *then* 6
entrar (a/en) *to go in, enter* 6
entregar (g > gu/e) *to hand in/over, turn in/over* 9
los entremeses *hors d'oeuvres* 3
entrometido *meddlesome* 12
entusiasmado *enthusiastic* 4
entusiasmarle a uno (*rev. constr.*) *to be/get excited about something* 9
entusiasmarse *to get excited, feel thrilled* 8
enviar (yo envío) *to send* 13
la época *time* 10
  en aquella época *at that time* 10
el equipaje *luggage* 9
  equipaje de mano *carry-on luggage* 9
el equipo *team* 11
equivocarse (c > qu/e) (al) *to be wrong* 11
  equivocarse de número *to get the wrong number* 11
las escaleras *stairs* 11
  la escalera mecánica *escalator* 11
escaparse *to escape* 11
escoger (g > j/o, a) *to choose* 15
escribir *to write* 6
el escritor, la escritora *writer* 3
escuchar *to listen*
la escuela *school* 4
ese, esa, esos, esas *that, those* 3
el esmalte de uñas *nail polish* 8
la espalda *back (anatomy)* 11
el espectáculo *show* 4
esperar *to hope; to wait for; to expect* 5
el espíritu *spirit* 12
  espíritu cívico *civic spirit* 12
espléndido *wonderful, splendid* 9
la esposa *wife* 3
el esposo *husband* 3
esquiar (yo esquío) *to ski* 15
la esquina *street corner* 1
la estación *station* 4; *season* 5
  estación de tren *train station* 4
el estacionamiento *parking lot* 4
estacionar *to park* 14
el estadio *stadium* 5
el estado civil *marital status* 4
estallar *to break out, explode* 11
el estante *shelf* 1
estar (*irreg.*) *to be* 4
  estar de acuerdo *to agree* 4
  estar de buen/mal humor *to be in a good/bad mood* 4
  estar de pie *to be standing* 4
  estar de vacaciones *to be on vacation* 4
  estar de viaje *to be on a trip* 4
  estar de visita *to be visiting* 15
  estar frito *to be done for / finished / doomed* 4
  estar seguro (de que) *to be sure (that)* 4
estatal (*adj.*) *state*
  la universidad estatal *state university* 10
el este *east* 9
este, esta, estos, estas *this, these* 3
el/la estilista *hair stylist* 3
el estilo de vida *lifestyle* 11
el estómago *stomach* 11
el estrés *stress* 11
estresado *stressed* 4
estricto *strict* 12
el/la estudiante *student* 3
estudiar *to study* 6
estupendo *terrific, great* 2
exactamente *exactly* 15
el examen *examination, test* 1
exasperar *to exasperate* 8
excelente *excellent* 7
exigente *demanding* 12
exigir (g > j/o, a) *to demand* 16
la experiencia *experience* 6
el experto *expert* 6
explicar (c > qu/e) *to explain* 9
la exposición de arte *art exhibit* 5
extranjero: en el extranjero *abroad* 11

la fábrica *factory* 13
fabuloso *fabulous* 7
fácil *easy* 2
la facilidad *ease, easiness* 8
  con facilidad *easily* 8
fácilmente *easily* 8
facturar *to check* 9
  facturar el equipaje *to check the luggage* 9
la facultad *school (within a university)* 12
  facultad de bellas artes *School of Fine Arts* 16
  facultad de ciencias *(school of) sciences* 12
la falda *skirt* 4
falso *two-faced* 12
faltarle a uno (*rev. constr.*) *to be short of something, not have something* 9
la familia *family* 3
familiar (*adj.*) *family* 16
famoso *famous* 4
el farmacéutico, la farmacéutica *pharmacist* 3
la farmacia *drugstore* 1
el favor *favor* 14
  favor de + *inf.* *please* 14
febrero *February* 5
la fecha de nacimiento *date of birth* 4
las felicidades *congratulations* 8
feo *ugly, nasty* 2
fiarse de (yo me fío) *to trust* 8
la fiebre *fever* 11
la fiesta *party* 2
fijarse (en) *to notice* 8
el film *film* 7
la filosofía *philosophy* 12
el filtro solar *sunblock, sunscreen* 11
el fin de semana *weekend* 6
la finca *farm* 10
fino *of better quality* 12
la física *physics* 12
el físico *physicist* 11
flaco *thin* 4

la flauta *flute* 5
la flor *flower* 1
el/la florista *florist* 3
el folleto *brochure* 2
el fondo *bottom, back* 4
el fontanero, la fontanera *plumber* (Spain) 3
la foto *photo* 5
tomar fotos *to take photos* 5
la frecuencia *frequency* 8
con frecuencia *frequently* 8
frecuentemente *frequently* 8
freír (e > i) (yo frío) *to fry* 14
frente a *in front of* 4
la fresa *strawberry* 15
el frijol *bean* 3
el frío *cold* (*weather*) 6
hace frío *it's cold* 6
frito *fried* 4
la fruta *fruit* 3
el fuego *fire* 14
a fuego lento *on a slow flame, over low heat* 14
fuera *out, outside* 5
fuerte *strong, hard* 6
fumar *to smoke* 10
funcionar *to work, function* 12
fundar *to found* 10
la furgoneta *van* 9
furioso *furious* 4
el fútbol *soccer* 5
fútbol americano *football* 5
jugar al fútbol *to play soccer* 6
jugar al fútbol americano *to play football* 6

la galería de arte *art gallery* 5
la galleta *cookie* 14
galleta con chispas/pepitas de chocolate *chocolate chip cookie* 3
la gallina *hen, chicken* 10
ganar *to earn* 5; *to win* 11
ganarse la vida *to earn a living* 16
la ganga *bargain* 6
el garaje *garage* 2
la gasolinera *gas station* 4
gastar *to spend* 5
los gastos *expenses* 13
el gato *cat* 4
la gaveta *drawer* 1
el gemelo *twin* 15
generalmente *generally* 8
generoso *generous* 10
la gente *people* 1
buena gente *good person* 16
el/la gerente *manager* 3
gerente de marketing (mercadeo) *marketing manager* 3
gerente de sucursal *branch manager* 11
gerente de ventas *sales manager* 3
el gimnasio *gym* 5
las golosinas *candy, sweets, treats* 3
goloso *sweet-toothed* 3
ser goloso *to have a sweet tooth* 3
gordo *fat* 4
el gorro *cap* 4
grabar *to record* 5
gracias *thank you* 1
muchas gracias *thank you very much* 1
gracioso *funny, witty* 4
graduarse (yo me gradúo) (en) *to graduate (from)* 8
grande *big* 2
el grano *grain* 10
grano integral *whole grain* 10
la grasa *fat* 11
la gripe *flu* 11
gris *gray* 2
el grito *shout, scream* 7
gruñón, gruñona *grouchy, grumpy* 12
el guante *glove* 4
guapo *good-looking, handsome* (*male*) 3
guardar *to save* 13
la guerra *war* 11
los guisantes *peas* 3
la guitarra *guitar* 5
gustarle a uno (*rev. constr.*) *to like* 9
el gusto *pleasure* 7
con gusto *gladly* 7

haber (*irreg.*) *to have* (auxiliary verb) 7
la habitación *room* 2
el habitante *inhabitant* 13
hablado (*p.p.* hablar) *spoken* 6
el francés hablado *spoken French* 6
hablar *to speak* 5
hacer (*irreg.*) *to do, make* 6
hace + *expression of time* + que + *verb in present tense* *have/has been doing something* 6
hace fresco *it's cool* 6
hace ___ grados *it's ___ degrees* 6
hace + *time* + *verb in preterit* ___ *ago* 9
hacer cola *to stand in line, line up* 7
hacer escala *to make a stopover* 9
hacer las maletas *to pack* 9
hacer maravillas *to do wonderful things* 13
hacer un papel *to play a role/part* 10
hacer preparativos *to prepare for, get ready* 9
hacer la tarea *to do homework* 16
hacer un viaje *to take a trip* 5
hacerle caso a alguien *to pay attention to someone* 16
hacerse *to become* 11
se hace tarde *it's getting/growing late* 8
la hacienda *estate* 15
haga el favor de *please* 14
el hambre *hunger* 6
la hamburguesa *hamburger* 3
hasta *even* 11
hay *there is, there are* 1
hay que *one must, one has to* 6
hecho *done* 4
hecho a la perfección *perfectly done* 4
muy hecho *too well done* 4
poco hecho *underdone* 4
la heladería *ice cream store* 1
el helado *ice cream* 1
helar (e > ie) *to freeze* 6
la herida *injury, wound* 11
herido *injured, wounded* 11
la hermana *sister* 4
el hermano *brother* 4
hermoso *beautiful* 2
la hija *daughter* 4
el hijo *son* 4
el hilo dental *dental floss* 8
la hipoteca *mortgage* 13
la historia *history* 2; *story* 9

histórico *historical* 16
la hoja de afeitar *razor blade* 8
el hombre *man* 6
hombre de negocios *businessman* 4
honrado *honest* 4
la hora *time (clock), hour* 4
a la misma hora *at the same time* 7
¿a qué hora? *at what time?* 4
es hora de *it's time to* 7
horas libres *free time* 5
las horas punta *rush hour* 9
media hora *half an hour* 9
horrendo *terrible, horrible* 9
horrible *horrible, terrible* 2
el hospital *hospital* 1
el hotel *hotel* 1
el hotelero, la hotelera *hotel manager* 3
hoy *today* 4
el huevo *egg* 3
huevo revuelto *scrambled egg* 6

la idea *idea* 6
no tener la menor idea *to have no idea at all* 15
el idioma *language* 1
la iglesia *church* 4
imaginarse *to imagine* 10
el imperio *empire* 10
la importancia *importance* 16
importante *important* 2
importarle a uno (*rev. constr.*) *to matter to someone* 9
imprescindible *crucial* 16
impresionante *impressive, awesome* 4
la impresora *printer* 4
imprevisto *impromptu, unforeseen, unexpected* 15
imprimir *to print* 6
los impuestos *taxes* 13
el incendio *fire* 11
incluir (yo incluyo) *to include* 13
la independencia *independence* 15
el Día de la Independencia *Independence Day* 15
indulgente *lenient* 12
la infección *infection* 11
inflexible *rigid, inflexible* 12
informar *to inform* 11
el informe *report* 1
el ingeniero, la ingeniera *engineer* 3
ingenuo *naïve* 12
los ingresos *income* 13
inmediatamente *immediately* 14
el/la inmigrante *immigrant* 10
inquieto *worried* 4
inscribirse *to register* 8
insistir en *to insist* 16
instalarse *to move in* 8
inteligente *intelligent* 2
interesante *interesting* 2
interesarle a uno (*rev. constr.*) *to be interested in something* 9
el interior *interior, inside* 2
interminable *unending* 9
el/la intérprete *performer, interpreter* 3
íntimo *intimate, close (relationship)* 16
el invierno *winter* 5
la invitación *invitation* 13
el invitado *guest* 7
invitar *to invite* 5

el iPod *iPod* 1
ir (*irreg.*) *to go* 5
ir a (+ *inf.*) *to be going to (do something)* 5
ir de compras *to go shopping* 5
irse *to go away* 8
la izquierda *left side* 4
a la izquierda de *to the left of* 4

el jabón *soap* 8
el jamón *ham* 3
el Jánuca *Hanukkah* 15
el jardín *garden, yard* 2
el jardinero, la jardinera *gardener* 3
el jetlag *jet lag* 9
el jogging *jogging* 5
hacer jogging *to jog, go jogging* 5
joven *young* 6
la joya *jewel* 1
la joyería *jewelry store* 1
el joyero, la joyera *jeweler* 3
jubilarse *to retire (stop working)* 11
judío *Jewish* 4
el jueves *Thursday* 4
el jugador, la jugadora *player* 6
jugar (u > ue, g > gu/e) *to play* 6
jugar al baloncesto / béisbol / fútbol / fútbol americano / tenis *to play basketball/baseball/soccer/football/tennis* 6
el jugo *juice* 3
el juguete *toy* 1
la juguetería *toy store* 1
julio *July* 5
junio *June* 5
juntos *together* 5

el kilómetro *kilometer* 4

la *the* (before a fem. noun) 1
la (*d.o.*) *her, it, you* (informal) 7
el labio *lip* 8
los lácteos *dairy* 3
el lado *side* 4
el ladrón *thief* 11
la lana *wool* 4
el lápiz *pencil* 1
lápiz para los labios *lipstick* 8
largo *long* 2
las (*d.o.*) *them, you* (pl.) 7
la lástima *pity, shame* 16
es una lástima que *it's a pity that* 16
latino *Latin*
la lavadora *washing machine* 7
el lavaplatos *dishwasher* 7
lavar(se) *to wash* 8
lavarse el pelo / la cabeza / la cara / las manos / los pies *to wash one's hair/hair/face/hands/feet* 8
le (*i.o.*) *him, her, you* 9
la leche *milk* 3
la lechuga *lettuce* 3
leer *to read* 6
la legumbre *vegetable* 3
lejos (de) *far (from)* 4
lentamente *slowly* 10
los lentes *glasses* 11
lentes de contacto *contact lenses* 11
lentes de sol *sunglasses* 11

lento *slow* 14
les (*i.o.*) *them, you* (pl.) 9
levantar *to lift* 5
levantarse *to get up* 8
leve *light, minor* 11
libre *free* (*time*) 5
la librería *bookstore* 1
el librero, la librera *bookseller* 3
el libro *book* 1
  libro de recetas de cocina *cookbook* 6
  libro de texto *textbook* 12
la licencia de manejar *driver's license* 15
la lima de uñas *nail file* 8
lindo *nice, lovely, pretty* (Spanish America) 2
la línea *line* 9
  en línea *online* 9
el lío *problem, complication, bit of trouble* 9
  lío de tráfico *traffic jam* 10
  nada de líos *no problems* 9
listo *ready* 4
llamar *to call* 5
llamarse *to be named* 8
la llave *key* 1
llegar (g > gu/e) *to arrive* 5
llevar *to take, carry, wear* 5
  lleva más tiempo *it takes longer* 9
  llevarse bien/mal con *to get along / not get along with* 8
llorón (< llorar) *given to crying, crybaby* 11
llover (o > ue) *to rain* 6
la lluvia *rain* 7
lo (*d.o.*) *him, it, you* (informal) 6
la loción para después del afeitado *aftershave* 8
el locutor, la locutora *newscaster* 3
lograr *to get, obtain* 6
  lograr + *inf. to succeed in (doing something), manage to (do something)* 6
los (*d.o.*) *them, you* (pl.) 7
la lucha *fight, struggle* 10
el lugar *place* 1
el lujo *luxury* 13
  el apartamento de lujo *luxury apartment* 13
el lunes *Monday* 4
la luz *light* 1

la madrastra *stepmother* 4
la madre *mother* 4
madrugar (g > gu/e) *to get up early* 9
la maestría *master's degree* 15
magnífico *great, terrific, magnificent* 2
el maíz *corn* 10
mal *ill, sick* 4
maleducado *rude* 12
la maleta *suitcase* 1
  hacer las maletas *to pack* 5
el maletín *attaché case* 1
malo *bad* 2
la mamá *mother, mom* 4
la mañana *morning* 4
mañana *tomorrow* 5
  pasado mañana *the day after tomorrow* 5
mandar *to send* 13
mandón (< mandar) *bossy* 11
manejar *to drive* 6
la manera *way* 14
el mango *mango* 15
la mano *hand* 1
mantener (*irreg.*) *to maintain* 8
  mantenerse en contacto *to stay in touch* 8
  mantenerse en forma *to stay in shape* 8
la mantequilla *butter* 3
  mantequilla de cacahuete *peanut butter* 3
la manzana *apple* 3
el mapa *map* 1
el maquillaje *makeup* 8
maquillarse *to put on makeup* 8
la máquina *machine* 9
  máquina (maquinilla) de afeitar *electric razor* 8
el mar *sea; seashore* 5
maravilloso *wonderful, marvelous, terrific* 2
mareado *dizzy* 9
el marido *husband* 3
la mariposa *butterfly* 10
los mariscos *shellfish* 3
marrón *brown* 2
el martes *Tuesday* 4
marzo *March* 5
las matemáticas *math, mathematics* 2
la materia *subject* (*school*) 12
la matrícula *registration, enrollment* 8
matricularse *to register, enroll* 8
mayo *May* 5
el MBA *Master's in Business Administration* 15
me (*d.o.*) *me* 6
me (*i.o.*) *me* 9
el mecánico, la mecánica *mechanic* 3
la medianoche *midnight* 4
la medicina *medicine* 2
el médico, la médico (la médica) *doctor* 3
medieval *medieval* 9
medio *half* 2
el mediodía *noon* 4
mejor *better, best* 2
  a lo mejor *maybe* 11
mejorar *to improve* 10
mejorarse *to get better* 8
menos *less* 6
  menos mal *fortunately* 6
mentiroso *deceitful* 12
el mercadeo *marketing* 9
el mercado *market* 6
la merienda *snack* 5; *afternoon snack* 10
  merienda campestre *picnic* 10
  tomar la merienda *to have a snack* 5
el mes *month* 1
  el mes próximo *next month* 6
la mesa *table* 2
la mesera *waitress* 3
el mesero *waiter* 3
meter *to put in, insert* 6
meterse (en) *to meddle, butt in* 8
el metro *subway* 5
la metrópolis *metropolis, capital (city), major city* 13
mi, mis *my* 2
el microondas *microwave* 7
el miembro *member* 15
el miércoles *Wednesday* 4
la milla *mile* 4
mirar *to look at* 5
miserable *paltry, miserable* 10
mismo *same* 2
la mochila *backpack* 1
moderno *modern* 2

modo: de ningún modo *not at all* 7
molestar *to annoy/bother (someone)* 8
molestarse *to get annoyed* 8
molesto *annoyed* 4
el momento *moment* 13
la montaña *mountain* 9
el monumento *monument* 4
morado *purple* 2
moreno *dark-haired, dark-skinned* 4
morir (o > ue, o > u) *to die* 6
morirse (o > ue, o > u) *to die* 8
el mosquito *mosquito* 11
mostrar (o > ue) *to show* 9
el móvil *cell phone* 1
mucho, mucha *much, a lot* 2
muchos, muchas *many, a lot of* 2
mudarse *to move (change residence)* 8
muerto *dead* 13
la mujer *woman, wife* 3
el mundo *world* 6
la muralla *wall* 10
el museo *museum* 1
museo de arte *art museum* 1
museo de ciencias *science museum* 4
la música *music* 2
el músico, la música *musician* 3
musulmán, musulmana *Muslim* 4
muy *very* 2

el nacimiento *birth* 11
la nacionalidad *nationality* 4
nada *nothing* 5
nada más *that's all, nothing else* 5
nada + *adj.* *not at all* +adj. 11
ni nada *nor anything* 6
nadar *to swim* 5
nadie *no one, nobody* 5
la naranja *orange* 3
la nariz *nose* 1
navegar (g > gu/e) *to surf* 5
navegar en la red *to surf the internet* 5
la Navidad *Christmas* 15
necesario *necessary* 16
necesitar *to need* 6
los negocios *business* 9
negro *black* 2
nervioso *nervous* 4
nevar (e > ie) *to snow* 6
ni *nor, neither* 6
ni nada *nor anything* 6
la niebla *fog* 10
la nieta *granddaughter* 4
el nieto *grandson* 4
la nieve *snow* 7
la niña *girl* 4
ningún, ninguno, ninguna, ningunos, ningunas *no, none, not any* 2
a ninguna parte *nowhere* 6
de ningún modo *not at all* 7
el niño *boy* 4
niño prodigio *child prodigy* 11
no *no* 1
¿no? *isn't it?* 4
¿no sabes? *you know?* (lit., *don't you know?*) 2
la noche *night* 4
esta noche *tonight* 5
la Noche Vieja *New Year's Eve* 15
el nombre *name* 8
el nordeste *northeast* 9
normalmente *normally* 8
el noroeste *northwest* 9
el norte *north* 9
nos (*d.o.*) *us* 7
nos (*i.o.*) *us* 9
notar *to notice* 12
la noticia *piece of news* 13
las noticias *news* 7
la novela *novel* 6
la novia *girlfriend, fiancée* 3
noviembre *November* 5
el novio *boyfriend, fiancé* 3
nublado: está nublado *it's cloudy* 7
nuestro, nuestra *our* 2
nuevo *new* 2
la nuez *nut* 3
el número *number* 1
número de teléfono *telephone number* 4
nunca *never* 9
como nunca *best ever* 9

la obra *work, play (theater)* 5
obra de teatro *play* 5
obra maestra *masterpiece* 12
octubre *October* 5
ocupado *busy* 4
ocuparse de *to take care of* 8
ocurrírsele a alguien *to dawn on someone, think of something* 11
el oeste *west* 9
ofender *to offend, insult* 8
ofenderse *to get insulted, be offended* 8
la oferta *sale* 6
las ofertas de enero *January sales* 6
la oficina *office* 2
oficina de turismo *tourist office* 1
el/la oficinista *office worker* 3
ofrecer (yo ofrezco) *to offer* 9
el oído *ear* 11
oiga *say* (lit., *hear, listen*) 1
oír (*irreg.*) *to hear, listen to* 7
oye *hey, say* 7
ojalá *I hope* 16
la ojera *dark circle under the eye* 11
el ojo *eye* 11
olvidadizo *forgetful* 10
olvidarse (de) *to forget* 8
olvidársele a uno *to forget (something)* 11
oponerse (*irreg.*) *to oppose* 16
optimista *optimistic* 12
el ordenador *computer* (Spain) 7
el organizador, la organizadora *organizer* 15
organizador de bodas *wedding planner* 15
organizar (z > c/e) *to organize* 9
el origen *origin, descent, background* 3
el oro *gold* 3
la orquesta *orchestra* 15
oscuro *dark* 2
el otoño *fall, autumn* 5
otro, otra *another, another one* 1
otra vez *again* 4
la oveja *sheep* 10

el padrastro *stepfather* 4
el padre *father* 4

los padres *parents* 4
pagar (g > gu/e) *to pay* 5
la página *page* 5
página web *web page* 5
el país *country* 3
el paisaje *landscape* 9
el pájaro *bird* 1
pajarito *little bird* 11
el pan *bread* 3
pan comido *piece of cake, easy as pie* 9
pan integral *whole grain bread* 3
el panadero, la panadera *baker* 3
la pantalla *screen* 4
el pantalón *pants* 4
los pantalones *pants* 2
el papá *father, dad*
los papás *parents* 4
la papa *potato* 3
papas fritas *French fries* 3
la papaya *papaya* 15
el papel *paper* 1
el paquete *package* 1
para *for* 1
estar para + *inf.* *to be about to (do something)* 6
para eso fuimos *that's why we went* 9
parado *standing* 4
el paramédico *paramedic* 11
parecer (yo parezco) *to seem* 7
el/la pariente *relative* 15
el parqueo *parking lot* 4
el parquímetro *parking meter* 6
la parte *part* 3
el partido *game* 4
pasado (*p.p.* pasar) *passed* 9
el año pasado *last year* 9
el mes pasado *last month* 9
la semana pasada *last week* 9
el pasajero *passenger* 9
la pasantía *internship* 10
el pasaporte *passport* 3
pasar *to spend* 6; *to pass, come by* 7
las pasas *raisins* 3
la Pascua *Easter* 15
Pascua judía *Passover* 15
pasear *to take for a walk* 5
pasearse *to stroll, go for a walk* 8
el paseo *boulevard* 2
el pasillo *aisle* 9
el asiento de pasillo *aisle seat* 9
la pasta *pasta* 3
la pasta de dientes *toothpaste* 8
el pastel *pastry, pie* 3
la patata *potato* (Spain) 3
patinar *to skate* 5
el patio *yard, patio* 2
el pavo *turkey* 3
la paz *peace* 1
el peatón *pedestrian* 11
peatonal (*adj.*) *pedestrian* 2
el/la pediatra *pediatrician* 11
pedir (e > i) *to ask for, order* 6
peinarse *to comb one's hair* 8
el peine *comb* 8
la película *film, movie* 3
el pelo *hair* 8
la pelota *ball* 6
la peluquería *hair salon, barber shop* 1
pensar (e > ie) *to think* 6
pensar + *inf.* *to intend to (do something)* 6
peor *worse, worst* 2
pequeño *small* 2
la pera *pear* 3
perder (e > ie) *to lose* 9
perderse *to get lost* 9
perdérsele *to lose* 11
perdón *excuse me* 1
perdonar *to forgive, pardon, excuse* 14
perezoso *lazy* 12
perfectamente *very well, great* 4
el perfume *perfume* 8
el periódico *newspaper* 2
el/la periodista *journalist* 3
permitir *to allow* 16
pero *but* 2
el perro *dog* 2
el perro caliente *hot dog* 3
la persona *person* 1
la pesa *weight* 5
pesado *heavy, boring* 2; *annoying, boring* 7
el pésame *expression of sympathy/condolences at someone's loss* 13
dar el pésame *to express one's sympathy/condolences* 13
las pesas *weights, dumbbells* 5
el pescado *fish* 3
pesimista *pessimistic* 12
el peso *weight* 11
aumentar de peso *to gain weight* 11
bajar de peso *to lose weight* 11
el petróleo *oil* 10
el pez *fish* 1
el piano *piano* 5
la picadura *bite (insect)* 11
picadura de abeja *bee sting* 11
picadura de mosquito *mosquito bite* 11
picante *spicy* 3
picar (c > qu/e) *to itch* 11
el pie *foot* 4
a pie *on foot* 11
la piel *skin* 1
la pierna *leg* 11
el pijama *pajamas* 14
la pimienta *pepper* 3
la piña *pineapple* 3
pintar *to paint* 5
pintarse *to put on makeup* 8
pintarse la cara / los labios / las uñas *to put on makeup / lipstick / nail polish* 8
el pintor, la pintora *painter* 3
la pintura *painting* 9
las pinzas *tweezers* 8
la pirámide *pyramid* 1
la piscina *swimming pool* 5
el piso *floor* 8
la pista *track* 5
la pizza *pizza* 3
la placa *license plate* 14
el plan *plan* 1
plan de mercadeo *marketing plan* 9
plan de negocios *business plan* 13
el plano *street map* 6
el plátano *banana* 3
el plato *dish* 3
plato acompañante/adicional *side dish* 3

la playa *beach* 4
la plaza *square* 4
plenamente *fully* 14
el plomero, la plomera *plumber* 3
la población *population* 13
pobre *poor* 2
pobre de mí *poor me* 12
la pobreza *poverty* 12
poco *little, not much* 2
pocos, pocas *few, not many* 2
poder (o > ue) *to be able, can* 6
el/la policía *policeman/policewoman* 3
la policía *police (force)* 11
el político, la política *politician* 3
el pollo *chicken* 3
la polución *pollution* 12
poner (*irreg.*) *to put; to put/turn on; to show (film)* 7
poner la mesa *to set the table* 13
ponerse *to put on (clothing)* 8
ponerse + *adj. to become* 11
ponerse a + *inf. to begin to (do something)* 8
ponerse de pie *to stand up* 9
ponerse en contacto *to get in touch* 8
ponerse en forma *to get into shape* 8
popular *popular* 12
por *for, around, along, on, in the area of* 1
por aquí *around here* 1
por la avenida *along the avenue* 6
por ciento *percent* 10
por desgracia *unfortunately* 6
por dónde *where* 6
por eso *therefore, that's why* 4
por favor *please* 1
por semana *weekly* 5
el postre *dessert* 3
potente *powerful* 12
practicar (c > qu/e) *to practice* 5
el precio *price* 13
precisamente *exactly* 5
preciso *necessary* 16
precolombino *pre-Columbian* 10
preferir (e > ie) *to prefer* 6
preguntar *to ask (a question)* 13
preguntón (< preguntar) *inquisitive, nosey* 11
prender *to turn on (appliance)* 9
preocupado *worried* 4
preocuparse *to worry* 8
preparar *to prepare* 5
prepararse para la prueba *to prepare for the quiz* 16
la presión *pressure* 11
presión sanguínea *blood pressure* 11
prestar *to lend* 10
presumido *conceited, full of oneself, arrogant* 11
el presupuesto *budget* 13
la primavera *spring* 5
primero *first* 2
los primeros auxilios *first aid* 11
el primo, la prima *cousin* 4
privado *private* 10
la universidad privada *private university* 10
probable *probable* 16
poco probable *improbable, not likely, unlikely* 16
probar (o > ue) *to try, taste* 6
el problema *problem* 1
producir (*irreg.*) *to produce* 10
el producto *product* 10
la profesión *profession* 4
el profesor, la profesora *professor, teacher* 3
profundamente *deeply* 11
el programa *program* 1
la programación *programming* 5
el programador, la programadora *programmer* 4
programar *to program* 6
prohibir (yo prohíbo) *to forbid, prohibit* 14
los prometidos *the fiancés, engaged couple* 8
pronto *soon* 5
la propina *tip (for service)* 10
proponer (*irreg.*) *to propose* 16
el protector solar *sunscreen* 9
protestante *Protestant* 4
el proyecto *project* 13
la prueba *quiz* 16
el público *audience* 7
el puente *bridge* 14
la puerta *door, gate* 9
puerta de embarque *boarding gate* 9
pues *then, well (then)* 3
el puesto *position, job* 10
puesto (*p.p.* poner) *put* 13
la pulsera *bracelet* 1
el punto *point* 4
puro *pure, just, nothing but* 13

¿qué? *what?* 1
quebrársele *to break* 11
quedar *to be located (permanent location)* 2
quedarle a uno (*rev. constr.*) *to have something left* 9; *to fit someone (clothing)* 11
quedarse *to stay, remain* 8
quedársele *to leave (something) behind* 11
quejarse (de) *to complain (about)* 8
la quemadura *burn* 11
quemadura de sol *sunburn* 11
quemarse *to burn* 14
querer (e > ie) *to want* 6; *to love* 10
quererse (e > ie) *to love each other* 8
la quesadilla *quesadilla* 3
¿quién? ¿quiénes? *who?* 1
¿para quién? *for whom?* 1
la química *chemistry* 2
el quiosco *kiosk* 14
quitarse *to take off (clothing)* 9
quizás *perhaps* 11

la radio *radio* 7
la raqueta de tenis *tennis racket* 6
raro *strange, weird* 4
el rascacielos *skyscraper* 13
rascarse (c > qu/e) *to scratch* 11
el rato *while (period of time)* 5
ratos libres *free time* 5
reaccionar *to react* 13
la realidad *reality*
realista *realistic* 12
realizar (z > c/e) *to achieve, realize* 10
realizarse (z > c/e) *to take place* 15
realmente *really* 2
rebasar *to exceed* 15
el/la recepcionista *receptionist* 3
la receta (de cocina) *recipe* 6
el libro de recetas de cocina *cookbook* 6
recetar *to prescribe, give a prescription* 11
recibir *to receive* 6
recibirse de + *profession to get one's ____ degree* 11

el reciclaje *recycling* 12
recientemente *recently* 8
recoger (g > j/o, a) *to pick up, gather* 9
recomendar (e > ie) *to recommend* 16
reconocido (*p.p.* reconocer) *recognized* 6
recorrer *to travel around, tour* 9
el recuerdo *memory* 9
la red *web, internet* 1
el refresco *soft drink* 3
regalar *to give as a gift* 15
el regalo *gift* 1
la región *region* 3
registrarse *to check in* 14
regresar *to come/go back, return* 6
regular *so-so* 4
reírse (e > i) (yo me río) (de) *to laugh (at)* 8
la relación *relation, relationship* 16
las relaciones familiares *family relations* 16
relajarse *to relax* 8
relativamente *relatively* 2
la religión *religion* 4
el reloj *wristwatch* 1
el repelente contra mosquitos *mosquito repellent* 11
la reservación *reservation* 9
reservar *to reserve* 9
el resfriado *cold (health)* 11
resfriarse (yo me resfrío) *to catch a cold* 8
resistir *to resist* 6
resolver (o > ue) *to solve* 6
respirar *to breathe* 13
el restaurante *restaurant* 1
el resultado *result* 11
retirar *to withdraw* 11
el retraso *delay* 9
reunido *having a meeting* 4
la reunión *meeting* 4
reunirse (yo me reúno) (con) *to get together (with)* 8
reventar (e > ie) *to explode* 6
la revista *magazine* 2
revuelto (*p.p.* revolver) *scrambled* 6
el huevo revuelto *scrambled egg* 6
ricachón (< rico) *very rich* 11
rico *delicious* 3
ridículo *ridiculous* 4
el río *river* 14
la rodilla *knee* 11
rogar (o > ue, g > gu/e) *to request* 16
rojo *red* 2
romper *to break, tear* 6
rompérsele *to break* 11
la ropa *clothing* 1
rotundamente *definitely, emphatically* 8
rubio *blond* 4
el ruido *noise* 2
ruido ambiental *noise pollution* 12
ruidoso *noisy* 2
la rutina *routine* 8
rutina diaria *daily routine* 8

el sábado *Saturday* 4
saber (*irreg.*) *to know* 6
saber + *inf.* *to know how to (do something)* 6
sabroso *tasty* 3
sacar (c > qu/e) *to take out, get out* 5
sacar billetes/boletos *to get tickets* 9
sacar buenas notas *to get good grades* 16
la sal *salt* 3
las sales de baño *bath salts* 8
la sala *room (public), living room* 4
sala de clase *classroom* 16
sala de conferencias *conference room* 4
sala de recepción *reception (area)* 15
el salario *salary* 13
la salchicha *sausage* 3
salir (*irreg.*) *to go out, leave* 2
el salón *ballroom* 15
salón de belleza *hair salon, beauty salon* 1
la salsa *salsa, sauce* 3
saludar *to say hello, greet, wave* 11
el sándwich *sandwich* 3
la sangre *blood* 11
sano *healthy* 10
el sarpullido *rash* 11
el/la sartén *frying pan* 13
el saxofón *saxophone* 5
el secador de pelo/cabello *hair dryer* 8
la secadora *dryer* 7
secar (c > qu/e) *to dry* 8
secarse el pelo *to dry one's hair* 8
el secretario, la secretaria *secretary* 3
la sed *thirst* 6
seguir (e > i, gu > g/o, a) *to follow, continue* 6
la seguridad *security* 9
seguro *sure, certain* 15
estar seguro de que *to be sure that* 15
el seguro de salud *health insurance* 13
la selva *forest, jungle* 10
el semáforo *traffic light* 14
el semáforo está en rojo / en verde / en amarillo / en naranja *the traffic light is red/green/yellow/yellow* 14
la semana *week* 5
la semana entrante *next week* 6
el semestre *semester* 6
la señal *sign* 14
señal de tráfico *traffic sign* 14
sencillo *simple* 6
el señor *man, Mr., sir* 1
la señora *woman, Mrs., ma'am* 1
la señorita *young woman, Ms., miss* 1
sensato *sensible* 12
sensible *sensitive* 11
sentado *sitting, seated* 4
sentarse (e > ie) *to sit down* 8
sentimental *sentimental* 15
sentir (e > ie) *to feel* 7
lo siento *I'm sorry* 7
sentirse (e > ie, e > i) *to feel* 8
sentirse mareado *to feel dizzy* 9
septiembre *September* 5
ser (*irreg.*) *to be* 1
serio *serious* 12
la servilleta *napkin* 13
servir (e > i) *to serve* 6
sí *yes* 1
la sierra *mountain range, mountains* 15
la siesta *nap* 10
dormir la siesta *to take a nap* 10
el sillón *armchair* 9
simpático *nice, likeable* 4
simple *simple* 2
la sinagoga *synagogue* 9
sincero *sincere* 12

el sistema *system* 1
el sitio web *website* 4
sobrarle a uno (*rev. constr.*) *to have more than enough of something* 9
sobresaltado *startled* 11
la sobrina *niece* 4
el sobrino *nephew* 4
el sofá *couch* 9
el software *software* 5
el sol *sun* 6
hace/hay sol *it's sunny* 6
solicitar *to apply for* 15
solicitar una beca *to apply for a scholarship* 15
solterón *confirmed bachelor* 11
el sombrero *hat* 4
sonar (o > ue) *to sound, ring* 11
soñar (con) (o > ue) *to dream (of/about)* 10
el sonido *sound* 7
la sopa *soup* 3
sorprender *to surprise* 16
sorprenderle a uno (*rev. constr.*) *to surprise* 16
la soya, la soja *soy* 3
su, sus *his, her, your, its, your* (pl.), *their* 2
el suavizante (para el pelo) *hair conditioner* 8
subir *to go up, take up* 6
subir al avión *to get on the airplane* 9
la sucursal *branch* (*business*) 11
el/la gerente de sucursal *branch manager* 11
el sudeste *southeast* 9
la suegra *mother-in-law* 15
el suegro *father-in-law* 15
el sueño *dream* 10
la suerte *luck* 1
por suerte *luckily* 11
el suéter *sweater* 4
suficiente, suficientes *enough* 2
sumamente *extremely* 2
superdotado *very gifted* 11
el supermercado *supermarket* 1
suponer (*irreg.*) *to suppose* 10
el sur *south* 9
el suroeste *southwest* 9
suscribirse *to subscribe* 8
suspender *to discontinue, suspend* 10
el susto *fright* 11

el taco *taco* 3
tal vez *perhaps, maybe* 16
el taller mecánico *mechanic's shop* 4
también *also, too* 1
tampoco *neither, not either* 4
tan *so* 4
las tapas *tapas, hors d'oeuvres* 3
la taquilla *ticket window* 9
tardar *to take long* 15
tardar en hacer algo *to take a long time to do something* 15
la tarde *afternoon* 4
tarde *late* 5
la tarjeta *pass, card* 1
tarjeta de crédito *credit card* 1
tarjeta de embarque *boarding pass* 1
el taxi *taxi cab* 4
el/la taxista *taxi driver* 3
la taza *cup* 13
te (*d.o.*) *you* (informal) 6
te (*i.o.*) *you* (informal) 9

el té *tea* 3
el teatro *theater* 1
el técnico, la técnica *technician* 4
la tele *TV* 7
el teléfono *telephone* 1
teléfono celular *cell phone* 1
la telenovela *TV serial drama* 7
la televisión *television* 4
el televisor *TV set* 4
el tema *topic* 1
temer *to fear* 16
la temperatura *temperature* 6
temprano *early* 5
el tenedor *fork* 13
tener (*irreg.*) *to have* 6
tener calor *to be warm* 7
tener celos *to be jealous* 7
tener frío *to be cold* 7
tener ganas de + *inf. to feel like (doing something)* 6
tener hambre *to be hungry* 7
tener lugar *to take place* 13
tener un niño *to have a child* 11
tener que + *inf. to have to (do something)* 7
tener sed *to be thirsty* 6
tenga la bondad de + *inf. please* 14
el tenis *tennis* 6
jugar al tenis *to play tennis* 6
la tentación *temptation* 6
resistir a la tentación *to resist temptation* 6
terco *stubborn* 12
la terminal *terminal* (*airport*) 9
terminar *to finish* 6
la ternera *veal* 3
la tía *aunt* 4
el tiempo *time* 6; *weather* 6
los tiempos que corren *nowadays* 16
la tienda *store* 1
tienda de campaña *tent* 11
tienda de cómputo *computer store* 1
tienda de deportes *sporting goods store* 1
tienda de electrodomésticos *appliance store* 1
tienda de ropa *clothing store* 1
tienda de zapatos *shoe store* 1
tienda por departamentos *department store* 1
la tierra *land, ground* 9
en la tierra *on the ground, landed* 9
tomar tierra *to touch down* (*airplane*) 9
el timbre *doorbell* 7
tímido *shy* 12
el tinte para el cabello *hair coloring* 8
el tío *uncle* 4
el tipo *guy* 4
el tobillo *ankle* 11
tocar (c > qu/e) *to play* (*a musical instrument*) 5; *to touch* 9
tocarle a uno (*rev. constr.*) *to be one's turn* 15
el tocino *bacon* 3
todo, toda, todos, todas *all, the whole* 2
todo el, toda la, todos los, todas las *all, every* 3
todo el día *all day* 4
tomar *to take; to drink* 5
tomar el almuerzo/desayuno *to have lunch/breakfast* 5
tomar apuntes *to take notes* 16

tomar una copa *to have a drink* 5
tomar el sol *to sunbathe* 11
tomar tierra *to touch down (airplane)* 9
el tomate *tomato* 3
tonto *silly, stupid* 4
la tormenta *storm* 10
la torre *tower* 1
la torta *cake* 3
la tortilla *tortilla* (Mexico), *omelet* (Spain) 3
la tos *cough* 1
trabajador(a) *hardworking* 4
trabajar *to work* 1
el trabajo *work, job* 4
traducir (*irreg.*) *to translate* 7
traer (*irreg.*) *to bring, have with one* 7
el tráfico *traffic* 11
el traje *suit* 4
el trámite *step* 9
hacer los trámites *to make arrangements* 9
tranquilizarse (z > c/e) *to calm down, stop worrying* 8
tranquilo *quiet* 2
transitado *heavily trafficked* 2
el tranvía *trolley* 1
trasladar *to transfer* 11
tratar de + *inf.* *to try to (do something)* 6
través: a través de *by means of, through* 9
tremendo *awful* 11
el tren *train* 1
tren de alta velocidad *high-speed train* 9
triste *sad* 4
triunfar *to succeed* 10
el triunfo *triumph, success* 10
tronar (o > ue) *to thunder* 6
tropical *tropical* 10
trotar *to jog* 5
tu, tus *your* (informal) 2
tumbado *lying* 4
el turismo *sightseeing* 5
hacer el turismo *to go sightseeing* 5

el/la uberista *Uber driver* 3
últimamente *lately* 8
último *last* 12
un *a, an* (before a masc. noun) 1
un poco *a little* 4
una *a, an* (before a fem. noun) 1
la uña *nail* 8
único *only* 2
la universidad *university* 4
universidad estatal *state university* 10
universidad privada *private university* 10
uno *one* 1
urgente *urgent* 16
urgir (g > j/o, a) *to be urgent/pressing* 16
usar *to use* 6
usted (Ud.) *you* (formal sing.) 3
ustedes (Uds.) *you* (pl.)
útil *useful* 2
la uva *grape* 15
las uvas pasas *raisins* 3

la vaca *cow* 10
las vacaciones *vacation* 4
ir de vacaciones *to go on vacation* 5
valer (*irreg.*) *to be worth, cost* 7
el valor *value* 15
varios, varias *several* 2
el vaso *glass* 13
el vecino *neighbor* 6
vegetariano *vegetarian* 5
la velocidad *speed* 9
el velorio *wake* 13
vender *to sell* 6
venir (*irreg.*) *to come* 7
la ventana *window* 9
el asiento de ventana *window seat* 9
ver (*irreg.*) *to see* 7
el verano *summer* 5
la verdad *truth* 1
¿verdad? *right?, isn't it?, don't you?* 4
verdaderamente *really* 2
verde *green* 2
las verduras *greens, green vegetables* 3
el vestido *dress* 4
vestirse (e > i) *to dress, get dressed* 8
la vez *time, occasion* 1
la última vez *the last time* 9
una vez *once* 9
viajar *to travel* 5
el viaje *trip* 4
hacer un viaje *to take a trip* 5
viaje de negocios *business trip* 6
la víctima *victim* 11
la vida *life* 10
el video *video* 7
el videojuego *video game* 14
viejo *old* 2
el viento *wind* 6
hace viento *it's windy* 6
el viernes *Friday* 4
el vino *wine* 3
violeta *purple* 2
el violín *violin* 5
la visita *visitor* 15
estar de visita *to be visiting* 15
la visita *visitor* 15
visitar *to visit* 5
la vitamina *vitamin* 11
la viuda *widow* 13
el viudo *widower* 13
la vivienda *housing, housing unit, dwelling* 13
vivir *to live* 6
vivo *alive* 11
volver (o > ue) *to return, go back* 6
volver a + *inf.* *to (do something) again* 11
la voz *voice* 1
el vuelo *flight* 9
vuelo de conexión *connecting flight* 9
vuelo directo *direct flight* 9
vuestro, vuestra *your* (Spain) 2

y *and* 1
ya *already* 4
ya no *no more, no longer* 6
yo *I* 3
el yoga *yoga* 5
hacer yoga *to do yoga* 5

la zanahoria *carrot* 3
la zapatería *shoe store* 1
el zapato *shoe* 1
la zona *area* 2
el zoológico *zoo* 4

Index